Shaping the Future:
Military and Veteran Health Research

Edited By

Alice B. Aiken and Stéphanie A.H. Bélanger

CANADIAN DEFENCE ACADEMY PRESS

Canadian Defence Academy Press
PO Box 17000 Stn Forces
Kingston, Ontario K7K 7B4

30747

Library and Archives Canada Cataloguing in Publication

Shaping the future : military and veteran health research / edited by
Alice B. Aiken and Stéphanie A.H. Bélanger.

Issued by: Canadian Defence Academy.
Available also on the Internet.
Includes bibliographical references.
ISBN 978-1-100-19408-0 (bound)
ISBN 978-1-100-19409-7 (pbk.)
Cat. no.: D2-287/1-2011E (bound)
Cat. no.: D2-287/2-2011E (pbk.)

1. Veterans--Services for--Canada--Congresses. 2. Veterans--Health and
hygiene--Canada--Congresses. 3. Veterans--Medical care--Canada--Congresses.
4. Soldiers--Services for--Canada--Congresses. 5. Soldiers--Health and hygiene
--Congresses. 6. Soldiers--Medical care--Canada--Congresses.
I. Bélanger, Stéphanie A. H., 1972- II. Aiken, Alice B., 1965- III. Canadian Defence Academy
IV. Title: Shaping the future : military and veteran health research.

U22 M54 2010   174'.9355   C2010-980188-1

Printed in Canada.

1 3 5 7 9 10 8 6 4 2

ACKNOWLEDGEMENTS

This volume was created in recognition of the extent of research that exists to benefit military personnel, veterans and their families. Through this collection of proceedings a diversity of research areas are explored and new ideas are generated.

Congratulations and thank you to each author. The researchers who contributed to this volume were part of the Military and Veteran Health Research (MVHR) Forum that took place in November 2010, hosted by Queen's University and the Royal Military College of Canada. This Forum was a stepping stone to launch the Canadian Institute for Military and Veteran Health Research (CIMVHR). This volume is one of the many ways CIMVHR is connecting researchers, government stakeholders, and, most importantly, the beneficiaries through knowledge exchange while also working towards our mission: to optimize the health and well-being of Canadian military personnel, veterans and their families by harnessing and mobilizing the national capacity for high-impact research, knowledge creation and knowledge exchange.

A special thank you is extended to our government stakeholders, especially the Canadian Forces Surgeon General, Commodore Hans Jung, Veterans Affairs Canada Director of the Research Directorate, Dr. David Pedlar, the Director of the Defence Security and Research Institute, Dr. Jacques Lavigne, and the scientists of Defence Research Development Canada. Without your support this volume would not have been possible to create.

The Editors would also like to thank the co-chairs of the CIMVHR Implementation Committee; Susan Marlin, Assistant Vice Principal Research at Queen's University, and Brigadier-General (Ret'd) William Richard who have dedicated endless hours to the development of CIMVHR, the MVHR Forum and engaging the Canadian community.

Many aspects of this project would not have been possible without the support of Queen's University, Principal Daniel Wolfe and Dr. Steven Liss, Vice-Principal Research, as well as of the Royal Military College of Canada, Principal Joel Sokolsky and Dr. Jean Fugère, Vice-Principal Research.

We would also like to acknowledge the support and patience of our 18 peer reviewers; Dr. Allan English, Department of History, Queen's University; Dr. Michael Greenwood, Department of Chemistry, Royal Military College of Canada; Dr. Dianne Groll, Department of Psychiatry, Queen's University; Dr. Kate Harkness, Department of Psychology, Queen's University; Dr. Cheryl King Van-Vlack, School of Rehabilitation Therapy, Queen's University; Dr. Joy Klammer, Department of Military Psychology and Leadership, Royal Military College of Canada; Dr. Mélanie Lavoie-Tremblay, School of Nursing, McGill University; Dr. Christian Leuprecht, Department of Politics and Economics, Royal Military College of Canada; Dr. Bob Martyn, Fellow, Queen's Centre for International and Defence Policy; Dr. Mary Ann McColl, Centre for Health Services and Policy Research, Queen's University; Dr. Bradford McFadyen, Centre

Interdisciplinaire de Recherche en Réadaptation et Intégration Sociale (CIRRIS), Laval University; Dr. Candice Monson, School of Psychology, Ryerson University; Dr. Richard Morchat, Defence Security and Research Institute, Royal Military College of Canada; Dr. Eric Ouellet, Sociology, Canadian Forces College; Dr. Lucie Pelland, School of Rehabilitation Therapy, Queen's University; Dr. Caroline Pukall, Department of Psychology, Queen's University; Dr. Heidi Sviestrup, School of Occupational Therapy, University of Ottawa; and Dr. Elizabeth Taylor, Faculty of Rehabilitation Medicine, University of Alberta.

The opportunity to create a volume such as this simply would not exist without the leadership and logistical support of the Canadian Defence Academy (CDA) Press, particularly the CDA Press Program Manager, Mélanie Denis. Colonel Bernd Horn is keenly aware of the importance of providing an opportunity for the academic community and our military members, past and present, to exchange knowledge and share experiences. He has provided ready access to the resources of CDA Press to see this volume through to completion.

We would like to thank the College Information Services section at the Royal Military College of Canada for the book editing process, with a special mention to the Information Management Services section head, Ms. France Couture and the two Graphic Artists, Mr. Terry Hutchinson and Mr. Darryl Berger, who collaborated with the production of this book.

As editors, we are very proud of the final product. The copy editing and layout were handled with expertise by Michelle Moore and Lauren Hanlon, their professionalism and attention to detail have made this final product the work that it is.

While any discrepancies are the sole responsibility of the co-editors, it is the combined efforts of Mélanie, Terry, Michelle and Lauren that have resulted in a volume in which we can all take great pride; thank you.

Alice B. Aiken and Stéphanie A.H. Bélanger

TABLE OF CONTENTS

TABLE OF CONTENTS

SECTION 2: MENTAL HEALTH

SECTION 3: SOCIAL HEALTH

FOREWORD

I am delighted to introduce the first volume of the Canadian Institute of Military and Veterans Health Research (CIMVHR) collective, *Shaping the Future: Military and Veteran Health Research*. This book represents the most current research being conducted across Canada on issues of military and veteran health. It provides a snapshot of the military health services, challenges, and research programs that are guiding the Canadian Forces' future strategic direction for military health – compiling the relevant health-related material that will be of use to active and veteran Canadian Forces personnel and their families.

Having been involved in the November Military and Veteran Health Research (MVHR) 2010 Forum, I am eager to see the new realms of research that will stem from this organization's founding. CIMVHR is uniting universities with research groups and military organizations to establish a pan-Canadian academic program dedicated to improving the health of military members not only during military service, but in the long-term life course of members who have experienced health issues as a result of past service.

With the abundance of Canadian Forces members serving overseas in the last several years, it was identified that the existing research priorities required updating. By incorporating the academic community into military research, Canadians will benefit from the greater coordination of efforts, and the expanded capacity to perform much needed research. This collaboration will create a bridge between the academic and government research environments to ensure that conclusions drawn are of the utmost quality for our dedicated military personnel.

Canadian researchers have made significant contributions to improving military and civilian health concerns. *Shaping the Future: Military and Veteran Health Research* highlights some of these advancements in health research, and explores the programs being developed to improve them further.

With the upcoming MVHR 2011 Forum, I am confident that the collaboration of these leaders in health research will provide the best health care and repair to our devoted military members who have served and are serving across Canada and worldwide, and to their families that have sacrificed immensely to make it possible for those members to serve.

Hugh Segal
Senator

INTRODUCTION

According to Lieutenant-General the Honourable Roméo A. Dallaire, (Retired), Senator,

> …the unique physical, mental and social context of military service intimately defines how military personnel, veterans and their families deal with health throughout their lives. Currently, the number of Canadian Forces casualties and the breadth of their health problems arising from military operations are greater than those at any time since the Korean War.[1]

This highlights the fact that there is an immediate need for health programs and research for Canadian Forces members, veterans and their families.

The veterans of the current war in Afghanistan have joined more than 700,000 living Canadians who have unselfishly served their nation in the Canadian Forces. Over the last 25 years, the Canadian government has called upon the Canadian military to deploy to war zones and humanitarian missions around the globe, including the former Yugoslavia, Kosovo, the Middle East, Central Africa, Sierra Leone, Lebanon, Sri Lanka, Pakistan, Haiti, and recently Libya. As a result of the consequences of high intensity training and operations associated with such missions, the life course health and well-being of these veterans can be seriously affected. The health implications range from battlefield injuries (mental and physical) and serious trauma to exposure to toxic chemicals, life-threatening diseases and viruses. Families of military members not only deal with the deployment of loved ones into "harm's way," but they become the primary care givers of injured veterans, and their own health is affected not only by this, but also the lack of continuity of care as they move about Canada.

In November 2010, Queen's University and the Royal Military College of Canada (RMCC) hosted the first Canadian Forum on Military and Veteran Health Research (MVHR Forum), with the objective of engaging and invigorating pan-Canadian support to establish a national academic research program related to protecting the health of soldiers and examining the health impacts that occur throughout the life course of the soldier and their families as a result of military service to Canada.

This initiative emerged from requirements identified by the Canadian Forces Surgeon General and liaison with senior government executives of Veterans Affairs Canada (VAC) and The Department of National Defence (DND).[2] A review of the best practices by our military allies and discussions with subject matter experts confirmed that the existing military and veteran[3] health research priorities, programs, and requirements could be substantially advanced through participation from the academic community. The broad scope and complexity of health issues facing military members, veterans, and their families calls for greater coordination of academic and government research efforts, as well as an expanded capacity to perform high-impact, relevant research. There is also a need for an independent academic focal point at arm's length from the government to make the most of national capabilities. It is clear that Canadians are immensely proud of their military, and they wish to reassure those who serve Canada so well, that in return Canada will meet the obligations inherent in the "social covenant" between the soldier and the nation.

This volume brings together the compilation of research presented at the MVHR 2010 Forum, addressing the health issues and needs of military members, veterans, and their families. The Canadian Forces Surgeon General, Commodore H.W. Jung, introduces the book with a snapshot of the kind of research that would be of value to Canadian Forces members by presenting the military health context and challenges, a sampling of the military health services' primarily clinical and epidemiological health research programs, and the Canadian Forces' future strategic direction. As a foundation for the articles to follow, Dr. David Pedlar and James Thompson, MD, identify the research challenges for veterans' health research in Canada from the VAC perspective. They provide a clear list of requirements for the successful advancement of veteran health research with an emphasis on the need to coordinate the national vision and partnerships with federal, provincial and university researchers in order to inform policy, programs and services to meet the needs of today's military veterans and their families.

The remainder of this book is organized into four sections: Physical Health, Mental Health, Social Health, and Program Description. This arrangement provides the reader with a clear guide to the various realms of research currently being conducted within the area of military health.

Major Vivian McAlister, MD, *et al.* begin the first section on Physical Health with an analysis of the potential for composite tissue allotransplantation (CTA) to overcome the barriers associated with amputee rehabilitation, such as the complexity of the injury, the associated injury, and the level of amputation. By examining medical literature and current programs, CTA was found to offer options for treatment to carefully selected veterans who are motivated to take part in an experimental limb transplantation program being developed in London, Ontario.

David Pichora, MD, *et al.*, present new means of planning fracture repair for orthopaedic surgery with precise computer navigation of fixation devices. Specifically, intraoperative imaging was found to improve outcomes and reduce in-hospital postoperative recovery time. This work is expected to translate into better fracture care and facilitate the integration of telesurgery and computer-assisted techniques into military medical centers and field units.

From Queen's School of Kinesiology and Health Studies, Dr. Brendon Gurd and Jasmin K. Ma present evidence that interval training increases aerobic capacity, exercise tolerance and exercise performance in both young adults and diseased populations, induces weight loss, improves insulin sensitivity and cardiovascular health in overweight/obese and diseased populations. According to their findings, improvements following interval training appear to match, or in some cases even exceed, those observed following endurance training. They recommend that interval training be adopted into the physical activity regimes of active military personnel and be utilized in life style interventions aimed at improving health in medically cleared veterans.

Dr. Alain Beaulieu *et al.* from RMCC teamed up with Queen's University to research and design a new generation of ambulatory medical telemetry systems. They aim to develop an open architecture using Real-Time Object Oriented Modeling that will allow wireless, wearable medical devices to join a dynamically configurable monitoring environment. The described system is intended to monitor patients' recovery by measuring biometrics and biomedical signals as they go about their daily activities in the comfort of their homes.

Danielle Salmon PhD, Dr. J. Patrick Neary *et al.*, from the University of Regina, attempt to mitigate the high prevalence of neck pain (81-84%)[1] in Canadian Forces CH-146 Griffon helicopter pilots and flight engineers. To do this, they quantified the adaptations of cervical musculature isometric strength using a 12 week exercise training program. The program resulted in a reduction in visual analogue scale self-reported neck pain scores coupled with a positive trend toward improvements in maximal voluntary contraction and muscular endurance of the cervical musculature, suggesting that exercise training can mitigate neck pain in this aircrew population.

Dr. Yushan Wang PhD and Tracy Weiss PhD, from Defence Research and Development Canada (DRDC) in Alberta, worked with researchers from the Naval Medical Research Center in Maryland and the Brain Research Centre at the University of British Columbia to investigate neuronal damages and changes in cell surface expression of glutamate receptors in the rat brain after blast. Traumatic brain injury has been a leading cause of morbidity and mortality in recent conflicts in Iraq and Afghanistan due to the increasing use of roadside improvised explosive devices. However, the mechanisms of blast induced traumatic brain injury are currently not known. Results from these experiments indicate that at 120 kPa, the blast wave produces consistent brain damage in the rat. Changes in the cell surface expression of glutamate receptors may contribute to neurodegeneration induced by blast.

Dr. Ayush Kumar, Kari Kumar, and Jenny Cortez-Cordova from the Antimicrobial Resistance Research Group at the University of Ontario Institute of Technology analyze the activity of the efflux pump inhibitor phenylalanine arginine β-naphthylamide against the AdeIJK RND efflux pump of *Acinetobacter baumannii*. *A. baumannii* is an important nosocomial pathogen responsible for serious multidrug resistant combat wound infections in soldiers serving in Iraq and Afghanistan.

Ann Nakashima, MASc, *et al.* from Defence Research and Development Canada examine the relationship between primary blast wave exposure and mild traumatic brain injury. Primary blast exposure could alter postural tremor, impair balance, and cause deficits in cognitive function. They assess the correlations and longitudinal stability of measures of postural tremor, balance, and cognitive function among neurologically healthy normal controls, and offer a comprehensive tool based on a normative database to assess performance following primary blast exposure.

The second section, Mental Health research, begins with Colonel Rakesh Jetly, MD and Major Alexandra Heber's, MD, article that explores the challenges of practicing "war zone psychiatry" through case examples and the description of the shared care approach in theatre, where the care team can include social workers, nurses, medical officers, medics, chaplains, and in some cases assistance from the patient's colleagues and chain of command. They provide an in-depth review of issue of mTBI in theatre, and discuss the controversy surrounding the relationship between mTBI and Post-traumatic Stress Disorder (PTSD).

Kate St. Cyr *et al.*, from St. Joseph's Health Care in London Ontario, explore the differences in treatment outcomes between three types of therapy offered at the Parkwood Hospital Operational Stress Injury Clinic: pharmacotherapy alone, combined pharmacotherapy and psychotherapy, and psychotherapy alone. Although differences between groups at baseline and various time increments were not statistically significant, the groups varied along the clinical pathway and some trends emerged, suggesting the need for further research to better understand the trends.

Dr. Deborah Norris and Sandra Pickrell Baker, MA, documented the experiences of female partners of male veterans diagnosed with PTSD. The Canadian Forces CF is acknowledging a corresponding increase in numbers of members diagnosed with PTSD. Family members, particularly partners, may themselves develop a secondary traumatic stress response. Semi-structured interviews were used to document the participants' experiences, revealing feelings of depression, loss of self, hyper-vigilance, and conscious accommodation that were complicated by the sense of ambiguous loss permeating the relationship. The authors hope this study will guide the development of educational programs and support services for family members of CF personnel diagnosed with PTSD.

Drs. Alla Skomorovsky and Kerry Sudom examined the roles of self-efficacy and coping strategies in psychological health of spouses of deployed military personnel. The link between deployments and psychological health problems among spouses of military personnel has revealed that families of military personnel face a number of unique challenges associated with the military lifestyle. These challenges can have adverse consequences on psychological well-being, but they found that individual characteristics can either buffer or increase the negative impact of stress, specifically that self-efficacy and coping play important and independent roles in the well-being of military spouses.

Drs. Shannon Gifford, James Hutchinson and Maggie Gibson explore the relevance of lifespan-related issues in the psychological treatment of Canadian veterans with PTSD. As part of a resident-training program, they used a collaborative process to identify lifespan-related treatment issues in three veteran cohorts of different ages and to synthesize evidence that speaks to the challenges of treating Canadian veterans at various stages of the life course.

The Mental Health section concludes with a study by Don Richardson, MD, *et al.*, on the need for careful assessment and treatment of PTSD. Due to the complex clinical presentation of PTSD, which can include symptoms across the continuum from adjustment disorder and sub threshold PTSD to "full-blown" PTSD, this issue of Mood and Anxiety Disorders Rounds is confined to a general overview of the psychiatric management of PTSD with comorbid psychiatric conditions. They demonstrate that, despite the challenges researchers face in conducting studies on the effectiveness of treatment of this disorder,[5] if evidence-based practices are utilized using established guidelines,[6] remission can be achieved in 30–50% of PTSD cases.

Dr. Allan English, from Queen's University, begins the third section, Social Health, by discussing the direct influence of the social convenant between Canada and its military on the resources Canadian governments and others allocated to military and veterans' health care (MVHC). This essay considers the nature of that social covenant and how its changing nature has affected resources allocated for the health care of military members and veterans. It concludes with an examination of how changes to the social covenant between Canada and its military impacts on strategic planning and organizational change issues related to MVHC.

Dr. Alice Aiken and Amy Buitenhuis, from Queen's University, use a comparison between financial packages offered by the Pension Act (PA) and the New Veterans Charter (NVC) to a veteran with severe disabilities to show that the PA provides better financial support than the NVC. This study demonstrates that changes to the NVC are needed so that veterans with severe disabilities are provided at least the same level of support as under the PA.

Dr. Stéphanie Bélanger, from RMCC, uses the case study of an injured veteran from Afghanistan to examine how the CF can optimize the mission-critical outcomes, while determining the extent of the organizational and individual forces, as CF personnel face the challenges of returning injured from combat in postmodern military warfare. The author explores how testimonies from CF members in combat arms (post-Cold War era) allow the exploration of new issues surrounding soldiers' identities (core soldiering values) and training in its full spectrum; from peacekeeping (Bosnia) to warfare (Afghanistan); from predeployment preparation to rehabilitation care.

Drs. Susan Ray and Cheryl Forchuk, from the Lawson Health Research Institute, aim to understand the experience of homelessness among veterans of the Canadian Forces and Allied Forces in an effort to discover the underlying causes of homelessness and to provide recommendations to improve services to veterans. Alcoholism was one of the major issues they found that led ultimately to homelessness many years after their release from the military. They also discuss recommendations to the Department of National Defence and Veterans Affairs Canada, and implications for education, practice and research.

Dr. Julie Salverson offers several case studies of group programs dealing with displacement, trauma, and violence: workshops with military students; a play developed with youth for the Canadian Red Cross on anti-personnel landmines; a theatre process with refugees; a theatre research project in South Africa. She frames the discussion in theory about the personal and social costs of listening and bearing witness, and the difficulty of limiting options for how traumatized individuals self-define and narrate their lives. The creative arts offer resources and methodologies to reconnect the individual with the community in therapeutics of integrated wellness. She discusses how research in this field can form the basis of a prevention program targeting the isolation that personnel and their family can experience as a consequence of trauma.

Mary Beth MacLean, MA, et al., also from VAC, discuss the Income Study and its objective to examine family income using Statistics Canada's low income measure. This study describes veteran income trends and income differences between sub-populations within a larger population of veterans. The study showed that VAC clients had experienced greater declines in income post-release than non-clients. Post-release veterans on average were found to experience a decline in income. VAC programs reach the groups with the largest declines. Small numbers of veterans experience low income. Unfortunately, most low income veterans are not clients of VAC.

Stephanie Cork ends this section by analyzing the literal deconstruction and then reconstruction of the modern soldier after acquired disability in an attempt to further assert that the disabled body, a casualty of war, makes use of advanced biomedical innovations in the way of prosthetics to transcend essential humanness. Using a Marxist sociological analysis of the construction of rehabilitation discourses, Stephanie Cork intends to place documented experiences of acquired disability along a spectrum of resiliency among casualties, specifically amputees. It becomes evident, through an analysis of literature, that some amputees embrace the way in which technology can improve their condition, while others wish only to return to their former state. This study looks to interrogate the social forces that act upon military bodies through the military discourses of the 'tactical athlete' that often govern rehabilitation goals.

The final section of this book provides various descriptions of current and potential programs for the advancement of veteran, military and family health. Linda VanTil, DVM, MSc(Epi), *et al.*, from VAC, describe the "Life After Service Studies (LASS)" program of population health research. This program aims to improve the health of veterans in Canada by understanding the ongoing effects of military service. LASS includes disability as the functional impact of barriers related to health impairment. Determinants of health include income, social support, education, employment, personal health practices, and access to health services. Changes that take place over the veterans' life course are important to consider in assessing the health of the veteran population. The LASS program of research is a vital resource to provide the research evidence-base for future policy directions that will prepare Veterans Affairs Canada to meet veterans' health needs in the future.

As part of a comprehensive evaluation of the New Veterans Charter, Occupational Therapist Marlee Franz provides a review of 350 Rehabilitation Program files to provide an overall assessment of the level of functioning and progress for clients who participated in the New Veterans Charter Rehabilitation Program. The purpose of the Rehabilitation Program is to provide former Canadian Forces members with a client-centred approach to restore physical, psychological, social and vocational functions to an optimal level following injury or illness through medical rehabilitation, psychosocial rehabilitation, vocational rehabilitation, and vocational assistance. The file review and analysis was done to provide an evaluation of progress for medical, psychosocial and vocational rehabilitation and to assess outcomes for clients who participated in the Rehabilitation Program.

Richard Birtwhistle, MD, and Anita Lambert-Lanning, MLS, describe the Canadian Primary Care Sentinel Surveillance Network (CPCSSN) and the methodological requirements for using de-identified primary care health data to study chronic disease in veterans and consideration of family health. CPCSSN is a network of nine primary care practice based research networks (PCPBRN) in six provinces in Canada. Its aim is to have representation across the country in five years. The health of military veterans and their families is affected by the individual's military experience, placing veterans at increased risk of a number of chronic diseases. In Canada, many of these veterans do not maintain contact with Veteran's Affairs Canada after they leave active duty and therefore are lost to follow-up. They propose a potential collaboration with the CPCSSN to provide longitudinal de-identified health information on military veterans.

Dr. Brenda Gamble and Olena Kapral, BHSc, explain why healthcare reform requires the implementation of interprofessional collaboration (IPC). Interprofessional teams (IPTs) include frontline providers (e.g., nurses, physiotherapists, doctors, physician assistants, etc.) who deliver direct patient care. However, a lack of management support has been identified as one of the key barriers to the implementation of IPTs. They surveyed Canadian College of Health Leaders' (CCHL) members to determine their views on the skills/competencies required to successfully manage in healthcare. While CCHL respondents reported they were not directly managing IPTs, they are aware of the skills/competencies that support the implement of IPC. They concluded that strategies to implement IPC must incorporate both top down and bottom up approaches with a clear understanding of how both managers and frontline workers can work together to facilitate the coordination of care.

Dr. Donna Pickering and Tara Holton from DRDC aimed to obtain a better understanding of an 'informal buddy support system' that was developed to provide peer support to deploying Reservists and their families. During a deployment, Canadian Forces members have a variety of support requirements that need to be met in order to ensure they remain connected with home and family. This role is fulfilled for Regular Force members by their unit's rear-party located at their home base in Canada, however is not typically available for Reservists who deploy. System implementers, deploying Reservists, and buddies were asked about their experiences and knowledge of the system. Overall, participants indicated that this type of system would be of benefit to all Reservists deploying.

Lieutenant-Colonel Peter Rowe, MRSc, and Major Luc Hébert, PhD, from the Canadian Forces Health Services Group Headquarters, provide a broad and strategized review of the impact of musculoskeletal conditions on the Canadian Forces. This literature review was conducted in order to develop support for a strategic plan of capturing necessary information, share information to facilitate integrated approaches for positive clinical outcomes, and develop integrated performance measurement strategies. They found that a more integrated musculoskeletal management program could lead to improved clinical outcomes.

To conclude the chapters of this book, R. Lee Kirby, MD, and Cher Smith, BScOT, sponsored by Lieutenant-Colonel Markus Besemann, MD, from the Canadian Forces Health Services Group Headquarters, provide details from their visit to the Nova Scotia Rehabilitation Centre in Halifax, where they participated in a Wheelchair Skills Program mini-workshop to assess the program's applicability to Canadian Forces' military personnel and veterans with mobility programs. They provide a detailed review of the skills acquired from the program, as well as requirements for implementing a similar program in various recommended locations.

As this book illustrates, through the Canadian Institute for Military and Veteran Health Research (CIMVHR), Canadian researchers specializing in the health of serving military members, of retired military members and their families are now more interconnected than ever. By working closely with the Department of National Defence (DND), VAC and a pan-Canadian array of university-based researchers, the CIMVHR unites existing research to promote, protect, and restore the health of soldiers and examine the numerous health complications that uniquely or commonly occur throughout the life course as a result of military service to Canada. The outcomes of this research institute will serve the Canadian Forces and VAC, as well as the thousands of Canadian military members, veterans and their families. The CIMVHR also serves to provide innovative research that is relevant to the health care of Canadians in general, particularly the health implications of service with "first responder", humanitarian, and non-governmental organizations, and for those who experience severe trauma or work in extreme environments. There will be a much greater understanding within the health care profession and broader Canadian community of the challenges and health issues facing the military, veterans, and their families.

Alice B. Aiken, Stéphanie A.H. Bélanger,
Michelle Moore and Lauren Hanlon.

[1]Debates of the Senate (Hansard) 3rd Session, 40th Parliament, Volume 147, Issue 78. Tuesday, 14 December 2010.

[2]The reference to National Defence in this Business Plan refers to the key stakeholders: the Surgeon General and the Canadian Forces Health Services Group Defence Research and Development Canada, and the Director General Military Personnel Research and Analysis (responsible for personnel and family support services).

[3]Veterans Affairs Canada and the Department of National Defence (DND) have extended veteran status to former Canadian Forces members and Reserve Force members who: meet DND's military occupational classification requirements (MOC-qualified); and have been released from the Forces with an honourable discharge. Veteran status recognizes the potential risk that Canadian Forces members assume by donning the uniform and pledging allegiance.

CHAPTER 1

Military and Veterans Health Research Forum:
CF Surgeon General's Keynote Address

*Commodore H.W. Jung, OMM, CD, Commander Health Services Group and
CF Surgeon General*

As Surgeon General, it gives me great pleasure to see such excitement and enthusiasm from such a diverse academic audience on the subject of enhancing the health of current and former members of the Canadian Forces through research. These selfless heroes truly merit your support for the tremendous personal sacrifices that they and their families make for Canada's defence and security at home and abroad. Queen's University and the Royal Military College of Canada should be acknowledged and praised for putting together such an outstanding agenda. By your presence at this forum, I'm sure that like me, you believe that it's time to create a viable, sustainable, national research agenda for military and veteran's health.

My aim in this keynote address is to provide you, the academic community, a snapshot of the kind of research that would be of value to Canadian Forces members by presenting the military health context and challenges, a sampling of the military health services' primarily clinical and epidemiological health research programs, and our future strategic direction.

It is important to understand that the notion of a health research agenda for military, veterans and their families in Canada is not new. With the support of many partners within and outside the defence department, we've been doing this for many decades, focusing primarily on military-essential research. In doing so, and in working with allies such as the US, UK and Australia, we have learned that we could greatly increase our capacity and impact by engaging the Canadian academic community through a coordinated national military, veteran and family health research agenda. By creating a national agenda that is open and transparent, I hope to break down the traditional boundaries that limited our ability to take a holistic approach to health research related to military service. Furthermore, the research should be at arms' length of government so that when controversial issues arise, such as Agent Orange, or Depleted Uranium, the science can take its true course and not be subject to potential misperception that the Government of Canada drove related research findings. Finally, it is critical to the relevance of such an agenda that the research directly addresses Canadian military and veteran health research interests, and does not simply duplicate the work and mandates of existing civilian health research efforts in addressing generic health interests. To be useful, the research must be tailored to address the specific needs of current and former Canadian Forces members, who consist of a unique population subset exposed to many unique occupational factors and facing many unusual health challenges, as well as their families.

Canadian Forces Health Services Mission and Role

The mission of the Canadian Forces Health Services (CFHS) is to provide full spectrum, high quality health services to Canada's fighting forces wherever we serve. Given the exclusion of CF members under the Canada Health Act and the responsibilities of the Defence Minister under the National Defence Act, the CFHS Group constitutes a comprehensive health system to promote, protect, and restore the health of Regular and full-time Reserve CF members. In partnership with allies, civilian entities, the CF chain of command, and individual CF patients, it provides medical, dental, public health, occupational health, educational, regulatory, research, administrative, and advisory functions and services. It also fulfils command and control, operational planning, and other operational support functions by virtue of its mission to provide health service support to shield and sustain military operations.

Like its civilian counterparts, the CF legally constitutes an independent jurisdiction akin to Canada's 14th provincial/territorial health care system. The CFHS differs in mandate; however, as we must ensure that military commanders have a fit and healthy fighting force to employ in military operations. In essence, our responsibility differs from that of other health jurisdictions in that our primary role is to protect the health and well-being of military personnel and to promote a healthy lifestyle. Secondary to this is the provision of treatment services through a network of facilities in Canada, at sea, and abroad. The CF Health Services consist of over 6300 military and civilian health personnel from a broad variety of health professions. Our units are mostly static clinics, but include manoeuvre units such as our deployable field hospital and field ambulances, health services units deployed overseas, and special units with training, research, dental, operational, hyperbaric medicine, aerospace medicine, health protection and medical supply functions. All require continuous research and analysis to maintain capabilities at the best level of readiness and effectiveness. The CFHS is comprised of a national headquarters in Ottawa, 7 national units, 2 Health Services Group Headquarters, 43 static local units, 77 detachments, plus mobile deployable elements (Figure 1.1).

Figure 1.1. CF Health Services Units[1]

Our role is not only to function as a military health organization, but also as a federal health organization. In addition to fulfilling military-specific functions such as personnel and administration, medical intelligence, operations, medical equipment and supply, plans, IM/IT, training, finance, public affairs, legal and research, the CFHS fulfils for the CF most functions of provincial/territorial ministries of health, the health-related functions of education and labour ministries, many functions of Health Canada and the Public Health Agency of Canada, industrial occupational health services, health research establishments, pharmaceutical and medical supply agencies, third party health insurers, workers compensation programs, and functions of organizations like the International Committee of the Red Cross with respect to our capability to rapidly deploy mobile field health capabilities anywhere in the world.

Over 200 CFHS personnel are presently deployed on 13 missions across the globe. As our major function is to support deployed military operations, we have a large Operations directorate and staff integrated with Canadian, US, and British operational headquarters, intelligence agencies, or training organizations. For some humanitarian, domestic, and stability operational scenarios, the health response could be the primary supported military or diplomatic "pointy end", such as our recent mission to Haiti and our annual deployment with the United States Navy on humanitarian assistance operations to South America & the South Pacific.

In Afghanistan, for example, we provide mobile battlefield support integral to Canadian units. In 2006, we assumed leadership of the North Atlantic Treaty Organization (NATO) field hospital providing tertiary care to all NATO coalition forces in southern Afghanistan for almost 4 years. Most staff were Canadians supported by allied staff from several other nations. Although it is now under US responsibility, the second-in-command remains a Canadian and we continue to provide about 30 clinical staff, as well as a much larger staff contingent to directly support the Canadian Task Force.

By North American standards, the physical structure of the field hospital in Kandahar was very basic and cramped before a new state-of-the-art hospital was built last year, but the standard of care provided was extremely high and described by the current NATO force commander General David Petraeus as world-class combat medicine. During those 4 years, approximately 42,000 trauma patients passed through its doors. Over 4500 surgeries were performed, almost all of these as a direct result of the conflict. Most have been Afghans, but over 3000 coalition troops were treated in this humble plywood facility.

Of primary importance has been our mentoring of Afghan health care providers to improve Afghan health capabilities. Our performance generated tremendous praise from NATO and individual allies like the US, and although we do not have the resources of the US, NATO now looks to Canada as a leader in combat medicine and in leading multinational medical operations.

In addition to our mentoring and combat medical roles in Afghanistan, 247 CFHS personnel from a variety of units deployed to Haiti on very short notice during this year's humanitarian assistance mission. The Disaster Assistance Response Team (DART) deployed to Jacmel, providing outpatient and limited inpatient hospital care. Aeromedical Evacuation crews also cared for about 5000 Canadian entitled persons and Haitian casualties who were evacuated to back to Canada. These deployments demonstrate our flexibility and versatility in operating in very distinct types of operations in very different parts of the world. Notwithstanding the deployment of the DART, 1 Canadian Field Hospital also rapidly deployed with a 100-bed capacity. In addition to primary, surgical, intensive, and intermediate care with support services, it provided obstetrical, dental, and preventive medicine care. Between all CFHS element, about 22,500 patients were treated during this brief mission.

What I have provided is a brief synopsis of our roles and responsibilities and is only a snapshot in time. Beyond the day-to-day activities, we must, as a military health care organization, look to the future. As a unique organization within Canada, we must increasingly strive for evidence-informed best practices through continuous advancement of knowledge and technology. For this reason, I am looking to both my own organization and externally to the Canadian academic community to support this effort.

Our many challenges include an obligation to optimally support and treat CF members with mental health conditions, a burden which is expected to grow after the end of operations in Afghanistan. We must also maintain a robust rehabilitation capability, deal with health conditions arising from a progressively older CF population that reflects the lifestyle practices of society in general, and do so responsibly within national fiscal realities.

A continual challenge given the changing nature of threats, missions, and medical technology is to maintain adequate leading-edge research to support the best possible capabilities in support of CF operations, particularly in combat casualty care, Chemical-Biological-Radiological-Nuclear (CBRN) medical defence, and other elements of military occupational and environmental health protection.

CF commanders are responsible for the health of their subordinates, but military medical personnel must provide them with the advice and services necessary to promote, protect, and restore health. Clinical quality improvement programs, clinical research, and epidemiology in particular are fundamental functions of health authorities. This is supported within the CF by the Surgeon General's Health Research Program, by various DRDC efforts, and by many other Canadian and allied partners contributing to military health research.

CANADIAN FORCES HEALTH RESEARCH

The Surgeon General Health Research Program is coordinated with the work of DRDC and our other partners. Most CF clinical and epidemiological research must, however, be conducted by CFHS staff who practice clinical and population health and have direct access to CF health information and a network of health institutional partners. The assumptions, conclusions and application of much military health research require a synthesis of many clinical, operational, privacy, resource, regulatory, and medico-legal factors that only come together within CFHS. This limits our military health research capacity since most of our clinicians and scientific staff have other military and clinical duties that limit the time available to conduct research.

Our military medical roles are unlike anything experienced by our civilian counterparts. For example, the Medical Service has suffered the highest rate of casualties in Afghanistan after the combat arms. This highlights that our imperative to conduct continuous research to improve CF health capabilities is partly driven by our own direct application of what we learn to the health protection of CF members. Whatever the research area, CFHS clinician-researchers may well be personally applying their findings to CF members and casualties shortly thereafter, and I am accountable for the results. Hostile operational and environmental threats evolve constantly, and in order to do the best we can to protect our country and ourselves, a robust national military health research capability is critical.

The past few years of intense operations have re-emphasized the operational and clinical importance of continuous military health research and scientific analysis. Combat operations with heavy casualties focus the efforts of those who must directly protect and treat our CF members. My mandates in this regard stimulated me to direct better formalization, coordination, and revitalization of the multiple Science and Technology (S&T) efforts of my directorates and clinician-scientists, better coordination with external partners to maximize benefits derived from limited S&T resources, and better articulate my research program's place within the broader Defence S&T enterprise. I therefore directed the development of a formal health research strategy, which was launched earlier this year and is now well underway in implementation. The mission of our research program is to direct, support and assist in the research, technology and analysis and the development, engineering and evaluation of outcome-based science and technology initiatives that affect the performance, health, and welfare of our fighting forces wherever we serve, protecting Canadians at home and abroad.

Virtually everything the CFHS does must be based on best practices derived from scientific evidence. For health professions and institutions, this is a requirement for licensing and accreditation, but in armed forces, failure to maintain a robust S&T capability would at best mean an ill-informed and inefficient health program, wasted money and loss of credibility, sub-optimal health care, and unnecessary absence from duty. At worst, it could mean serious medical and force protection capability gaps, unnecessary disability and casualties, loss of support from allies that do conduct adequate research, loss of public trust in the CF's ability to care for its personnel and, above all, constraints on the operational readiness and deployability of CF personnel.

Since the CFHS is primarily a health service delivery organization, our research efforts prioritize essential high-impact, lower-cost research, as well as close research collaboration with allies. While this approach is adequate, it can be significantly enhanced through supplementation by and coordination with the research capabilities of academia, particularly during periods of high intensity operations that present new, grave, and complex health threats and stresses to CF personnel.

The existing military health research program is supported by a network of organizations and activities that support CFHS requirements. Much of what CFHS routinely does internally to fulfil its mandate constitutes S&T, with portions of the program conducted by DRDC and our other partners. Our sources of S&T can be categorized into four groups:

1. CFHS personnel conduct research either through their faculty appointments in academic medical centres, their routine work within CFHS directorates, or in collaborative activities with DRDC. Most of our officers in post-graduate health programs also produce research theses that address CF health research interests.

2. Within DND, most DRDC 'Partnership Groups' (six specifically organized groups that formulate and manage the DND S&T enterprise) provide some health-related S&T. DRDC's medical interventions thrust (a subset of one partner group) has long worked collaboratively with CFHS in medical CBRN defence and military operational medicine. More recently and through another thrust, a collaborative psychological research effort has begun. Several other DND elements also contribute significant S&T through CFHS personnel embedded with them.

3. Key Canadian partners external to DND include civilian health research centres at various universities and community hospitals where CFHS clinicians are embedded, elements of Health Canada and the Public Health Agency of Canada, Statistics Canada, Veterans Affairs Canada, and industrial partners. Our ability and capacity to engage other elements of academia has, however, not yet progressed beyond the occasional small contract. Since this is primarily personality-based and not institutionally managed, the effort is not currently sustainable and remains personality driven.

4. Finally, many requirements are addressed in collaboration with our allies. For example, with the US we have an integrated officer with the National Center

for Medical Intelligence, representation on internal health science bodies like the Armed Forces Epidemiology Board and Institute of Surgical Research, and many other means to access the US defence department's vast network of health science research resources. Extensive S&T is also derived from participation in quadripartite alliance medical committees, NATO's Committee of the Chiefs of Military Medical Services (COMEDS), NATO Standardization Agency (NSA) committees, the NATO Research and Technology Organization's Health, Medicine, and Protection committee, and The (Quintepartite) Technical Cooperation Program.

Our strategy consists of eight Block areas for military health research; each led by a CFHS senior officer with relevant functional responsibilities. All CFHS research is assigned to a specific Block in accordance with our Health Research Strategy's Accountability Framework. The Army, Navy, Air Force and Special Operations Command Surgeons also participate with their respective DRDC research boards to help ensure that health-related research concerns are informed with clinical and operational health advice and coordinated within the Surgeon General Health Research Program.

The CFHS Blocks are: 1. Operational medicine (CBRN, aerospace medicine, hyperbaric medicine, personal and force protection equipment, extreme environments, medical intelligence); 2. Trauma Care (brain injury, haemorrhage control, resuscitation, combat casualty care, rehabilitation, diagnostics, critical care, etc); 3. Public/Occupational Health (tropical medicine, non-hostile health hazards, communicable diseases, health promotion); 4. Mental Health (deployment mental health, community mental health, specific treatments, resiliency, outcomes); 5. Health Care Resource Management (finance, health information management, health care utilization, system performance, supply chain management); 6. Primary Care (validation and outcome measurement, analysis and evaluation, pharmacy spectrum of care, quality of care, medical standards, clinic practice guidelines, patient safety); 7. Epidemiology / Population Health (validation of interventions, prospective health data analysis, retrospective data analysis, disease surveillance, deployment health outcomes, clinical preventive care outcomes, compliance rates – performance measurement); and, 8. Human Resources (learning systems, training validation, scope of practice, attraction and retention, employment models).

Through these Blocks, the Surgeon General Health Research Board identifies research requirements to address priority CF health research interests. Research issues are assigned to relevant directorates and clinicians where appropriate, and those that can be addressed by DRDC and other partners are communicated through partnership groups and other mechanisms. Examples of CFHS research interests include oxygen carrying resuscitation fluids, validated alternatives to live tissue models for training, fatigue countermeasures, field-friendly and non-sedating analgesic, chemical and biological therapeutics, and many others.

Since 2009, the CFHS has produced more than 43 peer reviewed publications and a far larger number of technical reports. Some currently funded studies include the following:

- Cesamet Study
- Rh-EPO – Effects on Septic Shock
- Rh-EPO – Effects on Hemorrhagic Shock
- Pneumonia – Post Surgery Study
- WWII Study – Stress Injuries
- Injury, Work and Health Study (Pilot)
- Organ Specific Biomarkers of Injury
- CF Cancer and Mortality Study
- MH Service Utilization
- Damage Control Resuscitation Study
- Prospective Randomized Optimal Platelet Plasma Ratio Clinical Trial
- fMRI and PTSD study
- Night Vision Goggle / Neck Strain Study
- HMCS Chicoutimi Crew Medical Monitoring

We're progressively improving our capture of all S&T undertaken across CFHS, but our list remains incomplete because so much S&T is done within the routine business mandates of clinicians, directorates, and others.

With respect to combat trauma research, its focus is guided by various databases, with an important focus on pre-hospital interventions that might make a difference in survival based on data such as summarized in Figure 1.2. Tension pneumothorax, for example, is the 2nd leading preventable cause of death on the battlefield, as seen in Figure 1.3.

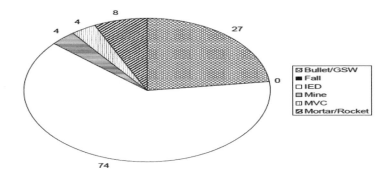

Figure 1.2: How People Die in Ground Combat [2]

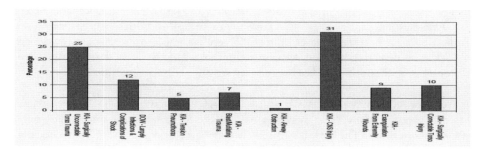

Figure 1.3. R3MMU % Casualty Distribution

Tactical Combat Casualty Care training was therefore expanded to permit trained personnel to decompress them far forward on the battlefield. An observant CFHS clinician-scientist in Kandahar studied the outcome, analyzed cases of under- and mis-use, and identified a training gap in that catheters were being applied too medially in the cardiac box. A new guideline for decompression at the nipple line was therefore recommended, was subsequently adopted by key Tactical Combat Casualty Care Committees and by the Pre-Hospital Trauma Life Support Course, and is now standard pre-hospital practice around the world.

While trying to understand trauma coagulopathy, a US military autopsy study found that 86% of potentially preventable deaths were from truncal hemorrhage, and that the development of coagulopathy contributes to exsanguination. In collaboration with Sunnybrook Health Sciences Centre and DRDC, CFHS researchers conducted the world's first prospective study to show a critical clotting factor deficiency related to the degree of shock that contributes to coagulopathy. Along the same lines, another US study demonstrated that a high ratio of Fresh Frozen Plasma to Packed Red Blood Cells was associated with lower mortality. This led CFHS researchers to establish the world's first feasibility Randomized Controlled Trial of transfusion practice to study if a 1 to 1 ratio of plasma to red cells improves survival.

The Trial on 1:1 Transfusion Practice (TRAP trial) helped inform the design of a larger US Army Damage Control Resuscitation trial called the Prospective, Randomized Optimal Platelets and Plasma Ratio Trial. With CFHS, Sunnybrook, and DRDC participation, it will examine whether a Damage Control resuscitation strategy using a pre-filled 1 to 1 ratio will reduce mortality from exsanguination in trauma patients compared to a traditional laboratory-driven massive transfusion protocol.

Continuing with a focus on combat trauma, it was generally accepted that the utility of ultrasound in the hands of non-specialists at far forward-deployed medical stations was ill-advised. Due to the potential benefits, a trial with 2-D FAST ultrasound was conducted by CFHS personnel at three Forward Operating Bases (FOBs). With specialist correlation at the Kandahar hospital of cases from FOBs, results showed over 95% sensitivity and specificity in detecting hemoperitoneum, hemothorax, and shrapnel injury, resulting in better triage and prioritization of limited forward air medical evacuation resources.

A fire aboard the submarine HMCS Chicoutimi in October 2004 tragically claimed one life and exposed many crew members to products of combustion under extremely stressful conditions. The CFHS subsequently embarked on a study to systematically monitor and study their health outcomes while serving in the CF and post-release. It is planned to evaluate health impacts through a retrospective records review this year, and prospective biennial assessments starting in 2011.

The Casualty Protective Equipment Analysis (CASPEAN) project is a collaborative effort between the Army, DRDC, the Ontario Coroner, and CFHS. The aim is to increase survivability by validating tactical procedures, equipment acquisition, and Research and Development (R&D) efforts by better understanding the mechanisms of battlefield trauma and by determining the relationship between threats, the environment, and the performance of in-service vehicle and personal protection systems. It is but one example of many highly successful collaborations between CFHS and DRDC in addressing major health threats. Medical staff in Afghanistan and at the Canadian Forces Environmental Medical Establishment in Toronto provide human factors investigation/analysis reports and clinical reports, autopsy reports for those Killed In Action, clinical injury data for Wounded In Action, and support in identifying casualties and conducting surveys. Among other things, it has guided the development and modification of protection systems and test methodologies, and informs equipment acquisition, design, and integration for the Army.

In addition to studying physical injuries, deploying troops receive pre-deployment resilience training and operational stress education, and are well supported in theatre by mental health staff. On return from Afghanistan, all continue to have access to extensive mental health care and undergo an Enhanced Post-deployment Screening Process to identify those who need help. Many with previously unrecognized problems are identified through this process, which includes four validated health questionnaires and clinical interviews. The results of screening show about 4% reporting PTSD symptoms, 4% major depression symptoms, and about 6% PTSD and/or major depression. About 13% reported any mental health problem. Most are thus identified at screening, although a minority have significant symptoms needing further evaluation. The database is updated and monitored with each rotation of forces and with changes in the condition of operationally-injured CF members. This data source is helping guide our research and mental health programs (Figure 1.4).

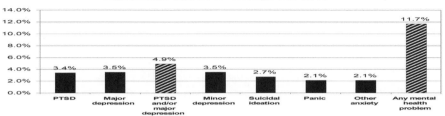

Figure 1.4. Enhanced Post-deployment Screening Findings.[3]

Understanding mental health and how it is manifested is a challenge. To help us better understand the relationship between mental health and brain function, CFHS personnel initiated a study that will use functional magnetic resonance imaging (fMRI) to explore the neuronal circuitry underlying PTSD. Subjects will include individuals involved in operations who developed PTSD or no psychiatric illness. Recent research has suggested that brain activity at rest is characterized by correlated, low frequency oscillations within the so-called "default mode network" parts of the brain, and has identified alterations in network activity during the resting state in psychiatric disorders. Recent results from a pilot study suggest that the network can be used to distinguish between those who will and will not develop PTSD. A greater understanding of the related neuronal circuitry at rest may allow the development of early detection and treatment.

Many allied and Canadian personnel in Afghanistan have suffered mild traumatic brain injury (mTBI) as a result of combat and exposure to blast. Since there are knowledge gaps regarding this kind of concussion, CFHS convened a multi-national mTBI expert panel in 2008 to critically assess available evidence in order to recommend a CF surveillance and clinical management strategy. Their conclusions and subsequent data affected our practices, as well as our research approach and priorities. Data has since confirmed the panel's expectation that the prevalence of self-reported TBI would be on the very mild end of the spectrum. The panel also determined that most cases would be due to causes in garrison such as sports, falls, car accidents, etc. Long-term non-specific symptoms such as headache, dizziness, fatigue, irritability, etc. were also found to be driven largely by psychosocial factors rather than mechanical injury. Data has shown that 86% of CF members with multiple post-concussive symptoms had not had a concussion while deployed, that symptoms were nearly as common in those who had a non-TBI injury, and were much more strongly associated with mental health problems

(Odds Ratio of 34). These findings thus validated our screening and management approach, which focuses on acute neurological care and a longer term focus on treatable mental health conditions.

Suicide is something the CF takes very seriously and it is an important focus area for our research. For the last 15 years, an average of 10.35 male regular force soldiers have committed suicide (female numbers are too low to permit valid studies) and a majority have been among CF members who have never been on an operational deployment. Last fall (2009), we convened an International civil-military suicide Expert Panel that examined prevention efforts in the CF and among allies, as well as evidence-based best practices to enhance our current program. It found that we have an effective program which compares favourably within and outside Canada, and most of its recommendations are already implemented or underway. The majority of suicides are a result of untreated mental health conditions. If caught early, effective care is the most reliable intervention to prevent the tendency towards suicide. The effectiveness of our program is evidenced by the fact that, even though we have been involved in combat for eight years, our suicide rates have not increased statistically and remain about 20% below the age- and sex-adjusted rate in the general population. Largely by enhancing the quality of care and by strengthening confidentiality and career protection, we are also seeing a reduction in stigma surrounding mental health conditions. Half of those returning from deployment with PTSD symptoms are in care within 5 months, versus a median treatment delay of 5.5 years in 2002. Other mental health research initiatives include determining the prevalence and co-variates of post-deployment mental health problems and the incidence of more severe forms in theatre, the prevalence of self-reported TBI, and co-variates of multiple post-concussive symptoms.

These are but some examples of the research conducted by CFHS or in collaboration with our key partners and allies.

The Future

The aim of the Surgeon General Health Research Strategy is to maximize the synergistic possibilities of closer collaboration within DND and with external partners. Although CFHS is rich with unexplored data, we rely heavily on DRDC's capabilities in many areas, on the capabilities of other partners in other areas, and we must work closely together to address CF health interests as we have in the past to produce tremendous results for CF health protection.

Our future vision also includes making greater use of data for analyses, quality improvement, and research through digitization and automation. Research using data in paper files requires a tremendous amount of staff effort, but the CF Health Information System for clinical and health services management data is already partly rolled out, and its Force Health Protection Information Management System sub-component will consolidate occupational and environmental hazard data. In combination with accurate personnel administrative data, studies linking people, occupational hazards, and clinical outcomes should become more timely and accurate.

As many of you know, the unique context of military threats, occupational exposures, environments, and operations often require very targeted and applied research in order to be applicable to the CF. CFHS and DRDC are well-resourced by DND to conduct such research, and we manage to conduct essential military health research independently or in collaboration with allied defence departments. CFHS is often approached, however, by civilian academics interested in researching military health issues. Unlike the US, UK and AUS, Canada does not have a centre that harnesses or coordinates academia's efforts in military and veteran health research. We welcome such interest since there are many complex issues that would benefit from civilian academic study and since much more elective research of military relevance might be conducted to enhance the formulation of military health policies, programs, and capabilities. Since the findings of some government-conducted research are occasionally perceived skeptically by elements of the public and media, the independence of an arms-length academic study can also be very helpful.

For these reasons, I have been pursuing the concept of a civilian academic network and institute, independent of government, to provide interested academics with a mechanism by which they could learn of militarily-relevant issues, obtain information, share research ideas and mutual program visibility, and seek collaboration from like-minded academics, the Department of National Defence, and Veterans Affairs Canada, all in the interests of serving the health research interests of current and former armed forces members and their families. Although ethics review and federal regulations regarding health data disclosure would have to be satisfied, I would encourage relevant research by academia through the provision of information and the assignment of a CFHS adviser or co-investigator for specific academic research projects.

In pursuing this over the last few years, it became clear that the diversity of academic interest and the breadth of military and veterans' health issues precluded any single university from having all the capabilities necessary to cover all military and veteran health research interests. RMCC and Queen's certainly cannot cover them all, but they have taken the initiative at their own expense to progress this concept through the organization of this Forum and of a broad network of researchers interested in supporting and supplementing the defence and veterans affairs health research programs. I hope to see the success of this great service to the health of our military personnel, for which I am deeply grateful and congratulate the leaders of this initiative on behalf of the armed forces. The Chief of Defence Staff's presence as a keynote dinner speaker is just one indication of the importance to the CF of this initiative and of the commitment of everyone in attendance.

I hope this overview has given you an outline of the breadth of military health issues, the consequent scope of my Health Research Program, and the opportunities for collaboration. Combined efforts with DRDC and other partners over the years continue to yield benefits to the health of CF members, and we hope to enjoy the health benefits that might result from broader collaboration with academia.

[1]National Defence, *Surgeon Generals Report: Building On Our Strategy*, Canadian Forces Health Services Group, DGM-10-04-00001, 2010, 4.

[2]Adapted from Colonel Ron Bellamy, "Presentation to the Joint Health Services Support Vision 2010 Working Group."

[3]Dr Mark Zamorski, "Report on the findings of the Enhanced Post-deployment Screening of those returning from OP ARCHER/TASK FORCE AFGHANISTAN/OP ATHENA as of 11 Feb 2011"

CHAPTER 2

Research in the Life Courses of Canadian Military Veterans and Their Families

David J. Pedlar, PhD, Director and James M. Thompson, MD CCFP(EM) FCFP, Medical Advisor, Research Directorate, Veterans Affairs Canada

ABSTRACT

This chapter aims at identifying research challenges for veterans' health research in Canada from the Veterans Affairs Canada perspective. Following World War II veterans' health research flourished in the Department of Veterans' Affairs (DVA) hospitals and facilities. Over time, Canadian veterans' health research capacity greatly diminished and research focus shifted from care of the recently ill and injured to care of the aging and elderly. Today, more Canadians have been affected by military service-related injuries and illnesses than any time since the Korean War. VAC research functions support innovation that is essential for VAC to meet its mandate. Four main challenges have been identified: (1) Veterans' health research must consider health, disability and the determinants of health status of all Canadian veterans, not just those receiving VAC benefits; (2) Determine effects of military service on the life courses of veterans and their families; (3) Identify optimum approaches to the care of veterans and their families; (4) Manage the explosion of expert opinion and research findings; and (5) Strengthen capacity in Canadian veterans' health research. A coordinated national vision and partnerships with federal, provincial and university researchers are needed to inform policy, programs and services to meet the needs of today's military veterans and their families.

INTRODUCTION

Transition to civilian life is a key step in the lives of military veterans and their families. While many do well, some whose health is affected by military service can face challenges throughout their life courses. Since Confederation, Canada has recognized veterans' services and sacrifices both by compensating them for health effects of military service, and by helping them to re-establish themselves in civilian life.[1] Canada, like other nations, has committed significant resources to assisting military personnel with transition to civilian life, but there is only sparse research literature on veterans' re-establishment experiences in Canada and around the world, particularly for those not receiving benefits from veterans' administrations.[2]

Veterans' health research plays a key role in providing sound evidence on which to base effective policy, programs and services. Immediately following both World Wars, the focus was on re-establishment, rehabilitation and the management of sub-acute complications of war injuries and illness.[3] When those cohorts reached middle age, the focus switched to chronic health conditions.[4] Throughout the last half of the 20th century, Canadian veterans' health research was dominated by the one million Canadians who served in uniform in WWII. The focus of both veterans' administration and research shifted with them as they aged to chronic health disorders and midlife issues, and then to care of the elderly.[5]

At the end of WWII, Canadians agreed on the importance of providing outstanding medical care to returning veterans, but Medicare was not yet in place and veterans' services were focused on aging WWI veterans.[6] To meet this challenge, the Department of Veterans Affairs (DVA) was established in 1944 and immediately developed a comprehensive rehabilitation, health care and financial benefits program called "The Veterans' Charter."[7] Under physician W.P. Warner's leadership following his appointment to lead Treatment Services in 1945, DVA developed the first national model for integrating medical care, education and research in Canada.[8] The 1963 DVA Annual Report listed 89 veterans' health research projects in DVA facilities.[9] Canadian veterans' health research capacity diminished greatly in the 1960s and 70s when DVA facilities were transferred to the provinces along with the health professionals who worked in them. Veterans' health research then had to compete for resources with diverse civilian interests.

Canada's recent military challenges have produced new generations of veterans and their families. More Canadians have been affected by military service-related injuries and illnesses in recent years than any era since the Korean War. These "new" veterans and their families live in a nation with very different health care and social support systems than had existed just after WWII, but Canadian research on the new generations of veterans and their families has been limited and not coordinated.

This chapter identifies the research challenges Veterans Affairs Canada (VAC) faces in meeting the needs of veterans and their families. Canada needs renewed capacity in veterans' health research. Veterans Affairs Canada congratulates Queen's University and the Royal Military College of Canada for hosting this first Canadian Military and Veterans' Health Research Forum. VAC was pleased to assist in planning the forum, and welcomes the opportunity to foster renewed Canadian veterans' health research.

INNOVATION THROUGH RESEARCH AT VETERANS AFFAIRS CANADA

VAC's mandate is to support "the care, treatment, or re-establishment in civil life of any person who served in the Canadian Forces or merchant navy or in the naval, army or air forces or merchant navies of Her Majesty, of any person who has otherwise engaged in pursuits relating to war, and of any other person designated ... and the care of the dependants or survivors of any person referred to ..."[10] VAC has several business lines to meet this mandate: compensation and financial support $2.13B, health care and re-establishment $1.14B, and remembrance and commemoration $46M.[11]

"Research" is systematic investigation to increase knowledge. Primary research collects and analyses data to discover new knowledge. Critical review of existing health-related expert opinion and scientific evidence (HRESE) can provide some answers. Expert opinion can fill gaps in primary research. Knowledge exchange is the process of getting research findings into the hands of those who write policy, design programs or work directly with veterans and their families.[12] The VAC Research Directorate engages in and supports research that supports and advances VAC priorities.

VAC research functions (Table 2.1) support the innovation that is essential for VAC to meet its mandate. Research informs effective programs, services and benefits that best fit the needs of veterans and their families. Research plays a key role in clarifying issues in controversial times: during the 1990s, when parliamentary committees and experts called for significant changes in how Canada provided for serving personnel, veterans and families, the Veterans Care Needs research program played a pivotal role in supplying evidence to shape new solutions.[13]

- Interpret and monitor military and veteran health issues.
- Conduct primary research linked to VAC priorities.
- Review expert opinion and scientific evidence to support decision-making for policy, programs and service delivery.
- Research partnerships with DND/CF, advisory bodies, universities, and allied countries.
- Promote leadership and capacity building in military and veteran health in Canada.
- Knowledge exchange.

Table 2.1. VAC Research Functions.

A FRAMEWORK FOR VETERANS' HEALTH RESEARCH

VAC's Research Directorate uses a framework with four core concepts: health including well-being, disability, determinants of health, and the life course perspective (Table 2.2). This framework recognizes that veterans seek support from VAC when they have problems with health, disability and the determinants of health throughout their life courses, and the diverse biopsychosocial dimensions of successful re-establishment in civilian life identified by VAC, DND/CF and Parliamentary committees.[14]

The framework accounts for current consensus expert opinion that physical and mental health conditions and their attendant impairments are not in themselves disabilities, but that a person with health impairments becomes "dis-abled" when encountering barriers to optimal function.[15] Determinants of health can also be outcomes of health, for example when physical or mental health impairments interfere with earning an income.

The life course core concept (Figure 2.1) recognizes that health and disability fluctuate over time as result of current and prior exposure to determinants of health.[16] Military service shapes future life courses in positive and negative ways.[17] Since Confederation, VAC and its predecessor agencies have served veterans applying for assistance throughout their post-service life courses (Figure 2.2).

The framework is broadly inclusive of diverse research activities, including quantitative versus qualitative methodologies; population health versus individual studies; primary versus applied research; and original research versus evidence synthesis. The framework proved useful in the work of the VAC Research Directorate, for example in the design and analysis of the Survey on Transition to Civilian Life.[18]

"Health" – Physical, mental and social well-being, with and without disorders.

"Disability" – Lessening of ability that occurs as result of barriers encountered by persons with health impairments, including coping or adapting internally, and barriers in the person's external social and physical environment.

"Determinants of health" – Range of personal, social, economic and environmental factors that determine the health status of individuals or populations.

1. Income, social status
2. Social support networks
3. Education, literacy
4. Employment/working conditions
5. Physical environments
6. Personal health practices
7. Healthy childhood development
8. Individual capacity and coping skills
9. Biology and genetic endowment
10. Health services
11. Gender
12. Culture

"Life course" – A perspective viewing a person's current health and disability status as fluctuating along a trajectory dependent on prior health, disability and determinants of health.

Table 2.2. Framework for veterans' research.

WHO, "Health Promotion Glossary," (Geneva: World Health Organization, 1998), 36, WHO/HPR/HEP/98.1; Public Health Agency of Canada, "What determines Health?" Government of Canada, (July, 2009), http://www.phac-aspc.gc.ca/ph-sp/determinants/index-eng.php, accessed 14 April 2011.

Adapted from: C. Hertzman and C. Power, "Health and human development: understandings from life-course research," DevNeuropsychol 24, no. 2-3(2003):719-744; D. Kuh, Y. Ben-Shlomo, J. Lynch, J. Hallqvist, and C. Power, "Life course epidemiology," J Epidemiol Community Health 57, 10 (2003): 778-783. Erratum in: J Epidemiol Community Health 57, 11, (2003): 914.

Adapted from "Definition of Health," Preamble to the Constitution of the World Health Organization as adopted by the International Health Conference, New York, 19-22 June, 1946; signed on 22 July 1946 by the representatives of 61 States (Official Records of the World Health Organization, 2, 100) and entered into force on 7 April 1948.

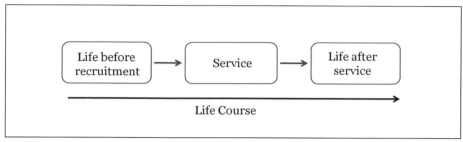

Figure 2.1. Life course view of veterans' research.

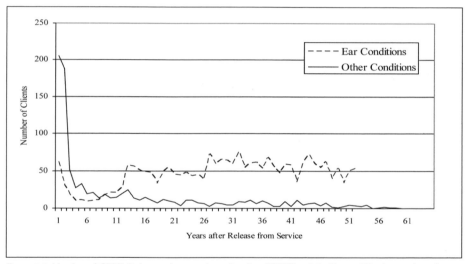

Figure 2.2. Number of CF VAC clients who served in other than WW II and the Korean War, by number of years after release from service when they were first found eligible for disability benefits in fiscal year 2008-09.

April 2008 to March 2009 fiscal year. Does not include CF personnel first found eligible for disability benefits prior to release.

CANADA'S VETERANS TODAY

Estimates of the number of veterans living in the Canadian general population are based on a variety of data, including self-report veteran identifier questions on the 1971 census,[19] in the 1988 Canadian Labour Force Survey to identify women veterans, and in the 2003 Canadian Community Health Survey.[20] As of March 2010, there were an estimated 749,400 Canadian military veterans alive in Canada, 155,700 who served in WWII or the Korean War, and 593,700 who served in the Canadian Forces outside those two wars, and about 83% of all veterans were not receiving benefits from VAC (Table 2.3). There were 78,100 survivors of deceased veterans receiving benefits through VAC, but there are no population estimates of family members of all veterans.

WWII and Korean War veterans are now very elderly, and for the first time their declining number is about to drop below the increasing number of CF veterans who served since Korea (Figure 2.3). Post-Korean War CF veterans receiving benefits from VAC range in age from young adults to very elderly (Figure 2.4).

Table 2.4 shows that veterans have received disability awards or pensions from VAC for a variety of physical and mental health conditions. These are counts of conditions for veterans currently in receipt of those types of benefits, not number of clients. The table shows only conditions for which veterans applied for and received benefits from VAC. It is not a measure of the prevalence of physical and mental health conditions in those veterans.

	Total Population	VAC Clients (Percent of Total Population)
World War II and Korean War (KW) Veterans	155,700[A]	68,800[A] (44%)
Veterans who served in other than WWII and KW Regular Force 314,200[A] Reserve Force 279,600[A]	593,700[A]	59,600[B] (10%)
Subtotal	*749,400*	*124,200 (17%)*
Canadian Forces Serving Personnel Regular Force 69,000[C] Primary Reserve Force 26,000[C]	95,000[C]	9,200[B] (10%)
Subtotal	*--*	*133,400*
Survivor family members of deceased Veterans WWII and Korean War 71,500[A] CF other than WWII and KW 6,600[A]	--[D]	78,100[A]
Total	*--[D]*	*211,500*

Notes: A – VAC Quarterly Fact Sheet March 2010.
B – Very approximate estimates: VAC does not require date-of-release records in many cases (VAC Statistics Directorate estimates for March 2010).
C – DND Plans and Priorities 2009-10 http://www.tbs-sct.gc.ca/rpp/2009-2010/inst/dnd/dnd01-eng.asp#sec1_e.
D – No data.

Table 2.3. Estimates of Canadian veteran populations, March 2010.

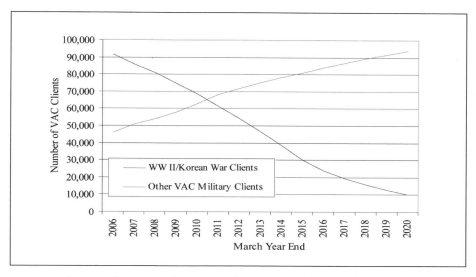

Figure 2.3. Projected trends in numbers of veterans receiving benefits through VAC.

VAC Statistics Directorate Client and Expenditure Forecast, August 2010. "Other VAC Military Clients" includes serving CF personnel as well as veterans.

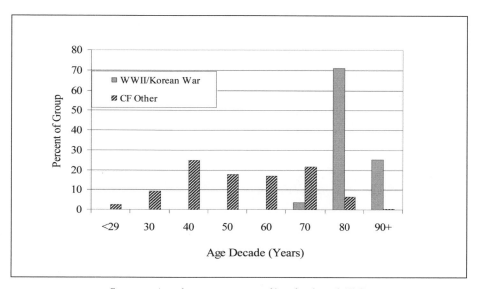

Figure 2.4. Age of veterans in receipt of benefits through VAC.

VAC Statistics Directorate, September 2010. "CF other" means serving and former CF personnel who served in other than WWII and the Korean War.

Medical Condition Category	Service in WWII and Korean War	Canadian Forces Service other than WWII and Korean War	Total
Ear	57.2%	27.4%	39.2%
Musculoskeletal	13.7%	47.8%	34.3%
Other Physical Trauma	10.9%	8.5%	9.5%
Psychiatric Conditions	3.0%	7.0%	5.4%
Digestive System	3.1%	2.2%	2.5%
Circulatory System	2.8%	1.6%	2.1%
Nervous System	0.5%	2.4%	1.7%
Bronchi and Lungs	2.1%	0.6%	1.2%
Skin/Subcutaneous Tissue	1.2%	0.5%	0.8%
Infectious and Parasitic Disease	1.5%	0.1%	0.7%
Eye	0.7%	0.5%	0.6%
Nose and Larynx	1.2%	0.2%	0.6%
Genitourinary System	0.7%	0.5%	0.6%
Cancer and Malignant Tumours	0.8%	0.3%	0.5%
Benign Tumours	0.2%	0.1%	0.1%
Other General Diseases	0.2%	0.2%	0.2%
Other	0.1%	0.0%	0.0%
Congenital Malformations	0.1%	0.0%	0.0%
Blood/Blood Forming Organs	0.0%	0.0%	0.0%
Ill-Defined Causes	0.0%	0.0%	0.0%
Poisoning and Intoxication	0.0%	0.0%	0.0%
Pregnancy/Childbirth/Puerperal	0.0%	0.0%	0.0%
Total – Percent	100.0%	100.0%	100.0%
Total – Number of conditions (not Veterans)	87,367	133,132	220,499

Table 2.4. Categories of medical conditions for which Veterans Affairs Canada clients were receiving disability benefits as of March 2010.

VAC Statistics Directorate. This is a count of conditions, not individuals: individuals can have two or more conditions entitling them to a disability pension or disability award.
Canadian Forces Service other than World War II and Korean War includes still-serving personnel.
Musculoskeletal includes Disc Disease and Spinal Conditions, Fractures and Amputations.
Other Physical Trauma includes Accidents/External Violence, Gunshot Wounds and Gunshot Wounds/Trauma (Accidental).

Challenge #1 – Understand all Canadian Veterans, not just those receiving Benefits through VAC

The needs of WWII and Korean War veterans remain a priority for VAC, but reviews conducted in the 1990s made it clear that VAC had to transform to meet the needs of veterans who served in other than WWII and the Korean War. An estimated 90% of these veterans are not receiving benefits from VAC, and little is known about them.

Since WWI, research focused on the health of veterans receiving care and benefits from DVA and its predecessor agencies. When conducting a mortality review prior to WWII to test the pre-aging hypothesis, Burke (1939) noted there was no data for veterans not receiving disability pensions. Woods (1953) described WWII veterans receiving care from DVA. Canadian veterans' research peaked in the 1960s, for example a study of geriatric veterans visiting an outpatient Edmonton DVA facility,[21] studies of Canadian veterans who had been prisoners of war in Hong Kong,[22] an analysis of inpatients in DVA facilities,[23] and a qualitative study of veterans with chronic mental health conditions.[24] VAC's 1997 Review of Veterans Care Needs survey (RVCN) and the 1999 VAC Canadian Forces client survey yielded ground-breaking information on VAC clients that supported transformation of VAC programs, but this work did not include veterans who were not VAC clients.[25]

Cycle 2.1 of the 2003 Canadian Community Health Survey included Veteran identifier questions, for the first time sampling veterans living in the general population. There were unexplained health differences between veterans and the general population, including higher rates of activity limitation and arthritis, but military service was identified by self-report.[26]

Life After Service Studies

The Life After Service Studies (LASS) program of research conducted by partnerships of VAC, DND/CF and Statistics Canada are beginning to shed greater light on Canadian veterans of recent eras. The LASS studies identified veterans by linking DND, VAC and Statistics Canada databases, and included veterans not receiving benefits through VAC.[27]

In the *Income Study*,[28] Statistics Canada linked release data with tax records for Regular Force CF veterans who released during 1998-2007. Average income decreased after release, then rose and exceeded pre-release average income by the end of the study decade (1998-2007). Although rates of low income were low, vulnerable subgroups were identified: those who released under age 20, or as recruits, or involuntarily. The Survey on Transition to Civilian Life (STCL) was a telephone survey conducted by Statistics Canada for CF Regular Force veterans who released during 1998-2007.[29] Although many had done well following transition to civilian life, the group was worse off than the general population for some aspects of health, disability and determinants of health. The

Canadian Forces Cancer and Mortality Study (CF-CAMS), led by CF Health Services, is studying mortality and cancer incidence among serving and released CF personnel who enrolled from 1972 to 2006.

IMPORTANCE OF POPULATION HEALTH STUDIES

While it is very important to qualitatively understand individual lived lives, quantitative population health studies provide measures of the health, disability and determinants of health status of all veterans necessary for supporting mitigation policies and programs. A series of ongoing, longitudinal population health studies rather than the occasional point-in-time cross-sectional studies like STCL provide the life course perspective necessary to identify and responsively mitigate causes of adverse Veteran health outcomes over time.

Better data systems are needed in Canada to identify veterans for population health research. Currently, nominal rolls of veterans have to be compiled retrospectively, a complex task rarely yielding complete lists.[30] In STCL, the response rate for non-clients (59%) was much lower than for VAC client groups (84%) owing to lack of current contact information.[31].

CHALLENGE #2 – DETERMINE IMPACT OF MILITARY SERVICE ON LIFE COURSES OF VETERAN AND THEIR FAMILIES

Much remains to be learned about the life course effects of military service. In the general population, advancing age is associated with acquiring chronic health conditions.[32] There is evidence that military service and combat exposure can be associated with positive as well as adverse health outcomes.[33] War veterans have long had controversial health concerns unique to warfare.[34]

The degree to which later life health and disability is attributable to prior military service remains unclear for many conditions arising later in life,[35] but there is good evidence that military service can impact some throughout their life courses.[36] Some later-life physical and mental health conditions have been associated with military service,[37] but association is not proof of causality.[38] There is some emerging evidence that the positive and adverse health effects of military service can be trans generational, impacting families and descendants of veterans.[39] Lack of research on determinants of veterans' health encountered both before and after military service is a significant gap.[40]

Challenge #3 – Identify Optimum Approaches to the Care of Veterans and their Families

WWI veterans' re-establishment programs ushered a new era of enhanced health care and management of disabilities for Canada's military veterans.[41] Free health care and broad social safety nets for all Canadians were decades away, but injured veterans were provided a greater degree of access to hospitals and rehabilitation services than most Canadians. The WWII Veterans Charter enhanced veterans' support significantly,[42] as did the New Veterans Charter of 2006.[43] The challenge of identifying optimum diagnostic and treatment approaches for chronic health conditions and the management of disabilities is greater today than ever before.

Challenge #4 – Manage Explosion of Expert Opinion and Research Findings

HRESE is accumulating at a rapid rate. The frequency of citations in the U.S. National Medical Library PubMed database found using the search word "Veteran" is a crude measure (Figure 2.5). Although the Medline database is incomplete historically and does not capture all Veteran's health research publications, the figure demonstrates both the very large numbers of research publications already available, and the rapidly increasing rate of publication. The research has helped to support better compensation, policy and services for veterans, but with opportunity comes the need to manage this ever-expanding pool of knowledge.

HRESE uncertainty challenges adjudication of claims for entitlement to disability benefits and decision-making about diagnostics and treatments. Expert opinions vary in quality and take divergent views. Scientific evidence varies in quality, quantity and consistency. Procedures for dealing with HRESE continue to evolve but have four common phases: acquire, assess, adapt and apply. In the U.S., an Institute of Medicine Committee recommended that certainty for causality be communicated using statements of probability not possibility.[44] In Australia, the Repatriation Medical Authority (RMA) was established by legislation to systematically assess HRESE to develop statements of principle (SOP) that become legally binding for adjudicating eligibility claims.[45]

The rate of production of Veteran-specific literature reviews is not keeping pace with the rate of publication of individual studies. Rigorously developed syntheses of HRESE are needed to deal with uncertainty and inform best practices in both disability compensation and the care of veterans and their families.

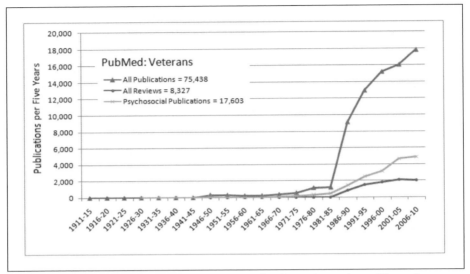

Figure 2.5: Five-year number of PubMed citations found using the search term "Veteran."

CHALLENGE #5 –STRENGTHEN CAPACITY IN CANADIAN VETERANS' HEALTH RESEARCH

A basic principle of health research is that the findings must apply to the population of interest, in this case Canadian veterans and their families. One dimension of this challenge is to determine what research can be applied in Canada, and another is to set priorities for both new primary research and reviews of existing HRESE pertaining to Canadian veterans.

WHY VETERAN-SPECIFIC HEALTH RESEARCH?

Many health and disability problems encountered by military personnel, veterans and their families are common to civilians, but there are differences owing to the unique contexts of military service. Anecdotally, many veterans and families speak of losing the "military family" when they transition to civilian life.[46] Others have concerns about potential health effects related to unique hazard exposures that might have occurred during service.[47] Civilians rarely encounter the military nature of service physical and psychological trauma, except police and others who support military operations or immigrants exposed to war in their home countries. The term "operational stress injury" was invented in the Canadian military,[48] and is not well known in the civilian world. Military vocabulary and values stay with veterans when they enter civilian life.

WHY CANADIAN VETERAN HEALTH RESEARCH?

International research is considered when reviews of HRESE are conducted, but while the Canadian context shares some similarities with other countries, it differs in many ways. Examples include age, education, genetics, length of service, deployments, nature of exposures, military personnel policies, military and civilian health care systems, comprehensiveness of veteran compensation and care systems, and civilian population attitudes toward military veterans. Canadian research is needed to better understand Canadian veterans and their families.

SUMMARY

Research has provided key support for innovation in Canadian veteran care and compensation since WWI. Today, Canada's veteran population is at a critical turning point, and research is needed more than ever to support responsive programs and policies. In this new era of global military challenges, a nationally coordinated vision for Canadian veteran health research priorities is necessary. The vision should use an inclusive research framework of health, disability, determinants of health and life course. The vision should address the five challenges: (1) Include all Canadian veterans, not just those receiving VAC benefits; (2) Determine effects of military service on the life courses of veterans and their families; (3) Identify optimum approaches to the care of veterans and their families; (4) Manage the explosion of expert opinion and research findings; and (5) Strengthen capacity in Canadian veterans' health research. Meeting these challenges requires nurturing partnerships between federal partners such as VAC, DND/CF, Statistics Canada and the Canadian Institute of Health Research; Provincial health care systems; and academic researchers in universities across Canada.

[1] P. Neary, "Without the stigma of pauperism": Canadian veterans in the 1930's," Br J Can Stud 22, 1 (2009): 31-62; P. Neary, "The origins and evolution of veterans' benefits in Canada 1914-2004" (Veterans Affairs Canada/Canadian Forces Advisory Council, Ottawa, 2004), 163 p; P. Neary and J.L. Granatstein, (editors). The Veterans Charter and Post-World War II Canada (Kingston: McGill-Queen's University Press, 1998), 298 p; S.R.G. Brown, "Re-establishment and rehabilitation Canadian Veteran Policy, 1933- 1946,"Submitted in partial fulfillment of the requirements for the degree of Doctor of Philosophy, (Faculty of Graduate Studies, University of Western Ontario, 1995), 379 p; E.M. Gee and A.M. Boyce, "veterans and veterans legislation in Canada: an historical overview," Can J Aging 7, 17 (1988): 204-217; M. Tremblay, "The right to the best medical care: Dr. W.P. Warner and the Canadian Department of Veterans Affairs, 1945-55," Can Bull Med Hist 15, 1 (1998): 3-25; R. England, Discharged: A Commentary on Civil Re-Establishment of veterans in Canada (Toronto, ON: Macmillan, 1943); J. Biggar, "The pensionability of the disabled soldier," CMAJ 9, 1 (1919): 28-33.

[2] J. Sweet and J.M. Thompson, "Literature review of military to civilian transition: Results of initial searches,"(Research Directorate Data Report, Veterans Affairs Canada, Charlottetown, 2009), 159 p; M.B. MacLean, L. Van Til, J.M. Thompson, D. Pedlar, A. Poirier, J. Adams, S. Hartigan, and K. Sudom, "Life After Service Study: Data Collection Methodology for The Income Study and The Transition to Civilian Life Survey"(Veterans Affairs Canada Research Directorate Technical Report, 2010), 79 p.

[3] R. England, Discharged: A Commentary on Civil Re-Establishment of veterans in Canada(Toronto, ON: Macmillan, 1943); R. Gault, "Physiotherapy in Department of Veterans Affairs Hospitals," Med Serv J Can 15, 2

(1959): 130-136; M. Tremblay, "The right to the best medical care: Dr. W.P. Warner and the Canadian Department of Veterans Affairs, 1945-55," Can Bull Med Hist 15, 1 (1998): 3-25; S.R.G. Brown, "Re-establishment and rehabilitation Canadian Veteran Policy, 1933-1946,"Submitted in partial fulfillment of the requirements for the degree of Doctor of Philosophy, (Faculty of Graduate Studies, University of Western Ontario, 1995), 379 p; P. Neary, "The origins and evolution of veterans' benefits in Canada 1914-2004" (Veterans Affairs Canada/Canadian Forces Advisory Council, Ottawa, 2004), 163 p.

[4]F.S. Burke, "Deaths among war pensioners," Can Med Assoc J 41, 5 (1939): 457-465.

[5]M.J. Hollander, J.A. Miller, M. MacAdam, N. Chappell, and D. Pedlar, "Increasing value-for-money in the Canadian health care system: New Findings and the case for integrated care for Seniors," Healthcare Quarterly 12, 1 (2009): 39-47; D. Pedlar and J. Walker, "The Overseas Service Veteran at home pilot: how choice of care may affect use of nursing home beds and waiting lists," Can J Aging 23, 4 (2004): 367-389; D. Pedlar, W. Lockhart, and S. Macintosh, "Canada's Veterans Independence Program: A Pioneer of "Aging at Home"," Healthcare Papers 10, 1 (2009): 72-77; J. Struthers, "Comfort, security, dignity: the Veterans Independence Program," (a policy history, Charlottetown, 2004), 242 p; S.R.G. Brown, "Re-establishment and rehabilitation Canadian Veteran Policy, 1933- 1946," Submitted in partial fulfillment of the requirements for the degree of Doctor of Philosophy, (Faculty of Graduate Studies, University of Western Ontario, 1995), 379 p; E.M. Gee and A.M. Boyce, "Veterans and veterans legislation in Canada: an historical overview," Can J Aging 7, 17 (1988): 204-217; F.S. Burke, "Deaths among war pensioners," Can Med Assoc J 41, 5 (1939): 457-465.

[6]M. Tremblay, "The right to the best medical care: Dr. W.P. Warner and the Canadian Department of Veterans Affairs, 1945-55," Can Bull Med Hist 15, 1 (1998): 3-25; P. Neary, "The origins and evolution of veterans' benefits in Canada 1914-2004" (Veterans Affairs Canada/Canadian Forces Advisory Council, Ottawa, 2004), 163 p.

[7]W.S. Woods, "Rehabilitation (A combined operation)," Being a history of the development and carrying out of a plan for the re-establishment of a million young veterans of World War II (Department of Veterans Affairs and its predecessor the Department of Pensions and National Health, Queen's Printer, Ottawa, 1953), 518 p.

[8]M. Tremblay, "The right to the best medical care: Dr. W.P. Warner and the Canadian Department of Veterans Affairs, 1945-55," Can Bull Med Hist 15, 1 (1998): 3-25.

[9]DVA, "Annual Report, Department of Veterans Affairs Canada," (Ottawa, ON: Government of Canada, 1963)

[10]Veterans Affairs Canada, "Canada. Department of Veterans Affairs Act," c. V-1, (R.S.C.: Ottawa, 1985), accessed from http://www.canlii.org/en/ca/laws/stat/rsc-1985-c-v-1/32115/rsc-1985-c-v-1.html.

[11]Planned spending in 2010-11 (Veterans Affairs Canada Report on Plans and Priorities 2010-11).

[12]Canadian Health Services Research Foundation, "Research dissemination: Actively bringing the research and policy worlds together," Insight and Action (Ottawa: CHSRF, 2007), 16, accessed from http://www.chsrf.ca/publicationsandresources/pastseries/insightandaction/07-07-01/798756b3-87af-4ede-9320-1880f32c790e.aspx.

[13]VAC-CF Advisory Council, "Honouring Canada's commitment: "Opportunity with Security" for Canadian Forces veterans and their families in the 21st century," Veterans Affairs Canada - Canadian Forces Advisory Council Discussion Paper, ed. Peter Neary, (Veterans Affairs Canada and Canadian Forces, Ottawa, 2004), 44, accessed from http://www.veterans.gc.ca/general/sub.cfm?source=pro_research/publications/reports, accessed 14 April 2011.

[14]Standing Committee on National Defence and Veterans Affairs, Moving forward: A strategic plan for the quality of life improvements in the Canadian Forces 1998, House of Commons, Report 3, 36th Parliament, 1st Session. (September 22, 1997 - September 18, 1999, October 1998; 92); VAC-CF Advisory Council, "Honouring Canada's commitment: "Opportunity with Security" for Canadian Forces Veterans and their families in the 21st century," Veterans Affairs Canada - Canadian Forces Advisory Council Discussion Paper, ed. Peter Neary, (Veterans Affairs Canada and Canadian Forces, Ottawa, 2004), 44, http://www.veterans.gc.ca/general/sub.cfm?source=pro_research/publications/reports, accessed 14 April 2011.

[15]J.M. Thompson and M.B. MacLean, "Evidence for best practices in the management of disabilities," (Research Directorate Technical Report, Veterans Affairs Canada, Charlottetown, 2009), 51 p; International Organization for Migration, "Improving the presumptive disability decision-making process for veterans," IOM Committee on Evaluation of the Presumptive Disability Decision-Making Process for Veterans, eds. Jonathan M. Samet and Catherine C. Bodurow (Washington DC: Institute of Medicine, 2007b), 789 p; WHO,

"International Classification of Functioning, Disability and Health (ICF)"(Resolution of the World Health Assembly, World Health Organization, 2001), WHA54.21.

[16]C. Hertzman and C. Power, "Health and human development: understandings from life-course research," Dev Neuropsychol 24, 2-3 (2003): 719-744; D. Kuh, Y. Ben-Shlomo, J. Lynch, J. Hallqvist, and C. Power, "Life course epidemiology," J Epidemiol Community Health 57, 10 (2003): 778-783. Erratum in: J Epidemiol Community Health 57, 11, (2003): 914.

[17]V. Marshall, and J.J. Dowd, "From officers to gentlemen: army generals and the passage to retirement," Restructuring work and the life course (Toronto, ON: U Toronto Press, 2001), 233-257; R.A. Settersten, "When nations call: how wartime military service matters for the life course and aging," Res Aging 28, 1 (2006): 12-36; R.A. Settersten and R.S. Patterson, "Military service, the life course, and aging; An Introduction," Research on Aging 28, 1 (2006): 5-11; R.J. Wright, "Why old soldiers cannot be allowed to simply fade away: life course epidemiology of war," J Epidemiol Community Health 63, 5 (2009): 338-339.

[18]M.B. MacLean, L. Van Til, J.M. Thompson, D. Pedlar, A. Poirier, J. Adams, S. Hartigan, and K. Sudom, "Life After Service Study: Data Collection Methodology for The Income Study and The Transition to Civilian Life Survey" (Veterans Affairs Canada Research Directorate Technical Report, 2010), 79 p; M.B. MacLean, L. Van Til, J.M. Thompson, A. Poirier, J. Sweet, D. Pedlar, J. Adams, K. Sudom, C. Campbell, B. Murphy, and C. Dionne, "Income Study: Regular Force Veteran Report" (Veterans Affairs Canada, Research Directorate and Department of National Defence, Director General Military Personnel Research and Analysis, Place of Publication, 2011), 70 p; J.M. Thompson, M.B. MacLean, L. Van Til, K. Sudom, J. Sweet, A. Poirier, J. Adams, V. Horton, C. Campbell, and D. Pedlar, "Survey on Transition to Civilian Life: Report on Regular Force Veterans," (Research Directorate, Veterans Affairs Canada, Charlottetown, and Director General Military Personnel Research and Analysis, Department of National Defence, Ottawa, 2011), 103 p.

[19]Veteran identifier questions were used in the Canadian census during 1951-1971.

[20]J. Thompson, J. Sweet, and D. Pedlar, Preliminary analysis of the CCHS 2.1 National Survey of the Health of Canadian Military Service Veterans," (Veterans Affairs Canada Data Report: Charlottetown).

[21]Richard G. Foulkes, "The geriatric DVA patient," Medical Services Journal 20, February (1964): 148-156.

[22]H.J. Richardson, "Report of a Study of Disabilities and Problems of Hong Kong veterans, 1964-1965" (Canadian Pension Commission, Ottawa, 1965), 92 p; J.D. Hermann, "Report to the Minister of Veterans Affairs of a study on Canadians who were prisoners of war in Europe during World War II" (Ottawa, ON: Queen's Printer, 1973), 60 p.

[23]A.J. Brunet and R.A. Tate, "An analysis of inpatients, Department of Veterans Affairs, at midnight, March 31, 1966," Med Serv J Can 23, 2 (196): 107-114.

[24]M.B. MacLean, L. Van Til, J.M. Thompson, D. Pedlar, A. Poirier, J. Adams, S. Hartigan, and K. Sudom, "Life After Service Study: Data Collection Methodology for The Income Study and The Transition to Civilian Life Survey"(Veterans Affairs Canada Research Directorate Technical Report, Charlottetown 2010), 79 p.

[25]J. Dumais and B. Belanger, "Veterans Care Needs Survey: sample design and questionnaire cognitive testing" (Catalogue no. 89-554-XPE, Social Survey Methods Division of Statistics Canada, Ottawa, 1997), 32 + app; G.J.G. Asmundson, VAC Canadian Forces Survey Analysis, Department of Veterans Affairs, Government of Canada, Mar 13, 2000, 40 p; V.W. Marshall and R.A. Matteo, "Canadian Forces clients of Veterans Affairs Canada: risk factors for post-release socio-economic well-being," (prepared for, Veterans Services Branch, Veterans Affairs Canada, Protected Status, 2004), 54 p; V.W. Marshall, R.A. Matteo, and M.M. Mueller, Canadian Forces clients of Veterans Affairs Canada: Employment status, career and retirement planning issues, (May 2000): 80 p; V.W. Marshall, R. Matteo, D. Pedlar, Post-military experiences of Veterans Affairs Canada clients: the need for military release readiness. Prepared for Veterans Affairs Canada. (January 2005a); V.W. Marshall, R. Matteo, D. Pedlar, "Work-related experience and financial security of Veterans Affairs Canada clients: contrasting medical and non-medical discharge," (Veterans Affairs Canada, Charlottetown, 2005b), 1-42.

[26]J. Thompson, J. Sweet, and D. Pedlar, Preliminary analysis of the CCHS 2.1 National Survey of the Health of Canadian Military Service Veterans," (Veterans Affairs Canada Data Report, Charlottetown).

[27]As per article published herein by Van Til, L.D., MacLean, M.B., Thompson, J., and Pedlar, D., "Life after Service Studies: a program of population health research at VAC."

[28]M.B. MacLean, L. Van Til, J.M. Thompson, A. Poirier, J. Sweet, D. Pedlar, J. Adams, K. Sudom, C. Campbell, B. Murphy, and C. Dionne, "Income Study: Regular Force Veteran Report" (Veterans Affairs Canada, Research

Directorate and Department of National Defence, Director General Military Personnel Research and Analysis, Place of Publication, 2011), 70 p.

[29]J.M. Thompson, M.B. MacLean, L. Van Til, K. Sudom, J. Sweet, A. Poirier, J. Adams, V. Horton, C. Campbell, and D. Pedlar, "Survey on Transition to Civilian Life: Report on Regular Force Veterans," (Research Directorate, Veterans Affairs Canada, Charlottetown, and Director General Military Personnel Research and Analysis, Department of National Defence, Ottawa, 2011), 103 p.

[30]J.M. Thompson, H. Gauthier, A. Poirier, S. Baglole, and S. MacIntosh, "Nominal Rolls: Lessons learned from developing the "Mustard Gas List"," (Veterans Affairs Canada Research Directorate Technical Report, Charlottetown, 2010), 26 p.

[31]J.M. Thompson, M.B. MacLean, L. Van Til, K. Sudom, J. Sweet, A. Poirier, J. Adams, V. Horton, C. Campbell, and D. Pedlar, "Survey on Transition to Civilian Life: Report on Regular Force Veterans," (Research Directorate, Veterans Affairs Canada, Charlottetown, and Director General Military Personnel Research and Analysis, Department of National Defence, Ottawa, 2011), 103 p.

[32]M. Fortin, G. Bravo, C. Hudon, A. Vanasse, and L. Lapointe, "Prevalence of multimorbidity among adults seen in family practice,"Ann Fam Med 3, 3 (2005): 223-228.; W.M. Hopman, M.B. Harrison, H. Coo, E. Friedberg, M. Buchanan, and E.G. VanDenKerdhof, "Associations between chronic disease, age and physical and mental health status," Chronic Diseases in Canada 29, 2 (2009): 108-116.

[33]M. Ardelt and S.D. Landes, "The long-term effects of World War II combat exposure on later life well-being moderated by generativity," Res Human Devel 7, 3 (2010): 202-220; Z. Solomon, and R. Dekel, "Posttraumatic stress disorder and posttraumatic growth among Israeli ex-pows," J Trauma Stress Vol. 20, No. 3 (2007): 303-312.

[34]E. Jones, R. Hodgins-Vermaas, H. McCartney, B. Everitt, C. Beech, D. Poynter, I. Palmer, K. Hyams and S. Wessely, "Post-combat syndromes from the Boer war to the Gulf: a cluster analysis of their nature and attribution," Br. Med. J., 7333 (2002): 321-324; K.C. Hyams, F.S. Wignall, and R. Roswell, "War syndromes and their evaluation: from the U.S. Civil War to the Persian Gulf War," Ann Intern Med 125 (1996): 398-405.

[35]S. Chatterjee, A. Spiro, L. King, D. King, and E. Davison, "Research on aging and military veterans," PTSD Research Quarterly 29, 3 (2009): 7 p.

[36]R.J. Wright, "Why old soldiers cannot be allowed to simply fade away: life course epidemiology of war," J Epidemiol Community Health 63, 5 (2009): 338-339; R.A. Settersten, "When nations call: how wartime military service matters for the life course and aging," Res Aging 28, 1 (2006):12-36.

[37]K.L. Dominick, Y.M. Golightly, and G.L. Jackson, "Arthritis prevalence and symptoms among US non-veterans, veterans, and veterans receiving Department of Veterans Affairs Healthcare," J Rheumatol 33, 2 (2006): 348-354; J.M. Thompson, M.B. MacLean, L. Van Til, K. Sudom, J. Sweet, A. Poirier, J. Adams, V. Horton, C. Campbell, and D. Pedlar, "Survey on Transition to Civilian Life: Report on Regular Force Veterans," (Research Directorate, Veterans Affairs Canada, Charlottetown, and Director General Military Personnel Research and Analysis, Department of National Defence, Ottawa, 2011), 103 p; A. Spiro, P.P. Schnurr, and C.M. Aldwin, "Combat-related posttraumatic stress disorder symptoms in older men," Psychology and Aging 9, 1 (1994): 17-26; J. Sareen, S.L. Belik, T.O. Afifi, G.J. Asmundson, B.J. Cox, and M.B. Stein, "Canadian military personnel's population attributable fractions of mental disorders and mental health service use associated with combat and peacekeeping operations," Am J Public Health 98, 12 (2008): 2191-2198; R.J. Wright, "Why old soldiers cannot be allowed to simply fade away: life course epidemiology of war," J Epidemiol Community Health 63, 5 (2009): 338-339.

[38]International Organization for Migration, "Improving the presumptive disability decision-making process for veterans," IOM Committee on Evaluation of the Presumptive Disability Decision-Making Process for veterans, eds. Jonathan M. Samet and Catherine C. Bodurow (Washington, DC: Institute of Medicine, 2007b), 789 p.

[39]A.C. McFarlane, "Military deployment: the impact on children and family adjustment and the need for care," CurrOpin Psychiatry 6, 22 (2009): 369-373; CMVH, "The intergenerational health effects of service in the military," Volume 2: Literature review. Australian Centre for Military and Veterans' Health (Herston, Australia: Australian Centre for Military and Veteran's Health, 2007), 134 p, accessed from http://www.dva.gov.au/aboutDVA/publications/health_research/effects_of_service/Pages/index.aspx.

[40]J.C. O'Donnell, "Military service and mental health in later life," Mil Med Vol. 165, No. 3 (2000): 219-23; O'Toole, B.I., Catts, S.V., Outram, S., Pierse, K.R., and Cockburn, J., "Factors associated with civilian mortality

in Australian Vietnam Veteran three decades after the War," Mil Med 175, 2 (2010):88-95.

[41]P. Neary, "The origins and evolution of veterans' benefits in Canada 1914-2004" (Veterans Affairs Canada/Canadian Forces Advisory Council, Ottawa, 2004), 163 p.

[42]P. Neary, "The origins and evolution of veterans' benefits in Canada 1914-2004" (Veterans Affairs Canada/Canadian Forces Advisory Council, Ottawa, 2004), 163 p.

[43]VAC-CF Advisory Council, "Honouring Canada's commitment: "Opportunity with Security" for Canadian Forces veterans and their families in the 21st century," Veterans Affairs Canada - Canadian Forces Advisory Council Discussion Paper, ed. Peter Neary, (Veterans Affairs Canada and Canadian Forces, Ottawa, 2004), 44, accessed from http://www.veterans.gc.ca/general/sub.cfm?source=pro_research/publications/reports, accessed 14 April 2011.

[44]International Organization for Migration, "Improving the presumptive disability decision-making process for veterans," IOM Committee on Evaluation of the Presumptive Disability Decision-Making Process for veterans, eds. Jonathan M. Samet and Catherine C. Bodurow (Washington, DC: Institute of Medicine, 2007b), 789 p.

[45]RMA, "Proceedings of the 2008 Canberra Forum Service & Science: Applying the evidence in the field of military and veterans' health to a contemporary military compensation system" (Repatriation Medical Authority, Australia, 2008), 75 p.

[46]T. Pranger, K. Murphy, and J.M. Thompson, "Shaken world - coping with transition to civilian life, veterans Health Files #2,"Canadian Family Physician 55, 2 (2009): 159-161, http://www.cfp.ca/cgi/content/full/55/2/159, accessed 12 October 2010.

[47]Y. Côté, "Heroism exposed: an investigation into the treatment of 1 combat engineer regiment Kuwait veterans (1991)," CF Ombudsman: Special report to the Minister of National Defence (Ottawa, ON: Government of Canada, 2006), 51 p.

[48]D. Richardson, K. Darte, S. Grenier, A. English, and J. Sharpe, "Operational Stress Injury Social Support (OSSIS): A Canadian innovation in professional peer support," Can Mil J 9, 1 (2008): 57-64.

CHAPTER 3

Composite Tissue Allotransplantation to Treat Veterans with Complex Amputation Injuries and Their Families

Major Vivian McAlister, Commander Ray Kao, Major Brian Church, Lieutenant-Colonel Markus Besemann, Lieutenant-Colonel Robert Stiegelmar, 1 Canadian Field Hospital, Canadian Forces Medical Service

ABSTRACT

Amputee rehabilitation may be limited by complexity of injury (e.g. bilateral arm amputation), associated injury (e.g. colostomy) or by the level of amputation (e.g. high above knee). To assess the potential for composite tissue allotransplantation (CTA) to overcome these barriers, medical literature was searched and programs were surveyed regarding the current status of CTA. CTA remains an experimental reconstructive option that involves a large collaborative (physiatry, orthopaedic, plastic and transplant surgeons). Limb transplantation has evolved out of limb reimplantation surgery and organ transplantation. Approximately 10 programs worldwide, with almost a decade of experience, report 90% success with good function. Most experience in forearm transplantation (50 grafts in 36 patients). Research in London Ontario, where a civilian CTA program is being developed, has demonstrated the protective effect immunologically of vascularized bone marrow so that the immunosuppressive requirements are equivalent or less than those for organ transplantation. A review of Canadian casualties suggests that relatively few will require forearm transplantation and more would benefit from above-knee leg replacement. Knee transplantation, permitting conversion to a below knee prosthesis, has been as successful as forearm transplantation. CTA may offer options for treatment of carefully selected veterans who are motivated to take part in an experimental reconstructive program. Carefully selected combat casualties with difficult amputations may be good candidates for a limb transplantation program being developed in London Ont. Worldwide experience suggests forearm transplantation is very successful with relatively low immunosuppressive drug requirements. Combat casualties will require leg as well as hand transplantation.

COMPOSITE TISSUE ALLOTRANSPLANTATION TO TREAT VETERANS WITH COMPLEX AMPUTATION INJURIES

The introduction of a new medical technology is fraught with difficulty. Not only must the technology survive its own growing pains but also it must withstand external criticism. This is particularly true of transplantation surgery where the complexity of surgery is matched by the interest of ethicists. The late Francis Moore who, as professor of surgery in Boston at the time that organ transplantation was developed into the routine clinical service it has become today, frequently addressed these issues. Moore believed that a central agency that makes rules for all could not substitute for flexibility and patient–focused decision making in the early days of a new procedure.[1] Limb transplantation is currently at the stage Moore faced in the 1960s with organ transplantation. There is a universal desire to help those disfigured by combat. In giving injured veterans access to innovative surgery, it is important to temper the desire to help with the caution not to harm. Even though limbs are not essential to life, in the way that a liver is, loss of a limb, even if it is a failed transplanted graft, will result in physical and psychological damage. The purpose of this chapter is to review the current status of limb transplantation so as to inform physicians who wish to research this treatment and soldiers who wish to consider it.

Extremity injury has always been a common combat injury but even more in the current conflict where improvised explosive devices are aimed at dismounted patrols wearing body armour.[2] These injuries often result in amputations. Amputee rehabilitation may be limited by complexity of injury (e.g. bilateral arm amputation), associated injury (e.g. colostomy) or by the level of the amputation (e.g. high above knee). Reintegration into active service life and full civilian activity, the goal of rehabilitation, is frequently achieved using conventional methods and advanced physiatry.[3] For those who fail conventional care the outlook is bleak. Options to improve outcome include limb transplantation and targeted muscle reinnervation, also known as the bionic arm. Limb transplantation is one form of CTA where the graft includes skin, bone, muscle, nerves and bone marrow. Limb transplantation has developed recently out of successful programs of replantation surgery (reattachment of severed limbs) and organ transplantation. CTA also involves transplantation of bone marrow. Limb transplantation therefore requires the specialized skills of orthopaedic, plastic, vascular and transplantation surgeons as well as those of bone marrow transplant physicians and rehabilitation experts. Alexis Carrel, a pioneer of experimental surgery who is often claimed as a progenitor of each of these specialties, performed limb transplantation in animals over a century ago.[4] The objective of this report is to assess the possibility for successful CTA and its potential to overcome the barriers to rehabilitation of patients with complex amputations.

METHOD

A descriptive report was generated from a review of published literature, supplemented by a survey of clinical programs of CTA.

RESULTS

Since 1998, 60 transplants in 42 patients at 14 centres have been reported. All of the patients are presumed to be civilians but the mechanisms of injury were not specified. No centres in Canada currently offer CTA. The two principal centres in the United States are located at Louisville, Kentucky and Pittsburgh, Pennsylvania. Two deaths occurred from sepsis in one face transplant recipient and one hand recipient. Three patients lost grafts to non-fatal thromboses (2 arterial, 1 venous). Of the patients with limb transplantations, 90% recovered tactile sensation, 72% discriminative sensation, and motor recovery was described as 'excellent'. The majority of limb transplants involved forearm or hand grafts (50 grafts in 36 patients). Twenty (90%) unilateral and seven (50%) bilateral hand transplant patients returned to work. Eight partial lower limb (knee) transplants have been performed to lower the level of amputation and thereby facilitate rehabilitation by prosthesis. Many of the reports and associated newspaper stories show recipients undertaking complex tasks requiring fine sensorimotor skills or activities requiring strength (such a push-ups).[5]

DISCUSSION

In the 1960's, soon after the advent of kidney allotransplantation, an arm transplant was attempted by a surgeon in Ecuador. Failure was ascribed to inadequate immunosuppression. It was believed that the CTA, made of bone, muscle, skin and marrow, induced rejection by the host that could not be prevented with safe doses of conventional immunosuppression. It was more than 30 years before another attempt was made. In 1998, Dubernard and colleagues performed the first successful hand transplantation.[6] It surprised everyone that routine doses of conventional immunosuppressive drugs used for successful kidney transplantation were adequate to prevent rejection of the limb.[7] Since then a series of successful transplantations using tacrolimus and mycophenolic mofetil have been reported.[8] A worldwide registry of CTA has reported a high rate of successful transplantation which is summarized in this report.[9] For limb transplantation to be considered successful, not only must the graft survive but sensory and motor function must be present. The series reported show remarkable return of strength, precise movement and sensation.[10] The following activities have been reported by hand recipients in the series from Louisville, Kentucky: open regular door knobs; pick up smaller objects, checkers, washers, small nuts, and bolts; lift gallon of milk or water from refrigerator; hold steering wheel with transplanted hand only; use wrench and other tools; use rake and other garden tools; take change in palm; use fork and knife; swing golf club or baseball bat; catch balls; tie shoes and assist in holding dishes and food items in buffet line.[11]

Not all the transplantations were successful. Two patients (0.9%) in the series died, not from immunological effects but from sepsis. Is this a risk worth taking for patients who do not have an immediately life threatening disease? The risk is comparable to that taken by patients on dialysis who undergo kidney transplantation. The disability faced by patients with complicated amputations is often worse than patients with renal failure. The issue has to be decided on a case-by-case basis as Francis Moore advised.[12] Alternatives such as targeted muscle reinnervation should be considered. A program of target muscle reinnervation is underway at Glenrose Amputee Program, Edmonton, Alberta, in which Canadian Forces Medical Service orthopaedic surgeons are participating.

Sepsis may be due to over-immunosuppression. Increasing confidence with respect to the prevention and control of rejection has allowed for the reduction in the doses of immunosuppressive drugs used in CTA. It is now believed that transplantation of vascularized bone marrow contributes a protective effect to the transplant.[13] Repopulation of the graft with native cells may also reduce the immunogenicity of the graft.[14] A program of experimental transplantation in London, Ontario has found that conditioning which specialized immunosuppression can induce transplant tolerance in the recipient so that the limb transplant is not rejected even though the immunosuppressive drugs have been discontinued.[15] A clinical limb transplant program is planned to start in London in the near future. The Armed Forces Institute of Regenerative Medicine is funding a clinical study of limb transplantation in the United States.[16]

Clearly there is optimism that limb transplantation will soon reach the same status as organ transplantation. The option will only be suitable for carefully selected military patients who have been fully apprised of the risks and effort required for success. The psychological stresses will have to be considered but there is a potential for a positive effect on residual non-physical effects of combat trauma. Unfortunately most CTA transplants today involve the distal upper limb. Soldiers who are most disabled and the least amenable to rehabilitation have high arm and high above knee amputations. The immunological barriers to lower limb transplantation are no different to the upper limb. Nerve regeneration and return of function have been seen with lower limb replantations. This may be due to a lack of demand for lower limb transplantation among civilians because lower level injuries most often seen in this population is highly amenable to modern prosthetic care. If transplantation becomes routinely successful using low doses of immunosuppressive drugs, the demand from injured soldiers with higher level or complicated amputations is likely to increase.

[1].D. Moore, A Miracle and a Privilege: Recounting a Half Century of Surgical Advance (Washington, DC: Joseph Henry Press, 1995).

[2]A. Ramasamy, A.M. Hill and J.C. Clasper, "Improvised explosive devices: pathophysiology, injury profiles and current medical management," J R Army Med Corps Vol. 155, No. 4 (2009): 265-72.

[3]B.M. Isaacson, S.R. Weeks, P.F. Pasquina, J.B. Webster, J.P. Beck and R.D. Bloebaum, "The road to recovery and rehabilitation for injured service members with limb loss: a focus on Iraq and Afghanistan," US Army Med Dep J. (July-September 2010): 31-6.

[4]A. Carrel, "Results of the transplantation of blood vessels, organs and limbs," (Nov 14, 1908, Nov 14, 1908: International registry on hand and composite tissue transplantation, http://www.handregistry.com/, accessed 25 April 2011.

[5]J.M. Dubernard, E. Owen, N. Lefrancois, et al., "First human hand transplantation," Case report. Transpl Int. 13, 1 (2000): S521-4.

[6]J.W. Jones Jr, E.T. Ustuner, M. Zdichavsky, et al., "Long-term survival of an extremity composite tissue allograft with FK506-mycophenolate mofetil therapy," Surgery Vol. 162, No. 2 (1999): 384–8.

[7]C.L. Kaufman, B. Blair, E. Murphy, W.B. Breidenbach, "A new option for amputees: transplantation of the hand," J Rehabil Res Dev. Vol. 46, No. 3 (2009): 395-404.

[8]T. Zhong, Y. Liu, J. Jiang, H. Wang, C.L. Temple, H. Sun, B. Garcia B, R. Zhong, and D.C. Ross, "Long-

term limb allograft survival using a short course of anti-CD45RB monoclonal antibody, LF 15-0195, and rapamycin in a mouse model," Transplantation,. Vol. 84, No. 12 (December 2007): 1636-43.

[9]Dubernard JM, Owen E, Lefrancois N, *et al.* First human hand transplantation. Case report. Transpl Int. 2000;13(suppl 1):S521–4.

[10]Dubernard JM, Owen E, Lefrancois N, *et al.* First human hand transplantation. Case report. Transpl Int. 2000;13(suppl 1):S521–4 T. Zhong, Y. Liu, J. Jiang, H. Wang, C.L. Temple, H. Sun, B. Garcia B, R. Zhong, and D.C. Ross, "Long-term limb allograft survival using a short course of anti-CD45RB monoclonal antibody, LF 15-0195, and rapamycin in a mouse model," Transplantation,. Vol. 84, No. 12 (December 2007):1636-43.

[11]T. Zhong, Y. Liu, J. Jiang, H. Wang, C.L. Temple, H. Sun, B. Garcia B, R. Zhong, and D.C. Ross, "Long-term limb allograft survival using a short course of anti-CD45RB monoclonal antibody, LF 15-0195, and rapamycin in a mouse model," Transplantation,. Vol. 84, No. 12 (December 2007):1636-43.

[12]F.D. Moore, A Miracle and a Privilege: Recounting a Half Century of Surgical Advance (Washington, DC: Joseph Henry Press; 1995).

[13]M. Pelzer, M. Larsen, P.F. Friedrich, R.A. Aleff, A.T. Bishop, "Repopulation of vascularized bone allotransplants with recipient-derived cells: detection by laser capture microdissection and real-time PCR," J Orthop Res, Vol. 27, No. 11 (2009):1514-20.

[14]A. Coombs, "Stem cells drafted for war on wounds", Nature Reports Stem Cells, (2008). doi:10.1038/stemcells.2008.148,
http://www.nature.com/stemcells/2008/0811/081113/full/stemcells.2008.148.html, accessed 25 April 2011.

[15]A. Coombs, "Stem cells drafted for war on wounds", Nature Reports Stem Cells, (2008). doi:10.1038/stemcells.2008.148,
http://www.nature.com/stemcells/2008/0811/081113/full/stemcells.2008.148.html, accessed 25 April 2011.

[16]"Research Clinical Trials" Armed Forces Institute of Regenerative Medicine, (last modified 18 March 2011), http://www.afirm.mil/index.cfm?pageid=research.clinical_trials.overview, accessed 25 April 2011.

CHAPTER 4

Advanced Real-Time 3D Imaging, Planning and Navigation in Orthopaedic Surgery

David Pichora, MD, Randy Ellis, PhD, Tim Bryant, PhD, and John Rudan, MD, Human Mobility Research Centre, Queen's University and Kingston General Hospital

ABSTRACT

The treatment of complex cases, such as periarticular fractures, remains a challenge despite recent advances in fixation technology. Improved minimally invasive surgical techniques are needed to, for example, obtain an anatomic reduction of the joint surface fracture. Advances in fracture surgery will benefit injured military and theatre civilian personnel who need repair and reconstruction of injuries to their limbs, pelvis or spine. The Queen's University Human Mobility Research Centre at Kingston General Hospital has North America's first image guided surgical suite. This advanced 3D suite supports research designed to integrate computer-assisted planning and optical-based navigation technologies, and to develop novel registration and calibration methods to permit 'real time' imaging, planning and surgery during a single anesthetic. We have successfully innovated navigated procedures based on volume rendered 3D imaging and planning; and performed pilot cases of navigated spinal surgery in this unit and have developed novel methods for navigated fracture surgery. One of the key findings is that intraoperative imaging improves outcomes and reduces in-hospital postoperative recovery time. We will present new means of planning fracture repair with precise navigation of fixation devices. We believe that this work will translate into better fracture care and facilitate the integration of telesurgery and computer-assisted techniques into military medical centers and field units.

ADVANCED REAL-TIME 3D IMAGING, PLANNING AND NAVIGATION IN ORTHOPAEDIC SURGERY

Musculoskeletal trauma is a major aspect of war injuries. The new Image-Guided Surgery Suite (ISS) at Kingston General Hospital has allowed us to develop, test and use 'real-time' computer planning and guidance methodologies to permit rapid, affordable intraoperative 3D imaging, image visualization and navigation of difficult and uncommon orthopedic procedures. In this chapter we will describe the clinical and technical advances to date and projects underway. We will relate their potential military applications.

An image-guided intervention uses computers to enhance the visualization of a surgical procedure. Assisting surgeons with intraoperative guidance results in increased precision for both open and less-invasive procedures. These systems use preoperative and intra-operative images to assist the surgeon in performing tasks for which direct vision is impossible or inappropriate. When this type of computer-assisted navigation is used, it is necessary to build a 3D surface model of the patient's anatomy. Automatically segmenting the anatomy directly from a Computerized Tomography (CT)/ Magnetic Resonnance Imaging (MRI) image and then applying a mathematical function achieves this.

There are several reasons why computer-assisted image guidance is able to optimize orthopaedic surgical procedures. Computer-guided technology is a minimally invasive approach that can improve the accuracy, precision and efficiency of surgeons in difficult procedures, where ordinarily a high level of experience and expertise is required. This is accomplished by the intra-operative navigational guidance of surgical instruments according to a pre-surgical plan. Most bone is rigid, enabling probing and drilling without collapse. This is important during the virtual modeling of the patient's anatomy. The technique has the added benefits of reducing radiation exposure to the patient and surgical team while serving as an excellent teaching tool for less-experienced surgeons.

A standard framework for image-guided surgery consists of four stages. A set of medical images (such as an x-ray, MRI or CT) is acquired of the relevant portion of the patient's anatomy. These images are segmented into distinct anatomical structures, yielding a 3D patient-specific model. The model is then registered to the actual position of the patient on the operating table. Surgical instruments are tracked relative to the patient and the model, allowing the surgeon to reliably place surgical devices, and avoid hidden, critical structures while performing the procedure.[1]

TECHNICAL ADVANCES TO DATE

We developed what is now an example of traditional CT-based optical navigation, in this case for the 3D correction of wrist fracture malunions.[2] Residual deformity (malunion) of a common wrist fracture (distal radius) causes persisting symptoms and impairment. Furthermore, conventional corrective surgical methods relying on intra-operative fluoroscopy have a risk of residual malunion. Various studies have shown that residual malunion[3] can have significant influences on the range of motion,[4] on grip strength[5] and on patient satisfaction.[6] Our innovative computer-assisted procedure showed excellent results with respect to accuracy, precision and reliability of surgical correction.[7]

In the first step of the computer-assisted process, a preoperative plan incorporates a CT-based 3D reconstructed surface mesh of both the malunited wrist and the mirrored contralateral normal wrist, and a digitized model of the wrist fixation plate. The preoperative planner produces a virtual bone cut and realignment to best fit the geometry of the normal template. The digitized fixation plate is then fitted to the corrected bone. Next the plan is reverse-engineered so that coordinates of the fixation screws are mapped onto the original malunion model. (See Figures 4.1 and 4.2).

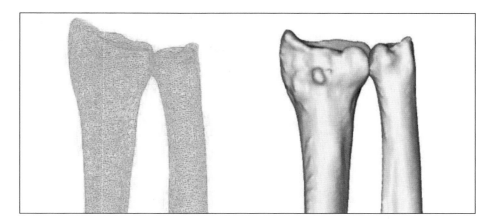

Figure 4.1: Osteotomy for wrist fracture malunion.

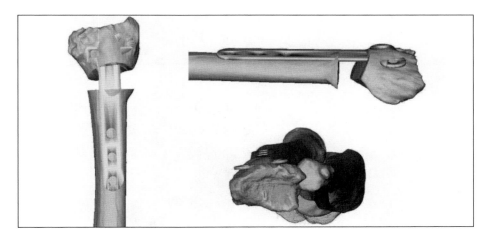

Figure 4.2: Virtual osteotomy to correct the malunion based on the normal template;
implant location is incorporated into the surgical plan.

The plan is imported into guidance software and is linked to the patient anatomy by
registering the preoperative plan to the landmarks on the patient's *in vivo* wrist using a
temporarily implanted tracking device with infrared emitting diodes (IRED)[8] which are
monitored by an optical tracking.[9] The IRED's are also attached to the surgical drill
enabling its location and orientation in space to be referenced to the preoperative plan

and to locations on the patient's exposed wrist bones. The surgeon is guided by virtual images of the user-computer interface showing the planned locations for the screw drill holes in the fixation plate. Intraoperative post procedure verification of the correction is obtained using fluoroscopic imaging. (Figure 4.3).

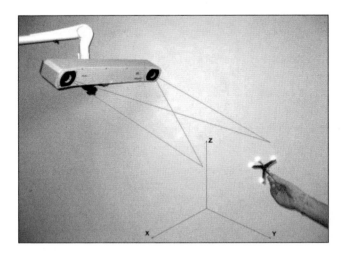

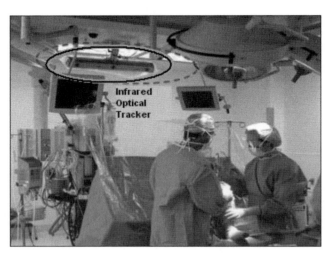

Figure 4.3: Infrared navigation principles

COMPUTER ASSISTED FLUOROSCOPY

Traditionally, intraoperative fluoroscopic x-ray is often employed for surgical guidance during the procedure. Fluoroscopy technology shows a continuous 2D x-ray image on a monitor in real-time. In computer assisted fluoroscopy, the computer integrates two or more images while optically tracking the location of the imager C-arm thereby approximating 3D imaging (with multiple 2D images) (Figure 4.4). As in CT-based navigation the optical tracking links 3D coordinates of images to the surgical tools, the patient's anatomy and a library of 3D objects or anatomical models.

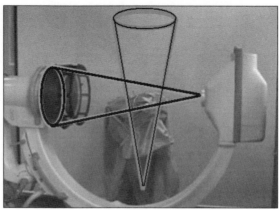

Figure 4.4: Fluoroscopic navigation: Approximates 3D with multiple 2D images.

While fluoroscopy provides good efficiency, technical difficulties often arise from its use. For example, image-intensifier nonlinearities along with visualization errors can provide distortions that compromise accuracy, and provide misleading angular and positional guidance.[10]

CT is the gold-standard imaging modality for 3D modeling and planning. Yet the surface models produced from CT sometimes lack information and clinically important indices revealed by conventional x-rays. We have developed computer algorithms for producing digitally rendered 'virtual' x-rays from CT data. As seen in Figure 4.5 it is possible to view and exploit the benefits of both surface models and virtual radiographs.

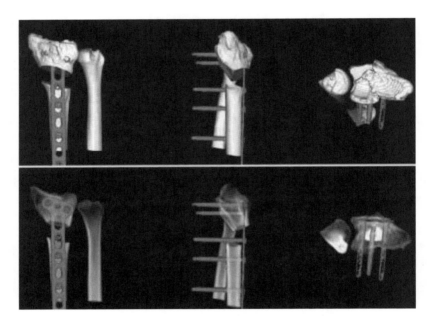

Figure 4.5: 2D and 3D images for planning.

Whilst fluoroscopic navigation is limited in its 3D capability and planning, there are also limitations to CT-based navigation. Considerable time prior to surgery is expended in segmenting the anatomy of interest from the CT scan of the patient. The registration phase is complicated and requires a dedicated technical support team. The rigid fixation of IRED's to the bone creates a more invasive surgical procedure. Also, because pre-operative planning is required, there is no ability to create or alter the plan intraoperatively. To address these shortcomings, intraoperative 2D and 3D imaging, modeling, and planning modalities have been introduced into the computer-assisted surgical workflow by a number of centers, including significant contributions by our team at Queen's. There is a continued focus on improving safety by reducing the exposure to ionizing radiation through the reduction in intensity of x-ray use.

Efforts continue to find simpler, more reliable and cost effective navigation technologies. Expensive optical or magnetic based navigation is not always required. Rademacher *et al.*, first introduced a method using computer-generated templates, which do not require optical navigation equipment and associated instrumentation.[11] They allow for the integration of small reference areas of the anatomy and precise intraoperative positioning without the need for additional or extended incisions for fixation of IRED trackers to the bone. More recently, patient-specific instrument guidance has been used for intra-operative navigation.[12] This method, however, used conventional alignment of the fragments and fixation of the plate.

Our research center has built on patient-specific instrument guidance technology to provide an alternative to optically navigated distal radius osteotomy by designing guides used to navigate the alignment of the correction with respect to a pre-operative plan, as well as to assist with the fixation of the plate to achieve the planned re-alignment.[13] The main advantage to a patient-specific instrument guidance system is that expensive intraoperative navigation equipment is no longer needed.

Patient-specific instrument guidance necessitates a two stage pre-operative planning phase. As before, the virtual correction of the wrist is planned using CT scans to create 3D surface models for affected and unaffected wrist bones. The next phase involves the creation of the patient specific instrument guide. Calculation of patient-specific guidance tools for drilling the screw hole into the malunited wrist bone is determined using custom made software. Intraoperative placement of the guidance tool on the selected registration area is then determined. For each screw location, a drill guide channel is inserted into the virtual template, which is located with respect to the pre-operative surgical plan. Once the design of the individualized drilling guide is complete, the computer model data is saved and a physical model of the guide is created using a Rapid Prototyping machine (dimension SST, Stratasys, Inc., USA). Thermo-plastic acrylonitrile butadiene styrene (ABS) is the material used during this 3D printing process.[14]

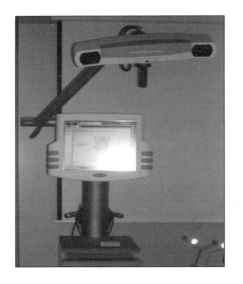
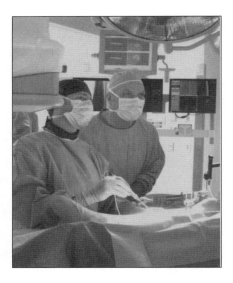
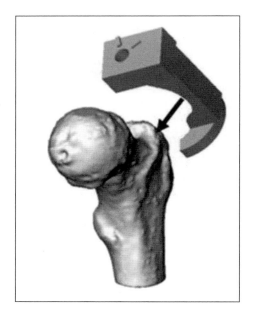

Figure 4.6: Surgical navigation versus patient-specific templates.

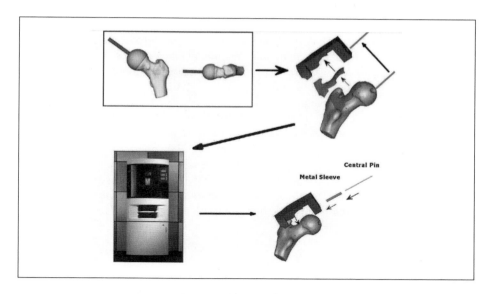

Figure 4.7: CT-Based 3D model.

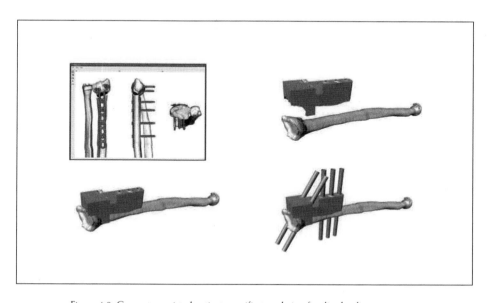

Figure 4.8: Computer-assisted patient-specific templating for distal radius osteotomy.

In order to compare the accuracy and precision of patient-specific instrument guidance compared to optical computer-assisted navigation, we conducted a laboratory experiment involving the use of CT scans, computer models, and planned corrections of wrist bones from seven patients who had previously received computer-assisted wrist fracture corrections. In this randomized study[15] senior and trainee orthopaedic surgeons compared optical-based computer-assisted and patient-specific guide procedures on plastic wrist bones. Outcome measures included ulnar variance, radial inclination and volar tilt. Using the patient-specific guides resulted in significantly more precise corrections for ulnar variance and radial inclination, but no significant differences between the groups on accuracy. The instrument guidance group also required significantly less time than computer-assisted navigation for this surgical procedure (Table 4.1). We also found that the guides provide an excellent training tool, whereby junior trainees achieved results typically only seen with experienced surgeons when using conventional techniques (Figure 4.9).

	Patient-specific Instrument Guidance	Optical Computer- assisted Navigation
Ulnar variance error, mm mean (SD)	-0.2 +/- 2.0	-0.7 +/- 0.6
Radial inclination error, degrees mean (SD)	-0.9 +/- 6.1	-1.0 +/- 1.4
Volar tilt error, degrees mean (SD)	-0.4 +/- 2.2	-0.9 +/- 1.9
Time, seconds mean (SD)	214 +/- 98	705 +/- 144

Table 4.1. Patient-specific versus Optical Computer Navigation.

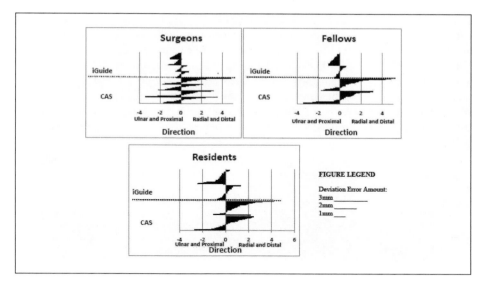

Figure 4.9: Drill position errors - Deviation between planned and final achieved screw hole position

Current Image Guided Surgery Research Activity

Notwithstanding the value of the forgoing technological advances, the requirement for preoperative imaging, image processing and planning is frequently time consuming, expensive and inefficient. Recent significant innovations have initiated the development and verification of highly accurate and robust methodologies for calibration of either a 3D fluoroscopy image, or a 3D CT image, to a ceiling mounted optical tracker.[16] Complementary to this calibration, advances in hardware rendering technology have made real-time visualization of large 3D image volumes feasible. This innovation eliminates the need for time-consuming preoperative image analysis. Work is ongoing to design, test and deploy novel real-time methodologies to permit rapid, affordable intraoperative 3D imaging and image visualization during the navigation of orthopaedic surgeries.

Image-Guided Surgery Suites

We are fortunate to have a state-of-the-art operating room at Kingston General Hospital. To our knowledge, this Image-guided Surgery Suite (ISS) is the only computer-assisted surgical suite in the world equipped with an angiography/computed-tomography (A/CT) unit. It is comprised of a mobile CT unit for real-time imaging at low radiation dosage CT and a floor-mounted L-arm/C-arm fluoroscope for angiography and cone-beam CT (CBCT).[17] Fluoroscopes emit a 'cone' shaped x-ray beam. When a computer driven spin of the C-arm is used to accumulate multiple sequential images, a CT-like image called a cone-beam CT is made possible. The locations of the ceiling-mounted camera and Innova™ imager are fixed, thereby allowing us to perform a preoperative calibration between the two systems. The systems produce accurate depictions of both soft tissue and bony anatomy. Because the 3D images from the mobile CT and the Innova™ C-arm can be viewed as they are acquired, they eliminate the need to transfer patients from table to table. This provides the opportunity for 3D imaging, virtual modeling of the region of interest, and planning and execution of the intervention all during one treatment episode. We believe this technology, with further development, can be translated onto conventional commercially available portable 3D fluoroscopy machines. (Figure 4.10).

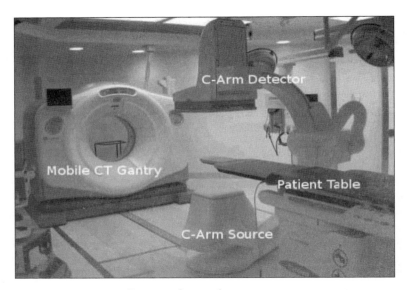

Figure 4.10: Integrated imaging suite.

In a recent proof of principle study at our center, the use of direct CBCT navigation in our ISS suite was evaluated for the purpose of drilling and pinning a fractured wrist bone. Our navigated approach was compared to two other approaches for percutaneous fixation: one using a standard portable 2D fluoroscopic C-arm and the second using the Innova™ C-arm in conventional 2D mode with anterior-posterior & lateral x-rays. Three surgeons performed 8 test trials for each approach technique, for a total of 24 trials, in which a K-wire was inserted along the central axis of the scaphoid. The hypothesis was that our direct navigation technique would lead to more accurate and precise positioning of a fixation wire along the central axis of the wrist bone when compared to conventional fluoroscopic techniques.[18]

For this study a plastic wrist model, based on a CT of a normal wrist, was created using a rapid prototyping printer. The model featured an exchangeable scaphoid wrist bone, which could be replaced following each trial. Our innovative navigation procedure made use of the Innova™ C-arm to obtain an intraoperative 3D CBCT scan of the wrist from which volume-rendered views were created. Preoperative calibration of the imaging and optical tracking systems permitted direct navigation of the drilling procedure using the CBCT image. An optically tracked drill guide was used to perform the procedure. Images of the guide and its orientation relative to the rendered images were displayed to the surgeon on monitors in the operating room.

A screenshot from the navigation software interface during one of the navigated trials is shown in Figure 4.11. The CBCT spin image was volume rendered, analogous to a digitally-rendered x-ray (DRR), and shown in anterior-posterior (A-P) and lateral views on the navigation interface. Unlike planar DRRs, however, the rendered CBCT images could be rotated in 3D in order to appreciate the complex geometry of the scaphoid. During a preoperative planning phase, the surgeon could rotate the images in order to position a target drill path on the scaphoid. During the drilling phase, the real-time orientation and projected drill path of the optically-tracked drill guide was overlaid on the A-P and lateral navigation views.

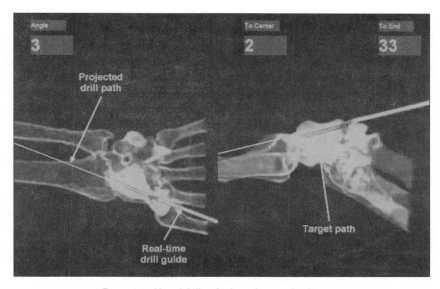

Figure 4.11: Virtual drill path planned on scaphoid bone.

After all trials were completed, each model scaphoid was imaged using high resolution CT (0.625mm slices) and carefully segmented to create a 3D digital surface mesh of the drilled scaphoid and the drill hole. The centricity or "safety" of screw placement was computed by fitting a straight line to the centre of the drill hole and finding the closest point from this line to the scaphoid surface mesh. Because the drill path and scaphoid mesh intersect, it was necessary to exclude a tolerance region of 2.5mm above and below the entry point of the drill path for this calculation. Other outcomes measures that were recorded for each trial were the number of drill passes, procedure time, and radiation dose recorded by an exposure meter.

Several key findings of this pilot study suggest that navigation may improve the ease and accuracy of percutaneous fixation in the scaphoid. First, the closest distance from the drill path to the scaphoid surface was considered to be a "safety factor" for the likelihood of screw breach. In the navigated group, the mean safe distance was 2.8 ± 0.5 mm which was significantly higher than the 2D Innova group which had a mean safe distance of 2.6 ± 0.5 mm ($p<0.05$). Second, navigation required an average of 1.5 ± 0.7 drill passes which was significantly less than the 2.2 ± 0.8 passes noted in the conventional C-arm group ($p<0.01$). Also, drilling during the navigated procedures took more than double the time using conventional C-arm or Innova imaging, although the overall time remained clinically acceptable at under 4 minutes. There was no significant difference in radiation exposure to the patient between the three methods. The 3D CBCT image was acquired remotely in the navigated approach, so conceivably the exposure to the surgeon was much less than the other techniques.

Image-guided surgery has resulted in better precision for difficult procedures, a superior learning tool for new surgeons, a reduction in intraoperative radiation exposure and is more efficient for some procedures. Currently, industries are working to develop better 3D portable fluoroscopic technology. Our hope is to translate our real-time imaging, planning and navigation techniques to this portable technology in order to support surgeons in many and varying settings.

[1] E. Grimson, M. Leventon, L. Lorigo, T. Kapur and R. Kikinis, "Image Guided Surgery," Michael Leventon 'Home Page', http://www.leventon.com/mit/pubs.html, accessed 17 January 2011.

[2] G.S. Athwal, R.E. Ellis, C.F. Small, and D.R. Pichora, "Computer-Assisted Distal Radius Osteotomy," *Journal of Hand Surgery* Vol. 28A, No. 6 (2003): 952.

[3] A. von Campe, L. Nagy, D. Arbab, and C.E. Dumont, "Corrective Osteotomy in Malunions of the Distal Radius - Do We Get What We Planned?" *Clinical Orthopaedics and Related Research* Vol. 450 (2006): 184.

[4] A. Abramo, M. Tagil, M. Geijer and P. Kopylov, "Osteotomy of Dorsally Displaced Malunited Fractures of the Distal Radius," Acta Orthopaedica Vol. 79, No. 2 (2008): 262–268.

[5] K.J. Prommersberger and U. Lanz. "Biomechanics of the Malunited Distal Radius fracture: A Literature Review," *Handchirurgie, Mikrochirurgie, Plastische Chirurgie* Vol. 31, No. 4 (1999): 221-226.

[6] H.T. Aro and T. Koivunen. "Minor Axial Shortening of the Radius Affects Outcome of Colles' Fracture Treatment," *Journal of Hand Surgery* Am. Vol. 16A, No. 3 (1991): 392-398.

[7] G.S. Athwal, R.E. Ellis, C.F. Small and D.R. Pichora, "Computer-Assisted Distal Radius Osteotomy," *Journal of Hand Surgery* Vol. 28A, No. 6 (2003): 951-58.

[8]Traxtal Technologies Inc., a subsidiary of Phillips Healthcare.

[9]OPTOTRAK 3020, Northern Digital Inc. Waterloo, Canada, http://www.ndigital.com/optotrak-techspecs.php, accessed 26 May 2011.

[10]R.E. Ellis, C.Y. Tso, J.R. Rudan and M.M. Harrison, "A Surgical Planning and Guidance System for High Tibial Osteotomy," *Computer Aided Surgery* Vol. 4, No. 5 (1999): 264-274.

[11]Klaus Radermacher, Frank Portheine, Marc Anton, Andreas Zimolong, Günther Kaspers, Günter Rau, and Hans-Walter Staudte, "Computer Assisted Orthopaedic Surgery with Image Based Individual Templates," *Clinical Orthopaedics and Related Research* Vol. 354 (1998): 28-38.

[12]K. Oka, H. Moritomo, A. Goto, K. Sugamato, H. Yoshikawa and T. Murase, "Corrective Osteotomy for Malunited Intra-Articular Fracture of the Distal Radius Using a Custom-Made Surgical Guide Based on Three-Dimensional Computer Simulation: A Case Report," *Journal of Hand Surgery* Vol. 33A, No. 6 (2008): 835-840.

[13]M. Kunz, J.F. Rudan, G.L. Xenoyannis and R.E. Ellis, "Computer-Assisted Hip Resurfacing Using Individualized Drill Templates," Journal of Arthroplasty Vol. 25, No. 4 (2010): 600-606.

[14]M. Kunz, B. Ma, R.E. Ellis, J.F. Rudan, and D.R. Pichora, "Distal Radius Osteotomy Using Patient-Specific Instrument Guides: A Clinical Trial," *The Journal of Hand Surgery* (submitted).

[15]B. Ma, M. Kunz, G. Fedorak, J. Rudan. H. Alsanawi, B. Smith, R. Ellis and D. Pichora, "Computer-assisted Navigation vs. Customized Jigs for Distal Radius Osteotomy" (proceedings, 9th Annual Meeting of the International Society for Computer Assisted Orthopaedic Surgery – CAOS, Boston, MA, June 17-20, (2009).

[16]R.E. Ellis, Toksvig-Larsen, S., Marcacci, M. *et al.* "Use of a Biocompatible Fiducial Marker in Evaluating the Accuracy of CT Image Registration," *Investigative Radiology* Vol. 31, No. 58 (1996): 658-67; P. Abolmaesumi, S.E. Salcudean, W.H. Zhu, M.R. Sirouspour and S.P. DiMaio, "ImageGuided Control of a Robot for Medical Ultrasound," *IEEE Transactions on Robotic Automation* 18, no.11 (2002): 11-23; Ma, B., and R.E. Ellis. "Robust registration for Computer-Integrated Orthopedic Surgery: Laboratory Validation and Clinical Experience," *Medical Image Analysis* Vol. 7, No. 237 (2003): 237-50.

[17]InnovaTM , GE Healthcare, W.I. Milwakee, GE Healthcare Surgery Suite Brochure, www.gehealthcare.com, accessed 26 May 2011.

[18]E.H. Smith, R.E. Al-Sanawi, P.J. Ellis, St. John and D.R. Pichora, "Accuracy and Precision of Percutaneous Scaphoid Fixation Using 3-D Volumetric Navigation: Level 2 Evidence," *Journal of Hand Surgery* Vol. 35, No. 10 (2010): 1-56.

CHAPTER 5

Potential Benefits of Interval Training for Active Military Personnel and Military Veterans

Brendon J Gurd, PhD and Jasmin K Ma, School of Kinesiology and Health Studies, Queen's University

ABSTRACT

Increasing incidences of overweight issues and obesity have impacted the military on two levels: 1) recruitment of future military personnel and the ability of current personnel to perform their duties, 2) development of obesity-associated disease in military veterans. Interval training may prove effective at reducing weight gain and associated disease in both active military personnel and veterans. This article aims at reviewing literature that examines the impact of interval training on aerobic fitness, exercise tolerance, exercise performance, body weight, insulin sensitivity, mitochondrial content and risk factors associated with cardiovascular disease. Whenever possible, we will attempt to compare the effects of interval training to traditional endurance training. This article presents evidence that interval training increases aerobic capacity, exercise tolerance and exercise performance in both young adults and diseased populations and induces weight loss and improves insulin sensitivity, and cardiovascular health in overweight/obese and diseased populations. Improvements following interval training appear to match, or in some cases even exceed those observed following endurance training. It is the recommendation of this review that interval training be adopted into the physical activity regimes of active military personnel and be utilized in life-style interventions aimed at improving health in medically cleared veterans. The recent increase in overweight issues and obesity in the North American population are well documented. The military is not exempt from these changes and is being affected on two levels: 1) increasing body weights in young adults is impacting both the recruitment of future military personnel and the ability of current personnel to perform their duties, and 2) incidences of overweight and obesity and the development of obesity associated disease are increasing in military veterans. While physical activity can both treat and prevent weight gain and its associated diseases, little is currently known about the specific amount and intensity of exercise that provides optimal benefit. Interval training represents a time efficient mode of exercise that may prove effective at reducing weight gain and disease. The current review will explore the potential benefits of interval training for both active military personnel and military veterans.

THE NEED FOR EFFECTIVE EXERCISE INTERVENTION IN MILITARY PERSONNEL

There is a minimum level of physical fitness that is required for military personnel to meet the physical demands associated with military service. As overweight issues and obesity increase in both the civilian and military populations there is a decreasing availability of appropriate recruits for military service.[1] Depending on the branch of the military, it is estimated that between 20-50% of the US population between 17 and 42 years of age does not qualify for military service. If this trend continues it is possible that entry standards for body mass index (BMI) may have to become more lenient in order to maintain current levels of recruitment.[2] Should this reduction in entry standards occur, there will be a need for effective interventions that both reduce body weight and, more importantly, increase physical fitness in new recruits such that they are capable of performing the physical tasks associated with military service.

The increasing incidence of overweight and obesity also has repercussions for retention of military personnel as active members of the military workforce.[3] Several reports indicate that close to 50% of military personnel in the US forces are overweight and, alarmingly, this percentage appears to be increasing.[4] These increases in weight gain are associated with a significant health care cost and a significant loss of productivity.[5] While a majority of military personnel surveyed between 1995 and 1998 reported regular participation in vigorous physical activity[6] this participation is clearly not adequate. There is a need for optimization of physical activity such that the required physical fitness and body weight can be achieved and maintained in military personnel.

As the military population ages and retires from active duty there are other, health related complications associated with an elevated body weight. These complications include impaired insulin sensitivity, type II diabetes, cardiovascular disease, heart failure and stroke. Importantly, the trend for high rates of overweight and obesity seen in military recruits and active personnel is also present in veteran populations. Indeed, rates of overweight and obesity in veteran populations are similar (overweight, men 73.3%, women 53.6%; obese, men 25.3%, women 21.2%) to those observed in the general population.[7] In particular, the incidence of diabetes, a disease also associated with cardiovascular complications, heart failure and stroke,[8] was equivalent or higher in veterans than non-veterans.[9] Further, the incidence of diabetes appears to be increasing in the veteran population.[10] As a result, the development of appropriate life-style interventions, incorporating exercise, should be a priority for the treatment of obesity and obesity related disease in veteran populations. There may be a role for interval training in these interventions.

INTERVAL TRAINING FOR MILITARY POPULATIONS

Regular physical activity is associated with reduced risk for development of obesity and diabetes[11] and life-style interventions utilizing exercise improve risk factors associated with disease in already obese populations.[12] In addition, exercise has long been associated with improved physical fitness[13] and optimized exercise intervention in military personnel will increase performance of activities associated with military service. Interval training is a time effective, stimulus for increasing both physical fitness and exercise performance and reducing the risk of obesity and its related diseases. While the study of interval training has included many different protocols, for ease of discussion, we will group these varied protocols into 3 different groups: 1) moderate intensity interval training (MIIT; 2-4 minute intervals at 80-95%, maximal aerobic capacity or VO_2max), 2) high intensity interval training (HIIT; 1-2 minute interval at 95-120% VO_2max), and 3) sprint interval training (SIT; 20-30 seconds maximal intensities).

This review will examine the effects of interval training on physical fitness and variables associated with obesity and obesity related disease. Specifically, we will examine the impact of interval training on aerobic fitness, exercise tolerance, exercise performance, body weight, insulin sensitivity, mitochondrial content and risk factors associated with cardiovascular disease. Whenever possible, we will attempt to compare the effects of HIIT to traditional endurance training.

Aerobic Fitness, Exercise Tolerance and Exercise Performance

As discussed above, physical fitness is an important determinant of an individual's ability to perform the physical tasks associated with military service. In military veterans, physical fitness can become a determining factor in the ability to perform tasks of daily living (getting out of chairs, climbing stairs, walking, etc.). In the following section we will discuss the impact of interval training on 3 markers of physical fitness: 1) maximal aerobic fitness (exercise capacity or the maximal ability to utilize oxygen; VO_2max), 2) exercise tolerance (ability to maintain a given task for an extended period of time), and 3) exercise performance (the level at which a given task can be performed).

Interval training and maximal aerobic fitness in military personnel. VO_2max is a measure of both cardiovascular/metabolic fitness and aerobic power. Importantly for military personnel, VO_2max sets the upper limit for sustainable exercise, as any exercise performed above VO_2max is associated with accumulations of metabolic bi-products and rapid fatigue. Thus, increasing VO_2max is an important target of any exercise intervention aimed at improving physical fitness in military recruits, or active military personnel that may be overweight and/or obese.

All intensities of interval training are associated with improvements in VO_2max in healthy adults. MIIT protocols increased VO_2max by 8-13% in men and women following as little as two weeks of training.[14] HIIT has proved equally effective at improving VO_2max with increases ranging from 5-16% in as little as three weeks of training.[15] One study demonstrated an increased VO_2max in men, but not women following 8 weeks of training utilizing a protocol of three, two minute intervals at 85-100%.[16] This may indicate a lower threshold for interval training induced adaptation in men and also suggests that three high-intensity intervals per training session may not be an adequate stimulus to increase aerobic fitness in all populations. Another study utilizing HIIT demonstrated a similar improvement in VO_2max when intervals were performed at 95% for either 30 seconds or two minutes.[17] This result suggests that intensity rather than interval length determines improvement in VO_2max following HIIT. Inconsistent with interval intensity being the primary determinant of adaptation are two reports that two weeks of SIT (four to six, 30 second intervals at maximal anaerobic power) did not increase VO_2max.[18] Two other studies, one utilizing the same SIT protocol as the aforementioned studies and another utilizing 20 second intervals at 170% did observe an increase in VO_2max following 6 weeks of training. While the two SIT studies that did not observe an increase in VO_2max were short (two weeks) increases in aerobic fitness have been observed following two week interventions of both MIIT[19] and HIIT.[20] Thus, it is not currently clear whether the effects of interval training on VO_2max is determined by interval intensity, interval duration, number of intervals per training session, or the length of a training program. Despite these uncertainties it is clear that interval training at any intensity can increase aerobic capacity. We recommended that any intervention aimed at improving aerobic fitness in military personnel either use MIIT or HIIT or be of a sufficient duration that the lack of improvements observed following two weeks of SIT would not be an issue. Further research is required to determine the optimal intensity or duration of intervals for maximal improvements in aerobic fitness.

Interval training and maximal aerobic fitness in military veterans. One of the criticisms of interval training has been that its inherent high intensity nature will not be tolerated by inactive individuals and will thus be ineffective at improving physical fitness in sedentary or diseased populations. Contrary to this commonly held belief several studies in diseased and overweight/obese populations utilizing both MIIT[21] and SIT[22] have demonstrated increases in physical fitness. In young overweight/obese men, two weeks of SIT increased VO_2max by 10%.[23] Much larger increases in VO_2max (18-53%) have been reported following MIIT in patients with coronary artery disease,[24] post myocardial infarct[25] and metabolic syndrome.[26] In these populations improvements in VO_2max following MIIT were greater than those induced by endurance exercise. Interval training would thus appear to be a tolerable alternative to traditional endurance type exercise for military veterans who are suffering from overweight, obesity and/or obesity related disease. In fact the available evidence would suggest that MIIT would produce greater benefit than endurance training, however, this hypothesis has yet to be tested in a population of military veterans.

Changes in exercise tolerance and performance. One benefit associated with exercise training is an increased tolerance for exercise at a given intensity. This is measured by determining the time to exhaustion, or time to fatigue (TTF) at a set work rate. Significant improvements in TTF have been observed following several intensities of interval training. For example, TTF for cycle exercise at 90% VO_2max was increased 111% following 6 weeks of MIIT[27] while 4 weeks of HIIT improved TTF at 100% VO_2max by 55%.[28] In the later study, improvements following HIIT were greater than those observed following endurance training (43%), however, this difference failed to reach statistical significance. Similar to MIIT and HIIT, SIT also improved exercise tolerance by 21% for exercise at 130% VO_2max[29] and by 100% for exercise at 80% VO_2max.[30] In a study with patients suffering from coronary artery disease TTF at 90% of heart rate reserve was increased 450%.[31] This increase in exercise tolerance was approximately double the increase observed in a matched group of subjects who completed endurance training.

Exercise performance (the time required to complete a task, or the ease with which a task is completed) is also improved by interval training. Time trial performance on a cycle ergometer was improved by SIT with the time required to complete both 250 kJ[32] and 750 kJ[33] of work being reduced by training. Increases in sport specific performance have also been observed in runners[34] and cyclists[35] while peak power was increased by SIT.[36] The ease with which a given exercise task is performed is also improved following exercise training. Increased ease of exercise is indicated by a decreased exercise heart rate for a set exercise intensity following both MIIT[37] and SIT[38]. In addition, a decreased reliance on energy systems associated with muscle fatigue is observed following interval training. This is indicated by both a decreased accumulation of lactate during exercise[39] and an increased reliance on fatty acid oxidation[40] following both MIIT and SIT. These improvements in substrate metabolism are likely due to increases in both the lactate and ventilatory thresholds, as increases in both of these thresholds have been observed following HIIT.[41] Interestingly, the increase in ventilatory threshold was observed to be greater following interval training than endurance training.[42] However, as will become a theme in this review, most of the studies comparing exercise performance following interval and endurance training were not adequately powered to detect differences. Thus, further research is needed to determine if differences in exercise performance following interval and endurance training exist.

Given the evidence discussed above, interval training appears to be an effective means of increasing exercise tolerance and exercise performance in both active military personnel and veterans. Increases in exercise performance in these populations will both improve the ability of active military personnel to perform tasks associated with military service and improve the ability of veterans to perform tasks associated with day-to-day living.

Interval training vs. endurance training. Several studies have compared increases in aerobic fitness following interval training and traditional endurance training in young, healthy adults. However, most of these studies were statistically powered to detect an improvement within training groups rather than between training groups; as a result few statistical differences between interval training and endurance training have been detected. The most common observation from these studies is that similar increases in physical fitness (VO_2max, exercise tolerance and exercise performance) are achieved following interval training despite a considerably smaller time commitment.[43] For example, equivalent improvements in VO_2max and time to fatigue at 100% were observed following four weeks of HIIT and endurance training despite total exercise time (including rest for interval training) being 160 minutes in the HIIT group and 825 minutes in the endurance group. Similarly, in a study that demonstrated equal increases in VO_2max and exercise performance following SIT and endurance training the weekly time commitment (including rest between intervals) was 90 minutes for SIT and 270 minutes for endurance training.[44] Across all six weeks of this study this meant a time savings for the SIT group of more than 18 hours. Interestingly, when time of exercise and total work performed were held constant, improvements in VO_2max were observed following HIIT but not endurance training.[45] There is a need for well controlled studies that are adequately statistically powered to determine if differences exist in improved physical fitness, exercise tolerance and exercise performance between interval and endurance training. Until these studies are performed, the major benefit associated with interval training, as it relates to physical fitness, appears to be the ability to induce improvements in fitness in a fraction of the time required for similar benefit to be achieved by endurance training.

Improved Health Outcomes Following Interval Training

As discussed above, the incidence of obesity is on the rise in military veterans[46] and the incidence of insulin resistance and type II diabetes in veterans is equal to or greater than that observed in the general population.[47] Perhaps of greater concern is the apparent trend for an increase in the incidence rate of diabetes in veteran populations.[48] The prevalence of obesity and diabetes in military veterans places them at high risk for obesity related health complications that include cardiovascular disease, heart failure and stroke. The introduction of regular exercise to military veterans has the potential to reduce the incidence of overweight and obesity, but more importantly, regular exercise is associated with improved insulin sensitivity[49] and reduced risk of cardiovascular disease.[50] In the following section, we will discuss the health benefits associated with interval training. Specifically we will discuss the impact of interval training on weight loss, insulin sensitivity, and cardiovascular disease.

Interval training and weight loss. Considering the mounting evidence that short-term exercise interventions rarely result in significant weight loss it is unfortunate that the main perceived benefit associated with regular exercise is weight loss.[51] This lack of effect may be due to increases in appetite, a masking of fat loss by gains in muscle mass, or by a myriad of other confounding factors. Because of this apparent failure, the many beneficial effects of exercise (including increases in aerobic capacity, exercise tolerance and performance, insulin sensitivity and cardiovascular health) that are independent of weight loss are often forgotten. Thus we would stress, as has been suggested elsewhere[52] that the emphasis on exercise benefit be shifted away from weight loss and onto the other beneficial effects induced by exercise training. We will however, provide a brief discussion of weight loss induced by interval training.

In general, the short duration and intermittent nature of interval training means that caloric expenditure is likely lower than would be expended during longer duration, constant load, endurance exercise. Interestingly, while the majority of research has failed to demonstrate weight loss following interval training in both young adults[53] and diseased populations,[54] the available evidence would suggest that interval training is at least as effective in inducing weight loss as endurance training. For example, four weeks of both HIIT and endurance training induced similar weight loss in young active men[55] while weight loss in patients with coronary artery disease and in overweight adults with metabolic syndrome[57] was similar between MIIT and endurance training. Thus, it would appear that interval training is equally effective at inducing weight loss as endurance training.

Interval training improves insulin resistance and mitochondrial content. Exercise has proven preventative and therapeutic effects on insulin resistance in diabetic individuals.[58] While the effects of exercise intensity on insulin resistance is controversial there is some evidence that improvements in insulin sensitivity and in symptoms associated with insulin resistance are greater following high intensity exercise.[59] It is therefore of interest if the relationship between exercise intensity and improved insulin sensitivity extends to interval training. In healthy adults, two weeks of SIT improved the response to an oral glucose tolerance test (decreased area under the curve for glucose and insulin).[60] However, somewhat surprisingly, a similar SIT intervention failed to improve insulin sensitivity in overweight and obese men.[61] The reason for these discrepant results is not currently clear and requires further research. In overweight and obese adults with metabolic syndrome, a 16-week intervention with MIIT improved insulin sensitivity and insulin action in skeletal muscle.[62] In this study, there were no improvements in insulin sensitivity following endurance training of the same duration. MIIT also reduced blood concentrations of C-reactive protein, a marker of insulin resistance, in patients with coronary artery disease.[63]

While there are few studies that have directly examined insulin sensitivity following interval training there is considerably more evidence surrounding the effects of interval training mitochondrial content, an important contributor to skeletal muscle insulin sensitivity. In support of mitochondrial content contributing to insulin sensitivity, increases in mitochondrial content are associated with improved metabolic health[64] and impairments in mitochondrial content are associated with decrements in muscle function, including insulin resistance.[65] Therefore, mitochondrial content is clinically relevant as an underlying mechanism of insulin resistance in obesity and type II diabetes. Increases in mitochondrial content have been repeatedly demonstrated following both MIIT and SIT. Citrate synthase activity, and bHAD activity, both markers of mitochondrial content, were increased 20-28% and 29-36% respectively following MIIT.[66] While no change in either citrate synthase[67] or bHAD[68] activities have been reported, these markers of mitochondrial content are consistently elevated following SIT (citrate synthase, +11-38%; bHAD, +25%).[69] SIT also induced increases in mitochondrial protein.[70]   Comparisons of increased mitochondrial content following SIT and endurance training demonstrate equivalent increases[71] however, it should be noted that these studies were not statistically powered to detect differences between training types. It is also important to note that the equivalent increases in mitochondrial content in these studies were accomplished with a considerably smaller time commitment in the interval training groups.

The available evidence suggests that interval training effectively improves insulin sensitivity and mitochondrial content, one mechanism responsible for determining insulin sensitivity. These results, combined with the tolerance for interval training demonstrated by overweight/diseased populations suggest that interval training is an appropriate exercise modality for life-style interventions aimed at improving health in military veterans.

Cardiovascular health following interval training. Incidence of cardiovascular disease is lower in populations of people who participate in regular physical activity. Further, it is accepted that the addition of exercise to an individual's life-style will improve cardiovascular health.[72] However, similar to other factors associated with overall health the optimal intensity of exercise for improving cardiovascular health is not known. Interval training is associated with improved cardiovascular function and may prove effective at increasing cardiovascular health in military veterans. Recent evidence has suggested that higher intensity exercise is associated with greater improvements in the cardiovascular z-score (an index of overall cardiovascular health).[73] Individual components of cardiovascular health are also improved following interval training. Cardiac function (ejection fraction and ability to deliver oxygen) is improved following MIIT in coronary artery disease patients.[74] There are also increases in vascular function following interval training; both endothelial function[75] and flow mediated dilation[76] are improved following MIIT and these increases were greater following interval training than endurance training. In overweight and obese adults SIT[77] and MIIT[78] decreased systolic and mean arterial blood pressure respectively. The improvements in mean arterial pressure in the later study were similar between MIIT and endurance training.[79] Finally, left ventricular remodelling observed in coronary artery disease patients was reversed to a greater extent following interval training.[80]

In an interesting study considering perceived exertion, time spent above 80% VO_2max, and patient comfort, investigators recommended a HIIT protocol consisting of 15-second intervals at 100% VO_2max for coronary artery disease patients.[81] This protocol was well tolerated by the patients examined and was preferred over intervals of different intensities and durations. To our knowledge, the impact of HIIT on cardiovascular health has not been examined but given the beneficial, and in many cases superior, impact of MIIT there is a need for studies examining the impact of HIIT on cardiovascular health in at risk populations. It would appear that interval training should be recommended for military veterans to improve cardiovascular health; however, there is a need for studies examining the impact of interval training and endurance training in this population before interval training should be exclusively recommended.

RECOMMENDATIONS AND FUTURE DIRECTIONS

It is clear that the benefits traditionally associated with endurance training are also observed following interval training. We have presented evidence that interval training increases aerobic capacity, exercise tolerance and exercise performance in both young adults and diseased populations. Further, improvements in weight loss, insulin sensitivity, and cardiovascular health following interval training appear to match, or even exceed those observed following endurance training. While these results are supportive of the beneficial effects of interval training, before interval training can be recommended to military populations unreservedly there is a need for studies examining, in military personnel, the impact of interval training on fitness and on performance in military specific tasks. There is also a need for studies examining the health benefits of interval training in military veterans.

These caveats aside, it is the recommendation of this review that interval training be adopted into the physical activity regimes of active military personnel and be utilized in life-style interventions aimed at improving health in medically cleared military veterans. At the least, there are considerable time savings associated with interval training, especially HIIT[82] and SIT[83] while at best, interval training may provide benefits in excess of endurance training, especially in overweight[84] and diseased[85] populations. While it is not currently clear whether or not benefits associated with interval training are superior to those induced by endurance training there is enough evidence to support further investigation examining this potential. Thus, there is a need for well-controlled, randomized trials that are statistically powered to detect differences in the adaptations induced by interval and endurance training.[86]

[1]R. Nolte, S.C. Franckowiak, C.J. Crespo, and R.E. Andersen "U.S. military weight standards: what percentage of U.S. young adults meet the current standards?" *Am J Med* Vol. 113, No. 6 (2002): 486-490; G.K. Yamane, "Obesity in civilian adults: potential impact on eligibility for U.S. military enlistment," *Mil Med* Vol. 172, No. 11 (2007): 1160-1165.

[2]R. McLaughlin and G. Wittert, "The obesity epidemic: implications for recruitment and retention of defence force personnel," *Obes Rev* Vol. 10, No. 6 (2009): 693-699.

[3]R. McLaughlin and G. Wittert, "The obesity epidemic: implications for recruitment and retention of defence force personnel," *Obes Rev* Vol.v10, No. 6 (2009): 693-699.

[4]C.H. Lindquist and R.M. Bray, "Trends in overweight and physical activity among U.S. military personnel, 1995-1998," *Prev Med* Vol. 32, No. 1 (2001): 57-65; R.M. Bray, L.L. Hourani, K.L. Rae Olmsted, M. Witt, J.M. Brown, M.R. Pemberton, M.E. Marsden, B. Marriott, and S. Scheffler, "2005 Department of Defense Survey of Health Related Behaviors among Active Duty Military Personnel," (Research Triangle Institute, Research Triangle Park: NC, 2006), 1-305.

[5]A.S. Robbins, S.Y. Chao, C.R. Russ, and V.P. Fonseca, "Costs of excess body weight among active duty personnel, U.S. Air Force, 1997," *Mil Med* Vol. 167, No. 5 (2002): 393-397.

[6]C.H. Lindquist and R.M. Bray, "Trends in overweight and physical activity among U.S. military personnel, 1995-1998," *Prev Med* Vol. 32, No. 1 (2001): 57-65.

[7]N. Almond, L. Kahwati, L. Kinsinger, and D. Porterfield, "Prevalence of overweight and obesity among U.S. military veterans," *Mil Med* Vol. 173, No. 6 (2008): 544-549.

[8]M.M. Engelgau, L.S. Geiss, J.B. Saaddine, J.P. Boyle, S.M. Benjamin, E.W. Gregg, E.F. Tierney, N. Rios-Burrows, A.H. Mokdad, E.S. Ford, G. Imperatore, and K.M. Narayan, "The evolving diabetes burden in the United States," *Ann Intern Med* Vol. 140, No. 11 (2004): 945-950.

[9]G.E. Reiber, T.D. Koepsell, C. Maynard, L.B. Haas, and E.J. Boyko, "Diabetes in nonveterans, veterans, and veterans receiving Department of Veterans Affairs health care," *Diabetes Care* Vol. 27, No. 2, (2004): B3-B9; C.P. Lynch, J.L. Strom, and L.E. Egede, "Variation in quality of care indicators for diabetes in a national sample of veterans and non-veterans," *Diabetes Technol Ther* Vol. 12, No. 10 (2010): 785-790.

[10]D.R. Miller, M.M. Safford, and L.M. Pogach, "Who has diabetes? Best estimates of diabetes prevalence in the Department of Veterans Affairs based on computerized patient data," *Diabetes Care* Vol. 27, No. 2, (2004): B10-B21.

[11]M.J. LaMonte, S.N. Blair, and T.S. Church, "Physical activity and diabetes prevention," *J Appl Physiol* 99, no. 3 (2005): 1205-1213; X. Zhang, L.S. Geiss, C.J. Caspersen, Y.J. Cheng, M.M. Engelgau, J.A. Johnson, R.C. Plotnikoff, and E.W. Gregg, "Physical activity levels and differences in the prevalence of diabetes between the United States and Canada," *Prev Med* Vol. 50, No. 5-6 (2010): 241-245.

[12]R. Ross and I. Janssen "Physical activity, total and regional obesity: dose-response considerations.," *Med Sci Sports Exerc* Vol. 33, No. 6 (2001): S521-S527; B.H. Goodpaster, A. Katsiaras, and D.E. Kelley, "Enhanced fat oxidation through physical activity is associated with improvements in insulin sensitivity in obesity," *Diabetes* Vol. 52, No. 9 (2003): 2191-2197; E.V. Menshikova, V.B. Ritov, F.G. Toledo, R.E. Ferrell, B.H. Goodpaster, and D.E. Kelley, "Effects of weight loss and physical activity on skeletal muscle mitochondrial function in obesity," *Am J Physiol Endocrinol Metab* Vol. 288, No. 4 (2005): E818-E825.

[13]J.O. Holloszy and E.F. Coyle, "Adaptations of skeletal muscle to endurance exercise and their metabolic consequences," *J Appl Physiol* Vol. 56, no. 4 (1984): 831-838.

[14]J.L. Talanian, S.D. Galloway, G.J. Heigenhauser, A. Bonen, and L.L. Spriet, "Two weeks of high-intensity aerobic interval training increases the capacity for fat oxidation during exercise in women," *J Appl Physiol* Vol. 102, No. 104 (2007): 1439-1447; C.G. Perry, G.J. Heigenhauser, A. Bonen, and L.L. Spriet, "High-intensity aerobic interval training increases fat and carbohydrate metabolic capacities in human skeletal muscle," *Appl Physiol Nutr Metab* Vol. 33, No.6 (2008): 1112-1123; B.J. Gurd, C.G.R. Perry, G.J.F. Heigenhauser, L.L. Spriet, and A. Bonen. "High-intensity interval training increases SIRT1 activity in human skeletal muscle," *Applied Physiology, Nutrition and Metabolism* Vol. 35, No. 3 (2010): 350-357.

[15]D.C. Poole and G.A. Gaesser, "Response of ventilatory and lactate thresholds to continuous and interval training," J Appl Physiol Vol. 58, No. 4 (1985): 1115-1121; E.M. Gorostiaga, C.B. Walter, C. Foster, and R.C. Hickson, "Uniqueness of interval and continuous training at the same maintained exercise intensity," *Eur J Appl Physiol Occup Physiol* Vol. 63, No .2 (1991): 101-107; J. Burke, R. Thayer, and M. Belcamino, "Comparison of effects of two interval-training programmes on lactate and ventilatory thresholds," *Br J Sports Med* Vol. 28, No. 1 (1994):18-21; C.L. Weber and D.A. Schneider, "Increases in maximal accumulated oxygen deficit after high-intensity interval training are not gender dependent," *J Appl Physiol* Vol. 92, No. 5 (2002): 1795-1801; B.R. McKay, D.H. Paterson, and J.M. Kowalchuk, "Effect of short-term high-intensity interval training vs. continuous training on O2 uptake kinetics, muscle deoxygenation, and exercise performance," *J Appl Physiol* Vol. 107, No. 1 (2009): 128-138; A.E. Smith, A.A. Walter, J.L. Graef, K.L. Kendall, J.R. Moon, C.M. Lockwood, D.H. Fukuda, T.W. Beck, J.T. Cramer, and J.R. Stout, "Effects of beta-alanine supplementation and high-intensity interval training on endurance performance and body composition in men; a double-blind trial," *J Int Soc Sports Nutr* Vol. 6, No.1 (2009): 5.

[16]C.L. Weber and D.A. Schneider, "Increases in maximal accumulated oxygen deficit after high-intensity interval training are not gender dependent," *J Appl Physiol* Vol. 92, No. 5 (2002): 1795-1801.

[17]J. Burke, R. Thayer, and M. Belcamino, "Comparison of effects of two interval-training programmes on lactate and ventilatory thresholds," *Br J Sports Med* Vol. 28, No.1 (1994):18-21.

[18]K.A. Burgomaster, S.C. Hughes, G.J. Heigenhauser, S.N. Bradwell, and M.J. Gibala, "Six sessions of sprint interval training increases muscle oxidative potential and cycle endurance capacity in humans," *J Appl Physiol* Vol. 98, No. 6 (2005): 1985-1990; K.A. Burgomaster, G.J. Heigenhauser, and M.J. Gibala, "Effect of short-term sprint interval training on human skeletal muscle carbohydrate metabolism during exercise and time-trial performance," *J Appl Physiol* Vol. 100, No. 6 (2006): 2041-2047.

[19]J.L. Talanian, S.D. Galloway, G.J. Heigenhauser, A. Bonen, and L.L. Spriet, "Two weeks of high-intensity

aerobic interval training increases the capacity for fat oxidation during exercise in women," *J Appl Physiol* Vol. 102, No. 104 (2007): 1439-1447.

[20]B.R. McKay, D.H. Paterson, and J.M. Kowalchuk, "Effect of short-term high-intensity interval training vs. continuous training on O2 uptake kinetics, muscle deoxygenation, and exercise performance," *J Appl Physiol* Vol. 107, No. 1 (2009): 128-138.

[21]O. Rognmo, E. Hetland, J. Helgerud, J. Hoff, and S.A. Slordahl, "High intensity aerobic interval exercise is superior to moderate intensity exercise for increasing aerobic capacity in patients with coronary artery disease," *Eur J Cardiovasc Prev Rehabil* Vol. 11, No. 3 (2004): 216-222; D.E. Warburton, D.C. McKenzie, M.J. Haykowsky, A. Taylor, P. Shoemaker, A.P. Ignaszewski, and S.Y. Chan, "Effectiveness of high-intensity interval training for the rehabilitation of patients with coronary artery disease," *Am J Cardiol* Vol. 95, No. 9 (2005): 1080-1084; U. Wisloff, A. Stoylen, J.P. Loennechen, M. Bruvold, O. Rognmo, P.M. Haram, A.E. Tjonna, J. Helgerud, S.A. Slordahl, S.J. Lee, V. Videm, A. Bye, G.L. Smith, S.M. Najjar, O. Ellingsen and T. Skjaerpe, "Superior cardiovascular effect of aerobic interval training versus moderate continuous training in heart failure patients: a randomized study," *Circulation* Vol. 115, No. 24 (2007): 3086-3094; A.E. Tjonna, S.J. Lee, O. Rognmo, T.O. Stolen, A. Bye, P.M. Haram, J.P. Loennechen, Q.Y. Al-Share, E. Skogvoll, S.A. Slordahl, O.J. Kemi, S.M. Najjar, and U. Wisloff, "Aerobic interval training versus continuous moderate exercise as a treatment for the metabolic syndrome: a pilot study," *Circulation* Vol. 118, No. 4 (2008): 346-354.

[22]L.J. Whyte, J.M. Gill, and A.J. Cathcart, "Effect of 2 weeks of sprint interval training on health-related outcomes in sedentary overweight/obese men," *Metabolism* Vol. 59, No. 10 (2010): 1421-1428.

[23]L.J. Whyte, J.M. Gill, and A.J. Cathcart, "Effect of 2 weeks of sprint interval training on health-related outcomes in sedentary overweight/obese men," *Metabolism* Vol. 59, No. 10 (2010): 1421-1428.

[24]O. Rognmo, E. Hetland, J. Helgerud, J. Hoff, and S.A. Slordahl, "High intensity aerobic interval exercise is superior to moderate intensity exercise for increasing aerobic capacity in patients with coronary artery disease," *Eur J Cardiovasc Prev Rehabil* Vol. 11, No. 3 (2004): 216-222; D.E. Warburton, D.C. McKenzie, M.J. Haykowsky, A. Taylor, P. Shoemaker, A.P. Ignaszewski, and S.Y. Chan, "Effectiveness of high-intensity interval training for the rehabilitation of patients with coronary artery disease," *Am J Cardiol* Vol. 95, No. 9 (2005): 1080-1084.

[25]U. Wisloff, A. Stoylen, J.P. Loennechen, M. Bruvold, O. Rognmo, P.M. Haram, A.E. Tjonna, J. Helgerud, S.A. Slordahl, S.J. Lee, V. Videm, A. Bye, G.L. Smith, S.M. Najjar, O. Ellingsen and T. Skjaerpe, "Superior cardiovascular effect of aerobic interval training versus moderate continuous training in heart failure patients: a randomized study," *Circulation* Vol. 115, No. 24 (2007): 3086-3094.

[26]A.E. Tjonna, S.J. Lee, O. Rognmo, T.O. Stolen, A. Bye, P.M. Haram, J.P. Loennechen, Q.Y. Al-Share, E. Skogvoll, S.A. Slordahl, O.J. Kemi, S.M. Najjar, and U. Wisloff, "Aerobic interval training versus continuous moderate exercise as a treatment for the metabolic syndrome: a pilot study," *Circulation* Vol. 118, No. 4 (2008): 346-354.

[27]C.G. Perry, G.J. Heigenhauser, A. Bonen, and L.L. Spriet, "High-intensity aerobic interval training increases fat and carbohydrate metabolic capacities in human skeletal muscle," *Appl Physiol Nutr Metab* Vol. 33, No.6 (2008): 1112-1123.

[28]B.R. McKay, D.H. Paterson, and J.M. Kowalchuk, "Effect of short-term high-intensity interval training vs. continuous training on O2 uptake kinetics, muscle deoxygenation, and exercise performance," *J Appl Physiol* Vol. 107, No. 1 (2009): 128-138.

[29]A.R. Harmer, M.J. McKenna, J.R. Sutton, R.J. Snow, P.A. Ruell, J. Booth, M.W. Thompson, N.A. Mackay, C.G. Stathis, R.M. Crameri, M.F. Carey, and D.M. Eager, "Skeletal muscle metabolic and ionic adaptations during intense exercise following sprint training in humans," *J Appl Physiol* Vol. 89, No. 5 (2000): 1793-1803.

[30]K.A. Burgomaster, S.C. Hughes, G.J. Heigenhauser, S.N. Bradwell, and M.J. Gibala, "Six sessions of sprint interval training increases muscle oxidative potential and cycle endurance capacity in humans," *J Appl Physiol* Vol. 98, No. 6 (2005): 1985-1990.

[31]D.E. Warburton, D.C. McKenzie, M.J. Haykowsky, A. Taylor, P. Shoemaker, A.P. Ignaszewski, and S.Y. Chan, "Effectiveness of high-intensity interval training for the rehabilitation of patients with coronary artery disease," *Am J Cardiol* Vol. 95, No. 9 (2005): 1080-1084.

[32]K.A. Burgomaster, G.J. Heigenhauser, and M.J. Gibala, "Effect of short-term sprint interval training on human skeletal muscle carbohydrate metabolism during exercise and time-trial performance," *J Appl Physiol* Vol. 100, No. 6 (2006): 2041-2047; K.A. Burgomaster, N.M. Cermak, S.M. Phillips, C.R. Benton, A. Bonen, and M.J. Gibala, "Divergent response of metabolite transport proteins in human skeletal muscle after sprint

interval training and detraining," *Am J Physiol Regul Integr Comp Physiol* Vol. 292, No. 5 (2007): R1970-R1976; J.A. Babraj, N.B. Vollaard, C. Keast, F.M. Gup py, G. Cottrell, and J.A. Timmons, "Extremely short duration high intensity interval training substantially improves insulin action in young healthy males," *BMC Endocr Disord* Vol. 9, No. 3 (2009): 3.

[33]M.J. Gibala, J.P. Little, E.M. van, G.P. Wilkin, K.A. Burgomaster, A. Safdar, S. Raha, and M.A. Tarnopolsky, "Short-term sprint interval versus traditional endurance training: similar initial adaptations in human skeletal muscle and exercise performance," *J Physiol Vol.* 575, (2006): 901-911.

[34]B.S. Denadai, M.J. Ortiz, C.C. Greco, and M.T. de Mello, "Interval training at 95% and 100% of the velocity at VO2 max: effects on aerobic physiological indexes and running performance," *Appl Physiol Nutr Metab* Vol. 31, No. 6 (2006):737-743.

[35]N.K. Stepto, J.A. Hawley, S.C. Dennis, and W.G. Hopkins, "Effects of different interval-training programs on cycling time-trial performance," *Med Sci Sports Exerc* Vol. 31, No. 5 (1999): 736-741.

[36]M.T. Linossier, C. Denis, D. Dormois, A. Geyssant, and J.R. Lacour, "Ergometric and metabolic adaptation to a 5-s sprint training programme," *Eur J Appl Physiol Occup Physiol* Vol. 67, No. 5 (1993): 408-414; J.D. MacDougall, A.L. Hicks, J.R. MacDonald, R.S. McKelvie, H.J. Green, and K.M. Smith, "Muscle performance and enzymatic adaptations to sprint interval training," *J Appl Physiol* Vol. 84, No. 6 (1998): 2138-2142; A.R. Harmer, M.J. McKenna, J.R. Sutton, R.J. Snow, P.A. Ruell, J. Booth. M.W. Thompson, N.A. Mackay, C.G. Stathis, R.M. Crameri, M.F. Carey, and D.M. Eager, "Skeletal muscle metabolic and ionic adaptations during intense exercise following sprint training in humans," *J Appl Physiol* Vol. 89, No. 5 (2000): 1793-1803; K.A. Burgomaster, S.C. Hughes, G.J. Heigenhauser, S.N. Bradwell, and M.J. Gibala, "Six sessions of sprint interval training increases muscle oxidative potential and cycle endurance capacity in humans," *J Appl Physiol* Vol. 98, No. 6 (2005): 1985-1990.

[37]J.L. Talanian, S.D. Galloway, G.J. Heigenhauser, A. Bonen, and L.L. Spriet, "Two weeks of high-intensity aerobic interval training increases the capacity for fat oxidation during exercise in women," *J Appl Physiol* Vol. 102, No. 104 (2007): 1439-1447; C.G. Perry, G.J. Heigenhauser, A. Bonen, and L.L. Spriet, "High-intensity aerobic interval training increases fat and carbohydrate metabolic capacities in human skeletal muscle," *Appl Physiol Nutr Metab* Vol. 33, No. 6 (2008): 1112-1123.

[38]K.A. Burgomaster, K.R. Howarth, S.M. Phillips, M. Rakobowchuk, M.J. Macdonald, S.L. McGee, and M.J. Gibala, "Similar metabolic adaptations during exercise after low volume sprint interval and traditional endurance training in humans," *J Physiol* Vol. 586, No.1 (2008): 151-160.

[39]A.R. Harmer, M.J. McKenna, J.R. Sutton, R.J. Snow, P.A. Ruell, J. Booth, M.W. Thompson, N.A. Mackay, C.G. Stathis, R.M. Crameri, M.F. Carey, and D.M. Eager, "Skeletal muscle metabolic and ionic adaptations during intense exercise following sprint training in humans," *J Appl Physiol* Vol. 89, No.5 (2000): 1793-1803; J.L. Talanian, S.D. Galloway, G.J. Heigenhauser, A. Bonen, and L.L. Spriet, "Two weeks of high-intensity aerobic interval training increases the capacity for fat oxidation during exercise in women," *J Appl Physiol* Vol. 102, No. 104 (2007): 1439-1447; C.G. Perry, G.J. Heigenhauser, A. Bonen, and L.L. Spriet, "High-intensity aerobic interval training increases fat and carbohydrate metabolic capacities in human skeletal muscle," *Appl Physiol Nutr Metab* Vol. 33, No. 6 (2008): 1112-1123; A.R. Harmer, D.J. Chisholm, M.J. McKenna, S.K. Hunter, P.A. Ruell, J.M. Naylor, L.J. Maxwell, and J.R. Flack, "Sprint training increases muscle oxidative metabolism during high-intensity exercise in patients with type 1 diabetes," *Diabetes Care* Vol. 31, No. 11 (2008): 2097-2102.

[40]J.L. Talanian, S.D. Galloway, G.J. Heigenhauser, A. Bonen, and L.L. Spriet, "Two weeks of high-intensity aerobic interval training increases the capacity for fat oxidation during exercise in women," *J Appl Physiol* Vol. 102, No. 104 (2007): 1439-1447; C.G. Perry, G.J. Heigenhauser, A. Bonen, and L.L. Spriet, "High-intensity aerobic interval training increases fat and carbohydrate metabolic capacities in human skeletal muscle," *Appl Physiol Nutr Metab* Vol. 33, No. 6 (2008): 1112-1123; A.R. Harmer, D.J. Chisholm, M.J. McKenna, S.K. Hunter, P.A. Ruell, J.M. Naylor, L.J. Maxwell, and J.R. Flack, "Sprint training increases muscle oxidative metabolism during high-intensity exercise in patients with type 1 diabetes," *Diabetes Care* Vol. 31, No.11 (2008): 2097-2102.

[41]D.C. Poole and G.A. Gaesser, "Response of ventilatory and lactate thresholds to continuous and interval training," *J Appl Physiol* 58, no.4 (1985): 1115-1121; J. Burke, R. Thayer, and M. Belcamino, "Comparison of effects of two interval-training programmes on lactate and ventilatory thresholds," *Br J Sports Med* 28, no.1 (1994):18-21; B.S. Denadai, M.J. Ortiz, C.C. Greco, and M.T. de Mello, "Interval training at 95% and 100% of the velocity at VO2 max: effects on aerobic physiological indexes and running performance," *Appl Physiol*

Nutr Metab Vol. 31, No.6 (2006):737-743.

[42]D.C. Poole and G.A. Gaesser, "Response of ventilatory and lactate thresholds to continuous and interval training," *J Appl Physiol* Vol. 58, No. 4 (1985): 1115-1121.

[43]D.C. Poole and G.A. Gaesser, "Response of ventilatory and lactate thresholds to continuous and interval training," *J Appl Physiol* Vol. 58, No. 4 (1985): 1115-1121; A.R. Harmer, D.J. Chisholm, M.J. McKenna, S.K. Hunter, P.A. Ruell, J.M. Naylor, L.J. Maxwell, and J.R. Flack, "Sprint training increases muscle oxidative metabolism during high-intensity exercise in patients with type 1 diabetes," *Diabetes Care* Vol. 31, No.11 (2008): 2097-2102; B.R. McKay, D.H. Paterson, and J.M. Kowalchuk, "Effect of short-term high-intensity interval training vs. continuous training on O2 uptake kinetics, muscle deoxygenation, and exercise performance," *J Appl Physiol* Vol. 107, No. 1 (2009): 128-138.

[44]A.R. Harmer, D.J. Chisholm, M.J. McKenna, S.K. Hunter, P.A. Ruell, J.M. Naylor, L.J. Maxwell, and J.R. Flack, "Sprint training increases muscle oxidative metabolism during high-intensity exercise in patients with type 1 diabetes," *Diabetes Care* Vol. 31, No.11 (2008): 2097-2102.

[45]E.M. Gorostiaga, C.B. Walter, C. Foster, and R.C. Hickson, "Uniqueness of interval and continuous training at the same maintained exercise intensity," *Eur J Appl Physiol Occup Physiol* Vol. 63, No.2 (1991): 101-107.

[46]N. Almond, L. Kahwati, L. Kinsinger, and D. Porterfield, "Prevalence of overweight and obesity among U.S. military veterans," *Mil Med Vol.* 173, No. 6 (2008): 544-549.

[47]G.E. Reiber, T.D. Koepsell, C. Maynard, L.B. Haas, and E.J. Boyko, "Diabetes in nonveterans, veterans, and veterans receiving Department of Veterans Affairs health care," *Diabetes Care* Vol. 27, No. 2, (2004): B3-B9; C.P. Lynch, J.L. Strom, and L.E. Egede, "Variation in quality of care indicators for diabetes in a national sample of veterans and non-veterans," *Diabetes Technol Ther* Vol. 12, No. 10 (2010): 785-790.

[48]D.R. Miller, M.M. Safford, and L.M. Pogach, "Who has diabetes? Best estimates of diabetes prevalence in the Department of Veterans Affairs based on computerized patient data," *Diabetes Care* 27, no. 2, (2004): B10-B21; R.M. Bray, L.L. Hourani, K.L. Rae Olmsted M. Witt, Brown, M.R. Pemberton, M.E. Marsden, B. Marriott, and S. Scheffler, "2005 Department of Defense Survey of Health Related Behaviors among Active Duty Military Personnel," (Research Triangle Institute, Research Triangle Park: NC, 2006), 1-305.

[49]M.J. LaMonte, S.N. Blair, and T.S. Church, "Physical activity and diabetes prevention," *J Appl Physiol* Vol. 99, No. 3 (2005): 1205-1213.

[50]G. O'Donovan, A.J. Blazevich, C. Boreham, A.R. Cooper, H. Crank, U. Ekelund, K.R. Fox, P. Gately, B. Giles-Corti, J.M. Gill, J.M. Hamer, I. McDermott, M. Murphy, N. Mutrie, J.J. Reilly, J.M. Saxton, and E. Stamatakis, 'The ABC of Physical Activity for Health: a consensus statement from the British Association of Sport and Exercise Sciences," *J Sports Sci* Vol. 28, No. 6 (2010): 573-591.

[51]N.A. King, M. Hopkins, P. Caudwell, R.J. Stubbs, and J.E. Blundell, "Beneficial effects of exercise: shifting the focus from body weight to other markers of health," *Br J Sports Med* Vol. 43, No. 12 (2009): 924-927.

[52]N.A. King, M. Hopkins, P. Caudwell, R.J. Stubbs, and J.E. Blundell, "Beneficial effects of exercise: shifting the focus from body weight to other markers of health," *Br J Sports Med* Vol. 43, No. 12 (2009): 924-927.

[53]E.M. Gorostiaga, C.B. Walter, C. Foster, and R.C. Hickson, "Uniqueness of interval and continuous training at the same maintained exercise intensity," *Eur J Appl Physiol Occup Physiol* Vol. 63, No. 2 (1991): 101-107; C.L. Weber and D.A. Schneider, "Increases in maximal accumulated oxygen deficit after high-intensity interval training are not gender dependent," *J Appl Physiol* Vol. 92, No. 5 (2002): 1795-1801; A.R. Harmer, D.J. Chisholm, M.J. McKenna, S.K. Hunter, P.A. Ruell, J.M. Naylor, L.J. Maxwell, and J.R. Flack, "Sprint training increases muscle oxidative metabolism during high-intensity exercise in patients with type 1 diabetes," *Diabetes Care* Vol. 31, no.11 (2008): 2097-2102; C.L. Weber and D.A. Schneider, "Increases in maximal accumulated oxygen deficit after high-intensity interval training are not gender dependent," *J Appl Physiol* Vol. 92, No. 5 (2002): 1795-1801.

[54]O. Rognmo, E. Hetland, J. Helgerud, J. Hoff, and S.A. Slordahl, "High intensity aerobic interval exercise is superior to moderate intensity exercise for increasing aerobic capacity in patients with coronary artery disease," *Eur J Cardiovasc Prev Rehabil* Vol. 11, No. 2 (2004): 216-222.

[55]B.R. McKay, D.H. Paterson, and J.M. Kowalchuk, "Effect of short-term high-intensity interval training vs. continuous training on O2 uptake kinetics, muscle deoxygenation, and exercise performance," *J Appl Physiol* Vol. 107, No. 1 (2009): 128-138.

[56]D.E. Warburton, D.C. McKenzie, M.J. Haykowsky, A. Taylor, P. Shoemaker, A.P. Ignaszewski, and S.Y. Chan, "Effectiveness of high-intensity interval training for the rehabilitation of patients with coronary artery disease," *Am J Cardiol* Vol. 95, No. 9 (2005): 1080-1084.

[57]A.E. Tjonna, S.J. Lee, O. Rognmo, T.O. Stolen, A. Bye, P.M. Haram, J.P. Loennechen, Q.Y. Al-Share, E. Skogvoll, S.A. Slordahl, O.J. Kemi, S.M. Najjar, and U. Wisloff, "Aerobic interval training versus continuous moderate exercise as a treatment for the metabolic syndrome: a pilot study," *Circulation* Vol. 118, No. 4 (2008): 346-354.

[58]M.J. LaMonte, S.N. Blair, and T.S. Church, "Physical activity and diabetes prevention," *J Appl Physiol* Vol. 99, No. 3 (2005): 1205-1213.

[59]N.G. Boule, G.P. Kenny, E. Haddad, G.A. Wells, and R.J. Sigal, "Meta-analysis of the effect of structured exercise training on cardiorespiratory fitness in Type 2 diabetes mellitus," *Diabetologia* Vol. 46, No. 10 (2003): 1071-1081.

[60]J.A. Babraj, N.B. Vollaard, C. Keast, F.M. Gup py, G. Cottrell, and J.A. Timmons, "Extremely short duration high intensity interval training substantially improves insulin action in young healthy males," *BMC Endocr Disord* Vol. 9, No. 3 (2009): 3.

[61]L.J. Whyte, J.M. Gill, and A.J. Cathcart, "Effect of 2 weeks of sprint interval training on health-related outcomes in sedentary overweight/obese men," *Metabolism* Vol. 59, No. 10 (2010): 1421-1428.

[62]A.E. Tjonna, S.J. Lee, O. Rognmo, T.O. Stolen, A. Bye, P.M. Haram, J.P. Loennechen, Q.Y. Al-Share, E. Skogvoll, S.A. Slordahl, O.J. Kemi, S.M. Najjar, and U. Wisloff, "Aerobic interval training versus continuous moderate exercise as a treatment for the metabolic syndrome: a pilot study," *Circulation* Vol. 118, No. 4 (2008): 346-354.

[63]P.S. Munk, E.M. Staal, N. Butt, K. Isaksen, and A.I. Larsen, "High-intensity interval training may reduce in-stent restenosis following percutaneous coronary intervention with stent implantation A randomized controlled trial evaluating the relationship to endothelial function and inflammation," *Am Heart J* Vol. 158, No. 5 (2009): 734-741.

[64]B.H. Goodpaster, A. Katsiaras, and D.E. Kelley, "Enhanced fat oxidation through physical activity is associated with improvements in insulin sensitivity in obesity," *Diabetes* Vol. 52, No. 9 (2003): 2191-2197; E.V. Menshikova, V.B. Ritov, F.G. Toledo, R.E. Ferrell, B.H. Goodpaster, and D.E. Kelley, "Effects of weight loss and physical activity on skeletal muscle mitochondrial function in obesity," *Am J Physiol Endocrinol Metab* Vol. 288, No. 4 (2005): E818-E825; E.V. Menshikova, V.B. Ritov, R.E. Ferrell, K. Azuma, B.H. Goodpaster, and D.E. Kelley, "Characteristics of skeletal muscle mitochondrial biogenesis induced by moderate-intensity exercise and weight loss in obesity," *J Appl Physiol* Vol. 103, No. 1 (2007): 21-27.

[65]V.K. Mootha, C.M. Lindgren, K.F. Eriksson, A. Subramanian, S. Sihag, J. Lehar, P. Puigserver, E. Carlsson, M. Ridderstrale, E. Laurila, N. Houstis, M.J. Daly, N. Patterson, J.P. Mesirov, T.R. Golub, P. Tamayo, B. Spiegelman E.S. Lander J.N. Hirschhorn D. Altshuler and L.C. Groop, "PGC-1alpha-responsive genes involved in oxidative phosphorylation are coordinately downregulated in human diabetes," *Nat Genet* Vol. 34, No. 4 (2003): 267-273.

[66]J.L. Talanian, S.D. Galloway, G.J. Heigenhauser, A. Bonen, and L.L. Spriet, "Two weeks of high-intensity aerobic interval training increases the capacity for fat oxidation during exercise in women," *J Appl Physiol* Vol. 102, No. 104 (2007): 1439-1447; C.G. Perry, G.J. Heigenhauser, A. Bonen, and L.L. Spriet, "High-intensity aerobic interval training increases fat and carbohydrate metabolic capacities in human skeletal muscle," *Appl Physiol Nutr Metab* Vol. 33, No. 6 (2008): 1112-1123; B.J. Gurd, C.G.R. Perry, G.J.F. Heigenhauser, L.L. Spriet, and A. Bonen. "High-intensity interval training increases SIRT1 activity in human skeletal muscle," *Applied Physiology, Nutrition and Metabolism* 35, no.3 (2010): 350-357.

[67]M.T. Linossier, C. Denis, D. Dormois, A. Geyssant, and J.R. Lacour, "Ergometric and metabolic adaptation to a 5-s sprint training programme," *Eur J Appl Physiol Occup Physiol* Vol. 67, No. 5 (1993): 408-414.

[68]M.T. Linossier, C. Denis, D. Dormois, A. Geyssant, and J.R. Lacour, "Ergometric and metabolic adaptation to a 5-s sprint training programme," *Eur J Appl Physiol Occup Physiol* Vol. 67, No. 5 (1993): 408-414; K.A. Burgomaster, G.J. Heigenhauser, and M.J. Gibala, "Effect of short-term sprint interval training on human skeletal muscle carbohydrate metabolism during exercise and time-trial performance," *J Appl Physiol* Vol. 100, No. 6 (2006): 2041-2047.

[69]J.D. MacDougall, A.L. Hicks, J.R. MacDonald, R.S. McKelvie, H.J. Green, and K.M. Smith, "Muscle performance and enzymatic adaptations to sprint interval training," *J Appl Physiol* Vol. 84, No. 6 (1998): 2138-2142; K.A. Burgomaster, S.C. Hughes, G.J. Heigenhauser, S.N. Bradwell, and M.J. Gibala, "Six sessions of sprint interval training increases muscle oxidative potential and cycle endurance capacity in humans," *J Appl Physiol* Vol. 98, No. 6 (2005): 1985-1990; K.A. Burgomaster, G.J. Heigenhauser, and M.J. Gibala, "Effect of short-term sprint interval training on human skeletal muscle carbohydrate metabolism during exercise and

time-trial performance," *J Appl Physiol* Vol. 100, No. 6 (2006): 2041-2047; A.R. Harmer, D.J. Chisholm, M.J. McKenna, S.K. Hunter, P.A. Ruell, J.M. Naylor, L.J. Maxwell, and J.R. Flack, "Sprint training increases muscle oxidative metabolism during high-intensity exercise in patients with type 1 diabetes," *Diabetes Care* Vol. 31, No.11 (2008): 2097-2102.

[70]M.J. Gibala, J.P. Little, E.M. van, G.P. Wilkin, K.A. Burgomaster, A. Safdar, S. Raha, and M.A. Tarnopolsky, "Short-term sprint interval versus traditional endurance training: similar initial adaptations in human skeletal muscle and exercise performance," *J Physiol* Vol. 575, No. 3 (2006): 901-911; K.A. Burgomaster, N.M. Cermak, S.M. Phillips, C.R. Benton, A. Bonen, and M.J. Gibala, "Divergent response of metabolite transport proteins in human skeletal muscle after sprint interval training and detraining," *Am J Physiol Regul Integr Comp Physiol* Vol. 292, No.5 (2007): R1970-R1976; A.R. Harmer, D.J. Chisholm, M.J. McKenna, S.K. Hunter, P.A. Ruell, J.M. Naylor, L.J. Maxwell, and J.R. Flack, "Sprint training increases muscle oxidative metabolism during high-intensity exercise in patients with type 1 diabetes," *Diabetes Care* Vol. 31, No. 11 (2008): 2097-2102.

[71]M.J. Gibala, J.P. Little, E.M. van, G.P. Wilkin, K.A. Burgomaster, A. Safdar, S. Raha, and M.A. Tarnopolsky, "Short-term sprint interval versus traditional endurance training: similar initial adaptations in human skeletal muscle and exercise performance," *J Physiol* Vol. 575, (2006): 901-911; A.R. Harmer, D.J. Chisholm, M.J. McKenna, S.K. Hunter, P.A. Ruell, J.M. Naylor, L.J. Maxwell, and J.R. Flack, "Sprint training increases muscle oxidative metabolism during high-intensity exercise in patients with type 1 diabetes," *Diabetes Care* Vol. 31, No. 11 (2008): 2097-2102.

[72]G. O'Donovan, A.J. Blazevich, C. Boreham, A.R. Cooper, H. Crank, U. Ekelund, K.R. Fox, P. Gately, B. Giles-Corti, J.M. Gill, M. Hamer, I. McDermott, M. Murphy, N. Mutrie, J.J. Reilly, J.M. Saxton, and E. Stamatakis, "The ABC of Physical Activity for Health: a consensus statement from the British Association of Sport and Exercise Sciences," *J Sports Sci* Vol. 28, No. 6 (2010): 573-591.

[73]J.L. Johnson, C.A. Slentz, J.A. Houmard, G.P. Samsa, B.D. Duscha, L.B. Aiken, J.S. McCartney, C.J. Tanner, and W.E. Kraus, "Exercise training amount and intensity effects on metabolic syndrome (from Studies of a Targeted Risk Reduction Intervention through Defined Exercise)," *Am J Cardiol* Vol. 100, No. 12 (2007): 1759-1766.

[74]D.E. Warburton, D.C. McKenzie, M.J. Haykowsky, A. Taylor, P. Shoemaker, A.P. Ignaszewski, and S.Y. Chan, "Effectiveness of high-intensity interval training for the rehabilitation of patients with coronary artery disease," *Am J Cardiol* Vol. 95, No. 9 (2005): 1080-1084; U. Wisloff, A. Stoylen, J.P. Loennechen, M. Bruvold, O. Rognmo, P.M. Haram, A.E. Tjonna, J. Helgerud, S.A. Slordahl, S.J. Lee, V. Videm, A. Bye, G.L. Smith, S.M. Najjar, O. Ellingsen and T. Skjaerpe, "Superior cardiovascular effect of aerobic interval training versus moderate continuous training in heart failure patients: a randomized study," *Circulation* Vol. 115, No. 24 (2007): 3086-3094.

[75]A.E. Tjonna, S.J. Lee, O. Rognmo, T.O. Stolen, A. Bye, P.M. Haram, J.P. Loennechen, Q.Y. Al-Share, E. Skogvoll, S.A. Slordahl, O.J. Kemi, S.M. Najjar, and U. Wisloff, "Aerobic interval training versus continuous moderate exercise as a treatment for the metabolic syndrome: a pilot study," *Circulation* Vol. 118, No. 4 (2008): 346-354.

[76]U. Wisloff, A. Stoylen, J.P. Loennechen, M. Bruvold, O. Rognmo, P.M. Haram, A.E. Tjonna, J. Helgerud, S.A. Slordahl, S.J. Lee, V. Videm, A. Bye, G.L. Smith, S.M. Najjar, O. Ellingsen and T. Skjaerpe, "Superior cardiovascular effect of aerobic interval training versus moderate continuous training in heart failure patients: a randomized study," *Circulation* Vol. 115, No. 24 (2007): 3086-3094; P.S. Munk, E.M. Staal, N. Butt, K. Isaksen, and A.I. Larsen, "High-intensity interval training may reduce in-stent restenosis following percutaneous coronary intervention with stent implantation A randomized controlled trial evaluating the relationship to endothelial function and inflammation," *Am Heart J* Vol. 158, No.5 (2009): 734-741.

[77]L.J. Whyte, J.M. Gill, and A.J. Cathcart, "Effect of 2 weeks of sprint interval training on health-related outcomes in sedentary overweight/obese men," *Metabolism* Vol. 59, No. 10 (2010): 1421-1428.

[78]A.E. Tjonna, S.J. Lee, O. Rognmo, T.O. Stolen, A. Bye, P.M. Haram, J.P. Loennechen, Q.Y. Al-Share, E. Skogvoll, S.A. Slordahl, O.J. Kemi, S.M. Najjar, and U. Wisloff, "Aerobic interval training versus continuous moderate exercise as a treatment for the metabolic syndrome: a pilot study," *Circulation* Vol. 118, No. 4 (2008): 346-354.

[79]A.E. Tjonna, S.J. Lee, O. Rognmo, T.O. Stolen, A. Bye, P.M. Haram, J.P. Loennechen, Q.Y. Al-Share, E. Skogvoll, S.A. Slordahl, O.J. Kemi, S.M. Najjar, and U. Wisloff, "Aerobic interval training versus continuous moderate exercise as a treatment for the metabolic syndrome: a pilot study," *Circulation* Vol. 118, No. 4 (2008): 346-354.

[80]U. Wisloff, A. Stoylen, J.P. Loennechen, M. Bruvold, O. Rognmo, P.M. Haram, A.E. Tjonna, J. Helgerud, S.A. Slordahl, S.J. Lee, V. Videm, A. Bye, G.L. Smith, S.M. Najjar, O. Ellingsen and T. Skjaerpe, "Superior cardiovascular effect of aerobic interval training versus moderate continuous training in heart failure patients: a randomized study," *Circulation* Vol. 115, No. 24 (2007): 3086-3094.

[81]T. Guiraud, M. Juneau, A. Nigam, M. Gayda, P. Meyer, S. Mekary, F. Paillard, and L. Bosquet, "Optimization of high intensity interval exercise in coronary heart disease," *Eur J Appl Physiol* 108, no. 4 (2010): 733-740.

[82]B.R. McKay, D.H. Paterson, and J.M. Kowalchuk, "Effect of short-term high-intensity interval training vs. continuous training on O2 uptake kinetics, muscle deoxygenation, and exercise performance," *J Appl Physiol* Vol. 107, No.1 (2009): 128-138.

[83]M.J. Gibala, J.P. Little, E.M. van, G.P. Wilkin, K.A. Burgomaster, A. Safdar, S. Raha, and M.A. Tarnopolsky, "Short-term sprint interval versus traditional endurance training: similar initial adaptations in human skeletal muscle and exercise performance," *J Physiol Vol.* 575, (2006): 901-911; A.R. Harmer, D.J. Chisholm, M.J. McKenna, S.K. Hunter, P.A. Ruell, J.M. Naylor, L.J. Maxwell, and J.R. Flack, "Sprint training increases muscle oxidative metabolism during high-intensity exercise in patients with type 1 diabetes," *Diabetes Care* Vol. 31, No.11 (2008): 2097-2102.

[84]A.E. Tjonna, S.J. Lee, O. Rognmo, T.O. Stolen, A. Bye, P.M. Haram, J.P. Loennechen, Q.Y. Al-Share, E. Skogvoll, S.A. Slordahl, O.J. Kemi, S.M. Najjar, and U. Wisloff, "Aerobic interval training versus continuous moderate exercise as a treatment for the metabolic syndrome: a pilot study," *Circulation* Vol. 118, No. 4 (2008): 346-354.

[85]D.E. Warburton, D.C. McKenzie, M.J. Haykowsky, A. Taylor, P. Shoemaker, A.P. Ignaszewski, and S.Y. Chan, "Effectiveness of high-intensity interval training for the rehabilitation of patients with coronary artery disease," *Am J Cardiol* Vol. 95, No. 9 (2005): 1080-1084.

[81]T. Guiraud, M. Juneau, A. Nigam, M. Gayda, P. Meyer, S. Mekary, F. Paillard, and L. Bosquet, "Optimization of high intensity interval exercise in coronary heart disease," *Eur J Appl Physiol* Vol. 108, No. 4 (2010): 733-740.

[82]B.R. McKay, D.H. Paterson, and J.M. Kowalchuk, "Effect of short-term high-intensity interval training vs. continuous training on O2 uptake kinetics, muscle deoxygenation, and exercise performance," *J Appl Physiol* Vol. 107, No. 1 (2009): 128-138.

[83]M.J. Gibala, J.P. Little, E.M. van, G.P. Wilkin, K.A. Burgomaster, A. Safdar, S. Raha, and M.A. Tarnopolsky, "Short-term sprint interval versus traditional endurance training: similar initial adaptations in human skeletal muscle and exercise performance," *J Physiol* 575, (2006): 901-911; A.R. Harmer, D.J. Chisholm, M.J. McKenna, S.K. Hunter, P.A. Ruell, J.M. Naylor, L.J. Maxwell, and J.R. Flack, "Sprint training increases muscle oxidative metabolism during high-intensity exercise in patients with type 1 diabetes," *Diabetes Care* Vol. 31, No.11 (2008): 2097-2102.

[84]A.E. Tjonna, S.J. Lee, O. Rognmo, T.O. Stolen, A. Bye, P.M. Haram, J.P. Loennechen, Q.Y. Al-Share, E. Skogvoll, S.A. Slordahl, O.J. Kemi, S.M. Najjar, and U. Wisloff, "Aerobic interval training versus continuous moderate exercise as a treatment for the metabolic syndrome: a pilot study," *Circulation* Vol. 118, No. 4 (2008): 346-354.

[85]D.E. Warburton, D.C. McKenzie, M.J. Haykowsky, A. Taylor, P. Shoemaker, A.P. Ignaszewski, and S.Y. Chan, "Effectiveness of high-intensity interval training for the rehabilitation of patients with coronary artery disease," *Am J Cardiol* Vol. 95, No. 9 (2005): 1080-1084.

CHAPTER 6

Wearable Wireless Medical Devices in a Dynamic and Open Architecture

Alain Beaulieu, PhD, Sandra Smith, Brittany van den Tillaart, & Jenifer Lindsay,
Royal Military College of Canada

ABSTRACT

Ambulatory and remote monitoring of biomedical signals have gained importance in the last decade as medical institutions try to reduce costs by discharging patients earlier while still requiring various levels of monitoring. Most of the systems currently on the market are bulky, closed architecture, static in configuration and use wired medical devices, all of which limit their usage. Most current devices provide only raw signals that are processed by a central-wearable computer limiting scalability. Queen's University and RMCC have teamed up to research and design a new generation of ambulatory medical telemetry systems. The aim of the research is to develop an open architecture using Real-Time Object-Oriented Modeling that will allow wireless, wearable medical devices to join a dynamically configurable monitoring environment. The intent of the system is to monitor patients' recovery by measuring biometrics and biomedical signals as they go about their daily activities in the comfort of their homes. The sensors that are being developed as part of this research are smart sensors that can provide pre-processed information, reducing the load on the wearable computer. This paper presents the preliminary analysis in the form of use cases that elaborate the requirements of the proposed system.

WEARABLE WIRELESS MEDICAL DEVICES IN A DYNAMIC AND OPEN ARCHITECTURE

With an aging population and steadily rising health care costs, it is increasingly important to provide systems and support for those elderly persons and patients with chronic impairments who wish to remain in their homes. Increases in conflicts overseas have also put an additional burden on the rehabilitation of our injured soldiers. The remote monitoring of patients undergoing rehabilitation will reduce stress on the health care system and provide these individuals with a better quality of life. The emergence of tele-health (mobile health) opens up the possibility of continuously monitoring the health status of elderly or at-risk individuals and how their health changes over time. Distance from major centers may sometimes keep a patient in recovery from returning to their daily lives in a timely fashion. In some cases, because of the increasing burden on the medical system, some patients return home and do not have the necessary medical follow-up in the community. This type of disparity in the quality of health care away from major centers is one of the central themes of the Romanow report, Building on Values: The future of health care in Canada.[1]

We present the initial results of our research to develop a new kind of monitoring system that will allow physicians and clinicians to monitor their patients away from major medical centers. The ambulatory medical telemetry system will be light, non-intrusive and flexible to allow many different kinds of sensors to be added or removed from the system with minimal effort. The system will allow healthcare professionals to use daily activities of the patients as part of the rehabilitation plan. Several papers have been published on the topic of using daily activities assessments including Casaburi (2007), Macfarlane *et al.*, (2006), and Najafi *et al.*, (2003).[2] Our research was initiated by a core of researchers in the domains of rehabilitation therapy, electrical and computer engineering, software engineering and software science from Queen's University, the Human Mobility Research Center at the Kingston General Hospital and the Royal Military College of Canada; all located in Kingston, Ontario. The idea behind the research is to leverage emerging lightweight wireless technology allowing small footprint sensors to be networked in a body worn network of intelligent devices. Apart from being wearable, the system will be designed to be scalable by providing an open architecture that is well documented through published interfaces available on -line.

REVIEW OF LITERATURE

REAL-TIME OBJECT-ORIENTED MODELING AND MODEL DRIVEN DEVELOPMENT

Real-Time Object-Oriented Modeling (ROOM) made its appearance in the early 1990s in the Canadian telecommunication industry and has evolved into a solid software engineering method over the years.[3] ROOM uses visual design components to model the architecture of the software. The behaviour of the software is modeled using the mathematical concept of Finite State Machines. ROOM was designed with the idea of using Model Driven Development (MDD), which is a software engineering method that uses models as the primary artefact.[4] MDD is supported by tools that allow models to be automatically converted to code allowing the system designers to work at a higher level of abstraction. ROOM and MDD have recently been brought into the fold of the Unified Modeling Language (UML), the international language of choice to communicate software engineering design, with the introduction of UML 2.0.

ROOM is well suited to our research because it is aimed at event-based, highly concurrent, message-based systems. ROOM uses bounded states to control the behaviour of the system and increase the integrity of the software. Software integrity is a quality of the software that encompasses reliability, availability, security and safety of safety critical software products. Although our research does not specifically address all facets of software integrity, we are setting a strong basis for future certification and market clearance by governmental authorities. By using wireless technology, we will be able to detect when a medical device enters the system and register it for use. We will be using current wireless device communication standards such as WiFi, ZigBee™ or Bluetooth™ and MDD to provide a system that is dynamically configurable and extendable as it can grow in functionality as devices enter and are registered to the system. By publishing which wireless communication protocols we are using and by publishing the software communication protocols as interfaces to our system any medical device manufacturer will be able to provide added capabilities to our system increasing the ability of the physicians and clinicians to monitor their patients at remote locations.

Wearable Biometric Sensors Literature and Market Survey

A (Wireless) Body Area Network (WBAN) consists of multiple interconnected mobile nodes, on, near or implanted into the human body, which provide sensing, processing and communication capabilities.[5] WBANs or BANs monitor physiological, body parameters and movements. Some discussions have focused around the proper name or acronym to use when discussing this form of sensor technology. For the remainder of the paper we use BAN as an all-encompassing category for these systems.

A comprehensive search of journals, commercially available systems, and sensors was conducted to identify significant developments, research, and technology covering the last five years. This survey provides researchers and clinicians with a compendium of research, devices, and analysis of the current state of BAN technology in hopes to increase the interdisciplinary communication to further advance the field.

As advances in sensor technology occur, the development of BANs and their possible use within the health care system have been rapidly becoming the forefront of sensor and health care research. In their paper Lymberis and Gatzoulis (2006)[6] report that most research in the field is currently conducted in physiological monitoring such as; electro cardiograms (ECG), heart rate (HR), respiratory rate (RR) and skin temperature. BANs could allow the possibility for long-term health monitoring at home and within the community. This would increase patient's independence and decrease the strain on the overall health care system. Furthermore, a BAN that permits individuals to view recorded data at home will enable them to play a more central role in the monitoring of their own health and well-being. A research review conducted by Koch and Hagglund (2009)[7] showed that the use of health informatics and BAN in elderly care is an expanding field but is still in its infancy. An interdisciplinary research approach is required for the development of a BAN that would be advantageous within the healthcare system.

The essential part of current BANs is the "node" or "mote". This platform is what allows the system to connect a number of sensors to a processing unit in order to collect multiple parameters of data from the patient within a single compact piece of hardware. These small motes are beneficial to a BAN as they are small in size and many offer open architecture designs. Research into the possibility of "Smart Dust," a hypothetical wireless network of tiny motes, is still advancing with the promise to reduce power consumption and the necessity of large batteries.[8] These motes will be the size of a dust particle with each mote having self-contained sensing, computation, communication and power.

There are several important considerations for sensors that are to be integrated into a BAN. Invisibility to the user is not only important to prevent any obstructions to activity or behaviour modification, but also to decrease any social stigma that may be associated with wearing such a system.[9] An open architecture design and multiple sensors compatibility are essential to the marketability of a BAN system. The system must have "plug and play" abilities and capabilities with a variety of sensors and algorithms. These qualities are essential for the transition of a BAN system into the commercial market such that manufacturers from a variety of application fields can all use the same system to fit their marketable needs.

Currently most commercially available sensors are wired while the development of wireless sensors is becoming more prevalent.[10] The development of wireless sensors is critical in order to create a decentralized health care system. Although sensors are used in multiple applications, their use in BAN systems typically range from five or fewer sensor types in a system.[11] It is predicted that the number of sensors per system will double in the next five years, while the different types of sensors will not increase as fast.[12] This increase in sensors per system may allow for more complex physiological parameter monitoring in the future.

Our market survey has uncovered many sensors, sensor systems and fully developed BANs. Obviously we cannot present the entire results of this survey here; however, we present some of the most interesting results. We identified 22 BANs that can be used to perform tele-health monitoring and rehabilitation tasks and 18 multi-sensor systems that have been used to develop biometrics measuring systems and BAN prototypes. Sensors in these systems can be classified as physiological (blood pressure (BP), electroencephalogram (EEG), electromyography (EMG), ECG, HR), biokinetic (acceleration, rotation, gait) and ambient (humidity, light, temperature, sound). The sensor table that we have developed illustrates a wide variety of sensor nodes that are currently circulating in the marketplace.

Many of the sensor nodes have specific applications to infrastructure and asset management, the SHIMMER sensor node developed by Intel however, is specifically targeted to human health monitoring. This sensor node is fully equipped with an accelerometer, gyroscope, temperature, ECG, tilt, and (PIR) passive infrared sensors allowing for many different human monitoring parameters to be measured continuously. A large number of the prototype studies also use the Crossbow Mica2Dot mote and other Crossbow products. These products all have the ability to add on several different types of sensors which also make them extremely attractive to work within BANs.

There are a few complex commercially available BAN systems that have the ability to monitor multiple parameters continuously. We have created a table of those products that are available for academic, commercial and/or industrial use. These systems extend from one specific use such as fitness monitoring, to a multi-faceted complex WBAN such as the BioHarness BT. There has yet to be widespread use of any one of these complex systems; this may be caused by the system's current level of obstruction to the user and a less than optimal battery life.[13] Improvements in sensor technology are required in order to increase the effectiveness of current systems. Further, many of these systems lack clinical research trials testing the accuracy, fidelity, and reliability in comparison to systems already used in hospital and rehabilitation settings to monitor patients.[14]

The literature and market surveys confirmed our initial hypothesis that most systems were single focus or usage, closed architecture, proprietary, provide no access to raw data if required, have unique interfaces, limit patients' movements, may easily get tangled, not comfortable for patients, dumb measuring devices with signals centralized for analysis, and most systems have a static configuration.

METHODOLOGY – THE HEALTH ACTIVITY ASSESSMENT SYSTEM

Requirements Elicitation

We chose to use a well-known method originating from software engineering and now used in a wide variety of domains to perform our requirements analysis. The method we used is called Use Case Analysis. The method can be employed in many different ways. Most often, Use Case Analysis is performed by software engineers who are very familiar with the method along with domain experts who know the application domain but in general are not cognizant of Use Case Analysis. Our approach was to initially train two kinesiologists in Use Case Analysis and to let them derive the initial requirements also using other domain experts in the process.

The initial requirements elicitation has 22 Use Cases and nine actors divided in three categories. Below we present the overview of the Use Case Analysis. Figure 6.1 (presented at the end of the chapter due to its size) shows the Use Case diagram displaying the relationships between the actors and the Use Cases. Each Use Case was further elaborated to include pre- and- post conditions, basic information flows as well as alternative flows describing exceptions.

Actors

Primary Actors. These are the people for whom the system is designed. They use the system as part of their regular work responsibilities
- Patient
- Health Provider
- Technician/Clinician

Secondary Actors. These actors (all systems) provide the system information or services that the system needs in order to serve the primary actors.
- Wearable System
- Base Station(s)
- Data Repository

Supporting Actors. These people keep the system going and ensure that it is configured to meet the needs of the primary actor.
- System Administrator
- Security Administrator
- Sensor Provider

PRIMARY ACTORS

Patient - Requires continuous medical monitoring and is responsible for wearing the system.

Health Provider - Responsible for determining the necessary needs of the patient and the response required from the system. The Health Provider analyzes the physical data and initiates medical care when system detects medical emergency.

Technician/Clinician - Views displayed physical data and analyzes data for use in patient care. The Technician/Clinician has the ability to add sensors to the wearable system as determined by the needs assessment of the Patient.

SECONDARY ACTORS

Wearable System - The Wearable System is worn by the patient and continually collects physical data.

Base Station(s) - The Base Station detects and registers active sensors on the Wearable System. Continually polls data from the wearable system and sends collected information to the Data Repository.

Data Repository - Processes data collected from the Base Station and displays data in a readable format for further analysis. The Data Repository also detects emergencies to alert necessary primary actors.

SUPPORTING ACTORS

System Administrator - Responsible for ensuring that the system is configured to function as needed. The System Administrator also maintains and submits necessary changes to the algorithms and sensory library.

Security Administrator - Responsible for ensuring the users have access and referenced data is up to date. The Security Administrator defines any privacy policies associated with the systems access and network.

Sensor Provider - The Sensor Provider is the manufacturer of the sensors and has access to the systems open architecture.

USE CASES

1.1 Medical Event - This Use Case determines whether the patient is in need of continuous medical monitoring and a good candidate for the system.

1.2 Needs Assessment - This Use Case will be utilized by the Health Provider to establish the medical needs of the patient to determine what the Wearable System continually monitors. This Use Case will also be used to determine what data analysis output and sensors will be required.

1.3 Request Emergency Help - The patient will be able to use this Use Case to request emergency assistance. This Use Case will allow for immediate medical care to be provided by the Health Provider or emergency care source, such as an ambulance.

1.4 View Data - The patient uses this Use Case to view collected physical data at home for their own monitoring. Data is displayed on a Base Station(s).

1.5 Collect Physical Data - The Wearable System uses this Use Case to acquire the physical data from the patient. The information is not stored here and must be detected by the Base Station.

1.6 Detect & Register Sensor - This Use Case provides the Base Station with the ability to detect and register a new sensor has been added to the Wearable System.

1.7 Poll Wearable System - The Base Station uses this Use Case to continuously gather data from the Wearable System. The Base Station has the ability to store this data.

1.8 Send Collected Data - This Use Case allows the Base Station to send the stored data to the data repository.

1.9 Process Data - The physical data is processed by the Data Repository. This Use Case allows the Data Repository to store the information in a readable format.

1.10 Detect Emergency - This Use Case allows the Data Repository to use the processed data in order to determine if an emergency is present and provide an alarm to the Health Provider and Technician/Clinician.

1.11 Contact Patient - The Technician/Clinician has the ability to contact the patient and engage in bi-directional communication in order to assess possible emergencies or patient non-compliance.

1.12 Display Physical Data - This Use Case allows the processed data to be continuously displayed for the review by the Health Provider and/or Technician/Clinician.

1.13 Configure Wearable System - The Technician/Clinician has the ability to use this Use Case to individualize the Wearable System based on the needs assessment of the Patient.

1.14 Analysis - This Use Case allows the Technician/Clinician to analyze the processed physical data displayed from the Data Repository and determine the necessary data collected for monitoring of the patient by the Health Provider.

1.15 Add Sensor - This Use Case is used by the Technician/Clinician to add any additional necessary sensors to the Wearable System as determined by the needs assessment.

1.16 Publish Open Architecture - The architecture for the system will be open in order that Sensor Manufacturers can access the information to develop sensors that confirm to the architecture and can be used within the wearable medical device telemetry system. The architecture must be publicly available in order that the most recent version of the architecture is openly available in a standard format.

1.17 Access Open Architecture - Anyone with an interest in the architecture of the wearable device telemetry system can access the most current version of the architecture in a standard format.

1.18 Maintain Library of Sensors - This Use Case allows the System Administrator to ensure that the library of sensors is compatible with the architecture in order to maintain proper functioning.

1.19 Maintain Library of Algorithms - This Use Case allows the System Administrator to ensure that the library of algorithms is compatible with the architecture in order to maintain proper functioning.

1.20 Maintain Library of Communication Protocols - This Use Case allows the System Administrator to ensure that the library of communication protocols is compatible with the architecture in order to maintain proper functioning.

1.21 Maintain Secure Access - Access to the system must be restricted to individuals who have been given official authorization to access information or functionality. System access is necessary to restrict individuals in the type of information or the types of things that they can do within the system. Every individual may have different levels of access that can change over time and the Security Administrator is the authoritative source in granting system privileges to users within the system.

1.22 Define Privacy Policy - In order to ensure that personal health information is properly protected according to provincial or federal standards, the system must have the capacity to enforce a specific privacy policy. The Security Administrator is responsible for ensuring that personal health information is properly retained and not used or disclosed for purposes other than those for which it was collected, except with the consent of the individual.

Device Prototyping. Two wireless biometric sensor systems were developed for use within the HAAS architecture. The two prototypes were designed, implemented and tested by two undergraduate groups as part of their fourth year design project academic requirement. Each of the two prototypes was developed for less than $300.00. The results and design of both prototypes have not yet been published; we briefly present them here to show the progress in the research.

The first prototype is a breathing monitor that was designed with a chest expansion/contraction sensor.[15] The breathing monitor uses a Differential Variable Reluctance Transducer (DVRT) to measure the expansion and contracting of the rib cage. The device also uses a signal conditioner to filter the raw signals. The entire system is controlled by a MC9S12DP256 microcontroller and uses ZigBee wireless technology.

The second system is a range of motion sensor system that uses a bend sensor on a joint.[16] The range of motion sensor was developed for a knee joint but the system was designed to incorporate up to sixteen sensors. The sensor is a flex sensor that changes its voltage as it is bent. This system also uses the MC9S12DP256 microcontroller and ZigBee wireless technology. Both systems were built to preprocess the measurements into usable data before transmission. Both systems provide the ability to also send raw data if required.

Validation

The requirements acquired during the Use Case Analysis went through several iterations and were validated by domain experts through document reviews and during two separate brainstorming sessions. The validation group was composed of researchers in the fields of biomechanics, ergotherapy, and physiotherapy, as well as an electrical engineer who is an expert in biomedical and biometrics device development.

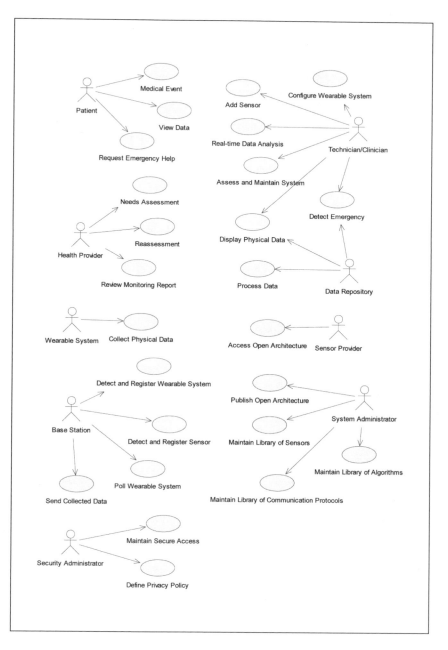

Figure 6.1: Use Case Analysis Diagram for HAAS.

CONCLUSION

Our initial literature review and market survey show a growing interest in decentralized health care monitoring and rehabilitation. The current state of the art for wearable devices and BANs is evolving rapidly. The main limitations of current systems are their lack of scalability and closed proprietary architectures. In this paper, we proposed to use ROOM and MDD to design an open architecture for a BAN of wearable monitoring devices; called the Health Activity Assessment System. The architecture will allow dynamic configuration of the BAN tailored to the needs of the patient and health care professionals. We have performed and validated our system requirements through Use Case Analysis. We also have developed two biometric wireless sensors. We are currently aiming to derive the software communication protocols using ROOM to be published and develop a low cost portable gate analysis system as part of HAAS.

[1] R.J. Romanow, *Building on values: The future of health care in Canada* (Ottawa, ON: Commission on the Future of Health Care in Canada, 2002), 16-20.

[2] R. Casaburi, "Activity monitoring in assessing activities of daily living," COPD: *Journal of Chronic Obstructive Pulmonary Disease* Vol. 4, No. 3 (2007): 251-255; D.J. Macfarlane, C.C.Y. Lee, E.Y.K. Ho, K.L. Chan and D. Chan, "Convergent validity of six methods to assess physical activity in daily life," *Journal of Applied Physiology* Vol. 101 (2006): 1328–1334; B. Najafi, K. Aminian, A. Paraschiv-Ionescu, F. Loew, C.J. Büla and P. Robert, "Ambulatory System for Human Motion Analysis Using a Kinematic Sensor: Monitoring of Daily Physical Activity in the Elderly," *IEEE Transactions On Biomedical Engineering* Vol. 50, No. 6 (2003): 711-723.

[3] B. Selic, G. Gullekson and P. Ward, *Real-Time Object-Oriented Modeling* (New York: Wiley, 1994), 36-358.

[4] D. Schmidt, "Model-Driven Engineering," *IEEE Computer* Vol. 39, No. 2 (2006): 25-31.

[5] M. Hanson, H.C. Powell, A.T. Barth, K. Ringgenberg, B.H. Clahoun, J.H. Aylor and J. Lach, "Body Area Sensor Networks: Challenges and Opportunities," *IEEE Computer Society* Vol. 42, No. 1 (2009): 58.

[6] A. Lymberis and L Gatzoulis, "Wearable health systems: from smart technologies to real applications," (Proceedings, 28th IEEE EMBS Annual International Conference, New York City, USA, August 30-September 3, 2006), 6789-6792.

[7] S. Koch and M. Hagglund, "Health informatics and the delivery of care to older people," *Maturitas* Vol. 63, No. 3 (2009): 198.

[8] Michael J. Sailor and Jamie R. Link, "Smart dust": nanostructured devices in a grain of sand," *Chemical Communications* Vol. 11 (2005): 1376; K. Pister, "Smart dust – Autonomous sensing and communication in a cubic millimeter," *UC Berkeley*, last modified in 2001 http://robotics.eecs.berkeley.edu/~pister/SmartDust/, accessed 26 May 2011.

[9] R. Steele, A. Lo, C. Secombe and Y.K. Wong, "Elderly persons' perception and acceptance of using wireless sensor networks to assist healthcare," *International Journal of Medical Informatics* Vol. 78, No. 12 (2009): 789

[10] K. Fowler, "Sensor survey: Part 2, sensor and sensor networks in five years," *IEEE Instrumentation & Measurement Magazine* Vol. 12, No. 2 (2009): 43.

[11] K. Fowler, "Sensor survey: Part 2, sensor and sensor networks in five years," *IEEE Instrumentation & Measurement Magazine* Vol. 12, No. 2 (2009): 43.

[12] K. Fowler, "Sensor survey: Part 2, sensor and sensor networks in five years," *IEEE Instrumentation & Measurement Magazine* 12, 2 (2009): 43.

[13] B. Gyselinckx, J. Penders and R. Vullers, "Potential and challenges of body area networks for cardiac monitoring," *Journal of Electrocardiology* Vol. 40, No. 6 (2007): S165-S168.

[14] A. Pantelopoulous and N. Bourbakis, "A survey on wearable biosensor systems for health monitoring." *30th Annual International IEEE EMBS Conference* (2008): 4887-4890.

[15] H. Venter and D. Priestley, "Detailed Design Document for the Wearable Breathing Monitor," (2009): Results to be published.

[16] D.P. Marson and C.A. Stockwell, "Detailed Design Document for the Range of Motion Sensor," (2010): Results to be published.

CHAPTER 7

The Effect of Neck Muscle Exercise Training on Self Reported Pain in CH-146 Griffon Helicopter Aircrew

Danielle M. Salmon, PhD(Cand), Michael F. Harrison, PhD, Donald Sharpe, PhD,
Darren G. Candow, PhD, and J. Patrick Neary, PhD;
Faculty of Kinesiology & Health Studies, University of Regina;
Wayne J. Albert, PhD, Faculty of Kinesiology, University of New Brunswick;

ABSTRACT

The prevalence of neck pain in Canadian Forces CH-146 Griffon helicopter pilots and flight engineers has been identified in the range of 81-84%.[2] In attempt to mitigate this problem we quantified the adaptations of cervical musculature isometric strength using a 12-week exercise training program. Subjects were recruited on a volunteer basis from the CF CH-146 Griffon aircrew at two air force bases, and randomized into either a general neck strength and muscle coordination training program (CTP; n=10), or a neck muscle endurance training program (ETP; n=11), or a non-treatment control (CON; n=8). Baseline assessments were performed to determine maximal voluntary contraction (MVC) for the cervical musculature using isometric contractions (flexion, extension, left lateral flexion and right lateral flexion), and the visual analog scale (VAS) to assess self-reported neck pain before and after exercise training. The ETP subjects performed dynamic contraction at 30% MVC in the four testing directions using a head harness and thera-band tubing. The CTP consisted of exercises that focused initially on strengthening the deep neck cervical flexors and extensors using weight of the head as resistance then progressed to exercises that incorporated more the superficial cervical muscles. Post-training CTP underwent a significant improvement in maximal force for flexion (13.8%) and right lateral flexion (15.9%). ETP achieved the only significant increase when compared to the CON for right lateral flexion (14.4%). Improved times to fatigue were achieved by the CTP for flexion, left lateral flexion, and right lateral flexion. Significant improvements were found in the VAS score for the CTP for "pain in general" ($t(9) = 2.47$, $p = 0.02$.) and "pain at worst" ($t(9) = 2.06$, $p = 0.04$) and "pain at worst" ($t(10) = 2.18$, $p = 0.03$) for ETP. The 12-week ETP and CTP resulted in a reduction in VAS self-reported neck pain scores coupled with a positive trend toward improvements in MVC and muscular endurance of the cervical musculature. These results suggest that exercise training can mitigate neck pain in this aircrew population.

THE EFFECT OF NECK MUSCLE EXERCISE TRAINING ON SELF REPORTED PAIN IN CH-146 GRIFFON HELICOPTER AIRCREW[3]

It has been reported that neck pain in the general population at any given time, is in the range of 10-20%,[4] but has also been reported to be as high as 67%.[5] Not only is neck pain a prevalent medical disorder in the general population, but it is an even larger concern for military air forces at an international level as it has the potential to interfere with an aircrew member's flying abilities, concentration, safety, overall health status and leisure time activity.[6] A survey conducted using CF CH-146 military helicopter pilots found 81% of the aircrew reported experiencing neck pain.[7] Although slightly lower than what has been documented in CF CH-146 aircrew, flight related neck pain in British helicopter pilots has been reported to be 56.6% with an even higher prevalence of 71.2% for airload masters (i.e., flight engineers).[8] The 3-month prevalence of neck pain in Swedish military helicopter pilots was 57%, including 32% that reported frequent neck pain.[9] Collectively, these results suggest that neck pain has a major impact on not only their occupational performance, but also their quality of life.

Furthermore, the technical report based on survey questionnaire data conducted by Adams (2004) for the Canadian Department of National Defence on night vision-goggle (NVG) induced neck strain found that those pilots who reported neck pain during flight, nearly 40% had experienced more than 10 episodes, suggesting that the pain was chronic. Of those reporting neck pains during flight, over 15% felt that their worst episode was severe enough during flight to be incapacitating. This was defined as "pain that rendered the respondent unable to perform normal duties."[10] Examination of the occurrence of neck pain after a flight found that 45% of pilots reported experiencing more than 10 episodes. Close to 50% of these pilots reported their worst episode of neck pain lasted in excess of a full day and in many cases up to four days.[11] These statistics function to highlight the impact neck pain is having on helicopter pilots during not only single isolated events but on a reoccurring basis.

Within the CH-146 Griffon flight engineers community, 84.5% reported neck pain related to flying. At least 50% reported experiencing more than 10 episodes. The most disturbing figure was that almost 100% reported neck pain after flight. Compared to the pilots, neck pain experienced after flight by flight engineers was severe enough to be considered incapacitating in 25% of cases.[12] This rate of pain occurrence is higher than was reported by their pilot counterparts.[13]

HELICOPTER FLIGHT AND THE DEVELOPMENT OF NECK PAIN

During flight, helicopter pilots encounter smaller +Gz forces than fighter pilots but are also exposed to low vibration frequencies with greater amplitudes.[14] The unique environment experienced during helicopter flight has led to the development of neck pain that is more chronic in nature. This chronic neck pain is defined as occurring over prolonged periods and is associated with a loss of function or in some cases premature degenerative changes in the cervical spine.[15] Research using radiographs of 732 Turkish flight personnel identified an increased number of cervical spondylarthritic/ spondylitic changes in helicopter pilots when compared to jet and transport pilots.[16] To determine the existence of predictive factors relating to neck pain in CF CH-146 helicopter aircrew, research was conducted examining fitness, flight history, and cervical isometric strength and endurance. The results of the data analysis suggest that only the height of the aircrew member and longest single NVG flight predicted which individuals would likely suffer from neck pain.[17] A questionnaire administered to Swedish military helicopter pilots found history of previous neck pain and recent shoulder pain were significant predictors for neck pain. Although not significant, NVG utilization and/or experience contributed to the overall risk of neck pain.[18] Wickes & Greeves (2005) also examined survey data from the British RAF and found that total number of NVG flying hours was associated with increased probability of having suffered flight related neck in helicopter pilots.[19]

MEASUREMENT OF NECK PAIN

A measurement tool widely used in both clinical and research settings is the VAS.[20] This scale requires subjects to rate the intensity or severity of their pain by placing a mark on a straight line anchored with verbal labels. VAS is a valid means for assessing the change in pain.[21] VAS has also been used in training studies to assess reductions in neck pain due to different cervical training programs.[22] Nikander *et al.* (2006) found that both a cervical strength and endurance training protocols were capable of a 40 mm decrease on the VAS (± 20 mm).[23] This is supported by Ylinen *et al.* (2003) who assessed strength and endurance training in women suffering from neck pain.[24] Ylinen *et al.* reported a reduction in both training programs relative to the control group; subjects in the endurance and strength programs achieved a mean reduction of 35 mm and 40 mm respectively.[25]

MITIGATING NECK PAIN

A number of factors have been implicated or related to neck pain and its development in helicopter aircrew during flight. Some of these factors include: NVG use,[26] adoption of sub-optimal postures during flight,[27] whole body vibrations resulting from the sustained low frequency (4-5Hz) vibration of the helicopter platform,[28] maintenance of low level contractions for extended periods,[29] and cockpit layout.[30] In attempt to minimize the force requirements of the neck extensors, some pilots place a counter-weight on the back of their helmet.[31] Thuresson *et al.*, (2003) found no significant difference in muscular activity using EMG measures between helmet with NVG compared to a helmet with NVG and a counter-weight when using a number of isolated postures.[32] In contrast, research during simulated night flights with NVG using near infrared spectroscopy (NIRS) found that counter-weights actually minimized the metabolic stress placed on the trapezius muscle.[33] Further research is needed to substantiate the effects of counter-weight use for military operations. Regardless of the factor(s) involved, countermeasures are needed to mitigate neck pain and disability in helicopter aircrew if they are to continue their profession.

It has been suggested that exercise training or therapy can provide a prophylactic effect.[34] Exercise therapy is cited as the most commonly used treatment modalities for non-specific neck disorders. Exercise therapy is defined as "therapy [that] involves the prescription of muscular contraction and bodily movement ultimately to improve the overall function of the individual and help meet the demands of daily living."[35] For the occupational environments associated with flight, research examining the role of exercise therapy in the alleviation of neck pain has focused mainly on fighter pilots, [36] with limited research available on helicopter pilots.

Furthermore, there is limited research to show that physical exercise training programs can have a positive influence on neck pain and disability. We hypothesized that specific exercise training programs would enhance physiological function of the neck musculature and reduce the perception of neck pain in helicopter aircrew that reported pre-existing neck pain as a result of their occupation. Thus, the purpose of this study was to determine whether exercise training programs can reduce the perception of neck pain in CF helicopter aircrew.

METHOD

SUBJECTS

Participants were recruited on a volunteer basis from the CH-146 Griffon aircrew in the 403 Squadron at the Canadian Forces Base (CFB) in Gagetown, NB, and from 430 Tactical Helicopter Squadron at CFB Valcartier, QC, for the Non-treatment Control group (NTC). Ethical approval was obtained from the University of Regina's Ethics Review Board. Prior to baseline data collection, each subject was fully briefed regarding the goals of the project by a member of the research team and CF personnel before providing their written informed consent. The voluntary nature of the project and the confidentiality of outcomes and medical information were emphasized to all participants. Participants were excluded if they exhibited any of the following: a) persistent signs and symptoms of a previous musculoskeletal injury to the cervico-thoracic spine; b) cervicobrachialgia or shoulder pain during neck movement; c) radiating pain when overloading the cervical spine; d) currently grounded.[37] All participants were required to fill out a Physical Activity Readiness Questionnaire (PAR-Q) which screened for any health problems.[38]

At the outset of the study, participants (n = 42: 39 males and 3 females; 29 pilots and 13 flight engineers) were assigned to one of three categories based on their total NVG hour flying time. A threshold value of 150 NVG hours flight time has been proposed for the onset of subjective neck pain in CF helicopter aircrew.[39] Based on this, total NVG hours were used as a blocking variable to equally distribute individuals who were at a higher risk of suffering from neck pain among the treatment groups. Three NVG hour categories were selected: <100hrs, 100-200hrs, and >200hrs. Subjects from each category at the base selected for the training programs were then randomly assigned to one of the two treatment groups. The initial subject cohort for each of the groups was the following: ETP n = 15 (females= 1), CTP n = 13 (females = 2) and NTC n = 14 (females = 0).

Eleven subjects did not complete the post-test assessment (4, ETP; 3, CTP; 6, NTC). Reasons for withdrawal were: time commitments, ongoing neck pain, posting to a different base, away on course and personal reasons. At the completion of the 12-week study, the attrition rates for the respective programs were 27% for the ETP, 23% for the CTP, and 43% for the NTC. The final cohort consisted of 11 participants (10m, 1f) in the ETP, 10 participants (8m, 2f) in the CTP and 8 participants (8m) in the NTC.

NECK PAIN AND DISABILITY QUESTIONNAIRES

Prior to the start of the training program, a familiarization session was conducted where each participant was asked to complete a Disability of Arm and Shoulder (DASH) Questionnaire and a Neck Disability Index Questionnaire. Participants were also asked to complete a questionnaire put together by the research team that inquired as to their basic anthropometric measurements such as height and weight, aircrew position, counterweight usage and dominant hand. Personal information regarding the subject's flight experience with fixed wing and rotary wing aircrafts as a function of years and hours, total NVG experience in hours, average NVG mission length in hours, and longest NVG mission length in hours were also collected.

Perceived neck pain was recorded using a VAS, which is based on a 0-100 mm scale with end points anchored on the left side with 'no pain at all' (0 mm) and on the right with 'worst possible pain' (100 mm).[40] The use of these verbal cues is a reliable and valid measure of sensory intensity relating to neck pain.[41] Three VAS scales representing 'pain at present', 'pain in general', and 'pain at worst' were used prior to the pre- and post-test assessment.[42]

TRAINING PROGRAM INTERVENTIONS

After the baseline assessment, subjects in each exercise intervention attended a familiarization session where the exercises that comprised their respective programs were demonstrated in detail. On the familiarization day, each participant was given a booklet outlining their respective programs with visual illustrations and written descriptions of each of the exercises. This was combined with a verbal explanation and physical demonstration of the exercises. Subjects were also asked to record their training progress in a training diary (i.e., the reps and sets of each exercise performed). Diaries were collected at the end of the training period to assess training attendance and ensure that each participant had progressively increased their training load. Supervision was provided during all training sessions. Supervision ensured that participants clearly understood the program, performed proper technique, and understood when to increase the resistance load.[43] All participants were asked to undertake their respective programs 3x per week in addition to any other exercise that they were doing in their daily routine. If they were unable to attend one of four sessions offered on the training days, they were asked to complete the session on their own.

Each treatment intervention began with 5 minutes of active warm-up where participants were guided through a series of movements of the cervical spine and shoulders. Each movement was repeated 10 times in each of the 3 sets and consisted of shoulder shrugs, shoulder circles, shoulder protraction and retraction and neck half circles performed in each direction. This was followed by approximately 15 minutes of specific neck exercises that varied depending on the treatment designation, concluding with approximately 15 minutes of abdominal exercises including abdominal curls with weights, the plank, core work with a Swiss ball, side plank, back bridges, and "good mornings" with weights (see Figure 7.1). These exercises initially began with 2 sets of 10 reps. The number of sets was increased to 3 sets after 5 weeks. Each session finished with approximately 5 minutes of stretching where each stretch was performed 3x and held for a total of 20 seconds. The stretching routine included: scalene muscle, upper trapezius muscle, sternocleidomastoid muscle, standing head drop stretch, and a dumb bell lateral stretch.

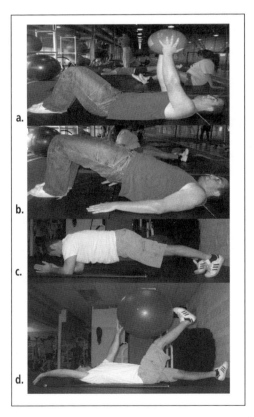

Figure 7.1: A selection of the exercises performed for the core strengthening component by both the CTP and the ETP. a. Abdominal curl with medicine ball; b. Back bridge; c. Plank; d. Core work with swiss ball.

Group A: Neck muscle endurance training program (ETP). Participants used elastic rubber tubing (Theraband, Hygiene Corp, Akron, OH) to resist the dynamic movements of cervical flexion, extension, right and left lateral flexion. Participants assumed a seated position wearing a 2.5 cm webbing head harness to which rubber tubing was attached via carabineers that was equivalent to their 30% MVC determined during baseline testing. The resistance was provided by rubber tubing that was cut to 70cm length. The approximate stretch of the rubber tubing that was predicted during the performance of the exercises was 25%. Given the predicted stretch, the tubing resistances were calculated to be: blue (3lbs), black (4lbs), and silver (5lbs). The resistance program was progressive in nature and thus all 3 color-coded bands were used to achieve the 30% MVC value used by the participants. For the extension direction, the tubing was attached via a carabineer to a weighted mount on the floor in front of the participant. For the flexion direction, the participants turned the chair in the opposite direction and the tubing was attached to a clip on the back of the head harness and the opposite end remained attached to the same floor mount. Left and right lateral flexion required the participants to attach the tubing to the clips located on the left and right sides of the head harness. For the lateral flexion directions, the participants were asked to hold the tubing with the same hand with their arm abducted and their elbow bent to 90° (see Figure 7.2). No specific directions were provided by the supervising member of the research team with regards to the movement patterns need to activate the deep neck flexors, in order to minimize any intentional effort to activate the deep neck stabilizers.

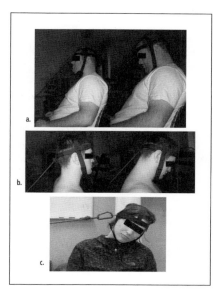

Figure 7.2: Exercises comprising the Endurance Training Program. a. Postures adopted for resisted extension; b. Postures adopted for resisted flexion; c. Bottom: Posture adopted for left and right lateral flexion.

For each of the four directions, participants performed 3 sets of 10 reps maintaining a resistance level of 30% MVC.[44] One minute of rest was given between each set.[45] If a participant was able to perform 12 consecutive reps of an exercise, the load was increased by 5% as necessary to maintain 10RM on subsequent performed sets. A rhythmic cadence of 2 sec for concentric and eccentric contractions was maintained. At the end of range of motion, the contraction was held for 1 sec.[46] Timing for the cadence was provided by the supervisor.

Group B: General neck strength and muscle coordination training program (CTP). The purpose of this program was muscle control. Low load exercises were used to train the coordination between the layers of cervical muscle.[47] The motor control aspect "is based on biomechanical evidence of the functional interplay of the deep and superficial neck muscles and on the physiological and clinical evidence of impairments in these muscles in neck pain patients."[48] Based on their moment-generating capacity, the muscles of the cervical spine can be classified as either segmental stabilizers or prime movers. The musculature surrounding the cervical vertebrae of the spinal column are classified as segmental stabilizers, whose role is to provide the postural support for cervical lordosis and the cervical joints.[49] The deep cervical flexors are the longus colli, longus capitis, rectus capitis anterior and rectus capitis lateralis.[50] The deep cervical extensors are the semispinalis capitis, semispinalis cervicis, longissimus cervicis and the posterior suboccipitals.[51] The superficial and intermediate layers of the cervical muscles are known as prime movers, whose primary role is movement of the head and cervical spine.[52] Fall, Rainoldi, Merletti, and Jull (2003) identified the SCM and anterior scalene muscles as the prime movers of cervical flexion.[53] Based on MRI technology the splenius capitis, semispinalis capitis, semispinalis cervicis and multifidus muscles are the primary head extensors.[54] This exercise regime uses low load exercises to place specific emphasis on strengthening and re-educating the deep postural cervical musculature. Once the imbalance between deep and the superficial muscle was addressed, general neck strengthening exercises were introduced.[55]

Three stages of progression were used in this program. Stage 1 extended for the first two weeks of the training program and focused on isolating the deep segmental stabilizers of the cervical spine. The primary exercises of this stage used isometric contractions to maintain a neutral cervical spine (slight lordosis of the cervical spine) in supine, standing and sitting. Other exercises in this initial stage focused on proper segmental movement of the deep extensor cervical musculature in a return to neutral posture in four point kneeling and a sitting position. Stage 2 occurred during weeks 2-6 and focused primarily on maintaining a neutral cervical spine while integrating limb motion into the exercises. The exercises consisted of the windmill, internal and external shoulder rotation and return to neutral posture in four-point kneeling with pure rotation. Stage 3, weeks 7-12, the programs focus changed to include only two exercises that focused specifically on the deep cervical musculature: the deep neck flexor head nod with a head lift in supine and the return to a neutral posture in four-point kneeling with pure rotation (see Figure 7.3). During this phase of the program, the emphasis changed to strengthening the superficial muscles of the neck through resisted flexion, extension, and left and right lateral flexion through a controlled segmental movement pattern, which incorporated the deep cervical muscle through the maintenance of proper posture and a slight chin nod. Resistance was applied using the same method used in the neck muscle endurance training program. Resistance was increased when subjects were able to perform 3 sets of 10 reps while maintaining segmental control throughout the movement.

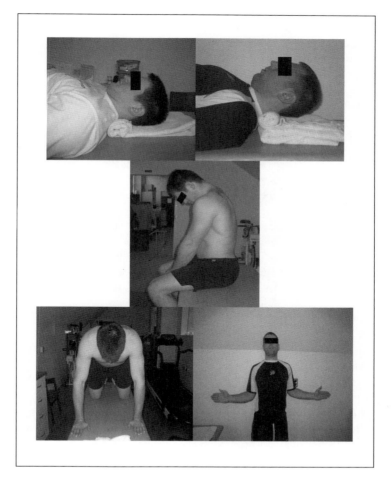

Figure 7.3: Exercises used in the Coordination Training Program: Top left deep neck flexor head nod, top right deep neck flexor head nod with head lift, middle seated return to neutral, bottom left return to neutral in four point kneeling, bottom right external shoulder rotation.

The exercise schedule for this program was progressed on an individual basis based upon each participant's progress. All participants were given continual feedback in regard to exercise performance and posture by the supervisor. Between each set, 1 min of rest was given.[56] If the participant was able to perform 12 consecutive reps for 3 sets of an exercise, the resistance was increased by approximately 5% as necessary to maintain 10RM on subsequent performed sets. A rhythmic cadence of 2 seconds for concentric and eccentric contractions was maintained for each exercise. At the end of range of motion, an isometric contraction was held for 1 second.[57]

Group C: Non-treatment control group (NTC). The participants in this control group were asked to refrain from initiating or from participating in any neck specific strength or endurance exercise training. However, they were encouraged to continue with their normal daily exercise routine. They were given no information about the potential benefits of neck specific exercises or stretching until after the completion of the study.

DATA ANALYSIS

Statistical analysis was performed using SPSS 16.0 (SPSS Inc. Chicago, IL). Descriptive statistics are reported as mean ± one standard deviation (SD). All results were examined for the presence of outliers exceeding ± 2 SDs. A baseline comparison of MVCs, anthropometric measures and neck pain VAS scores was made between the two treatment groups and the control using a one-way analysis of variance (ANOVA). VAS pain scores for the treatment groups were analyzed using within-subjects ANOVA. Visual inspection of the mean pre- and post-test values for the VAS scores was used to identify interaction contrasts of interest which were then tested using methods described by Jaccard and Guilamo-Ramos (2002).[58] Single degree-of-freedom contrasts were used to determine significant changes for either of the two treatment groups or the control.[59] An alpha value of ≤0.05 was used to determine statistical significance.

RESULTS

CHARACTERISTICS OF SUBJECT SAMPLE

The anthropometric values, personal characteristics and flight experience for the subjects in the ETP, CTP and NTC are presented as sample means and standard deviations in Table 7.1. At baseline, the ETP, CTP and NTC were found to be equivalent for all personal, anthropometric and flight experience variables measured ($p > 0.05$). Based on training diaries, compliance with the exercise programs was 52.78% ± 32.39% for the ETP and 76.11% ± 20.75 for the CTP.

	ETP		CTP		NTC	
	M	*SD*	*M*	*SD*	*M*	*SD*
Age (yrs)	37.18	4.5	35.40	8.22	37.12	6.31
Height (m)	1.80	0.08	1.74	0.077	1.79	0.07
Weight (kg)	86.03	12.28	77.33	24.07	90.05	11.24
Total Years Flying	8.09	6.76	7.67	7.14	9.69	7.59
Total Hours Flying	1664.66	1696.82	1676.70	1741.06	2348.28	2115.19
Rotary Wing Years	5.73	5.35	5.61	6.63	8.75	7.64
Rotary Wing Hours	1210.00	1184.64	1281.60	1611.08	2225.09	2083.23
NVG Hours	167.91	165.86	148.50	153.84	225.49	186.69
Average NVG Flight (hrs)	1.36	1.12	1.58	0.83	1.59	0.76
Maximum NVG Flight (hrs)	2.55	2.29	2.45	1.64	3.25	2.04

Table 7.1: Baseline anthropometric values, personal characteristics and flight experience for the endurance (ETP), coordination (CTP) training groups and control group (NTC) subjects.

VAS Self-Seported Neck Pain Scores

In the familiarization session the first baseline self-reported neck pain scores were collected for 'pain at present', 'pain in general' and 'pain at worst' on a VAS scale for both treatment groups. The control group was asked to rate their baseline neck pain on VAS sheets during their baseline assessment, but only three of the 14 volunteers completed the required form. Due to the large amount of missing data, we were unable to include the NTC data in the analysis of neck pain scores. With the data collected, the analysis of the self-reported neck pain scores was limited to the baseline and post-test assessment for the ETP and the CTP.

Based on previous research analyzing self-reported neck pain on a 100mm VAS pre- and post-training intervention, a 10mm decrease in the neck pain VAS score was viewed as a clinically important finding.[60] The ETP produced a 10mm drop in self-reported neck pain scores in 1 individual in the 'pain at present' category, 2 individuals in the 'pain in general' category and 6 individuals in the 'pain at worst' category. For the CTP, a 10mm reduction was achieved by 2 individuals in the 'pain at present' category, 3 individual in the 'pain in general' category and 5 individuals in the 'pain at worst' category.

Pain at present. A 2 (Group) x 2 (Time) ANOVA was conducted for the self-reported neck pain scores for 'pain at present' and showed a no statistically significant main effect for Time, $p = 0.15$, or Group, $p = 0.67$. The Time x Group interaction was also statistically non-significant, $p = 0.20$, indicating no statistical difference in the neck pain scores for 'pain at present' between the two treatment groups from the pre- to the post-test assessment. The mean VAS scores for the ETP for pre-test were $\bar{x} = 4.09 \pm 9.17$mm and post-test were $\bar{x} = 3.60 \pm 5.04$mm. The pre- and post-test mean VAS score for the CTP were $x^- = 8.50 \pm 13.75$mm and $x^- = 1.7 \pm 3.94$mm, respectively. The decrease seen in CTP was examined using a paired t-test, but was not statistically significant, $p = 0.07$ (see Figure 7.4).

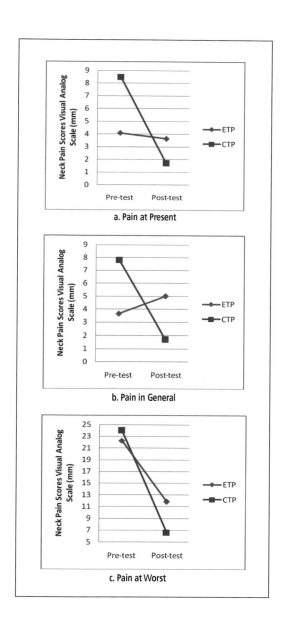

Figure 7.4: Mean pre- and post-test scores of self-reported neck pain on a visual analog scale for 'pain at present', 'pain in general' and 'pain at worst' for the ETP, CTP, and NTC groups.

Pain in General. The neck pain score results for the main effect for Time and the main effect for Group from the 2 x 2 ANOVA for 'pain in general' were p = 0.16, and p = 0.87, respectively. These results indicated that with respect to 'pain in general', there was no statistical difference from pre- to post-test assessment or between the ETP and the CTP. A statistically significant Time x Group interaction was produced, p = 0.03 (see Figure 7.4). This interaction was the result of the increase seen for pre-test ($\bar{x}$ =3.64 ±5.04mm) to post-test ($\bar{x}$ = 5.00 ±7.42mm) for the ETP compared to the decrease from pre-test ($\bar{x}$ = 7.8 ±9.58mm) to post-test ($\bar{x}$ = 1.7 ±3.94mm) for the CTP. The results of a paired t-test for CTP from pre- to post-test statistically decreased, p = 0.02 (see Figure 7.4).

Pain at Worst. The 2 x 2 ANOVA 'pain at worst' VAS scores relating to the self-reported neck pain of the treatment population produced a statistically significant result for the main effect for Time, p = 0.01, indicating a difference from the pre- to post-test assessment. However, there was no statistically significant main effect for Group, p = 0.81, indicating that no statistical difference existed between the two treatment conditions. There was no statistically significant result for Time x Group interaction, p = 0.47. Visual inspect revealed that both treatment conditions underwent large decreases in the self-report 'pain at worst': the CTP decreased from $\bar{x}$ = 22.27 ± 22.73 mm to $\bar{x}$ =11.82 ±18.34mm, and the ETP decreased from $\bar{x}$ = 24 ± 24.13mm to $\bar{x}$ = 6.6 ± 8.58mm. Single degree-of-freedom contrasts were conducted for both the CTP and the ETP using paired t-tests to determine if the respective decreases were statistically significant. Both CTP and ETP revealed statistically significant decreases in 'pain at worst', p = 0.04, and p = 0.03, respectively (see Figure 7.4). Figure 7.5 shows the comparison between training groups for each pain category.

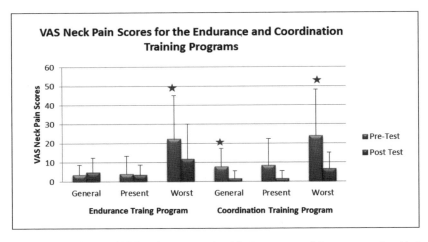

Figure 7.5: Mean self reported VAS neck pain scores (mm) for 'pain in general', 'pain at present', and 'pain at worst' pre- and post-intervention for the ETP and CTP treatment groups.

Discussion

Previous research has established that neck pain is a medical concern with occupational relevance for the Canadian Forces CH-146 helicopter aircrew.[61] The provision of cervical exercise training programs has been found to reduce in-flight muscle strain[62] and workdays lost,[63] and to improve isometric and dynamic strength[64] in the cervical musculature of military populations with an emphasis on fighter pilots. The purpose of this study was to evaluate the effects of two different cervical exercise training programs on reducing self-reported neck pain in a cohort of CH-146 aircrew. The results indicate that both a low load muscular endurance training program and a muscular coordination training program achieved clinically and statistically significant reductions in self-reported neck pain for 'pain at worst' on a visual analog scale. However, only those subjects in the CTP showed statistically significant reductions in 'pain in general' on the VAS.

At baseline, 76.2% of the treatment population in the present study reported some form of neck pain, comparable to values reported by Adam (2004)[65]; 81.2% for CH-146 helicopter pilots and 84.5% flight engineers, but higher than the 53% reported by Harrison (in press-b).[66] Previous research on flight related neck pain has been conducted using dichotomized scales to identify participants as either suffering from neck pain or pain free.[67] To our knowledge, the use of a VAS for assessing neck pain is a novel approach for studies of aircrew. This scale has been used to examine the effects of different neck training modalities on self-reported neck pain in female office workers with chronic neck pain. Niklander *et al.* (2006), Randlov *et al.* (1998) and Ylinen *et al.* (2006) all found the greatest decreases in self-reported neck pain using the VAS occurred in subjects who performed high load resistance training.[68] The model used in the present study was based on Ahlgren *et al.* (2001), who used 'pain at present', 'pain in general' and 'pain at worst' to assess the effects of three dynamic training programs on women with work-related *trapezius myalgia*. No differences between the treatment interventions in the reducing perceived 'pain at present' and 'pain in general' were found. However, in comparison to the endurance and coordination training programs, the strength training program produced the greatest reductions in 'pain at worst'.[69]

The findings from our study differed from those of Ahlgren *et al.* (2001) who found that individuals in the coordination and endurance groups reported lower scores for all three VAS scales, but isolated no differences in the reductions between the two groups. Over the course of our training intervention, the results for 'pain at present' did not significantly change for either the CTP or the ETP. However, for the CTP group the 'pain at present' from pre- to post-test approached significance (p-value of 0.07). The two treatment groups differed in response to 'pain in general' and the ETP mean scores actually increased relative to the significant decrease produced by CTP as seen by the statically significant interaction effect. Both training programs elicited statistically significant decreases in 'pain at worst' over the 12-weeks. Thus, based on

VAS scores, CTP subjects reported the greatest reduction in overall neck pain for all three categories (i.e., 'pain at present', 'pain in general' and 'pain at worst').

Research examining the self-reported risk factors related to the prevalence and development of neck pain in helicopter pilots illustrates that those who engage in regular aerobic exercise[70] and muscle strength training[71] were at a decreased risk. When examining the effect of posture, head mounted equipment, and vibration in the neck muscle of helicopter pilots, exercise therapy could potentially reduce the impact of these stressors.[72] The provision of an exercise program consisting of strength and endurance components has the capacity to increase the isometric strength and endurance of the flexors and extensor muscles of the cervical spine.[73] Given that the cervical muscles provide 80% of cervical stabilization, improving the force production from these muscles should theoretically lead to enhanced stabilization of the cervical spine.[74]

Alricsson et al. (2004) tested the effects of a supervised cervical strength training program on the occurrence of neck pain in fighter pilots.[75] In contrast to our results, Alricsson et al. found that despite improved maximal force in the neck extensors and flexors, and improved endurance in the neck extensors, there was no change in the frequency of self-reported neck pain.[76] However, neck pain was determined using a frequency scale with possible responses ranged from 0-3 based on the number of neck pain occurrence during the past 3 months.

The reduction in 'pain at worst' for both the ETP and CTP and 'pain in general' for the CTP were significant, but the impact of these in a clinical environment is unknown. Linton (1986) suggested that a reduction of 10mm on the VAS is the minimum value required to indicate clinical importance.[77] This contradicts Forouzanfar et al., (2003) who found a relative pain reduction of 50% or more and an absolute pain reduction of at least 30mm on the VAS was needed to accurately predict pain reduction after a treatment.[78] Given that the mean reported baseline value for 'pain at present' and 'pain in general' in our population did not exceed 8.5mm, a 30mm decrease was not possible. Therefore a 10mm decrease was taken to indicate whether a reduction was clinically important.[79] Twenty percent of the individuals in the CTP achieved a 10mm decrease for 'pain at present', 30% of subjects for 'pain in general' and 50% of subjects for 'pain at worst'. A 10mm reduction for 'pain at present', 'pain in general' and 'pain at worst' for the ETP occurred in 9%, 18%, and 54% of the group subjects, respectively. In comparison to the 10 mm decrease, a relative pain reduction of 50% was also used to determine whether the treatment was successful. Based on this criteria, ETP achieved a 50% reduction in VAS scores in 18% of the subjects for both 'pain at present' and 'pain in general' and in 45% of the subjects for 'pain at worst'. This decrease was achieved by 30% of the CTP cohort for 'pain at present', 40% for 'pain in general', and 60% for 'pain at worst'. The decrease in self-reported neck pain scores seen in conjunction with the improved maximal cervical force and muscular endurance is consistent with the statement "chronic non-specific neck pain is to a considerable extent neuromuscular in origin."[80] However, Falla *et al.*, (2006) found reductions in self-reported neck pain in a treatment intervention with no coinciding improvement in cervical flexor strength or endurance suggesting the existence of other physiological or psychological mechanisms which contribute to reductions in neck pain.[81] Alricsson *et al.*, (2004) improved neck strength and endurance in fighter pilots with a supervised training program, but found no reductions in reported neck pain.[82] Other studies have reported reduced neck pain symptoms in non-treatment control subjects and have linked this improvement to spontaneous recovery.[83] These findings illustrate the complexities surrounding the experience of neck pain and the role psychological and physiological factors may play in its reduction.

FUTURE DIRECTIONS

This study demonstrated that both an ETP and a CTP reduced self-reported neck pain in CH-146 aircrew. The greatest reductions in neck pain scores occurred for the CTP group. Future research should therefore expand upon the finding of this investigative study and examine the effects in a larger population over an extended time frame. It would also be useful to examine the effects of the two treatment programs on in-flight muscle strain. At the end of the training intervention, a survey was given to each participant to allow any opportunity for feedback and suggestions to improve the training programs (see Appendix 1). Some of the general comments were that training sessions should be made mandatory part of daily schedule, sessions should be shorter (15 minutes was suggested) and more frequent, and re-design of the head gear was suggested for greater comfort. Therefore, based on the feedback we received and the results from this study, it is our recommendation that training sessions be made a mandatory part of the daily schedule for CF aircrew, and that the sessions be conducted daily for a period of 15min alternating between CTP and a core strengthening program.

The first six weeks of the CTP focused on strengthening the deep cervical musculature and muscle coordination, before progressing to general endurance exercises for the neck. Given the change in focus of the CTP, the degree of activation of the deep cervical flexors needs to be determined pre- and post-intervention compared to the level in the ETP. Additional analysis of the prime movers of flexion, extension, left and right lateral flexion is needed to assess the two treatment interventions with neuromuscular and metabolic measurements.

CONCLUSION

Flight related neck pain has been identified as a major concern with high prevalence in CH-146 aircrew.[84] The provision of an ETP and CTP three times per week for 12 weeks resulted in improvements in maximal isometric force and muscular endurance in the cervical spine. The greatest improvements occurred for those subjects in the

CTP. These improvements in cervical muscular function reduced self-reported neck pain based on a VAS for 'pain in general' and 'pain at worst'. Reductions in self-reported neck pain for the ETP were limited to 'pain at worst'. These results suggest that exercise training can mitigate neck pain in this aircrew population.

ACKNOWLEDGEMENTS

We would like to thank the volunteers from 403 Squadron in CFB Gagetown, NB and the 430 Squadron in CFB Valcartier, QC, for their participation, which was greatly appreciated. Special thanks to 1 Wing in Kingston, Ontario for their support in this project, to Major Mario Coutu, Captain Dan O'Neil, Captain Cheryl A. Elvidge, Master Corporal Joseph L. Hussey, Dr. Luc Hébert, Captain Robin Richer, and Carol Kennedy, BSc PT, DipManipPT, FCAMT, for their assistance with this project. This research was funded by the Department of National Defence Canada, Canadian Forces (Canadian Forces Quality of Life Grant #1725981 & Military Health Program #W3931-050513-001/SV).

APPENDIX 1

NVG Neck Strain Post Test Questionnaire

1. With regards to your training program in general, did you?

| 1 | 2 | 3 | 4 | 5 | 6 | 7 | 8 | 9 | 10 |
| Disliked | | | | Neutral | | | | | Enjoyed |

Response:

Score	Response
5	1 person
6	0
7	5 people
8	3 people
9	6 people
10	2 people

2. How did you feel about the exercises you were given?

| 1 | 2 | 3 | 4 | 5 | 6 | 7 | 8 | 9 | 10 |
| Disliked | | | | Neutral | | | | | Enjoyed |

Responses:

Score	Response
4	1 person
5	0
6	1 person
7	1 person
8	6 people
9	7 people
10	0

3. In your personal opinion did you find your training program beneficial?

1	2	3	4	5	6	7	8	9	10
Do Not Agree				Neutral					Agree

Responses:

Score	Response
4	0
5	1 person
6	0
7	3 people
8	2 people
9	2people
10	9 people

4. Is there anything that you disliked about your training program?

Responses:

-Sessions were a bit long.
-Lack of training time and schedule conflicts.
-Head gear may require redesigning to maximize, and improve comfort and efficiency.
-The head harness was somewhat awkward.
-Was not crazy about the planks but got a lot out of them.
-The head straps could fit a bit better
-The frequency and/or length of the experience. Also the seated flexion exercise was not convenient since it required special equipment (harness and tubing) to take on the road with us.
-Side stretch was painful.
-Erratic schedule from operations.
-No really it was good.

5. Is there anything that you would like to see changed?
Responses:

-Shorter daily sessions
-A training device tailored to the neck exercise (ie. A helmet type contraption that
  would allow for a more structured exercise regime).
-Mandatory ASSIGNED training time to attend (example: You must attend @ time-X
therefore can go on daily schedule).
-Head gear may require redesign to maximize/improve comfort and efficiency.
-No
-Better head harness.
-Head straps could fit a little better.
-No seated flexion
-Shorter exercise time (but more frequently if required) ie. A 15 min daily routine.
-Side stretch was painful
-Continue
-A more comfortable head harness
-No

6. Do you have any suggestion on how we can make the training
program more successful?

Responses:

-Mandated sessions at specific times.
-Make it compulsory for all to participate. This is beneficial to our health in the long
term.
-Mandatory assigned times to attend.
-I found it beneficial
-Do not rest feet on ground as it helps during testing. In the helicopter feet would be
of the rudder pedals.
-Thank you for making my quality of life better.
-As proposed above, shorter exercises instead of the 1 hour commitment 3 hours per
  week. A 15 min daily routine option would be excellent for me.
-Don't schedule us for other work duties.
-No

[1]Support: DND Canada (Canadian Forces Quality of Life Grant #1725981, and Military Health Program #W3931-050513-001/SV).

[2]J. Adam, *Results of NVG-induced neck strain questionnaire study in CH-146 Griffon aircrew* (Toronto, ON: DRDC Toronto TR 2004), 1-75.

[3]Support: DND Canada (Canadian Forces Quality of Life Grant #1725981, and Military Health Program #W3931-050513-001/SV).

[4]E.B. Holmstrom, J. Lindell, and U. Moritz, "Low back and neck/shoulder pain in construction workers: occupational workload and psychosocial risk factors. Part 2: Relationship to neck and shoulder pain," Spine Vol. 17, No. 6 (1992): 672-677.

[5]P. Côté, J.D. Cassidy, and L. Carroll, "The Saskatchewan health and back pain survey: The prevalence of neck pain and related disability in Saskatchewan adults," *Spine* Vol. 23, No. 15 (1998): 1689-1698.

[6]M. Alricsson, K. Harms-Ringdahl, B. Larsson, J. Linder, and S. Werner, "Neck muscle strength and endurance in fighter pilots: effects of a supervised training program," *Aviat Space Environ Med* Vol. 75, No. 1 (2004): 23-28; B. Ang, J. Linder, and K. Harms-Ringdahl, "Neck strength and myoelectric fatigue in fighter and helicopter pilots with a history of neck pain," *Aviat Space Environ Med* Vol. 76, No. 4 (2005): 375-380; O. Hamalainen, "Thoracolumbar pain among fighter pilots," *Mil Med* Vol. 164, No. 8 (1999): 595-596.

[7]J. Adam, *Results of NVG-induced neck strain questionnaire study in CH-146 Griffon aircrew* (Toronto, ON: DRDC Toronto TR 2004), 1-75.

[8]S. Wickes and J. Greeves, "Epidemiology of flight-related neck pain in Royal Air Force (RAF) aircrew," *Aviat Space Environ Med* Vol. 76, No. 3 (2005): 298-311.

[9]B. Ang, J. Linder, and K. Harms-Ringdahl, "Neck strength and myoelectric fatigue in fighter and helicopter pilots with a history of neck pain," *Aviat Space Environ Med* Vol. 76, No. 4 (2005): 375-380.

[10]J. Adam, *Results of NVG-induced neck strain questionnaire study in CH-146 Griffon aircrew* (Toronto, ON: DRDC Toronto TR 2004), 40.

[11]J. Adam, *Results of NVG-induced neck strain questionnaire study in CH-146 Griffon aircrew* (Toronto, ON: DRDC Toronto TR 2004), 1-75.

[12]J. Adam, *Results of NVG-induced neck strain questionnaire study in CH-146 Griffon aircrew* (Toronto, ON: DRDC Toronto TR 2004), 1-75.

[13]J. Adam, *Results of NVG-induced neck strain questionnaire study in CH-146 Griffon aircrew* (Toronto, ON: DRDC Toronto TR 2004), 1-75.

[14]Y. Chen, V. Wickramasinghe, and D. Zimcik, "Adaptive mount approaches for helicopter seat vibration control" (presentation, Proceedings of ICAST, Ottawa: Canada, October 3-5, 2007).

[15]B. Ang and K. Harms-Ringdahl, "Neck pain and related disability in helicopter pilots: A survey of prevalence and risk factors," *Aviat Space Environ Med* Vol. 77, No. 7 (2006): 713-719; N.D. Green and L. Brown, "Head positioning and neck muscle activation during air combat," *Aviat Space Environ Med* 75, no. 8 (2004): 676-680; S. Wickes and J. Greeves, "Epidemiology of flight-related neck pain in Royal Air Force (RAF) aircrew," *Aviat Space Environ Med* Vol. 76, No. 3 (2005): 298-311.

[16]S.T. Aydog, E. Turbedar, A.H. Demirel, O. Teti·k, A. Akin, and M.N. Doral, "Cervical and lumbar spinal changes diagnosed in four-view radiographs of 732 military pilots," *Aviat Space Environ Med* Vol. 77, No. 7 (2004): 713-719.

[17]M.F. Harrison, "The investigation of muscular factors in night vision goggle induced neck strain in Canadian forces helicopter aircrew," (Regina, SK: University of Regina; 2009), 1-117.

[18]B. Ang and K. Harms-Ringdahl, "Neck pain and related disability in helicopter pilots: A survey of prevalence and risk factors," *Aviat Space Environ Med* Vol. 77, No. 7 (2006): 713-719.

[19]S. Wickes and J. Greeves, "Epidemiology of flight-related neck pain in Royal Air Force (RAF) aircrew," *Aviat Space Environ Med* Vol. 76, No. 3 (2005): 298-311.

[20]D.D. Price, P.A. McGrath, A. Rafii, and B. Buckingham, "The validation of visual analogue scales as ratio scale measures for chronic and experimental pain," Pain Vol. 17, No. 1 (1983): 45-56.

[21]J.S. Dixon and H.A. Bird, "Reproducibility along a 10-cm vertical visual analogue scale," Ann Rheum Dis 40, (1981): 87-89; P. Goolkasian, "Neck pain and disability scale: A critical evaluation," *Expert Rev Pharmacoecon Outcomes Res* 3 (2003): 379-382; D.D. Price, P.A. McGrath, A. Rafii, and B. Buckingham, "The validation of visual analogue scales as ratio scale measures for chronic and experimental pain," Pain 17, no. 1 (1983): 45-56.

[22]C. Ahlgren, W. Kerstin, F. Kadi, M. Djupsjobacka, L. Thornell, and G. Sundelin, "Effects on physical persformance and pain from three dynamic training programs for women with work-related trapezius myalgia," *J Rehabil Med* Vol. 33, No. 4 (2001): 162-169; R. Nikander, E. Malkia, J. Parkkari, A. Heinonen, H. Starck, and J. Ylinen, "Dose-response relationship of specific training to reduce chronic neck pain and disability," *Med Sci Sports Exerc* Vol. 38, No. 12 (2006): 2068-2074; J.J. Ylinen, A.H. Hakkinen, E.P. Takala, M.J. Nykanen, H.J. Kautiainen, E.A. Malkia, *et al.*, "Effects of neck muscle training in women with chronic neck pain: one-year follow-up study," *J Strength Cond Res* Vol. 20, No. 1 (2006): 6-13.

[23]R. Nikander, E. Malkia, J. Parkkari, A. Heinonen, H. Starck, and J. Ylinen, "Dose-response relationship of specific training to reduce chronic neck pain and disability," *Med Sci Sports Exerc* Vol. 38, No. 12 (2006): 2068-2074.

[24]J.J. Ylinen, E.P. Takala, M. Nykanen, A. Hakkinen, E. Malkia, T. Pohjolainen, *et al.*, "Active neck muscle training in the treatment of chronic neck pain in women: a randomized controlled trial," *JAMA* Vol. 289, No. 19 (2003): 2509-2516.

[25]J.J. Ylinen, E.P. Takala, M. Nykanen, A. Hakkinen, E. Malkia, T. Pohjolainen, *et al.*, "Active neck muscle training in the treatment of chronic neck pain in women: a randomized controlled trial," *JAMA* Vol. 289, No. 19 (2003): 2509-2516.

[26]B.P. Butler, "Helmeted head and neck dynamics under whole-body vibration" (PhD dissertation, University of Michigan, 1992), 13-24; B.T. Weirstra, *Ergonomic assessment of flight engineers at 403 SQN* (Camp Gagetown, New Brunswick: Physiotherapy Report, 2001), 6600-1; S. Wickes and J. Greeves, "Epidemiology of flight-related neck pain in Royal Air Force (RAF) aircrew," *Aviat Space Environ Med* 76, no. 3 (2005): 298-311.

[27]K.A. Forde, W.J. Albert, M.F. Harrison, J.P. Neary, J. Croll, and J.P. Callaghan, "Neck loads and posture exposure of helicopter pilots during simulated day and night flights," *International Journal of Industrial Ergonomics*, In Press, Corrected Proof. doi: DOI: 10.1016/j.ergon.2011.01.001, (2011): 128-135; T.W. Pelham, H. White, L.E. Holt, and S.W. Lee, "The etiology of low back pain in military helicopter aviators: prevention and treatment," Work Vol. 24, No. 2 (2005): 101-110.

[28]Y. Chen, V. Wickramasinghe, and D. Zimcik, "Adaptive mount approaches for helicopter seat vibration control" (presentation, Proceedings of the 18th International Conference of Adaptive Structures and Technologies, Ottawa, ON, October 3-5, 2007).

[29]K.A. Forde, W.J. Albert, M.F. Harrison, J.P. Neary, J. Croll, and J.P. Callaghan, "Neck loads and posture exposure of helicopter pilots during simulated day and night flights," *International Journal of Industrial Ergonomics*, In Press, Corrected Proof. doi: DOI: 10.1016/j.ergon.2011.01.001, (2011): 128-135; M.F. Harrison, J.P. Neary, W.J. Albert, D.W. Veillette, N.P. McKenzie, and J.C. Croll, "Trapezius muscle metabolism measured with NIRS in helicopter pilots flying a simulator," *Aviat Space Environ Med* Vol. 78, No. 2 (2007b): 110-116; M. Thuresson, B. Ang, J. Linder, and K. Harms-Ringdahl, "Neck muscle activity in helicopter pilots: effect of position and helmet-mounted equipment," *Aviat Space Environ Med* Vol. 74, No. 5 (2003): 527-532.

[30]M.F. Harrison, J.P. Neary, W.J. Albert, D.W. Veillette, N.P. McKenzie, and J.C. Croll, "Helicopter cockpit seat side and trapezius muscle metabolism with night vision goggles," *Aviat Space Environ Med* Vol. 78, No. 10 (2007a): 995-998.

[31]K. Harms-Ringdahl, J. Linder, C. Spångberg, and R.R. Burton, "Biomechanical considerations in the development of cervical spine pathologies" (NATO Research and Technology Organization: RTO-TR RTO-TR-4, 1999), 49-65; M.F. Harrison, J.P. Neary, W.J. Albert, M.D. Veillette, N.P. McKenzie, and J.C. Croll, "Physiological effects of night vision goggle counterweights on neck musculature of military helicopter pilots," *Mil Med* Vol. 172, No. 8 (2007c): 864-870.

[32]M. Thuresson, B. Ang, J. Linder, and K. Harms-Ringdahl, "Neck muscle activity in helicopter pilots: effect of position and helmet-mounted equipment," *Aviat Space Environ Med* Vol. 74, No. 5 (2003): 527-532.

[33]M.F. Harrison, J.P. Neary, W.J. Albert, M.D. Veillette, N.P. McKenzie, and J.C. Croll, "Physiological effects of night vision goggle counterweights on neck musculature of military helicopter pilots," *Mil Med* Vol. 172, No. 8 (2007c): 864-870.

[34]B. Ang, "Impaired neck motor function and pronounced pain-related fear in helicopter pilots with neck pain - a clinical approach," *J Electromyogr Kinesiol* Vol. 18, No. 4 (2008): 538-549; B. Ang, J. Linder, and K. Harms-Ringdahl, "Neck strength and myoelectric fatigue in fighter and helicopter pilots with a history of neck pain," *Aviat Space Environ Med* Vol. 76, no. 4 (2005): 375-380; B. Ang, A. Monnier, and K. Harms-Ringdahl, "Neck/shoulder exercise for neck pain in air force helicopter pilots: a randomized controlled trial," *Spine* (Phila Pa 1976) Vol. 34, No. 16 (2009): E544-551.

[35]N. Smidt, H.C. de Vet, L.M. Bouter, J. Dekker, J.H. Arendzen, R.A. de Bie, *et al.*, "Effectiveness of exercise therapy: a best-evidence summary of systematic reviews," *Aust J Physiother* Vol. 51, No. 2 (2005): 71-85.

[36]M. Alricsson, K. Harms-Ringdahl, B. Larsson, J. Linder, and S. Werner, "Neck muscle strength and endurance in fighter pilots: effects of a supervised training program," *Aviat Space Environ Med* Vol. 75, No. 1 (2004): 23-28; A.F. Burnett, F.L. Naumann, and E.J. Burton, "Flight-training effect on the cervical muscle isometric strength of trainee pilots," *Aviat Space Environ Med* Vol. 75, No. 7 (2004): 611-615; O. Hamalainen, H. Heinijoki, and H. Vanharanta, "Neck training and +Gz-related neck pain: a preliminary study," *Mil Med* Vol. 163, No. 10 (1998): 707-708; O. Hamalainen, S.K. Toivakka-Hamalainen, and P. Kuronen, "+Gz associated stenosis of the cervical spinal canal in fighter pilots," *Aviat Space Environ Med* Vol. 70, No. 4 (1999): 330-334; J.A. Jones, S.F. Hart, D.S. Baskin, R. Effenhauser, S.L. Johnson, M.A. Novas, *et al.*, "Human and behavioral factors contributing to spine-based neurological cockpit injuries in pilots of high-performance aircraft: recommendations for management and prevention," *Mil Med* Vol. 165, No. 1 (2000): 6-12.

[37]D. Falla, G. Jull, P. Hodges, and B. Vicenzino, "An endurance-strength training regime is effective in reducing myoelectric manifestations of cervical flexor muscle fatigue in females with chronic neck pain," *Clin Neurophysiol* Vol. 117, No. 4 (2006): 828-837; R. Nikander, E. Malkia, J. Parkkari, A. Heinonen, H. Starck, and J. Ylinen, "Dose-response relationship of specific training to reduce chronic neck pain and disability," *Med Sci Sports Exerc* Vol. 38, No. 12 (2006): 2068-2074.

[38]S. Thomas, J. Reading, and R.J. Shephard, "Revision of the Physical Activity Readiness Questionnaire (PAR-Q)," *Can J Sport Sci* Vol. 17, No. 4 (1992): 338-345.

[39]J. Adam, Results of NVG-induced neck strain questionnaire study in CH-146 *Griffon aircrew* (Toronto, ON: DRDC Toronto TR 2004), 1-75.

[40]C. Ahlgren, W. Kerstin, F. Kadi, M. Djupsjobacka, L. Thornell, and G. Sundelin, "Effects on physical persformance and pain from three dynamic training programs for women with work-related trapezius myalgia," *J Rehabil Med* Vol. 33, No. 4 (2001): 162-169; R. Nikander, E. Malkia, J. Parkkari, A. Heinonen, H. Starck, and J. Ylinen, "Dose-response relationship of specific training to reduce chronic neck pain and disability," *Med Sci Sports Exerc* Vol. 38, No. 12 (2006): 2068-2074; J.J. Ylinen, A.H. Hakkinen, E.P. Takala, M.J. Nykanen, H.J. Kautiainen, E.A. Malkia, *et al.*, "Effects of neck muscle training in women with chronic neck pain: one-year follow-up study," *J Strength Cond Res* Vol. 20, No. 1 (2006): 6-13.

[41]P. Goolkasian, "Neck pain and disability scale: A critical evaluation," *Expert Rev Pharmacoecon Outcomes Res* Vol. 3 (2003): 379-382.

[42]C. Ahlgren, W. Kerstin, F. Kadi, M. Djupsjobacka, L. Thornell, and G. Sundelin, "Effects on physical persformance and pain from three dynamic training programs for women with work-related trapezius myalgia," *J Rehabil Med* Vol. 33, No. 4 (2001): 162-169.

[43]M. Alricsson, K. Harms-Ringdahl, B. Larsson, J. Linder, and S. Werner, "Neck muscle strength and endurance in fighter pilots: effects of a supervised training program," *Aviat Space Environ Med* Vol. 75, No. 1 (2004): 23-28.

[44]M.S. Conley, M.H. Stone, M. Nimmons, and G.A. Dudley, "Resistance training and human cervical muscle recruitment plasticity," *J Appl Physiol* Vol. 83, No. 6 (1997): 2105-2111; R. Nikander, E. Malkia, J. Parkkari, A. Heinonen, H. Starck, and J. Ylinen, "Dose-response relationship of specific training to reduce chronic neck pain and disability," *Med Sci Sports Exerc* Vol. 38, No. 12 (2006): 2068-2074.

[45]M.S. Conley, M.H. Stone, M. Nimmons, and G.A. Dudley, "Resistance training and human cervical muscle recruitment plasticity," *J Appl Physiol* Vol. 83, No. 6 (1997): 2105-2111; R. Nikander, E. Malkia, J. Parkkari, A. Heinonen, H. Starck, and J. Ylinen, "Dose-response relationship of specific training to reduce chronic neck pain and disability," *Med Sci Sports Exerc* Vol. 38, No. 12 (2006): 2068-2074; J.J. Ylinen, A.H. Hakkinen, E.P. Takala, M.J. Nykanen, H.J. Kautiainen, E.A. Malkia, *et al.*, "Effects of neck muscle training in women with chronic neck pain: one-year follow-up study," *J Strength Cond Res* Vol. 20, No. 1 (2006): 6-13.

[46]M.K. Taylor, J.A. Hodgdon, L. Griswold, A. Miller, D.E. Roberts, and R.F. Escamilla, "Cervical resistance training: effects on isometric and dynamic strength," *Aviat Space Environ Med* Vol. 77, No. 11 (2006): 1131-1135.

[47]D. Falla, "Unravelling the complexity of muscle impairment in chronic neck pain," *Man Ther* Vol. 9, No. 3 (2004): 125-133.

[48]D. Falla, "Unravelling the complexity of muscle impairment in chronic neck pain," *Man Ther* Vol. 9, No. 3 (2004): 171.

[49]J.M. Winters and J.D. Peles, *Neck muscle activity and 3-D head kinematics during quasi-static and dynamic tracking movements*, ed. J.M. Winters and S.L. Woodworth (New York, NY: Springer, 1990), 35-41.

[50]D. Falla, "Unravelling the complexity of muscle impairment in chronic neck pain," *Man Ther* Vol. 9, No. 3 (2004): 125-133.

[51]C. Kennedy, "Exercise interventions for the cervical spine," *Orthopaedic Division Review, Nov/Dec*, (1998): 13-29.

[52]C. Kennedy, "Exercise interventions for the cervical spine," *Orthopaedic Division Review, Nov/Dec*, (1998): 13-29.

[53]D. Falla, A. Rainoldi, R. Merletti, and G. Jull, G., "Myoelectric manifestations of sternocleidomastoid and anterior scalene muscle fatigue in chronic neck pain patients," *Clin Neurophysiol* Vol. 114, No. 3 (2003): 488-495.

[54]M.S. Conley, R.A. Meyer, J.J. Bloomberg, D.L. Feeback, and G.A. Dudley, "Non-invasive analysis of human neck muscle function," *Spine* Vol. 20, No. 23 (1995): 2505-2512.

[55]G. Jull, "Deep cervical flexor muscle dysfunction in whiplash," *J Musculoskeletal Pain* Vol. 8, No. 1 (2000): 143-154.

[56]M.S. Conley, M.H. Stone, M. Nimmons, and G.A. Dudley, "Resistance training and human cervical muscle recruitment plasticity," *J Appl Physiol* Vol. 83, No. 6 (1997): 2105-2111; R. Nikander, E. Malkia, J. Parkkari, A. Heinonen, H. Starck, and J. Ylinen, "Dose-response relationship of specific training to reduce chronic neck pain and disability," *Med Sci Sports Exerc* Vol. 38, No. 12 (2006): 2068-2074.

[57]M.K. Taylor, J.A. Hodgdon, L. Griswold, A. Miller, D.E. Roberts, and R.F. Escamilla, "Cervical resistance training: effects on isometric and dynamic strength," *Aviat Space Environ Med* Vol. 77, No. 11 (2006): 1131-1135.

[58]J. Jaccard, and V. Guilamo-Ramos, "Analysis of variance frameworks in clinical child and adolescent psychology: issues and recommendations," *J Clin Child Adolesc Psychol* Vol. 31, No. 1 (2002): 130-146.

[59]M.F. Harrison, "The investigation of muscular factors in night vision goggle induced neck strain in Canadian forces helicopter aircrew," (Regina, SK: University of Regina; 2009), 1-117.

[60]S. Linton, "A critical review of methods for analysis of behaviour in chronic pain," *Scand J Behav Ther* Vol. 5, No. 2 (1986): 31-48.

[61]J. Adam, *Results of NVG-induced neck strain questionnaire study in CH-146 Griffon aircrew* (Toronto, ON: DRDC Toronto TR 2004), 1-75; K.A. Forde, W.J. Albert, M.F. Harrison, J.P. Neary, J. Croll, and J.P. Callaghan, "Neck loads and posture exposure of helicopter pilots during simulated day and night flights," *International Journal of Industrial Ergonomics*, In Press, Corrected Proof. doi: DOI: 10.1016/j.ergon.2011.01.001, (2011): 128-135; M.F. Harrison, J.P. Neary, W.J. Albert, M.D. Veillette, N.P. McKenzie, and J.C. Croll, "Physiological effects of night vision goggle counterweights on neck musculature of military helicopter pilots," *Mil Med* Vol. 172, No. 8 (2007c): 864-870; M.F. Harrison, "The investigation of muscular factors in night vision goggle induced neck strain in Canadian Forces helicopter aircrew," (Regina, SK: University of Regina; 2009), 1-117.

[62]R. Sovelius, J. Oksa, H. Rintala, H. Huhtala, J. Ylinen, and S. Siitonen, "Trampoline exercise vs. strength training to redcue neck strain in fighter pilots," *Aviat Space Environ Med* 77, no. 1 (2006): 20-25.

[63]O. Hamalainen, H. Heinijoki, and H. Vanharanta, "Neck training and +Gz-related neck pain: a preliminary study," *Mil Med* Vol. 163, No. 10 (1998): 707-708.

[64]A.F. Burnett, F.L. Naumann, R.S. Price, and R.H. Sanders, "A comparison of training methods to increase neck muscle strength," *Work* Vol. 25, No. 3 (2005): 205-210; M.K. Taylor, J.A. Hodgdon, L. Griswold, A. Miller, D.E. Roberts, and R.F. Escamilla, "Cervical resistance training: effects on isometric and dynamic strength," *Aviat Space Environ Med* Vol. 77, No. 11 (2006): 1131-1135.

[65]J. Adam, *Results of NVG-induced neck strain questionnaire study in CH-146 Griffon aircrew* (Toronto, ON: DRDC Toronto TR 2004), 1-75.

[66]M.F. Harrison, "The investigation of muscular factors in night vision goggle induced neck strain in Canadian forces helicopter aircrew," (Regina, SK: University of Regina; 2009), 1-117.

[67]M. Alricsson, K. Harms-Ringdahl, B. Larsson, J. Linder, and S. Werner, "Neck muscle strength and endurance in fighter pilots: effects of a supervised training program," *Aviat Space Environ Med* Vol. 75, No. 1 (2004): 23-28; B. Ang, J. Linder, and K. Harms-Ringdahl, "Neck strength and myoelectric fatigue in fighter and helicopter pilots with a history of neck pain," *Aviat Space Environ Med* Vol. 76, No. 4 (2005): 375-380; M.F. Harrison, "The investigation of muscular factors in night vision goggle induced neck strain in Canadian forces helicopter aircrew," (Regina, SK: University of Regina; 2009), 1-117.

[68]R. Nikander, E. Malkia, J. Parkkari, A. Heinonen, H. Starck, and J. Ylinen, "Dose-response relationship of specific training to reduce chronic neck pain and disability," *Med Sci Sports Exerc* Vol. 38, No. 12 (2006): 2068-2074; A. Randlov, M. Ostergaard, C. Manniche, P. Kryger, A. Jordan, S. Heegaard, and B. Holm, "Intensive dynamic training for females with chronic neck/shoulder pain. A randomized controlled trial," Clin Rehabil Vol. 12, No. 3 (1998): 200-210; J.J. Ylinen, A.H. Hakkinen, E.P. Takala, M.J. Nykanen, H.J. Kautiainen, E.A. Malkia, *et al.*, "Effects of neck muscle training in women with chronic neck pain: one-year follow-up study," *J Strength Cond Res* Vol. 20, No. 1 (2006): 6-13.

[69]C. Ahlgren, W. Kerstin, F. Kadi, M. Djupsjobacka, L. Thornell, and G. Sundelin, "Effects on physical persformance and pain from three dynamic training programs for women with work-related trapezius myalgia," *J Rehabil Med* Vol. 33, No. 4 (2001): 162-169.

[70]S. Wickes and J. Greeves, "Epidemiology of flight-related neck pain in Royal Air Force (RAF) aircrew," *Aviat Space Environ Med* Vol. 76, No. 3 (2005): 298-311.

[71]B. Ang and K. Harms-Ringdahl, "Neck pain and related disability in helicopter pilots: A survey of prevalence and risk factors," *Aviat Space Environ Med* Vol. 77, No. 7 (2006): 713-719.

[72]M.F. Harrison, J.P. Neary, W.J. Albert, D.W. Veillette, N.P. McKenzie, and J.C. Croll, "Trapezius muscle metabolism measured with NIRS in helicopter pilots flying a simulator," *Aviat Space Environ Med* Vol. 78, No. 2 (2007b): 110-116; Thuresson, M., On neck load among helicopter pilots effects of head-worn equipment, whole-body vibration and neck position (Stockholm: Sweden, Karolinska Institutet, 2005), 17-45.

[73]M. Alricsson, K. Harms-Ringdahl, B. Larsson, J. Linder, and S. Werner, "Neck muscle strength and endurance in fighter pilots: effects of a supervised training program," *Aviat Space Environ Med* Vol. 75, No. 1 (2004): 23-28; O. Hamalainen, H. Heinijoki, and H. Vanharanta, "Neck training and +Gz-related neck pain: a preliminary study," Mil Med Vol. 163, No. 10 (1998): 707-708; R. Sovelius, J. Oksa, H. Rintala, H. Huhtala, J. Ylinen, and S. Siitonen, "Trampoline exercise vs. strength training to redcue neck strain in fighter pilots," *Aviat Space Environ Med* Vol. 77, No. 1 (2006): 20-25.

[74]M.M. Panjabi, J. Cholewicki, K. Nibu, J. Grauer, L.B. Babat, and J. Dvorak, "Critical load of the human cervical spine: an in vitro experimental study," *Clin Biomech* Vol. 13, No. 1 (1998): 11-17.

[75]M. Alricsson, K. Harms-Ringdahl, B. Larsson, J. Linder, and S. Werner, "Neck muscle strength and endurance in fighter pilots: effects of a supervised training program," *Aviat Space Environ Med* Vol. 75, No. 1 (2004): 23-28.

[76]M. Alricsson, K. Harms-Ringdahl, B. Larsson, J. Linder, and S. Werner, "Neck muscle strength and endurance in fighter pilots: effects of a supervised training program," *Aviat Space Environ Med* Vol. 75, No. 1 (2004): 23-28.

[77]S. Linton, "A critical review of methods for analysis of behaviour in chronic pain," *Scand J Behav Ther* Vol. 5, No. 2 (1986): 31-48.

[78]T. Forouzanfar, W. Weber, M. Kemler, and M. van Kleef, "What is a meaningful pain reduction in patients with complex regional pain syndrome type 1," *Clin J Pain* Vol. 19, No. 5 (2003): 281-285.

[79]S. Linton, "A critical review of methods for analysis of behaviour in chronic pain," *Scand J Behav Ther* Vol. 5, No. 2 (1986): 31-48.

[80]J.J. Ylinen, A.H. Hakkinen, E.P. Takala, M.J. Nykanen, H.J. Kautiainen, E.A. Malkia, *et al.*, "Effects of neck muscle training in women with chronic neck pain: one-year follow-up study," *J Strength Cond Res* Vol. 20, No. 1 (2006): 6-13.

[81]D. Falla, G. Jull, P. Hodges, and B. Vicenzino, "An endurance-strength training regime is effective in reducing myoelectric manifestations of cervical flexor muscle fatigue in females with chronic neck pain," *Clin Neurophysiol* Vol. 117, No. 4 (2006): 828-837.

[82]M. Alricsson, K. Harms-Ringdahl, B. Larsson, J. Linder, and S. Werner, "Neck muscle strength and endurance in fighter pilots: effects of a supervised training program," *Aviat Space Environ Med* Vol. 75, No. 1 (2004): 23-28.

[83]C. Ahlgren, W. Kerstin, F. Kadi, M. Djupsjobacka, L. Thornell, and G. Sundelin, "Effects on physical performance and pain from three dynamic training programs for women with work-related trapezius myalgia," *J Rehabil Med* Vol. 33, No. 4 (2001): 162-169.

[84]J. Adam, *Results of NVG-induced neck strain questionnaire study in CH-146 Griffon aircrew* (Toronto, ON: DRDC Toronto TR 2004), 1-75; K.A. Forde, W.J. Albert, M.F. Harrison, J.P. Neary, J. Croll, and J.P. Callaghan, "Neck loads and posture exposure of helicopter pilots during simulated day and night flights," *International Journal of Industrial Ergonomics*, In Press, Corrected Proof. doi: DOI: 10.1016/j.ergon.2011.01.001, (2011): 128-135; M.F. Harrison, J.P. Neary, W.J. Albert, U. Kuruganti, J.C. Croll, V.C. Chancey, and B.A. Bumgardner, "Measuring neuromuscular fatigue in cervical spinal musculature of military helicopter aircrew," *Mil Med* 174, no. 11 (2009): 1183-1189; M.F. Harrison, "The investigation of muscular factors in night vision goggle induced neck strain in Canadian forces helicopter aircrew," (Regina, SK: University of Regina; 2009), 1-117; M.F. Harrison, J.P. Neary, W.J. Albert, D.W. Veillette, N.P. McKenzie, and J.C. Croll, "Trapezius muscle metabolism measured with NIRS in helicopter pilots flying a simulator," *Aviat Space Environ Med* 78, no. 2 (2007b): 110-116; M.F. Harrison, J.P. Neary, N.P. McKenzie, D.W. Veillette, and J.C. Croll, "Cytochrome oxidase changes in trapezius muscles with night vision goggle usage," *Int J Ind Ergon* Vol. 40, No. 2 (2009): 140-145.

CHAPTER 8

Blast Exposure Induced Neurodegeneration and Changes in the Expression of Cell Surface Glutamate Receptors in the Rat Brain

Yushan Wang, PhD, and Tracy Weiss, PhD, Defense R&D Canada Suffield, Medicine Hat, Alberta; Mikulas Chavko, PhD, Saleena Adeeb, Richard McCarron, PhD, Naval Medical Research Center, MD, USA; Taesup Cho, Brain Research Centre, University of British Columbia.

ABSTRACT

Traumatic brain injury (TBI) has been a leading cause of morbidity and mortality in recent conflicts in Iraq and Afghanistan due to the increasing use of roadside improvised explosive devices (IEDs). However, the mechanisms of blast induced TBI are currently not known. Here we investigated neuronal damages and changes in cell surface expression of glutamate receptors in the rat brain after blast. Animals were exposed to a 120 kPa blast wave in a pneumatic-pressure driven shock tube and observed for 24 hours, 1 week and 3 weeks after blast. At the end of each observation period, animals were euthanized and their brains harvested. Frontal cortices and hippocampi of both sides of the brain were processed to separate synaptic membranes. The expression of α-amino-3-hydroxy-5-methyl-4-isoxazolepropionic acid (AMPA) receptor subunits on synaptic membranes were analyzed using western blot analysis. Immunohistochemistry was used to investigate neuronal and glial degeneration in both sides of the hippocampi. Results showed that the synaptic expression of AMPA receptor subunits, GluR1 and GluR2, were dramatically reduced 24 hours after blast injury. These changes became less significant 1 week after blast. However, both GluR1 and GluR2 were significantly increased 3 weeks after blast. Immunohistochemistry results showed that within 24 hours of blast, axonal damage was apparent in the dentate gyrus and CA1 regions of both sides of the hippocampi, as stained by the neuronal marker Neurofilament H (NFH). The blast-induced reduction in NFH staining persisted for at least three weeks. In contrast, glial fibrillary acidic protein (GFAP) staining showed a transient decrease 24 hours after blast, but fluorescence intensity increased 1 week and 3 weeks after blast, indicating gliosis. Together, results from these experiments indicate that at 120 kPa, the blast wave produces consistent brain damage in the rat. Changes in the cell surface expression of glutamate receptors may contribute to neurodegeneration induced by blast.

BLAST EXPOSURE INDUCED NEURODEGENERATION AND CHANGES IN THE EXPRESSION OF CELL SURFACE GLUTAMATE RECEPTORS IN THE RAT BRAIN

Increasing use of IEDs and other explosives during conflicts in Afghanistan and Iraq have led to mass casualties.[1] As a result, TBI caused by IEDs has become a major focus of casualty care in combat areas. One of the confounding issues is that soldiers who initially had no immediate trauma from exposure to blasts are now showing signs of cognitive impairments and behavioural changes.[2] For this reason, mild-to-moderate traumatic brain injury (mTBI) has garnered attention as one of the most significant injuries of the recent conflicts in these two countries. Traditionally it was believed that the blast waves only affected air containing organs such as the lungs and the ear. However, recent evidence shows that the brain is one of the most important organs affected by blast waves, although the exact mechanism(s) by which the blast wave damages the brain are still under investigation.[3] Recent reports have suggested several possibilities regarding how the blast wave is transmitted to the brain.[4] These include acceleration of the head, direct passage of the blast wave via the cranium, and propagation of the blast wave to the brain via a thoracic mechanism.[5] Moreover, these possibilities do not mutually exclude each other. In addition to primary brain injury due to acceleration, blast waves can cause victims to fall or be struck by objects, resulting in secondary or tertiary injuries.[6] There is currently no standard treatment for TBI or mTBI due to the complexity and the lack of understanding on the mechanisms of these injuries.[7]

In blast-induced TBI, hippocampus and the frontal cortex are most vulnerable to blast damage.[8] The most common types of damage are diffuse axonal injury, contusion, and subdural haemorrhage and hypoxia.[9] Collectively, these damages lead to biochemical and metabolic changes that eventually result in tissue damage and associated cell death.[10] In addition to neurodegeneration, gliosis in the brain has been shown to exist in various models of TBI.[11] Gliosis happens as a result of inflammatory responses to blast damage and has been considered the hallmark of TBI.[12]

Glutamate and aspartate are the most important excitatory neurotransmitters acting in the central nervous system.[13] Their interactions with specific membrane receptors, which are divided into NMDA, kainate, AMPA and metabotropic receptors, are responsible for many neurological functions such as cognition, learning, memory and sensation.[14] In addition, these receptors, especially NMDA and AMPA receptors, are involved in the developmental plasticity of synaptic connections in the nervous system.[15] However, excessive glutamate release and consequent overstimulation of its receptors can lead to excitotoxicity. The latter has been associated with a wide range of neurological disorders, including trauma and stroke damage, epilepsy, Alzheimer's and Huntington's diseases.[16] Numerous reports showing massive glutamate release and subsequent over-activation of its receptors after various models of TBI have been published in the past 30 years.[17] Most current treatment strategies against TBI are based on the hypothesis that glutamate receptors are over-activated,[18] regardless of the model used to induce TBI. However, NMDA or AMPA receptor antagonists rarely show effectiveness in clinical settings,[19] suggesting that other complicating factors exist during TBI. In the present report, we hypothesize that in addition to excessive glutamate release, cell surface expression of glutamate receptor subunits are also changed during blast induced TBI, therefore changing their efficiencies on the synapse.

METHOD

ANIMAL PREPARATION AND EXPOSURE TO BLAST

In conducting experiments with animals, the authors adhered to the principles set forth in the "Guide for the Care and Use of Laboratory Animals", Institute of Laboratory Animal Resources, National Research Council, National Academy Press, 1996, and was approved by WRAIR/NMRC IACUC Committee. Male Sprague-Dawley rats (250-300g) were anaesthetized with isoflurane (2% in air, 2.5 min in a sealed box) and exposed to blast. To restrict body movement from the blast impact and prevent subsequent secondary blast injuries, animals were secured into a holder placed 30 cm inside the compressed air-driven shock tube with Mylar membranes rupturing at predetermined pressure thresholds.[20] Animals were placed in such a way that the right side facing the blast wave and subjected to blast with a mean peak overpressure of 120 kPa. Control animals underwent the same anaesthetization procedure and placement in the blast tube, but were returned to their respective cages without exposure to a blast wave. After blast exposure, animals were closely observed for 24 hours, 1 week and 3 weeks before being sacrificed and their brains harvested. For experiments involving immunohistochemistry, animals were sacrificed at the end of each observation period and immediately perfused with 4% formaldehyde and placed in formaldehyde solution for fixation before histological preparations. For experiments involving expression of glutamate receptors, animals were sacrificed at the end of each observation period and their brains removed and immediately placed in dry ice and stored at -800C until analysis.

IMMUNOHISTOCHEMISTRY

Both sides of rat hippocampi were stained with antibodies against the axonal marker Neurofilament H (NFH) and the glial marker glial fibrillary acidic protein (GFAP). Briefly, fixed brains were dehydrated in 30% sucrose (dissolved in 0.1 M phosphate buffer) and frozen at -800C. Horizontal sections containing the hippocampus (30 µM thickness) were processed for sequential staining with antibodies against NFH (1: 500, Millipore) and GFAP (1: 500, Millipore). At the end of the staining process, all slices were counter-stained with DAPI (Invitrogen) to view nucleus.

PREPARATION OF SYNAPTONEUROSOMES

Synaptoneurosomes (SN) are purified synaptic membranes that contain both the pre- and post-synaptic termini and enriched in post synaptic density protein 95 (PSD95).[21] The procedure of making SNs is based on Williams *et al.* with slight modifications.[22] Briefly, frozen brains were thawed on ice; hippocampi and frontal cortices were dissected from both sides of the brain. The dissected brain structures were then homogenized in HEPES buffer containing (in mM: HEPES 10, EDTA 1, Dithiothreitol

0.25 and sucrose 350) using a Teflon glass homogenizer (5 strokes for each homogenization). Homogenates were centrifuged at 4^{0C} (1000 × g) for 10 min. The resulting supernatants were then sequentially filtered through a 100 μm, an 8 μm and a 5 μm filter (Millipore). The resulting filtrates were enriched with SNs, which were further characterized with antibodies against PSD-95 and tubulin using western blot analysis.

WESTERN BLOT ANALYSIS

SNs (10 – 15 μg protein) were separated on a 4–20% gradient pre-cast gel[23] and transferred onto polyvinylidene difluoride (PVDF) membranes. The membranes were blocked with 5% skim milk, 0.1% Tween 20 in phosphate buffered saline and then probed with antibodies against GluR1 and GluR2 receptors (1:1000; Invitrogen) (overnight at 4^{0C}. After washing, the membranes were incubated with a secondary antibody; donkey anti-rabbit or mouse IgG-HRP[24] diluted 1:5000. Detection was carried out by using ECL advanced detection reagents[25] and imaged using a Molecular Imager VersaDoc MP 4000 system.[26] To confirm equal protein loading, blots were re-probed with anti-pan-actin antibody.[27]

DATA ANALYSIS

Western blot bands corresponding to each receptor subunit or pan-actin were identified and quantified for optical density using the Quantity One software.[28] The ratio between optical densities of each receptor subunit and pan-actin was then calculated and normalized against control (the ratio for control arbitrary set at 100%). One-way analysis of variance and post hoc Tukey's multiple comparison tests were used to examine the statistical differences between groups.

RESULTS

BLAST-INDUCED NEURODEGENERATION AND GLIOSIS IN THE RAT HIPPOCAMPUS

Horizontal sections of the brain containing both sides of the hippocampi were stained with the neuronal marker NFH and the glial marker GFAP after various periods of post exposure. Although the rat is blasted from the right side, brain damages were apparent on both sides of the brain. For the ease of illustration, only one side of the staining was shown in Figures 8.1 and 8.2. Figure 8.1 showed changes in the staining patterns of NFH and GFAP in the dentate gyrus region of the hippocampus. Figure 8.2 showed the same staining in the CA1 region of hippocampus with a higher magnification. NFH staining was dramatically decreased as early as 24 hours after blast exposure, and the decrease in NFH staining persisted for at least 3 weeks after blast, indicating neurodegeneration. In contrast, GFAP staining showed an initial decrease 24 hours after blast exposure but was dramatically increased 1 week and 3 weeks after exposure.

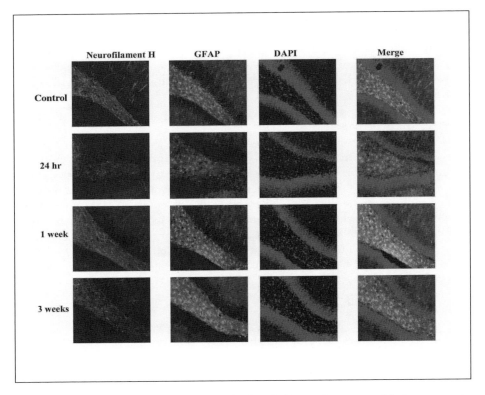

Figure 8.1: Blast-induced damage in neurons and glial cells in the Dentate Gyrus region of the hippocampus in the rat (Magnification: 100 X).

Both NFH and GFAP staining were dramatically reduced 24 h blast. However, starting from 1 week after blast, NFH staining remained reduced while GFAP staining was increased, indicating gliosis.

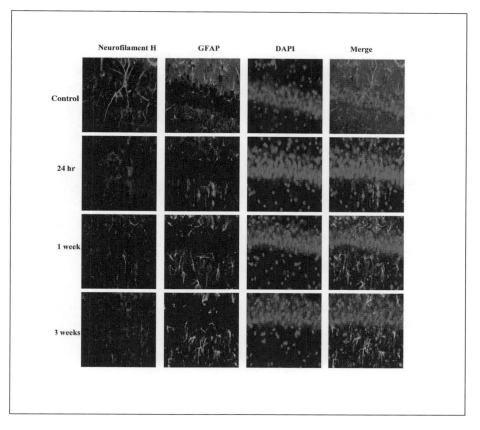

Figure 8.2: Blast-induced damage in neurons and glial cells in the CA1 region of the hippocampus
in the rat (Magnification 200 X).

Both NFH and GFAP staining were dramatically reduced 24 hours after blast. However, starting from 1 week after blast, NFH staining remained reduced while GFAP staining was increased, indicating gliosis.

BLAST-INDUCED CHANGES IN THE CELL SURFACE EXPRESSION OF GLUTAMATE RECEPTORS

In order to study the changes in the synaptic expression of glutamate receptors, we performed multi-step filtrations of rat hippocampus and frontal cortex to isolate synaptoneurosomes. As shown in Figure 8.3, the specific synaptic marker PSD-95 was significant enriched, while the intracellular protein tubulin was greatly decreased in synaptoneurosomes. These observations were evidence in both the frontal cortex and the hippocampus.

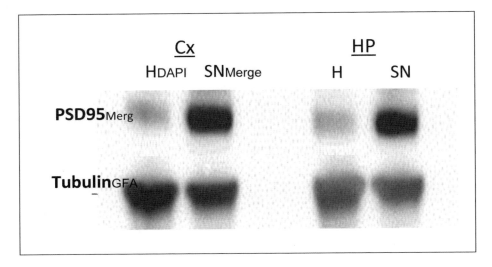

Figure 8.3: Characterization of rat synaptoneurosomes.

Rat brain frontal cortices (Cx) and hippocampi (HP) were quickly excised from deep frozen and thawed brain, homogenized and processed by multi-filtration steps to prepare synaptoneurosomes (SN). Western blots show the comparison of homogenates (H) and SN in the expression of PSD-95, a post-synaptic protein and tubulin, a cytosolic protein. PSD-95 is enriched while tubulin is reduced in SN.

Figure 8.4 showed the changes in the expression the AMPA receptor subunit GluR1 in synaptoneurosomes after different period of blast. In both hippocampus and frontal cortex, the synaptic expression of GluR1 was significantly reduced ($p < 0.01$ compared with control). However, at 3 weeks after blast, the number of GluR1 receptors was dramatically increased ($p < 0.05$ compared to control).

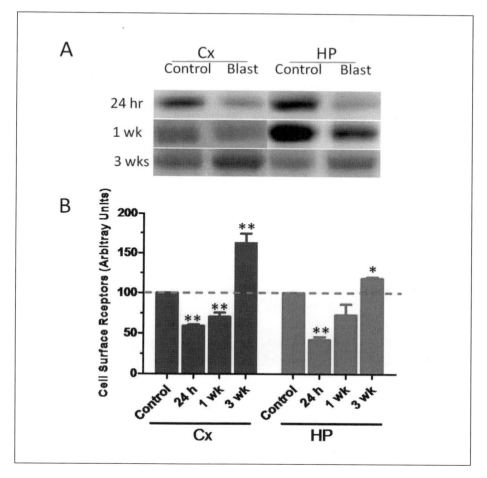

Figure 8.4: Changes in the cell surface expression of GluR1 in frontal cortex (Cx) and hippocampus (HP) after blast injury.

1 = control, 2 = blast. A: Representative western blot bands after different periods of blast exposure. B: Summarized data comparing the synaptic expression of GluR1 after different periods of blast exposure. * $p < 0.05$; ** $p < 0.01$ compared with control. Data were Mean ± SEM from 4 experiments.

Figure 8.5 showed the changes in the expression the AMPA receptor subunit GluR2 in synaptoneurosomes after different periods post blast. Similar to the expression of GluR1, the synaptic expression of GluR2 was significantly reduced in both the frontal cortex and hippocampus. At 3 weeks after blast, the synaptic expression of GluR2 was dramatically increased.

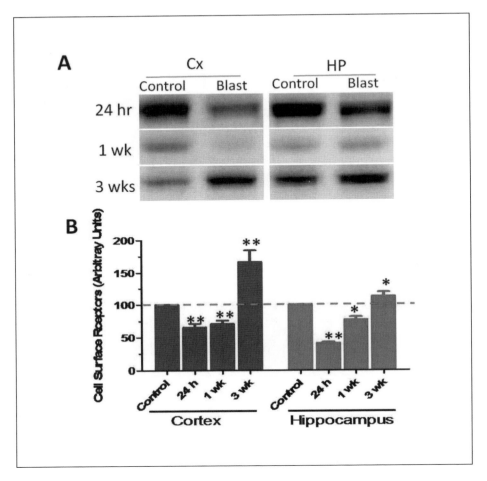

Figure 8.5: Changes in the cell surface expression of GluR2 in frontal cortex (Cx) and hippocampus (HP) after blast injury.

1 = control, 2 = blast. A: Representative western blot bands after different periods of blast exposure. B: Summarized data comparing the synaptic expression of GluR2 after different periods of blast exposure. * $p < 0.05$; ** $p < 0.01$ compared with control. Data were Mean ± SEM from 4 experiments.

DISCUSSION

The present report demonstrates that neurodegeneration was apparent as early as 24 hours after blast exposure, as shown by the reduction in the fluorescent intensity in NFH staining. In addition, the staining for GFAP was initially decreased but was enhanced starting 1 week after blast in the dentate gyrus region of the hippocampus, indicating gliosis. These findings are consistent with previous reports that neurodegeneration is a common pathology in various models of traumatic brain injury.[29] Moreover, the hypothesis that synaptic expression of glutamate receptor subunits would be altered by blast exposure was supported by our experimental data. The synaptic expression of both GluR1 and GluR2 were dramatically decreased 24 hours and 1 week after blast but were significantly enhanced 3 weeks after blast in the frontal cortex and hippocampus. To the best of our knowledge, this is the first report to show changes in AMPA receptor trafficking after blast-induced TBI in animal models.

Neurofilaments are the most abundant cytoskeletal components of large myelinated axons in both central and peripheral nervous systems. They are heteropolymers consisting of at least four subunits, a heavy (NFH), medium (NFM), light (NFL) chain and alpha-internexin.[30] Their functions include increasing the conductivity of axons, contributing to the dynamic properties of axonal cytoskeleton during neuronal differentiation, axon outgrowth, regeneration and guidance.[31] Disruption of the neurofilament structures has been implicated in a variety of neurodegenerative diseases such as amyotrophic lateral sclerosis (ALS) and Alzheimer's diseases. Changes in the levels of neurofilaments in the brain have been considered a sign of neurodegeneration. The present report showed that the fluorescence intensity of NFH staining was dramatically reduced at all time points after blast exposure, indicating that neurodegeneration is evident as early as 24 hours after blast injury, and the loss of NFH on the axons may contribute to neuronal cognitive symptoms in patients suffering from TBI. Furthermore, GFAP, a specific glial marker in the brain, showed a transient reduction in the hippocampus but later increased, indicating gliosis in this region. Long term gliosis is another indicator for neurodegeneration.[32]

During basal excitatory synaptic transmission, glutamate binds to the extracellular domains of AMPA receptors and gates channel opening. Opened AMPA receptor channels permit the entrance of sodium into the intracellular space, resulting in the depolarization of the synaptic membrane. The depolarized synaptic membrane will then remove the magnesium block of NMDA receptor channels, allowing NMDA receptors to be activated.[33] NMDA receptor activation is crucial for brain cognitive functions and cell survival. Therefore, changes in the synaptic expression of AMPA receptors will lead to malfunctions and possibly cell death in the brain. There are four subunits of AMPA receptors, GluR1-R4. They usually form tetramers to form a complete functional receptor. AMPA receptor trafficking is controlled by the c-terminus of the GluR2 subunit. Because GluR1 often forms poly dimmers with GluR2, it generally follows the trafficking patterns of GluR2.[34] Our results in the current report also showed similar trafficking patterns between GluR1 and GluR2 on the synaptic membrane after TBI, further proving that these two receptor subunits move into and out of the synaptic membrane together.

Both decreases and increases in the synaptic expression of AMPA receptors have been implicated in the development of brain malfunctions. In a previous report, we have shown that endocytosis of AMPA receptors causes cell death in cultured rat hippocampal neurons; and blockade of this process by a mimetic peptide corresponding to the GluR2 c-terminus prevent NMDA-induced apoptosis.[35] More recently, it has been shown that GluR2 endocytosis mediated events may involve the activation of caspase-3 in the brain.[36] Based on our current findings that synaptic AMPA receptors were significantly reduced within 1 week after blast injury, it is plausible to speculate that reduction of synaptic AMPA receptors may contribute to neurodegeneration after blast injury in the rat. On the other hand, previous reports have shown that in addition to mediating fast excitatory synaptic neurotransmission, some AMPA receptors are calcium permeable, and excess number of AMPA receptors are capable of inducing cell death through excessive calcium entry and subsequent calcium overload.[37] Therefore, the fact that both GluR1 and GluR2 expression on the synapse were up-regulated 3 weeks after blast exposure suggest that the increase in AMPA receptors may contribute to long term neurodegeneration after blast-induced TBI.

In conclusion, our present report shows that blast exposure causes significant neurodegeneration and gliosis in the hippocampus within 3 weeks after exposure. Moreover, the synaptic expression of AMPA receptors was dramatically changed after blast. The exact mechanism(s) by which blast induced AMPA receptor changes needs further investigation. However, regardless of the exact mechanism(s), intervention in the AMPA receptor trafficking pathway may provide a novel therapeutic target to treat blast-induced TBI in both military and civilian populations.

[1]Y. Bhattacharjee, "Shell shock revisited: solving the puzzle of blast trauma," *Science* 319, 5862 (2008): 406-408; E. Park, J.D. Bell and A.J. Baker, "Traumatic brain injury: can the consequences be stopped?" *Canadian Medical Association Journal* Vol. 178, No. 5 (2008): 1163-1170.

2C.W. Hoge, D. McGurk, J.L. Thomas, A.L. Cox, C.C. Engel and C.A. Castro, "Mild traumatic brain injury in U.S. Soldiers returning from Iraq," *N Engl J Med* Vol. 358, S. 8 (2008): 453-463.

3A.I. Faden, "Neuroprotection and traumatic brain injury: the search continues," *Arch Neurol* Vol. 58, No. 10 (2001): 1553-1555; M. Chavko, W.A. Koller, W.K. Prusaczyk and R.M. McCarron, "Measurement of blast wave by a miniature fiber optic pressure transducer in the rat brain," *J Neurosci Methods* Vol. 159, No. 2 (2007): 277-281; G. Ling, F. Bandak, R. Armonda, G. Grant and J. Ecklund, "Explosive blast neurotrauma," *J Neurotrauma* 26, 6 (2009): 815-825; D.J. Loane, A. Pocivavsek, C.E. Moussa, R. Thompson, Y. Matsuoka, A.I. Faden, G.W. Rebeck and M.P. Burns, "Amyloid precursor protein secretases as therapeutic targets for traumatic brain injury," *Nat Med* Vol. 15, No. 4 (2009): 377-379; M. Chavko, T. Watanabe, S. Adeeb, J.

Lankasky, S.T. Ahlers and R.M. McCarron, "Relationship between Orientation to a Blast and Pressure Wave Propagation inside the Rat Brain," *J Neurosci Methods* Vol. 5, No. 1 (2010): 61-66; C.J. Gibson, R.C. Meyer and R.J. Hamm, "Traumatic brain injury and the effects of diazepam, diltiazem, and MK-801 on GABA-A receptor subunit expression in rat hippocampus," *J Biomed Sci* Vol. 17, No. 1 (2010): 38; K. Nagamoto-Combs, R.J. Morecraft, W.G. Darling and C.K. Combs, "Long-term gliosis and molecular changes in the cervical spinal cord of the rhesus monkey after traumatic brain injury," *J Neurotrauma* Vol. 27, No. 3 (2010): 565-585.

4A.C. Courtney and M.W. Courtney, "A thoracic mechanism of mild traumatic brain injury due to blast pressure waves," *Med Hypotheses* Vol. 72, No. 1 (2009): 76-83; Chavko *et al.*, "Relationship between Orientation," 61-66.

5Courtney and Courtney, "A thoracic mechanism," 76-83.

6M.F. Finkel, "The neurological consequences of explosives," *J Neurol Sci* 249, 1 (2006): 63-67.

7I. Cernak and L.J. Noble-Haeusslein, "Traumatic brain injury: an overview of pathobiology with emphasis on military populations," *J Cereb Blood Flow Metab* Vol. 30, No. 2 (2010): 255-266.

8K.H. Taber, D.L. Warden and R.A. Hurley, "Blast-related traumatic brain injury: what is known?" *J Neuropsychiatry Clin Neurosci* 18, 2 (2006): 141-145; B.A. Stoica and A.I. Faden, "Cell death mechanisms and modulation in traumatic brain injury," *Neurotherapeutics* Vol. 7, No. 1 (2010): 3-12.

9A. Saljo, F. Bao, K.G. Haglid and H.A. Hansson, "Blast exposure causes redistribution of phosphorylated neurofilament subunits in neurons of the adult rat brain," *J Neurotrauma* Vol. 17, No. 8 (2000): 719-726; Taber *et al.*, "Blast-related traumatic," 141-145.

10D.J. Loane and A.I. Faden, "Neuroprotection for traumatic brain injury: translational challenges and emerging therapeutic strategies," *Trends Pharmacol Sci* Vol. 31, No. 12 (2010): 596-604.

11K. Nagamoto-Combs, R.J. Morecraft, W.G. Darling and C.K. Combs, "Long-term gliosis and molecular changes in the cervical spinal cord of the rhesus monkey after traumatic brain injury," *J Neurotrauma* Vol. 27, No. 3 (2010): 565-585.

12D. Cederberg and P. Siesjo "What has inflammation to do with traumatic brain injury?" *Childs Nerv Syst* 26, 2 (2010): 221-226; I. Cernak and L.J. Noble-Haeusslein, "Traumatic brain injury: an overview of pathobiology with emphasis on military populations," *J Cereb Blood Flow Metab* Vol. 30, No. 2 (2010): 255-266; K. Nagamoto-Combs, R.J. Morecraft, W.G. Darling and C.K. Combs, "Long-term gliosis and molecular changes in the cervical spinal cord of the rhesus monkey after traumatic brain injury," *J Neurotrauma* Vol. 27, No. 3 (2010): 565-585.

[13]D.T. Monaghan, R.J. Bridges and C.W. Cotman, "The excitatory amino acid receptors: their classes, pharmacology, and distinct properties in the function of the central nervous system," *Annu Rev Pharmacol Toxicol* Vol. 29, No. 1 (1989): 365-402.

[14]G.P. Gasic and M. Hollmann, "Molecular neurobiology of glutamate receptors," *Annu Rev Physiol* Vol. 54, No. 1 (1992): 507-536.

[15]S.A. Lipton and S.B. Kater, "Neurotransmitter regulation of neuronal outgrowth, plasticity and survival," *Trends Neurosci* Vol. 12, No. 7 (1989): 265-270.

[16]S.A. Lipton and P.A. Rosenberg, "Excitatory amino acids as a final common pathway for neurologic disorders," *N Engl J Med* Vol. 330, No. 9 (1994): 613-622; E. Besancon, S. Guo, J. Lok, M. Tymianski, and E.H. Lo, "Beyond NMDA and AMPA glutamate receptors: emerging mechanisms for ionic imbalance and cell death in stroke," *Trends Pharmacol Sci* Vol. 29, No. 5 (2008): 268-275.

[17]A.I. Faden, P. Demediuk, S.S. Panter and R. Vink, "The role of excitatory amino acids and NMDA receptors in traumatic brain injury," *Science* Vol. 244, (1989): 798-800; E. Park, J.D. Bell and A.J. Baker, "Traumatic brain injury: can the consequences be stopped?" *Canadian Medical Association Journal* Vol. 178, No. 5 (2008): 1163-1170; R. Chamoun, D. Suki, S.P. Gopinath, J.C. Goodman J.C., and Robertson C., "Role of extracellular glutamate measured by cerebral microdialysis in severe traumatic brain injury," *J Neurosurg* Vol. 113, No. 3 (2010): 564-570.

[18]E. Park, J.D. Bell and A.J. Baker, "Traumatic brain injury: can the consequences be stopped?" *Canadian Medical Association Journal* Vol. 178, No. 5 (2008): 1163-1170.

[19]N. Marklund, A. Bakshi, D.J. Castelbuono, V. Conte and T.K. McIntosh, "Evaluation of pharmacological treatment strategies in traumatic brain injury," *Curr Pharm Des* Vol. 12, No. 13 (2006): 1645-1680.

[20]N.M. Elsayed, "Toxicology of blast overpressure," *Toxicology* Vol. 121, No. 1 (1997): 1-15; Chavko *et al.*, "Relationship between Orientation," 61-66.

[21]E.B. Hollingsworth, E.T. McNeal, J.L. Burton, R.J. Williams, J.W. Daly and C.R. Creveling, "Biochemical characterization of a filtered synaptoneurosome preparation from guinea pig cerebral cortex: cyclic adenosine 3':5'-monophosphate-generating systems, receptors, and enzymes," *J Neurosci* Vol. 5, No. 8 (1985): 2240-2253.

[22]C. Williams, R. Mehrian Shai, Y. Wu, Y.H. Hsu, T. Sitzer, B. Spann, C. McCleary, Y. Mo and C.A. Miller, "Transcriptome analysis of synaptoneurosomes identifies neuroplasticity genes overexpressed in incipient Alzheimer's disease," *PLoS One* Vol. 4, No. 3 (2009): e4936.

[23]Bio Rad, Missisauga ON

[24]GE Health Care Biosciences, Quebec, Canada

[25]GE Health Care Biosciences, Quebec, Canada

[26]Bio Rad, Missisauga ON

[27]1:1000; Cell Signaling, Massachusetts, USA

[28]Bio Rad, Missisuga ON

[29]A.I. Faden, "Neuroprotection and traumatic brain injury: the search continues," *Arch Neurol* Vol. 58, No. 10 (2001): 1553-1555; I. Cernak and L.J. Noble-Haeusslein, "Traumatic brain injury: an overview of pathobiology with emphasis on military populations," *J Cereb Blood Flow Metab* Vol. 30, No. 2 (2010): 255-266.

[30]R. Perrot, R. Berges, A. Bocquet and J. Eyer, "Review of the multiple aspects of neurofilament functions, and their possible contribution to neurodegeneration," *Mol Neurobiol* Vol. 38, No. 1 (2008): 27-65.

[31]R. Perrot, R. Berges, A. Bocquet and J. Eyer, "Review of the multiple aspects of neurofilament functions, and their possible contribution to neurodegeneration," *Mol Neurobiol* Vol. 38, No. 1 (2008): 27-65.

[32]K. Nagamoto-Combs, R.J. Morecraft, W.G. Darling and C.K. Combs, "Long-term gliosis and molecular changes in the cervical spinal cord of the rhesus monkey after traumatic brain injury," *J Neurotrauma* Vol. 27, No. 3 (2010): 565-585.

[33]T. Nakagawa, "The biochemistry, ultrastructure, and subunit assembly mechanism of AMPA receptors," *Mol Neurobiol* Vol. 42, No. 3 (2010): 161-184.

[34]P.V. Migues, O. Hardt, D.C. Wu, K. Gamache, T.C. Sacktor, Y.T. Wang and K. Nader, "PKMzeta maintains memories by regulating GluR2-dependent AMPA receptor trafficking," *Nat Neurosci* Vol. 13, No. 5 (2010): 630-634.

[35]Y. Wang, W. Ju, L. Liu, S. Fam, S. D'Souza, C. Taghibiglou, M. Salter and Y.T. Wang, "alpha-Amino-3-hydroxy-5-methylisoxazole-4-propionic acid subtype glutamate receptor (AMPAR) endocytosis is essential for N-methyl-D-aspartate-induced neuronal apoptosis," *J Biol Chem* Vol. 279, No. 40 (2004): 41267-41270.

[36]Z. Li, J. Jo, J.M. Jia, S.C. Lo, D.J. Whitcomb, S. Jiao, K. Cho and M. Sheng, "Caspase-3 activation via mitochondria is required for long-term depression and AMPA receptor internalization," *Cell* Vol. 141, No. 5 (2010): 859-871.

[37]J.R. Brorson, P.A. Manzolillo, R.J. Miller, "Ca2+ entry via AMPA/KA receptors and excitotoxicity in cultured cerebellar Purkinje cells," *J Neurosci* Vol. 14, No. 1 (1994): 187-197.

CHAPTER 9

Phenylalanine arginine β-naphthylamide (PAβN) Inhibits the AdeIJK Multidrug Efflux Pump of *Acinetobacter baumannii*

Ayushi Kumar, PhD, Jenny Cortez-Cordova, and Kari Kumar, Antimicrobial Resistance Research Group (ARRG), Applied Bioscience Program, Faculty of Health Sciences, University of Ontario Institute of Technology[1]

Abstract

Acinetobacter baumannii is an important nosocomial pathogen responsible for serious multidrug resistant combat wound infections in soldiers serving in Iraq and Afghanistan. Multidrug efflux pumps belonging to the Resistance-Nodulation-Division (RND) family are an important contributor to the multidrug resistance of this organism. In this study we analyzed the activity of the efflux pump inhibitor (EPI) phenylalanine arginine β-naphthylamide (PAβN) against the AdeIJK RND efflux pump of *A. baumannii*. The *adeIJK* operon was cloned in single copy into a surrogate *Pseudomonas aeruginosa* strain devoid of its six native efflux pumps. The sensitivity of the surrogate strain expressing the *adeIJK* operon to PAβN was analyzed and compared with that of clinical isolates of *A. baumannii* for chloramphenicol, tetracycline, ciprofloxacin, trimethoprim, and sodium dodecyl sulfate (SDS). PAβN was found to inhibit the ability of the AdeIJK pump to efflux trimethoprim and SDS in the surrogate *P. aeruginosa* strain, but not in the clinical isolates of *A. baumannii*. Our results show that PAβN is capable of inhibiting the AdeIJK pump and also underscore the importance of the use of a strain devoid of efflux pumps for the screening of EPI's.

Phenylalanine arginine β-naphthylamide (PAβN) Inhibits the AdeIJK Multidrug Efflux Pump of Acinetobacter baumannii

Acinetobacter baumannii is recognized as the most significant bacterial species responsible for nosocomial war-wound infections, causing deep wound infections, respiratory infections, and bacteremia.[2] A Gram-negative non-fermentative bacillus, *A. baumannii* is one of the most common bacterial species isolated from the wounds of soldiers injured in war zones in Afghanistan and Iraq.[3] Since most of the infections caused by this organism are multidrug resistant, therapy options are often limited. Antibiotic resistance of *A. baumannii* can be attributed to its impressive ability to acquire resistance genes and it has been shown to exhibit a wide array of resistance mechanisms including -lactamase production,[4] the presence of aminoglycoside-modifying enzymes,[5] target-site mutations,[6] and multidrug efflux systems.[7]

Multidrug efflux pumps belonging to the RND family have been shown to play an important role in the intrinsic antibiotic resistance of various Gram-negative bacterial species.[8] These pumps form a tripartite complex with proteins belonging to the outer membrane (OMP) and membrane fusion (MFP) family to ensure the extrusion of antibiotics directly into the external media, against the concentration gradient, across the Gram-negative cell envelope.[9] Three different RND pumps have been characterized in *A. baumannii*, namely, AdeABC,[10] AdeIJK,[11] and most recently, AdeFGH.[12] The AdeABC system effluxes amikacin, chloramphenicol, cefotaxime, erythromycin, gentamicin, kanamycin, norfloxacin, netilmicin, ofloxacin, perfloxacin, sparfloxacin, tetracycline, tobramycin, and trimethoprim,[13] while the AdeIJK pump has been shown to efflux -lactams, chloramphenicol, tetracycline, erythromycin, lincosamides, fluoroquinolones, fusidic acid, novobiocin, rifampin, trimethoprim, acridine, pyronine, safranin, and SDS.[14] The AdeFGH pumps effluxes chloramphenicol, trimethoprim, ciprofloxacin, and clindamicin.[15]

As observed with the AdeABC, AdeIJK, and AdeFGH pumps of *A. baumannii*, RND pumps exhibit very broad substrate specificity, effectively effluxing various structurally-unrelated compounds.[16] Collectively, these three pumps are capable of effluxing almost all antibiotics currently in clinical use, including some of the antibiotics such as tigecycline that has only recently approved for clinical use.[17] Moreover, there is mounting evidence that the activity of these pumps is a major hindrance in the search for new antibacterial compounds with studies showing that a large number of lead compounds with antibacterial activity are likely to be missed in primary screening because of the activity of RND pumps.[18] It is therefore becoming increasingly clear that for therapeutic efforts to be effective against *A. baumannii*, new antimicrobial agents that are poor substrates of these pumps and/or approaches to inhibit the activity of the RND pumps are required. Inhibition of RND pumps of *A. baumannii* is indeed a promising approach since it can potentially allow increased efficacy of antibiotics that are currently rendered ineffective because of they are substrates of RND pumps. However, a major challenge associated with this approach is that clinical isolates of *A. baumannii*, like other Gram-negative pathogens, are known to express more than one efflux pump. Due to the overlapping substrate profiles of the pumps, it is difficult to search for a specific inhibitor of any one pump. In this study, we utilize novel genetic tools to overcome these challenges and show the inhibition of the AdeIJK pump by the EPI PAβN. The data presented in this work shows that our approach of using a clean genetic background for the screening of EPIs can prove to be very effective in searching for novel therapeutic options for treatment of *A. baumannii* infections.

METHOD

BACTERIAL STRAINS, GROWTH MEDIA, AND PLASMIDS

All bacterial strains and plasmids used in this study are listed in Table 9.1. Clinical isolates of A. baumannii were provided by George Zhanel, University of Manitoba.[19] Bacterial cells were grown routinely in LB-broth (Bioshop, Burlington, ON, Canada) at 37°C with shaking. The following antibiotics were used in order to maintain respective plasmids in *E. coli* or *P. aeruginosa* hosts: ampicillin (Amp) (Bioshop, Burlington, ON, Canada) (100 mg/L), gentamicin (Gen) (Bioshop, Burlington, ON,

Canada) (30 mg/L), and carbenicillin (Car) (Duchefa Biochemie, Haarlem, Netherlands) (200 mg/L). LB supplemented with 5% sucrose (w/v) was used for curing plasmids containing the sacB counterselection marker. Mueller-Hinton broth (BD-Canada, Mississauga, ON, Canada) was used to perform the antibiotic susceptibility assays.

PRESENCE AND EXPRESSION OF THE adeJ GENE IN CLINICAL ISOLATES OF *A. BAUMANNII*

The presence and expression of the *adeJ* gene in the clinical isolates of *A. baumannii* was determined by PCR using the genomic DNA and cDNA, respectively, as templates. DNA was extracted from *A. baumannii* strains using the DNeasy kit from Qiagen (Qiagen, Mississauga, ON, Canada) following the manufacturer's instructions.

The RNeasy kit (Qiagen, Mississauga, ON, Canada) was used for the purification of total RNA. Briefly, one ml of late log phase (A600nm≈0.8) culture was harvested and the pellet frozen at -80°C for 15 min to facilitate cell lysis. Synthesis of the cDNA was performed using the Quantitect Reverse transcription kit (Qiagen, Mississauga, ON, Canada) following the manufacturer's instructions. Minus-RT control reactions were included to rule out genomic DNA contamination of RNA samples, and were prepared by excluding the reverse transcriptase enzyme in the reaction mix.

PCR was performed to amplify a 99 bp sequence within the *adeJ* gene using Taq DNA polymerase from New England Biolabs (Pickering, ON, Canada). DNA amplification was carried out for 30 cycles using the following steps: denaturation: 95°C for 30 sec; annealing: 60°C for 30 sec; and extension: 72°C for 30 sec. A no-template control and the minus-RT control were used in all RT-PCR reactions. Primers were designed using the OligoPerfect primer designing tool from Invitrogen[20] to anneal to the RND component-encoding gene of each operon. The 23S rRNA gene was used as the housekeeping control. Oligonucleotides used for PCR reactions are listed in Table 9.2.

CLONING OF THE adeIJK OPERON

The cloning strategy for the *adeIJK* operon is shown in Fig. 9.1. Briefly, primers were designed to amplify 4051 and 1983 bp regions of the *adeIJK* operon. PCR amplification was carried out using the Taq DNA polymerase (New England Biolabs, Pickering, ON, Canada) using the following conditions: for the 4051 bp fragment, denaturation at 94°C (30 sec), annealing at 59°C (30 sec), and extension at 72°C (4 min); and for the 1983 bp fragment, denaturation at 94°C (30 sec), annealing at 55°C (30 sec), and extension at 72°C (1.5 min). Both fragments, 4051 bp and 1983 bp, were cloned in the PCR cloning vector pGEMT-easy separately to construct plasmids pPLS001 and pPLS002, respectively. Assembly of the entire operon was carried out by purifying a 4061 bp fragment, using a gel purification kit (Biobasic, Markham, ON, Canada), from pPLS001 (containing the *adeI* and the partial *adeJ* gene) using AatII and KpnI, and ligating it in pPSL002 digested with the same enzymes, yielding the plasmid pPLS007. Sequencing of the *adeIJK* operon was carried out at the Genome Quebec sequencing facility at McGill University, Montreal, QC, Canada. Table 9.2 contains the list of primers used to clone the *adeIJK* operon.

Subcloning of the *adeIJK* operon was accomplished by digesting pPLS007 with *SpeI* and *XhoI* (New England Biolabs, Pickering, ON, Canada) to obtain the complete operon, which was then cloned into the pUC18T-mini-Tn7T-Gm-LAC plasmid digested with the same enzymes to yield the recombinant plasmid pPLS009. The resulting plasmid pPLS009 therefore contains the *adeIJK* operon, expression of which is driven from the tac promoter, controlled by the *lacI*q-encoded Lac repressor. Expression of the operon is thus inducible by the addition of 1mM IPTG (isopropyl-β-D-thiogalactopyranoside) (Biobasic, Markham, ON) to the growth medium.

INSERTION OF THE adeIJK OPERON IN SINGLE COPY IN THE SURROGATE *P. aeruginosa* STRAIN

Insertion of the *adeIJK* operon in the surrogate *P. aeruginosa* strain PAO750 in single copy was carried out by a method previously described[21] and is shown in Figure 9.2. Briefly, electrocompetent *P. aeruginosa* cells were prepared[22] and electroporated with 50 ng each of pPLS009 and the helper plasmid pTNS2. [23] Transformants were selected on LB agar supplemented with gentamicin (30mg/L). The Genr-marker was subsequently removed using the Flp-recombinase to obtain *P. aeruginosa* PA006.

PCR was used to confirm the insertion of the mini-Tn7 element in *P. aeruginosa* PA006 using primers PaglmS_Dn and Tn7R, described previously, [24] that bind to the *glmS* gene in the *P. aeruginosa* genome and the mini-Tn7 element, respectively. The positive insertion resulted in an amplicon of 272 bp.[25]

ANTIBIOTIC SUSCEPTIBILITY ASSAYS AND ACTIVITY OF PAβN AGAINST THE AdeIJK PUMP

Antibiotic susceptibility assays were performed for chloramphenicol, tetracycline, ciprofloxacin, trimethoprim, and SDS (substrates of AdeIJK pump) using the two-fold microdilution method from the Clinical Laboratory Standard Institutes.[26] Induction of the *adeIJK* operon in *P. aeruginosa* PA006 was achieved by supplementing the MH broth with 1mM IPTG. PAβN was added to a final concentration of 10 g/mL in order to assess its activity against the AdeIJK pump.

RESULTS

PRESENCE AND EXPRESSION OF THE adeJ gene IN CLINICAL ISOLATES OF *A. baumannii*

PCR was used to determine the presence and expression of *adeJ*, the RND component-encoding gene of the *adeIJK* operon, in *A. baumannii* isolates. We found that all clinical isolates showed the presence of the *adeJ* gene (Figure 9.3.B.i). Endpoint RT-PCR, used to determine the expression of the adeJ gene in these isolates, revealed the expression of the gene in four out of 11 clinical isolates (Figure 9.3.B.ii), namely *A. baumannii* AB008, *A. baumannii* AB009, *A. baumannii* AB012, and *A. baumannii* AB014. *A. baumannii* ATCC19606 was also found to express the gene.

Antibiotic susceptibility assays

Results from the antibiotic susceptibility assays are presented in Table 9.3. Induction of expression of the *adeIJK* pump in *P. aeruginosa* PA006 resulted in a 2-fold increase in resistance to ciprofloxacin and SDS, a 4-fold increase in that of tetracycline and trimethoprim, and an 8-fold increase in resistance to chloramphenicol. Addition of PAβN resulted in the potentiation of chloramphenicol, tetracycline, ciprofloxacin, trimethoprim, and SDS by 2-, 1-, 2-, 4-, and 4-fold, respectively. Of the two clinical isolates of *A. baumannii* tested for the activity of PAβN, *A. baumannii* AB005 (the strain that was found not to express the *adeJ* gene) showed 8-fold potentiation to SDS, while no significant potentiation was observed for any other antibiotics tested for this strain. *A. baumannii* AB006 (the strain found to express the *adeJ* gene), showed no significant potentiation of the activity of any of the antibiotics tested, upon addition of PAβN.

DISCUSSION

In the last few decades, *A. baumannii* has shown a remarkable capacity to acquire and accumulate various resistance genes. As a result, extremely high antibiotic resistance of this organism makes treatment of infections very difficult. With *A. baumannii* isolates exhibiting resistance to every drug currently in clinical use, there is an urgent need for newer therapeutic options. Characterization of three efflux pumps belonging to the RND family in this organism namely, AdeABC,[27] AdeIJK,[28] and AdeFGH,[29] suggests an important role of efflux pumps in the antibiotic resistance of *A. baumannii*. It is accepted that an effective therapeutic approach against Gram-negative pathogens like *A. baumannii* must take into account the activity of RND efflux pumps. In order to achieve this, approaches may involve designing of antibiotics that bypass RND efflux pumps or finding inhibitors of RND pumps that can be used in combination with existing drugs and thus improve their efficacy. One of the challenges associated with finding specific inhibitors of RND pumps is that clinical isolates of *A. baumannii* that overexpress RND pumps are likely to contain resistant mutations thus masking the effect of the inhibitor. In addition, these isolates may also be expressing pumps belonging to other families with overlapping substrate profiles with the RND pump of interest, once again making interpretation of the activity of the inhibitor difficult. However, as we have shown in this study, use of suitable genetic tools can help circumvent this problem. In this study we use a clean background with no interference from other RND pumps to show the inhibition of the AdeIJK pump with PAβN, a compound that has been shown to inhibit RND pumps in other Gram-negative bacterial species.[30]

We used PCR to analyze the prevalence of AdeIJK pump in the clinical isolates of *A. baumannii* from Canadian hospitals and found that it was present in all of the isolates tested. RT-PCR analysis showed that more than one-third of the clinical isolates expressed the *adeJ* gene (Figure 9.3), thus making the AdeIJK pump an ideal candidate for inhibition.

In order to test the activity of PAβN against the AdeIJK pump, we cloned and expressed the *adeIJK* operon in the surrogate *P. aeruginosa* PA006 strain and that resulted in increased resistance to chloramphenicol, tetracycline, ciprofloxacin, trimethoprim, and SDS. All of these compounds are substrates of the AdeIJK pump, and decreased susceptibility of the *P. aeruginosa* PA006 to these antimicrobials upon the expression of this pump indicates that it is active in the surrogate strain. Addition of the EPI, PAβN, resulted in the MIC values decreasing to the values of that seen for uninduced expression of the AdeIJK pump for ciprofloxacin, trimethoprim, and SDS, indicating that the EPI inhibits the ability of the pump to efflux these three compounds. No significant decrease in the MIC values was observed for chloramphenicol and tetracycline. We also tested the activity of PAβN against the clinical isolates of *A. baumannii*. We found that *A. baumannii* AB006, the strain that expressed the *adeJ* gene, was unaffected by the presence of PAβN in the media with no potentiation observed for any of the antimicrobials tested. *A. baumannii* AB005, the strain that did not exhibit the expression of *adeJ* gene, showed an 8-fold potentiation for the activity of SDS but not for any antibiotic tested. Potentiation of the activity of SDS by PAβN in *A. baumannii* AB005 does not indicate that the outer membrane permeability of *A. baumannii* serves as a barrier for the EPI. However, not surprisingly, neither the antibiotic susceptibility nor the potentiation of SDS by PAβN could be correlated to the expression of the *adeJ* gene in the two clinical isolates tested (Table 9.3 and Figure 9.3). This suggests the activity of other RND efflux pumps with similar substrate profiles may mask the effect of PAβN, since even *A. baumannii* AB005 that was found not to express the *adeJ* gene exhibited the potentiation of SDS activity in the presence of PAβN. Additionally, susceptibilities of both *A. baumannii* AB005 and *A. baumannii* AB006 to chloramphenicol, tetracycline, and trimethoprim were not found to differ in spite of the fact that only *A. baumannii* AB006 expressed the *adeJ* gene. This is most likely due to the presence of other resistance mechanisms and/or efflux pumps with similar substrate profiles. For example, AbeM,[31] a pump belonging to the MATE family, has been shown to efflux trimethoprim and chloramphenicol in *A. baumannii*, while another pump belonging to the MFS family, AmvA,[32] has been shown to efflux SDS. Neither MATE nor MFS family pumps are inhibited by PAβN. However, in the surrogate *P. aeruginosa* PA006 strain, induction of the *adeIJK* pump led to a significant increase in resistance to the same three antibiotics, therefore underscoring the importance of a genetically clean system for such studies.

To summarize, in this study, using single copy gene expression, we have shown that the EPI PAβN is active against the AdeIJK pump of *A. baumannii*. However, its activity and that of other potential inhibitors against the pump can be overlooked if not tested in a clean background, in the absence of other efflux pumps with overlapping substrate profiles. This study also highlights the importance of appropriate genetic tools in the search for specific inhibitors of RND pumps, and thus novel and effective therapeutic agents, in *A. baumannii*.

Plasmid or strain	Relevant characteristics	Source
Plasmids		
pGEMT-Easy	Ap^r, PCR cloning vector	Promega
pTNS2	Ap^r; helper plasmid encoding the site-specific TnsABCD Tn7 transposition pathway	(Choi, et al., 2005)
pFLP2	Ap^r; source of *Flp* recombinase	(Hoang, Karkhoff-Schweizer, Kutchma, & Schweizer, 1998)
pUC18T-mini-Tn7T-Gm-LAC	Ap^r Gen^r; mini-Tn7 expression vector containing *lacI^q* and *tac* promoter	(Choi, et al., 2005)
pPLS001	pGEMT-Easy containing the 4051 bp of the *adeI* and *adeJ* genes	This study
pPLS002	pGEMT-Easy containing the 1983 bp of the *adeJ* and *adeK* genes	This study
pPLS007	Ap^r, pGEMT-easy containing the *adeIJK* operon of *A. baumannii* ATCC19606	This study
pPLS009	Ap^r, pUC18T-mini-Tn7T-Gm-LAC containing the *adeIJK* operon of *A. baumannii* ATCC19606	This study
***A. baumannii* strains**		
A. baumannii ATCC19606	*A. baumannii* reference strain	American Type Culture Collection
A. baumannii AB004	Clinical isolate	(Zhanel, et al., 2008)
A. baumannii AB005	Clinical isolate	(Zhanel, et al., 2008)
A. baumannii AB006	Clinical isolate	(Zhanel, et al., 2008)
A. baumannii AB007	Clinical isolate	(Zhanel, et al., 2008)
A. baumannii AB008	Clinical isolate	(Zhanel, et al., 2008)
A. baumannii AB009	Clinical isolate	(Zhanel, et al., 2008)
A. baumannii AB010	Clinical isolate	(Zhanel, et al., 2008)
A. baumannii AB011	Clinical isolate	(Zhanel, et al., 2008)
A. baumannii AB012	Clinical isolate	(Zhanel, et al., 2008)
A. baumannii AB013	Clinical isolate	(Zhanel, et al., 2008)
A. baumannii AB014	Clinical isolate	(Zhanel, et al., 2008)
***P. aeruginosa* strains**		
PAO1	*P. aeruginosa* prototroph	(Holloway & Zhang, 1990)
PAO750	PAO1: Δ(mexAB-oprM), Δ(mexCD-oprJ), Δ(mexEF-oprN), Δ(mexJK), Δ(mexXY), ΔopmH, ΔpscC	(Kumar, et al., 2006)
PA005	Gen^r; PAO750 with chromosomally integrated mini-Tn7T-LAC-*adeIJK*	This study
PA006	PA005 without the Gen^r-marker	This study
***E. coli* strains**		
JM109	*endA1, recA1, gyrA96, relA1, supE44, Δ(lac-proAB) [F⁻ traD36, proAB, laqI^{q}ZΔM15]*	Promega
DH5α	F- φ80*lacZ*ΔM15 Δ(*lacZYA-argF*)U169 *recA1 endA1 hsd*R17(r$_k$⁻, m$_k$⁺) *phoA supE44 thi-1 gyrA96 relA1* λ⁻	Invitrogen

Table 9.1: Bacterial strains and plasmids used in this study.

Name	Sequence	Features/purpose	Source
adeJ_R_RT	AATCCGGCAGTTACACCAAG	RT-PCR of adeJ gene	This study
adeJ_F_RT	TTCAGCGTGGTATGGCATTA		This study
23S_R_RT	GGGAGAACCAGCTATCACCA	RT-PCR of 23S rRNA	This study
23S_F_RT	GCAGGTTGAAGGTTGGGTAA	gene	This study
AdeI_For_Sp	TTActagTTATCTAAACGAGGTG	Cloning of adeIJ' fragment (4051 bp) with engineered SpeI and native KpnI sites (underlined, base changes introduced shown in lowercase)	This study
AdeJ_Rev_Kp	TCAATACGATTGCACCAATGAC		This study
AdeJ_For_Kp	TATATGAAAGCTGGTCAATTCCG	Cloning of adeJ'K fragment (1983 bp) with engineered XhoI and native KpnI sites (underlined, base changes introduced shown in lowercase)	This study
AdeK_Rev_Xh	CCCACCGActcGAGCTTTTATAAG		This study
PaglmS_Dn	GCACATCGGCGACGTGCTCTC	Confirmation of the insertion of mini- Tn7 element in P. aeruginosa	(Choi & Schweizer, 2006)
Tn7R	CACAGCATAACTGGACTGATTTC		(Choi & Schweizer, 2006)

Table 9.2: List of oligonucleotides used in the study.

	P. aeruginosa PA006			A. baumannii AB005			A. baumannii AB006		
adeIJK expression	(-)	(+)		(-)			(+)		
Treatment/ Antibiotic	None	IPTG	IPTG, PAβN	Potentiation	None	PAβN	Potentiation	PAβN	PAβN	Potentiation
Chl	0.256	2	1	2	32	16	2	32	32	1
Tet	0.125	0.5	0.5	1	0.5	1	-2	0.5	1	-4
Cip	0.002	0.004	0.002	2	0.25	0.25	1	0.064	0.128	-2
Tmp	0.5	4	1	4	16	16	1	16	16	1
SDS	32	64	16	4	1024	128	8	>1024	>1024	1

Chl, chloramphenicol; Tet, tetracycline; Cip, ciprofloxacin; Tmp, trimethoprim; SDS, sodium dodecyl sulfate; PAβN, phenylalanine-arginine-β-naphthylamide

Table 9.3: Antibiotic susceptibilities (mg/L) of surrogate P. aeruginosa PA006 and the A. baumannii clinical isolates.

Figure 9.1

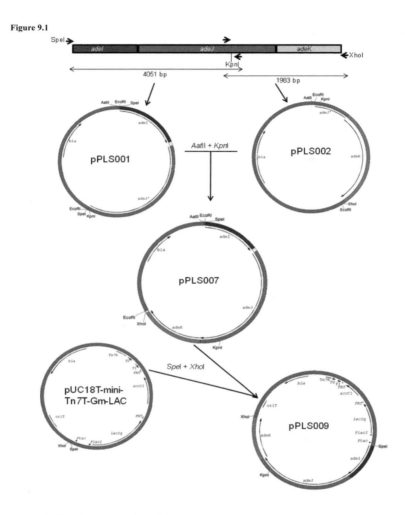

Figure 9.1: PCR cloning of the *adeIJK* operon. Amplification of the *adeIJK* operon was carried out in two steps amplifying 4051 and 1983 bp regions of the *adeIJK* operon. Both PCR products were cloned in the PCR cloning vector pGEMT-easy to derive plasmids pPLS001 and pPLS002, respectively. Assembly of the entire operon yielded the plasmid pPLS007. *aacC1*, gentamycin acetyl transferase–encoding gene; *bla*, beta-lactamase–encoding gene; *FRT*, Flp recombinase target; MCS, multiple cloning site; *ori*, ColE1-derived origin of replication; *oriT*, origin of conjugative transfer; P_{tac}, tac promoter; *lacIq*, lac operon repressor-encoding gene with q promoter-up mutation; T0T1, transcriptional terminators T_0 and T_1 from bacteriophage lambda and *E. coli rrnB* operon, respectively; Tn7L and Tn7R, left and right end of Tn7, respectively.

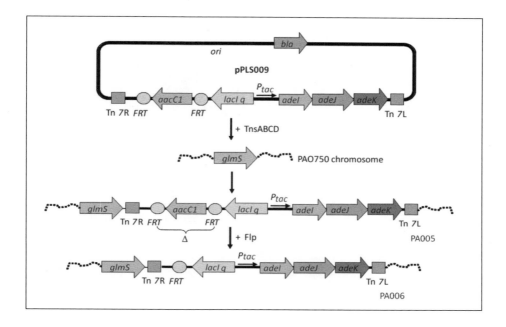

Figure 9.2: Cloning of the *adeIJK* operon in single copy in the surrogate *P. aeruginosa* strain. A mini-Tn7-based expression system (Choi *et. al.*, 2005 and Kumar *et. al.*, 2010) was used to insert the *adeIJK* operon into *P. aeruginosa* PAO750, a strain lacking six different native RND pumps. Expression of the operon was achieved by supplementing the growth medium with 1mM IPTG.

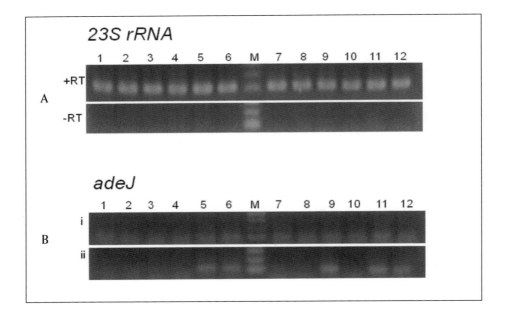

Figure 9.3: Analysis of the presence and expression of the *adeJ* gene in *A. baumannii* isolates (B). 1, *A. baumannii* AB004; 2, *A. baumannii* AB005; 3, *A. baumannii* AB006; 4, *A. baumannii* AB007; 5, *A. baumannii* AB008; 6. *A. baumannii* AB009; 7, *A. baumannii* AB010; 8, *A. baumannii* AB011; 9, *A. baumannii* AB012; 10, *A. baumannii* AB013; 11, *A. baumannii* AB014; 12, *A. baumannii* ATCC19606; M, 100 bp molecular weight marker. PCR was performed using genomic DNA (i) and cDNA as template (ii). Amplification of cDNA was performed for 30 cycles. 23S rRNA (A) was used as the housekeeping control gene and amplified using the cDNA preparations with minus-RT (-RT) samples as controls to rule out contamination of the samples with genomic DNA.

[1]Acknowledgements: This work was supported by grants from NSERC and University of Ontario Institute of Technology to AK.

[2]K.A. Davis, K.A. Moran, K.A. McAllister, and P.J. Gray, "Multidrug-resistant *Acinetobacter* extremity infections in soldiers," *Emerg Infect Dis*, Vol. 11, No. 8 (2005): 1218-1224; K.M. Hujer, A.M. Hujer, E.A. Hulten, S. Bajaksouzian, J.M. Adams, C.J. Donskey, and R.A. Bonomo, "Analysis of antibiotic resistance genes in multidrug-resistant *Acinetobacter* sp. isolates from military and civilian patients treated at the Walter Reed Army Medical Center," *Antimicrob Agents Chemother* Vol. 50, No. 12, (2006): 4114-4123; Centers for Disease Control and Preventation. "*Acinetobacter baumannii* infections among patients at military medical facilities treating injured U. S. service members, 2002-2004," *Morb Mortal Wkly Rep* Vol. 53, No. 45 (2004): 1063-1066; T.L. Stuart, M. Mulvey, A.E. Simor, H.C. Tien, A. Battad, G. Taylor, J.V. Vayalumkal, C. Weir, M. Ofner, D. Gravel, and S. Paton, "*Acinetobacter baumannii* in casualties returning from Afghanistan," *Can J Infect Control* Vol. 22, No. 3, (2007): 152-154.; H.C. Tien, A. Battad, E.A. Bryce, J. Fuller, M. Mulvey, K. Bernard, R. Brisebois, J.J. Doucet, S.B. Rizoli, R. Fowler, A. Simor, "Multi-drug resistant *Acinetobacter* infections in critically injured Canadian Forces soldiers," *BMC Infect Dis* Vol. 7, (2007): 95.

[3]Centers for Disease Control and Preventation. "*Acinetobacter baumannii* infections among patients at military medical facilities treating injured U. S. service members, 2002-2004," *Morb Mortal Wkly Rep* Vol. 53, No. 45 (2004): 1063-1066.

[4]K.M. Hujer, A.M. Hujer, E.A. Hulten, S. Bajaksouzian, J.M. Adams, C.J. Donskey, and R.A. Bonomo, "Analysis of antibiotic resistance genes in multidrug-resistant *Acinetobacter* sp. isolates from military and civilian patients treated at the Walter Reed Army Medical Center," *Antimicrob Agents Chemother* Vol. 50, No. 12, (2006): 4114-4123.

[5]K.S. Akers, C. Chaney, A. Barsoumian, M. Beckius, W. Zera, X. Yu, C.K. Murray, "Aminoglycoside resistance and susceptibility testing errors in *Acinetobacter baumannii-calcoaceticus complex*," *J Clin Microbiol* Vol. 48, No. 4 (2010): 1132-1138.

[6]A. Hamouda and S.G.B. Amyes, "Novel *gyrA* and *parC* point mutations in two strains of *Acinetobacter baumannii* resistant to ciprofloxacin," *J Antimicrob Chemother*, Vol. 54, No. 3 (2004): 695-696.

[7]L. Lin, B.-D. Ling, and X.-Z. Li, "Distribution of the multidrug efflux pump genes, *adeABC*, *adeDE* and *adeIJK*, and class 1 integron genes in multiple-antimicrobial-resistant clinical isolates of *Acinetobacter baumannii-Acinetobacter calcoaceticus* complex," *Int J Antimicrob Agents* Vol. 33, No. 1 (2009): 27-32.

[8]X.-Z. Li and H. Nikaido, "Efflux-mediated drug resistance in bacteria: an update," *Drugs* Vol. 69, No.12 (2009): 1555-1623; K. Poole, "Efflux-mediated multiresistance in Gram-negative bacteria," *Clin Microbiol Infect* Vol. 10, (2004):12-26.

[9]A. Kumar and H.P. Schweizer, "Bacterial resistance to antibiotics: active efflux and reduced uptake," *Adv Drug Deliv Rev* Vol. 57, No. 10 (2005): 1486-1513.

[10]S. Magnet, P. Courvalin, and T. Lambert, "Resistance-nodulation-cell division-type efflux pump involved in aminoglycoside resistance in *Acinetobacter baumannii* strain BM4454," *Antimicrob Agents Chemother* Vol. 45, No. 12 (2001): 3375-3380.

[11]L. Damier-Piolle, S. Magnet, S. Bremont, T. Lambert, and P. Courvalin, "AdeIJK, a resistance-nodulation-cell division pump effluxing multiple antibiotics in Acinetobacter baumannii," *Antimicrob Agents Chemother*, 52, no. 2 (2008): 557-562.

[12]S. Coyne, N. Rosenfeld, T. Lambert, P. Courvalin, and B. Perichon, "Overexpression of resistance-nodulation-cell division pump AdeFGH confers multidrug resistance in Acinetobacter baumannii," *Antimicrob Agents Chemother* Vol. 54, No. 10 (2010): 4389-4393.

[13]S. Magnet, P. Courvalin, and T. Lambert, "Resistance-nodulation-cell division-type efflux pump involved in aminoglycoside resistance in Acinetobacter baumannii strain BM4454," Antimicrob Agents Chemother Vol. 45, No. 12 (2001): 3375-3380.

[14]L. Damier-Piolle, S. Magnet, S. Bremont, T. Lambert, and P. Courvalin, "AdeIJK, a resistance-nodulation-cell division pump effluxing multiple antibiotics in Acinetobacter baumannii," *Antimicrob Agents Chemother*, Vol. 52, No. 2 (2008): 557-562.

[15]S. Coyne, N. Rosenfeld, T. Lambert, P. Courvalin, and B. Perichon, "Overexpression of resistance-nodulation-cell division pump AdeFGH confers multidrug resistance in Acinetobacter baumannii," *Antimicrob Agents Chemother* Vol. 54, No. 10 (2010): 4389-4393.

[16]A. Kumar and H.P. Schweizer, "Bacterial resistance to antibiotics: active efflux and reduced uptake," *Adv Drug Deliv Rev* Vol. 57, No. 10 (2005): 1486-1513.

[17]J.-R. Sun, M.-C. Chan, T.-Y. Chang, W.-Y. Wang, and T.-S. Chiueh, "Overexpression of the *adeB* gene in clinical isolates of tigecycline-nonsusceptible Acinetobacter baumannii without insertion mutations in adeRS," Antimicrob Agents Chemother Vol. 54, No. 11, (2010): 4934-4938.

[18]X. Li, M. Zolli-Juran, J.D. Cechetto, D.M. Daigle, G.D. Wright, and E.D. Brown, "Multicopy suppressors for novel antibacterial compounds reveal targets and drug efflux susceptibility," *Chem Biol* Vol. 11, No. 10 (2004): 1423-1430.

[19]G.G. Zhanel, M. Decorby, K.A. Nichol, A. Wierzbowski, P.J. Baudry, J.A. Karlowsky, P. Lagace-Wiens, A. Walkty, M.R. Mulvey, and D.J. Hoban, "Antimicrobial susceptibility of 3931 organisms isolated from intensive care units in Canada: Canadian National Intensive Care Unit Study, 2005/2006," *Diagn Microbiol Infect Dis* Vol. 62, No. 1, (2008): 67-80.

[20]http://www.invitrogen.com, accessed 14 April 2011.

[21]A. Kumar, K.L. Chua, and H.P. Schweizer, "Method for regulated expression of single-copy efflux pump genes in a surrogate Pseudomonas aeruginosa strain: identification of the BpeEF-OprC chloramphenicol and trimethoprim efflux pump of *Burkholderia pseudomallei* 1026b," Antimicrob Agents Chemother Vol. 50, No. 10, (2006): 3460-3463.

[22]K.H. Choi, A. Kumar, and H.P. Schweizer, "A 10-min method for preparation of highly electrocompetent Pseudomonas aeruginosa cells: application for DNA fragment transfer between chromosomes and plasmid transformation," *J Microbiol Methods* Vol. 64, No. 3, (2006). 391-397.

[23]K.H. Choi, J.B. Gaynor, K.G. White, C. Lopez, C.M. Bosio, R.R. Karkhoff-Schweizer, and H.P. Schweizer, "A Tn7-based broad-range bacterial cloning and expression system," *Nat Methods* Vol. 2, No. 6 (2005): 443-448.

[24]K.H. Choi, J.B. Gaynor, K.G. White, C. Lopez, C.M. Bosio, R.R. Karkhoff-Schweizer, and H.P. Schweizer, "A Tn7-based broad-range bacterial cloning and expression system," *Nat Methods* Vol. 2, No. 6 (2005): 443-448.

[25]K.H. Choi, and H.P. Schweizer, "mini-Tn7 insertion in bacteria with single attTn7 sites: example Pseudomonas aeruginosa," *Nat Protocols* Vol. 1, No. 1 (2006): 153-161.

[26]Clinical and Laboratory Standards Institute, "M7-A7", *Methods for dilution antimicrobial susceptibility tests for bacteria that grow aerobically, approved standard seventh edition* (Wayne, PA. 2006).

[27]S. Magnet, P. Courvalin, and T. Lambert, "Resistance-nodulation-cell division-type efflux pump involved in aminoglycoside resistance in *Acinetobacter baumannii strain* BM4454," Antimicrob Agents Chemother Vol. 45, No. 12, (2001): 3375-3380.

[28]L. Damier-Piolle, S. Magnet, T. Bremont, T. Lambert, and P. Courvalin, "AdeIJK, a resistance-nodulation-cell division pump effluxing multiple antibiotics in Acinetobacter baumannii," *Antimicrob Agents Chemother*, Vol. 52, No. 2 (2008): 557-562.

[29]S. Coyne, N. Rosenfeld, T. Lambert, P. Courvalin, and B. Perichon, "Overexpression of resistance-nodulation-cell division pump AdeFGH confers multidrug resistance in Acinetobacter baumannii," *Antimicrob Agents Chemother* Vol. 54, no. 10 (2010): 4389-4393.

[30]L. Mamelli, J.P. Amoros, J.M. Pages, and J.M. Bolla, "A phenylalanine-arginine beta-naphthylamide sensitive multidrug efflux pump involved in intrinsic and acquired resistance of *Campylobacter* to macrolides," *Int J Antimicrob Agents* 22, no. 3 (2003): 237-241; Renau, T. E., Leger, R., Flamme, E. M., Sangalang, J., She, M. W., Yen, R., Gannon, C. L., Griffith, D., Chamberland, S., Lomovskaya, O., Hecker, S. J., Lee, V. J., Ohta, T., and Nakayama, K. "Inhibitors of efflux pumps in *Pseudomonas aeruginosa* potentiate the activity of the fluoroquinolone antibacterial levofloxacin," *J Med Chem* Vol. 42, No. 24 , (1999): 4928-4931.

[31]X-Z. Su, J. Chen, T. Mizushima, T. Kuroda, and T. Tsuchiya, "AbeM, an H+-coupled *Acinetobacter baumannii* multidrug efflux pump belonging to the MATE family of transporters," *Antimicrob Agents Chemother* Vol. 49, No. 10 (2005): 4362-4364.

[32]G. Rajamohan, V.B. Srinivasan, and W.A. Gebreyes, "Molecular and functional characterization of a novel efflux pump, AmvA, mediating antimicrobial and disinfectant resistance in *Acinetobacter baumannii*," *J Antimicrob Chemother* 65, no. 9, (2010): 1919-1925; K.H. Choi, A. Kumar, and H.P. Schweizer, "A 10-min method for preparation of highly electrocompetent *Pseudomonas aeruginosa* cells: application for DNA fragment transfer between chromosomes and plasmid transformation" *J Microbiol Methods* Vol. 64, no. 3 (2006): 391-397; T.T. Hoang, R.R. Karkhoff-Schweizer, A.J. Kutchma, and H.P. Schweizer, "A broad-host range *Flp*-FRT recombination system for site-specific excision of chromosomally-located DNA sequences: application for isolation of unmarked *Pseudomonas aeruginosa* mutants," Gene Vol. 212, No.1 (1998): 77-86; B.W. Holloway, and C. Zhang, "Genetic maps," *Locus Maps of Complex Genomes 5th Edition*, ed. S. J. O'Brien (Cold Spring Harbor: Cold Spring Harbor Laboratory Press, 1990), 2, 71, 72, 78.

CHAPTER 10

A Test Battery for the Assessment of Psychological and Physiological Performance Following Primary Blast Wave Exposure

Ann Nakashima, MASc, Oshin Vartanian, PhD, Fethi Bouak, PhD, Kevin Hofer, MA, and Bob Cheung, PhD, DRDC Toronto

ABSTRACT

Primary blast exposure could alter postural tremor, impair balance, and cause deficits in cognitive function. It is purported that injury due to exposure to primary blast wave could also result in mTBI. Here we assess the correlations and longitudinal stability of measures of postural tremor, balance, and cognitive function among neurologically healthy normal controls, and offer a comprehensive tool based on a normative database to assess performance following primary blast exposure.

A TEST BATTERY FOR THE ASSESSMENT OF PSYCHOLOGICAL AND PHYSIOLOGICAL PERFORMANCE FOLLOWING PRIMARY BLAST WAVE EXPOSURE

Primary blast wave injury can be defined as an injury caused by direct blast energy or pressure- a form of barotrauma. Closed head injuries due to primary blast are most insidious, elusive and difficult to diagnose. In the absence of open or penetrating wounds to the head or other obvious immediate signs of impairment, it has been suggested that an alteration of consciousness or mental status should be considered in the assessment of this type of injury.[1] If so, a field-deployable assessment tool would be ideal to determine whether the exposed soldier can continue with duties or must seek medical attention instead. A critical question concerns the composition of the specific measures for such a field-deployable assessment tool. A review of the literature indicates that three types of indices can be used to detect an alteration of mental status: postural stability,[2] tremor,[3] and cognitive function.[4] Therefore, this paper describes the construction and evaluation of a tripartite instrument designed to assess psychological and physiological performance following primary blast wave exposure.

POSTURAL STABILITY

Transient vestibular balance dysfunction following primary blast injuries without tympanum rupture has been reported, although the mechanism remains unknown.[5] With recent escalation of IED in the military and civilian environments, it is estimated that 25–30% of the patients subjected to blast injury were diagnosed as suffering from balance disorders.[6] There is a large body of literature discussing the use of balance testing to assess the effects of and recovery from closed head injuries, particularly in sports medicine.[7] The instruments range from variations of a basic Romberg test[8] to computerized systems that challenge the subject's visual, vestibular, and somatosensory systems to obtain a detailed analysis of postural stability.[9]

Despite the apparent heterogeneity of the available measures, a review of the literature suggests that three categories of postural stability or balance tests can be identified. The first category can be referred to as subjective static testing, which includes the Romberg test and its variations.[10] These tests require only a flat surface, no specialized equipment, and can be administered with minimal training. It has been argued that such static tests are insensitive to subtle changes in balance.[11] The second category involves subjective dynamic balance tests which may involve introducing an unstable surface, thereby forcing the subject to adapt to dynamic changes at the base of support. For example, the Balance Error Scoring System (BESS) includes conditions in which the subject stands on a foam surface.[12] A third category which may be considered more objective can be used for static or dynamic testing. Specifically, tests in this category offer a quantitative analysis of postural stability using specialized equipment. These tests are often performed in a clinical setting, and require a computer-interfaced platform that measures the center of the vertical forces exerted by the subject.[13] In the current study, balance tests in each of the three categories were included to assess their relative efficacy.

POSTURAL TREMOR

Physiological tremor is present in all humans, but it also manifests itself as a pathological symptom.[14] Specifically, tremor has also been reported as one of the physiological indices affected following blast exposure. Postural tremor can be measured by recording the movement of an extremity (e.g., an extended index finger) as it is held in position against gravity. It has been shown that there are distinguishing frequency domain characteristics in the postural tremor of subjects with Parkinson's disease.[15] Subjects with altitude-induced hypoxia have shown increased tremor in the 6–12 Hz frequency range compared to the control condition.[16] Little research has been done on the assessment of postural tremor in subjects who have incurred head trauma. It is therefore of interest to include postural tremor measurements in the current study to determine whether they contribute uniquely to the physiological effects of blast exposure.

COGNITIVE FUNCTION

The cognitive effects of head trauma have been studied extensively by clinical and neuropsychological researchers.[17] Generally speaking, the findings are very heterogeneous, making reliable inferences about the effects of head trauma on cognitive function difficult. However, two conclusions have been borne out by the available evidence. First, the effects of head trauma on cognitive performance vary as a function of the specific cognitive task under consideration.[18] Thus, the proper procedure for measuring cognitive impairment following primary blast wave exposure must involve multiple tests that measure different abilities (e.g., memory, reasoning, etc.). Second, the effects of head trauma on cognitive performance vary as a function of the time of measurement (i.e., delay) following the trauma.[19] Thus, interpreting results from patients can be made meaningful only if test results can be compared to norms from a neurologically healthy population *collected longitudinally*. In other words, researchers must know how variable test scores are longitudinally in normal controls to quantify the extent of impairment in patients following primary blast wave exposure.

STUDY AIMS

The tests described above are usually administered cross-sectionally, based on the assumption that in neurologically healthy, normal controls, postural stability, postural tremor and cognitive function are stable indices. Furthermore, although many studies have tested subjects using these tests, few have combined all three indices into a single study, and even fewer have attempted to correlate the indices when the respective tests were available. Using data from neurologically healthy subjects, the main objectives of this study were (a) to measure each of the indices at three time points where testing sessions were separated by a week to determine their longitudinal stability, and (b) to assess the correlations among the indices at a single time point. The results will be used to determine which tests should be included in the test battery for the assessment of blast-wave induced head trauma in the field.

DESCRIPTION OF THE TEST BATTERY AND APPARATUS

VESTIBULAR ATAXIA TEST BATTERY

It has been shown that a floor ataxia test battery can detect differences in performance between normal subjects and those with vestibular deficits.[20] A variation of the vestibular ataxia test battery was used in this study. For all of the tests, the eyes were closed and the arms were crossed in front of the chest, with the elbows held parallel to the floor. Gross movements of the arms or either leg resulted in termination of the trial. The tests were administered in the following order:

(a) Standing on Preferred Leg (SOPL): The subjects stood on their preferred (dominant) leg with the free foot resting on the back of the preferred leg. The subject was scored according to how many seconds the position was held (maximum 30 sec), and up to three attempts were allowed. If the maximum score was attained on the first attempt, the maximum total score was given (90 sec). If the position was held successfully on the second attempt, maximum scores were awarded for trials two and three (60 sec) plus the time for the first trial. Otherwise, the number of seconds for each of the three attempts was added to obtain the total score. The test was then performed on the non-preferred leg (SONL).

(b) Sharpened Romberg (SR): The subject stood heel-to-toe (heel of front foot touching the toe of the back foot) with the weight equally distributed on both feet.

This position was held for 60 sec. The test was performed first with the preferred foot in front (SRP), then with the non-preferred foot in front (SRN). The scoring was similar to that of SOPL, except that the maximum total score was 180 sec (3 × 60 sec) for the SRP and SRN.

(c) Walking on Floor Eyes Closed (WOFEC): The subject stood heel-to-toe with the preferred foot in front, and walked 12 steps. With each step, the subject must touch the heel of the stepping foot to the toe of the supporting foot. The scoring method was similar to that of the SOPL, except that the maximum total score was 36 (3 × 12 steps), measured in steps rather than time.

BALANCE ERROR SCORING SYSTEM

The BESS was developed as a method for quickly evaluating postural stability without the use of computerized force platform technology.[21] Briefly, the BESS test battery consists of three different stances (double leg, single leg and tandem) performed on two different surfaces (firm and foam). In this study, an Airex balance pad[22] was used as the foam surface. The Airex balance pad is a fitness training aid made of medium-density foam (dimensions: 50 × 40 × 6 cm^3, 0.7 kg). In the single leg condition, subjects stood on the non-dominant foot. The tandem condition was the same as the SR in the vestibular ataxia test battery, with the non-dominant foot in the rear. For each condition, the subject stood with their hands on their hips and eyes closed for 20 sec. Each time the subject committed an error, a point was added to their score. The errors were described as follows: hands lifted off of iliac crests (hips), opening eyes, stumble or fall, moving hip into more than 30° of flexion or abduction, and lifting of forefoot or heel.[23] The maximum error score for each of the six conditions was 10, and the scores were added together to obtain the composite BESS score. Because points were given for the number of errors, a higher score indicated poorer performance.

FORCE PLATFORM

Postural stability can be assessed quantitatively through the use of force platform technology. We used the Accusway^{PLUS} system[24] which is a 50cm × 50cm platform that measures the forces and moments of balance in three directions: x (medial-lateral), y (anterior-posterior) and z (dorsal-ventral). Balance Clinic software[25] was used to calculate the center of pressure (COP) coordinates over time, from which a number of sway parameters were obtained. The sway velocity was chosen for analysis because it has been suggested that it shows the most consistent difference between test conditions.[26] The data were acquired at a sampling rate of 100 Hz. The same stances as the BESS were used, with eyes open and closed. The six tests were performed in the following order: double leg (eyes open, then closed), tandem and single leg. Each position was held for 20 sec.

Postural tremor

Postural tremor data were acquired using a device that has been used in a previous study.[27] The device consisted of a Class II laser diode (Micro laser sensor LM10, series ARN12821[28]) from which data was sampled at a rate of 1000 Hz (Figure 10.1). The laser was located 8cm above white cardboard disk that was fixed on the tip of the dominant index finger. The cardboard disk was 5cm in diameter and weighed about 1g. Vertical finger displacements were recorded by the laser beam, which was directed downwards onto the cardboard disk. The laser is an analog output sensor using an optical triangulation with a ±2 cm range of measurement. It has a resolution of ±5 μm after filtering out high frequencies. Since a change in tremor amplitude and frequency concentration can indicate pathology,[29] these characteristics were chosen for analysis. Both values are calculated using the filtered time series data (2–20 Hz). For the tremor amplitude, larger values correspond to worse performance. The frequency concentration is the width of the interval containing 68% of the power spectrum, with smaller values corresponding to worse performance.[30]

During the measurements, the subject was seated with the dominant arm resting on the table with the palm of the hand resting on a moulded support. The subject was instructed to relax and to point the dominant index finger forward without hyper-extending it. The subject received a visual feedback of the position of their finger represented by a horizontal line displayed on a LCD screen in front of them: each subject had to maintain this line steady, aligned with the "zero" position displayed on the screen. Data were recorded three times each with eyes open and eyes closed. For each trial, data were recorded for one minute, with one minute of rest between trials.

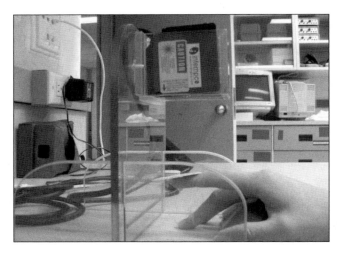

Figure 10.1: Postural tremor device.

Cognitive function

Cognitive function was assessed using the Cognitive Test Software.[31] This test battery is a reconfigurable package of cognitive tests for measuring various cognitive functions of interest. This test battery has been used in the past to collect data in laboratory studies of cognitive performance.[32] In this study we administered a combination of four tests, for a total of 45 minutes for the entire package of tests.

(a) Four-choice Reaction Time Test

The Four-choice Reaction Time Test assesses the ability to respond rapidly and accurately to simple visual stimuli. A series of visual stimuli at 1 of 4 different spatial locations are presented. The subject must indicate the correct spatial location of each stimulus by pressing 1 of 4 adjacent keys on the keyboard. Correct and incorrect responses, reaction time, premature errors (responding before stimulus presentation), and time-out errors are recorded. The key dependent variable in this test is reaction time (RT), given that accuracy is at ceiling levels.

(b) Grammatical Reasoning Test

The Grammatical Reasoning Test assesses language-based logical reasoning. It has been used to assess the effects of various treatments on cognitive function. On each trial, the letters AB or BA follow a statement. The subject must decide whether or not each statement correctly describes the order of the 2 letters. The "T" key on the keyboard is pressed for correct (statement is true), and the "F" key is pressed for incorrect (statement is false). Correct and incorrect responses, RT, and time-out errors are recorded.

(c) Two-choice Test

This is a test developed to assess deductive reasoning ability. On each trial the subject is presented with two premises (e.g., A > B and B > C) followed by a conclusion (e.g., A > C), and must judge whether the conclusion follows necessarily from the premises (i.e., the argument is valid). Correct and incorrect responses, RT, and time-out errors are recorded.

(d) Matching-to-sample Test

This test assesses short-term spatial memory (working memory) and pattern recognition skills. An 8 by 8 matrix of a red and green checkerboard pattern is presented for 10 sec, then removed, and then followed by a variable delay of 8 or 16 sec. Two matrices are then presented side-by-side: the original matrix and a matrix with the color of 2 squares reversed. The subjects must select the original matrix. Correct and incorrect responses, RT, and time-out errors are recorded.

Experimental Protocol

Subjects

Forty subjects completed the first session of the study (20 males and 20 females, age 29.3±9.3 years [range 18 to 50], height 169.6±9.6 cm [range 150 to 192], weight 70.1±14.7 kg [range 47.7 to 105.8]). The data from the first session was used to calculate the correlations between physiological and psychological measures. In addition, twenty of the subjects (10 males and 10 females) completed an additional two sessions. The data from these twenty subjects across the three sessions was used to calculate the longitudinal stability of each physiological and psychological measure across the three time points. Subjects were screened by a physician for a history of head trauma, neurological disease, vestibular dysfunction and carpal tunnel syndrome, and were compensated for their participation according to DRDC guidelines. All of the subjects were right-handed.

The average WAIS-R IQ for the sample was 109.53 (SD = 6.61), measured using the Shipley Institute of Living Scale[33] in combination with WAIS-R IQ estimation.[34]

Procedure

All subjects participated in a familiarization session prior to their first session. During the familiarization, an experimenter directed the subject to stand in the three basic positions (double leg, single leg, tandem), both on the force platform (firm surface) and on the foam. The outlines of the subject's feet in all three positions were traced onto paper. The tracings were used during the experimental sessions to allow for consistency of foot placement during the force platform measurements. The tremor device was shown to the subjects and a practice measurement was taken. The cognitive test battery was not shown to the subjects prior to their first session, but subjects received thorough instructions in advance of each test.

Half of the subjects completed the physiological test batteries (BESS, postural tremor, vestibular ataxia, force platform) before the cognitive tests, whereas the other half of the subjects completed the cognitive tests first. In each experimental session, the subjects completed the physiological test batteries in the following order: BESS, postural tremor, vestibular ataxia, force platform. The order of physiological tests was not counterbalanced because performance (i.e., test-retest reliability) was to be analyzed independently for each test. The order of the four tests of cognitive functions was reversed for half of the subjects (i.e., d-a versus a-d). All of the sessions were completed in the morning. For the twenty subjects who completed three sessions, the sessions were completed at the same time of day, separated by one week. For those twenty subjects the order of the four cognitive tests was reversed at each session.

The BESS was performed with bare feet. All of the subjects were videotaped during the BESS test for scoring purposes. There were five experimenters in total who were trained on scoring the BESS, and each subject was scored independently by three experimenters: one during the experimental session and two others after the session, using the video. During the session, one experimenter rated the subject and timed the tests using a stopwatch, and a second experimenter was positioned as a spotter for the safety of the subject.

Postural tremor was recorded with the subject seated with their forearms resting on the desk. The right hand was placed on the moulded support with the index finger extended, and a cardboard disk was placed on the fingertip (see Figure 10.1). After aligning the index finger such that the laser position was zeroed on the LCD screen, tremor was recorded for one minute with eyes open. The subject was then instructed to relax their index finger. The procedure was repeated three times with eyes open, then three times with eyes closed.

The vestibular ataxia test battery was performed on a non-slip, tiled floor surface, with the subjects wearing socks. One experimenter used a stopwatch to time the subject for the SOPL, SONL, SRP and SRN tests, recording the number of seconds for each trial.

The subjects performed the force platform test battery with bare feet, standing on a sheet of paper on top of the platform. One experimenter observed the subject while a second experimenter operated the software and noted any errors (e.g., if the subject stepped off the platform). All of the subjects were videotaped for data verification (e.g., to confirm if the subject put the other foot down during the single-leg stance). A trial was considered to be incomplete if the subject did not hold the position for 20 sec. In the case of an incomplete trial, the subject was allowed a second attempt.

In each session the cognitive task battery was completed in a single sitting. The experimenter started the program, which in turn navigated the subject through all four tests. Each test included its own set of instructions. Subjects were prompted to ask questions from the experimenter in case the instructions were unclear.

RESULTS

The data was analyzed employing repeated-measures (within-subjects) ANOVAs. For all analyses, $p < 0.05$ was considered statistically significant.

POSTURAL STABILITY

A reliability analysis was performed on the BESS scores given by each of the five raters (three for each subject), for five of the BESS conditions. The analysis could not be done for the double leg condition for both surfaces because almost all of the subjects were given a score of zero error by all raters. The reliability results are shown in Table 10.1. The Cronbach's alpha values ranged from 0.90 (single leg, foam surface) to 0.95 (single leg, firm surface), indicating a high level of consistency among the five raters.

Stance	Surface	Alpha
Double leg	Firm	*
Single leg	Firm	0.95
Tandem	Firm	0.94
Double leg	Foam	*
Single leg	Foam	0.90
Tandem	Foam	0.94

*could not be calculated because variance ≈ 0

Table 10.1. Reliability analysis of scores given by five possible raters (three raters for each subject; n = 20).

The median of the three ratings for each condition was added to obtain the composite BESS scores for each subject. Lower scores indicate better performance. T-tests showed no significant differences between males and females for any of the sessions; therefore data were collapsed across this variable. For the 40 subjects who completed one session, the mean score was 18.5±6.7. For the 20 subjects who completed three sessions, the mean scores for each session were 18.0±6.6, 18.6±6.4 and 16.1±7.6, respectively (Figure 10.2). A repeated-measures ANOVA showed no main effect for session.

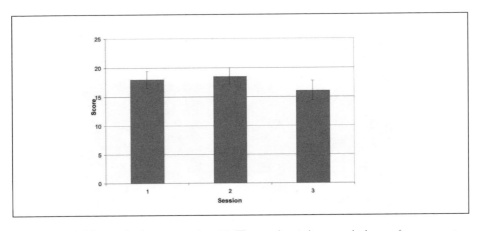

Figure 10.2: BESS scores for three sessions (n = 20). The error bars indicate standard error of measurement.

The scores for the vestibular ataxia test battery did not have a normal distribution. A Mann-Whitney test showed no significant differences between the scores for males and females for any of the tests; therefore, the data were collapsed across gender for further analysis. The mean ataxia test battery scores for the 40 subjects who completed at least one session are shown in Table 10.2. For these tests, a higher score indicates better performance. The average scores for the SOPL, SONL, SRP and SRN tests, for each session, are shown in Figure 10.3; the results for WOFEC are shown in Table 10.3. The Friedman test showed no main effect of session on the scores for any of the tests.

Test	Mean score (Max score)	SD
SOPL	49.9 (90)	29.4
SONL	54.5 (90)	29.5
SRP	143.9 (180)	53.4
SRN	144.9 (180)	53.5
WOFEC	32.0 (36)	7.9

Table 10.2. Mean scores and Standard Deviation (SD) for the ataxia test battery (one session; n = 40).

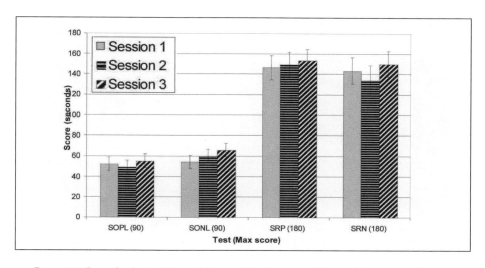

Figure 10.3: Scores for the single-leg and sharpened Romberg tests of the vestibular ataxia test battery (n = 20). The error bars indicate standard error of measurement.

Session	WOFEC score (steps)	SD
1	32.8	7.7
2	32.9	6.6
3	32.2	8.3

Table 10.3. Average scores and standard deviations for Walking on Floor Eyes Closed (WOFEC). The error bars indicate standard error of measurement.

The mean sway velocities for each of the force platform measurements are shown in Table 10.4. A higher sway velocity indicates poorer performance. If the subject did not hold the position for 20 seconds, the trial was excluded from the analysis.

Test	Velocity (cm/s)	SD
Double leg, eyes open	2.11	0.31
Double leg, eyes closed	2.83	0.69
Single leg, eyes open[1]	4.71	0.89
Single leg, eyes closed[2]	7.82	1.79
Tandem, eyes open	4.09	0.99
Tandem, eyes closed[3]	6.54	1.81

Note. $N = 40$ except 1 ($N = 39$), 2 ($N = 26$), and 3 ($N = 33$).

Table 10.4. Velocity data for the subjects who completed at least one session.

The mean sway velocities for the subjects who completed three sessions are shown in Figure 10.4. Because there was no gender difference, data was collapsed across this variable. There were eight incomplete trials for the single leg with eyes closed condition, and five for the tandem with eyes closed condition. A repeated-measures ANOVA showed a significant main effect of session for the single leg, eyes open condition, $F(2, 38) = 5.40$, $p = 0.009$, partial $\eta^2 = 0.22$. *Post hoc* comparisons using Bonferroni correction revealed a significant difference between the first and third sessions ($p = 0.007$). The decreasing sway velocity for this condition over time indicated an improvement in performance.

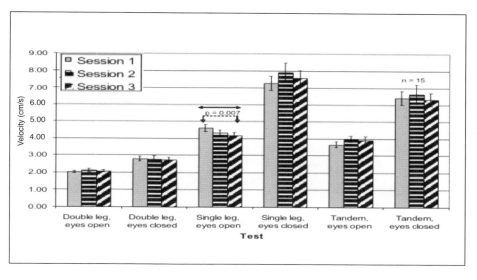

Figure 10.4: Sway velocity for the force platform test battery for subjects who completed three sessions (n = 20 unless otherwise indicated). The dashed arrow indicates significance between sessions 1 and 3.

POSTURAL TREMOR

The mean amplitude and frequency concentration data for 40 subjects are shown in Table 10.5. The tremor amplitude and frequency data for the subjects who completed three sessions are shown in Figures 10.5 and 10.6, respectively. Two t-tests indicated that there was no significant difference for gender for either dependent variable. Therefore, data were collapsed across this variable. A repeated-measures ANOVA showed no effect of session on the amplitude or frequency concentration data.

	Amplitude (mm)		Frequency Concentration (Hz)	
	Average	SD	Average	SD
Eyes open	0.069	0.058	5.059	1.071
Eyes closed	0.062	0.039	5.543	1.950

Table 10.5. Postural tremor data for 40 subjects.

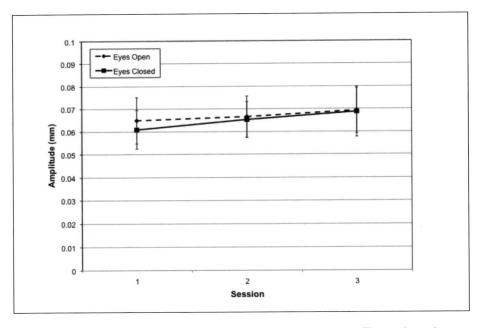

Figure 10.5: Tremor amplitude for the 20 subjects who completed three sessions. The error bars indicate standard error of measurement.

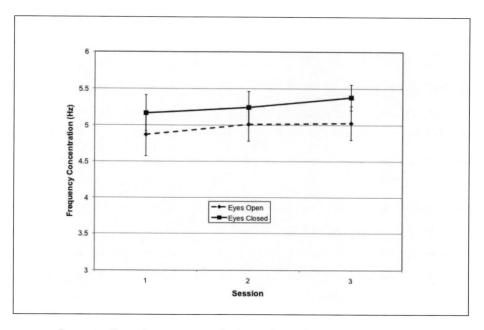

Figure 10.6: Tremor frequency content for the 20 subjects who completed three sessions.
The error bars indicate standard error of measurement.

COGNITIVE FUNCTION

For tests of cognitive function, accuracy and RT represented the two dependent variables of interest.

(a) Four-choice Reaction Time Test

Given that average accuracy across Session 1 ($M = 99\%$, $SD = 1$), Session 2 ($M = 98\%$, $SD = 2$), and Session 3 ($M = 97\%$, $SD = 3$) was at ceiling with little variance, we did not conduct a repeated-measures ANOVA for accuracy. However, a repeated-measures ANOVA on the RT data was significant, $F(2, 38) = 14.01$, $p < 0.001$, partial $\eta^2 = 0.42$. *Post hoc* tests demonstrated that subjects were significantly faster in Session 2 ($M = 435ms$, $SD = 82$) and Session 3 ($M = 425ms$, $SD = 77$) than they were in Session 1 ($M = 461$, $SD = 92$) ($p < 0.01$).

(b) Grammatical Reasoning Test

A repeated-measures ANOVA on the accuracy data was significant, $F(2, 38) = 9.45$, $p < 0.01$, partial $\eta^2 = 0.33$. *Post hoc* tests demonstrated that all pairwise differences between Session 1 (M = 69%, SD = 12), Session 2 (M = 76%, SD = 18), and Session 3 (M = 80%, SD = 18) were significant (p < 0.05). A repeated-measures ANOVA on the RT data was not significant, $F(2, 38)$ = .35, ns.

(c) Two-choice Test

A repeated-measures ANOVA on the accuracy data was not significant, $F(2, 38)$ = 1.83, ns. However, a repeated-measures ANOVA on the RT data was significant, $F(2, 38)$ = 20.52, p < 0.001, partial η^2 = 0.53. *Post hoc* tests demonstrated that all pairwise differences between Session 1 (M = 11020ms, SD = 3729), Session 2 (M = 7827, SD = 4182), and Session 3 (M = 6798, SD = 4592) were significant (p < 0.05).

(d) Matching-to-sample Test

A repeated-measures ANOVA on the accuracy data was not significant, $F(2, 38)$ = 3.11, ns. A repeated-measures ANOVA on the RT data was also not significant, $F(2, 38)$ = 2.99, ns.

CORRELATIONS BETWEEN PHYSIOLOGICAL AND PSYCHOLOGICAL MEASURES

To determine whether there are relationships between physiological and psychological measures, we computed the correlations between all dependent variables for balance, postural tremor, and cognitive function at Session 1 (N = 40). Note that our focus here was on correlations between measures of balance, postural tremor, and cognitive function, rather than within various measures in each category. The correlations are reported in Table 10.A1.

DISCUSSION

There are several factors that need to be considered when selecting measures for a test battery. Because we were interested in the effects of primary blast wave exposure, two criteria drove test selection. First, *logistic* considerations dictated that the tests must be field-deployable, easily administrable, and must require minimal training prior to data collection. Second, *psychometric* considerations dictated that practice effects be minimal such that the tests must show a flat performance gradient over successive measurement. Each of the tests that were used in the current study will be discussed in terms of these two factors.

The BESS has been used for repeated testing of athletes who have suffered from a closed-head injury to determine the rate and extent of recovery.[35] However, it has been suggested that repeated administration results in an improvement in the BESS scores, depending on the time between the tests.[36] In the current study, there was no main effect of session, suggesting that a one week lag may be long enough to offset practice effects. A practice effect was seen for the single leg with eyes open condition on the force platform (Figure 10.4). No main effect of session was found for any of the tests in the vestibular ataxia test battery. Thus, with the exception of one of the force platform tests (single leg with eyes open), test-retest reliability was found to be high for all three of the balance test batteries.

As for field use, it has been shown that administration of the BESS in the field led to higher total scores (i.e., poorer performance) than when the test was performed in the locker room.[37] Tests that require sensitive equipment, such as a force platform, may not be suitable for certain environments. The test results are also sensitive to the way the test is administered. Scoring of the BESS is subjective, although it has been shown to have high inter-rater reliability.[38] The reliability coefficients for the five different experimenters in the current study (0.90 to 0.95) were high and similar to those found by Riemann *et al* (0.78 to 0.96), despite having most of the scoring based on video recording. This suggests that in the absence of a trained clinician or experimenter (as may be the case in a non-clinical environment), the BESS could be recorded onto video and scored remotely. However, there is still the issue of determining baseline performance. Despite the high inter-rater reliability shown in this study, our BESS scores were relatively higher than scores found in the literature. Scores of 10.97±5.05 for normal subjects aged 20 to 39 years (N = 104) and 11.88±5.40 for 40 to 49 year olds (N = 172) have been reported,[39] compared to our scores of 16.1±7.6 to 18.0±6.6 for subjects in the same age range. The same foam surface (Airex Balance Pad[40]) was used in both studies. It is unknown how the training of the experimenters differed between the two studies. Based on our findings and the limitations imposed by the operational environments, the vestibular ataxia battery appears to be the best option for balance testing.

For the postural tremor test, amplitude and frequency concentration were chosen for analysis in this study. These characteristics have been measured reliably in previous studies.[41] The average values shown in Table 10.5 can serve as baseline values for future work on postural tremor in injured subjects. Both the amplitude and frequency concentration data were shown to be stable across the three sessions (see Figures 10.5 and 10.6). Preliminary data based on a study of "Breachers" in a field setting have suggested that it may be feasible to deploy and use our postural tremor apparatus in the operational environment, although additional data are required to evaluate its effectiveness in that setting.

The four tests of cognitive function demonstrated little learning effects across the three sessions. Specifically, in terms of accuracy, only the Grammatical Reasoning Test demonstrated a learning effect across the three sessions (i.e., higher accuracy in later sessions), whereas in terms of RT only the Four-choice Reaction Time Test and Two-choice Test demonstrated a learning effect across the three sessions (i.e., lower RT in later sessions). Importantly, we did not assess the potential of this cognitive battery for deployment in this study, nor are aware of other studies that have assessed this specific package of tests in the filed. This critical feature must be tested in future field studies.

Critically, we also computed the correlations between our physiological and psychological measures. As stated above, our focus here was on correlations *between* measures of balance, postural tremor, and cognitive function, rather than *within* various measures in each category. The correlations demonstrated that there was no systematic correlation between physiological and psychological measures in this study (Table 10.1). In other words, the measures appear to tap into different abilities, suggesting that a comprehensive battery must include measures of balance, postural tremor, and cognitive functions to address relevant aspects of performance.

CONCLUSION

Primary blast exposure can alter postural tremor, impair balance, and cause deficits in cognitive function. In this study we assessed the longitudinal stability of measures of postural tremor, balance, and cognitive function as well as their correlations among neurologically healthy normal controls. The data provide the normative database for the assessment of performance using this battery of tests following primary blast exposure. The following conclusions can be drawn: First, our results suggest that a comprehensive assessment of psychological and physiological performance following primary blast wave exposure will benefit from the inclusion of measures that assess balance, postural tremor, and cognitive function. Second, the vestibular ataxia battery appears to be the best option for balance testing. Third, amplitude and frequency concentration are satisfactory indices to assess postural tremor using the device described here. Fourth, cognitive testing must include tests of elementary as well as higher-order cognitive function. Having established a normative database for these measures here, proper standards now exist for comparing data collected in the field to data collected from neurologically healthy normal controls.

Table 10.1: Correlation matrix of the neurocognitive, tremor, and balance tests.

	GR ACC	GR RT	MS ACC	MS RT	FC ACC	FC RT	TC ACC	TC RT	Tremor AEO	Tremor AEC	Tremor FEO	Tremor FEC	FP DLEO	FP DLEC	FP TEO	FP TEC	FP SLEO	FP SLEC	VTB SOPL	VTB SONL	VTB SRP	VTB SRN	VTB WOFEC	BESS
GR ACC	1.00	-0.13	**0.37**	0.19	-0.11	-0.25	0.06	0.00	**0.31**	**0.29**	0.05	-0.02	-0.18	0.05	-0.06	0.02	-0.06	0.02	0.16	0.26	0.12	0.16	0.13	-0.16
GR RT	-0.13	1.00	-0.04	0.10	-0.07	0.21	**-0.33**	**0.49**	-0.09	-0.05	0.08	0.07	-0.15	-0.15	0.05	0.02	-0.06	0.02	0.02	-0.09	0.18	0.10	-0.09	-0.19
MS ACC	**0.37**	-0.04	1.00	0.14	0.10	0.10	0.20	-0.19	0.16	0.06	0.03	0.12	0.18	0.09	0.04	0.04	0.22	0.12	-0.10	-0.25	0.21	-0.01	0.09	-0.07
MS RT	0.19	0.10	0.14	1.00	0.20	0.20	0.28	0.00	0.18	0.18	0.14	0.23	0.06	0.08	0.03	-0.02	0.12	0.12	-0.09	-0.25	-0.01	-0.17	-0.04	0.02
FC ACC	-0.11	-0.07	0.10	0.20	1.00	**-0.29**	0.28	0.00	0.17	0.09	0.04	0.06	-0.03	0.08	-0.11	-0.05	0.08	-0.01	-0.05	-0.12	-0.01	-0.17	-0.06	0.24
FC RT	-0.25	0.21	0.10	0.20	**-0.29**	1.00	**-0.29**	-0.17	-0.08	0.06	0.19	0.28	-0.11	-0.09	-0.21	-0.25	0.17	-0.30	-0.36	0.24	-0.09	0.04	-0.13	0.24
TC ACC	0.06	**-0.33**	0.20	0.28	0.28	**-0.29**	1.00	-0.17	-0.06	-0.08	0.06	0.19	-0.21	-0.09	-0.16	-0.05	-0.01	-0.17	-0.04	-0.09	0.13	0.04	-0.12	-0.11
TC RT	0.00	**0.49**	-0.19	0.00	0.00	-0.17	-0.17	1.00	-0.04	-0.19	0.01	0.11	0.12	0.13	0.01	0.00	0.13	-0.05	0.27	0.13	0.04	0.13	-0.01	-0.24
Tremor AEO	**0.31**	-0.09	0.16	0.18	0.17	-0.08	-0.06	-0.04	1.00	**0.85**	**-0.53**	**-0.49**	0.20	**0.46**	0.16	**0.63**	0.26	**0.53**	0.08	-0.07	0.22	0.18	-0.13	-0.01
Tremor AEC	**0.29**	-0.05	0.06	0.18	0.09	0.06	-0.08	-0.19	**0.85**	1.00	**-0.41**	**-0.57**	0.25	0.26	0.26	**0.57**	0.21	0.22	0.02	-0.09	0.18	0.28	-0.01	0.02
Tremor FEO	0.05	0.08	0.03	0.14	0.04	0.19	0.06	0.01	**-0.53**	**-0.41**	1.00	**0.76**	-0.09	0.25	0.26	**0.61**	0.26	**0.53**	0.21	-0.10	0.18	0.28	-0.13	0.18
Tremor FEC	-0.02	0.07	0.12	0.23	0.06	0.28	0.19	0.11	**-0.49**	**-0.57**	**0.76**	1.00	-0.24	-0.24	**-0.37**	-0.25	-0.32	-0.28	-0.13	-0.21	-0.27	-0.36	-0.08	-0.05
FP DLEO	-0.18	-0.15	0.18	0.06	-0.03	-0.11	-0.21	0.12	0.20	0.25	-0.09	-0.24	1.00	**0.49**	**0.63**	**0.50**	**0.47**	**0.65**	-0.33	**-0.53**	-0.19	0.02	-0.06	**0.30**
FP DLEC	0.05	-0.15	0.09	0.08	0.08	-0.09	-0.09	0.13	**0.46**	0.26	0.25	-0.24	**0.49**	1.00	**0.51**	**0.42**	**0.40**	**0.71**	**-0.38**	-0.26	-0.05	0.00	-0.23	**0.38**
FP TEO	-0.06	0.05	0.04	0.03	-0.11	-0.21	-0.16	0.01	0.16	0.26	0.26	**-0.37**	**0.63**	**0.51**	1.00	**0.50**	**0.71**	**0.62**	-0.24	**-0.50**	-0.26	-0.05	-0.13	**0.44**
FP TEC	0.02	0.02	0.04	-0.02	-0.05	-0.25	-0.05	0.00	**0.63**	**0.57**	**0.61**	-0.25	**0.50**	**0.42**	**0.50**	1.00	**0.43**	**0.62**	-0.21	**-0.50**	-0.24	0.14	-0.23	**0.39**
FP SLEO	-0.06	-0.06	0.22	0.12	0.08	0.17	-0.01	0.13	0.26	0.21	0.26	-0.32	**0.47**	**0.40**	**0.71**	**0.43**	1.00	**0.59**	-0.33	**-0.39**	-0.04	0.01	-0.26	**0.54**
FP SLEC	0.02	0.02	0.12	0.12	-0.01	-0.30	-0.17	-0.05	**0.53**	0.22	**0.53**	-0.28	**0.65**	**0.71**	**0.62**	**0.62**	**0.59**	1.00	-0.32	**-0.39**	0.01	0.01	-0.07	**0.54**
VTB SOPL	0.16	0.02	-0.10	-0.09	-0.05	-0.36	-0.04	0.27	0.08	0.02	0.21	-0.13	-0.33	**-0.38**	-0.24	-0.21	-0.33	-0.32	1.00	**0.62**	**0.57**	**0.59**	**0.50**	**-0.62**
VTB SONL	0.26	-0.09	-0.25	-0.25	-0.12	0.24	-0.09	0.13	-0.07	-0.09	-0.10	-0.21	**-0.53**	-0.26	**-0.50**	**-0.50**	**-0.39**	**-0.39**	**0.62**	1.00	**0.62**	**0.53**	**0.51**	**-0.54**
VTB SRP	0.12	0.18	0.21	-0.01	-0.01	-0.09	0.13	0.04	0.22	0.18	0.18	-0.27	-0.19	-0.05	-0.26	-0.24	-0.04	0.01	**0.57**	**0.62**	1.00	**0.74**	**0.59**	**-0.41**
VTB SRN	0.16	0.10	-0.01	-0.17	-0.17	0.04	0.04	0.13	0.18	0.28	0.28	-0.36	0.02	0.00	-0.05	0.14	0.01	0.01	**0.59**	**0.53**	**0.74**	1.00	**0.41**	**-0.31**
VTB WOFEC	0.13	-0.09	0.09	-0.04	-0.06	-0.13	-0.12	-0.01	-0.13	-0.01	-0.13	-0.08	-0.06	-0.23	-0.13	-0.23	-0.26	-0.07	**0.50**	**0.51**	**0.59**	**0.41**	1.00	**-0.29**
BESS	-0.16	-0.19	-0.07	0.02	0.24	0.24	-0.11	-0.24	-0.01	0.02	0.18	-0.05	**0.30**	**0.38**	**0.44**	**0.39**	**0.54**	**0.54**	**-0.62**	**-0.54**	**-0.41**	**-0.31**	**-0.29**	1.00

Note. Correlations in bold are significant at $p < .05$ (2-tailed). VTB = Vestibular, FP = Force platform, MS = Matching-to-sample test, FC = Four choice reaction time test, TC = Two-choice test. ACC – accuracy, AEO – amplitude eyes open, AEC – amplitude eyes closed, FEO – frequency eyes open, FEC = frequency eyes closed, DLEO – double leg eyes open, DLEC – double leg eyes closed, TEO – tandem eyes open, TEC – tandem eyes closed, SLEO – single leg eyes open, SLEC – single leg eyes closed.

[1]M. McCrea, K.M. Guskiewicz, S.W. Marshall, W. Barr, C. Randolph, R.C. Cantu, J.A. Onate, J Yang, and J.P. Kelly, "Acute effects and recovery time following concussion in collegiate football players," *Journal of the American Medical Association* Vol. 290, No. 19 (2003): 2556-2563.

[2]M. McCrea, K.M. Guskiewicz, S.W. Marshall, W. Barr, C. Randolph, R.C. Cantu, J.A. Onate, J Yang, and J.P. Kelly, "Acute effects and recovery time following concussion in collegiate football players," *Journal of the American Medical Association* Vol. 290, No. 19 (2003): 2556-2563.

[3]A. Legros, H.R. Marshall, A. Beuter, J. Gow, B. Cheung, A.W. Thomas, F.S. Prato, and R.Z. Stodilka, "Effects of acute hypoxia on postural and kinetic tremor," *Eur J Apl Physiol* Vol. 110, No. 1 (2010): 109-119.

[4]M. McCrea, K.M. Guskiewicz, S.W. Marshall, W. Barr, C. Randolph, R.C. Cantu, J.A. Onate, J Yang, and J.P. Kelly, "Acute effects and recovery time following concussion in collegiate football players," *Journal of the American Medical Association* Vol. 290, No. 19 (2003): 2556-2563.

[5]F.R. Sylvia, A.J. Drake, and D.C. Wester, "Transient vestibular dysfunction after primary blast injury," *Mil Med* 166, Vol. No. 10 (2001): 918-920.

[6]J. Cohen, G. Ziv, J. Bloom, D. Zikk, Y. Rapoport, and M. Himmelfarb, "Blast injury of the ear in a confined space explosion: Auditory and vestibular evaluation," *Israeli Journal of Military Medicine* Vol. 4, No. 7 (2002): 559-562.

[7]M. McCrea, K.M. Guskiewicz, S.W. Marshall, W. Barr, C. Randolph, R.C. Cantu, J.A. Onate, J Yang, and J.P. Kelly, "Acute effects and recovery time following concussion in collegiate football players," *Journal of the American Medical Association* Vol. 290, No. 19 (2003): 2556-2563; J.R. Basford, L-S. Chou, K.R. Kaufman, R.H Brey, A. Walker, J.F. Malec, A.M. Moessner, and A.W. Brown, "An assessment of gait and balance deficits after traumatic brain injury," *Arch Phys Med Rehabil* Vol. 84, No. 3 (2003): 343-349; K.M. Guskiewicz, D.H. Perrin, and B.M. Gansneder, "Effect of mild head injury on postural stability in athletes," *Journal of Athletic Training* 31, no. 4 (1996): 300-306; B.L. Riemann, and K.M. Guskiewicz, "Effects of mild head injury on postural stability as measured through clinical balance testing," *Journal of Athletic Training* Vol. 35, No. 1 (2000): 19-25; J.J Sosnoff, S.P. Broglio, and M.S. Ferrara, "Cognitive and motor function are associated following mild traumatic brain injury," *Exp Brain Res* Vol. 187, No. 4 (2008): 563-571; T.C. Valovich, D.H. Perrin, and B.M. Gansneder, "Repeat administration elicits a practice effect with the balance error scoring system but not with the standardized assessment of concussion in high school athletes," *Journal of Athletic Training* Vol. 38, No. 1 (2003): 51-56.

[8]A.R. Fregly, and A. Graybiel, "An ataxia test battery not requiring rails," *Aerospace Medicine* Vol. 39, No. 3 (1968): 277-282.

[9]R.J. Peterka, and F.O. Black, "Age-related changes in human posture control: Sensory organization tests," *Journal of Vestibular Research* Vol. 1, No. 1 (1990): 73-85.

[10]A.R. Fregly, M.J. Smith, and A. Graybiel "Revised normative standards of performance of men on a quantitative ataxia test battery," *Acta Otolaryngol* Vol. 75, No. 1 (1973):10-16.

[11]K.M. Guskiewicz, "Impaired Postural Stability: Regaining Balance," in *Techniques in Musculoskeletal Rehabilitation*, eds. W.E. Prentice and M.L. Voight (New York: McGraw Hill Medical Pub. Division, 2001), 125-150.

[12]B.L. Riemann, K.M. Guskiewicz, and E.W. Shields, "Relationship between clinical and forceplate measures of postural stability," *Journal of Sport Rehabilitation* 8, no. 2 (1999): 71-82.

[13]K.M. Guskiewicz, "Postural stability assessment following concussion: One piece of the puzzle," *Clinical Journal of Sport Medicine* Vol. 11, No. 3 (2001): 182-189.

[14]J.H. McAuley, and C.D. Marsden, "Physiological and pathological tremors and rhythmic central motor control," *Brain* Vol. 123, Pt. 8 (2000): 1545-1567.

[15]A. Beuter, and R. Edwards, "Using frequency domain characteristics to discriminate physiologic and Parkinsonian tremors," *J Clin Neurophysiol* Vol. 16, No. 5 (1999): 484-494.

[16]A. Legros, H.R. Marshall, A. Beuter, J. Gow, B. Cheung, A.W. Thomas, F.S. Prato, and R.Z. Stodilka, "Effects of acute hypoxia on postural and kinetic tremor," *Eur J Apl Physiol* 110, no. 1 (2010): 109-119.

[17]T. Tanielian, and L.H. Jaycox, eds. *Invisible wounds of war: Psychological and cognitive injuries, their consequences, and services to assist recovery*, eds. (Santa Monica, CA: RAND Corporation 2008).

[18]Petchprapai, N. and Winkelman, C., "Mild traumatic brain injury: Determinants and subsequent quality of life," *Journal of Neuroscience Nursing* Vol. 39, No. 5 (2007): 260-272.

[19]McCrea, Acute effects and recovery time following concussion in collegiate football players, 2556-2563; Masel, B.E. and DeWitt, D., "Traumatic brain injury: A disease process, not an event," *Journal of Neurotrauma* Vol. 27, No. 8 (2010): 1529-1540.

[20]A.R. Fregly, and A. Graybiel, "An ataxia test battery not requiring rails," *Aerospace Medicine* Vol. 39, No. 3 (1968): 277-282.

[21]B.L. Riemann, K.M. Guskiewicz, and E.W. Shields, "Relationship between clinical and forceplate measures of postural stability," *Journal of Sport Rehabilitation* Vol. 8, No. 2 (1999): 71-82.

[22]Alcan Airex AG, Switzerland.

[23]B.L. Riemann, K.M. Guskiewicz, and E.W. Shields, "Relationship between clinical and forceplate measures of postural stability," *Journal of Sport Rehabilitation* Vol. 8, No. 2 (1999): 71-82.

[24]Advanced Mechanical Technology Inc, Watertown, MA.

[25]Advanced Mechanical Technology Inc, Watertown, MA.

[26]J.A. Raymakers, M.M. Samson, and H.J.J. Verhaar, "The assessment of body sway and the choice of stability parameter(s)," *Gait and Posture* Vol. 21, No. 1 (2005): 48-58.

[27]A. Legros, H.R. Marshall, A. Beuter, J. Gow, B. Cheung, A.W. Thomas, F.S. Prato, and R.Z. Stodilka, "Effects of acute hypoxia on postural and kinetic tremor," *Eur J Apl Physiol* Vol. 110, No. 1 (2010): 109-119.

[28]Matsushita Electronic Work, Ltd., Osaka, Japan.

[29]J.H. McAuley, and C.D. Marsden, "Physiological and pathological tremors and rhythmic central motor control," *Brain* Vol. 123, Pt. 8 (2000): 1545-1567; A. Beuter, and R. Edwards, "Using frequency domain characteristics to discriminate physiologic and Parkinsonian tremors," *J Clin Neurophysiol* Vol. 16, No. 5 (1999): 484-494.

[30]A. Legros, H.R. Marshall, A. Beuter, J. Gow, B. Cheung, A.W. Thomas, F.S. Prato, and R.Z. Stodilka, "Effects of acute hypoxia on postural and kinetic tremor," *Eur J Apl Physiol* Vol. 110, No. 1 (2010): 109-119.

[31]NTT Systems Inc., North York, Ontario.

[32]H.R. Lieberman, C.M. Caruso, P.J. Niro, G.E. Adam, M.D. Kellogg, B.C. Nindl, and F.M. Kramer, "A double-blind, placebo-controlled test of 2 d of calorie deprivation: effects on cognition, activity, sleep, and interstitial glucose concentrations," *Am J Clin Nutri* Vol. 88, No. 3 (2008):667–676.

[33]R.A. Zachary, *Shipley Institute of Living Scale: Revised manual*. (Los Angeles: Western Psychological Services 1986).

[34]R.A. Zachary, E. Crumpton, and D.E. Spiegel, "Estimating WAIS-R IQ from the Shipley Institute of Living Scale," *Journal of Clinical Psychology*, Vol. 41, No. 4 (1985):532-540.

[35]M. McCrea, K.M. Guskiewicz, S.W. Marshall, W. Barr, C. Randolph, R.C. Cantu, J.A. Onate, J Yang, and J.P. Kelly, "Acute effects and recovery time following concussion in collegiate football players," *Journal of the American Medical Association* Vol. 290, No. 19 (2003): 2556-2563; B.L. Riemann, K.M. Guskiewicz, and E.W. Shields, "Relationship between clinical and forceplate measures of postural stability," *Journal of Sport Rehabilitation* Vol. 8, No. 2 (1999): 71-82.

[36]T.C. Valovich, D.H. Perrin, B.M. Gansneder, "Repeat Administration Elicits a Practice Effect With the Balance Error Scoring System but Not With the Standardized Assessment of Concussion in High School Athletes", *Journal of Athletic Training* Vol. 38, No. 1 (2003): 51-56.

[37]J.A. Onate, B.C. Beck, and B.L.V. Lunen, "On-field testing environment and balance error scoring system performance during preseason screening of healthy collegiate baseball players," *Journal of Athletic Training* Vol. 42, No. 4 (2007): 446-451.

[38]B.L. Riemann, K.M. Guskiewicz, and E.W. Shields, "Relationship between clinical and forceplate measures of postural stability," *Journal of Sport Rehabilitation* Vol. 8, No. 2 (1999): 71-82.

[39]G.L. Iverson, M.L. Kaarto, and M.S. Koehle, "Normative data for the balance error scoring system: Implications for brain injury evaluations," *Brain Injury* Vol. 22, No. 2 (2008): 147-152.

[40]Alcan Airex AG, Switzerland.

[41]A. Beuter, and R. Edwards, "Using frequency domain characteristics to discriminate physiologic and Parkinsonian tremors," *J Clin Neurophysiol* Vol. 16, No. 5 (1999): 484-494.

CHAPTER 11

Mental Health Care for Canadian Forces Members in Afghanistan

Colonel Rakesh Jetly, OMM, CD, MD, FRCPC, Psychiatry and
Mental Health Advisor to Surgeon General;
Major Alexandra Heber, MD, FRCPC, Clinical Leader of Mental Health,
Canadian Forces Health Services Centre (Ottawa)

ABSTRACT

Members of the Canadian Forces have been exposed to greater physical and psychological stressors during their current mission in Kandahar than any conflict in recent memory. Because of this, a robust multidisciplinary mental health team now deploys on each rotation. Contrary to popular thought only about one half of all cases presenting to mental health are related to psychological trauma. The remaining cases represent other illnesses and likely reflect the base rate of these illnesses in the population. Most cases fit into four categories: pre-existing conditions; new onset of illness; trauma related disorders and psychosocial issues. While treatment of these disorders is well outlined in current literature, a significant challenge is adapting or translating treatment approaches to a war zone.

mTBI is an emerging topic in the military medical community. The term includes concussion, and possible persistent neuropsychiatric symptoms in some. The Canadian Forces have developed clinical guidelines for the management of acute concussions during operations.

This chapter explores the challenges of practicing "war zone psychiatry" through case examples, and the description of the shared care approach in theatre. The care team can include social workers, nurses, medical officers, medics, chaplains, and in some cases assistance from the patient's colleagues and chain of command. The issue of mTBI in theatre is reviewed, and the controversy surrounding the relationship between mTBI and PTSD is discussed.

MENTAL HEALTH CARE FOR CANADIAN FORCES MEMBERS IN AFGHANISTAN

Not since the Korean War, have the CF engaged in combat missions like those in Afghanistan. Combat, asymmetric warfare, violent insurgency and the constant threat of IEDs all contribute to the psychological stressors experienced by Canadian soldiers. The psychiatric and neuropsychiatric causalities, like their physical counterparts, present unique challenges to leadership and the clinicians responsible for the management of these mental health conditions in theatre.

In 2008, the RAND Corporation published a report raising awareness of the so-called invisible "signature wounds" of the current conflicts. RAND predicted that PTSD and mTBI would account for a very large number of psychologically and cognitively impaired veterans.[1]

A multidisciplinary clinical team (psychiatrists, social workers and mental health nurses) is deployed with the soldiers to the base in Kandahar Airfield (KAF). This self-contained team has the capability to diagnose and treat soldiers with both medication and psychotherapy, with the objective of helping them complete their tour, whenever possible.

It is interesting to note that trauma-related conditions such as Combat Stress, Acute Stress Disorder (ASD) and PTSD account for, at most, 50% of cases presented to the mental health team in theatre. Given the high prevalence rates for mental illness in the general population, (lifetime prevalence for mood and anxiety disorders approaching 20%),[2] the presence of these mental illnesses in the deployed CF population is understandable. Presentations to the Kandahar Mental Health Clinic generally fit into one of four categories.

The first large group is soldiers with pre-existing mental illness. The spectrum of illness in this group is very broad, covering mood disorders such as Major Depressive Disorder, anxiety disorders such as PTSD or Obsessive Compulsive Disorder (OCD), and substance abuse disorders. Many in this category may not have been previously diagnosed, but the illness becomes apparent in theatre, as it causes difficulty in the member's functioning. Others may have received a diagnosis and treatment in the past, but the illness was in remission and was not expected to interfere with deployment.

The second group is one in which the illness presents itself for the first time during deployment. This could include the above examples or illnesses typically not seen in active military members, such as schizophrenia or severe bipolar disorder. The emergence of these illnesses may be entirely coincidental to deployment and explained by epidemiological risk or deployment factors such as stress and sleep deprivation, which may unmask an otherwise dormant condition.

Trauma-specific conditions comprise the third category. From a diagnostic perspective, these include Adjustment Disorder, ASD and PTSD.[3] A nonclinical term commonly used by soldiers to describe their symptoms is combat operational stress reaction (COSR). The clinical term that best describes this condition is Adjustment Disorder or ASD. These conditions pose the greatest challenge to the treatment team as they are often present in large numbers of troops, often days after a significant event (such as an IED explosion with loss of life). The challenge is to apply or adapt best practices from our largely civilian literature to these soldiers. The cornerstone of treating psychological trauma in civilian practice is exposure based therapy which "exposes" patients to feared situations, while at the same time cognitively helping them to realize the trauma is part of the past. In theatre, we can certainly expose soldiers to feared situations; however, the actual trauma and risk is still present. Treating trauma-related disorders in the face of ongoing risk is a challenge. It is in this group that our most novel pharmacological approaches are most useful. Beta-blockers in the acute aftermath of trauma bring almost immediate relief from tremor and panic. Prazosin, a traditional antihypertensive, is often effective for PTSD-related nightmares.

The final category is one in which psychosocial issues, commonly family problems from the home front, dominate and interfere with the functioning of the member. Marital or relationship problems are the most frequent examples in this category. These issues are typically not in the realm of psychiatry; however, they can be a significant distraction for the individual and may jeopardize a mission. Therefore the psychiatrist's clinical leadership will be called upon to organize a solution. Management of these issues often involves creative approaches such as clinicians conducting couples therapy simultaneously in Kandahar and at the home base.

The above categories encompass the types of conditions that we often see in garrison. The challenge is to adapt the best practices and treatment guidelines that psychiatry has developed over the years to the very difficult setting found in a war zone. For example, it is not always clear that our civilian-centred treatment guidelines for Major Depression or PTSD are applicable to soldiers at war.

The psychiatrist and mental health team working in theatre must be flexible. Much of the work occurs outside of the clinical office. After arriving in KAF on each new rotation, one of the priorities of the mental health team members is to get themselves known, and to get to know the troops. Because conditions change so quickly in a war zone, it is imperative that members of the mental health team are easily available at all times. Much of the work occurs in informal settings, such as having coffee with a distressed member on the boardwalk in KAF. The "helping network" of the psychiatrist expands in the arena of war, and becomes more inclusive. The medical officer, the nurse and the medic, frequently in conjunction with a chaplain and a suffering member's chain of command, become members of this "helping network". Often a concerned senior NCO (non-commissioned officer) is the one to bring a soldier in to be seen by the mental health team. Similarly, Commanding Officers often call to request a mental health worker to travel "outside the wire" to offer support and assess CF members following a mortar attack or an IED that left some of his troops dead or injured. Educational sessions on topics such as "How to Recognize Combat Stress" are delivered to reinforce pre-deployment mental health training. Mental health clinicians may also provide education to other health care providers, for example by providing medical assistants training on the use of the MACE (Military Acute Concussion Evaluation) for suspected concussions. These approaches allow the mental health team to reach out to make themselves and their expertise known and available.

mTBI is another area that has received a lot of attention. This disorder can include long-term cognitive and neurological symptoms, and is currently an area of much research and debate. Here the challenge has been to translate and adapt lessons learned from sports concussions. Is the concussion from a blast comparable to having one's "bell rung" playing hockey or football? The challenge to explain the very significant psychiatric component of mTBI also challenges the attribution of long-term sequelae to the head injury.[4]

In May of 2008, the Canadian Forces Health Services convened an international expert panel to develop clinical guidelines for head injury during deployed operations.[5] The meeting resulted in a consensus paper that discussed the approach to concussions that is now applied in theatre, a plan for surveillance through utilization of post-deployment screening and guidance for in-garrison care of persistent post-deployment symptoms.

An algorithm describing the in-theatre management (see Figure 11.1) has been in use since 2008. Essentially a soldier exposed to a blast is assessed as soon as it is safe to do so. Any trained clinician, including the medical technicians who accompany soldiers on all missions, may conduct the assessment. The algorithm is applied to all suspected or confirmed head injuries. The immediate priority is to assess for any "red flags," such as declining levels of consciousness, pupillary asymmetry and vomiting. If these symptoms are present, the soldier is evacuated to a higher level of care. Symptoms such as headache, dizziness, nausea and vertigo are noted. After history of head injury is confirmed and red flags are ruled out the MACE is administered.[6] This scale, adapted from sports medicine, is a rapid screen for concussions by assessing orientation, immediate memory, concentration and memory recall. A positive history of head injury and significant deficits on MACE leads to a soldier being forced to rest and avoid risk of further head trauma. Frequent re-evaluation is suggested and a soldier is not returned to combat until MACE score normalizes and there is a complete absence of symptoms even after provocation through physical exertion.

The best scientific studies in the sports literature (primarily dealing with impact injuries) suggests that in the majority of cases of mTBI, symptoms and measurable neurological deficits resolve within a week,[7] and most other studies show resolution within a few weeks to months.[8] This fact leads to a significant debate amongst experts with regards to an explanation of persistent symptoms months or years after the initial concussion. Hoge *et al.*, suggest a very strong association between PTSD and mTBI.[9]

A recent examination of Canadian Forces post deployment screening data found that mental health conditions such as PTSD were a greater predictor of "mTBI symptoms" than concussion or head injury. The screening utilizes screening questionnaires that ask respondents to describe amongst other things a history of head injury, physical symptoms and mental health problems. Preliminary results from 1,817 screenings performed three to six months after deployment show that 6.4% reported mTBI/concussion while deployed. Most of these were on the mild end of the mTBI/concussion spectrum in that only four individuals (0.2%) reported mTBI/concussion with loss of consciousness of more than 20 minutes. Blast was a mechanism of injury in 67% of those reporting mTBI/concussion.162 (9%) of those screened reported three or more "post-concussive" symptoms (e.g., headache, dizziness, irritability). Such symptoms were seen in 26 (22%) of those reporting mTBl/concussion, in 45 (14%) of those reporting injuries other than mTBl/concussion, and in 91 (7%) of the uninjured. It is noteworthy that 84% of cases with post-concussive symptoms occurred in those without mTBl/concussion. The association of these symptoms with mental health problems was far stronger than their association with mTBl/concussion (odds ratios of 32 and 4.0, respectively).[10]

The above suggests a mechanism other than head injury to explain the chronic symptoms attributed to concussion. The nonspecificity of these symptoms and strong overlap with mental health disorders such as PTSD suggest that the mental health condition may have mediating affect on the expression of late and persistent symptoms. The lack of specificity of symptoms and a lack of specific treatments for post concussive syndrome suggest an aggressive treatment of the mental health disorders that do have evidence-based treatments. The in-theatre approach is to treat symptoms such as headache with analgesics and use therapies such as cognitive behaviour therapies and medications to treat any mental health conditions present.

In conclusion, Canadian Forces mental health professionals are being challenged in Afghanistan in a manner unlike any mission in recent memory. Trauma-specific psychiatric conditions represent a significant proportion of cases, although another very large proportion is not attributable to trauma and may reflect the base rate of mental illness in the CF population. mTBl/concussion also presents a unique challenge, as cases must be immediately identified to prevent further injury. The lack of specific symptoms and treatment approaches, coupled with significant psychiatric symptoms in chronic mTBI, challenge the simple attribution of symptoms solely to the head injury.

In a war zone, psychiatrists and the rest of the mental health team need to be creative and flexible in their approach, and to apply due diligence and excellent clinical care in the constantly changing and high-risk environment.

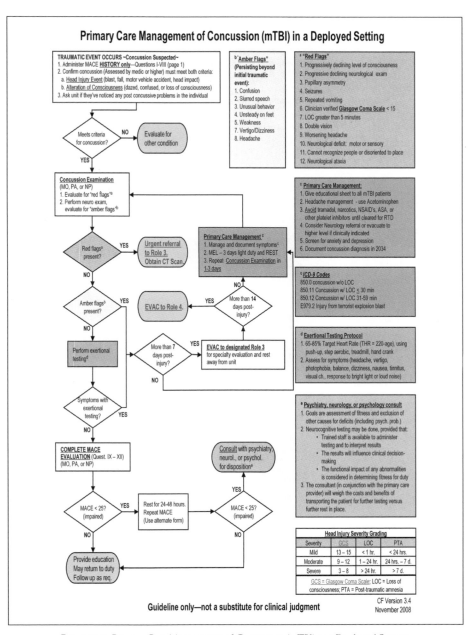

Figure 11.1: Primary Care Management of Concussion (mTBI) in a Deployed Setting.

Canadian Forces, "Canadian Forces Health Services Advisory Panel on Management of Mild Traumatic Brain Injury in Military Operational Settings," May 2008, accessed from http://www.forces.gc.ca/health-sante/ps/dh-sd/tbi-tcl-eng.asp

[1]Center for Military Health Policy Research, *Invisible Wounds of War: Psychological and Cognitive Injuries, their Consequences, and Services to Assist Recovery* (Santa Monica, CA: RAND Corportation; 2008).

[2]R.C. Kessler *et al.*, "Lifetime and 12-month Prevalence of DSM-III-R Psychiatric Disorders in the United States: Results from the National Comorbidity Survey," *Arch Gen Psychiatry* 51, 1 (1994): 8-19.

[3]American Psychiatric Association. *Diagnostic and Statistical Manual of Mental Disorders*: DSM-IV-TR (Washington, DC: American Psychiatric Association; 2000).

[4]C.W. Hoge *et al.*, "Mild Traumatic Brain Injury in U.S. Soldiers Returning from Iraq," *New England Journal of Medicine* 358, 5 (31 January 2008): 453-63.

[5]Canadian Forces Health Services Advisory Panel on Management of Mild Traumatic Brain Injury in Military Operational Settings, "Clinical Practice Guidelines and Recommendations," Canadian Forces Web Site 2009, accessed from http://www.forces.gc.ca/health-sante/ps/dhsd/pdf/mildtraumaticbraininjury-traumatismecerebralleger-eng.pdf, accessed 14 April 2011.

[6]Defense and Veterans Brain Injury Center Working Group, "On the Acute Management of Mild Traumatic Brain Injury in Military Operational Settings: Clinical Practice Guidelines and Recommendations," Defense and Veterans Brain Injury Center Web Site, 22 Dec 2006, http://dvbic.org/public_html/pdfs/clinical_practice_guideline_recommendations.pdf, accessed 14 April 2011.

[7]M. McCrea *et al.*, "Acute Effects and Recovery Time Following Concussion in Collegiate Football Players: The NCAA Concussion Study," *JAMA* 290, 19 (2003): 2556-2563; J. Bleiberg *et al.*, "Duration of cognitive impairment after sports concussion. *Neurosurgery* 54, 5 (2004): 1073-1078; L.J. Carroll *et al.*, "Prognosis for mild traumatic brain injury: results of the WHO Collaborating Centre Task Force on Mild Traumatic Brain Injury," *J Rehabil Med* 43 (2004): 84-105.

[8]L.J. Carroll *et al.*, "Prognosis for Mild Traumatic Brain Injury: Results of the WHO Collaborating Centre Task Force on Mild Traumatic Brain Injury," *J Rehabil Med* 43 (2004): 84-105.

[9]C.W. Hoge *et al.*, "Mild Traumatic Brain Injury in U.S. Soldiers Returning from Iraq," *New England Journal of Medicine* 358, 5 (31 January 2008): 453-63.

[10]M.A. Zamorski, *Preliminary Report on the Self-Reported Incidence of Mild Traumatic Brain Injury/Concussion in CF Members Deployed in Support of the Mission in Afghanistan* (Ottawa: Department of National Defence (Canada); 2009).

CHAPTER 12

Treatment Outcomes of Canadian Military Personnel Receiving Pharmacotherapy, Psychotherapy, or Both for an Operational Stress Injury: A Pilot Study

Kate St. Cyr, MSc, Maya L. Roth, PhD, J.Don Richardson, M.D., Alexandra McIntyre-Smith, PhD, & Nancy Cameron, Parkwood Hospital Operational Stress Injury Clinic, St. Joseph's Health Care London

ABSTRACT

Research shows that some military personnel experience mental health problems such as Post Traumatic Stress Disorder, depression, and anxiety following deployment, and recent studies show that a number of these individuals seek treatment. The objective of the current study is to explore differences in treatment outcomes between three types of therapy offered at the Parkwood Hospital Operational Stress Injury Clinic: pharmacotherapy alone, combined pharmacotherapy and psychotherapy, and psychotherapy alone. A retrospective chart study of thirty individuals receiving either pharmacotherapy (n=10), pharmacotherapy and individual psychotherapy (n=10), or individual psychotherapy (n=10) and who completed the Posttraumatic Stress Checklist – Military version (PCL-M), the Beck Depression Inventory-II (BDI-II), and the Beck Anxiety Inventory (BAI) at intake and one, three, and six months of treatment was conducted. A repeated measures general linear model was used to compare differences in mean PCL-M, BDI-II, and BAI scores of each group. Differences in mean PCL-M, BDI-II, and BAI scores between groups at baseline and one, three, and six months of treatment were not statistically significant; however these mean scores varied between groups along the clinical pathway and some trends emerged. Further research and a larger sample are required to better understand trends within groups.

TREATMENT OUTCOMES OF CANADIAN MILITARY PERSONNEL RECEIVING PHARMACOTHERAPY, PSYCHOTHERAPY, OR BOTH FOR AN OPERATIONAL STRESS INJURY: A PILOT STUDY

The association between deployment experiences, particularly exposure to combat, and adverse mental health outcomes known as operational stress injuries, such as depression and PTSD, has been well documented in the literature for many years.[1] Estimates of the prevalence of PTSD and depression in military personnel vary, but recent studies show that between 1.4 and 31.1% of American soldiers deployed to Iraq will go on to develop PTSD or depression with moderate to serious functional impairment;[2] however, most studies report a more consistent rate of 10-17%.[3] The lifetime prevalence rate of PTSD in deployed Canadian peacekeepers (approximately 11%)[4] continues to be higher than in the Canadian civilian population (9.2%).[5] Previous research demonstrates that not only is there a self-perceived need for mental health service utilization following deployment among CF personnel, a substantial proportion of military personnel who acknowledge a need for treatment will seek it.[6]

Current treatment modalities for PTSD fall largely into two categories: pharmacotherapy, and psychotherapy. The primary objectives of pharmacotherapy for PTSD are to: 1) reduce the severity of core symptoms of PTSD, such as hyperarousal, avoidance and emotional numbing, and re-experiencing; 2) improve daily functioning and disability stemming from PTSD; and 3) increase resilience and adaptive coping abilities.[7] A number of pharmacologic agents are available to treat PTSD, and literature shows a range in the effectiveness of each on the reduction of PTSD symptomatology. However, methodological issues inherent to pharmacological studies complicate both the interpretation of the results of the study and the generalization of results to a broader population; therefore, it is important for clinicians to keep this in mind when considering the inclusion of a pharmacologic agent in a treatment plan.

Pharmacologic treatment of PTSD with selective serotonin reuptake inhibitors (SSRIs) has been shown to reduce the severity of a number of central symptoms of PTSD including avoidance, depression, hyperarousal, and intrusive thoughts[8] in randomized clinical trials of civilians,[9] but has been shown to be slightly less effective in samples of military veterans with chronic PTSD.[10] Response rates to SSRIs are moderate - Stein and colleagues (2002) demonstrated that they rarely exceed 60%, and that a mere 20-30% of SSRI users will achieve remission of their PTSD symptoms by using SSRIs alone.[11] Additionally, a meta-analysis of treatment modalities for PTSD revealed that effect sizes noted in pharmacologic trials for PTSD were, for the most part, smaller than effects for psychotherapeutic modalities, though effect sizes for the most effective psychotherapeutic (cognitive-behavioural therapy and eye-movement desensitization and reprocessing) and pharmacologic modalities (SSRIs and carbamazepine) were similar.[12] SSRIs such as sertraline, paroxetine, and citalopram have demonstrated reasonable effectiveness at reducing PTSD symptomatology and continue to be used, both alone and in conjunction with psychotherapy, to treat PTSD.[13]

Dual action serotonin-norepinephrine reuptake inhibitors (SNRIs) have also been shown to reduce PTSD symptomatology more effectively than placebo in two large-scale studies; however, similarly to studies involving SSRIs, observed effect sizes were small.[14] Other pharmacologic agents that have been used to treat PTSD symptoms include tricyclic antidepressants, monoamine oxidase inhibitors (MAOIs), novel antidepressants such as bupropion, benzodiazepines, anticonvulsants, and atypical antipsychotics.[15] Tricyclic antidepressants, such as amitryptiline and imipramine, prevent the uptake of the neurotransmitters serotonin and norepinephrine, and have been demonstrated to reduce anxious and depressive symptoms, flashbacks, feelings of guilt, and sleep difficulties such as insomnia and nightmares.[16] MAOIs such as phenelzine increase serotonin, dopamine, and norepinephrine in the brain by preventing the breakdown of the neurotransmitter monoamine, and have typically been used in the treatment of depression and anxiety.[17] Both positive and negative outcomes have been reported for MAOIs in controlled trials.[18] Novel antidepressants such as bupropion, mirtazapine, venlafaxine, and trazodone may contribute to the reduction of PTSD and anxious symptoms, as well as nightmares and sleep disturbance. However, similarly to SSRIs, studies have shown novel antidepressants to be somewhat less effective in military trauma samples compared to civilian cohorts.[19] Few studies to date have examined the efficacy of benzodiazepines in the treatment of PTSD though the results of these studies demonstrate that benzodiazepines may reduce symptoms of anxiety that often accompany PTSD without actually improving the symptoms of PTSD itself.[20] As such, benzodiazepines are not often recommended as a monotherapeutic treatment option for PTSD.[21] Anticonvulsants have been demonstrated to be effective at reducing impulsive and aggressive behaviours, as well as intrusive thoughts and hypervigilance in individuals with PTSD.[22] While controlled trials of anticonvulsants for PTSD are, at this point in time, limited, one study demonstrated a response rate to an anticonvulsant of 50%, compared to a response rate of 25% for placebo.[23] As such, anticonvulsants may be particularly effective when used in conjunction with first-line treatment options. Lastly, a small number of open trials have demonstrated the usefulness of atypical antipsychotics as augmentation in the treatment of PTSD. Though not routinely used to treat individuals with PTSD until recently, the results of these studies have shown atypical antipsychotics contribute to reductions in the severity of depressive and PTSD symptomatology, as well as nightmares and flashbacks.[24]

While a considerable number of studies have shown pharmacotherapy to be effective in treating PTSD,[25] there remains debate about whether pharmacotherapy is more than or as effective as trauma-based psychotherapy, which has been traditionally viewed as the gold-standard in the treatment of PTSD.[26] Psychotherapy for PTSD can be offered both as individual psychotherapy and in group session. Currently, trauma-focused cognitive-behavioural therapy (CBT) is considered the optimal treatment modality for PTSD.[27] Trauma-focused CBT, which includes prolonged exposure (PE) therapy, aims to accomplish three objectives: 1) to engage the client emotionally with the memory of the traumatic event; 2) to organize the traumatic event into a narrative; and 3) to restructure dysfunctional thoughts related to the memory of the traumatic event;[28] and often includes *in vivo* "homework" assignments to improve coping with reminders of the trauma.[29] The efficacy of trauma-based therapy for PTSD, especially PE, has been established in numerous settings, and has been assessed as both a monotherapeutic treatment and in concurrence with other forms of treatment.[30] While not all individuals respond positively to PE, [31] it remains one of the most widely used forms of therapy for victims of trauma.

Both published research and clinical experience suggests that combined pharmacotherapy and psychotherapy may be reciprocally beneficial. Otto and colleagues (2003) found that, in a controlled trial, combined sertraline and CBT was more effective than sertraline alone.[32] Hollon and colleagues (1992) found that combined pharmacotherapy and psychotherapy for depression produced improved responses than either treatment modality alone, though the differences were not statistically significant.[33]   However, no study to date has explored differences in treatment outcomes for PTSD, depression, and anxiety in CF members.   Therefore, the aims of the current study are to 1) determine whether differences exist in treatment outcomes between three types of therapy (pharmacotherapy alone, combined pharmacotherapy and psychotherapy, and psychotherapy alone); and 2) identify trends within groups along the clinical pathway. The authors of this study hypothesize that there will be differences both within and between groups along the clinical pathway.

METHOD

A retrospective chart review of thirty individuals receiving treatment for an Operational Stress Injury (OSI) at the Parkwood Hospital OSI Clinic was conducted; ten of these individuals were receiving pharmacotherapy services only, ten more were receiving both pharmacotherapy and individual psychotherapy, and the remaining ten participants were receiving individual psychotherapy only.

INCLUSION CRITERIA

Participants were deemed eligible for inclusion in the pharmacotherapy group if they were: 1) a currently serving or former Canadian Forces members who experienced a military-related trauma; 2) had been diagnosed with an OSI; and 3) were receiving or had received pharmacotherapy at the Parkwood Hospital OSI Clinic. Participants were excluded from enrolment in this group if they were receiving any concurrent psychotherapeutic services, either at the OSI clinic or in their home community. Participants were deemed eligible for inclusion in the pharmacotherapy and psychotherapy combined group if they were: 1) a currently serving or former Canadian Forces members who experienced a military-related trauma; 2) had been diagnosed with an OSI; and 3) were receiving or had received pharmacotherapy and psychotherapy at the Parkwood Hospital OSI Clinic. Participants were excluded from enrolment in this group if they were receiving either concurrent psychotherapeutic or psychiatric services in their home community. Finally, participants were deemed eligible for inclusion in the psychotherapy group if they were: 1) a currently serving or former Canadian Forces members who experienced a military-related trauma; 2) had been diagnosed with an OSI; and 3) were receiving or had received psychotherapy at the Parkwood Hospital OSI Clinic. Participants were excluded from enrolment in this group if they were receiving any concurrent psychiatric services, either at the OSI clinic or in their home community.

MEASURES

Participants completed three psychological assessment tools at baseline and one, three, and six months of treatment: the Beck Anxiety Inventory (BAI; Beck *et al*, 1988),[34] the Beck Depression Inventory – II (BDI-II; Beck *et al*, 1996),[35] and the PTSD Checklist -

Military Version (PCL-M; Weathers *et al*, 1993).[36] Scores from these measures were extracted at commencement and one, three, and six months of treatment from participants' testing charts.

The BAI is a 21-item self-report measure that assesses anxiety symptom severity. Respondents rate items on a scale of 0 to 3 according to how much they are bothered by each item, where 0 = "not at all" and 3 = "severely, I could barely stand it". The BAI is positively correlated with the revised Hamilton Anxiety Inventory ($r = 0.51$) and has demonstrated excellent internal consistency ($\alpha = 0.94$) and acceptable reliability ($r = 0.67$).[37]

The BDI is a 21-item self-report measure that measures the presence and severity of depressive symptoms. Respondents rank each item on a 4-point scale, where 0 = less severe symptomatology and 3 = most severe. Total scores range from 0-63.[38] The BDI is strongly correlated with the revised Hamilton Psychiatric Rating Scale for Depression (Riskind, Beck, Brown, & Steer, 1987) ($r = 0.71$),[39] and has demonstrated high internal consistency ($\alpha = 0.92$ among outpatients; $\alpha = 0.91$ among undergraduate students) and adequate content and factorial validity.[40]

The PCL-M is a self-administered, 17-item scale that provides an estimate of PTSD symptom severity related to a distressing military-specific traumatic experience. Using a 5-point scale, respondents rank how affected they have been by each of 17 symptoms over the past month; a total score indicating the severity of PTSD symptoms is tabulated by summing all 17 item responses (range = 17-85).[41]

Data Analysis

Data was analyzed with PASW Statistics 17.0 (SPSS Inc, Chicago, Illinois). A repeated measures general linear model (GLM) was conducted to compare differences between and within groups at baseline and one, three, and six months of treatment. Effect sizes were measured as partial eta-squared ($\eta^2 p$) using previously utilized values of 0.01, 0.06, and 0.14 to reflect small, medium, and large effect sizes, respectively.[42]

Participant Data

The mean age of participants at entry into the study was 42.9 years (SD = 12.7). All but one participant were male (96.7%; n = 29), and two-thirds were CF veterans (66.7%; n = 20); the remaining ten individuals (33.3%) were currently serving Regular or Reserve Force members.

93.3% (n = 28) of participants met Diagnostic and Statistical Manual for Mental Disorders - IV (DSM-IV) criteria for PTSD, and 60% (n = 18) met DSM-IV criteria for MDD. 20% (n=6) also had a substance use disorder diagnosis. Other Axis I diagnoses including various anxiety disorders (n = 4), obsessive-compulsive disorder (OCD; n = 3), attention deficit hyperactivity disorder (ADHD; n = 2), and panic disorder (n = 2). 86.7% (n = 26) of participants had more than one Axis I diagnosis, with PTSD and MDD being the most common comorbidities, while the remaining 4 individuals (13.3%) had a single psychiatric diagnosis. Diagnoses were made following an interview with a OSI clinic psychologist or psychiatrist, and were confirmed using the results of the Clinician-Administered PTSD Scale (CAPS) and, in some instances, the Structured Clinical Interview for DSM Disorders (SCID).

Treatment sessions for individuals with multiple psychiatric diagnoses focused on treating the primary diagnosis, or the diagnosis causing the most distress for the client, first. On average, participants received 12.58 sessions of therapy over the course of the current study (SD = 3.34; range = 7-18); however participants in the pharmacotherapy group received fewer treatment sessions over the course of the study (n = 9.3) than those in either the combined therapy or psychotherapy group (14.0 and 14.4 sessions, respectively). Treatment was administered by one of five OSI clinicians – either a psychiatrist, psychologist, or clinical nurse specialist. Each participant was assigned a primary clinician who delivered all treatment sessions for that participant, with the exception of the individuals in the combined therapy group, who received treatment from both a psychiatrist and either a psychologist or clinical nurse specialist.

RESULTS

ATTRITION

Four individuals (40%) in the pharmacotherapy group did not complete the screening measures on at least one occasion, while one individual (10%) in the combined pharmacotherapy/psychotherapy group did not complete all screening measures on all four occasions. Seven individuals (70%) in the psychotherapy group did not complete the screening measures on all four occasions. Reasons for not completing measures may have been the result of a missed appointment, clinician error, or discontinuation of therapy entirely. Individuals who did not complete all three screening measures at all four points in time were excluded from any further analyses, leaving a final sample size of 18. The exclusion of these individuals ensured that missing data did not contaminate the results.

PTSD SYMPTOM SEVERITY

PTSD symptom severity, as measured by mean PCL-M scores, decreased for all three treatment groups from baseline to six months of treatment (M = 60.39, SD = 13.88 vs. M = 56.33, SD = 15.71). Some differences within treatment groups were evident (see Table 12.1). Within the pharmacotherapy group, two peaks in symptom severity can be observed: at baseline, and at three months of treatment. Within the pharmacotherapy and psychotherapy combined and psychotherapy alone groups, a steady decrease in symptom severity is evident until six months of treatment, when a slight increase in symptom severity is noted (see Table 12.1). When we tested for between-group effects, a substantial effect size was noted [$F(2, 15) = 1.339, p = 0.292, \eta^2p = 0.151$]. A moderate effect size was noted for time ($p = 0.319, \eta^2p = 0.074$). An analysis of the Group x Time interaction was also moderate ($p = 0.669, \eta^2p = 0.083$). The observed power for the effect sizes ranged from 0.241 to 0.301.

DEPRESSIVE SYMPTOM SEVERITY

Depressive symptom severity, as measured by mean BDI-II scores, decreased for all three treatment groups from baseline to six months of treatment ($M = 34.11, SD = 10.50$ vs. $M = 30.33, SD = 11.24$). When differences within treatment groups were examined, similar patterns to PTSD symptom severity were observed in all groups (see Table 12.1). Within the pharmacotherapy group, symptom severity continued to decrease from baseline to six months of treatment, with a evident increase in symptom severity at three months of treatment. Within the pharmacotherapy and psychotherapy group, a slow decline in symptom severity continues over the course of treatment, with a slight plateau in symptom severity at six months of treatment. Finally, in the psychotherapy group, no noticeable difference is apparent between mean scores at baseline and one month of treatment; however a significant increase in symptom severity is evident at six months of treatment (see Table 12.1). When between-group effects was tested, a moderate effect size was revealed [$F(2, 17) = 0.559, p = 0.583, \eta^2p = 0.069$]. A much smaller effect size was observed for time ($p = 0.793, \eta^2p = 0.021$); however, the Group x Time interaction for BDI scores was substantial ($p = 0.320, \eta^2p = 0.139$). Observed power for effect sizes ranged from 0.104 to 0.402.

ANXIETY SYMPTOM SEVERITY

Anxiety symptom severity, as measured by mean BAI scores, decreased for all three treatment groups from baseline to six months of treatment ($M = 24.78, SD = 11.85$ vs. $M = 22.44, SD = 13.40$). Within the pharmacotherapy group, a fairly noticeable increase in symptom severity is observable between one and three months of treatment (see Table 12.1). Within both the pharmacotherapy and psychotherapy group, and psychotherapy group, only small gains were made between anxiety symptom severity at baseline and six months of treatment, with a slight increase in symptom severity at one month of treatment (see Table 12.1). When between-group effects was tested, the effect size was substantial [$F(2, 17) = 1.517, p = 0.251, \eta^2p = 0.168$], however the effect size of time was quite small ($p = 0.9, 17 \eta2p = 0.011$). When the Group x Time interaction was examined, the effect size was small ($p = 0.963, \eta^2p = 0.030$). Observed power for effect sizes ranged from 0.079 to 0.272.

Measure	Treatment Group	Base-line	One month	Three months	Six months	Group (η^2_p)	Time (η^2_p)	Group x Time (η^2_p)
PCL-M	Pharmacotherapy alone	66.17 (12.27)	57.50 (12.96)	64.67 (10.11)	58.17 (16.77)	0.151	0.074	0.083
	Pharmacotherapy + psychotherapy	59.22 (14.64)	56.44 (17.38)	54.44 (15.89)	58.78 (14.64)			
	Psychotherapy alone	52.33 (14.19)	47.67 (14.64)	43.67 (7.57)	45.33 (18.01)			
BDI-II	Pharmacotherapy alone	34.17 (10.34)	29.83 (8.84)	35.00 (6.93)	27.00 (13.24)	0.069	0.021	0.139
	Pharmacotherapy + psychotherapy	36.33 (11.06)	34.67 (9.67)	31.89 (12.69)	31.56 (10.33)			
	Psychotherapy alone	27.33 (9.50)	27.00 (10.58)	23.67 (2.08)	33.33 (11.59)			
BAI	Pharmacotherapy alone	22.33 (7.71)	18.67 (4.80)	23.17 (6.62)	19.33 (15.25)	0.168	0.011	0.030
	Pharmacotherapy + psychotherapy	28.44 (12.78)	28.67 (13.60)	27.22 (12.78)	26.11 (12.84)			
	Psychotherapy alone	18.67 (16.01)	19.00 (14.93)	16.00 (8.54)	17.67 (12.66)			

Table 12.1. Mean PCL-M, BDI-II, and BAI scores (standard deviations in parentheses) by treatment group at baseline and one, three, and six months of treatment.

Discussion

Some interesting patterns were revealed when mean scores over time and by treatment group were examined. Within the pharmacotherapy group, a noticeable increase in symptom severity occurred at three months of treatment for all three measures. This increase in symptom severity at three months was followed by a clear decrease in symptom severity at six months of treatment. This may be explained by the provision of pharmacologic agents, which result in an immediate effect on symptom severity but require a dose escalation around three months of treatment.[43] This elucidation could also explain the decrease in symptom severity at six months of treatment.

Within the pharmacotherapy and psychotherapy combined group, slow and steady declines can be observed for mean BDI-II and BAI scores. While no large increases or decreases in symptom severity are evident over time within this treatment group, treatment gains are apparent when mean baseline and six months of treatment scores are inspected. Previous research suggests that the efficacy of combined pharmacotherapy and psychotherapy further along the clinical pathway may be the result of independent rather than synergistic mechanisms of action; meaning that apparent increases in treatment gains may actually be the result of an additive effect of one modality of therapy, rather than the two therapies mutually complementing each other to produce improved treatment outcomes.[44]

Finally, within the psychotherapy group, treatment gains are most noticeable around three months of treatment. The delay in achieving perceptible treatment gains may be attributed to the time required to build a therapeutic alliance.[45] Once this bond of trust has been established, patients can begin to work on their treatment goals in earnest. However, small increases in symptom severity can be observed at six months of treatment in both mean PCL-M and BAI scores. This may be attributed to more frequent engagement in reminders of the index trauma as trauma-based psychotherapy becomes more intense, or other confounding factors such as primary or other interpersonal relationship issues, which were not controlled for in this study.

There were some limitations inherent to the design of this study. The small sample size has important implications for the interpretation of the results and the generalizability of these results to other military populations. It is widely accepted that larger sample sizes typically produce more precise results and truer estimates of effect size.[46] A formal sample size calculation was not used for this study because a) it is a pilot study; and b) the authors hoped to include as many individuals as possible in order to increase the power of the study. However, the initial sample size (n = 30) was limited by the number of potential participants who met inclusion criteria for one of the three groups studied. It was further reduced (n = 18) because of incomplete data. As such, the final sample size did not produce enough power for the results to be interpreted as true effects rather than chance variations (range from 0.079 to 0.402), as a minimum power estimate of 0.80 is typically required in clinical studies.[47] It is likely because of the small sample size that moderate and substantial effect sizes were revealed in the analysis; these results should be interpreted with caution. Additionally, the final sample size of the psychotherapy group was substantially smaller than the pharmacotherapy and pharmacotherapy and psychotherapy combined groups (n = 3 vs. n = 6 and n = 8, respectively); therefore it is difficult to draw any conclusions about the effectiveness of psychotherapy alone based on these results.

A number of potentially significant baseline differences may exist between groups. Mean baseline scores for the combined therapy group tended to be higher than those of the pharmacotherapy or psychotherapy groups; likely because these individuals were experiencing more complex symptomatology than those whose treatment needs could be met with only one kind of therapy. Additionally, differences in the medications being prescribed for those in the pharmacotherapy group and the combined therapy group may have contributed to differences in symptom severity scores. Of those receiving psychiatric medication, 30% (n = 6) were receiving an SSRI while 85% (n = 17) were being prescribed a dual-acting antidepressant. Further to that, 60% (n = 12) were receiving an antipsychotic and 45% (n = 9) were taking an anticonvulsant; 35% (n = 7) were taking other psychiatric medication, such as benzodiazepines, stimulants, or hypnotics. All individuals (n = 20) were receiving more than one type of medication. The wide array of medications being prescribed to participants in the current study may have significant implications; namely that the effects of these medications may vary depending on a number of physiological and independent factors (e.g., adherence to medication dosage, tolerance of side effects, etc.) and these effects were not examined in the current study.

Furthermore, because treatment was administered to each participant by one of five therapists, there may have been differences in the types of therapy provided and the means in which they were provided. Future studies should further explore differences between modalities of psychotherapy, and compare each unique form of psychotherapy to both pharmacotherapy and combination therapy in order to better understand their efficacies.

The retrospective design of this study has some disadvantages. In particular, it is limited by its uncontrolled design, and the availability and accuracy of the data. Retrospective studies are typically considered less useful than prospective studies, due to a number of inherent design issues, such as difficulty controlling bias and confounding, and reliance on the accuracy of the existing data.[48] However, preliminary retrospective studies such as this one may be useful in hypothesis-generating and the planning of a similar prospective study, in which the authors are able to control the intervention.[49]

Additionally, the use of partial eta-squared for measuring effect sizes ($\eta2p$) is somewhat controversial. Most commonly used for factorial ANOVA designs, Levine and Hullett

(2002) suggest that the partial eta-squared estimate often produces inflated effect sizes, especially when the sample size is small.[50] Moreover, "effect size interpretation should be context specific, weighing the merits and potential unreliability of the study methodology against potential real-world impact of small or large effects."[51] Therefore, the effect sizes reported in this study should be interpreted with caution.

The results of this study show that differences in treatment outcomes exist between pharmacotherapy, pharmacotherapy and psychotherapy combined, and psychotherapy along the clinical pathway, and these findings warrant further investigation in a larger, prospective sample of Canadian military personnel. By increasing the sample size and therefore the power of the study, any true differences in treatment outcomes between therapeutic modalities may become evident, and the results may be more generalizable to other military populations. In addition, a sudden gains analysis could be conducted to provide further insight to the trends observed in this study; however, this would require a larger quantity of prospective longitudinal data.

A prospective study design would provide the authors with the opportunity to develop a stronger methodology and reduce the amount of missing data, thereby increasing the generalizability of any novel research findings to other military samples and the ability to make recommendations for modified treatment guidelines for military personnel with complex chronic PTSD.

[1]J.D. Richardson, J. Peveski, and J.D. Elhai, "Posttraumatic stress disorder and health problems among medically ill Canadian peacekeeping veterans," *Australian and New Zealand Journal of Psychiatry* 43, 4 (2009): 370; C.W. Hoge, C.A. Castro, S.C. Messer, D. McGurk, D.I. Cotting, and R.L. Koffman, (2004). "Combat duty in Iraq and Afghanistan, mental health problems, and barriers to care," *NEJM* 351, 1 (2004): 14.

[2]P.D. Bliese, K.M. Wright, A.B. Adler, J.L. Thomas, and C.W. Hoge, "Timing of Postcombat Mental Health Assessments," *Psychological Services* 4, 3 (2007): 144-146; C.W. Hoge, A. Terhakopian, C.A. Castro, S.C. Messer, and C.C. Engel, "Association of posttraumatic stress disorder with somatic symptoms, health care visits, and absenteeism among Iraq war veterans," *The American Journal of Psychiatry* 164 (2007): 151; J.L. Thomas, J.E. Wilk, L.A. Riviere, D. McGurk, C.A. Castro, and C.W. Hoge, "Prevalence of mental health problems and functional impairment among Active Component and National Guard soldiers 3 and 12 months following combat in Iraq," *Arch Gen Psychiatry* 67, 6 (2010): 618-61.

[3]J. Sundin, N.T. Fear, A. Iversen, R.J. Rona, and S. Wessely, "PTSD after deployment to Iraq: conflicting rates, conflicting claims," *Psychological Med* 40, 3 (2010): 367-382.

[4]Gordon J.G. Asmundson, PhD, Murray B. Stein, M.D., and Donald R. Mccreary, PhD. "Posttraumatic Stress Disorder Symptoms Influence Health Status of Deployed Peacekeepers and Nondeployed Military Personnel," *Journal of Nervous and Mental Disease* 190, 12 (2002): 807-815.

[5]Michael Van Ameringen, Catherine Mancini, Beth Patterson, and Michael H. Boyle. "Post-traumatic stress disorder in Canada," *CNS Neuroscience and Therapeutics* 14, 3 (2008): 171-181.

[6]D. Fikretoglu, A. Brunet, S. Guay, and D. Pedlar, "Mental health treatment seeking by military members with posttraumatic stress disorder: findings on rates, characteristics, and predictors from a nationally representative Canadian military sample," *Can J Psychiatry* 52, 2 (2007): 103-110; J. Sareen, B.J. Cox, T.O. Afifi, M.B. Stein, S.L. Belik, G. Meadows, and G.J.G. Asmundson, "Combat and peacekeeping operations in relation to prevalence of mental disorders and perceived need for mental health care: findings from a large representative sample of military personnel," *Arch Gen Psychiatry* 64, 7(2007): 843-852.

[7]Rosario B. Hidalgo and Jonathan R. T. Davidson "Selective serotonin reuptake inhibitors in post-traumatic stress disorder," *Journal of Psychopharmacology* 14, 1 (2000): 70-76.

[8]Klaus Peter Lesch MD and Ursula Merschdorf "Impulsivity, aggression, and serotonin: a molecular psychobiological perspective," *Behavioral Sciences and the Law* 18, 5 (2000): 581-604.

[9]Brady, K., Pearlstein, T., Asnis, G.M., Baker, D., Rothbaum B.O., Sikes C.R., and Farfel, G.M. "Efficacy and safety of sertraline treatment of posttraumaticstress disorder: a randomized controlled trial," *JAMA* 283, 14 (2000): 1837-1844; J.R. Davidson, B.O. Rothbaum, B.A. van der Kolk, C.R. Sikes, and G.M. Farfel, "Multicenter, double-blind comparison of sertraline and placebo in the treatment of posttraumatic stress disorder," *Arch GenPsychiatry* 58, 5 (2001): 485-492.

[10]M.J. Friedman, C.R. Marmar, D.G. Baker, C.R. Sikes, and G.M. Farfel, "Randomized, double-blind comparison of sertraline and placebo for posttraumatic stress disorder in a Department of Veterans Affairs setting," *J Clin Psychiatry* 68, 5 (2007): 711-720; J. Zohar, D. Amital, C. Miodownik, M. Kotler, A. Bleich, R.M. Lane, and C. Austin, "Double-blind placebo-controlled pilot study of sertraline in military veterans with posttraumatic stress disorder," *J Clin Psychopharmacol* 22, 2 (2002): 190-195.

[11]Murray B. Stein, MD, Neal A. Kline, MD, and Jeffrey L. Matloff, PhD. "Adjunctive olanzapine for SSRI-resistant combat-related PTSD: a double-blind, placebo-controlled study," *American Journal of Psychiatry* 159, (2002): 1777–1779.

[12]Michelle L. Van Etten and Steven Taylor. "Comparative efficacy of treatments for post-traumatic stress disorder: a meta-analysis," *Clinical Psychology and Psychotherapy* 5, 3 (1998): 126-144.

[13]G.M. Asnis, S.R. Kohn, M. Henderson, and N.L. Brown, "SSRIs versus non-SSRIs in post-traumatic stress disorder: an update with recommendations," *Drugs* 64, 4 (2004): 383-404.

[14]J. Davidson, D. Baldwin, D.J. Stein, E. Kuper, I. Benattia, S. Ahmed, R. Pederson, J. Musgnung, "Treatment of posttraumatic stress disorder with venlafaxine extended release: a 6-month randomized controlled trial," *Arch Gen Psychiatry* 63, 10 (2006): 1158-1165; J. Davidson, B.O. Rothbaum, P. Tucker, G. Asnis, I. Benattia, and J.J. Musgnung, "Venlafaxine extended release in posttraumatic stress disorder: a sertraline- and placebo-controlled study," *Journal of Clinical Psychopharmacology* 26, 3 (2006): 259-267.

[15]G. Sullivan, and Y. Neria "Pharmacotherapy of PTSD: current status and controversies," *Psychiatric Annals* 39, 6 (2009): 342-347.

[16]B.S. McEwen, "The neurobiology of stress: from serendipity to clinical relevance," *Brain Research* 886, 1-2 (2000): 172-189.

[17]G.M. Asnis, S.R. Kohn, M. Henderson and N.L. Brown, "SSRIs versus non-SSRIs in post-traumatic stress disorder: an update with recommendations," *Drugs* 64, 4 (2004): 383-404.

[18]J.B. Frank, T.R. Kosten, E.L. Giller, and E. Dan, "A randomized clinical trial of phenelzine and imipramine for posttraumatic stress disorder," *American Journal of Psychiatry* 145, 10 (1988): 1289–1291; Shestatzky, M., Greenberg, D. and Lerer, B. "A controlled trial of phenelzine in posttraumatic stress disorder," *Psychiatry Research* 24, 2 (1988): 149–155.

[19]F.B. Schoenfeld, C.R. Marmar, and T.C. Neylan, "Current concepts in pharmacotherapy for posttraumatic stress disorder," *Psychiatric Services* 55, 5 (2004): 519-531.

[20]J. Cooper, J. Carty, and M. Creamer, "Pharmacotherapy for posttraumatic stress disorder: empirical review and clinical recommendations," *Australian and New Zealand J Psychiatry* 39, 8 (2005): 674-682.

21##1 J.R. Davidson, "Use of benzodiazepines in social anxiety disorder, generalized anxiety disorder, and posttraumatic stress disorder," *Journal of Clinical Psychiatry* 65, Suppl. 5 (2004): 29-33.

[22]Ronald C. Albucher and Israel Liberzon "Psychopharmacological treatment in PTSD: a critical review," *Journal of Psychiatric Research* 36, 6 (2002): 355-367.

[23]M.A. Hertzberg, M.I. Butterfield, M.E. Feldman, J.C. Beckham, S.M. Sutherland, K.M. Connor, and J.R. Davidson, "A preliminary study of lamotrigine for the treatment of posttraumatic stress disorder," *Biological Psychiatry* 45, 9 (1999):1226–1229.

[24]M.B. Stein, N.A. Kline, and J.L. Matloff, "Adjunctive olanzapine for SSRI-resistant combat-related PTSD: a double-blind, placebo-controlled study," *American Journal of Psychiatry* 159, 10 (2002): 1777–1779; M.B. Hamner, R.A. Faldowski, H.G. Ulmer, B.C. Frueh, M.G. Huber, and G.W. Arana, "Adjunctive risperidone treatment in post-traumatic stress disorder: a preliminary controlled trial of effects on comorbid psychotic symptoms," *Int Clin Psychopharmacology* 18, 1 (2003): 1–8.

[25]J. Ipser, S. Seedat, and D.J. Stein, "Pharmacotherapy for post traumatic stress disorder - a systematic review and meta-analysis," *S Afr Med J* 96, 10 (2006): 1088-1096.

[26]E.B. Foa, T.M. Keane, M.J. Friedman, and J.A. Cohen, *Effective treatments for PTSD: Practice guidelines from the International Society for Traumatic Stress Studies* (New York: Guildford, 2009), 622; J.I. Bisson, A. Ehlers, R. Matthews, S. Pilling, D. Richards, and S. Turner, S. "Psychological treatments for chronic post-traumatic stress disorder: Systematic review and meta-analysis," *British Journal of Psychiatry* 190 (2007): 97-104; R. Bradley, J. Greene, E. Russ, L. Dutra, and D. Westen, "A multidimensional meta-analysis of psychotherapy for PTSD," *American Journal of Psychiatry* 162, 2 (2005): 214-227.

[27]B.O. Rothbaum, E.A. Meadows, P. Resick, and D.W. Foy, "Cognitive-behavioral therapy." *Effective treatments for PTSD*, eds E.B. Foa, T.M. Keane, and M.J. Friedman (New York: Guilford, 2000), 60-83.

[28]E.A. Hembree, and E.B. Foa, Posttraumatic stress disorder: psychological factors and psychosocial intervention," *J Clin Psychiatry* 61, 7 (2000): 33-39.

[29]M.B. Powers, J.M. Halpern, M.P. Ferenschak, S.J. Gillihan, and E.B. Foa, "A meta-analytic review of prolonged exposure for posttraumatic stress disorder," *Clin Psychology Rev* 30, 6 (2010): 635-641.

[30]N. Nacasch, E.B. Foa, J.D. Huppert, D. Tzur, L. Fostick, Y. Dinstein, M. Polliack, and J. Zohar, "Prolonged exposure therapy for combat- and terror-related posttraumatic stress disorder: a randomized control comparison with treatment as usual," *Journal of Clinical Psychiatry*, (2010), http://www.ncbi.nlm.nih.gov/pubmed/21208581, accessed 14 April 2011; P.P. Schnurr, M.J. Friedman, D.W. Foy, M.T. Shea, F.Y. Hsieh, P.W. Lavori, S.M. Glynn, M. Wattenberg, and N.C. Bernardy, "Randomized trial of trauma-focused group therapy for posttraumatic stress disorder: results from a development of veterans affairs cooperative study," *Arch Gen Psychiatry* 60, 5 (2003): 481-489; I. Marks, K. Lovell, H. Noshirvani, M. Livanou, and S. Thrasher, "Treatment of posttraumatic stress disorder by exposure and/or cognitive restructuring: a controlled study," *Arch Gen Psychiatry* 55 4 (1998): 317-325.

[31]E.B. Foa, E.A. Hembree, S.P. Cahill, S.A.M. Rauch, D.S. Rigg, N.C. Feeny, and E. Yadin, "Randomized trial of prolonged exposure for posttraumatic stress disorder with and without cognitive restructuring: outcome at academic and community clinics," *J Consult Clin Psychol* 73, 5 (2005): 953-964; P.A. Resick, P. Nishith, T.L. Weaver, M.C. Astin, and C.A.Feuer, "A comparison of cognitive-processing therapy with prolonged exposure and a waiting condition for the treatment of chronic posttraumatic stress disorder in female rape victims," *J Consult Clin Psychol* 70, 4 (2002): 867-879; P.P. Schnurr, M.J. Friedman, C.C. Engel, E.B. Foa, M.T. Shea, B.K. Chow, P.A. Resick, V. Thurston, S.M. Orsillo, R. Haug, C. Turner, and N.C. Bernardy, "Cognitive behavioral therapy for posttraumatic stress disorder in women: a randomized controlled trial," *JAMA* 297, 8 (2007): 820-830.

[32]M.W. Otto, D. Hinton, N.B. Korbly, A. Chea, P. Ba, B.S. Gershuny, and M.H. Pollack, "Treatment of pharmacotherapy-refractory posttraumatic stress disorder among Cambodian refugees: a pilot study of combination treatment with cognitive-behavior therapy vs sertraline alone," *Behav Res Ther* 41, 11 (2003): 1271–1276.

[33]S.D. Hollon, R.J. DeRubeis M.D. Evans, M.J. Wiemer, M.J. Garvey, W.M. Grove, and V.B. Tuason, "Cognitive therapy and pharmacotherapy for depression," *Arch Gen Psychiatry* 49, 10 (1992): 774-781.

[34]A.T. Beck, N. Epstein, G. Brown, and R.A. Steer, "An inventory for measuring clinical anxiety: psychometric properties," *Journal of Consulting Clinical Psychology* 56, 6 (1988): 893-897.

[35]A.T. Beck, R.A. Steer, R. Ball, W. Ranieri, "Comparison of Beck Depression Inventories-IA and -II in psychiatric outpatients," *J Pers Assess* 67, 3 (1996): 588-597.

[36]F. Weathers, B.T. Litz, D.S. Herman, J.A. Huska, and T.M. Keane, "The PTSD checklist (PCL): reliability, validity, and diagnostic utility" (presentation, International Society of Traumatic Stress Studies, San Antonio, TX, October 1993).

[37]T. Fydrich, D. Dowdall, and D.L. Chambless, "Reliability and validity of the Beck Anxiety Inventory," *Journal of Anxiety Disorder* (1992): 55-61.

[38]R.C. Arnau, M.W. Meagher, M.P. Norris, and R. Bramson, "Psychometric Evaluation of the Beck Depression Inventory-II with Primary Care Medical Patients," *Health Psychology* 20, 2 (2001): 114.

[39]R.A. Steer, R. Ball, W.F. Ranieri, and A.T. Beck, "Dimensions of the Beck Depression Inventory-II in Clinically Depressed Patients," *Clin Psychol* 55, 1 (1999): 117-128.

[40]D.J.A. Dozois, K.S. Dobson, and J.L. Ahnberg, "A psychometric evaluation of the Beck Depression Inventory-II," *Psychological Assess* 10, 2 (1998): 83-89.

[41]P. D. Bliese, K.M.Wright, A.B. Adler, O. Cabrera, C.A. Castro, and C. Hoge, "Validating the primary care posttraumatic stress disorder screen and the posttraumatic stress disorder checklist with soldiers returning from combat," *J Consult Clin Psychol* 76, 2 (2008): 272-281.; Weathers, F., Litz, B.T., Herman, D.S., Huska, J.A., and Keane, T.M., "The PTSD checklist (PCL): reliability, validity, and diagnostic utility" (presentation, International Society of Traumatic Stress Studies, San Antonio, TX, 1993).

[42]J.J. Barnette, *Effect Size and Measures of Association.* (University of Alabama at Birmingham: 2006), http://www.eval.org/summerinstitute/06SIHandouts/SI06.Barnette.TR2.Online.pdf, accessed 14 April 2011.

[43]M.T. Smith, M.L. Perlis, A. Park, M.S. Smith, J.M.Pennington, D.E.Giles, and D.J. Buyesse, "Comparative meta-analysis of pharmacotherapy and behavior therapy for persistent insomnia," *American Journal of Psychiatry* 159 (2002): 5-11.

[44]M.B. Keller, J.P. McCullough, D.N Klein, B.Arnow, D.L Dunner, A.J Gelenberg, *et al.* "A comparison of nefazodone, the cognitive behavioral-analysis system of psychotherapy, and their combination for the treatment of depression," *New England Journal of Medicine* 342 (2000): 1462-1470.

[45]J.L. Krupnick, S.M. Sotsky, I. Elkin, S. Simmens, J. Moyer, J. Watkins, and P.A. Pilkonis, "The role of the therapeutic alliance in psychotherapy and pharmacotherapy outcome: findings in the National Institute of Mental Health treatment of depression collaborative research program," *J Consult Clin Psychol* 64, 3 (1996): 532-539.

[46]Hackshaw, A. "Small studies: strengths and limitations," *Eur Respir J* 32, 5 (2008): 1141-1143.

[47]D. Machin, M. Campbell, P. Fayers, and A. Pinol, *Sample size tables for clinical studies*, 2nd edition (Malden, MA: Blackwell Science Ltd., 1997), 4.

[48]A. Aschengrau, G.R Seague, 3rd. *Essentials of epidemiology in public health* (Mississauga, ON: Jones and Bartlett Publishers, Ltd., 2003), pp. 237, 246, 253.

[49]D.R. Hess, "Retrospective studies and chart reviews," *Respir Care* 49, 10 (2004): 1171-1174.

[50]T.R. Levine, and C.R Hullett, "Eta squared, partial eta squared, and misreporting of effect size in communication research," *Human Commun Res* 28, 4 (2002): 612-625.

[51]C.J. Ferguson, "An Effect Size Primer: A Guide for Clinicians and Researchers," *Professional Psychology: Practice and Research* 40, 5 (2009): 532-538.

CHAPTER 13

The Experiences of Female Partners of Canadian Forces Veterans Diagnosed with Post-Traumatic Stress Disorder

Sandra Pickrell Baker, MA, MSW, Dalhousie University; Deborah Norris, PhD, Department of Family Studies and Gerontology, Mount Saint Vincent University, Halifax, Nova Scotia

ABSTRACT

Members of the CF engage in active combat in locations including Rwanda, Bosnia, and more recently, Afghanistan. The CF is acknowledging a corresponding increase in numbers of members diagnosed with PTSD. Family members, particularly partners, may themselves develop a secondary traumatic stress response (STSR). Little is known about how the partners of military members diagnosed with PTSD experience this phenomenon. The objective of this study was to document the experiences of female partners of male CF veterans diagnosed with PTSD. Questions guiding the study were: What are the experiences of women with male partners diagnosed with PTSD? What is the meaning of these experiences, particularly within the partner relationship? An interpretive/constructivist framework formed the theoretical and methodological foundation for this qualitative study. First-voice accounts emerged from the sharing of participants' experiences through eight semi-structured interviews. Participating women described experiences of depression, loss of self, hyper- and conscious-accommodation that were complicated by the sense of ambiguous loss permeating the relationship. This study has the potential to guide the development of educational programs and support services for family members of CF personnel diagnosed with PTSD.

THE EXPERIENCES OF FEMALE PARTNERS OF CANADIAN FORCES VETERANS DIAGNOSED WITH POST-TRAUMATIC STRESS DISORDER

Military members, veterans and their families are challenged by institutional imperatives that test their capacity for healthy functioning. For serving members, deployment-related family separations are an operational requirement that affect their well-being[1] require psychological adjustment for female military members balancing motherhood and the expectations of the military[2] and are managed through the ongoing daily work of female military partners[3]. Veterans diagnosed with severe service-related disabilities and their families may experience economic, health and social consequences[4]. These stresses may compound the impact of normative change common to all contemporary families across the life course. For military members, veterans and their families, providing care to children and/or aging family members, managing a dual-work household and supporting adult or vulnerable family members are family tasks potentially complicated by the requirements or consequences of military service.

Segal[5] refers to both the military and the family as "greedy" institutions. This description is particularly apt now that military service has extended to include deployments in war-torn areas of the globe. Members of the CF and other militaries are now more engaged than in the past in active combat in locations such as Rwanda, Bosnia, and more recently, Afghanistan. The level of stress for military members, veterans and their families has intensified such that the numbers of members and veterans diagnosed with PTSD has increased.[6]

PTSD is a significant health outcome resulting from the shift to active combat for military members. The personality and behavioural changes associated with PTSD sometimes affect the military's member's capacity to maintain active service.[7] Evidence of this can be discerned through examination of the increase in numbers of CF members who leave the military because of a diagnosis of PTSD. In 2005, 1142 soldiers were pensioned out of the military due to complications of PTSD compared to 25 soldiers in 1995.[8] This increase in the diagnosis of PTSD and the resultant effect on retention has prompted research and the development of clinical interventions for those directly affected.

PTSD AND STSR AND THE MILITARY

The consequences of PTSD for the military member and veterans are profound. A study examining the impact of a diagnosis of a service-related disability on Canadian veterans of the Vietnam War exposed ongoing problems with family and marital adjustment.[9] These findings are corroborated by other studies[10] that reveal issues with expressiveness, self-disclosure and establishing intimacy. Moreover, Kulka, Schlenger, Fairbank, Hough, Jordan & Marmar,[11] in one of the largest studies of mental health and veterans of the Vietnam War, found that rates of divorce are twice as high for veterans with PTSD compared to veterans without PTSD.

Research is also revealing a chain reaction within the families of those diagnosed. Couples in which the male serving member sustained a combat stress injury (PTSD) report more conflict, less intimacy, less consensus, less cohesion and less expressiveness than other couples.[12] Partners of veterans with PTSD experience higher levels of emotional distress and lower levels of marital adjustment than the general population.[13] Increased mental health problems in partners have also been documented.[14] Some partners have to cope with physical and psychological violence perpetrated by the veteran diagnosed with PTSD.[15] Partners may become enmeshed[16] in the relationship, organizing their lives around the primary sufferer's traumatic experience and his/her needs. Exhibiting some of the same symptoms as the primary sufferer[17] such as depression, lack of self-care, hostility, withdrawal, difficulty maintaining concentration, and sexual dysfunction are also detected in some instances. Ambiguous loss[18] may result from the sense that the primary sufferer, as he or she was once known, no longer exists. Social isolation and self-blame[19] are also discussed as outcomes noted among some partners of military veterans diagnosed with PTSD as is a tendency to avoid opportunities to receive social support.[20]

In some cases, partners, children and other family members, risk being consumed by the "burden of care"[21] with PTSD and struggle to maintain a sense of self[22] and their independence and autonomy.[23] Where this proves to be difficult, a STSR[24] may result. STSR is now recognized as a health outcome for partners and family members of military members/veterans diagnosed with PTSD.

The research cited presents a compelling account of a "greedy" institution. It appears that the consequences of military service on the member, the veteran and the families, whether those consequences emerge in response to balancing military service with customary life course transitions and/or from a diagnosis of an acute response to combat (PTSD or STSD), are deeply experienced, pervasive and potentially detrimental. Little is known about how partners of military members and veterans diagnosed with PTSD experience this. This qualitative study was designed as a step toward addressing this gap in knowledge.

Purpose of Study

The central questions guiding the study were: What are the experiences of female partners of Canadian military veterans diagnosed with PTSD? What meanings do the women ascribe to this experience? What is the relationship between the experience of the diagnosis and daily life?

Seven female partners of CF veterans were recruited through a snowball sampling technique initiated through contacts with the DND treatment facility, VAC and the Operational Stress and Injury Support Services (OSSIS) program.

Participants ranged in age from thirty to sixty. The duration of their relationships with their partners ranged from seven to forty years. Two women were separated from their partners. The range in rank held by the male partner was also broad, spanning from enlisted members to a commanding officer. All of the veterans had served in "hot spots" (a location involving active military engagement) at some time in their careers. All the women were Caucasian and had grown up in Canada. The education level of the women was varied, as was their employment status. One participant was retired, but all had been, or were currently, primary providers for their families. One woman was on maternity leave at the time the study was conducted. Children ranged in age from newborn to adult.

THEORY/METHOD

Participating women were interviewed using a semi-structured interview guide after receiving detailed information about the research and agreeing to participate through an informed consent process. Questions were designed to garner first-voice accounts of experience including their perceptions of processes and outcomes related to the diagnosis and treatment of PTSD both for their partner and themselves. The interviews took place over a six-month period. Field notes and a reflexive journal were kept throughout the process to supplement the interviews. The interviewing process continued until saturation was achieved. The research protocol received ethics approval from the University Research Ethics Board at Mount Saint Vincent University.

An interpretive/constructivist theoretical framework was used to design the study and analyze the results. Interpretive/constructivist research proceeds from the epistemological position that multiple truths are created through individual action in daily life.[25] Within this framework, cultural and historical contexts are considered to be significant to the meanings inherent in experience. Interpretive/constructivist researchers strive to understand and interpret these meanings through an understanding of the individual's life view of their situation.

Interviews were transcribed and imported into MAXQDA, a qualitative data analysis software program. Open coding[26] brought general themes into view such as the redefinition of roles in the women's relationships with their partners following the diagnosis of PTSD and related coping strategies and resources. Axial coding[27] enabled the identification of sub-themes and linkages between and among themes and sub-themes. For example, the experience of ambiguous loss emerged as the relationships between role changes and accommodations were analyzed. Emergent themes were compared against existing data until saturation was attained in a process described as "working up from the data".[28] Rich accounts of the experiences of female partners of CF veterans diagnosed with PTSD and the meanings associated with those experiences resulted.

RESULTS

Accommodation and Adaptation

As participating women shared experiences related to their partner's diagnosis of PTSD, subsequent treatment and ongoing experiences, efforts to adapt and accommodate were visible. Previous patterns of interaction were modified, routines altered and strategies devised and implemented to accommodate the impact of the symptoms experienced by the veteran. Some women refer to "role reversal" in the interviews noting that they now assume responsibility for key functions in the family, including switching to being the sole or main provider in some instances.

For some, the accommodations follow from acute sensitivity to factors in physical spaces and social settings thought to provoke stress for the partner living with PTSD. Discomfort in open spaces or in crowded rooms is acknowledged by partners and accommodated. Relationships with friends and family are also adjusted. Carol shares her experience with strained social relationships, the ensuing isolation and steps she takes to increase her partner's comfort in the external world:

> Social relationships changed big time, he was always a do anything, go anywhere kind of guy, now he's not. I mean we were very upfront that he had PTSD, a lot of people I know aren't, but this is not something we kept a secret but um - socially we don't go out a lot anymore. Um, (sigh) we have to plan to go to children's graduations because he has to sit at the very back by a door. We don't go to concerts. If we go to a restaurant, he has to sit with his back to the thing, so he doesn't - he doesn't really enjoy going out with a lot of people anymore...I have to do all the planning. I have to scout everything out and say ok, this is where we'll go, this is where we'll sit and, you know the exit is right there if you need to leave...

Tammy describes her new experience as the primary wage-earner in the family:

> ... people don't understand – I'm the one who picks up – all... every piece. It's like – I don't want to say it's like having another child but when you have somebody that's disabled and not capable, basically all the responsibilities fall on me. I pay the bills, I worry about the bills, I make all the doctor's appointments, you know. I was filling out his Veterans Affairs papers because they come in and sit on the desk for weeks and weeks because he wasn't even capable of even filling them out. And, just the day-to-day things, you know. Laundry, I work 40 hours a week and then I come home and have to do it all, so I'm being a single parent even though we're in a relationship. So it's really hard.

Hyper

There is a reciprocal relationship between accommodation and adaptation and a hypervigilent attention paid to the partner and his/her environment. Hypervigilance facilitates the processes of accommodation and adaptation and, in turn, accommodation and adaptation require hypervigilance. The interdependence between the two processes is a particularly meaningful result of this research.

Participating women report that their concern for their partner's welfare and the awareness of the stress associated with the escalation of symptoms of PTSD are constant preoccupations. Maintaining this level of watchfulness is a day-to-day reality. Tammy states that she worries about what is happening at home, even when she is working:

I call a couple of times [a day]. It's on my mind. I've been trying to back away from calling – but it's tough because I worry about him…. I know I'm depressed…. It's been hell. Really. There's some days I don't want to get out of bed myself, you know…there's going to be times when I'm going to be angry with him but I can't be. I don't feel that I can be - I can't be - I can't be normal. You have to walk on eggshells, you know…

Other women discuss the effort expended in proactively managing the conditions that could potentially precipitate acute symptoms of PTSD. Natalie has lived with her husband's injury for thirty years and describes her efforts to minimize the stress and create a stable life for them both. She notes:

It's - it's - non-stop. You're always watching but you don't even really think about it. It just becomes a way of life. I watch for triggers, like too much news on bombings and earthquakes and it's like, oh you know what dear, it's a really nice day, let's go for a car ride and we really don't need the satellite radio on, you know. Because he becomes like when there's an earthquake or something like that, he's just transfixed. And he watches the military channel. And I said, that's great dear, but you really don't need to be watching bombings. He says, well, it doesn't really bother me. And I said, you don't probably think it does, but I said, there's a reason you are drawn to that. You know…

Ambiguous Loss

Women participating in this study discuss their partners as physically present, but psychologically different from the person known before the diagnosis. Some speak of changes in personality and unhealthy coping strategies, such as addictions and violence. The women describe how they miss the person they knew before the diagnosis and the support they once received from their partners. They mourn the loss of dreams and goals once shared. These responses are consistent with the experience of ambiguous loss.[29]

Carol discusses her loss through reference to the person she married as being "replaced" by another and feels the loss acutely. She articulates the ways in which she has adapted to being with a very different person:

The above-normal anger was a little hard to deal with. A lot of the personalities he had which were, you know, in normal amounts became huge, with the drinking which was - kind of - goes with the territory for a lot of it. Um, like I said - very jumpy, very skittish - I lit a candle in the house one day and it was like he came out of nowhere, - God, just almost magnified, all the personality traits just totally magnified, out of control, um the personality that really would change that was disturbing as was his lack of wanting to be social. That's totally out of character. That wasn't a magnification of him that's complete turnaround of normal. Um, things have kind of shrunk back to normal to a certain extent, but yeah, that, that -you're looking at the total person, you can see the pieces of the person from before but it's totally different. And just way out of proportion. It's like ah -applying for a job as a cook and going in and discovering that you're the floor washer. It's like, you know, this is my job. This is what I signed up for. What happened here? Why am I in something totally foreign and - It wasn't a gradual thing; it's like he went to the store and came back a totally different person -And that's hard. Some of the things he says, you kind of look and say, yeah, okay, just go away and leave me alone...

Janet adds:

> When I got married and part of the reason I said yes was that I, I thought he is a great guy that is an honourable man and will always do the right thing, and will treat me well. Every…everything that I thought he is is now gone. The respectful, wonderful guy is gone.

This sentiment is poignantly echoed in Tammy's remarks:

> It's like where did he go? He's gone. And I've said that to him, I miss you, I'd like to have you back. I find it very, very, very lonely. And that's - I think the grief if that is, is something that's harder than the physicality, like if he wasn't physically there.

The experience of ambiguous loss can be complicated by guilt and anger. While the women are grateful that their partners returned home when others did not, they still refer to "losing" the person and the relationship once known and then feel guilty for not being glad that "…at least he is still alive."

Secondary Trauma

All of the participants in this study report difficulty with differentiating between their partner's symptoms and signs of depression detected in themselves. Some wonder if they have unwittingly absorbed the impact of PTSD and taken on the symptoms as their own. Janet states:

> Like I mean you wonder sometimes where the line is. I will tell you the doctor swears I have PTSD. I have some of the same symptoms, so – it's kind of a little weird…. Not so much that as, you know, you have to take care of yourself or you'll get really tired. But, I - you kind of – osmosis…because you're tired of dealing with everything, you do get kind of shell-shocked...

Denise adds some compelling observations about her behaviour which she describes as secondary traumatic stress:

> I'm very high functioning but you don't realize the little – why do I jump all the time? I kind of have an idea now, before I'm just like oh I'm a nervous person. But there's stuff I don't - I don't do well with anger.... You know you can't live on what ifs but it - for me it was painful because it opened it; I mean you recognize a lot of things. Like startling or whatever... It's similar...nightmares, um waking up and being unable to run. I still don't sleep.

All of the participating women are confused as they struggle to discern if their symptoms are valid indicators of their own "injuries" resulting from secondary trauma or extensions of what they see and live with every day with their partners. Regardless, it is clear that these women are profoundly affected by the experience of PTSD in their partners.

Discussion

This research proceeded from first-voice accounts of an experience deemed to be challenging at best and catastrophic at worst. The themes emerging from these accounts can be integrated by considering the changes ongoing within the relationships affected by the veteran's diagnosis of PTSD.

Redefining Relationships

It is clear from this study that traumatic injuries induce significant changes to the relationships affected. In part, these changes are propelled by the behavioural consequences of PTSD for the veteran. Women participating in this study are struggling to come to terms with a different partner. Some are witnessing the former "life of the party" no longer wanting to leave the house. In some cases, the partner with PTSD is engaging in addictive behaviours. Some with no history of violent behaviour are suddenly having dangerous outbursts. All had been proud members of the military but are no longer able to work, feel ashamed about the injury and reluctant to seek help. In some instances, this has resulted in isolation from peers and social networks as well as isolation within the relationship.

Most women participating in this study are working to redefine the relationship through adaptation and accommodation. Women who previously had worked at home are now thrust into the role of primary provider. Others are learning to manage the symptoms of PTSD in their partners through hypervigilant attention to the "triggers" thought to provoke acute attacks. Hypervigilance and the processes of accommodation and adaptation that follow from the experience of PTDS in the partner are reciprocally related.

Some women choose to accommodate because of the love felt for their partners and the desire to maintain a cohesive relationship while others were compelled by duty. Some run the risk of over-investing in the relationship[30] and de-selfing[31] particularly if meeting the needs of their partner assumes a greater priority then their own.

Ambiguous loss[32] also alters the relationship. The accounts of ambiguous loss offered by participating women resonate with meaning. The women refer to the loss of the person they had married and the loss of hopes and dreams for the future. These emotions were difficult to express and complicated by ambiguity. On the one hand, the women are mourning the loss of the person once known, but, on the other hand, they know that they should be grateful that their partners returned home alive. All of the women participating in this study acknowledge that life, as they had known it, has changed forever. The relationship they had with their partner has been redefined.

RECOMMENDATIONS

This study provides a descriptive account of the experiences of female partners of CF veterans diagnosed with PTSD and the meanings ascribed to those experiences. Guided by the interpretive/constructivist framework, the study proceeded from the voices of the women participating. The themes resulting from the analysis provide a starting point for further study. In particular, questions emerge about the impact of differential access to formal and informal supports, community resources and needs-based policies and programs on the capacity for resilience for women supporting veterans with PTSD over the life course spanning active service, which may include combat, to post-military life.

A recent report commissioned by VAC entitled *Wounded Veterans, Wounded Families* authored by Fast, Yacyshin and Keating[33] succinctly outlines the economic, health and social needs of veterans diagnosed with severe service-related disabilities and their families and substantiates the requirement for a "needs-based philosophy of services" in response to gaps in service provision. Further research focusing on the experiences, attributes and contexts of military members, veterans and families will help fulfill this objective through the development of deeper and more extensive understandings of the life course impacts of military service, the multi-dimensional character of that experience and the transitions that occur over time. From this, it will be possible to develop an analysis of the pathways to resilience for members, veterans and families throughout the life course.

[1]Amy Alder, Ann Huffman, Paul Bliese, and Carl Castro, "The Impact of Deployment and Experience on the Well Being of Male and Female Soldiers," *Journal of Occupational Health and Psychiatry* 10, 2 (2005): 121-137.

[2]Michelle L. Kelley, Peggy A. Herzog-Simmer, and Marci A. Harris, "Effects of military induced separation on the parenting stress and family functioning of deployed mothers," *Military Psychology* 6, 1 (1994): 125-138; Michelle I. Kelley, Ellen Hock, Melinda S. Jarvis, Kathleen M. Smith, Monica A. Gaffney and Jennifer F. Bonney, "Psychological Adjustment of Navy Mothers Experiencing Deployment," *Military Psychology* 14. 3, (2002): 199-216.

[3]Deborah Norris, "Working them out ...Working them in: Ideology and the everyday lives of female military partners experiencing the cycle of deployment," *Atlantis* 26, 1 (2001): 55-63.

[4]Janet E. Fast, Norah Keating, and Alison Yacyshyn, "Wounded veterans, wounded families," (presented at, the National Council on Family Relations 70th Annual Conference, Little Rock, AR, November 5-8, 2008).

[5]Mady W. Segal, "The military and the family as greedy institutions," *Armed Forces & Society* 13, 1 (1986): 9-38.

[6]Mary McFadyen, "A long road to recovery: Battling operational stress injuries," http://www.ombudsman.forces.gc.ca/rep-rap/sr-rs/osi-tso-3/doc/osi-tso-3-eng.pdf, accessed 28 June 2009.

[7]C.W. Hoge, H.E. Toboni, S.C. Messer, N. Bell, P. Amoroso, and D.T. Orman, "The Occupational Burden of Mental Disorders in the U.S. Military: Psychiatric Hospitalizations, Involuntary Separations, and Disability," *American Journal of Psychiatry* 162, 3 (2005): 585-591.

[8]Canadian Press "Number of ex-soldiers on disability soars," *Chronicle Herald*, 15 May2005.

[9]Robert H. Stretch, "Psychosocial readjustment of Canadian Vietnam veterans," *Journal of Consulting and Clinical Psychology* 59, 1 (1991): 188-9.

[10]Edward E. Carroll, Drue B. Rueger, David W. Foy, and CP Donahue, "Vietnam combat veterans with posttraumatic stress disorder: Analysis of marital and cohabitating adjustment," *Journal of Abnormal Psychology* 94, 3 (1985): 329-37; Davis S. Riggs, Christina A. Byrne, Frank W. Weathers, and Brett T. Litz, "The quality of the intimate relationships of male Vietnam veterans: Problems associated with posttraumatic stress disorder," Journal of Traumatic Stress 11, 1 (2005): 87-101; William Roberts, W. Penk, M. Gearing, E. Patterson, and Dolan, M., "Interpersonal Problems of Vietnam Combat Veterans With Symptoms of Posttraumatic Stress Disorder," *Journal of Abnormal Psychology* 91, 6 (1982) 444-450.

[11]Richard A. Kulka, William E. Schlenger, John A. Fairbank Richard L. Hough, B. Kathleen Jordan, and Charles R. Marmar, *Trauma and the Vietnam War generation: Report of findings from the National Vietnam Veterans Readjustment Study* (New York: Brunner/Mazel, 1990), 1-332.

[12]Zahava Solomon, Mark Waysman, Ruth Belkin, Gaby Levy, Mario Mikulincerm, and Dan Enoch, "Marital relations and combat stress reaction: The wives' perspective," *Journal of Marriage and the Family* 54, 2 (1992): 316-326.

[13]Rachel Dekel, Zahava Solomon, and Avi Bleich, "Emotional distress and marital adjustment of caregivers: Contribution of level of impairment and appraised burden," *Stress, Anxiety and Coping* 18, 1 (2005): 71-82.

[14]B. Kathleen Jordon, Charles R. Marmar, John A. Fairbank, William E. Schlenger, Richard A. Kulka, Richard L. Hough, and Daniel S. Weiss, "Problems in families of male Vietnam veterans with posttraumatic stress disorder," *Journal of Consulting and Clinical Psychology* 60, 6 (1992): 916-26.

[15]T. Galovsky and J. Lyons, "Psychological sequelae of combat violence: A review of the impact of PTSD on the veteran's family and possible interventions," *Aggression and Violent Behavior* 9 (2004): 477-501.

[16]David Johnson, Susan Feldman, and Hadar. Lubin, "Critical interaction therapy: Couplestherapy in combat-related post traumatic stress disorder," *Family Process* 34, 4 (2005): 401-402.

[17]Margaret Lyons, "Living with post-traumatic stress disorder; the wives'/female partners' perspective," *Journal of Nursing* 34, 1 (2001): 69-77.

[18]Pauline Boss, "Family stress: Perception and context," *Handbook of Marriage and the Family*, eds. Marvin Sussman and Suzanne Steinmetz (New York: Plenum Press, 1987), 695-723.

[19]Zahava Solomon, Mark Waysman, Ruth Belkin, Gaby Levy, Mario Mikulincerm, and Dan Enoch, "Marital relations and combat stress reaction: The wives' perspective," *Journal of Marriage and the Family* 54, 2 (1992): 316-326.

[20]C. Rabin and C. Nardi, "Treating post traumatic stress disorder couples: A psychoeducational program," *Community Health Journal* 27, 1 (1991): 209-224.

[21]Rachel Dekel, Zahava Solomon, and Avi Bleich, "Emotional distress and marital adjustment of caregivers:

Contribution of level of impairment and appraised burden," *Stress, Anxiety and Coping* 18, 1 (2005): 71-82.

[22]Harriet Lerner, *Women in therapy* (Northvale, NJ: Jason Aronson, 1998), 1-266.

[23]Rachel Dekel, Hadass Goldblatt, Michal Keidar, Zahava Solomon, and Michael Polliack, "Being a wife of a veteran with posttraumatic stress disorder," *Family Relations* 54, 1 (2005): 24-36.

[24]Juliet Corbin and Marvin Strauss, "Analytic ordering for theoretical purposes," *Qualitative Inquiry* 2, 2 (1996): 139-151.

[25]Jane Ritchie and Jane Lewis, *Qualitative Research Practice* (Thousand Oaks, CA: Sage, 2003), 1-331.

[26]Juliet Corbin and Marvin Strauss, "Analytic ordering for theoretical purposes," *Qualitative Inquiry* 2, 2 (1996): 139-151.

[27]Juliet Corbin and Marvin Strauss, "Analytic ordering for theoretical purposes," *Qualitative Inquiry* 2, 2 (1996): 139-151.

[28]Norman Denzin and Yvonna Lincoln, *Handbook of qualitative research* (Thousand Oaks CA: Sage, 1994), 1-1099.

[29]Pauline Boss, "Family stress: Perception and context," *Handbook of Marriage and the Family*, eds. Marvin Sussman and Suzanne Steinmetz (New York: Plenum Press, 1987), 695-723.

[30]Charles R. Figley, "Compassion fatigue as secondary traumatic stress disorder: An Overview," *Compassion fatigue: Coping with secondary traumatic stress disorder in those who treat the traumatized*, ed. Charles R. Figley (New York: Brunner/Mazel, 1995), 1-20.

[31]C. Rabin and C. Nardi, "Treating post-traumatic stress disorder couples: A psychoeducational program," *Community Health Journal* 27, 1 (1991): 209-224.

[32]Pauline Boss, "Family stress: Perception and context," *Handbook of Marriage and the Family*, eds. Marvin Sussman and Suzanne Steinmetz (New York: Plenum Press, 1987), 695-723.

[33]Janet E. Fast, Norah Keating, and Alison Yacyshyn, "Wounded veterans, wounded families," (presented at the National Council on Family Relations 70th Annual Conference, Little Rock, AR, November 5-8, 2008).

CHAPTER 14

The Roles of Self-Efficacy and Coping in the Well-Being of Military Spouses

Alla Skomorovsky, PhD and Kerry A. Sudom, PhD, Defence Research and Development Canada

Abstract

Families of military personnel face a number of unique challenges associated with military lifestyle, which can have adverse consequences on psychological well-being. The link between deployments and psychological health problems among spouses of military personnel has been documented. Previous research suggests that individual characteristics can either buffer or increase the negative impact of stress on psychological well-being. This study examined the roles of self-efficacy and coping strategies in psychological health of spouses of deployed military personnel ($N = 254$). Self-efficacy played an important role in psychological well-being, predicting both greater health and lower depression scores among spouses. Furthermore, emotional and humour coping strategies played a unique role in well-being, over and above that of self-efficacy. Finally, both self-efficacy and coping buffered the negative impact of deployment stress on psychological well-being. These results suggest that self-efficacy and coping play important and independent roles in the well-being of military spouses.

The Roles of Self-Efficacy and Coping in the Well-Being of Military Spouses

Many organizations have come to recognize the importance of family life on workplace productivity and organizational well-being.[1] Perhaps more than any other organization, the military has a pervasive influence on the lifestyle of its members and their families.[2] Spouses of military members face unique challenges associated with the military lifestyle, including frequent relocations, temporary housing, spousal unemployment and underemployment, separations, and deployments of the military member to potentially dangerous situations.[3] Furthermore, previous research has documented the adverse effects of deployments on spouses, including marital dissatisfaction, unemployment, psychological health problems, adjustment disorders, and divorce.[4] Evidence suggests that while military factors can have a pervasive influence on family life, the family can also have a profound impact not only on the serving member (e.g., psychological well-being) but also on the organization as a whole (e.g., retention).[5] Therefore, knowledge of the individual characteristics that can buffer families against the negative impact of stress would be especially valuable in the military context, due to its potentially stressful demands.[6] The ability to predict psychological well-being of spouses of deployed military personnel would have important practical implications for military organizations, including reduced attrition and increased organizational well-being.

Psychological well-being is a key element of mental functioning. It is believed that the quality of psychological well-being is influenced by a number of antecedent factors, including negative early life events. Stressful life events, both major stressors (traumatic events) and more minor stressors (circumstances that create personal distress but do not constitute a life threat), are linked to health problems, including depression and PTSD.[7] Despite strong evidence of a link between negative life events and psychological well-being, research has demonstrated that not all individuals who experience a negative life event develop a psychological health problem. In fact, it has been found that some individuals exposed to traumatic events experience no negative health consequences.[8] There may be certain individual characteristics that buffer these individuals against the negative impact of stressful events on psychological health, making them more resilient.[9]

SELF-EFFICACY AND WELL-BEING

A key element in social learning theory, self-efficacy refers to an individual's belief in his or her capability to organize and execute a course of action needed to meet the demands of a situation and/or to produce a desired outcome.[10] Poor perceptions of self-efficacy play a detrimental role in the amount of effort and persistence people apply under stress. High self-efficacy represents a sense of mastery that is linked with better quality of life and general psychological well-being.[11] Consistent with this, self-efficacy was linked to psychological health outcomes in empirical studies.[12] For example, greater self-efficacy was associated with greater quality of life and psychological well-being among chronically ill patients (e.g., asthma, diabetes, and heart failure conditions).[13] In addition, greater self-efficacy was associated with lower depression among rheumatoid arthritis patients.[14] In the organizational context, self-efficacy significantly predicted both psychological well-being (affect and satisfaction with life) and engagement (vigour and dedication).[15]

In addition to its direct effects, there is evidence that high self-efficacy can buffer the negative influence of stress on psychological well-being in relation to stressful experiences.[16] Perceived self-efficacy was found to be the key factor in posttraumatic recovery following such traumatic experiences as natural disasters, technological catastrophes, terrorist attacks, military combat, and sexual and criminal assaults.[17] In addition, high self-efficacy differentiated between individuals with and without chronic PTSD following the Yom Kippur attack among Israeli veterans, such that those with higher levels of this characteristic had no PTSD symptomatology.[18] In addition, self-efficacy moderated several stressor-strain relations among military personnel.[19]

One of the main explanations for the path between self-efficacy and psychological well-being was proposed to be feelings of hopelessness and passivity among individuals with lower self-efficacy.[20] Indeed, individuals who are passive will make fewer attempts to cope with or change situations because they perceive such attempts as futile.[21]

It was suggested that, in order to more accurately predict the impact of self-efficacy on health outcomes under stress, individuals' use of coping should be taken into account.[22] Specifically, it was suggested by the authors that if high self-efficacy is not accompanied by effective coping styles, self-efficacy alone may not help individuals adapt to stressors more effectively. Although low self-efficacy may negatively influence coping choices,[23] it is also possible that coping strategies and self-efficacy are independent predictors of psychological well-being. Indeed, Gowan, Craft, & Zimmermann[24] found that self-efficacy was not significantly related to the use of particular coping strategies. Whether coping is a function of individual characteristics or an independent predictor, the role of coping in the interrelationships between stress, self-efficacy, and psychological well-being deserves research attention.

COPING AND WELL-BEING

Coping refers to the constantly changing cognitive and behavioural efforts to manage external and/or internal demands when an event is perceived as stressful (i.e., the event is appraised as taxing or exceeding the resources of the person).[25] Coping involves strategies for dealing with what the person perceives as a threat. The way a person copes is determined in part by his or her resources, which include health and energy, positive beliefs, problem-solving skills, social skills, social support, and material resources.[26]

The relationship between coping and health outcomes has been established.[27] Researchers have demonstrated that a failure to cope with stressful or traumatic situations leads to psychological problems, including depression, ASD and subsequent PTSD.[28] Coping effectiveness is based on two functions: the regulation of distress (emotion-focused) and the management of the problem that is causing distress (problem-focused).[29] A person who manages a problem effectively but at great emotional cost cannot be viewed as coping effectively. Thus, effective coping includes both problem solving and the management of related emotions.

While some researchers argue that coping strategies are not inherently good or bad, and the effectiveness of a strategy depends on the extent to which it is appropriate to the internal and/or external demands of the situation,[30] other researchers argue that some strategies can be more effective than others.[31] However, among those who argue that there are more effective strategies to cope with stressful events, there is no consensus as to which coping techniques should be viewed as most adaptive and leading to a healthy mental state. Coyne, Aldwin and Lazarus[32] found the effective coping efforts of depressed persons to be characterized by seeking emotional and informational support and by wishful thinking. Billings and Moos[33] found that depressive mood was positively correlated with avoidant coping, whereas active cognitive coping was correlated with a less depressive mood. Research suggests that active coping, and specifically problem-solving, is associated with lower mental distress, whereas passive coping, such as withdrawal and avoidance, is associated with higher mental distress. In addition, social support seeking is believed to be the most adaptive coping strategy against mental distress, particularly among women.[34] Based on the evidence demonstrating that coping can buffer the negative impact of stress on psychological well-being, the coping strategies adopted by spouses of military personnel might buffer the negative impact of deployment-related stressors.

The goal of the study was to examine the roles of self-efficacy and coping in the psychological well-being and depressive symptoms of spouses of deployed military personnel. It was expected that self-efficacy would significantly predict psychological health, such that greater self-efficacy would be associated with better psychological well-being and fewer depressive symptoms. In addition, it was hypothesized that coping strategies would play an independent role in predicting psychological health of spouses. Finally, it was hypothesized that both self-efficacy and coping would moderate the path between deployment stress and psychological health.

METHOD

Participants and Procedure

The sample consisted of spouses of deployed military personnel ($N = 254$). The data was collected as part of a larger survey examining impacts of military life on families. The majority of the military personnel were deployed to Afghanistan (N = 195, 76.8%). Most of the spouses were female (92.9%) and spoke English as their first language (89.4%). In addition, 54 (21.3%) of the spouses were CF members themselves, the majority of these being part of the Regular Force. Among those who provided rank information for their spouse, the majority of spouses in the study (69.7%) were married to junior officers or Non-Commissioned Members (NCMs). In addition, most respondents (70.5%) had children living in their home, and the majority of these were living in the home on a full-time basis.

Measures

Psychological well-being. The abbreviated version of the General Health Questionnaire[35] was used to measure psychological well-being. This scale measures non-psychotic psychological distress and is a valid and reliable indicator of distress in the general population. The scale focuses on recent interruptions in normal healthy functioning (e.g., "Have you recently lost much sleep over worry?"). Items were rated on a scale ranging from 1 ("not at all") to 4 ("much more than usual"). The mean rating across the twelve items was used as the overall score (Cronbach's $\alpha = .78$).

Depressive symptoms. A shortened (nine-item) version of the Center for Epidemiologic Studies Depression Scale (CES-D)[36] was used to assess symptoms of depression. Participants rated the frequency with which they experienced each of the nine symptoms on a scale ranging from 1 ("rarely or none of the time") to 4 ("most or all of the time"). The mean rating across all of the items was used as the overall score (Cronbach's α = .93).

Self-efficacy. The 10-item General Self-Efficacy Scale[37] was used to measure self-efficacy, or the belief that one's own actions lead to positive outcomes. Perceived self-efficacy refers to optimistic beliefs that one can perform difficult tasks or cope with stressors, and facilitates perseverance in the face of obstacles and recovery from setbacks. Responses to the items (e.g., "I can always manage to solve difficult problems if I try hard enough") ranged from 1 ("not at all true") to 4 ("exactly true"). Responses were averaged to create a single score for each respondent (Cronbach's α = .91).

Coping. Coping strategies were measured using the Brief COPE,[38] a 28-item scale based on the COPE Inventory.[39] The Brief COPE contains 14 subscales of coping responses: self-distraction, active coping, denial, substance use, use of emotional support, use of instrumental support, behavioural disengagement, venting, positive reframing, planning, humour, acceptance, religion, and self-blame. Responses ranged from 1 ("I usually don't do this at all") to 4 ("I usually do this a lot"). Responses were averaged to create a score for each of the 14 subscales for each respondent. Following a principal component analysis of the 14 subscales using varimax rotation, and retaining items which loaded greater than 0.45, five main dimensions explaining 51.8% of the variance were identified. The first factor comprised four items assessing active coping strategies (active, problem-solving) (Cronbach's α = .85). The second factor comprised 10 items assessing emotional coping strategies (avoidance, denial, substance use, disengaging, self-blaming) (Cronbach's α = .74). The third factor comprised 4 items reflecting social support seeking strategies (emotional and instrumental social support) (Cronbach's α = .89). The fourth factor comprised 2 items reflecting humour coping (Cronbach's α = .84). Finally, the fifth factor comprised 2 items reflecting religious coping strategies (Cronbach's α = .90). Scores for each of the five factors were created by taking the unit-weighted mean of the relevant items.

Deployment stress. Deployment stress was assessed using one item from the modified version of the Family Issues Scale:[40] "The deployment was stressful for me". The responses to the item were rated on a scale of 1 ("strongly disagree") to 5 ("strongly agree"). Higher score indicated higher levels of post-deployment stress.

RESULTS

The analyses examined the roles of self-efficacy and coping in psychological well-being and depression of spouses of deployed military personnel. For these purposes, two multiple regression analyses were conducted wherein the domains of psychological health (psychological well-being and depressive symptoms) were regressed onto self-efficacy and coping, which were entered simultaneously. Second, two sets of hierarchical regression analyses were conducted where the domains of psychological health were regressed onto deployment stress and individual characteristics (self-efficacy and coping) at the first step, followed by their interaction terms at the second step.

Psychological Well-Being

Overall, self-efficacy and coping significantly predicted health symptoms, R2 = .262, F (6, 239) = 14.18, p < .001 (Table 14.1). Self-efficacy was uniquely and positively predictive of health symptoms over and above the impact of coping. In addition, although three coping scales, active, emotional, and humour, were correlated with well-being scores, only emotional coping and humour were uniquely predictive of well-being over and above the impact of other coping strategies and self-efficacy. Specifically, emotional coping was negatively correlated with well-being, while humour was positively correlated with well-being. Both self-efficacy and coping were found to have important and independent roles in the well-being of spouses of military personnel.

	Pearson r	*B*	R^2
			.262***
Self-efficacy	.44***	.35***	
Active coping	.22***	-.05	
Emotional coping	-.39***	-.26***	
Social support coping	.08	.01	
Humour coping	.15*	.14*	
Religious coping	.02	.03	

*p<.05;***p<.001

Table 14.1: Role of self-efficacy and coping in psychological well-being.

Given that self-efficacy and coping were found to be independent predictors of well-being, the moderating roles of self-efficacy and coping were examined in two separate regression analyses. The first hierarchical regression examined the moderating effect of self-efficacy on the relationship between deployment stress and well-being. The interaction between deployment stress and self-efficacy was significant, R^2 change = .034, F (1, 239) = 11.72, p < .01 (Table 14.2). Specifically, the interaction between stress and self-efficacy was positively predictive of well-being (β = .89, p < .01). Follow-up analyses demonstrated that for low levels of self-efficacy, the negative effect of deployment stress on well-being was significant (β = -.42, p < .01), whereas for high levels of self-efficacy, the negative effect of deployment stress on well-being was not significant (β = -.16, ns). In other words, self-efficacy served as a buffer against deployment stress.

	Pearson r	*B*	R^2_{change}
Step 1			.293***
Deployment stress	-.33***	-.33***	
Self-efficacy	.44***	.46***	
Step 2			.034**
Deployment Stress x Self-Efficacy	.46***	.89**	

p<.01;*p<.001

Table 14.2: Moderating role of self-efficacy in the path between deployment stress and psychological well-being.

The second hierarchical regression examined the moderating role of coping on the relationship between deployment stress and well-being. The interaction between deployment stress and coping was significant, R^2 change = .036, F (5, 259) = 2.40, p < .05 (Table 14.3). Specifically, the interaction between deployment stress emotional coping was negatively predictive of health symptoms (β = -.70, p < .05). Follow-up analyses demonstrated that for low levels of emotional coping, the negative effect of deployment stress on health scores was weaker (β = -.26, p < .01) than for high levels of self-efficacy (β = -.39, p < .001). In other words, the use of emotional coping was associated with poor well-being among spouses already experiencing deployment stress.

	Pearson r	B	R^2_{change}
Step 1			.269***
Deployment stress	-.35***	-.33***	
Active coping	.21**	-.26	
Emotional coping	-.39***	.38	
Social support coping	.08	.38	

Table 14.3: Moderating role of coping in the path between deployment stress and psychological well-being.

DEPRESSIVE SYMPTOMS

Overall, self-efficacy and coping significantly predicted depressive symptoms, R^2 = .323, F (6, 239) = 19.02, $p < .001$ (Table 14.4). Self-efficacy was uniquely predictive of depressive symptoms over and above the impact of coping. Specifically, self-efficacy was negatively correlated with depressive symptoms. In addition, although four coping scales (active, emotional, social support, and humour) were correlated with depressive symptoms, emotional coping was the only unique predictor over and above the impact of other coping strategies and self-efficacy, and was positively correlated with depressive symptoms. Both self-efficacy and coping had important and independent roles in the depressive symptoms of spouses of military personnel.

	Pearson r	B	R^2
			.323***
Self-Efficacy	-.46***	.32***	
Active coping	-.24***	.05	
Emotional coping	.47***	.34***	
Social support coping	-.17**	-.11	
Humour coping	-.11*	-.10	
Religious coping	-.03	-.01	

*$p<.05$; **$p<.01$;***$p<.001$

Table 14.4: role of self-efficacy and coping in depressive symptoms.

Given that self-efficacy and coping were found to be independent predictors of depressive symptomatology, the moderating roles of self-efficacy and coping were examined in two separate regression analyses. The first hierarchical regression examined the moderating effect of self-efficacy on the relationships between deployment stress and depressive symptoms. In this analysis, the interaction between deployment stress and self-efficacy was significant, R^2 change = .013, $F (1, 239) =$ 4.53, $p < .05$ (Table 14.5). Specifically, the interaction between stress and self-efficacy was negatively predictive of depressive symptoms (β = -.55, $p < .05$). For low levels of self-efficacy, the negative effect of deployment stress on depressive scores was slightly stronger (β = .40, $p < .001$) than for high levels of self-efficacy (β = .36, $p <$ .05). Although the difference in the coefficients was small, the interaction was statistically significant, suggesting that self-efficacy served as a buffer against deployment stress in predicting depressive symptoms among spouses of military personnel.

	Pearson r	B	R^2_{change}
Step 1			.293***
Deployment stress	.35***	.33***	
Self-efficacy	-.45***	.13	
Step 2			.013*
Deployment Stress x Self-Efficacy	-.45***	-.55*	

*p<.05;***p<.001

Table 14.5: Moderating role of self-efficacy in the path between deployment stress and depressive symptoms.

The second hierarchical regression examined the moderating effect of coping on the relationships between deployment stress and depressive symptoms. In this analysis, the interaction between deployment stress and coping did not significantly predict depressive symptoms over and above the effects of deployment stress and coping, R^2 change = .017, $F (5, 259) = 1.22$, ns (Table 14.6).

	Pearson r	B	R^2_{change}
Step 1			.337***
Deployment stress	.36***	.31***	
Active coping	-.23***	-.26	
Emotional coping	.47***	-.11	
Social support coping	-.16**	-.04	
Humour coping	-.10	-.20	
Religious coping	-.02	-.58	
Step 2			.017
Deployment stress x active coping	-.23***	.18	
Deployment stress x emotional coping	.47***	.52	
Deployment stress x social support coping	-.16**	-.09	
Deployment stress x humour coping	-.10	.13	
Deployment stress x religious coping	-.01	.58	

$p<.01$;*$p<.001$

Table 14.6: Moderating role of coping in the path between deployment stress and depressive symptoms.

DISCUSSION

Individuals with greater self-efficacy have been found to experience less stress and to have better psychological well-being than those with lower self-efficacy.[41] Furthermore, certain coping strategies are associated with better psychological well-being.[42] Given that deployment can have a negative impact on the well-being of spouses of military personnel[43] and that the family can also have a profound impact on both military personnel and the organization as a whole,[44] it is important to be able to predict spouses' psychological well-being. However, limited research has been conducted to examine the factors that can protect families from the negative impact of military stressors.

The present study examined the role of self-efficacy and coping in psychological health of spouses of deployed military personnel. It was found that self-efficacy played an important role in the well-being of spouses of deployed military personnel over and above the impact of coping. Consistent with previous research,[45] individuals who reported greater self-efficacy were consistently found to have better psychological well-being and fewer depressive symptoms. Furthermore, self-efficacy buffered the negative impact of deployment stress on well-being, consistent with the suggestion of previous researchers that self-efficacy would serve as a buffer against psychological health problems during stressful conditions.[46] As well, coping significantly predicted variance in psychological health over and above the impact of self-efficacy. Specifically, emotional coping was associated with poorer psychological well-being and greater depressive symptoms, in line with previous research which demonstrated that the use of emotion-focused coping methods was associated with negative outcomes under stress.[47] The finding is also consistent with previous research on the link between emotional coping and greater depressive symptoms among spouses of deployed military personnel.[48] Furthermore, humour was found to buffer individuals against psychological health problems. This finding is consistent with previous research,[49] which demonstrated that humour buffered the negative impact of basic training stress on well-being of military recruits, as well as other contemporary research that has recognized the valuable role of humour in psychological well-being.[50] In addition, emotional coping was found to moderate the negative impact of deployment stress on psychological health. Specifically, individuals who experienced greater deployment stress and used an emotional coping strategy in an attempt to deal with their negative emotions experienced lower well-being and greater depressive symptoms than those who did not use this type of coping. This finding is consistent with previous research conducted among military personnel, [51] which demonstrated that emotional coping increased the perception of stress and psychological health problems. Although emotional coping strategies may be effective in the short term, they are usually dysfunctional as long-term solutions because they only allow individuals to temporarily escape from stressors.

The results of the study suggest that coping effectiveness depends on a combination of factors, which are the beliefs about the self and coping methods adopted. In the light of these findings, it may be advantageous for organizations to focus on developmental activities that aim to increase perceptions of self-efficacy among military families. Consistent with the view that self-efficacy is amenable to training efforts, it was found that resilience training increased perceived self-efficacy among veterans with substance abuse problems.[52] Self-efficacy training would provide individuals with greater perceptions of mastery to deal with stressful situations, thereby reducing the negative psychological impacts of stressors. Furthermore, coping strategies uniquely predicted psychological well-being and depressive symptoms among spouses of deployed military personnel, and buffered the impact of stress. Therefore, it may be beneficial to provide coping training to the families of deployed military personnel. For example, research has demonstrated that problem-solving coping could be enhanced with training,[53] and coping skills training has been found to increase self-efficacy in dealing with stressful situations.[54] However, future research should consider and examine the best coping training method, such as whether the intervention should focus on helping individuals choose effective coping strategies, or on increasing the effectiveness of the coping strategies already employed.[55]

The results of the present study suggest that providing self-efficacy and coping training to spouses of deployed military personnel would be beneficial, as it would reduce stress and improve psychological health outcomes. Spouses of military members face a number of unique challenges associated with the military lifestyle, including frequent relocations, temporary housing, spousal unemployment and underemployment, and separations.[56] Furthermore, deployments, which may be compounded by significant and realistic concerns about the service member's safety,[57] have been found to contribute to psychological health problems among spouses.[58] Therefore, it is crucial to help spouses of military personnel maintain resiliency in the face of stressors associated with military life, such as deployment. Stress and coping training should provide military families with information on the adaptive coping strategies that may be used to deal with military-related stressors.

LIMITATIONS

There are a number of limitations in this study. First, it is possible that some spouses of military personnel may have self-selected into the study. That is, some respondents who chose to complete the survey may have done so due to their experiences (either positive or negative) with the CF. However, it is not possible to determine the extent to which this may have been the case in this study, or what the impacts of such bias may be. For example, if a disproportionate number of individuals with negative experiences responded to the study, higher rates of depression may have been found in comparison to the general population of spouses.

Second, although the results are presented overall, regardless of the military status of the respondent, it will be of interest in future analyses of the data to look specifically at the experiences of dual-service couples, in which the respondent is also a member of the CF. As well, since the survey included only the spouses and common-law partners of Regular Force members, the results cannot be generalized to the population of families of Reservists. It is possible that families of Reservists face unique challenges that are not captured in the present study, and it would be of benefit for future research to include reserve families.

Third, although previous evidence is supportive of the role of coping in psychological well-being, [59] given the correlational nature of the present study, caution should be merited, especially in making cause and effect interpretations. It is also possible that individuals with psychological health problems (e.g., poor psychological health or greater depressive symptomatology) develop emotion-focused strategies for coping (e.g., avoiding their own health problems or dissatisfaction or rumination about them), and, alternatively, these processes might be both caused by a third factor resulting in a spurious relation.

Finally, future research should expand the findings by introducing other important factors that may contribute to the process of coping with stress (e.g., availability and usage of social support) and examining other types of outcomes, such as physical health and job and training performance. In addition, the mediating role of stress appraisals should be incorporated into the current personality, coping, and psychological well-being models. It is possible that the paths between self-efficacy, coping, and psychological well-being differ based on the level of stress experienced. As well, the study did not examine the potential positive effects of military service. Although individual resilience has been studied in terms of the resources that enable adaptation to the adverse impacts of stress, less research has been conducted on resilience of families, particularly families that are exposed to unique stressors such as those associated with military life. It has been suggested that although military separations are challenging for families, they can also serve to strengthen families by increasing their resiliency.[60] Identifying the protective factors which enable families to maintain well-being despite stressors such as the deployment of a spouse, will provide information about ways to increase resiliency (e.g., by way of family-related programs and policies). It must be recognized that the effects of experiences such as deployment are not entirely negative. For example, deployments may involve a sense of pride in the military member for having completed meaningful work. It would be beneficial for future research with military spouses to include measures of the positive impacts of military service, and to link these with individual factors such as coping strategies and self-efficacy, in order to be better able to focus on the variables associated with positive adaptation to stressors.

CONCLUSIONS

The demands of military service on its members can have numerous effects at the family, individual, and organizational levels.[61] In the current climate of increasing intensity and frequency of military operations combined with decreased resources, it is particularly important to assess how families adapt to the demands of military life. Since spousal support plays an important role in both the well-being of serving members and the organization as a whole, it is crucial to examine how spouses of military personnel can maintain resiliency in the face of the stressors associated with military life. The main goal of this study was to examine the roles of self-efficacy and coping in the psychological health of spouses of deployed military personnel. The results suggest that the protective role of high self-efficacy may be strongest among those who use effective coping strategies and do not use emotional coping. Psychological health problems of spouses of military personnel are costly to both the military family and the organization. Practical implications point towards the value of heightening families' perceptions of self-efficacy in order to assist them in coping with the demanding aspects of military life and to embrace new opportunities.

[1]E.E. Kossek and C. Ozeki, "Work-family conflict, policies, and the job-life satisfaction relationship: A review and directions for organizational behavior/human resources research," *Journal of Applied Psychology* 83 (1998): 139-149.

[2]S. Dursun, and K. Sudom, *Impacts of military life on families: results from the Perstempo survey of Canadian Forces spouses*, Director General Military Personnel Operational Research and Analysis Technical Report 2009-001, 2009.

[3]K. Sudom, *Quality of Life among Military Families: Results from the 2008/9 Survey of Canadian Forces Spouses*, Director General Military Personnel Operational Research and Analysis, 2010.

[4]J.D. Angrist and J.H. Johnson, "Effects of work-related absences on families: evidence from the Gulf War," *Industrial and Labor Relations Review* 54, 1 (2000) 41-58; W.G. Black, "Military-induced family separation: a stress reduction intervention," Social Work 38 (1993): 273-80; P.S. Jensen, D. Martin, and H. Watanabe, "Children's response to parental separation during Operation Desert Storm," *Journal of the American Academy of Child and Adolescent Psychiatry* 35, (1996): 433-441; A.J. Mansfield, J.S. Kaufman, S.W. Marshall, B.N. Gaynes, J.P. Morrissey, and C.C. Engel, "Deployment and the Use of Mental Health Services among U.S. Army Wives," *The New England Journal of Medicine* 362, (2010): 101-109; W.R. Schumm, D.B. Bell, and P.A. Gade, "Effects of a military overseas peacekeeping deployment on marital quality, satisfaction, and stability," *Psychological Reports* 87, (2000): 815-821.

[5]S. Dursun, "Results of the 2005 spouse Perstempo survey" (presentation, Military Family National Advisory Board, Ottawa, ON, November 7, 2006); D.R. McCreary, M.M. Thompson, and L. Pasto, "Predeployment family concerns and soldier well-being: the impact of family concerns on the predeployment well-being of Canadian Forces personnel," *The Canadian Journal of Police and Security Services* 1, (2003): 33 40; D.K. Orthner, "Family Impacts on the Retention of Military Personnel," Research Report 1556, *U.S. Army Research Institute for the Behavioral and Social Sciences* (April 1990).

[6]S.R. Maddi, "Relevance of Hardiness Assessment and Training to the Military Context," *Military Psychology* 19, 1, (2007): 61-70; E.R. Fiedler, T.F. Oltmanns, and E. Turkheimer, "Traits associated with personality disorders and adjustment to military life: Predictive validity of self and peer reports," *Military Medicine* 169, (2004): 207-211; D.C. Scholtz, "The validity of psychological screening measures across the performance domain in the Canadian Forces", Sponsor Research Report 2003-03, *Director Human Resources Research and Evaluation, National Defence Headquarters*, 2003.

[7]I.M. Engelhard, and M.A. van den Hout, "Preexisting neuroticism, subjective stressor severity, and posttraumatic stress in soldiers deployed to Iraq," *The Canadian Journal of Psychiatry* 52, 8 (2007): 505-509.

[8]J.R. Rundell, and R.J. Ursano, "Psychiatric responses to war trauma," in *Emotional Aftermath of the Persian Gulf War*, ed. R.J. Ursano, and A.E. Norwood, (Washington, DC: American Psychiatric Press, 1996), 43-81.

[9]P.T. Bartone, "Hardiness protects against war-related stress in Army Reserve Forces," *Consulting Psychology Journal: Practice and Research* 51 (1999): 72-82.

[10]A. Bandura, "Self-efficacy," *Encyclopedia of human behavior* 4, ed. V. S. Ramachaudran (New York: Academic Press, 1994), 71-81.

[11]S. Rosenfield, "Factors contributing to the subjective quality of life of the chronically mentally ill," *Journal of Health and Social Behaviour* 33, (1992): 299-315.

[12]M.M. Barry, and A. Zissis, "Quality of life as an outcome measure in evaluating mental health services: A review of the empirical evidence," *Social Psychiatry and Psychiatric Epidemiology* 32, (1997): 38-47; L. Hansson, T. Middelboe, L. Merinder, and O. Bjarnason, "Predictors of subjective quality of life in schizophrenic patients living in the community. A nordic multicentre study," *The International Journal of Social Psychiatry* 45, (1999): 247-258; M.K. Kentros, K. Terkelsen, J. Hull, T.E. Smith, and M. Goodman, "The relationship between personality and quality of life in persons with schizoaffective disorder and schizophrenia," *Quality of Life Research* 6 (1997): 118-122.

[13]K. Joekes, T. Van Elderen, and K. Schreurs, "Self-efficacy and overprotection are related to quality of life, psychological well-being and self-management in cardiac patients" *Journal of Health Psychology* 12, 1, (2007): 4-16; R.G. Kuijer, and D.T.D. De Ridder, "Discrepancy in illness-related goals and quality of life in chronically ill patients: The role of self-efficacy," *Psychology and Health* 18 (2003): 313-330.

[14]J.H. Barlow, B. Williams, and C. Wright, "The generalized self-efficacy scale in people with arthritis," *Arthritis Care & Research* 9 (1996): 189-196; K.M. Schiaffino, and T.A. Revenson, "The role of perceived self-

efficacy, perceived control, and causal attributions in adaptation to rheumatoid arthritis: Distinguishing mediator vs. moderator effects," *Personality and Social Psychology Bulletin* 18 (1992): 709-718.

[15]S. Williams, M. Wissing, S. Rothman, and M. Themane, "Self efficacy, work, and psychological outcomes in a public service context," *Journal of Psychology in Africa* 20 (2010): 53-60.

[16]P. Arnstein, M. Caudill, C.L. Mandle, A. Norris, and R. Beasley, "Self-efficacy as a mediator of the relationship between pain intensity, disability and depression in chronic pain patients," *Pain 80*, (1999): 483-491; A. O'Leary, "Self-efficacy and health: behavioral and stress physiological mediation," *Cognitive Therapy and Research* 16 (1992): 229–245; K.M. Schiaffino, and T.A. Revenson, "The role of perceived self-efficacy, perceived control, and causal attributions in adaptation to rheumatoid arthritis: Distinguishing mediator vs. moderator effects," *Personality and Social Psychology Bulletin* 18 (1992): 709-718.

[17]C.C. Benight and A. Bandura, "Social cognitive theory of posttraumatic recovery: The role of perceived self-efficacy," *Behaviour Research and Therapy* 42 (2004): 1129-1148.

[18]K. Ginzburg, Z. Solomon, R. Dekel, and Y. Neria, "Battlefield functioning and chronic PTSD: Associations with perceived self- efficacy and causal attribution," *Personality and Individual Differences* 34, (2003): 463-476.

[19]S.M. Jex and P.D. Bliese, "Efficacy beliefs as a moderator of the impact of work-related stressors: A multilevel study," *Journal of Applied Psychology* 84 (1999): 349–361.

[20]S. Rosenfield, "Factors contributing to the subjective quality of life of the chronically mentally ill," *Journal of Health and Social Behaviour* 33 (1992): 299-315.

[21]H. Murphy and E.K. Murphy, "Comparing quality of life using the World Health Organization Quality of Life measure (WHOQOL-100) in a clinical and non-clinical sample: exploring the role of self-esteem, self-efficacy and social functioning," *Journal of Mental Health* 15 (2006): 289-300.

[22]S.M. Jex and P.D. Bliese, "Efficacy beliefs as a moderator of the impact of work-related stressors: A multilevel study," *Journal of Applied Psychology* 84 (1999): 349–361.

[23]G.F. Keoske, S.A. Kirk, and R.D. Keoske, R.D. "Coping with job stress: Which strategies work best?" *Journal of Occupational and Organizational Psychology* 66 (1993): 319-335; A.J. Kinicki and J.C. Latack, "Exploration of the construct of coping with involuntary job loss," *Journal of Vocational Behavior* 36 (1990): 339-360.

[24]M.A. Gowan, S.L. Craft, S L., and R.A. Zimmermann, "Response to work transitions by United States Army personnel: effects of self-esteem, self-efficacy, and career resilience," *Psychological Reports* 86 (2003): 911-921.

[25]R.S. Lazarus and S. Folkman, *Stress, appraisal, and coping* (New York: Springer, 1984), 141.

[26]R.S. Lazarus and S. Folkman, *Stress, appraisal, and coping* (New York: Springer, 1984), 157-164.

[27]M. Olff, J.F. Brosschot, and G. Godaert, "Coping styles and health," *Personality and Individual Differences* 15 (1993): 81-90.

[28]E.E. Beckham and R.L. Adams, "Coping behaviour in depression: report on a new scale," *Behavior Research and Therapy* 22, (1984): 71-75; C.R. Brewin, B. Andrews, and J.D.Valentine, "Meta-analysis of risk factors for posttraumatic stress disorder in trauma-exposed adults," *Journal of Consulting and Clinical Psychology* 68, (2000): 748-766; R.A. Bryant, J.E. Marosszeky, J. Crooks, I.J. Baguley, and J.A. Gurka, "Posttraumatic stress disorder and psychosocial functioning after severe traumatic brain injury," *The Journal of Nervous and Mental Disease* 189, (2001): 109-113; R.A. Bryant, J.E. Marosszeky, J. Crooks, and J.A. Gurka, J.A. "Posttraumatic stress disorder after severe traumatic brain injury," *American Journal of Psychiatry* 157, (2000): 629 631; S. Cohen and T.A. Wills, "Stress, social support, and the buffering hypothesis," *Psychological Bulletin* i 98, (1985): 310 357; J. Griffiths, A.V. Ravindran, Z. Merali, and H. Anisman, "Dysthymia: neurochemical and behavioral perspectives," *Molecular Psychiatry* 5, (2000): 242-261; S.M. Monroe and R.A. Depue, "Life stress and depression," in *Psychosocial Aspects of Depression* eds. J. Becker and A. Kleinman, (Hillsdale, NJ, US: Lawrence Erlbaum Associates, Inc., 1991), 101-130; S.D. Solomon, and E.M. Smith, "Social support and perceived control as moderators of responses to dioxin and flood exposure," in *Individual and community responses to trauma and disaster: the structure of human chaos*, eds. R.J. Ursano, and B.G. McCaughey, (NY, US: Cambridge University Press, 1994), 179-200.

[29]R.S. Lazarus and S. Folkman, *Stress, appraisal, and coping* (New York: Springer, 1984), 188.

[30]R.S. Lazarus and S. Folkman, *Stress, appraisal, and coping* (New York: Springer, 1984), 185.

[31]A.G. Billings and R.H. Moos, "The role of coping responses and social resources in attenuating the stress of life event," *Journal of Behavioural Medicine* 4 (1981): 139 157; L.A. Doerfler, and C.S. Richards, "Self-initiated attempts to cope with depression," Cognitive Therapy and Research 5 (1981): 367 371.

[32]J. Coyne, C. Aldwin, and R.S. Lazarus, "Depression and coping in stressful episodes," *Journal of Abnormal Psychology* 90 (1981): 439-447.

[33]J. Coyne, C. Aldwin, and R.S. Lazarus, "Depression and coping in stressful episodes," *Journal of Abnormal Psychology* 90 (1981): 439-447.

[34]S. Claerhout, J. Elder, and C. Janes, "Problem-solving skills of battered women," *American Journal of Community Psychology* 10, (1982): 605-612; D. Funabiki, N.C. Bologna, M. Pepping, and K.C. Fitzgerald, "Revisiting sex differences in the expression of depression," *Abnormal Psychology* 89 (1980): 194-202; R.E. Mitchell, and C.A. Hodson, "Coping with domestic violence: Social support and psychological health among battered women," *American Journal of Community Psychology* 11 (1983): 629-654.

[35]M.H. Banks, C.W. Clegg, P.R. Jackson, N.J. Kemp, E.M. Stafford, and T.D. Wall, "The use of the general health questionnaire as an indicator of mental health in occupational settings," *Journal of Occupational Psychology* 53 (1980): 187-94.

[36]L.S. Radloff, "The CES-D scale: a self-report depression scale for research in the general population," *Applied Psychological Measurement* 1, (1990): 385-401.

[37]R. Schwarzer and M. Jerusalem, "Generalized self-efficacy scale," in *Measures in health psychology: a user's portfolio*. Causal and control beliefs, eds. J. Weinman, S. Wright, and M. Johnston (Windsor, England: NFER-NELSON, 1995), 35-37.

[38]C.S. Carver, "You want to measure coping but your protocol's too long: Consider the Brief COPE," *International Journal of Behavioral Medicine* 4 (1997): 92-100.

[39]C.S. Carver, M.F. Scheier, and J.K. Weintraub, "Assessing coping strategies: A theoretically based approach," *Journal of Personality and Social Psychology* 56 (1989): 267 283.

[40]M.M. Thompson and L. Pasto, "Psychometric assessment and refinement of the family issues scale of the Human Dimensions of Operations (HDO) project," *Defence and Civil Institute of Environmental Medicine*, TR 2001-049. 2001.

[41]P. Arnstein, M. Caudill, C.L. Mandle, A. Norris, and R. Beasley, "Self-efficacy as a mediator of the relationship between pain intensity, disability and depression in chronic pain patients," *Pain* 80 (1999): 483-491; A. O'Leary, "Self-efficacy and health: behavioral and stress physiological mediation," *Cognitive Therapy and Research* 16 (1992): 229–245; K.M. Schiaffino, T.A. Revenson, and A. Gibofsky, "Assessing the impact of self-efficacy beliefs on adaptation to rheumatoid arthritis," *Arthritis Care & Research* 4 (1991): 150-157.

[42]M. Olff, J.F. Brosschot, and G. Godaert, "Coping styles and health," *Personality and Individual Differences* 15, (1993): 81-90.

[43]J.D. Angrist and J.H. Johnson, "Effects of work-related absences on families: evidence from the Gulf War," *Industrial and Labor Relations Review* 54, 1 (2000) 41-58; A.J. Mansfield, J.S. Kaufman, S.W. Marshall, B.N. Gaynes, J.P. Morrissey, and C.C. Engel, "Deployment and the Use of Mental Health Services among U.S. Army Wives," *The New England Journal of Medicine* 362 (2010): 101-109.

[44]S. Dursun, and K. Sudom, *Impacts of military life on families: results from the Perstempo survey of Canadian Forces spouses*, Director General Military Personnel Operational Research and Analysis Technical Report 2009-001, 2009; D.R. McCreary, M.M. Thompson, and L. Pasto, "Predeployment family concerns and soldier well-being: the impact of family concerns on the predeployment well-being of Canadian Forces personnel," *The Canadian Journal of Police and Security Services* 1 (2003): 33-40; D.K. Orthner, "Family Impacts on the Retention of Military Personnel," Research Report 1556, *U.S. Army Research Institute for the Behavioral and Social Sciences*, (April 1990).

[45]M.M. Barry and A. Zissis, "Quality of life as an outcome measure in evaluating mental health services: A review of the empirical evidence," *Social Psychiatry and Psychiatric Epidemiology* 32, (1997): 38-47; L. Hansson, T. Middleboe, L. Merinder and O. Bjarnason,"Predictors of subjective quality of life in schizophrenic patients living in the community. A nordic multicentre study," *The International Journal of Social Psychiatry* 45 (1999): 247-258; M.K. Kentros, K. Terkelsen, J. Hull, T.E. Smith, and M. Goodman, "The relationship between personality and quality of life in persons with schizoaffective disorder and schizophrenia," *Quality of Life Research* 6 (1997): 118 – 122.

[46]P. Arnstein, M. Caudill, C.L. Mandle, A. Norris, and R. Beasley, "Self-efficacy as a mediator of the relationship between pain intensity, disability and depression in chronic pain patients," *Pain* 80 (1999): 483-491; O'Leary, A. "Self-efficacy and health: behavioral and stress physiological mediation," *Cognitive Therapy and Research* 16 (1992): 229–245; K.M. Schiaffino, and T.A. Revenson, "The role of perceived self-efficacy, perceived control, and causal attributions in adaptation to rheumatoid arthritis: Distinguishing mediator vs. moderator effects," *Personality and Social Psychology Bulletin* 18 (1992): 709-718.

[47]T.A. Beehr, L.B. Johnson, and R. Nieva, "Occupational stress: Coping of police and their spouses," *Journal of Organizational Behavior* 16, (1995): 3-26; G.F. Keoske, S.A. Kirk, and R.D. Keoske, "Coping with job stress: Which strategies work best?" *Journal of Occupational and Organizational Psychology* 66 (1993): 319-335.

[48]E.E. Dimiceli, M.A. Steinhardt, and S.E. Smith, "Stressful experiences, coping strategies, and predictors of health-related outcomes among wives of deployed military servicemen," *Armed Forces & Society* 36 (2010): 351-373.

[49]A. Skomorovsky, "Personality and psychological well-being of Canadian Forces officer candidates: the role of coping", Technical Memorandum 2010-022, *Director General Military Personnel Research and Analysis*, 2010.

[50]L. Franzini, "Humor in Therapy: The case for training therapists in its uses and risks," *The Journal of General Psychology* 128 (2001): 170-193.

[51]A. Skomorovsky, "Personality and psychological well-being of Canadian Forces officer candidates: the role of coping", Technical Memorandum 2010-022, *Director General Military Personnel Research and Analysis*, 2010, 20-45.

[52]D. Sadow, and B. Hopkins, "Research Communications in Psychology," *Psychiatry & Behavior* 18 (1993): 121-134.

[53]J.A. Blumenthal, F.J. Keefe, M.A. Babyak, C.V. Fenwick, J.M. Johnson, K. Stott, R. Funk, N.J. McAdams, S. Palmer, T. Martinu, D. Baucom, P.T. Diaz, and C.F. Emery, "Caregiver-assisted coping skills training for patients with COPD: background, design, and methodological issues for the INSPIRE-II study," *Clinical Trials* 6 (2009): 172-184.

[54]R.E. Smith, "Effects of coping skills training on generalized self-efficacy and locus of control," *Journal of Personality and Social Psychology* 56, (1989): 228-233; E.A. Gammon and S.D. Rose, "The coping skills training program for parents of children with developmental disabilities: An experimental evaluation," *Research on Social Work Practice* 1, (1991): 244-256; S.D. Rose, "Coping skills training in groups," *International Journal of Group Psychotherapy* 39 (1989): 59-78.

[55]N. Bolger and A. Zuckerman, "A framework for studying personality in the stress process," *Personality Processes and Individual Differences* 69, (1995): 890-902.

[56]K. Sudom, *Quality of Life among Military Families: Results from the 2008/9 Survey of Canadian Forces Spouses*, Director General Military Personnel Operational Research and Analysis, 2010.

[57]M.W. Segal, "The military and the family as greedy institutions," *The Armed Forces & Society* 1 (1986): 9-38.

[58]J.D. Angrist and J.H. Johnson, "Effects of work-related absences on families: evidence from the Gulf War," *Industrial and Labor Relations Review* 54, 1 (2000) 41; W.G. Black, "Military-induced family separation: a stress reduction intervention," Social Work 38 (1993): 273-80; P.S. Jensen, D. Martin, and H. Watanabe, "Children's response to parental separation during Operation Desert Storm," *Journal of the American Academy of Child and Adolescent Psychiatry* 35 (1996): 433-441; A.J. Mansfield, J.S. Kaufman, S.W. Marshall, B.N. Gaynes, J.P. Morrissey, and C.C. Engel, "Deployment and the Use of Mental Health Services among U.S. Army Wives," *The New England Journal of Medicine* 362 (2010): 101-109; W.R. Schumm, D.B. Bell, and P.A. Gade, "Effects of a military overseas peacekeeping deployment on marital quality, satisfaction, and stability," *Psychological Reports* 87 (2000): 815-821.

[59]N. Bolger, "Coping as a personality process: A prospective study," *Journal of Personality and Social Psychology* 59 (1990): 525-537; N. Bolger, and A. Zuckerman, "A framework for studying personality in the stress process," *Personality Processes and Individual Differences* 69 (1995): 890-902; C.S. Carver, C. Pozo, S.D., Harris, V. Noriega, M.F. Scheier, D.S. Robinson, A.S. Ketcham, F.L. Moffat, and K.C. Clark, "How coping mediates the effect of optimism on distress: A study of women with early stage breast cancer," *Journal of Personality and Social Psychology* 65 (1993): 375-390; C.J. Holahan and R.H. Moos. "Personality, coping, and family resources in stress resistance: A longitudical analysis," *Journal of Personality and Social Psychology* 51 (1986): 389-395.

[60]W.T. Wiens and P. Boss, "Maintaining family resiliency before, during, and after military separation," in *Military life: the psychology of serving in peace and combat* 3, The military family, eds. C.A. Castro, A.B. Adler, and T.W. Britt, (Westoport, Connecticut: Praeger Security International, 2006), 13-38.

[61]S. Dursun, "Results of the 2005 spouse Perstempo survey" (presentation, Military Family National Advisory Board, Ottawa, ON, November 7, 2006). .

CHAPTER 15

Lifespan Considerations in the Psychological Treatment of Canadian Veterans with Post Traumatic Stress Disorder

Shannon Gifford, PhD, C.Psych, Operational Stress Injury Clinic, Parkwood Hospital, St. Joseph's Health Care London;
James G. Hutchinson, PhD, C.Psych, Trillium Health Centre - West Toronto, WSIB Specialty Hand Program;
Maggie Gibson, PhD, CPsych, Veterans Care Program, Parkwood Hospital, St. Joseph's Health Care London; Aging, Rehabilitation and Geriatric Care, Lawson Health Research Institute

Abstract

This chapter explores the relevance of lifespan-related issues in the psychological treatment of Canadian veterans with PTSD. As part of a resident-training program, a collaborative process was undertaken to identify lifespan-related treatment issues in three veteran cohorts of different ages and to synthesize evidence that speaks to the challenges of treating Canadian veterans at various stages of the life course. Where the state of the current literature allows, recommendations regarding adapting general principles of PTSD treatment to the unique circumstances of each cohort are made. In the absence of empirical information about the suitability of trauma-focused therapies for older adults with PTSD, clinicians may hesitate to employ first-line psychological treatments with veterans from the eldest cohort (Second World War and the Korean War), however, this decision should be made on an individual basis. Age-related adaptations to treatment are available. Services should be made available to provide contextually sensitive, timely intervention to veterans of the second cohort (veterans of United Nations peacekeeping missions) and the third cohort (current Afghanistan veterans).

Lifespan Considerations in the Psychological Treatment of Canadian Veterans with Post Traumatic Stress Disorder

The term operational stress injury encapsulates a wide range of potential difficulties in functioning, including but not limited to problems with substance use, anxiety, and mood. This chapter addresses Post Traumatic Stress Disorder, an OSI that has been the focus of particular attention and concern within military and veteran health services. Our purpose is to explore the adaptation of psychological services to the needs of individuals with PTSD within three groups of Canadian veterans, representing different generations, cohorts and age groups: now elderly veterans who fought in the Second World War and the Korean War, veterans of United Nations (UN) peacekeeping operations, and veterans of the current war in Afghanistan.

Our interest in considering the needs of these three veteran groups independently is aligned with current thinking at the policy level. Governmental organizations responsible for veterans care are becoming increasingly aware of the need to think in terms of the life course when planning mental health services. In Canada, the New

Veterans Charter asserts that Canada has a moral obligation to provide veterans who have been physically or psychologically injured while serving their country with programs and care that will minimize injury-related losses and optimize quality of life. The recent Charter review[1] emphasizes that properly honouring this "social contract" will require a lifespan perspective on service planning. In the mental health domain, it argues for continued efforts to make government-funded, empirically supported treatments for military-related psychological difficulties, or "operational stress injuries," available to veterans across the life course. Similar policy perspectives are found in the United States. A recent assessment of the needs of veterans of the wars in Afghanistan and Iraq flagged several lifespan-related issues, including the likely chronicity of deployment-related mental health concerns and the likelihood that many years may pass before some soldiers first request help.[2]

We begin with a necessarily brief overview of PTSD and its treatment to set the stage. We then consider each of the three veteran cohorts in turn, with a focus on applying general principles of treatment for PTSD to the unique circumstances of each cohort. Where the current literature is sufficiently developed to allow for recommendations, these are offered.

Post Traumatic Stress Disorder

It has long been recognized that traumatic events, including traumatic military experiences, can have marked effects on psychological functioning. Until recently, however, a lack of diagnostic consistency hindered the development and evaluation of psychological treatments for traumatic stress reactions. The inclusion of PTSD as a diagnosis in the third edition of the American Psychiatric Association's Diagnostic and Statistical Manual of Mental Disorders (DSM-III)[3] contributed to a surge of research interest in treatments for traumatic stress.

According to the current version of the DSM (DSM-IV-TR),[4] a diagnosis of PTSD requires a person to have been exposed to a traumatic event in which both of the following were present: (1) experiencing or witnessing events involving actual or threatened death or serious injury, or threat to the physical integrity of self or others; and (2) an emotional response of intense fear, helplessness, or horror. A specified number of post-event criterion symptoms from each of three symptom subsets must be present for more than one month and must cause significant distress or impairment in social, occupational or other important areas of functioning. These three symptom subsets include persistent re-experiencing of the traumatic event, persistent avoidance of stimuli associated with the trauma and numbing of general responsiveness, and persistent symptoms of increased arousal.

Thorough reviews of the psychological treatment outcome literature on PTSD are widely available, [5] and we provide only a brief summary here. A variety of CBT approaches have been shown to be effective in the treatment of this disorder. PE treatment[6] has been more extensively studied than any other form of CBT treatment for PTSD, and has been shown to be highly effective in reducing the symptoms of PTSD.[7] A recent study demonstrated that PE was more effective than treatment as usual in reducing combat- and terrorism-related PTSD.[8] PE emphasizes imaginal exposure to trauma memories to a greater extent than any other approach. It includes psychoeducation and breathing retraining components as well as repeated, detailed retellings of trauma stories.

Other CBT approaches for PTSD also incorporate exposure to traumatic memories, though typically not as extensively as in PE. These therapies tend to focus more on exploring and challenging trauma-related cognitions and emotions, with exposure to traumatic memories occurring in the natural course of this work. For example, Cognitive Processing Therapy (CPT)[9] involves psychoeducation, writing about the meaning and implications of the traumatic experience, and identifying and challenging rigidly held and potentially distorted trauma-related beliefs. In one head-to-head study, CPT was shown to be equally effective to PE in treating assault-related trauma[10]; it has also shown significant promise in treating military-related PTSD.[11] Other treatments for PTSD with some empirical support include stress inoculation training,[12] cognitive therapy, assertiveness training, and eye movement desensitization and reprocessing (EMDR).[13]

Feeny and Foa (2005) recommend several strategies for reducing risk of relapse following cognitive-behavioural PTSD treatment. These include normalizing and anticipating brief symptom exacerbations, using skills learned in sessions to manage symptom spikes, and scheduling booster sessions.[14] Therapists are advised to review the steps to take if symptoms reappear, such as re-initiating *in vivo* and imaginal exposure, applying relaxation strategies, and seeking social support. To date, research into the efficacy of psychological treatments for PTSD has tended to examine short-term outcomes (i.e., less than one year), and studies that have incorporated relapse prevention have typically been vague about what these interventions involve. Although relapse prevention strategies make intuitive sense, their incremental value in PTSD treatment has not yet been established empirically.[15]

The treatment outcome literature shows that CBT for PTSD is effective when used in general adult veteran samples, although effect sizes tend to be smaller than those found in civilian samples.[16] Creamer & Forbes (2004) outline possible reasons for this discrepancy, including potential differences between military and civilian populations on personality, gender, or personal history variables, the fact that traumatic military events tend occur in the context of prolonged, stressful deployments, the chronicity and comorbidity associated with military-related PTSD, and the influence of compensation-related issues. [17]

Veterans of the Second World War and the Korean War

The demonstrably effective treatments available today were not available to our Second World War and Korean War veterans in the decades following their exposures to wartime trauma. Veterans of these conflicts currently presenting for treatment are now elderly, and issues of age may influence treatment planning decisions. Are current first-line psychological interventions for PTSD appropriate regardless of the stage the person has reached in his (or her) life course, or does treatment need to be modified on the basis of age? It is worth noting that the vast majority of veterans in this cohort are male, reflecting military recruitment policies in effect at the time of service.

On the one hand, the selection of PTSD treatment options for the elderly veteran should be based on a broad assessment of how a given intervention fits with general recommendations for psychological care of older adults. An excellent resource to guide this decision-making process can be found in the *Guidelines for Psychological Practice with Older Adults*.[18] A key recommendation is for clinicians to continuously evaluate whether their treatment decisions might be unduly influenced by inaccurate stereotypes about the elderly. These include beliefs that most older adults are frail, ill, or have significant cognitively impairments, that they are inflexible or stubborn, or that they are too old to change or are otherwise unlikely to benefit from treatment. The American Psychiatric Association (APA) guidelines emphasize the importance of recognizing that older adults are a heterogeneous group with variability in rate and types of cognitive and physical decline. They emphasize that cognitive impairment in older adults is typically mild, and that it rarely impairs daily functioning to a significant degree. The ability to engage intellectually with people and problems and benefit from new learning is typically retained in older adults, except in cases of severe dementia that become much more frequent in the very old.[19] Moreover, the APA guidelines highlight the importance of recognizing positive aspects of aging when treating older adults.

On the other hand, while age categories are at best a rough proxy for functional status, for the purposes of illustration older adults are often characterized categorically, for example as young old (ages 65-74), middle old (ages 75-84) and old old (ages 85 and over).[20] While heterogeneity within these groups is the norm and older adults demonstrate functional and behavioural plasticity across their lifespan, there are somewhat predictable age-related changes that can inform our understanding of how to adapt PTSD treatment to meet the changing needs of older adults as they age.

Developmental processes of aging may lead to the emergence or worsening of PTSD symptoms in late life.[21] These processes include greater time for reflection, normal increases in reminiscence, breakdown of established coping strategies due to age-related changes in habits and health, cumulative social network losses, cognitive changes, increased threats to personal control and privacy arising from dependence on others, and changes in sleep patterns and sensory abilities. In general, as adults transition from the young old to the middle old phase of their lives they may begin to experience mild declines in attention, concentration, processing speed, and memory.[22] Individuals in the middle old group may experience an escalation in challenges related to declining health and mobility, shrinking social networks, and role changes. With increasing age comes an increase in the prevalence of cognitive impairment and dementia. Adults who have reached advanced age and suffer from PTSD and dementia often must rely on others to help them identify trauma symptoms, avoid or cope with stressors, and access social support. Serious illness, increasing reliance on others for assistance with activities of daily living, and marked losses to the social support network can compromise emotional resources.

From the evidentiary perspective, treatment guidelines based on studies conducted with young and middle-aged adults advocate exposure-based CBT methods as the first line treatment for PTSD. However, research on the efficacy and suitability of these methods for older adults is lacking. There are two published case studies in which exposure therapy is used with older adults, [23] but no instances of randomized control trials of this treatment in an elderly sample have been published. This lack of research is problematic because the best-supported psychological treatments for PTSD involve confronting traumatic memories, and as such are inherently distressing and physiologically arousing. In the absence of empirical information on the efficacy and tolerability of trauma-focused therapies for older adults with PTSD, clinicians may worry that older veterans are not physically equipped to tolerate and benefit from exposure therapy.

A second concern is that cognitive changes more common in older adults may potentially affect the efficacy or tolerability of exposure therapy in elderly populations. For example, loss of specific memories due to diminished episodic memory may complicate efforts to recall events with precision.[24] However, traumatic events are typically encoded more deeply than less emotionally salient or striking events, and may resist this more general pattern of memory loss. Age-related declines in attentional control can make inhibition of trauma-related memories more difficult.[25] It is therefore possible that older adults may have more difficulty inhibiting intrusive traumatic memories after leaving an exposure therapy session, leading to higher-than-anticipated distress between sessions, although this issue has not been investigated empirically. Likewise, to the extent that exposure-based therapies require the formation of new memories incorporating information about current safety that compete with older fearful memories, the hypothesized mechanism of exposure treatment may be less likely to be effective, although this issue also requires study. Other evidence suggests that advanced age is often accompanied by heightened emotional intelligence and wisdom.[26] These qualities would seem to be of great potential utility in trauma therapy; again, research needed to evaluate this potential has not yet been conducted.

Good clinical practice, whether with young, middle-aged, or elderly patients, involves establishing first that the patient is ready and willing to confront the trauma memory. If and when the patient is ready to do direct exposure work (which may follow a lengthy "stabilization" period involving psychoeducation, development of emotion-regulation and other skills, and targeting of concurrent problems), the therapist carefully attends to the emotional intensity of the patient's experience, such that he or she stays in the optimal "therapeutic window."[27] This helps to ensure that patients are emotionally engaged enough with the trauma memory for the experience to be meaningful, but not so overwhelmed that they are re-traumatized. These standard considerations may be sufficient when planning exposure work with healthy, cognitively well-functioning older veterans. Additional considerations arise if the older veteran presents with significantly compromised physical or cognitive abilities.

Certain aspects of age-related physical decline have been identified as particular areas of concern in the use of exposure treatment with older adults.[28] It has been suggested that exposure therapies could be physically unsafe in individuals with pre-existing health problems because they typically involve elicitation of sympathetic response such as accelerated heart rate and increased respiration.[29] In support of this idea, there is evidence to suggest that acute emotional stress is related to sudden cardiac death (SCD).[30] However, the literature is unclear about whether older adults with PTSD are at increased risk of adverse health reactions to exposure therapy. Morse, Martin, and Moshonov (1992) reviewed the literature on stress-induced SCD and found that this phenomenon was more likely to occur in individuals suffering from a pre-existing heart condition or hypertension, and who possess psychosocial risk factors such as trait anxiety, hostility, anger repression, socially isolation, and recent major loss.[31] The authors make no mention of age as an independent risk factor. No empirical evidence could be found to indicate that healthy older adults are at increased risk of adverse physical outcomes relating to the experience of acute sympathetic response of the magnitude that is characteristically elicited during prolonged exposure therapy. It is also worth considering that untreated intrusive recollections and nightmares can result in panicky sensations involving intense physiological stress, and that this stress occurs in less predictable and controllable circumstances than those provided in exposure therapy. Health-related concerns about exposure therapy should be balanced against concerns over the health impact of recurrent episodes of trauma-related anxiety.

Recommendations. Individuals with health conditions that may be reactive to stress should receive a medical consultation prior to commencing intensive exposure therapy. The therapist should take the responsibility of screening for this early in the assessment process, in a manner that does not create unwarranted fears in the patient. With older patients who may be vulnerable to the effects of high physiological arousal, or who are expected to have more difficulty shifting attention away from traumatic memories after a session, a slower and gentler approach to exposure is indicated. The clinician may spend more time getting to know the patient and teaching emotion regulation skills prior to initiating any form of trauma-focused work, and less time per session might be spent in direct discussion of the traumatic events. Additional time might be given to discussion of more positive past and current events. Hyer and Sohnle (2001) offer specific guidelines and good practical suggestions for making decisions about exposure work and managing its "dosage" in work with older patients.[32]

If, after carefully considering an older veteran's presentation and history, the clinician has lingering doubts about the appropriateness of prolonged exposure therapy, he or she may elect to adopt a milder approach that contains some exposure-based elements. Maercker (2002) presents a promising approach to treating PTSD in older adults using a modified version of Life Review Therapy.[33] In this structured, time-limited approach, patients are guided through a chronological process of reminiscing about life events, with the aim of enhancing ego integrity and wisdom. Positive as well as traumatic events are discussed in the course of the life review, and patients are encouraged to reflect on personal strengths as well as on problems experienced during the life course. Discussion of a traumatic event involves a review of the event itself, followed by an exploration of how the experience affected the individual, how others responded to help him or her, what lessons were taken from it, and how he or she successfully coped with the experience over the years.

VETERANS OF UNITED NATIONS PEACEKEEPING MISSIONS

More than 125,000 CF members have participated in international peacekeeping missions, including those in Cyprus, Syria, the Persian Gulf, the former Yugoslavia, Rwanda, Somalia, Egypt, Ethiopia, East Timor, and Haiti. The original concept of peacekeeping involved placing a neutral force between opposing factions in order to supervise cease-fires and the withdrawal of opposing forces. These duties rapidly evolved as UN forces adapted to the particular demands of the specific conflicts. As a result, Canadian peacekeepers have been tasked with such diverse activities as delivering humanitarian aid, repatriating refugees, disarming hostile factions, clearing land-mines, conducting body exchanges, engaging in active combat, and training local police forces. CF members have also been charged with "peace-making" duties in active war zones. CF veterans deployed to such regions (e.g. Rwanda in 1994; areas of the Balkans in the early 1990s) witnessed the occurrences or aftermaths of atrocities inflicted on civilian populations and were often in great personal danger.

A CF veteran who has participated in multiple peacekeeping deployments is likely to have risked exposure to numerous traumatic events of varying type and intensity, occurring not just in early adulthood but across the adult life span. The impact of prolonged stress and periodic trauma may accumulate over the course of years, leading to gradual, insidious "personality change" as well as more clear-cut traumatic reactions to particularly stressful tours. Perhaps in contrast to most Second World War veterans, peacekeeping veterans may feel a lack of broad societal recognition or appreciation for the intensity of the work they have done. Although Canadians profess pride in our country's peacekeeping reputation, CF veterans may well feel that most Canadians know little about the physical and psychological risks this work entails.

For middle-aged veterans who have spent most of their adult lives within the "military family," adjusting to retirement can involve the added stress of transitioning into civilian culture. Decisions about retiring into civilian life can be difficult at the best of times. At this point in Canadian history, these decisions are further complicated by the Afghan war, as a decision about releasing from the CF likely involves deciding whether or not to accept a tour to Afghanistan. Clinical observation suggests that the war often affects how this cohort of veterans think about their own military experiences – for example, some veterans from the peacekeeping era report feeling ashamed to seek help for their debilitating post traumatic stress symptoms because they believe "they're going through so much worse in Afghanistan."

Recommendations. Veterans of UN peacekeeping missions have served during a period of great change in both our understanding of military-related traumatic stress and in the availability of services addressing these issues. These veterans may have been exposed to many different ideas about what post traumatic stress looks like, what it means to suffer from these symptoms, the social and occupational consequences of seeking help, and the availability of effective treatment. Special efforts ought to be made to draw these veterans in need of assistance into treatment or into less intensive relapse-prevention style interventions before they face the transitions and losses of advancing age.

VETERANS OF THE WAR IN AFGHANISTAN

Canadian veterans of the war in Afghanistan are better positioned to access effective, timely interventions for PTSD than their counterparts have been in the past. Our knowledge about best practices continues to evolve. Empirically supported interventions are increasingly available through clinics run by DND and VAC. Peer support initiatives such as the OSISS program are helping to ease veterans into treatment, as well as providing invaluable support from understanding and knowledgeable peers. However, significant barriers to treatment remain, despite advances in the availability of care. Many of these challenges are detailed in the 2008 DND/CF Ombudsman's Report[34] on the status of mental health care services in the Canadian military. Among other issues, the report discusses continued stigma associated with mental health issues, a lack of overarching leadership for mental health services within the CF, and geographic inequities in the availability of services across Canada. One issue the report does not address concerns the specific challenges in identifying reserve force members who may be experiencing deployment-related post traumatic stress. The issue is significant given the large number of reservists who have served in Afghanistan; it has been reported that at any given time reservists comprise

20-30% of the Canadian brigade forces in Afghanistan.

Chief Warrant Officer (CWO) Craig Grant, a 24-year veteran of the Regular Force currently serving with the Reserves as Officer Commanding, 7 Field Squadron, Combat Engineers, has advocated for the needs of reservists returning from Afghanistan. He points to a number of factors that reduce the chances that a reservist suffering a traumatic stress reaction will be identified and helped into treatment. Reservists returning to their home communities rather than to large military bases are less likely to have people in their family, social, and occupational circles who are well-briefed on OSIs and who are aware of services available to soldiers. At the reserve unit itself, there may be few individuals with the kind of deployment experiences that increase sensitivity to signs of combat-related post traumatic stress in others. Even when reserve leadership is motivated and able to spot warning signs of post traumatic stress, opportunities to do so may be severely limited. Reservists can choose to have minimal contact with their units post-deployment; when they do attend weekly parade nights, circumstances may not provide opportunities for others to recognize signs of stress.

As CWO Grant describes it, "Parade nights are a jam-packed four hours... and you don't find out that a soldier's having problems during training - it's when you're changing a tire, when stories come out in the mess, when things are more informal." More generally, he said, reservists suffer from being "more alone." He described the circumstances that many reservists return to as follows: "You come back in February. You're not going back to university or college right away because your semester's shot. From February till May, there's nothing for you, unless you find a job – and it's difficult finding a job in February. Chances are your family is off doing their own work. So you're stuck at home with a lot of time on your hands to replay things and no one to interact with." His suggestion for enhancing detection of reservists with traumatic stress reactions is to hire them for a few months upon their return, so "they come to the unit, and we have that time to watch, to hear, to listen." His unit actually attempted this solution after one deployment rotation, with good results: two soldiers whose post traumatic stress problems might otherwise have gone unnoticed were identified and linked up with mental health services. Innovative solutions such as this, which involve personal contact with influential military members, may be required if reservists are to access available treatments.

Recommendations. Accessing effective treatment in a timely manner is of key importance for veterans with PTSD, and innovative solutions may be needed to ensure all veterans of conflicts such as the Afghanistan war have the opportunity to take advantage of treatment options. It has been argued that it is also highly important to teaching relapse prevention strategies towards the end of treatment, especially those that involve coping with trauma-related triggers.[35]
Questions about whether relapse prevention strategies enhance long-term treatment outcome are part of a larger set of questions about how treatment moderates the course

of PTSD over time. Following veterans after an initially effective course of treatment could help answer questions about the impact of treatment on PTSD symptoms across the lifespan, such as whether symptom reductions persist over time, or whether one-time CBT can protect against symptom exacerbations in old age. It could also help us understand whether and how key life transitions (e.g., release from the military; retirement from working life) might interact with PTSD symptomatology. Thus, we recommend that modern treatment services for PTSD routinely consider the inclusion of a research component.

Conclusion

We explored how lifespan-related issues can affect the planning and delivery of psychological treatment for PTSD in three cohorts of Canadian veterans: elderly veterans of the Second World War and the Korean War, veterans of UN peacekeeping operations, and veterans of the current war in Afghanistan. Today's effective psychological interventions were not available to now elderly veterans in the decades following their exposures to wartime trauma. Decisions about how best to treat these veterans can be complicated by age-related declines in cognitive and physical functioning, and by a lack of empirical evidence about the efficacy and appropriateness of first-line psychological treatments when used with older adults. The heightened challenges of treating veterans in old age should inspire increased efforts to provide timely, effective treatment to veterans of UN peacekeeping missions and to recent veterans of Afghanistan. Working to ensure that veterans who have incurred psychological injuries through military service receive treatment across the life-course will honour Canada's social contract with its CF members, while creating research opportunities through which we may better understand the impact of treatment on PTSD symptoms across the lifespan.

[1]New Veterans Charter Advisory Group, *Honouring our commitment to new veterans and their families: the "living" charter in action*, (2009).

[2]Institute of Medicine, *Returning home from Iraq and Afghanistan: preliminary assessment of readjustment needs of veterans, service members, and their families* (Washington, DC: National Academies Press, 2010), 192.

[3]American Psychiatric Association, *Diagnostic and statistical manual of mental disorders 3rd ed.*, (Washington, DC: American Psychiatric Association, 1980), 494.

[4]American Psychiatric Association, *Diagnostic and statistical manual of mental disorders 4th ed.*, text rev., (Washington, DC: American Psychiatric Association, 2000), 886.

[5]E.B. Foa, Keane, T.M., and Friedman, M.J., *Effective treatments for PTSD: practice guidelines for the international society for traumatic stress studies* (New York, NY: Guilford Press, 2000), 385; V.M. Follette, J.I. Ruzek, and F.R. Abueg, *Cognitive-behavioral therapies for trauma* (New York, NY: Guilford Press, 2006), 472; C.B. Nemeroff, J.D. Bremner, E.B. Foa, H.S. Mayberg, C.S. North, and M.B. Stein, "Posttraumatic stress disorder: a state-of-the-science review," *Journal of Psychiatric Research* 40, 1 (2006): 1-21.

[6]E.B. Foa, and B.O. Rothbaum, *Treating the trauma of rape: Cognitive-behavioral therapy for PTSD treatment manual for practitioners*, (New York, NY: Guilford Press, 1998), 286; E.B. Foa, C.V. Dancu, E.A. Hembree, L.H. Jaycox, E.A. Meadows, and G.P. Street, "A comparison of exposure therapy, stress inoculation training, and their combination for reducing posttraumatic stress disorder in female assault victims," *Journal of Consulting and Clinical Psychology* 67, 2 (1999): 194-200.

[7]E.B. Foa, B.O. Rothbaum, D.G. Riggs, and T.B. Murdock, "Treatment of posttraumatic stress disorder in rape victims: a comparison between cognitive-behavioral procedures and counseling," *Journal of Consulting and Clinical Psychology* 59, 5 (1991): 715-723; E.B. Foa, C.V. Dancu, E.A. Hembree, L.H. Jaycox, E.A. Meadows, and G.P. Street, "A comparison of exposure therapy, stress inoculation training, and their combination for reducing posttraumatic stress disorder in female assault victims," *Journal of Consulting and Clinical Psychology* 67, 2 (1999): 194-200; I. Marks, K. Lovell, H. Noshirvani, M. Livanou, and S. Thrasher, "Treatment of posttraumatic stress disorder by exposure and/or cognitive restructuring: A controlled study," *Archives of General Psychiatry* 55, 4 (1998): 317-325.

[8]N. Nacasch, E.B. Foa, J.D. Huppert, D. Tzur, L. Fostick, Y. Dinstein, M. Pollack, and J. Zohar, "Prolonged exposure therapy for combat- and terror-related Posttraumatic Stress Disorder: A randomized control comparison with treatment as usual," *Journal of Clinical Psychiatry*, (in press).

[9]P.A. Resick, and M.K. Schnicke, "Cognitive processing therapy for sexual assault victims," *Journal of Consulting and Clinical Psychology* 60, 5 (1992): 748-756.

[10]P.A. Resick, and M.K. Schnicke, "Cognitive processing therapy for sexual assault victims," *Journal of Consulting and Clinical Psychology* 60, 5 (1992): 748-756.

[11]C.M. Monson, P.P. Schnurr, P.A. Resick, M.J. Friedman, Y. Young-Xu, and S.P. Stevens, "Cognitive processing therapy for veterans with military-related posttraumatic stress disorder," *Journal of Consulting and Clinical Psychology* 74, 5 (2006): 898.

[12]D.H. Meichenbaum, and J.L. Deffenbacher, "Stress inoculation training," *Counseling Psychologist* 16, 1 (1988): 69.

[13]Shapiro, F., *Eye Movement Desensitization and Reprocessing* (New York: Guilford Press, 1995), 473; For a comprehensive review see: B.O. Rothbaum, E.A. Meadows, P. Resick, and D.W. Foy, "Cognitive-behavioral therapy," in *Effective treatments for PTSD: practice guidelines from the international society for traumatic stress studies*, eds. E.B. Foa, T.M. Keane, and M.J. Friedman (New York, NY: Guilford Press, 2000), 60-83.

[14]N.C. Feeny, and E.B. Foa, "Posttraumatic stress disorder," in *Improving outcomes and preventing relapse in cognitive-behavorial therapy*, eds, M.M. Antony, D.R. Ledley and R.G. Heimberg (New York, NY: Guilford Press, 2005), 174-203.

[15]M.J. Dugas, A.S. Radomsky, and P. Brillon, "Tertiary intervention for anxiety and prevention of relapse," in *The prevention of anxiety and depression: theory, research, and practice*, eds. D. J. Dozois and K. S. Dobson, (Washington, DC: American Psychological Association, 2004), 161-184.

[16]M. Creamer and D. Forbes, "Treatment of posttraumatic stress disorder in military and veteran populations," *Psychotherapy: Theory, Research, Practice, Training* 41, 4 (2004): 388-398.

[17]M. Creamer and D. Forbes, "Treatment of posttraumatic stress disorder in military and veteran populations," *Psychotherapy: Theory, Research, Practice, Training* 41, 4 (2004): 388-398.

[18]American Psychological Association, Washington, DC., "Guidelines for psychological practice with older adults," *American Psychologist* 59, 4 (2004): 236-260.

[19]P.B. Baltes, and J. Smith, "New frontiers in the future of aging: from successful aging of the young old to the dilemmas of the fourth age," *Gerontology* 49, 2 (2003): 123-135.

[20]R. Schulz, L.S. Noelker, K. Rockwood, K., and R.L. Sprott, *The encyclopedia of aging: A comprehensive resource in gerontology and geriatrics* 4th ed. (New York: Springer, 2006), 1440.

[21]F.I. Snell, and E. Padin-Rivera, "Post-traumatic stress disorder and the elderly combat Veteran," *Journal of Gerontological Nursing* 23 (1997): 13-19.

[22]A.D Smith and J.L. Earles, "Memory changes in normal aging," in Perspectives on cognitive change in adulthood and aging, eds. F. Blanchard-Fields, and T.M. Hess, *Perspectives on cognitive change in adulthood and aging* (New York, NY: McGraw-Hill, 1996), 192-220.

[23]T.L. Cornelius, and R. Kenyon-Jump, "Application of cognitive-behavioral treatment for long-standing posttraumatic stress disorder in law enforcement personnel: a case study," *Clinical Case Studies* 6, 2 (2007): 143; Markowitz, J.D., "Post-traumatic stress disorder in an elderly combat veteran: a case report," *Military Medicine* 172, 6 (2007): 659-662.

[24]A.D Smith and J.L. Earles, "Memory changes in normal aging," in *Perspectives on cognitive change in adulthood and aging*, eds. F. Blanchard-Fields, and T.M. Hess, Perspectives on cognitive change in adulthood and aging (New York, NY: McGraw-Hill, 1996), 192-220.

[25]M. Floyd, J. Rice, and S.R. Black, "Recurrence of posttraumatic stress disorder in late life: a cognitive aging perspective," *Journal of Clinical Geropsychology* 8, 4 (2002): 303-311.

[26]P.B. Baltes and J. Smith, "New frontiers in the future of aging: from successful aging of the young old to the dilemmas of the fourth age," *Gerontology* 49, 2 (2003): 123-135.

[27]J. Briere and C. Scott, *Principles of trauma therapy: A guide to symptoms, evaluation, and treatment* (Thousand Oaks, CA: Sage Publications, Inc., 2006), 312.

[28]L. Hyer, and M.G. Woods, "Phenomenology and treatment of trauma in later life," in *Cognitive-behavioral therapies for trauma*, eds.V.M. Follette, J.I. Ruzek, and F.R. Abueg (New York, NY: Guilford Press, 1998), 383-414.

[29]J.M. Cook, and C. O'Donnell, "Assessment and psychological treatment of posttraumatic stress disorder in older adults," *Journal of Geriatric Psychiatry and Neurology* 18, 2 (2005): 61.

[30]A. Myers, and H.A. Dewar, "Circumstances attending 100 sudden deaths from coronary artery disease with coroner's necropsies," British Medical Journal 37, 11 (1975): 1133-1143; V. Rissanen, M. Romo, and P. Siltanen, "Prehospital sudden death from ischaemic heart disease. A postmortem study," *British Medical Journal* 40, 9 (1978): 1025-1033.

[31]D.R. Morse, J. Martin, and J. Moshonov, "Stress induced sudden cardiac death: Can it be prevented?" *Stress Medicine* 8, 1 (1992): 35-46.

[32]L.A. Hyer, and S.J. Sohnle, *Trauma among older people: issues and treatment.* (New York, NY: Brunner-Routledge, 2001), 376.

[33]A. Maercker, "Life-review technique in the treatment of PTSD in elderly patients: rationale and three single case studies," *Journal of Clinical Geropsychology. Special Issue: Traumatic Exposure and PTSD in Older Adults* 8, 3 (2002): 239-249; B.K. Haight, and J.D. Webster, *The art and science of reminiscing: theory, research, methods, and applications* (Philadelphia, PA: Taylor & Francis, 1995), 323.

[34]M. McFadyen, *A long road to recovery: Battling operational stress injuries*, Second Review of the Department of National Defence and Canadian Forces' Action on Operational Stress Injuries, Government of Canada, 2008.

[35]B.T Litz, "Research on the impact of military trauma: Current status and future directions," *Military Psychology* 19 (2007): 217-238.

CHAPTER 16

Post-traumatic Stress Disorder: Guiding Management with Careful Assessment of Comorbid Mental and Physical Illness[1]

Don Richardson MD, FRCPC, Department of Psychiatry, University of Western Ontario,
Diane McIntosh MD, FRCPC, Department of Psychiatry, University of British Columbia
Jitender Sareen, MD, FRCPC, Professor of Psychiatry, Psychology and
Community Health Sciences, University of Manitoba
Murray B. Stein, MD, FRCPC, Family & Preventive Medicine, University of California, San Diego

ABSTRACT

PTSD is a common and serious psychiatric condition in the civilian and veteran population. The lifetime prevalence of PTSD in the Canadian general population is 9.2%,[2] which, surprisingly, is not significantly different from the 7.2% lifetime prevalence rate within the Canadian Regular Forces.[3] In Canadian veterans pensioned with a medical condition, the 1-month prevalence was 10.3%.[4] Given the serious functional impairment and impaired quality of life[5] associated with PTSD, careful assessment and treatment of PTSD is warranted. Due to the complex clinical presentation of PTSD, which can include symptoms across the continuum from adjustment disorder and sub threshold PTSD to "full-blown" PTSD, this issue of Mood and Anxiety Disorders Rounds is confined to a general overview of the psychiatric management of PTSD with comorbid psychiatric conditions. Despite the challenges researchers face in conducting studies on the effectiveness of treatment of this disorder,[6] if evidence-based practices are utilized using established guidelines,[7] remission can be achieved in 30%–50% of PTSD cases.[8]

COMORBIDITY: THE RULE RATHER THAN THE EXCEPTION

Over 90% of individuals with PTSD will have another Axis I disorder. Major depression, another anxiety disorder (social phobia, generalized anxiety disorder, obsessive-compulsive disorder, and panic disorder), alcohol and substance use disorders,[9] and suicidality[10] are common comorbid conditions (Figure 16.1). Careful assessment for personality disorders, especially border-line[11] and antisocial,[12] is required because Axis II pathology may substantially affect management. Bipolar disorder is an important consideration, because bipolar II disorder is often difficult to recognize and can be an important barrier to response to treatment. Emerging evidence shows a strong relationship between PTSD and physical health problems.[13] The most common medical complaints associated with PTSD include chronic pain syndromes, asthma, gastrointestinal complaints and cardiovascular disease.[14] These conditions should be considered when planning the management of PTSD.

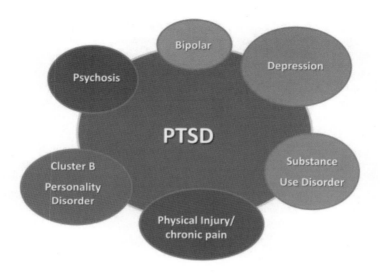

Figure 16.1: Important comorbid conditions to consider in the management of post-traumatic stress disorder.

Don Richardson *et al.*, "Post-Traumatic Stress Disorder: Guiding Management with Careful Assessment of Comorbid Mental and Physical Illness," *Mood and Anxiety Disorders Rounds* 1, 6 (2010).

PSYCHIATRIC ASSESSMENT

The psychiatric assessment should detail the presenting symptoms and elicit a trauma history, including childhood and adolescent trauma, and exposure to military trauma (combat or peacekeeping operations).[15] It should be noted that minute detail related to a traumatic event should only be gathered if absolutely necessary; the recounting of an extremely traumatic event may be highly triggering and lead to significant symptom exacerbation. If possible, history gathering should be limited to information that clarifies the diagnosis.

Patients with PTSD present with 4 symptom clusters: re-experiencing the traumatic events, avoidance of reminders, emotional numbing, and hyper arousal symptoms.[16] Avoidance of reminders and emotional numbing are grouped together as a symptom cluster in the Diagnostic and Statistical Manual of Mental Disorders, Fourth Edition (DSM-IV),[17] but are seen as distinct and will likely be denoted as such in DSM-V. Patients may relive their trauma via intrusive recollections during the day, including flashbacks, or at night as bad dreams or nightmares. Many complain of both physical and emotional symptoms of anxiety when exposed to reminders of their traumatic event. They may avoid reminders of the trauma and describe emotional numbness or an inability to experience a normal range of emotions. Common hyper arousal symptoms include insomnia, irritability, poor concentration, and hyper vigilance. According to the DSM-IV-TR, acute PTSD has a duration of 1–3 months, and the disorder is considered to be chronic if its duration exceeds three months.[18]

The Primary Care PTSD Screen, a 4-item self-report yes/no instrument, is easy to use in clinical practice. The instrument has a sensitivity of 78% and specificity of 87% for PTSD in patients who answer 'yes' to ≥3 items (Table 16.1).[19] Patients who screen positive should be assessed for PTSD using the DSM-IV-TR diagnostic criteria, or by using a more specific screening instrument. The Clinician Administered PTSD Scale (CAPS)[20] may be too detailed for most clinicians and is more commonly used in research centres. A more practical approach is to use a self-rating scale such as the PTSD Checklist, which has a military and a civilian version,[21] and then to confirm the self-report rating and the nature of the traumatic experience(s) with a clinical interview. Some patients may present with some symptoms of PTSD without meeting the full diagnostic criteria.[22] Even if the full criteria are not met, studies indicate that these individuals may experience significant functional impairment,[23] and may also benefit from treatment.

> In your life, have you ever had any experience that was so frightening, horrible, or upsetting that, in the past month, you:
>
> 1. Have had nightmares about it or thought about it when you did not want to?
> 2. Tried hard not to think about it or went out of your way to avoid situations that reminded you of it?
> 3. Were constantly on guard, watchful, or easily startled?
> 4. Felt numb or detached from others, activities, or your surroundings?
>
> Screen is positive if patient answers "yes" to any three items.

Table 16.1: Primary Care PTSD Screen

Prins A, Ouimette PC, Kimerling R, *et al*. The Primary Care PTSD Screen (PC-PTSD): development and operating characteristics. *Primary Care Psychiatry*. 2004;9(1):9-14.

Determining the presence of psychiatric comorbidity, as part of a thorough PTSD assessment, is critical.[24] PTSD often presents with comorbidities such as depression and substance abuse and dependence.[25] Studies have estimated that >50% of PTSD patients have symptoms of a major depressive disorder,[26] but in the veteran population the percentage may be much higher.[27]

A risk assessment for both suicidal and homicidal ideation is essential. The presence of PTSD increases suicidal ideation and the risk of completed suicide.[28] The presence of comorbid depression further increases suicide risk.[29] In the veteran population, aggression and anger are well documented.[30] During the initial PTSD assessment, military members may report violent thoughts and aggressive behaviour, including homicidal thoughts. Assessing comorbidity, suicidal or homicidal ideation, and extent of social support is imperative in order to determine the need for urgent, inpatient treatment.[31] In particular, a high risk for suicidal behaviour should prompt strong consideration for inpatient admission. Enquiry should also be made into family functioning as the family plays an important role in the treatment process.[32]

TREATMENT

Table 16.2 describes the initial steps in the management of PTSD. Substantial comorbidities, whether psychiatric or physical, should be managed simultaneously with the PTSD.

1. Develop a therapeutic alliance
2. Assess the safety and suicide risk
3. Consider the setting of treatment (outpatient, inpatient, or day program)
4. Assess and manage physical conditions that could exacerbate PTSD symptoms (eg, thyroid problems, chronic pain conditions)
5. Conduct careful psychoeducation related to PTSD
6. If there is a current comorbidity (eg, substance use disorder, mood disorder, or borderline personality disorder), prioritize treatment of this/these condition(s)
7. Choose pharmacotherapy based on the presence of any comorbidities
8. Once the comorbid condition(s) has/have been stabilized, then consider a trauma-focussed cognitive behaviour therapy.

Table 16.2: Important principles in the management of PTSD

Canadian Psychiatric Association Clinical Guidelines. Can J Psychiatry. 2006(5(Suppl 2):61S.

PSYCHOEDUCATION

Once a firm diagnosis has been established, psychoeducation regarding diagnosis and treatment is critical for both patients and their families. Educating patients regarding the phases of treatment and understanding of what is to be expected, particularly when to expect treatment benefits, helps to avoid frustration and hopelessness associated with inappropriate treatment expectations.

SYMPTOM STABILIZATION

The main goal of stabilization is to manage acute symptoms and improve current functioning. Stabilization usually requires psychoeducation, anxiety management training, and medication. Once symptoms stabilize, patients are more able to engage in psychotherapy,[33] such as prolonged exposure and other evidence-based forms of CBT. Regardless of the treatment modality, stabilization is critical. The initiation of "trauma-focussed psychotherapy" prior to stabilization may exacerbate both PTSD symptoms and pre-existing or comorbid symptoms of depression and substance abuse.

For mild to moderate PTSD without significant comorbidity, and where minimal stabilization is required, CBT may be initiated prior to medication. However, for the typically more severe and chronic cases referred to psychiatrists, CBT should follow acute symptom stabilization with medication. CBT requires the ability to learn and apply new information. When severe depression or anxiety symptoms are present, cognitive impairment is common and often has a significant impact on new learning. CBT specifically for PTSD typically involves close to 20 sessions emphasizing a combination of cognitive restructuring of maladaptive trauma-related beliefs and exposure techniques.[34]

PHARMACOLOGICAL MANAGEMENT

As demonstrated in Table 16.3, a number of medications have been employed to treat PTSD. SSRIs and the SNRI venlafaxine have the most empirical evidence for efficacy in the treatment of PTSD and are usually considered as a first-line treatment for PTSD.[35] SSRIs and venlafaxine are also effective agents for the treatment of comorbid mood and anxiety disorders commonly associated with PTSD. Education about the potential risk of increased suicidal thoughts associated with antidepressant medication, particularly at the time of initiation of treatment, should also be reviewed with the patient.[36]

First line	Fluoxetine, paroxetine, sertraline, venlafaxine XR
Second line	Citalopram, fluvoxamine, mirtazapine, moclobemide, phenelzine
	Adjunctive: risperidone, olanzapine
Third line	Amitriptyline, imipramine
	Adjunctive: carbamazepine, gabapentin, lamotrigine, valproate, tiagabine, topiramate, quetiapine, clonidine, trazodone, buspirone, bupropion, prazosin
Not recommended	Monotherapy with alprazolam, clonazepam, olanzapine, naltrexone, cyproheptadine

Table 16.3: Recommendations for pharmacotherapy for PTSD

Reproduced with permission from the Canadian Psychiatric Association Clinical Guidelines.
Can J Psychiatry. 2006(5(Suppl 2):61S.

Other dual acting antidepressants such as mirtazapine, bupropion, and, more recently, duloxetine are widely used to treat major depression and other anxiety disorders, but have less empirical data demonstrating their efficacy for the specific treatment of PTSD.[37] In PTSD they are considered as second- and third-line treatment options for patients who have failed to respond to first-line treatment. However, since SSRIs have not demonstrated their efficacy in subpopulations of combat-related PTSD[38] and due to the high rate of comorbid major depression and other anxiety disorders, dual-acting antidepressants should also be considered as first-line treatments, especially in PTSD with comorbid major depression.

Benzodiazepines are not recommended as monotherapy for the treatment of PTSD,[39] but are sometimes used for the treatment of insomnia[40] or, in combination with an antidepressant, to treat acute anxiety. They might also be useful to manage early side effects associated with some antidepressants or antipsychotics, including restlessness, jitteriness, or agitation. There is a risk of rebound insomnia or anxiety when a benzodiazepine is discontinued, especially after long-term use.[41] The use of benzodiazepines among patients with PTSD who have comorbid substance abuse should be avoided.

COMBINING PSYCHOTHERAPY AND PHARMACOTHERAPY

Although there is limited research evaluating combination treatment,[42] many clinicians prescribe psychotherapy and pharmacotherapy either concurrently or sequentially during the course of treatment. There is also evidence that psychotherapy improves outcomes in patients with chronic PTSD who have demonstrated a partial response to pharmacotherapy.[43]

ASSESSING TREATMENT RESPONSE

Despite the lack of a generally accepted definition for recovery or remission in PTSD, assessing treatment response remains critical. Response to treatment for PTSD can be assessed objectively, using the self-rated PTSD Checklist (Military or Civilian Version) and comorbid depression can be assessed objectively using the Hamilton rating scale for Depression (HAMD-7)44 or the self-rated Patient Health Questionnaire (PHQ-9).[45]

DOSING CONSIDERATIONS

PTSD patients often present with marked anxiety, and they may be very sensitive to the potential heightened anxiety or agitation sometimes associated with early antidepressant treatment. Patients benefit from a "start low, go slow" approach to medication titration. Consider initiating treatment at 25–50% of the usual starting dose and then gradually increasing to a therapeutic level.[46] While the initiation of medication might be slow and cautious, ultimately the dose should be titrated to full symptom remission, at maximum tolerated doses.

TREATMENT ADHERENCE/COMPLIANCE

Medication compliance is crucial for treatment to be effective. False beliefs or fears about medications should be explored and confronted prior to starting treatment and addressed regularly during treatment follow-up. Providing a safe environment and a positive doctor-patient interaction will help develop trust and improve medication compliance.[47] Engaging and educating all care providers, including the family, is essential. Peer social support programs can play a valuable role in encouraging treatment adherence.[48]

Patients may wish to discontinue their medication once they start to feel better or can no longer tolerate side effects such as weight gain or sexual dysfunction. However, studies have demonstrated that patients with PTSD continued to show improvement with pharmacotherapy up to 36 weeks after treatment initiation and early discontinuation leads to a high rate of relapse.[49] Therefore, in most cases, long-term medication treatment may be recommended.[50]

There are no published guidelines specifying the length of pharmacological treatment for anxiety disorders; however, existing guidelines for major depression suggest that the medication should be continued for at least 6 months to 1 year after symptom remission has been reached.[51]

MANAGING TREATMENT-RESISTANT PTSD

In cases of treatment-resistant PTSD, it is important to reassess the patient to ensure that the diagnosis is correct and that comorbid conditions have been considered in the management. Although there is no treatment algorithm for the pharmacological treatment of PTSD, for patients who demonstrate a partial response (25–50% improvement) after 6-8 weeks of treatment with the first antidepressant trial, optimization of monotherapy is a critical first step. This generally entails titrating the agent to maximally tolerated doses, so long as each dose increase produces some benefit. If after dose optimization a response to treatment (≥50% improvement) is not evident, the initial agent should be switched to another first-line agent. If optimizing the initial agent leads to treatment response but not full remission, combination strategies may be considered. There is some evidence to suggest that combining 2 agents early in the treatment of depression might be more effective than monotherapy to induce remission,[52] but it is unclear if this strategy would be similarly effective in PTSD.

When considering combination strategies, discuss potential risks as well as expected benefits with the patient.[53] Common combination treatments include adding an antidepressant with a different mechanism (e.g., mirtazapine or bupropion) to an SSRI or SNRI. The utility of adding an atypical antipsychotic (e.g., risperidone, quetiapine, aripiprazole, or olanzapine) in combination with a primary antidepressant has been suggested in several small studies.[54] These agents appear to be beneficial in managing hyper arousal symptoms such as hyper vigilance and irritability, as well as for severe dissociation symptoms.[55] There is significant evidence for the addition of an atypical antipsychotic for treatment-resistant depression,[56] which often presents as a complicating factor in PTSD. There is no established role for the use of conventional antipsychotics in the treatment of PTSD.

Anticonvulsant medications (e.g., carbamazepine, valproate, topiramate, and lamotrigine) are increasingly used in combination with antidepressants to treat symptoms of depression, mood instability, and impulsivity;[57] however, controlled trials have, to date, failed to confirm the utility of these agents for PTSD.[58] These agents are generally reserved as third-line agents, and used in combination with first- or second-line agents.

Insomnia is extremely common, persistent, and severe for most PTSD patients. If symptoms of insomnia persist with the use of therapeutic doses of antidepressants, a trial of low-dose mirtazapine (15 mg) or trazodone (50-100 mg) may be helpful. Alternative non-benzodiazepine hypnotics include zopiclone. There is also some evidence demonstrating the benefits of using prazosin, an adrenergic inhibitor specifically to reduce nightmares.[59] A sleep study should also be considered in cases where a specific comorbid sleep disorder such as sleep apnea is suspected.

CASE 1: MILITARY-RELATED PTSD WITH PHYSICAL INJURY AND DEPRESSION

A 27-year-old veteran was referred with persistent depressed mood, insomnia, and panic attacks. He was nonresponsive to citalopram 30 mg daily. He was recently released from the CF after serving 8 years. He first noticed symptoms after returning home from his deployment in Afghanistan where he was exposed to major combat. He was the driver in the second vehicle of a convoy when the lead vehicle hit a roadside bomb. He tried to rescue his comrade from the burning vehicle, but they were ambushed by the Taliban. During the firefight he was shot in his right leg; he was evacuated first to the Kandahar Airfield and was transferred to an American hospital in Germany, then back to Canada.

Within 6 months of returning to Canada, the patient reported reliving the events in Afghanistan in intrusive recollections and recurrent nightmares. He became preoccupied with the safety of his family, especially his children. He started to fear going to bed and was drinking increasing amounts of alcohol to help him sleep and smoking marijuana to control pain. He started to become nervous in crowds and became afraid to leave his home. He was irritable, frequently getting into fights at work and at home with his wife. His moods were low; he had lost interest in most activities and complained of fatigue, low energy, diminished appetite, and no sex drive. After his release from the military, he finally went to see his family doctor who started him on citalopram and zopiclone to help him sleep. At first he noticed some improvement in anxiety, but these periods were short-lived. He continued to use alcohol regularly for sleep and he was still having frequent anger outbursts. Finally, after losing his job and reporting increased thoughts of suicide, his family doctor convinced him to see a psychiatrist.

Following a comprehensive psychiatric evaluation, the initial plan was to focus on stabilization by aggressively treating his comorbid addiction and major depression. An initial first step, as the patient was concerned with potential sexual side effects, was to add bupropion XL 150 mg in combination with citalopram and start low-dose (15 mg) mirtazapine RD at bedtime to assist with his sleep. He was also provided with extensive psychoeducation and psychotherapy focussing on depression and addiction. Once his symptoms were better controlled, he could benefit from trauma-focussed psychotherapy.

CASE 2: PTSD WITH SOCIAL PHOBIA

A 28-year-old single woman was referred for assessment of anxiety symptoms. She described worrying throughout the day, and was experiencing nightmares and concentration problems. She had experienced intimate-partner violence from her ex-boyfriend, who had hit her and forced her to have sex with him on a number of occasions. She reported nightmares about these attacks. She could not sleep in her own bedroom, where the attacks had occurred. The anxiety symptoms were so disabling she had difficulty functioning at work. She also described a long history of being shy and described high anxiety in social situations. She was not suicidal, and denied a history of drug or alcohol abuse. Her mother had life-long social phobia. There was no childhood history of sexual or physical abuse.

The patient was treated with a combination of pharmacotherapy and psychotherapy. She responded to individual cognitive behaviour therapy with a focus on exposure and response prevention. She also found that the anxiety symptoms were substantially reduced with a combination of venlafaxine XR 300 mg per day, trazodone 25 mg at bedtime, and clonazepam 1 mg at bedtime. This approach not only improved the PTSD symptoms, but also reduced her social phobia. With her symptoms of anxiety better controlled, the patient was now ready for trauma-focussed psychotherapy.

CONCLUSION

The presentation of PTSD is often complicated by comorbidity. Understanding the impact of trauma can help the clinician appreciate the challenges faced by the patient, which is essential to establishing a trusting therapeutic alliance. Treatment often involves a combination of medications, making compliance more challenging. Although remission is not always possible, pharmacological interventions assist with symptom reduction and improve functioning and quality of life. Pharmacological interventions, especially with comorbidity, can also assist with stabilization and facilitate psychotherapeutic interventions such as trauma-focussed psychotherapy.[60]

[1]The author has obtained permission from the Canadian Network of Mood and Anxiety Treatment, through Dr. Sagar Parikh, for the CANMAT psychiatric Rounds article to be reprinted; Don Richardson *et al.*, "Post-Traumatic Stress Disorder: Guiding Management with Careful Assessment of Comorbid Mental and Physical Illness," *Mood and Anxiety Disorders Rounds* 1, 6 (2010).

[2]M. Van Ameringen, C. Mancini, B. Patterson, M.H. Boyle,"Post-traumatic stress disorder in Canada," *CNS Neurosci Ther*, 14, 3 (2008): 171-181.

[3]Statistics Canada, Canadian Community Health Survey Cycle 1.2 – Mental Health and Well-being (Canadian Forces Supplement), 2002.

[4]J.D. Richardson, J. Elhai, D. Pedlar, "Association of PTSD and depression with medical and specialist care utilization in modern peacekeeping veterans in Canada with health-related disabilities," *J Clin Psychiatry* 67, 8 (2006): 1240-1245.

[5]J.D. Richardson, M.E. Long, D. Pedlar, J.D. Elhai, "Posttraumatic stress disorder and health related quality of life (HRQol) among a sample of treatment- and pension-seeking deployed Canadian Forces peacekeeping veterans," *Can J Psychiatry* 53, 9 (2008): 594-600; J. Richardson, M.E. Long, D. Pedlar, J.D. Elhai, "Posttraumatic stress disorder and health related quality of life (HRQol) in pension-seeking Canadian WW II and Korean veterans," *J Clin Psychiatry* 71, 8 (2010): 1099-1101.

[6]Institute of Medicine, *Treatment of Posttraumatic Stress Disorder: An Assessment of the Evidence*, (Washington, DC: The National Academies Press, 2008).

[7]R.J. Ursano, C. Bell, S. Eth, *et al.*, "Practice guidelines for the treatment of patients with acute stress disorder and posttraumatic stress disorder," *Am J Psychiatry* 161, 11 (2004): 3-31; Australian Centre for Post Traumatic Mental Health, *Australian Guidelines for the Treatment of Adults with Acute Stress Disorder and Post Traumatic Stress Disorder*, (Melbourne, Victoria; ACPMH, 2007).

[8]M.J. Friedman, "Posttraumatic stress disorder among military returnees from Afghanistan and Iraq," *Am J Psychiatry* 163, 4 (2006): 586-593.

[9]R. Kessler, A. Sonnega, E. Bromet, M. Hughes, and C. Nelson, "Posttraumatic stress disorder in the National Comorbidity Survey," *Arch Gen Psychiatry* 52, 12 (1995): 1048-1060.

[10]J.L. Gradus, P. Qin, A.K. Lincoln, *et al.*, "Posttraumatic stress disorder and completed suicide," *Am J Epidemiol* 171, 6 (2010): 721-727.

[11]J. Pagura, M.B. Stein, J.M. Bolton, B.J. Cox, B. Grant, J. Sareen, "Comorbidity of borderline personality disorder and posttraumatic stress disorder in the U.S. population," *J Psychiatr Res*. 2010 May 25.

[12]J. Sareen, M. Stein, B. Cox, and S. Hassard, "Understanding comorbidity of anxiety disorders and antisocial behavior: Findings from two large community surveys," *J Nerv Ment Dis* 192, 3 (2004): 178-186.

[13]M. Jakupcak, J. Luterek, S. Hunt, D. Conybeare, and M. McFall, "Posttraumatic stress and its relationship to physical health functioning in a sample of Iraq and Afghanistan war veterans seeking postdeployment VA health care," *J Nerv Ment Dis* 196, 5 (2008): 425-428; J. Sareen, B.J. Cox, M.B. Stein, T.O. Afifi, C. Fleet, and G.J.G. Asmundson, "Physical and mental comorbidity, disability, and suicidal behavior associated with posttraumatic stress disorder in a large community sample," *Psychosom Med* 69, 3 (2007): 242-248.

[14]J. Sareen, B. Cox, I., Clara, G. Asmundson, "The relationship between anxiety disorders and physical disorders in the U.S. National Comorbidity Survey," *Depress Anxiety* 21, (2005): 193-202.

[15]M.J. Friedman, "Posttraumatic stress disorder among military returnees from Afghanistan and Iraq," *Am J Psychiatry* 163, 4 (2006): 586-593.

[16]R.J. Ursano, C. Bell, S. Eth, *et al.*, "Practice guidelines for the treatment of patients with acute stress disorder and posttraumatic stress disorder," *Am J Psychiatry* 161, 11 (2004): 3-31; American Psychiatric Association, *Diagnostic and Statistical Manual of Mental Disorders, Fourth Edition, Text Revision*, (Arlington, VA: American Psychiatric Association Press, 2000).

[17]American Psychiatric Association, *Diagnostic and Statistical Manual of Mental Disorders, Fourth Edition, Text Revision*, (Arlington, VA: American Psychiatric Association Press, 2000).

[18]American Psychiatric Association, *Diagnostic and Statistical Manual of Mental Disorders, Fourth Edition, Text Revision*, (Arlington, VA: American Psychiatric Association Press, 2000).

[19]A. Prins, P.C. Ouimette, R. Kimerling, *et al.*, "The Primary Care PTSD Screen (PC-PTSD): development and operating characteristics," *Primary Care Psychiatry* 9, 1 (2004): 9-14.

[20]D.D. Blake, F.W. Weathers, L.M. Nagy, *et al.*, "The development of a clinician- administered PTSD scale," *J Trauma Stress* 8, 1 (1995): 75-90.

[21]F.W. Weathers, B.T. Litz, D.S. Herman, J.A. Huska, and T.M. Keane, "The PTSD checklist: Reliability, validity, & diagnostic utility," (presented, 9th Annual Meeting of the International Society for Traumatic Stress Studies, San Antonio, Texas: October, 1993).

[22]C. Zlotnick, C.L. Franklin, and M. Zimmerman, "Does "subthreshold" posttraumatic stress disorder have any clinical relevance?" *Compr Psychiatry* 43, 6 (2002): 413-419; M.B. Stein, J.R. Walker, A.L. Hazen, and D.R. Forde, "Full and partial posttraumatic stress disorder: Findings from a community survey," *Am J Psychiatry* 154, 8 (1997): 1114-1119.

[23]Marshall, R.D., Olfson, M., Hellman, F., Blanco, C., Guardino, M., Struening, E.L., "Comorbidity, impairment, and suicidality in subthreshold PTSD," *Am J Psychiatry* 158, 9 (2001): 1467-1473.

[24]R.D. Marshall, M. Olfson, F. Hellman, C. Blanco, M. Guardino, and E.L. Struening, "Comorbidity, impairment, and suicidality in subthreshold PTSD," *Am J Psychiatry* 158, 9 (2001): 1467-1473.

[25]R. Kessler, A. Sonnega, E. Bromet, M. Hughes, and C. Nelson, "Posttraumatic stress disorder in the National Comorbidity Survey," *Arch Gen Psychiatry* 52, 12 (1995): 1048-1060; D. Forbes, M. Creamer, G. Hawthorne, N. Allen, and T. McHugh, "Comorbidity as a predictor of symptom change after treatment in combat-related posttraumatic stress disorder," *J Nerv Ment Dis* 191, 2 (2003): 93-99.

[26]R. Kessler, A. Sonnega, E. Bromet, M. Hughes, and C. Nelson, "Posttraumatic stress disorder in the National Comorbidity Survey," *Arch Gen Psychiatry* 52, 12 (1995): 1048-1060.

[27]T.M. Keane and J. Wolfe, "Comorbidity in post-traumatic stress disorder: An analysis of community and clinical studies," *J Appl Soc Psychol* 20, 21 (1990): 1776-1788; S. Southwick, R. Yehuda, and E.J. Giller, "Characterization of depression in war-related posttraumatic stress disorder," *Am J Psychiatry* 148, 2 (1991): 179-183.

[28]J.L. Gradus, P. Qin, A.K. Lincoln, *et al.*, "Posttraumatic stress disorder and completed suicide," *Am J Epidemiol* 171, 6 (2010): 721-727; Marshall, R.D., Olfson, M., Hellman, F., Blanco, C., Guardino, M., Struening, E.L., "Comorbidity, impairment, and suicidality in subthreshold PTSD," *Am J Psychiatry* 158, 9 (2001): 1467-1473.

[29]J.L. Gradus, P. Qin, A.K. Lincoln, *et al.*, "Posttraumatic stress disorder and completed suicide," *Am J Epidemiol* 171, 6 (2010): 721-727; Kaufman, J. and Charney, D., "Comorbidity of mood and anxiety disorders," *Depress Anxiety* 12, 1 (2000): 69-76.

[30]D. Forbes, M. Creamer, G. Hawthorne, N. Allen, and T. McHugh, "Comorbidity as a predictor of symptom change after treatment in combat-related posttraumatic stress disorder," *J Nerv Ment Dis* 191, 2 (2003): 93-99; Forbes, D., Hawthorne, G., Elliott, P., *et al.*, "A concise measure of anger in combat-related posttraumatic stress disorder," *J Trauma Stress* 17, 3 (2004): 249-256.

[31]R.J. Ursano, C. Bell, S. Eth, *et al.*, "Practice guidelines for the treatment of patients with acute stress disorder and posttraumatic stress disorder," *Am J Psychiatry* 161, 11 (2004): 3-31.

[32]R.J. Ursano, C. Bell, S. Eth, *et al.*, "Practice guidelines for the treatment of patients with acute stress disorder and post traumatic stress disorder," *Am J Psychiatry* 161, 11 (2004): 3-31.

[33]J. Davidson and B.A. Van Der Kolk, "The psychopharmacological treatment of posttraumatic stress disorder," *Traumatic Stress: The Effects of Over whelming Experience on Mind, Body, and Society*, eds. B.A. Van Der Kolk, A.C. McFarlane, and L. Weisaeth (New York, NY: The Guilford Press, 1996), 521.

[34]K. Ponniah and S.D. Hollon, "Empirically supported psychological treatments for adult acute stress disorder and post traumatic stress disorder: a review," *Depress Anxiety* 26, 12 (2009): 1086-1109.

[35]R.J. Ursano, C. Bell, S. Eth, *et al.*, "Practice guidelines for the treatment of patients with acute stress disorder and post traumatic stress disorder," *Am J Psychiatry* 161, 11 (2004): 3-31; A. Smajkic, S. Weine, Z. Djuric-Bijedic, E. Boskailo, J. Lewis, and I. Pavkovic, "Sertraline, paroxetine, and venlafaxine in refugee posttraumatic stress disorder with depression symptoms," *J Trauma Stress* 14, 3 (2001): 445-452; M. Hopwood, P.L.P. Morris, P. Debenham, *et al.*, "An open label trial of venlafaxine in war veterans with chronic post traumatic stress disorder," *Aust N Z J Psychiatry* 34, s1 (2000): A31; J. Davidson, D. Baldwin, D.J. Stein, *et al.*, "Treatment of post traumatic stress disorder with venlafaxine extended release: a 6-month randomized controlled trial," *Arch Gen Psychiatry* 63, 10 (2006): 1158-1165.

[36]National Institute for Clinical Excellence, *Post-traumatic Stress Disorder (PTSD): The Management of PTSD in Adults and Children in Primary and Secondary Care*, (London, UK: National Institute for Clinical Excellence, 2005).

[37]J.R. Davidson, R.H. Weisler, M.I. Butterfield, *et al.*, "Mirtazapine vs placebo in post traumatic stress disorder: a pilot trial," *Biol Psychiatry* 53, 2 (2003): 188-191. M.Y. Chung, K.H. Min, Y.J. Jun, S.S. Kim, W.C. Kim, and E.M. Jun, "Efficacy and tolerability of mirtazapine and sertraline in Korean veterans with post traumatic stress disorder: a randomized open label trial," *Hum Psychopharmacol* 19, 7 (2004): 489-494; K.M. Connor, J.R. Davidson, R.H. Weisler, and E. Ahearn, "A pilot study of mirtazapine in post-traumatic stress disorder," *Int Clin Psychopharmacol* 14, 1 (1999): 29-31; M.E. Becker, M.A. Hertzberg, S.D. Moore, M.F. Dennis, D.S. Bukenya, and J.C. Beckham, "A placebo-controlled trial of bupropion SR in the treatment of chronic post-traumatic stress disorder," *J Clin Psychopharmacol* 27, 2 (2007): 193-197; E. Walderhaug, S. Kasserman, D. Aikins, D. Vojvoda, C. Nishimura, and A. Neumeister, "Effects of duloxetine in treatment-refractory men with posttraumatic stress disorder," *Pharmacopsychiatry* 43, 2 (2010): 45-49.

[38]F.B. Schoenfeld, C.R. Marmar, and T.C. Neylan, "Current Concepts in Pharmacotherapy for Posttraumatic Stress Disorder," *Psychiatr Serv* 55, (2004): 519-531; M. Friedman, C. Marmar, D. Baker, C. Sikes, and G. Farfel, "Randomized, double-blind comparison of sertraline and placebo for posttraumatic stress disorder in a Department of Veterans Affairs setting," *J Clin Psychiatry* 68, 5 (2007): 711-720.

[39] M.J. Friedman, "Posttraumatic stress disorder among military returnees from Afghanistan and Iraq," *Am J Psychiatry* 163, 4 (2006): 586-593; P. Braun, D. Greenberg, H. Dasberg, and B. Lerer, "Core symptoms of posttraumatic stress disorder unimproved by alprazolam treatment," *J Clin Psychiatry* 51, 6 (1990): 236-238; E. Gelpin, O. Bonne, T. Peri, D. Brandes, and A.Y. Shalev, "Treatment of recent trauma survivors with benzodiazepines: a prospective study," *J Clin Psychiatry* 57, 9 (1996): 390-394.

[40] R.J. Ursano, C. Bell, S. Eth, *et al.*, "Practice guidelines for the treatment of patients with acute stress disorder and posttraumatic stress disorder," *Am J Psychiatry* 161, 11 (2004): 3-31.

[41] J. Cooper, J. Carty, and M. Creamer, "Pharmacotherapy for posttraumatic stress disorder: empirical review and clinical recommendations," *Aust N Z J Psychiatry* 39, 8 (2005): 674-682.

[42] R.P. Swinson, M.M. Antony, P. Bleau, *et al.*, "Canadian Psychiatric Association, Clinical Practice Guidelines: Management of Anxiety Disorders," *Can J Psychiatry* 51, 2 (2006): 57S-63S; R.D. Marshall and M. Cloitre, "Maximizing treatment outcome in post-traumatic stress disorder by combining psychotherapy with pharmacotherapy," *Curr Psychiatry Rep* (2000): 2.

[43] B. Rothbaum, S. Cahill, E. Foa, *et al.*, "Augmentation of sertraline with prolonged exposure in the treatment of posttraumatic stress disorder," *Journal of Traumatic Stress* 19, (2006).

[44] R.S. McIntyre, J.Z. Konarski, D.A. Mancini, *et al.*, "Measuring the severity of depression and remission in primary care: validation of the HAMD-7 scale," *Canadian Medical Association Journal* 173, 11 (2005): 1327-1334.

[45] K. Kroenke, R.L. Spitzer, and J.B. Williams, "The PHQ-9: validity of a brief depression severity measure," *Journal of General Internal Medecine* 16, 9 (2001): 606-613.

[46] J. Cooper, J. Carty, and M. Creamer, "Pharmacotherapy for posttraumatic stress disorder: empirical review and clinical recommendations," *Aust N Z J Psychiatry* 39, 8 (2005): 674-682; M.B. Stein, M.K. Goin, M.H. Pollack, *et al.*, "Work Group on Panic Disorder," *American Psychiatric Association Practice Guideline: Treatment of Patients with Panic Disorder, Second Edition*, October 12, 2010, http://www.psychiatryonline.com/pracGuide/pracGuideChapToc_9.aspx, accessed 14 April 2011.

[47] P.J. Weiden and N. Rao, "Teaching medication compliance to psychiatric residents: placing an orphan topic into a training curriculum," *Acad Psychiatry* 29, 2 (2005): 203-210; R.P. Kluft, "Negotiating the therapeutic alliance: a relational treatment guide," *Am J Psychiatry* 159, 5 (2002): 885.

[48] Veterans Affairs Canada, "Operational Stress Injury Social Support Program," *Veterans Affairs Canada*, October 12, 2010, http://www.vac-acc.gc.ca/remembers/sub.cfm?source= mental-health/support/ossis-support.

[49] P.D. Londborg, M.T. Hegel, S. Goldstein, *et al.*, "Sertraline treatment of post-traumatic stress disorder: results of 24 weeks of open label continuation treatments," *J Clin Psychiatry* 65, 5 (2001): 325-331.

[50] R.P. Swinson, M.M. Antony, P. Bleau, *et al.*, "Canadian Psychiatric Association, Clinical Practice Guidelines: Management of Anxiety Disorders," *Can J Psychiatry* 51, 2 (2006): 57S-63S.

[51] Canadian Psychiatric Association, "Canadian Network for Mood and Anxiety Treatments (CANMAT). Clinical Practice Guidelines for the Treatment of Depressive Disorder," *Can J Psychiatry* 46, 1 (2001): 5S-90S.

[52] P. Blier, H.E. Ward, P. Tremblay, L. Laberge, C. Hebert, and R. Bergeron, "Combination of antidepressant medications from treatment initiation for major depressive disorder: a double-blind randomized study," *Am J Psychiatry* 167, 3 (2010): 281-288.

[53] J. Cooper, J. Carty, and M. Creamer, "Pharmacotherapy for posttraumatic stress disorder: empirical review and clinical recommendations," *Aust N Z J Psychiatry* 39, 8 (2005): 674-682.

[54] M.B. Stein, N.A. Kline, and J.L. Matloff, "Adjunctive olanzapine for SSRI-resistant combat-related PTSD: a double-blind, placebo-controlled study," *Am J Psychiatry* 159, 10 (2002): 1777-1779; G. Bartzokis, T. Freeman, and V. Roca, "Risperidone for patients with chronic combat-related posttraumatic stress disorder" (presentation, 154th Annual Meeting of the American Psychiatric Association, New Orleans, LA, May 9, 2001), abstract NR562:152; M.B. Hamner, R.A. Faldowski, H.G. Ulmer, B.C. Frueh, M.G. Huber, and G.W. Arana, "Adjunctive risperidone treatment in post-traumatic stress disorder: a preliminary controlled trial of effects on comorbid psychotic symptoms," *Int Clin Psychopharmacol* 18, 1 (2003): 1-8; E.P. Monnelly, D.A. Ciraulo, C. Knapp, and T. Keane, "Low-dose risperidone as adjunctive therapy for irritable aggression in post traumatic stress disorder," *J Clin Psychopharmacol* 23, 2 (2003): 193-196.

[55]F.B. Schoenfeld, C.R. Marmar, and T.C. Neylan, "Current Concepts in Pharmacotherapy for Posttraumatic Stress Disorder," *Psychiatr Serv* 55, (2004): 519-531.

[56]S. Kennedy, R. Lam, S. Parikh, *et al.*, "Canadian Network for Mood and Anxiety Treatments (CANMAT) clinical guidelines for the management of major depressive disorder in adults," *J Affect Disord* 117, 1 (2009): S1-S2.

[57]S. Lipper, J.R. Davidson, T.A. Grady, *et al.*, "Preliminary study of carbamazepine in post-traumatic stress disorder," *Psychosomatics* 27, 12 (1986): 849-854; P.E. Jr. Keck, S.L. McElroy, and L.M. Friedman, "Valproate and carbamazepine in the treatment of panic and posttraumatic stress disorders, withdrawal states, and behavioral dyscontrol syndromes," *J Clin Psychopharmacol* 12, 1 (1992): 36S-41S; F.A. Fesler, "Valproate in combat-related posttraumatic stress disorder," *J Clin Psychiatry* 52, 9 (1991): 361-364; J. Berlant and D.P. Van Kammen, "Open-label topiramate as primary or adjunctive therapy in chronic civilian post traumatic stress disorder: a preliminary report," *J Clin Psychiatry* 63, 1 (2002): 15-20; M.A. Hertzberg, M.I. Butterfield, M.E. Feldman, *et al.*, "A preliminary study of lamotrigine for the treatment of posttraumatic stress disorder," *Biol Psychiatry* 45, 9 (1999): 1226-1229; M.B. Hamner, P.S. Brodrick, and L.A. Labbate, "Gabapentin in PTSD: a retrospective, clinical series of adjunctive therapy," *Ann Clin Psychiatry* 13, 3 (2001): 141-146.

[58]L.N. Ravindran and M.B. Stein, "Pharmacotherapy of PTSDS: premises, principles, and priorities," *Brain Res* 1293, (2009): 24-39.

[59]M.A. Raskind, C. Thompson, E.C. Petrie, *et al.*, "Prazosin reduces nightmares in combat veterans with post traumatic stress disorder" *J Clin Psychiatry* 63, 7 (2002): 565-568; M.A. Raskind, E.R. Peskind, E.D. Kanter, *et al.*, "Reduction of nightmares and other PTSD symptoms in combat veterans by prazosin: a placebo-controlled study," *Am J Psychiatry* 160, 2 (2003): 371-373.

[60]7 L.N. Ravindran and M.B. Stein, "Pharmacotherapy of PTSDS: premises, principles, and priorities," *Brain Res* 1293, (2009): 24-39.

CHAPTER 17

Not Written in Stone: Social Covenants and Resourcing Military and Veterans Health Care in Canada

Allan English, PhD, History Department, Queen's University

ABSTRACT

The social covenant between Canada and its military has had a direct effect on the resources Canadian governments and others have been prepared to allocate to MVHC. This chapter considers the nature of that social covenant and how its changing nature has affected resources allocated for the health care of military members and veterans. It concludes with an examination of how changes to the social covenant between Canada and its military impacts on strategic planning and organizational change issues related to MVHC.

SOCIAL COVENANTS AND RESOURCING MILITARY AND VETERANS HEALTH CARE IN CANADA

One might ask what a historian could contribute to this collective - an activity designed to showcase a new initiative in Canadian Military and Veterans Health Research (MVHR). The short answer is found in a quote attributed to the German statesman Otto von Bismarck: "Fools say they learn by experience. I prefer to profit from the experience of others."[1] As he implies, to avoid making the same mistakes over and over again we must go beyond personal experience and take advantage of historical analysis of our collective experiences.

In the context of military health care, the Deputy Surgeon General of the Canadian Forces noted that we must be constantly aware of our past not only to make progress, but also to avoid losing gains that we have made:

> ...history teaches that we often do not learn from our past...Although low injury and disease rates are usually the fruit of persistent and prolonged health protection and promotion efforts, their achievement is often seen as justification to scale back such programs... Should the CF's current commitment to these efforts wane as recent problems recede from memory, the cycle will predictably repeat itself.[2]

His statement speaks to the focus of this paper – that the state of our knowledge of the constantly changing political and social climate in Canada has consequences for our ability to obtain resources for MVHC. Now this might seem like an obvious statement, but I chose this topic because I have observed in my interactions with individuals and groups involved with MVHC that a significant number of people seem to be convinced that the current situation of high levels of support and resourcing for the CF and MVHC will continue indefinitely, and, therefore no serious planning needs to take place to anticipate possible fluctuations in resources available for MVHC. Whereas, I argue that the changing nature of the social covenant between Canada and its military and veterans has caused in the past, and will continue to cause in the future, significant variations in the amount of resources governments and others are prepared to allocate to MVHC.

SOCIAL COVENANTS AND SOCIAL CONTRACTS

Related to this theme is the widespread use of the term "social covenant" in discussions of MVHC to infer that these current high levels of support will be stable or even increase and can be used as a basis for long term plans. In contrast, I argue that the relationship between Canadians and their military and veterans is more in the nature of a contract, which can be amended, rather than a covenant; therefore, future resource levels cannot be reliably predicted.

A social covenant is often taken to be, in the context of MVHC, a solemn promise by governments and the Canadian people to provide adequate, and if necessary increasing, levels of support to MVHC. It is usually perceived to be enduring and unchangeable.[3] The historical record demonstrates, however, that such commitments are more like a social contract than a covenant.[4] In this context, a social contract can be seen as a commitment that, while durable, is subject to modification over time according to prevailing circumstances. The concern I have with the use of the term "covenant" in the phrase "social covenant" in the MVHC context is that it conveys to many the impression that Canadian governments have made an enduring and unchangeable promise to fund MVHC at today's levels or higher, when this may not be the case.[5] The following two statements, made only two years apart by Sir Robert Borden a Canadian prime minister who wrestled with MVHC issues almost 100 years ago, are but one example that shows that government promises are more in the nature of a contract that is subject to periodic renegotiation depending on changing conditions:

> The government and the country will consider it their first duty to ... prove to the returned men its just and due appreciation of the inestimable value of the services rendered to the country and Empire...[6] (1917)

> Canada has done all she could for her soldiers...this country is face to face with a serious financial situation which will call for a rigid economy and careful retrenchment.[7] (1919)

These statements allude to the fact that reasons for changes in the MVHC social contract are numerous and they interact in complex ways, and this issue will be examined next.

REASONS FOR CHANGES IN THE MVHC SOCIAL CONTRACT

Three important factors that influence changes in the MVHC social contract are perceptions of the causes of disease, national culture, and changing decision makers.

Different perceptions of the causes of disease is in part a cultural issue since various societies at different times in their history have had diverse explanations for the causes of illnesses, for example, organisms like bacteria, bad luck, divine retribution for misconduct, carelessness, character flaws (especially for psychological disorders like Operational Stress Injuries), etc. Not surprisingly, whenever injury and illness among military personnel are perceived as being due to personal failings of any kind, support for MVHC decreases.[8]

Under the heading of national culture, three factors can be highlighted: perceptions of the military in a society, perception of the conflict in which injuries occurred, and perceptions of how military personnel and veterans are being treated in relation to others in society.

Extremes of perceptions of the military in a society can be illustrated by these contrasting views held by two prominent Kingston politicians, Sir John A. MacDonald (Canada's first prime minister) and W.F. Nickle (Kingston's Member of Parliament 1911-19), respectively:

> ...'regulars' are useful only for hunting, drinking and chasing women...they are soldiers because they are no good at anything else.[9]

> ...this war has clearly demonstrated ...that the hero is to be found under practically every jacket...[10]

It does not take a great deal of imagination to deduce how each man might differ in his views on the allocation of resources to MVHC. Perceptions of a society's military are also related to society's perception of the conflict in which injuries occurred. For example, as we shall see, Canadians today are much more sympathetic to compensating military personnel injured in ongoing operations in Afghanistan than they were to compensating those who were disabled as a result of service in Somalia or the Former Yugoslavia in the 1990s. However, perceptions of any given conflict can change over time as new interpretations of conflicts appear or as the demographics of a society change.[11]

Lastly, under national culture perceptions of how military personnel and veterans are being treated in relation to others in society has also been an important factor in determining levels of support for MVHC. Economic conditions are an important influence in this regard as MVHC is in competition with other demands for government and private funds. For example, between the First and Second World Wars, the annual cost of veterans' programs and pensions was the second largest government expense next to servicing the national debt. Furthermore, by 1939, in trying economic times, those outwardly uninjured veterans pensioned in Canada for "shellshock" represented 50 percent of the over 70,000 veterans receiving pensions, causing many to think that veterans' pensions were too generous.[12]

Changing decision makers is the third important factor that can precipitate changes in the MVHC social contract. Any time there are changes in key decision makers, at any level, there can be changes in beliefs, attitudes, and actions that affect MVHC. Two brief examples of how these factors contributed to significant change in the MVHC social contract follow.

TWO EXAMPLES OF CHANGES IN THE MVHC SOCIAL CONTRACT

The two examples selected to illustrate changes in the MVHC social contract in Canada come from the period during and immediately after the First World War and from the 1990s, the so-called "Decade of Darkness" for the Canadian Forces.

The period during and immediately after the First World War was a critical period in our history as the enormous human cost of the war facilitated paradigm shifts that were unimaginable before the war. In the context of MVHC, assumptions and practices developed in that era persist today.

The huge human cost of the war to Canada was a critical influence on how the public perceived the war. There were approximately 65,000 military personnel killed and 150,000 wounded in the First World War, for a total casualty count of about 215,000. Based on a population of 7.2 million of whom 600,000 served in uniform, those numbers represent losses of almost 1% of the population and 11% of those who served killed and approximately 2% of the population and 25% of those who served wounded. To see those figures today the way they might have been viewed by Canadians after the war, consider that if Canada then had today's population of 34 million, using the percentages given above, casualties would have been 306,000 killed and 680,000 wounded for almost 1 million total casualties.[13]

In the Canadian postwar debate over what the nation's unprecedented loss meant, there were competing interpretations. Two explanations, "for what?" based on the idea that the nation's loss was in vain and "death so noble" based on the idea that the sacrifice of Canada's youth had helped to make a better world, were two competing parts of the national postwar discourse. The "death so noble" interpretation that the sacrifice was worthwhile became the dominant interpretation for a period of time and contributed significantly to support for high levels of public and government expenditures on veterans' health care.[14]

The second example chosen is the period from what has been called the CF's "Decade of Darkness," the 1990s, because of its impact on current and future MVHC issues. During that era, cuts to the CF during the Defence retrenchment at the end of the Cold War were exacerbated by public perceptions of wrong doing in the Somalia mission and by widespread distrust in the senior leadership of the CF – all of which had an impact on public support for MVHC.[15] This situation began to change gradually in 1997 and the publication in 2000 of the findings of the Board of Inquiry - Croatia was a major milestone in the effort to re-establish public support for the CF and in particular for MVHC.[16] Recent operations in Afghanistan have magnified that support considerably.[17]

These two examples represent the wave-like nature of support for MVHC in this country. The first example shows how a powerful wave of public and government support for MVHC developed based on the widely held belief among Canadians that they owed a debt to the surviving veterans who had sacrificed so much for their country. However, Sir Robert Borden's comments during the 1919 financial crisis and the perception among many during the Great Depression and its aftermath, that veterans' pensions were too generous, show that support for MVHC is not unconditional. The second example, the "Decade of Darkness," illustrates a trough or low point in public and government support for MVHC based on public perceptions that Canada's military had brought dishonour upon itself in Somalia and on public ambivalence at the time about the CF's role and performance in its operations in the tumultuous Former Yugoslavia in the 1990s.

Therefore, we can see that, from a historical perspective, support for MVHC will rise and fall periodically, and that just because things are good (or bad) does not mean that they will stay that way.

When I started my involvement with these issues during the "Decade of Darkness," there were serious deficiencies in MVHC; however, over the past 10 years due to the dedication, empathy and energy of senior leaders in the CF and Veterans Affairs Canada many significant improvements have been made to MVHC.[18] Nevertheless, any system can be improved and must adapt to changing circumstances. Consequently, two of the most important skills for senior decision makers involved in MVHC to possess are leading change and the art of understanding the possible at any given time – both key elements of strategic planning and of change strategies.

STRATEGIC PLANNING AND CHANGE STRATEGIES

Given the changeable and unpredictable nature of support for MVHC over time, some suggestions for strategic planning and change strategies based on "understanding the possible" follow.

One way of conceptualizing the strategic environment in which MVHC planning and policy development and implementation take place is to visualize surfers on an ocean on a windy day. The waves they surf represent the periodic rise and fall in support for MVHC; the waves also represent times of maximum opportunity for obtaining resources for MVHC (wave peaks) and times when there are fewer opportunities (troughs between the waves). If we picture three surfers, one riding a surfboard just under the crest of the wave going at maximum speed, one riding a surfboard half way down the wave and losing speed, and one surfer laying on a board in the trough between waves positioning to catch the next wave, we can get an idea of the three main situations MVHC strategic planners and policy makers can find themselves in.

Based on this metaphor of the surfers, I offer these principles based on work colleagues and I have done on strategic planning and culture change in military organizations.[19] A key principle is patience. MVHC leaders have to be able to work within the existing strategic environment (peak, trough, or somewhere in between) while positioning their organizations to ride the next wave. In periods of opportunity they need to exploit those opportunities that present themselves, and while in troughs they need to make or revise plans to be ready for the next wave, which will inevitably come. At all times, MVHC leaders should be engaged and connected with the public, shapers of public opinion, and decision makers in society. This engagement will allow them, among other things, to be attuned to the strategic environment, the equivalent of surfers understanding the wind and waves of their ocean environment.

An important, and often ignored, issue in implementing change strategies is succession planning among organizational leaders. At some points in a change process, organizations need visionaries to create visions and change strategies. At others they need leaders who are implementers of visions. A series of visionary leaders with constantly changing visions often leads to chaos and meaningful change is rarely achieved.[20]

While these principles are not a guarantee of success in planning and implementing change in organizations, they can optimize chances of success by helping leaders grasp the art of "understanding the possible" at any given time. In other words, there are times to plan and restructure, there are times to consolidate gains and protect hard-won advances, and there are times to exploit opportunities for growth. To reiterate an earlier statement, these may sound like statements of the obvious, but recent experience has shown that many organizations have forgotten or are not aware of these basic principles. For example, in the past two decades the CF has been so preoccupied with "transformational" change that it has been unable to assess which changes have merit and which do not. From an organizational perspective, the CF has not made adequate efforts to learn from its "transformational" changes since the end of the Cold War, and change has become an end in itself, rather than a process used to reach a desired endstate. The result has been uncoordinated, sometimes chaotic, change, and "change fatigue," coupled with cynicism about constant change, among members of the organization.[21]

THE FUTURE

Historians have not been noted for their ability to predict the future; their predictions tend to be wrong more often than not. However, there are general trends and patterns from the past that can guide us in our future plans and actions.

As we have seen, opportunities for resourcing MVHC will rise and fall over time, like the waves on the ocean. Knowing this, as in the surfer in the analogy above, we can position ourselves to wait out troughs and exploit peaks of support. Today, in the West, the wave of support for MVHC seems to be cresting, from what we can discern in the public forum.

For example, in the US, the Chairman of the Joint Chiefs of Staff recently described military health care costs as "unsustainable," based on the fact, reiterated by the Secretary of Defense, that "annual military health-care costs, which have risen from $19 billion a decade ago to roughly $50 billion today, are 'eating the department alive.'"[22] Similarly, the chair of the Veterans' Affairs Committee of the US House of Representatives declared that veterans health care will "break the bank" in the future.[23] And in Britain, massive spending cuts, averaging almost 20 percent to all government departments in the next 5 years, will no doubt impact MVHC, as the British government has already announced plans to reduce pensions for disabled veterans and war widows.[24]

We seem to be still at a high point of support for MVHC now in Canada, but there is no way to predict how long it will last. One factor to consider is that cuts to government budgets are just starting with the aim of reducing and eliminating the deficit. However, based on Canada's experience in the 1990s in trying to pay down, rather than just reduce, the deficit, the real cuts may still be some years in the future.[25] Based on this type of scenario, the best approach for those planning MVHC initiatives may be to exploit current opportunities, but to be prepared for whatever comes in the future.

LEARNING FROM THE PAST – PREPARING FOR THE FUTURE

One obstacle to using general trends and patterns from the past to guide us in future plans and actions is the state of our knowledge of the past related to Canadian MVHC issues. At the beginning of the essay, I quoted the Deputy Surgeon General of the CF to illustrate the potential contribution of history to MVHC initiatives. However, the ability to take advantage of lessons from our past in this area is predicated on us actually having a history of Canadian MVHC. After literature searches and in conversations with those attending the 2010 MVHR conference, it is clear to me that Canadian MVHC does not have an adequate history. Not only do very few historical studies of the development, implementation, and outcomes of military and veteran health care policies exist, but even scholarly accounts of more recent events, like the operations of CF health care units overseas, are not available to the health care community and general public. Therefore, if we are to learn from our past in order to optimize our future efforts for MVHC, we must invest in documenting, analyzing, and disseminating the successes, failures, and wisdom of our forbears.

[1]B.H. Liddell Hart, Strategy (New York: Frederick A. Praeger, 1954), 23.

[2]Jean Robert Bernier, "Threats to Operational Force Health Protection," The Operational Art - Canadian Perspectives: Health Service Support, eds Allan English and James C. Taylor (Kingston, ON: Canadian Defence Academy Press, 2006), 41.

[3]Jonathan Sacks, "Address by Chief Rabbi Sir Jonathan Sacks to The Lambeth Conference 28th July 2008," Lambeth Conference 28 July 2008, http://www.chiefrabbi.org/UploadedFiles/Articals/lambethconference28july08.pdf, accessed 18 December 2010. The address of the Chief Rabbi of Britain to a major conference of the worldwide Anglican Communion highlights the salient differences between a covenant and a contract; "Social Contract," Wikipedia, the Free Encyclopedia, http://en.wikipedia.org/wiki/Social_contract, accessed 18 December 2010; Rosie DiManno, "Pity the Walking Wounded Among Our Vets," Toronto Star (4 January 2010). http://www.thestar.com/news/canada/afghanmission/casualties/article/745501--dimanno-pity-the-walking-wounded-among-our-vets, accessed 4 January 2010.

[4]Veterans Affairs Canada - Canadian Forces Advisory Council, "Honouring Canada's Commitment: 'Opportunity with Security' for Canadian Forces Veterans and Their Families in the 21st Century-Discussion Paper" http://www.vac-acc.gc.ca/content/forces/nvc/discuss_paper.pdf, accessed 18 December 2010.

[5]Eugene Lang, "When the Government Fights a Deficit the Military has no Friends," Globe and Mail Mar 9, 2010, http://www.theglobeandmail.com/news/opinions/if-ottawa-fights-a-deficit-the-military-has-no-allies/article1495359, accessed 18 December 2010.

[6]Veterans Affairs Canada - Canadian Forces Advisory Council, "The Origins and Evolution of Veterans Benefits in Canada, 1914-2004 Reference Paper" http://www.vac-acc.gc.ca/clients/sub.cfm?source=forces/nvc/reference, accessed 18 December 2010.

[7]Desmond Morton and Glenn Wright, Winning the Second Battle: Canadian Veterans and the Return to Civilian Life (Toronto: University of Toronto Press, 1987), 124.

[8]Allan English, "Leadership and Operational Stress in the Canadian Forces," Canadian Military Journal 1, 3 (2000): 33-38.

[9]Allan English, Understanding Military Culture: A Canadian Perspective (Montreal & Kingston: McGill-Queen's University Press, 2004), 87.

[10]James Wood, Militia Myths: Ideas of the Canadian Soldier, 1896-1921 (Vancouver: UBC Press, 2010), 259.

[11]Allan English, Understanding Military Culture: A Canadian Perspective (Montreal & Kingston: McGill-Queen's University Press, 2004), 111-114.

[12]Desmond Morton, "Military Medicine and State Medicine: Historical Notes on the Canadian Army Medical Corps in the First World War 1914-1919," Canadian Health Care and the State, ed. David C. Naylor, (Montreal & Kingston: McGill-Queen's Univ. Press, 1992), 38-66; Desmond Morton, A Military History of Canada:3rd edition. (Toronto: McClelland & Stewart, 1992), 167.

[13]Desmond Morton, A Military History of Canada: 3rd edition. (Toronto: McClelland & Stewart, 1992), 165; G.W.L. Nicholson, Official History of the Canadian Army in the First World War (Ottawa: Queen's Printer, 1962), 535; Shane Schreiber, Shock Army of the British Empire: The Canadian Corps in the Last 100 Days of the Great War (Westport, CT: Praeger, 1997), 232-33; Commonwealth War Graves Commission Annual Report 2007-2008 Jul 31 2008, 53. http://www.cwgc.org/admin/files/Finances,%20Statistics%20and%20Service.pdf, accessed 18

December 2010; "World War I Casualties," *Wikipedia, the Free Encyclopedia*, last modified on 19 December 2010. http://en.wikipedia.org/wiki/World_War_I_casualties accessed 19 December 2010.

[14]Jonathan F. Vance, *Death So Noble: Memory, Meaning and the First World War* (Vancouver: UBC Press, 1997), 29-34, 257-67.

[15]Veterans Affairs Canada - Canadian Forces Advisory Council, "The Origins and Evolution of Veterans Benefits in Canada, 1914-2004", op.cit; G.E. Sharpe and Allan English, "The Experience of the Senior Leadership of the Canadian Forces in the 1990s," *The Decade of Darkness* paper written for CF Leadership Institute, 24 Feb 2004.

[16]R.R. Henault, *et al.*, "Operational-Level Leadership and Command in the CF – General Henault and the DCDS Group at the Beginning of the 'New World Order,'" *The Operational Art Canadian Perspectives: Leadership and Command*, ed. Allan English (Kingston, ON: Canadian Defence Academy Press, 2006), 135-161; Allan English, "Leadership and Operational Stress in the Canadian Forces." *Canadian Military Journal* 33, (2000), abbreviated version.

[17]Michael Valpy, "Canada's military: Invisible no more," *Globe and Mail*, Nov. 20, 2009 http://www.theglobeandmail.com/news/politics/canadas-military-invisible-no-more/article1372117/, accessed 18 December 2010.

[18]J. Don Richardson, *et al.*, "Operational Stress Injury Social Support: A Canadian Innovation in Professional Peer Support," *Canadian Military Journal* 9, 1 (2008): 57-64.

[19]Allan English, "Understanding Military Culture," *The Decade of Darkness*, paper written for CF Leadership Institute, 24 February 2004; T.F.J. Leversedge, "Transforming Canada's Air Force: Creating a Strategic Planning Process," Allan D. English, ed., *Air Campaigns in the New World Order, Silver Dart* - Canadian Aerospace Studies Series, 2 (Winnipeg: Centre for Defence and Security Studies, 2005), 123-55; Michael Barzelay and Colin Campbell, *Preparing for the Future – Strategic Planning in the U.S. Air Force* (Washington, DC: Brookings Institution Press, 2003).

[20]Allan English, "Outside Canadian Forces Transformation Looking In," *Canadian Military Journal* 11, 2 (2011) at http://www.journal.forces.gc.ca/vo11/no2/04-english-eng.asp. accessed 18 December 2010.

[21]Lieutenant-Colonel Michael Rostek, "A Framework for Fundamental Change? The Management Command and Control Re-engineering Initiative," *Canadian Military Journal* 5, 4 (Winter 2004-2005): 65-72; Allan English, "Outside Canadian Forces Transformation Looking In," Canadian Military Journal 11, 2 (2011) at http://www.journal.forces.gc.ca/vo11/no2/04-english-eng.asp., accessed 25 May 2011.

[22]Francine Kiefer, "Admiral Mike Mullen: Cost of military health care is 'not sustainable,'" *Christian Science Monitor* (Boston, Mass.), September 29, 2010, http://www.csmonitor.com/Commentary/Editorial-Board-Blog/2010/0929/Admiral-Mike-Mullen-Cost-of-military-health-care-is-not-sustainable, accessed 26 May 2011; Nathan Hodge, "The Pentagon Would Take $100 Billion Hit," *Wall Street Journal*, 11 November 2010, http://online.wsj.com/article/SB10001424052748704804504575606961144468530.html, accessed 18 December 2010.

[23]Shaun Waterman, "War veterans' care to cost $1.3 trillion," *Washington Times*, September 29, 2010, http://www.washingtontimes.com/news/2010/sep/29/war-veterans-care-to-cost-13-trillion/, accessed 18 December 2010.

[24]Richard Norton-Taylor, "War pensions reform row played down by defence chief," *The Guardian* (London, UK, Nov. 14, 2010, http://www.guardian.co.uk/uk/2010/nov/14/war-pensions-reform-defence-chief. accessed 18 December 2010.

[25]Martin Shadwick, "Darkness Revisited?" *Canadian Military Journal* 9, 3 (2008): 95-97.

CHAPTER 18

A Comparison of Financial Programs Offered to 'Traditional' Versus 'New' Veterans with Severe Disabilities: A New Class of Veteran?[1]

Amy Buitenhuis, BScE, BA, Canadian Disability Policy Alliance, Queen's University and
Alice B. Aiken, CD, PhD, MSc, BScPT, BSc(Kin), Centre for Health Services and Policy Research,
Queen's University

Abstract

The New Veterans Charter (NVC) aims to improve services available to veterans. It was enacted in 2006 to replace the Pension Act (PA). A comparison between financial packages offered by both policies to a veteran with severe disabilities shows that the PA provides better financial support than the NVC. Therefore, changes to the NVC are needed so that veterans with severe disabilities are provided at least the same level of support as under the PA.

A Comparison of Financial Programs Offered to 'Traditional' Versus 'New' Veterans with Severe Disabilities: A New Class of Veteran?

Every veteran released from the military before April 2006 was entitled to benefits according to the Pension Act. Depending on eligibility, the veterans received a number of financial benefits and services administered by VAC. Veterans would go through a disability assessment where their disabilities would be assessed in terms of severity and relatedness to service and given a percentage. The disability assessment would determine the amounts for various disability pensions available. Other factors that affected financial benefits include marital status and number of children. These pensions were paid monthly to veterans from release to death, and were paid to the veterans spouse or dependent children after death.

In 2006, the Canadian Forces Members and veterans Re-establishment and Compensation Act, referred to as the New Veterans Charter, was enacted, changing the way veterans receive benefits and services from VAC. Services such as rehabilitation, career counselling, and vocational training were restructured. Financial benefits were also reorganized into some lump-sum payments and some monthly pensions. These benefits were divided into two categories: benefits related to financial losses due to disability, and benefits related to non-financial losses due to injury. The amounts are based on eligibility for work, pre-release salary (and therefore, rank), and disability of the veteran. The purpose of the redesign was to shift the focus of VAC programs and benefits from disability management, which was the aim of the Pension Act, to one of reintegration.[2]

Since its implementation, the NVC's effectiveness has been the focus of much discussion and debate within VAC and other government bodies and from veterans and veterans' organizations around Canada. Two major reports have been written, one by the NVC Advisory Group,[3] commissioned by VAC, and the other by the Senate Subcommittee on Veterans Affairs.[4] These reports provided over 300 recommendations, some relating to large 'framework' suggestions, others giving specific recommendations. The recommendations focused on all aspects of the NVC, relating to strengthening family support services, ensuring financial security, improving rehabilitation services and outcomes, actively promoting NVC programs and services, and establishing performance measures to monitor and evaluate the impact of the program.[5] Other specific suggestions include increase collaboration between VAC, the DND and SISIP regarding health care, rehabilitation, and career transition programs; increase Earnings Loss Benefit to 100% of pre-release salary instead of 75%; make Earnings Loss Benefit non-taxable and adjust it for inflation without cap; improve financial benefits offered after age 65, including the re-examination of Supplementary Retirement Benefits; improve supports for families who are care-givers for severely disabled veterans; and change options available for the receipt of the lump-sum Disability Award.

VAC began its own three phase review into the NVC in April 2009 and published Phase 1 of this review in December 2009[6] and Phase 2 in December 2010.[7] Phase 1 discussed the relevance and rationale of the NVC and its programs. It looked at the overlap between VAC and other government agencies and found that there are some overlaps between VAC programs and DND Programs, specifically relating to rehabilitation and job placement. The report provided recommendations including: explore the overlap between VAC and other government agencies; review the current services offered to families; and examine veterans' access to health and dental care. Phase 2 focused on the service delivery framework of the NVC and provided recommendations specific to service provision by VAC. Phase 3 will focus on the successes and unintended consequences of the NVC.

In this chapter, rather than proposing further recommendations related solely to the NVC, we compare the financial benefits of the Pension Act and the NVC for a case study of a 40-year-old Captain with a focus on veterans with severe disabilities. Such a comparison has not been done thus far, and we feel that it will illuminate some of the weaknesses in the financial aspects of the NVC, particularly for veterans with severe disabilities, who are the most financially vulnerable. We compare the net present values of the benefits from each program for a Captain released from the military at the age of 40. We vary the veteran's disability assessment percentage, age of death, family size and rank at release to see how these factors affect the total net present value provided by each program. This paper is part of a larger study that takes a more comprehensive look at this and two other case studies.[8]

The definition of veterans with disabilities used in this study is the definition used by VAC. Veterans with severe disabilities are those veterans with a disability assessment of 78% or greater.[9] Although the disability assessment is complex, as a simplified example, hearing loss could be a 10% disability or a 100% disability depending on severity and cause. A lower limb, below-the-knee amputation might be 52% disability, regardless of cause because it is a defined disability. Some disabilities, such as post-traumatic stress disorder, are difficult to define accurately and may be assessed through a range of percentages depending on the severity.[10] As of June 30, 2010, 4% (n=832) of veterans served by the NVC (n=20796) are assessed with a disability of 78% or greater.[11]

The objectives of this report are first to conduct a direct comparison between the NVC and the PA with respect to the total amount of financial compensation for veterans with severe disabilities, and second, to determine the effects of factors such as degree of disability, rank, and family status on the total financial benefits available from the NVC compared to the PA for veterans with severe disabilities.

METHOD

CASE STUDY

To facilitate the comparison of the net present values of the benefits provided by the Pension Act and NVC, a case study of a 40-year-old Veteran was chosen. A case study was necessary because the Pension Act and NVC have a number of programs with different eligibility criteria; a case study of a particular Veteran allows us to see how the financial benefits available from VAC differ under the two policies.

A number of assumptions were made about the case study veteran. The veteran was male, and assumed to be married with two children. A majority of veterans be served by the Pension Act are married or in a common-law relationship (72%), although data is not available for the average number of children of veterans.[12] This assumption is important because under the Pension Act, the veteran is given a pension for her or his spouse and children. The veteran was assumed to be living in Ontario so that Ontario provincial income tax rates would be used for deducting taxes from the programs that are not tax-exempt.[13] The age of release was chosen to be 40 years old because it is the average age of all medically released CF members as of March 2009.[14] The rank of Captain was chosen to look at a CF member with a medium/high rate of pay. The veteran was assumed to have entered the military at the age of 18, and was assumed to have died at the age of 78, which is the average age of death for men in Canada.[15] Finally, a disability assessment of 100% was chosen because this comparison is focusing on veterans with severe disabilities.

Inclusion of Programs in Analysis

All programs available under the Pension Act and NVC were considered for comparison. Because of the assumptions made about the case study veteran, not all programs could be included. The programs are described in Table 18.1 and Table 18.2 and in the case that a program was not included in the analysis, the rational for exclusion was provided. In September 2010 changes were made to the NVC16 and these changes are also included in Table 18.2.

Subprogram	Description	Amount	Included?	Rationale for exclusion
PENSION ACT				
Disability Pension	Monthly pension until one year after death. Based on disability assessment. Non-taxable.	Max: $2,397.83/month†	Yes	
Spousal Pension	Monthly pension until one year after death, award only if Veteran has spouse or common-law partner. Based on disability assessment. Non-taxable.	Max: $599.46/month†	Yes	
Children's Pension	Monthly pension, awarded based on number of children, given from birth of child until child turns 18, or 25 if child pursues post-secondary education. Non-taxable.	1st child: $311.72/month 2nd child: $227.79/month Other children: $179.84/month per child†	Yes	
Attendant Allowance	Monthly pension until one year after death. Provided for Veterans who are in need of assistance with daily living, often to compensate family caregivers. Non-taxable.	Max: $1,586.66/month‡	Yes	
Clothing Allowance	Monthly pension until death. Provided when a Veteran's disability causes extraneous wear-and-tear on clothing. Non-taxable.	Max: $179.79/month‡	No	The same program exists under the NVC, so no comparison is needed.
Exceptional Incapacity Allowance	Monthly pension until death. For Veterans who are exceptionally incapacitated, in whole or part by their disability. Non-taxable.	Max: $1,269.36/month‡	Yes	
Prisoner of War Compensation	Monthly pension until death. For Veterans who spend a certain amount of time as a Prison of War or in a similar situation. Non-taxable.	Max: $1,989.23/month‡	No	It was assumed the Veterans in the case study had not been prisoners of war.
Survivor Benefits	Monthly pension awarded to survivors of a Veteran beginning one year after Veteran's death. Non-taxable.	Max for a Veteran with a spouse: $34,528.68/year‡	Yes	

† Veterans Affairs Canada. (2009a). Disability Pensions. Retrieved from http://www.vac-acc.gc.ca/clients/sub.cfm?source=dispen
‡ Pension Rates Rise with Cost of Living. (2010, Mar - April). Legion Magazine, 68.

Table 18.1: Description and rationale for the inclusion and exclusion of programs available through the Pension Act.

A. Aiken, & A. Buitenhuis, *Supporting Canadian Veterans with Disabilities: A Comparison of Financial Benefits*, (Kingston: Claxton Papers, Defence Management Studies Program School of Policy Studies, Queen's University and Canadian Institute for Military and Veterans Health Research (2011), 14.

Program	Description	Amount	Included?	Rational for exclusion
NEW VETERANS CHARTER				
Disability Award	Lump-sum amount paid at release. Paid to compensate for the non-economic impacts of disability (pain and suffering). Non-taxable.	Max: $276,079.70†	Yes	
Earning Loss Benefit	Monthly amount based on 75% of the Veteran's pre-release salary minus other income including employment income, Canadian Forces Superannuation, Canada/Quebec Pension Plan. Ends when Veteran finishes rehabilitation program, or when Veteran turns 65 if deemed Totally and Permanently Incapacitated. Changes made to program in September 2010 ensure that the minimum income is approximately $40 000‡. Taxable.	75% of pre-release salary	Yes	
Permanent Impairment Allowance	Monthly amount paid until death. For Veterans who are permanently and severely impaired. Taxable.	Max: $19,200/year‡	Yes	
Extended Permanent Impairment Allowance	A program that was promised in September 2010 but not implement. Monthly amount paid until death. For Veterans who receive Permanent Impairment Allowance and have catastrophic injuries. Non-taxable.	$1000/month‡	Yes	

Table 18.2: Description and rationale for the inclusion and exclusion of programs available through the New Veterans Charter.

A. Aiken, & A. Buitenhuis, *Supporting Canadian Veterans with Disabilities: A Comparison of Financial Benefits*, (Kingston: Claxton Papers, Defence Management Studies Program School of Policy Studies, Queen's University and Canadian Institute for Military and Veterans Health Research (2011), 15.

In addition to the VAC programs described above, veterans are eligible for programs provided by the DND, the federal government, and private insurance companies. Table 18.3 describes these programs and gives reasons for which these programs were included or excluded from analysis.

Program	Description†	Included?	Rationale for inclusion/exclusion
Canadian Forces Superannuation	Pension paid to all Canadian Forces members who served for 10 years or more and are medically released from the CF. Dependent on years of service and pre-release salary.	Yes	This benefit is considered income and therefore is deducted from Service Income Security Insurance Plan Long Term Disability payments and Earning Loss Benefits (ELB) payments. It is included because it is important in the calculation of the total Service Income Security Insurance Plan Long Term Disability and ELB received by Veterans.
Service Income Security Insurance Plan Long Term Disability	Monthly payment of 75% of pre-release salary, minus other income. Provided to former CF members who are medically released and undergoing rehabilitation. Can be extended if member is deemed to be Totally and Permanently Incapacitated.	Yes	This benefit is similar to ELB. Therefore, under the Pension Act, this benefit was available to Veterans if their total income, including Pension Act Disability Pensions and CFSA, is less than 75% of the pre-release salary. However, under the NVC, Veterans are not eligible for the Service Income Security Insurance Plan Long Term Disability payment because they are receiving ELB.
Canada Pension Plan Disability	A monthly pension for Canadian with disabilities ends at 65.	No	These benefits were not included in the analysis because it was assumed that these payments would be similar for the Veteran whether under the Pension Act or the NVC. For income-dependent benefits, the payments available under both the NVC and Pension Act would be over the maximum amount for eligibility in most cases.
Canada Pension Plan/Quebec Pension Plan	Retirement benefit paid monthly after retirement. Amount is dependent upon contribution throughout working life.	No	
Old Age Security	Monthly pension paid after retirement. Amount is dependent upon income.	No	
Guaranteed Income Supplement	Monthly pension paid after retirement. Amount is dependent upon income.	No	

† The amounts of each program are not included in this table because they are highly case-dependent and cannot be determined based on the assumptions made within this study.

Table 18.3: Description of Programs not offered by Veterans Affairs Canada and reasons for exclusion.

A. Aiken, & A. Buitenhuis, *Supporting Canadian Veterans with Disabilities: A Comparison of Financial Benefits,* (Kingston: Claxton Papers, Defence Management Studies Program School of Policy Studies, Queen's University and Canadian Institute for Military and Veterans Health Research (2011), 16..

METHODS OF ANALYSIS

The comparison of the Pension Act and the NVC was completed by calculating the net present value of the financial programs for each program and then completing a sensitivity analysis to determine how certain assumptions affected the outcome of the comparison. The net present value calculation was done by summing all payments available to veterans under each program and discounting for the time value of money at a rate of 3%, compounded annually. Inflation was not included in this analysis.

A single variable sensitivity analysis was completed by varying disability assessment, rank, number of children, age of death, and eligibility for Exceptionally Incapacitated Allowance (EIA) and Permanent Impairment Allowance (PIA). Varying these parameters changed the case study veteran's eligibility for certain programs under the Pension Act and the NVC and shows how the net present values of each policy changes with different assumptions. The changes to the NVC proposed in September 2010 are considered in the sensitivity analysis varying disability assessment.

RESULTS

Based on the eligibility of our case study Veteran for different programs under both the Pension Act and the NVC, we determined the total amount of financial benefits that the Veteran would receive under each policy. Figure 18.1 shows the net present values of the Pension Act and New Veterans Charter financial benefits for the case study Veteran, indicating that under the assumptions described in section 2.1, the NVC offers 58% of the money offered by the Pension Act over the Veteran's life. The figure also shows how the programs within each policy contribute to the net present value. Under the Pension Act, the Disability Pension, Spousal Pension and Children's Pension amount to just over half (52%) of the total benefits. Under the NVC, the Earning Loss Benefit and the Permanent Impairment Allowance each amount to around 40% of the total.

Figure 18.1 shows that using the assumptions previously described, the Veteran receives more financial support over his lifetime under the Pension Act than under the NVC. The following results examine how this result changes as four characteristics are varied: age of death, rank at release, number of children and disability assessment. Each characteristic was varied independently, meaning this is a simple, single-variable sensitivity analysis.

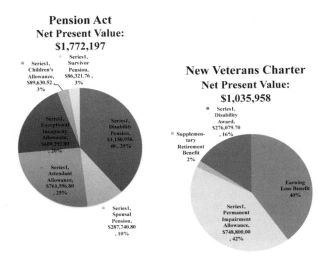

Figure 18.1: Net present value comparison of the Pension Act and the NVC with program breakdown.

A. Aiken, & A. Buitenhuis, *Supporting Canadian Veterans with Disabilities: A Comparison of Financial Benefits*, (Kingston: Claxton Papers, Defence Management Studies Program School of Policy Studies, Queen's University and Canadian Institute for Military and Veterans Health Research (2011), 26.

First, the age of death of the veteran was varied between 65 and 90 years old, and the net present values of financial benefits of the Pension Act and NVC are shown in Figure 18.2. In all cases, the Pension Act has a higher net present value than the NVC. A linear regression was completed on the data and the slopes of the lines of best fit were calculated. The slopes of the lines of best fit for the Pension Act and the NVC are 16 (R^2=0.992) and 5 (R^2=0.988), respectively. This means that the veteran receives more per year lived after 65 under the Pension Act than under the NVC.

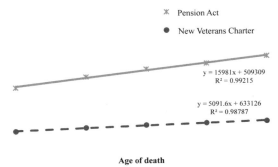

Figure 18.2: The net present value of the financial benefits offered by the Pension Act and the NVC, varying the age of death of the Veteran.

A. Aiken, & A. Buitenhuis, *Supporting Canadian Veterans with Disabilities: A Comparison of Financial Benefits*, (Kingston: Claxton Papers, Defence Management Studies Program School of Policy Studies, Queen's University and Canadian Institute for Military and Veterans Health Research (2011), 27.

Second, the rank at release of the veteran was varied between senior Private and Colonel, and the net present values of financial benefits of the Pension Act and NVC for different ranks are shown in Figure 18.3. The rank and salary at release determines the amount of the Earning Loss Benefit (ELB) under the NVC. The ELB amount is 75% of the veteran's pre-release salary, minus any other income such as employment income or pension payments.[17] The rank at release does not affect any of the programs under the Pension Act. Thus, as shown in Figure 18.3, the net present values for the Pension Act for ranks are the same, while those for the NVC increase as salary increases.

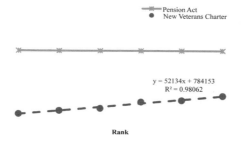

Figure 18.3: The net present value of the financial benefits offered by the Pension Act and the NVC, varying the rank at release of the veteran.

A. Aiken, & A. Buitenhuis, *Supporting Canadian Veterans with Disabilities: A Comparison of Financial Benefits*, (Kingston: Claxton Papers, Defence Management Studies Program School of Policy Studies, Queen's University and Canadian Institute for Military and Veterans Health Research (2011), 31.

Third, the veteran's number of children was varied between 0 and 4, and the net present values of financial benefits of the Pension Act and NVC for different ranks are shown in Figure 18.4. The number of children determines the Children Allowance that is given under the Pension Act, but does not change the amount of any programs under the NVC. Thus, as shown in Figure 18.4, the net present values for the Pension Act increase as number of children increases, while those for the NVC remain the same.

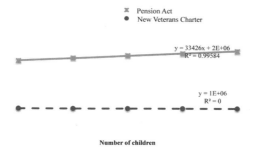

Figure 18.4: The net present value of the financial benefits offered by the Pension Act and the NVC, varying the veteran's number of children.

A. Aiken, & A. Buitenhuis, *Supporting Canadian Veterans with Disabilities: A Comparison of Financial Benefits*, (Kingston: Claxton Papers, Defence Management Studies Program School of Policy Studies, Queen's University and Canadian Institute for Military and Veterans Health Research (2011), 29.

Fourth, the net present values of the Pension Act and the NVC were calculated as the veteran's disability assessment was varied between 75% and 100%. This shows how different veterans with severe disabilities (those with a disability assessment of 78% or greater) would be financially supported under each policy. The comparison is shown in Figure 18.5. Also included in the comparison is an examination of some of the changes proposed to the NVC in September 2010. One proposed change was to create an Extended Permanent Impairment Allowance which would provide veterans with "catastrophic injuries" who were eligible for PIA with a monthly payment of $1,000.[18] Another change was to increase access to PIA, since on 0.01% (16) of veterans were receiving it as of June 30th, 2010.[19]

Figure 18.5 shows the net present values for the Pension Act and the NVC as disability assessment is varied from 75% to 100%. It also shows the net present values of the NVC with the Extended Permanent Impairment Allowance, and the net present values of the NVC excluding PIA and Extended PIA. It was important to show the net present values of the NVC excluding PIA because a very small number of veterans are receiving it.

The results show that the net present values of the Pension Act are significantly higher than those of the NVC excluding PIA. The net present values of the NVC when PIA is included are higher, but still not as high as those of the Pension Act. A linear regression was completed on the data and the slopes of the lines of best fit were calculated. The slopes of the lines of best fit for the Pension Act and the NVC are 32 ($R^2 = 1$) and 25 ($R^2 = 1$), respectively. This means that the veteran receives more per percentage of disability assessment under the Pension Act than under the NVC.

Increasing access to PIA would improve access to financial benefits, but would not bring the net present values of the NVC up to those of the Pension Act. However, when Extended PIA is included in the NVC net present value calculation, the net present values of both policies are similar with the exception of the net present value at a disability assessment of 100%. This is because veterans under the Pension Act with a disability assessment of 98% or greater are able to receive Exceptional Incapacity Allowance, a monthly payment paid until death, meaning that the net present value of the Pension Act at that disability assessment is much greater.

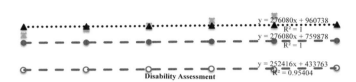

Figure 18.5: The net present value of the financial benefits offered by the Pension Act and the NVC, varying the disability assessment, and accounting for changes to the NVC made in September 2010.

A. Aiken, & A. Buitenhuis, *Supporting Canadian Veterans with Disabilities: A Comparison of Financial Benefits*, (Kingston: Claxton Papers, Defence Management Studies Program School of Policy Studies, Queen's University and Canadian Institute for Military and Veterans Health Research (2011), 36.

DISCUSSION

This section discusses the results of our study and examines what these results show about how the NVC will affect veterans with severe disabilities. It first discusses the differences between different programs under both policies and how these programs affect the net present value of the NVC and the Pension Act. It then discusses the results of the sensitivity analysis and how different veterans will be affected based on age of death, rank at release, number of children and disability assessment.

NET PRESENT VALUE COMPARISON

The results of the net present value comparison of the NVC and the Pension Act, shown in Figure 18.1, show that the net present value of the NVC is 58% of that of the Pension Act. One of the reasons for this difference is that under the Pension Act, the veteran receives a monthly disability, spousal pension and children's pension from the day of release until one year after the veteran's death. This accounts for 52% of the net present value of the Pension Act. These programs are not available under the NVC. Instead, the lump sum disability award and Earning Loss Benefit are available. Together, these programs make up 56% of the net present value of the NVC, but they do not amount to as much as the pensions available under the NVC.

One important difference between the Pension Act and the NVC is the cancelling of the Exceptional Incapacity Allowance from the Pension Act and the creation of the Permanent Incapacity Allowance under the NVC. Under the Pension Act, the amount of EIA "is based on the extent of the helplessness, pain, loss of enjoyment of life and shortened life expectancy of the pensioner."[20] One criteria of EIA is that the veteran must have a disability assessment of 98% or higher. Under the NVC, PIA is available to veterans who have a permanent and severe impairment.[21] This is defined by the type of disability that the veteran has, but is not officially tied to any minimum disability assessment percentage. Both programs are paid monthly until the veteran's death, although PIA is a slightly larger allowance than EIA (PIA: $1500 monthly, EIA: $1269 monthly). However, it is important to note that under the NVC, 16 veterans are in receipt of PIA, as of June 30, 2010.[22] This represents around 0.1% of the veteran population who have been assessed with a disability under the NVC. Thus, in comparing the net present values of the NVC and the Pension Act, it is important to note that very few veterans would have PIA, and therefore the net present value of their benefits would be much lower.

Another important difference between the two policies is that most programs available under the NVC are taxable, whereas most under the Pension Act are tax-free. The net present value of the NVC is reduced significantly by taxes, and this contributes to the large different between them.

SENSITIVITY ANALYSIS

Our sensitivity analysis varied four characteristics of the case study veteran: age of death, rank at release, number of children, and disability assessment. These results show that the Pension Act is more sensitive to factors that may increase the financial need of the veteran, such as a longer life, a great number of children, and a greater disability assessment. They also show that veterans released at a higher rank benefit much more from VAC programs under the NVC than those released at a lower rank. There were no benefits to being released at a higher rank under the Pension Act.

Figure 18.2 compares the net present values of the NVC and Pension Act while varying age of death. As previously discussed, under the Pension Act the veteran receives more per year lived after 65 than he would under the NVC. This is because under the Pension Act, all programs begin at release and end at the veteran's death. Under the NVC, the Disability Award and the Supplementary Retirement Benefit are lump-sum payment that do not depend on the number of years lived by the veteran, and the ELB is a monthly payment but it ends when then veteran turns 65. Thus, the only VAC program the veteran receives after 65 is PIA. This is important because in general, veterans who live longer lives would need more financial support than those who live shorter lives.

Figure 18.3 compares the net present values of the NVC and Pension Act while varying rank at release. The net present value of the Pension Act is not affected by the veteran's rank at release because none of the programs offered by the Pension Act depend on the veteran's pre-release salary. However, since ELB is dependent on the veteran's pre-release salary, the net present value of the NVC increases as rank (pre-release salary) increases. This basic concept is consistent with private insurance policy, but marks a change in the way that VAC provides veterans with benefits, since VAC has not used rank in the past to determine the amount or type of benefits or services available to veterans. Additionally, the authors feel that there should be some discussion about whether or not veterans should be provided financial benefits according to policies that are used by private insurance companies who aim to profit from the provision of insurance. A proposed change was made to the NVC in September 2010 so that the ELB would be calculated as the greater of $40,000 or 75% of the veteran's pre-release salary (minus all other income). This change would affect veterans released as senior Privates, since their salary is $44,364.00, and 75% of that salary is $33,273.00.[23] While this change would improve the financial benefits for low-ranking veterans, it does not affect any ranks above Senior Private. This change was promised but not implemented at the time of publication of this chapter.

Figure 18.4 compares the net present values of the NVC and Pension Act while varying the number of children. The Pension Act provides a pension for veterans based on the number of dependent children that the veteran has. No programs under the NVC are dependent on the veteran's number of children. This is significant because veterans who have more children would need more financial aid to support their children than veterans with fewer or no children.

Figure 18.5 compares the net present values of the NVC and Pension Act while varying the disability assessment of veterans, and also considers the changes to the NVC proposed in September 2010 (but not implemented). These results show that the net present value of the Pension Act increases more per percentage disability assessment than the NVC. This is important because veterans with a higher disability assessment would need more financial support than those with a lower disability assessment, and financial security is a strong predictor of improved health outcomes in people with severe disabilities.[24] The results also show that as the by increasing access to PIA and by providing an Extended PIA to veterans, the net present value of the NVC is approximately the same as that of the Pension Act. Thus, these results strongly support the implementation of the changes to the NVC proposed in September 2010.

CONCLUSIONS

Several conclusions arise from this study. The first and most obvious is that the Pension Act provides a significant financial advantage over the NVC for veterans with severe disabilities. The difference between the Pension Act and the NVC compensations is greatest for veterans who live longer, those who have more children, those with a higher disability assessment, and those released at a lower rank. These groups are financially disadvantaged under the NVC compared to the Pension Act.

Changes need to be made to the NVC to ensure that veterans with severe disabilities receive compensation equivalent to that under the Pension Act. The most obvious discrepancies come from programs or benefits that were eliminated under the NVC. It would benefit veterans with severe disabilities if spousal and child benefits were added back into the plan. In this way, the veteran's family is seen to be part of the NVC, and their new life circumstances of living with a seriously disabled Veteran are also acknowledged.

It can be seen from this analysis that the majority of the benefits offered under the NVC are taxable. This puts NVC veterans at a serious disadvantage over their life course since the net amount they take home each month is less than the gross amount they are pensioned. Over the life course of the veteran, this can amount to a significant amount of money.

One limitation to this study was that it focused on a case study veteran (a 40-year-old Captain with a disability assessment of 100%) and completed a simple, single-variable sensitivity analysis around that case study. As previously mentioned, this study was part of a larger project that looked in more depth at a number of cases to better compare the two policies.[25]

It is important to note that this study was a comparison of two policies, and does not examine the NVC financial benefits in any 'absolute' sense. Thus, our conclusion is not that veterans do not receive adequate financial benefits for a good quality of life under the NVC, but rather that under the NVC they receive far less financial compensation than under the Pension Act. It would be of benefit to compare the payments under the NVC to the poverty line in Canada to see in veterans would be able to maintain a good quality of life with the benefits available from the NVC. It would also be of benefit to consider programs such as the Canada Pension Plan and Old Age Security to see how they work for veterans receiving NVC benefits. Finally, a comparison should be made between the NVC and civilian disability insurance schemes.

Overall, to change the NVC to accommodate veterans with severe disabilities would not be very costly since only 4% of all NVC veterans are considered seriously disabled. One of the most important recommendations that comes out of this study is that creating separate standards and pension categories for veterans with severe disabilities may ensure that the NVC supports veterans who are most in need.

[1]This article is a partial summary of the monograph: A. Aiken, & A. Buitenhuis, *Supporting Canadian Veterans with Disabilities: A Comparison of Financial Benefits*, (Kingston: Claxton Papers, Defence Management Studies Program School of Policy Studies, Queen's University and Canadian Institute for Military and Veterans Health Research (2011).

[2]New Veterans Charter Advisory Group, *Honouring Our Commitment to New Veterans and Their Families: The "Living" Charter in Action*, Veterans Affairs Canada 2009, 7, http://www.veterans.gc.ca/eng/sub.cfm?source=forces/nvc/2009-oct-nvcag, accessed 12 April 2011.

[3]New Veterans Charter Advisory Group, *Honouring Our Commitment to New Veterans and Their Families: The "Living" Charter in Action*, Veterans Affairs Canada 2009, 7, http://www.veterans.gc.ca/eng/sub.cfm?source=forces/nvc/2009-oct-nvcag, accessed 12 April 2011.

[4]Standing Committee on Veterans Affairs. (2010). A Timely Tune-Up for the Living New Veterans Charter: Parliament of Canada.

[5]New Veterans Charter Advisory Group, *Honouring Our Commitment to New Veterans and Their Families: The "Living" Charter in Action*, Veterans Affairs Canada 2009, 2-5, http://www.veterans.gc.ca/eng/sub.cfm?source=forces/nvc/2009-oct-nvcag, accessed 12 April 2011.

[6]Veterans Affairs Canada, *New Veterans Charter Evaluation - Phase I*, Veterans Affairs Canada 2009b, http://www.veterans.gc.ca/eng/sub.cfm?source=department/reports/deptaudrep/2009-dec-nvc/1-0, accessed 12 April 2011.

[7]Veterans Affairs Canada, *New Veterans Charter Evaluation Phase II*, Government of Canada 2010b, http://www.veterans.gc.ca/eng/sub.cfm?source=department/reports/deptaudrep/2010-aug-nvcep-ph2, accessed 12 April 2011.

[8]A. Aiken, & A. Buitenhuis, *Supporting Canadian Veterans with Disabilities: A Comparison of Financial Benefits*, (Kingston: Claxton Papers, Defence Management Studies Program School of Policy Studies, Queen's University and Canadian Institute for Military and Veterans Health Research (2011).

[9]Canada Gazette, "Regulations Amending the Veterans Health Care Regulations," *Canada Gazette* 135, no. 25 (2001), part C, http://canadagazette.gc.ca/archives/p1/2001/2001-06-23/html/reg3-eng.html, accessed 12 April 2011.

[10]Veterans Affairs Canada, *Table of Disabilities*, Government of Canada 2006b, http://www.vac-acc.gc.ca/content/dispen/2006tod/pdf_files/tod_total_2006.pdf, accessed 19 November 2010.

[11]According to email correspondence between the authors and Robert MacDonald, Senior Communications Advisor for the Ontario Regional Office of VAC, 4 August 2010.

[12]According to email correspondence between the authors and Robert MacDonald, Senior Communications Advisor for the Ontario Regional Office of VAC, 4 August 2010.

[13]Canada Revenue Agency, *What are the income tax rates in Canada?*, Government of Canada 2010, http://www.cra-arc.gc.ca/tx/ndvdls/fq/txrts-eng.html, accessed 15 October 2010.

[14]New Veterans Charter Advisory Group, *Honouring Our Commitment to New Veterans and Their Families: The "Living" Charter in Action*, Veterans Affairs Canada 2009, 10.

[15]Statistics Canada, *Life expectancy at birth, by sex, by province*, Government of Canada 2010, http://www40.statcan.gc.ca/l01/cst01/health26-eng.htm, accessed 17 August 2010.

[16]Veterans Affairs Canada, *Speaking Notes for The Honourable Jean-Pierre Blackburn on Proposed Changes for Service to Canadian Veterans*, Government of Canada 2010c, http://www.vac-cc.gc.ca/general/sub.cfm?source=department/press/viewspeech&id=523, accessed 19 September 2010.

[17]Veterans Affairs Canada, *The New Veterans Charter: Services and Benefits* Government of Canada 2006a, http://vac-acc.gc.ca/content/Forces/nvc/infoKits/ServiceBenefits, 18 August 2010.

[18]Veterans Affairs Canada, *Backgrounder: New Veterans Charter Services and Benefits*, Government of Canada 2010a, http://www.veterans.gc.ca/eng/sub.cfm?source=department/press/nvc-media-kit/backgrounder, accessed 18 April 2011.

[19]According to email correspondence between the authors and Robert MacDonald, Senior Communications Advisor for the Ontario Regional Office of VAC, August 4, 2010.

[20]Veterans Affairs Canada, *Disability Pensions*, Government of Canada 2009a, http://www.vac-acc.gc.ca/clients/sub.cfm?source=dispen, accessed 12 April 2011.

[21]Veterans Affairs Canada, *The New Veterans Charter: Services and Benefits* Government of Canada 2006a, http://vac-acc.gc.ca/content/Forces/nvc/infoKits/ServiceBenefits, accessed 18 April 2011.

[22]According to email correspondence between the authors and Robert MacDonald, Senior Communications Advisor for the Ontario Regional Office of VAC, 4 August 2010.

[23]New Veterans Charter Advisory Group, *Honouring Our Commitment to New Veterans and Their Families: The "Living" Charter in Action*, Veterans Affairs Canada 2009, 32, http://www.veterans.gc.ca/eng/sub.cfm?source=forces/nvc/2009-oct-nvcag, accessed 12 April 2011.

[24]McColl, M. A. and Jongbloed, L. Disability and Social Policy in Canada (2nd ed.), (Concord, Ont: Captus University Publications, 2006), 254-256.

[25]A. Aiken, & A. Buitenhuis, *Supporting Canadian Veterans with Disabilities: A Comparison of Financial Benefits*, (Kingston: Claxton Papers, Defence Management Studies Program School of Policy Studies, Queen's University and Canadian Institute for Military and Veterans Health Research (2011).

CHAPTER 19

The Testimony of a War Amputee From Afghanistan: Discursive Myths and Realities[1]

Stéphanie A.H. Bélanger, PhD, Department of French Studies, Royal Military College of Canada

Abstract

Testimonies from CF members in combat arms (post cold war era) allow the exploration of new issues surrounding soldiers' identities (core soldiering values) and training in its full spectrum; from peacekeeping (Bosnia) to warfare (Afghanistan); from predeployment preparation to rehabilitation care. This proposal is based on a case study of an injured veteran from Afghanistan and aims at determining the extent of the organizational and individual forces, as CF personnel face the challenges of returning injured from combat in postmodern military warfare.

To Testify

Testimonies of war were first analyzed by Jean Norton Cru, who wrote the founding book on the study of testimonies as a genre, based on the experience of soldiers who survived the First World War.[2] He explains that the goal of testimonies is to offer "a true image of war from the ones who have closely seen it; to make known the emotions of the soldiers, which are not acquired by imitation or influence, but instead a direct reaction to the contact of war."[3] The value of the testimony would be dependent on the view from the veteran of the First World War, on the capacity of the testifier to say all that it was. If it is true that testimony as a genre can be distinguished from a novel, for example, with regards to its relationship with reality, then only the Poilu[4] would have this capacity. It is also true, nevertheless, that the testimony is far from being true enough to be acceptable to the eyes of the historian: similarly its aesthetical qualities, including the recourse to the metaphor that will be analyzed here, precludes it from being considered as a non-fiction discourse to the eyes of the literary specialist. Current research stipulates that the testimony constitutes, unbeknownst to the testifier, a reconstruction of reality.[5] With all the discursive work that is involved in the transposition from the lived experience to a total memory, the testimony would not be the narration of "what is", as argued by Cru, but the evocation of what matters.[6] I postulate that, far from being naïve in his approach, the testifier sometimes voluntarily, more often involuntarily, reconstructs reality; an intention that is even mentioned or at least traceable in his discourse: it seems that the testifier tries to construct a narration that offers the audience an ethic, a way of behaving and seeing the world. Like the testifier at court who tells of what he saw in order to convince the jury to make a judgment on a specific event, the testifier of war tells what he saw in order to convince the audience to make a precise judgment on one or the other dimensions of warfare. It will contribute to a better understanding of the link between what is lived and what is told, without judgment of what is true and what is exaggerated. An analysis of the work of memory that is put to the test, an analysis of the body sacrificed on the altar of ideologies, and an analysis of the challenges undertaken by the sacrificed body will contribute, I hope, to shining a pale light onto the discursive darkness that haunts the testimonies of the war injured.

MEMORY PUT TO TEST

The problem is not one of truth, even less one of a perception of truth. The goal is not to review the facts that are said, or come to a verdict[7] on the memory of the testifier, but rather to analyze the meaning of their testimonies, their internal consistency, and also their consistency within a discursive network. If the testifier tells his experience to offer a specific meaning to the experienced events, the warrior is also speaking to a specific public; to other warriors who are still there on the battlefield with all the uncertainty surrounding their return home;[8] to give a voice to the efforts, to the sacrifice of health, body, and life, of his brothers and sisters in arms. In the precise context of interest here, the testimony under study is that of Master Corporal (Retired) Paul Franklin[9], an amputee of the war in Afghanistan, which was presented by the media as an institutional discourse, as the ultimate symbol of the sacrifices made by Canada in the war efforts linked to the so-called "war against terror". War amputees in general, including MCpl (Ret'd) Franklin, are considered here as the pars pro toto (the few for the many), the figurehead of what they would wish to be the values of their country:[10] "This is what Canada's about."[11] MCpl (Ret'd) Franklin stated this quote while talking about the Provincial Reconstruction Team, founded by the United States in 2001, one of which Canada has been in charge of in Kandahar since 2005. It is in this ambiguity that one can situate the discourse of this veteran who returned home from war amputated.

Because the war amputee's image is ambiguous, he represents a wounded country that provided unnecessary sacrifices for a cause that doesn't belong to it, but he also represents a country that is courageous and ready to sacrifice its youth to promote peace in the world.[12] If this veteran is of particular interest, it is because he endorses himself into this role of becoming a Canadian icon: the idea of a country that is making many efforts for the reconstruction of peaceful nations around the world. In the same manner as the institutional media discourse, he sees himself as the symbol of the Canadian peacekeeper, and he presents himself as such in every public appearance he makes. His experience has been told in many television interviews and many newspapers, as well as in a book written by journalist Liane Faulder as a biography entitled *The Long Walk Home*: Paul Franklin's Journey from Afghanistan, published in 2007 by Brindle Glas, a Canadian editor specializing in non-fiction books. MCpl (Ret'd) Franklin has promoted this book in the many presentations he has made since the explosion of his vehicle (a G-wagon green all-terrain vehicle, 4 wheel drive, from Mercedes) has caused him to lose his two legs in Afghanistan. MCpl (Ret'd) Franklin is one of the first casualties from the war in Afghanistan since the scandal of friendly fires in 2002. Since then, nearly 100 military personnel, out of the 152 (and counting) who lost their lives in combat, were victims of these explosives, including Sgt Martin Goudreault, who died 6 June, 2010 during the drafting of the first words that were to become this chapter.

If, on the one hand, this hyper contemporary subject allows an understanding of the discourse at the moment that its aesthetical and narrative parameters are being formed, then on the other hand, to undertake the study of the war veterans who are still active on the public scene is an enterprise that can be perilous. We recall the magician Erichtho who excelled in the morbid art of the reanimation of the soul of soldiers still lying on the battlefield so that they would unveil the outcome of the civil war in which Caesar and Pompeius confronted one another.[13] They were conjured forth just at the moment when they were to cross the inferno river that would allow them to rest eternally after paying tribute to life by dying courageously with sword in hand. These dead soldiers were taken away from their just death by threats and incantations recited by the Thessalian Witch, and were then obliged to reanimate their pale corpse, bruised and putrid, in order to unveil their knowledge about the future, of which only the dead have the secret. To testify corresponds to the same insistence forced upon these dead, or more precisely upon the past events that are at every testimony revived from silence, from forgetfulness. To tell of an experience, to testify this experience, is an occasion to re-live the experience, like the dead soldier who saw hell and returned from it staggering and trembling, in order to unveil the secrets from the dead. The soldier who comes back injured from war tells, in his broken and trembling body, a knowledge that is unique because he has the privilege of being a survivor of the greatest secret of war – the ultimate encounter with death, from which he barely escaped.

In that sense to undertake the analysis of testimony is comparable to making the autopsy of a memory that was outrageously pulled away from silence. If MCpl (Ret'd) Franklin voluntarily performs this courageous exercise, as per suggested by the number of public appearances he has done,[14] he is nevertheless a human being before a subject of study. His experience is as real to his eyes as it is a reconstruction to the eyes of the researcher who analyzes his discourse. For instance, when he uses the analogy of the mountain to explain his rehabilitation, he undertakes this comparison in the true sense of the term: to heal for him is not a challenge that is as grand as climbing the mountain, but to heal for him is to actually climb that mountain. In one way, it is only the day that he will have been able to climb that mountain that he will be able to feel as though he has become the person he was before he was seriously injured by the IED. It is this tension between the experience told in a narration and the analysis of the many interpretations of the narration that the present study examines.

If the authors from antiquity were using witchcraft to reanimate their soldiers after a deadly battle, then modern science is not totally detached from this sorcery as it is still using the expression 'phantom limb' to talk about the impression that a mutilated member is still there. This illusionary impression is well incurred in the spirit of the amputees because it continues to give them painful sensations. The phantom limb is a reconstruction of the body before the accident, but it is also a painful reminder of the missing limb. This phenomenon is widely spread among amputated people, and MCpl (Ret'd) Franklin is not an exception.[15] The brain gives life, shape, and sensation to a limb that was nevertheless shattered by an IED. The brain gives the impression, a painful impression, that the body is whole again. Similarly, the brain creates a "memory" of events that will allow the injured to create coherence in their recollection of the chaotic sequence of events surrounding the circumstances that caused the amputation. A few days after his incident, MCpl (Ret'd) Franklin tells how it was he, himself, who saved his life through the use of his own medical instruments, more precisely, a tourniquet that was used to stop the haemorrhaging. This action that he remembered in all its details was not to make a hero out of himself, but rather to portray a soldier who did what he was trained to do; defending one's country cannot be done without first defending oneself, explained Faulder. The medic was portrayed as a hero by the reporters who were spreading out this heroic story, although for the medic, he was simply doing his job: he used his medical skills when it mattered to save his own life. The problem is that the tourniquet was in reality many meters away from MCpl (Ret'd) Franklin, in the boot of the leg that was pulverized, which means that it was actually a brother in arms, also a medic, trained by MCpl (Ret'd) Franklin, who used another tourniquet to save his life. To learn the true sequence of events was like a cold shower for MCpl (Ret'd) Franklin, for two reasons: he realized his memory failed him due to a mTBI, and he also had the impression that he failed at his job as a medic to save his own life: "I didn't do the job", noted the soldier.[16] He then reinterpreted the events to his own advantage; after all he did his job well because he's the one who trained his brother in arms how to react in a crisis situation. This anecdote is very important to MCpl (Ret'd) Franklin and he revisits it often during his interviews, always insisting on the necessity of doing his job well until the end.[17] This episode demonstrates the importance for a military member to do his job properly. He considers himself as a "soldier" and must put the "soldier first" mentality ahead of everything he does; he must behave as a soldier in all circumstances. A homemade bomb made him lose his legs, but it did not make him lose his dignity as a soldier. Analyzed from this angle, the lived experience is transformed into a narration that lends a new coherence, a story that is more acceptable to the eyes of the soldier. This episode also illustrates the ambiguity of the recollection of events even though the recollection was done by the actors. The memory transformed the lived events into a coherent whole. In the same way that his body cannot accept being disintegrated, his spirit cannot accept that his identity has broken. The brain rebuilds the memory of events in a way that offers an acceptable representation of the identity. What is acceptable in the eyes of the MCpl is to have done everything possible to have saved his life, to have behaved as a good soldier. In the way he tells the event, his memory constructed an event that never occurred; the attempt to save his own life, and then transferred this fictive narration into another character: this brother in arms who saved him. It is as if he did it himself since this other medic did exactly what he would have done. There is a transfer from a tale where the subject is himself, into another tale constructed under identical parameters but where the subject is another person.

This discourse was then submitted to a third transformation. Indeed, in a more recent interview with CBC, he said that he saved his own life by using respiratory techniques during shock, a technique that he learned during his training to be a medic.[18] He doesn't talk anymore about the pulverized limb or of the tourniquet in the distanced boot, but he is now talking about his own lungs, that were never affected by the incident. The story is now complete: the MCpl, the medic saved his own life, and he eliminated from his discourse everything that reminds him of the breakdown of his body. The enemy did not destroy his first quality of being a good soldier, being able to save his own life. The transposition of the experience into a coherent narration implies the act of creating, and this creation has an aesthetical dimension that is intimately linked with the ethic of the soldier's honour.

THE SACRIFICED BODY ON THE ALTAR OF IDEALS

For most soldiers, the ethics of their honour, their fundamental values, are shaken when compared to that of their enemies. They come to a point where the only wish they have is to protect their brothers and sisters in arms[19]: "Paul wanted Canadians to know what soldiers were made of. He also wanted his country to support the mission as the pressure grew on his command in Afghanistan."[20] The more people who become injured, the more soldiers who become casualties, leads to more ways to overcome the fact that their numbers are increasing; for MCpl (Ret'd) Franklin to show his injuries, to talk about his sufferings, to show the world his mutilated body, becomes an act of bravery; a way to participate in this war and to make his own contribution to the mission. It is a way to win this war against the enemy by showing the world the moral superiority Canada has over her enemy: "To show the world how Canadian families are strong."[21]

In December 2009, another Jeep all-terrain vehicle had a similar fate as that of MCpl (Ret'd) Franklin. Newspapers were producing numerous articles, and on their electronic versions, the readers would express their opinions: strongly affirming that it was time for Canada to pull out its troops; that Canada had enough victims. When the contrast between the public opinion and the opinion of the military members who went to war became obvious, most of the military members would say the same thing as MCpl (Ret'd) Franklin: that they chose to enrol because they believe in the superiority of Canada's values, and they would insist on the fact that when they are fighting shoulder to shoulder, they need to know that the Canadian public is behind them:

> As for their moral ground, you tell me, sarcastically, that we are rational and valid, and all that jazz, well let's have a little lesson in their morals. On a foot

patrol, when we were attacked by what we thought was a suicide bomber, well apparently it was, only he was 12 or 13 yrs old, and you wanna know who pushed the button? His own father, from about 200-300 yards away, so don't sit there on your couch and judge anyone of us who CHOOSE to go and fight for the guys next to us, because that's all we're doing, we don't care why we are there, and what the plan is in the long run, we only care about the men and women next to us, who know that at any given moment in the time of need, ALL of us will be there...[22]

This discourse questions the values and the first motivations to fight; the impact of having to use weapons in a country where everything is dangerous, there is no authority of law, there is no control over the population; where the shared values, at least the ones of the insurgents, are incompatible with the ones of the occupying forces. Following MCpl (Ret'd) Franklin's example, the soldiers are choosing to fight with the hopes that they can bring their own values (political, economic, etc.) to a failing state.[23] Testimonies on war seem to polarize opposite opinions. For the 'civilian', war is unacceptable, the armed forces should not exist, and casualties are unnecessary. For the warriors, to fight and to believe in the importance of fighting is the sole way to win against an enemy who has different values and war tactics, which are morally unacceptable to them. Therefore, these two discursive positions do not have the same presupposition, one aiming for peace, and the other for dignity, and MCpl (Ret'd) Franklin is not an exception.

The discourse surrounding war experience seems to be less a means to tell what happened than to share a point of view, an ideal; in that sense, it is a reconstruction of that experience: a way to give order to chaos, to make sense, ideologically speaking. For instance, the MCpl would refer to himself as a medic accompanying a Provincial Reconstruction Team (PRT), and will often insist on the importance of things like training the local police forces to solidify the local infrastructures. These PRTs play a significant role in the ideological discourse surrounding war. PRTs replaced the blue helmets in UN Peacekeeping, and offer a dignified meaning to warfare in Afghanistan: "Today, these new capabilities [Provincial Reconstruction Teams and Strategic Advisory Teams] are helping to strengthen Afghan capacity to deliver quality governance, both centrally and locally,"[24] said a Lieutenant-Colonel who published in the Canadian Military Journal. Such teams are what most Canadian warriors refer to when discussing their role in this mission; MCpl (Ret'd) Franklin is an example of this. For instance, he agrees to say that he spent most of his time driving diplomats and flag officers, and providing the high level of security necessary when going outside the wire,[25] but nevertheless will insist on the importance of rebuilding Afghanistan after decades of war. There is a discrepancy between what they believe they are doing and the reality of the war theatre. The mandate of this medic is more frequently to drive around, in either armoured or highly protected vehicles, flag officers, diplomats and other civilians, who are going from one place to another in order to bring humanitarian aid.

It was while driving a Canadian diplomat with an army contingent that his vehicle was hit by an IED:

> I think the suicide bomber took away my innocence, he took away the thought that someone would try to kill me and I represented something that is so abhorrent to someone else that they would destroy their own lives to kill me and that is a very confusing concept that someone would look at me and see such a horror that they would be willing to destroy their own life to destroy mine. Shocking.[26]

It is a shock for the medic, and he is always trying to justify these contradictory and traumatizing events ('shocking') by insisting on the importance of the mission. His physical condition gives him a unique presence: it is because he participated in this mission, at the sacrifice of his legs; it is because he met death face to face, that his story is now the epitome of truth. It is because he is injured that his discourse gains credibility, in the same way as the soldiers returning from the dead through Erichtho's sorcery.[27] Many injured soldiers almost consciously play that role of bearing truth. For instance, Captain Simon Mailloux, during a talk show interview, was explaining that the purpose of his public appearance was not to showcase his agility with his prosthesis: "I did not come here to show how good I am at going down the stairs, but to say a message."[28] For Mailloux, for MCpl (Ret'd) Franklin, for many injured soldiers and veterans, their injury does not make them question the validity of the mission, but rather it reinforces their belief in the importance of the mission:

> Paul's motivation increased as the number of dead and wounded soldiers rose in the early months of 2006. Polls suggested Canadians were growing more concerned about the military role in Afghanistan. [...] More than ever, Paul wanted Canadians to know what soldiers were made of. He also wanted his country to support the mission as the pressure grew on his comrades in Afghanistan.[29]

The difference between the Canadian public's point of view and that of the military cannot be more obvious. To be sacrificed gives a moral superiority that transforms the testimony into a discourse of truth in the public's eyes – similar to how Christ showed his stigmata to Thomas as a proof of his resurrection; the warrior can talk about and show his injuries as a proof that the mission persists and that he still supports it. More than just rhetoric, it is a tradition for people who live in the extremes, for instance, there is a long tradition of Christian martyrs who will testify of their faith by the scars that are left on their bodies.[30]

Similarly, most CF members deployed in Afghanistan are not fighting solely to eliminate the enemy, but also for an ideal, the ideal of peace. Serving members who come back from war without any medical diagnosis, and serving or retired members diagnosed with single or multiple injuries, mental or physical, all say the same thing: if Canada wants to send them back in the field, they would go back in a heartbeat, because the work is not finished yet. The work? One may ask… To this question, the answer is automatically the same: they still kill each other over there, the situation is not stabilized, the presence of the CF is still required: "For one, we never got to finish the job, and that's a big thing in the military, to finish what you started."[31] The same way the Christian martyrs would proudly display the marks on their bodies as a proof of the inner strength they possess to ward off evil for the advent of peace: "Paul truly believed in the Canadian mission. He thought his efforts would help lead the Afghan people toward a peaceful future."[32]

The way CF members perceive the enemy is in line with that same way of thinking: they endure the pain, they endure the "shock" of being shot at even though they are there to help, by trying to understand the mindset of the enemy as they do this: "he could see the world from the bomber's perspective,"[33] insists the author of *The long walk home*, as she was explaining how MCpl (Ret'd) Franklin, after going through a journey comparable to a descent to hell, was still not angry at the ones who injured him, displaying, there again, a Christian figure: "Father, forgive them, for they do not know what they are doing."[34] Similarly, war veterans diagnosed with physical and psychological injuries will typically answer, when asked about how they think the Canadian population perceives them, that "civilians" (because in the military jargon, the world is split up in two parts, the military and the civilians) do not support them because they are ignorant of the political situation. "It is not their fault, they [have] never been there, they cannot imagine what it is unless they went there", referring to the combat zone.[35] The wounded soldier displays a wounded body that allows him to talk in the name of a greater good: the same way Christians would suffer in order to participate in the upcoming of a peaceful world, the injured war veterans are suffering for their country because they too believe in the importance of participating in the upcoming of a peaceful world. In that same sense, Simon Mailloux, who lost a leg in his first tour in Afghanistan, did all the training he could to achieve the universality of service standard and be deployed again in 2010 with his prosthetic leg: "By coming back here, I think I have defeated the IED that blew me up."[36] For him, what is to be defeated is the IED, the bombs aimed at the soldiers who were sent there to bring peace. For him, the fact that he can go back there as a Canadian soldier is proof that there is still a will to stabilize the situation; his mission was not in vain, his sacrifice was worth it. Was it?

THE CHALLENGES OF THE SACRIFICED BODY

Serving members who offer the ultimate sacrifice or who come back wounded from combat are given, these days, the tribute of heroism. Since 2008, the Governor General has recognized, with the Sacrifice Medal, any member of the CF, or of allied forces, or civilians working for the CF, who was killed or wounded in honourable circumstances in combat, retroactive to October 2001. Himself a recipient of the Sacrifice Medal, MCpl (Ret'd) Franklin was invited twice to dine at the table of the Governor General at Rideau Hall. He was also invited to dine in a dignitary event beside Gen Hillier, whom he had met after his return from Afghanistan after his accident. According to the Northern Alberta Amputee Program, he is among the 10 most inspiring Canadians of the country. Canada is pulling numerous efforts in 'return from war' programs and does not hesitate to transform its wounded military members into heroes. This escalation, or is it just an attitude that is typical to soldiers, makes them competitive for the tribune of heroism even among themselves: "we tend to compare", says MCpl (Ret'd) Franklin to the Legion Magazine.[37]

These struggles for recognition, where one deserves the palms of glory more than the other, are not always positive and can even become noticeable when it comes to grievances.[38] "I did not lose two legs to shred paper,"[39] explains MCpl (Ret'd) Franklin when talking about the rehabilitation program he was put into as he was struggling to return to work in uniform. Wearing the uniform is also wearing the proof of the confidence their country put into them while sending them to war. Most soldiers take pride in their war exploits; the same way they always insist on the importance of putting the soldier first, they also like to insist on the importance of their reliability while doing so. The first chapter of *The Long Walk Home* starts with "The Attack", but even before it actually talks of the accident, it describes the vehicle in which the accident happened: "the G-Wagon was most fun to drive when he was off-road, bumping along riverbeds … Where else can you drive a two hundred thousand dollar vehicle like you stole it?"[40] How can one ask a MCpl, to whom they gave the responsibility of such a valuable vehicle, to suddenly only be shredding paper? This lesson was taught thirty years ago by Rambo at the end of the movie First Blood:[41] "Over there I was in charge of many million dollar tanks, back here I can't even hold a job", wails the Vietnam War American veteran just before he surrenders to the authorities. And this lesson, that became a topos in war literature, was also taught by Jean Vaillancourt in his war novel *Les Canadiens errants*.[42] After the war, while walking along Ste-Catherine Street in downtown Montreal, instead of being received as a hero, his main character, a Second World War Canadian veteran, causes people to fear him and walk away from him because he is poor, he is dressed in a fashion from before the war, and he is wounded, which makes him walk in a crippled, or simply different, manner: "Civilians were walking away from him and bypass him […], by consideration, undoubtedly, for his cane that did not look elegant, for these decorations that were evoking less the honour of glory than the sweating and the blood."[43] If, at the dawn of the 21st Century, the Canadian government is now giving official dignity to soldiers with the recent Sacrifice Medal, the Canadian population is still ambivalent in the way they interpret and receive these marks of honor. The whole book from Liane Faulder on MCpl (Ret'd) Franklin seems to be written to rehabilitate the soldier, who is erected as a hero, or at least as a model of inspiration to the Canadian population.[44] Most public appearances made by the soldier himself seem to go in that same direction, to fight for recognition. As long as

MCpl (Ret'd) Franklin was a MCpl, this standpoint was obvious. But when the soldier became a "civilian", when the MCpl became Paul Franklin, the struggle for recognition took a different stand. In the Proceedings of the Subcommittee on Veterans Affairs, that was held in Ottawa,[45] and where among the main players were Senator Romeo Dallaire, as well as personnel from VAC, from DND, and MCpl (Ret'd) Franklin, it is possible to read for the first time another constituent of Paul Franklin's journey. As important as it was for him to heal so he could show to all Canadians "what Canadian soldiers are made of"; his will to heal was also explained by a less ideal, more practical consideration, that is, to gain as many advantages as he could while he was still in the Forces:

> If I may, I stayed for three years as a wounded soldier to ensure that all the parts and pieces of my future life would be intact. I knew that DND would cover me. They would buy the wheelchairs and the prosthetics and modify the house. I knew that DND would always be there for me. Many soldiers tend to say that they are doing great because they are still at work. In reality, they do not want a 25 per cent pay cut, and they want to ensure that they get all their stuff and have an employer that completely understands their state of mind and their well-being.[46]

But when his contract ended in 2009, MCpl (Ret'd) Franklin had to fill out paperwork with the VAC and fight for every compensation gained; struggles that brought him to Parliament to fight against the latest reform of the Disability Award, a "one-time, tax-free cash award designed to compensate for the non-economic impacts of a service-related disability such as pain and suffering."[47] Even though this Award was recently amended with a $2M injection into the program by the Federal Government,[48] many still see major problems related to its accessibility.

For instance, Corporal (Ret'd) Pascal Lacoste, who participated in the Special Forces, in the war in the Balkans and in East Timor, explains how the administrative steps are so extensive that they discourage any potential recipient who is too physically and psychologically wounded to be able to sort himself out: "Is it these values that I defended, me? Is it for these values that I am dying? [...] Their paperwork is given to you to discourage you from being able to complete it. They hope to save money this way,"[49] explains the bitter retired corporal. Nevertheless, the last sentence of his interview is "If it was to be done again, I would do it again."[50] Every single veteran who is interviewed, regardless of the extent of their injuries, regardless if these are physical or mental, will say the same thing: "I would go back there in a heartbeat". Yes, they try to stay in as long as they can in order to receive some benefits, but they also stay in because this is where they feel they belong. Their sacrifice to the nation is total, and they do not accept that there is not a reciprocal understanding that they should receive total benefit and social recognition from their efforts and sacrifice. Instead, they need to fight to prove their injury is combat related, or, even harder, they need to argue to prove they do have an injury. The amount of paperwork to fill out and the bureaucracy to go through make this journey as hard as climbing a mountain.

CONCLUSION: THE BROKEN BODY, THE ABRUPT MOUNTAIN

More than a tool of construction of identity,[51] it seems that testimonies are now tools of reconstruction of a broken identity: "Paul's goal is to return to being the man he was on January 12, 2006, the day he hiked up the mountain in Afghanistan."[52] A medically released war veteran interviewed in November 2010 said "Give us a chance to prove we can be the soldier we were."[53] The voices of these soldiers resonate like the pale echo of the warrior's litany: "I will always place the mission first. I will never accept defeat. I will never quit. I will never leave a fallen comrade."[54] They are a reminder of the legendary figure of the ancient Hellenised world, Orpheus, when he descended into death. The life of his fiancée Eurydice was taken away too soon. The Gods pitied the sorrow that Orpheus expressed by beautifully playing his lyre. Seduced by the shepherd's talent, they promised him he could meet the beautiful Eurydice again under one condition: while walking in the Underworld, he could not look at her, as no living being can look death in the face. He used his lyre to enchant the gods of the Underworld and was able to cross the Acheron twice, the dreadful river that was a passage of no return to everyone. Eurydice was following him on his way back, but he could not see her, not even feel her presence or her breath. In the moments before he was to leave Hades, he turned back to hold his loved one, but a fraction of a second too early. She vanished. He never played the instrument again and died shortly after. The voice of the testifiers reminds us of the sound of Orpheus' lyre. As long as they are talking, explaining, expressing their sorrow, they feel alive and claim back the better half of themselves that stayed in Hades, the war theater. The variations of their stories are numerous and the logical arguments behind their discourse is frail, but the words are constantly expressing their desire to come back to who they were before, to the holiness that defined their soldier identity before their mental or physical injury. As long as they talk and as long as they are listened too, their discourse is constructing the image they believe represent them the best as warriors.

[1] This paper would not have been possible without the help of Ms Michelle Moore, my research assistant.

[2] Jean Norton Cru, *Du Témoignage* (Paris: Allia, 2008[1930]), 195 p.

[3] Original French text: "une image de la guerre d'après ceux qui l'ont vue de plus près; de faire connaître les sentiments du soldat, qui ne sont pas des sentiments acquis par imitation ou par influence, mais qui sont sa réaction directe au contact de la guerre."; Jean Norton Cru, *Du Témoignage* (Paris: Allia, 2008[1930]), 25.

[4] "Poilu" is the expression used to relate to men who experienced the trenches, meaning they had beard and long hair.

[5] Frédéric Rousseau, *Le procès des Témoins de la Grande Guerre* (Paris: Seuil, 2003), 288 p.

[6] Jean Norton Cru, *Du Témoignage* (Paris: Allia, 2008[1930]), 160 p.

[7] Frédéric Rousseau, *Le procès des Témoins de la Grande Guerre* (Paris: Seuil, 2003), 288 p.

[8] Régine Waintrater, *Sortir du Génocide* (Paris: Payot & Rivages, 2003), 27 p.

[9] Herein referred to as MCpl (Ret'd) Franklin.

[10] S. Chivers, "Disabled Veterans in the Americas: Canadians « Soldier On » after Afghanistan – Operation

Enduring Freedom and the Canadian Mission," *Canadian Review of American Studies* 39, 3 (2009): 321-342.

[11]Liane Faulder, *The Long Walk Home. Paul Franklin's Journey From Afghanistan. A Soldier's Story* (Winnipeg: Windle and Glass, 2007), 47.

[12]This bi-polar opinion was expressed in mass media at every public appearance of military personnel returning home injured. See, for example, the reactions to the interviews made with MCpl (Ret'd) Franklin: MCpl Paul Franklin, "Leaving military to further cause," interviewed by *The Canadian Press* and posted on the *Army.ca Forums*, 24 September 2009, http://forums.army.ca/forums/index.php?topic=89358.0, accessed 17 May 2011; MCpl. Paul Franklin, interviewed by Mark Kelly, *Connect with Mark Kelly,* CBCNews, 11 November 2009, http://www.cbc.ca/connect/2009/11/interview-master-cpl-paul-franklin.html, accessed 17 May 2011; see, also, the public reactions of the interviews made with Captain (then Lieutenant) Simon Mailloux while returning from Afghanistan, where he lost one foot: Simon Mailloux, interviewed by Guy A. Lepage at the television weekly show *Tout le monde en parle*, 2 March 2008, posted on the Dailymotion website, http://www.dailymotion.com/video/x4x1e7_tlmep-lieutenant-simon-mailloux-ret_news, accessed 17 May 2011; see public opinion from people who commented the interview that was recorded at *Tout le monde en parle* on 2 March 2008 on the *Army.ca* Forums, http://forums.army.ca/forums/index.php?topic=71543.0, accessed 17 May 2011; See also a comment from a blogger "L'avocat du diable", on Michel Fugain's appearance at the interview recorded at *Tout Le Monde en Parle*, titled Objection Votre Honneur, 3 mars 2008, http://objection_votre_honneur.monblogue.branchez-vous.com/2008/3/3/, accessed 17 May 2011.

[13]Lucain, "La Guerre civile," *La Pharsale*, ed. and trans. by A. Bourgery, 1993, 2nd Edition ed. Paul Jal. (Paris : Belles Lettres, 1997), 2T, 16 9 p, 213 p.

[14]He appeared publically almost immediately after was transferred in a hospital in Germany, right after his injury. His picture is on the promotion poster of the 2010 International Day for Persons with Disabilities.

[15]Liane Faulder, *The Long Walk Home. Paul Franklin's Journey From Afghanistan. A Soldier's Story* (Winnipeg: Windle and Glass, 2007), 224 p.; see also testimonies presented by war amputees at the Subcommittee on Veterans Affairs of the Standing Senate Committee on National Security and Defence, heard 12 May 2010, http://www.parl.gc.ca/40/3/parlbus/commbus/senate/com-f/vete-f/48187-f.htm?Language=F&Parl=40&Ses=3&comm_id=79, accessed 16 May 2011.

[16]Liane Faulder, *The Long Walk Home. Paul Franklin's Journey From Afghanistan. A Soldier's Story* (Winnipeg: Windle and Glass, 2007), 74.

[17]N. Salat, "The Quiet Fight: Master Corporal Paul Franklin," *Legion Magazine*, November 6, 2007, http://www.legionmagazine.com, accessed 17 May 2011; Liane Faulder, *The Long Walk Home. Paul Franklin's Journey From Afghanistan. A Soldier's Story* (Winnipeg: Windle and Glass, 2007), 224 p.; Paul Franklin, "Canada's engagement in Afghanistan," Video, Canadian Forces Medic and CEO, *Northern Alberta Amputee Program*, 3 December 2007, http://www.afghanistan.gc.ca/canada-afghanistan/multimedia/franklin.aspx, accessed 17 May 2011.

[18]Paul Franklin, [Co-Founder] "Board Profiles Paul Franklin," *Northern Alberta Amputee Program*, 2009, http://www.naap.med.ualberta.ca/board_paul_fr.html, accessed 9 June 2010.

[19]Leonard Wong, *Why they fight: Combat Motivation in the Iraq War* (Strategic Studies Institute, 2003), 2; Samuel Lyman Atwood Marshall, *Men Against Fire: The Problem of Battle Command* (University of Oklahoma Press, 2000), 161; Lieutenant-Colonel K.J. Hamilton, "Unit Cohesion," *Canadian Army Journal* 12, 3 (Winter 2010): 18.

[20]Liane Faulder, *The Long Walk Home. Paul Franklin's Journey From Afghanistan. A Soldier's Story* (Winnipeg: Windle and Glass, 2007), 139.

[21]Liane Faulder, *The Long Walk Home. Paul Franklin's Journey From Afghanistan. A Soldier's Story* (Winnipeg: Windle and Glass, 2007), 97.

[22]the_madness, Re: "CBC News Article: 5 Canadians Killed in Afghanistan: Roadside Bomb Hits Armoured Vehicle," web log message, 30 December 2009, http://www.cbc.ca/news/world/story/2009/12/30/kandahar-soldiers.html, accessed 17 May 2011.

[23]Rubin, B.R., "Peace Building and State-Building in Afghanistan: Constructing Sovereignty for whose Security?" *Third World Quarterly* 17, 1 (2006): 175-185.

[24]Lieutenant-Colonel M.-H. St-Louis, "The Strategic Advisory Team in Afghanistan – Part of the Canadian Comprehensive Approach to Stability Operations," Canadian Military Journal 9, 3 (2009), available on line at http://www.journal.forces.gc.ca/vo9/no3/09-stlouis-eng.asp, accessed 17 May 2011.

[25]Liane Faulder, *The Long Walk Home. Paul Franklin's Journey From Afghanistan. A Soldier's Story* (Winnipeg: Windle and Glass, 2007), 224 p.

[26]Liane Faulder, *The Long Walk Home. Paul Franklin's Journey From Afghanistan. A Soldier's Story* (Winnipeg: Windle and Glass, 2007), 72.

[27]Lucain. La Guerre civile. « La Pharsale ». 2 T. Ed and trad by A. Bourgery, 2ne ed reviewed by Paul Jal. Paris : Belles Lettres, 1993, 1997, 339 p, 434 p.

[28]Original French text: "Je ne suis pas venu ici pour descendre les marches et faire un show, mais pour passer un message": Simon Mailloux, interviewed by Guy A. Lepage at the tv show *Tout le monde en parle*, 2 March 2008, posted on the *Dailymotion* website, http://www.dailymotion.com/video/x4x1e7_tlmep-lieutenant-simon-mailloux-ret_news, accessed 17 May 2011.

[29]Liane Faulder, *The Long Walk Home. Paul Franklin's Journey From Afghanistan. A Soldier's Story* (Winnipeg: Windle and Glass, 2007), 139.

[30]Stéphanie Bélanger, *Guerres, sacrifices et persécutions : Une relecture de Garnier, Hardy, Corneille et Rotrou à la lumière des théories thomistes de la guerre juste*, Commentaires philosophiques (Paris: l'Harmattan, 2010), 142 and passim.

[31]Liane Faulder, *The Long Walk Home. Paul Franklin's Journey From Afghanistan. A Soldier's Story* (Winnipeg: Windle and Glass, 2007), 170; This point of view is so widespread that it has recently been used by the Prime Minister as a justification to prolong the stay of CF in Afghanistan until 2014, instead of 2012 as previously stated: I do not want to risk our gains by withdrawing too early" (Translated from French), "Harper decide de prolonger la mission en Afghanistan", Hugo de Grandpré, "Harper decide de prolonger la mission en Afghanistan", *La Presse* (Quebec, Canada), November 10, 2010, http://www.cyberpresse.ca/actualites/quebec-canada/politique-canadienne/201011/10/01-4341465-harper-decide-de-prolonger-la-mission-en-afghanistan.php accessed 17 May 2011. Interestingly enough, the journalist also quotes a Korean War veteran, who says the exact same thing about his presence in Korea: "Le pays a grandi et il s'est développé, on se dit: on n'est pas venu se battre pour rien" ("the country has grown and developed, se we tell ourselves, we did not come to fight for nothing").

[32]Liane Faulder, *The Long Walk Home. Paul Franklin's Journey From Afghanistan. A Soldier's Story* (Winnipeg: Windle and Glass, 2007), 47.

[33]Liane Faulder, The Long Walk Home. Paul Franklin's Journey From Afghanistan. A Soldier's Story (Winnipeg: Windle and Glass, 2007), 101.

[34](Luke 23:34); Georges St-Pierre, a Canadian professional mixed martial artist known as "a warrior of another type", also likes to display some feelings of compassion for his enemy just before entering the cage, as per the interview from Frédérick Garcia, "Georges St-Pierre à Tout le monde en parle" *MMA Nouvelles*, 12 Novembre 2010, http://mmanouvelles.com/2010/11/12/georges-st-pierre-a-tout-le-monde-en-parle/, accessed 17 May 2011.

[35]Stéphanie A.H. Bélanger, *Personal Interviews #KINOCT 10-02*, in the context of a sponsored research project on "Warrior culture and Soldier identity," conducted in Kingston, October 2010.

[36]Capt Simon Mailloux as cited in C. Perkel, "Canadian soldier first amputee at Afghan mission," *The Star*, 11 Jan 2010, retrieved from http://www.thestar.com/, accessed 17 May 2011.

[37]Natalie Salat, "The Quiet Fight: Master Corporal Paul Franklin," *Legion Magazine*, November 6, 2007, http://www.legionmagazine.com/en/index/php/2007/11/the-quiet-fight, accessed on June 2, 2010.

[38]Alex Honneth, Struggle for recognition, (Great Britain: Polity Press, 1995), 127-128.

[39]Natalie Salat, "The Quiet Fight: Master Corporal Paul Franklin," *Legion Magazine*, November 6, 2007, http://www.legionmagazine.com/en/index/php/2007/11/the-quiet-fight, accessed 17 May 2011.

[40]Liane Faulder, *The Long Walk Home. Paul Franklin's Journey From Afghanistan. A Soldier's Story* (Winnipeg: Windle and Glass, 2007), 11.

[41]*First Blood*, movie, Ted Kotcheff, Dir, 1982, 93 mins.

[42]Jean Vaillancourt, *Les Canadiens Errants* (Montréal: Cercle du libre de France, 1954), 250 p.

[43]Jean Vaillancourt, *Les Canadiens Errants* (Montréal: Cercle du libre de France, 1954), 228; Original French text: "Les civils s'écartaient et le contournaient comme un drôle d'îlot sur ce drôle de fleuve, par égard sans doute pour cette canne qui ne ressemblait pas à un jou jou d'élégance, ces décorations qui disaient moins l'honneur et la gloire que la sueur et le sang."

[44]Liane Faulder, *The Long Walk Home. Paul Franklin's Journey From Afghanistan. A Soldier's Story* (Winnipeg: Windle and Glass, 2007), 11.

[45]The proceedings can be found at http://www.parl.gc.ca/40/3/parlbus/commbus/senate/com-e/vete-e/03mn-e.htm?Language=E&Parl=40&Ses=3&comm_id=79, accessed 17 May 2011.

[46]Subcommittee on Veterans Affairs of the Standing Senate Committee on National Security and Defence, heard 12 May 2010, http://www.parl.gc.ca/40/3/parlbus/commbus/senate/com-e/vete-e/03mn-e.htm?Language=E&Parl=40&Ses=3&comm_id=79, accessed 17 May 2011.

[47]Veterans Affairs Canada, "Current or Former Canadian Forces Members: Services and Benefits," site modified 17 Nov 2010, http://www.vac-acc.gc.ca/general/sub.cfm?source=information-canadian-forces/services-benefits/disability-benefits, accessed 17 May 2011.

[48]L. Millette, "Ottawa bonifie les sommes aux vétérans blessés, " *CyberPresse* (Montreal, QB) 18 September 2010, http://www.cyberpresse.ca, accessed 17 May 2011.

[49]Corporal (Ret'd) Pascal Lacoste, "Forgotten Veterans," video, 14 April 2009, accessed on http://www.youtube.com/watch?v=n2af5YIwaho&feature=player_embedded#, accessed 17 May 2011; the same idea was also recently expressed by a journalist, Daniel Baird, "Ottawa turns a blind eye to invisible wounds of war", *Globe and Mail*, 24 September 2010 : http://www.theglobeandmail.com/news/politics/ottawa-turns-a-blind-eye-to-invisible-wounds-of-war/article1724924/, accessed 17 May 2011: "Those who end up having their voluminous paperwork organized into neat piles in a cabinet near the door in Mike Newcombe's London office are fortunate. But many other depressed, anxious and confused veterans suffering from PTSD and the long-term effects of MTBI will not get that far. For any new program to be fair and effective, the method of identifying and aiding the veterans who deserve benefits needs to become flexible enough to accommodate those with injuries that do not leave a physical mark, but whose long-term damage runs deep".

[50]Corporal (Ret'd) Pascal Lacoste, "Forgotten Veterans," video, 14 April 2009, http://www.youtube.com/watch?v=n2af5YIwaho&feature=player_embedded#, accessed 17 May 2011.

[51]Hélène Wallenborn, *L'Historien, la Parole des Gens et l'Écriture de l'Histoire* (Paris: Labor, 2006), 195 p.

[52]Liane Faulder, *The Long Walk Home. Paul Franklin's Journey From Afghanistan. A Soldier's Story* (Winnipeg: Windle and Glass, 2007), 178.

[53]Stéphanie A.H. Bélanger, *Personal Interviews #KINOCT 10-02*, in the context of a sponsored research project on "Warrior culture and Soldier identity," conducted in Kingston, October 2010.

[54]Elizabeth D. Samet, "Leaving No Warriors Behind: The Ancient Roots of a Modern Sensibility," *Armed Forces & Society* 37, 2 (2005): 626.

CHAPTER 20

The Experience of Homelessness among Canadian Forces and Allied Forces Veterans: Preliminary Findings

Susan L. Ray, PhD, University of Western Ontario, Faculty of Health Sciences, and Cheryl Forchuk, PhD, Lawson Health Research Institute

Abstract

Little is known about homelessness among CF and Allied Forces (AF) veterans. The purpose of this first national study was to understand the experience of homelessness among veterans of the CF and AF, to discover the underlying causes of homelessness and to provide recommendations to improve services to veterans. An interpretative phenomenological methodology guided the study to focus on understanding the experience of homelessness among the CF and AF population. A purposive sample of 54 homeless CF and AF veterans in three provinces and five cities (London, Toronto, Vancouver, Victoria and Calgary) were interviewed who met the inclusion criteria. Thirty- two transcriptions were analyzed to identify common themes until an understanding of the experience of homeless veterans was attained. Three themes were identified: A long journey from the military home to homelessness; the best and the worst of the system, and; two different worlds: like being on Mars and coming to Earth. Alcoholism was one of the major issues identified that lead ultimately to homelessness many years after their release from the military. Recommendations from participants for the DND and VAC and implications for education, practice and research will be discussed.

The Experience of Homelessness among Canadian Forces and Allied Forces Veterans: Preliminary Findings

There is a lack of research concerning homeless CF and AF veterans and whether or not they are homeless as a result of military service. International research indicates that the number of homeless people in the veteran community is quite significant. In the United States for example, veterans comprise 11% of the total male population aged 18 and over, but account for more than 26% of the male homeless population.[1] In Australia, it is estimated that there are at least 3,000 homeless veterans representing approximately 3% of the homeless population.[2] UK study found that an estimated 6% of London's current nonstatutory ('single') homeless population has served in the Armed Forces.[3] If the international research is placed in a Canadian context, it can be inferred that the number of homeless CF and AF veterans could range from 3% to 26% of the homeless population. Factors such as alcoholism and social isolation contributing to homelessness among CF and AF veterans remain unknown.

REVIEW OF THE LITERATURE

Presently, there have been no studies and no statistics conducted on the homeless veteran population in Canada. Most published studies of homeless veterans are American based on samples from the 1980s. While there are some inconsistencies, these studies tend to show that homeless veterans are older and better educated than homeless nonveterans. In the groups that have been studied, white men were also overrepresented among homeless veterans when compared to other homeless men who had not served in the Armed Forces.[4] Recent research studies from the United States have indicated a complex pattern of influences which predispose veterans to homelessness including extreme poverty as well as post military psychiatric disorder and social isolation.[5] It appears that at least some of the problems which put veterans at risk of homelessness were not present when they were screened for military services, but instead developed later. On the other side of the ledger, there is more evidence of alcohol dependence and abuse among the homeless veterans than among the homeless nonveterans. A recent British study found that veterans' vulnerabilities and support needs are, on the whole, very similar in nature to those of other homeless people, but a greater proportion of ex-service personnel have alcohol, physical and/or mental health problems.[6]

The CF releases approximately 5,000 personnel a year, of which 20-25% are released medically. This includes both those with service related medical conditions and those whose medical condition is not attributable to service. The number of releases appears to be increasing due to demographics (CF slowed recruiting in the 90's and cut personnel as directed by government for deficit reduction) and increased operational tempo, which creates more casualties and wears personnel out. It is estimated that 30 percent of CF veterans transitioning to civilian life have an OSI described as "any persistent psychological difficulty resulting from military service" such as PTSD, addictions and other mental health problems.[7] Many of these returning veterans have undiagnosed mental health problems and suffer in silence.[8] Despite VAC's provision of transition services, the re-adjustment experience and transition back into civilian life especially for the younger generation of returning veterans can be very difficult.[9] Internationally, veterans make up 3% to 26% of the homeless population.[10] If the international research is placed in a Canadian context, it can be inferred that many CF veterans become part of the homeless population.[11] However, until quantitative research is done for the Canadian situation, no inferences about the exact proportion of veterans in the total Canadian homeless population can be safely made. In addition, there is no research on approximately 24,000 AF war veterans in Canada many of whom may be part of the homeless veteran population.

SIGNIFICANCE

There is a gap in the research literature regarding homelessness among CF and AF veterans. Research on understanding the experience of homelessness among CF and AF veterans, its underlying causes, and the supports needed are required to close the knowledge gap. The knowledge gained from this research will help to inform how best to provide the supports and services needed to prevent and reduce homelessness among the CF and AF Veteran population.

PURPOSE

This study aims to understand the experience of homelessness, the underlying causes of homelessness and the supports needed to prevent and reduce homelessness among veterans of the CF regular forces, and/or reservists who have served in Special Duty Areas (SDA's) and AF, in order to assist them in optimizing their health and productive contribution to Canadian society. This will be addressed through the following objectives: to engage with CF and AF veterans in focus groups or individual interviews to understand their experience of homelessness and to address the underlying causes of homelessness; to identify the supports needed to prevent and reduce homelessness among the CF and AF veteran population; to begin the development of appropriate supports needed to prevent and reduce homelessness among the CF and AF veteran population; to put strategies in place for future evaluation of supports within the communities for the ongoing improvement of services delivered to CF and AF veterans; to increase strategic engagement of partners such as AC and the community agencies in London, Toronto, Victoria, Vancouver and Calgary and surrounding areas to improve coordination and delivery of services to CF and AF veterans and to increase knowledge about homelessness among the CF and AF veteran population in order to support better informed policies, investment decision making and provision of services.

METHODOLOGY

The methodology for the study was an interpretative phenomenological approach. There is limited knowledge about the experience of homelessness among veterans of the CF and AF. The reasons why and the supports and services needed to reduce and prevent homelessness among veterans of the CF and AF remain unknown. An interpretative phenomenological approach is a methodology used when little is known about the research topic.[12] An interpretative phenomenological methodology focuses on understanding the perceptions and attitudes toward everyday lived experience, the importance of shared social meanings, and the value of embodied experience for the purpose of understanding the human experience.[13] Such a methodological framework is appropriate for this study as it will focus on understanding the experience of homelessness among CF and AF veterans from the perspective of the participants. An interpretative phenomenological approach will be used to first uncover the experience of homelessness among CF and AF veterans then secondly to identify underlying causes and supports needed to prevent or reduce homelessness among this population. The goals of this methodology are to enter another's world to discover the practical wisdom, possibilities, and embodied understandings found there. Moreover, such a methodology is justified when attempting to elicit the meaning of a phenomenon from the participants themselves.

An interpretative phenomenological study is credible when it represents an accurate account of the participants' experiences, as defined by the participants themselves. This type of approach is particularly important in that it helps to ensure that the study findings will have meaning and relevance in the lives of homeless CF and AF veterans. The significance of an interpretative phenomenological approach rests with the opportunity to provide a richer and deeper understanding of the experience of homelessness among CF and AF veterans, the underlying causes of homelessness and the supports needed to prevent or reduce homelessness among this population.

METHOD

Ethics approval was obtained from the Research Ethics Board for Health Sciences Research Involving Human Subjects at the University of Western Ontario. The research team was comprised of the two principal investigators and graduate student research assistants. In addition, some members of the team were affiliated in various ways, as volunteers, staff, and/or board members, with the agencies that are included in the research.

INCLUSION AND EXCLUSION CRITERIA

Potential participants had to be veterans of the CF regular forces, and/or reservists who have served in SDA's or AF veterans. They had to be presently homeless or homeless within the past year. For the purpose of this study, homeless was defined as accessing the shelter system, living in the rough such as parks or under bridges, living in abandoned buildings, a tent or car and /or couch surfing with friends or family. Participants had to be able to give a written informed consent related to the research and needed to be able to speak and understand English to the degree necessary to participate in the interview. CF and AF members who were neither currently homeless nor homeless within the past year were excluded.

SAMPLING

Initially, a purposive sample of 30 to 36 homeless CF and AF veterans who met the inclusion criteria in a mid-size city (London, Ontario) and its catchment area were to be interviewed in either focus groups of 6 to 8 participants or individual interviews. Three months into implementing the study, it was decided to expand the sample to

30-60 participants and to expand the locations to Toronto, Hamilton, Vancouver, Victoria, Calgary and surrounding areas. In each city, one of the principal investigators made contact with the various shelters and other community agencies serving the homeless population to discuss the study. An in service about the study was held at the local London VAC office and flyers were left with the VAC counsellors to hand out to potential participants to contact the research team if interested in participating in the study. In addition, one of the principal investigators contacted local VAC representatives in Hamilton, Toronto, Vancouver, Victoria and Calgary to discuss the study.

When the study was implemented it was decided that a focus group would be arranged when six to eight veterans had agreed to participate after contacting the researchers. However, three months into the study, only one or two potential participants contacted the research team directly and both requested an individual interview. Therefore, flyers were sent to the various shelters and community agencies with specific times and dates for either one of the principal investigators or the research assistants to conduct individual interviews or focus groups rather than waiting for potential participants to call the research team. Nine months into the study, 32 individual interviews had been conducted with 32 homeless veterans in London, Toronto and the surrounding areas. By the 10th month of the study, 16 more homeless veterans were interviewed individually in Vancouver and Victoria. Six more interviews were conducted in Calgary at two homeless shelters and one drop in centre.

The interview guide was semi-structured to allow for the exploration of the experience and circumstances that led participants to their current situation of homelessness, the underlying causes of homelessness and the supports and services needed to prevent and reduce homelessness among the veteran population. As well, participants were asked what would have been helpful that they did not receive. All participants received an honorarium of $20 for each data collection session. Prior to the start of the interview, the researchers asked the potential participants for their service number to ensure that they were a veteran of either the CF or the AF. The researcher reviewed the letter of information, any questions were addressed, and consent was obtained from those who agreed to participate.

Data was collected through individual interviews lasting 20 to 60 minutes and a demographic questionnaire was completed. Each individual interview was audiotaped and notes were taken by the researcher. Audio tapes were transcribed *verbatim* by the research assistants. Confidentiality was ensured and all original data is locked in a file in which only the primary researchers and research assistants have access. The list of identifiers will be destroyed once data collection is complete. However, data with no identifying information will be retained for further analysis in the future.

As analysis of successive transcripts proceeded, common themes among the various descriptions were noted. Data analysis will proceed until understandings of the experience of homeless veterans are attained. The following are the preliminary findings from the 32 interviews transcribed and analyzed.

DEMOGRAPHICS

Of the 32 participants interviewed, all were male with an average age of 52.4 years. On average, they had served in the CF for 7.11 years and had been released 24.25 years ago from the CF. Eighty-four percent had served in the Regular CF and 15.6 percent in the Reserves. Forty three percent were either separated or divorced and 40.6% were single. The majority (56.3%) had a high school education and 71.9% identified themselves as Caucasian Canadian. On average, they had experienced their first episode of homelessness 8.58 years ago and had spent a total of 5.71 years homeless. Sixty-two percent were in shelters, 31.3 percent were presently housed and 6.3 percent were no fixed address (NFA). Additional demographic information is provided in Tables 20.1-20.4.

RESULTS

There was one overarching analytical interpretation and three themes that emerged from the inquiry based on the 32 analyzed transcriptions. *A downward spiral that can become a vicious circle* is the overarching analytical interpretation and the three underlying themes are: *A long journey from the military home to homelessness; the best and the worst of the system and two different worlds...like being on Mars & coming to earth.* Each theme will be followed by excerpts from the participants and then, comparisons with prior studies and recommendations for practice, education and research will be discussed.

Theme I: A long journey from the military home to homelessness

Alcoholism, other drug addictions and mental health problems were some of the major issues identified by the participants that lead ultimately to homelessness many years after their release from the military. The following excerpts illustrate this theme.

Participant 4:

> I would say the number one cause...alcoholism & drug addiction, that's how I dealt with the problems when I came out of the military. There isn't enough help for you to make the transition...you resort to drugs & alcoholism because it makes you forget.

Participant 17:

> A real hard adjustment from getting out of the service for me was the loss of all that structure…a lot of bouncing around from jobs, changing a lot of addresses…I was suffering from depression and I was drinking a lot….a lot of heavy drinking went on in the military. That's what ultimately helped to lead to my homelessness was undiagnosed depression…and you still continue to drink and the depression takes over…it's a real downward spiral…

Participant 5:

> Lack of support…family issues…the PTSD I suffered through my service. I've become cold and unapproachable…distant, closed off…

On average, the participants had been released 24.25 years ago from the military. Many stated that their drinking started or increased during their military service as at the time drinking off duty was very much part of the military culture. Many found the transition to civilian life very difficult and resorted to drinking or other drugs to cope with their problems. For many these problems lead to depression and further drinking and drugs to cope. Ultimately, this lead to a downward spiral of broken relationships, inability to find work or losing jobs, no income to retain a place to live and finally, homelessness many years after their release from the military. Because these problems and homelessness occurred many years after their release, no causal link can be made between military service and homelessness. If addictions, mental health problems or physical health problems cannot be attributed to military service, then the veteran is not eligible for benefits. In addition, if a veteran leaves the military with less than 10 years service, any compensation or pension is limited.

These findings were very similar to the results from a recent UK study whereby homeless veterans were divided into four different groups.[14] Some had had experienced difficulties from childhood (i.e. fraught relationships with parents, problematic drinking) that followed them into the armed forces and later civilian life. Approximately one quarter of the ex-service personnel interviewed fell into this group. Others encountered difficulties within the armed forces, such as the onset of alcohol or mental health problems which continued to affect them after discharge. A further one quarter of the ex-service personnel interviewed reported these experiences. The third group included those who had a successful career in the armed forces but found the adjustment to civilian life (particularly employment and 'normal' family life) very difficult. This was the smallest group, comprising approximately one in six ex-service interviewees. The fourth group had successful careers in the armed forces and did not encounter difficulties until an apparently unrelated event later in life – such as relationship breakdown, bereavement, or financial crisis. This was the most widespread experience, reported by one third of ex-service interviewees.

Many of the service providers in the UK study were cautious of implying causality, but all unanimously agreed there was a link between military service and alcohol problems within the homeless veteran population.[15] This finding was similar to the findings from this study and other studies that found there was more evidence of alcohol dependence and abuse among the homeless veterans than among the homeless nonveterans.[16]

Theme II: The best and the worst of the system

The participants were asked about the best services received and what they liked the least about the services they were presently receiving. Services included those provided by VAC and other services including the shelter system. The following excerpts illustrate this theme:

Participant 3:

> I went to the detox place to get some treatment finally for my drug & alcohol abuse. I have nothing bad to say it has been a good experience for what I needed it for. I am happy here (shelter) for them telling me how to go about it & showing me how to do the referrals to all the places.

Participant 2:

> Two & a half years after my injury, I'm receiving enough money to go to pay rent and have enough to eat... also received a pension settlement from VAC which is allowing me to pay for my tuition for college for two years.

For the majority of veterans in this study, the best services were provided by the shelter system. The shelter staff and services offered a variety of resources and referrals including those who needed detox and follow up treatment for drug and alcohol abuse. One veteran stated that he had received the best services from VAC as illustrated in the above excerpt. On the other hand, several veterans stated that they had had no contact or follow up from VAC since their release from the military. The following two excerpts illustrate this theme:

Participant 6:

> I have never been contacted by VAC...Forgotten & abandoned. I screwed up my knees in the forces...Both cartilages are gone. I have had two operations. It wasn't bad enough for them to give me a pension. I would have liked a little bit of follow- up.

Participant 7:

> If there is somebody there who's like a liaison…the military is not in the
> business of helping ex-military people to deal with reality. You're controlled
> 24/7 on the base…To have it all gone…you're on your own completely. I've
> heard a lot of guys that are having trouble getting things done with VAC or
> getting to be heard…. I haven't had contact with them at all.

Regardless of the best and worst of the system, many of the veterans stated that the
shelters were run like businesses and that there needed to be affordable descent
housing. Because of substandard housing, many veterans were forced back into the
shelter system thereby, setting up a vicious repeating cycle. The following excerpt
illustrates this situation:

Participant 18:

> What tends to happen is a vicious circle, people are going to filthy housing
> with the bed bugs…they come back to the system again, because they get fed
> up with it. There definitely should be a better housing situation.

Substandard housing and lack of affordable housing is a common theme for the
homeless population whether or not they are a veteran. A person's ability to live in
affordable good quality housing is important to their health and well-being. In Canada,
the lack of a National Housing Policy and access to affordable and adequate housing
is a critical problem contributing to poorer health for many. Extensive literature exists
on the powerful and adverse relationship between homelessness and poor mental and
physical health.[17] The evidence, both at a national and international level, indicates
that individuals that are homeless tend to have multiple, complex health needs that
are often exacerbated by periods of homelessness and/or stays in marginal or temporary
accommodation.[18] Affordable decent housing is needed for homeless veterans not only
to break the vicious cycle of being forced back into the shelter system but also for their
health and well-being.

Theme III: Two different worlds…like being on Mars & coming to earth

The majority of the veterans expressed how different it was from the military to the
civilian world and therefore, found transitioning to civilian life to be one of the major
problems that lead to homelessness. The following excerpt illustrates this theme:

Participant 13:

> I was trying to set up a business at the time with no financial presence in the civilian world ... Which made it hard to get loans...I wound up at that time homeless...As a military person living in barracks I wasn't entirely prepared for what real finances in the real world was like...all of my expenses came out of my pay check...boiled down to never having been exposed to the reality of civilian finances... I was rather coddled in the military. Big, big difference... Like two completely different worlds...

The participants were asked what would have been helpful in transitioning to civilian life that they have not received. They were also asked about the supports needed to prevent and reduce homelessness among the veteran population. The following are some of the recommendations made by the veterans.

Participant 2:

> DND/VAC services need early identification of specific problems related to alcoholism.

Participant 13:

> No one from VAC contacted me. A transitional program definitely...My family has been full of military people...for generations and every one of them has had trouble adjusting to the civilian world.

Participant 17:

> A staffed call centre for people going through a transition period and have VAC staff who have the training that are equipped to know the paper work.

Participant 20:

> VAC needs to follow up for a certain period. Most of the problems happen pretty fast usually within the first year but after three years you are probably dealing with other chronic problems...just follow up for three years.

Participant 5:

> In depth family counseling.... to help not only the soldier returned from active duty to adapt to civilian life, but also for the family members to learn how to better adapt to the fact that the man or woman they knew no longer exists.

Participant 15:

> If they had somebody from VAC show up at the shelters twice a week…it'll make a big difference. There are a lot of us now on the street.

Participant 8:

> VAC needs to design a shelter to deal with ex-military not just for those suffering from a drug addiction…suffering from mental illnesses, post-traumatic stress that are caused by military.

Participant 18:

> Veterans as a group should be kept separate and dealt with separately… have their own shelters…Should have their own housing.

As illustrated in the above excerpts the veterans made several recommendations that they felt would have helped in easing their transition to civilian life and thereby, may have prevented or reduced homelessness among this particular veteran population. Many felt that the DND/VAC needed early identification and screening of specific problems especially alcohol and drug related either prior to their release or immediately upon their release. Since the 1980s, the Second Career Assistance Network (SCAN) seminars about programs and services offered has been in place for CF members transitioning to civilian life. However, none of the veterans interviewed mentioned the SCAN program. Perhaps since on average their release from the CF was over twenty years ago, they may have forgotten that information about the SCAN program had been given to them. Regardless, at the time of their release from the military, the majority of veterans felt that there was inadequate transitioning services and follow up offered by either the DND and /or VAC. Many of the veterans felt that a structured transitional program over several months would have assisted them to adapt to civilian life. In particular, they suggested a transitional program that included such topics as financing, budgeting, writing resumes, and vocational rehabilitation. Many of the veterans suggested family counseling not only to help with assisting the veteran to adapt to civilian life but also to help families to adjust to the changes in the veteran. Several suggested the need for a stream lined VAC staffed call-in centre for veterans during the transitional period that would help them with the paper work in regards to eligibility for benefits or a pension. Many of the veterans recommended that VAC follow-up with veterans at least three years after their release from the military as many chronic problems including mental health issues begin to emerge at that time.

In Canada, the DND is responsible for monitoring the health of personnel for six months after their release from service.[19] The preliminary findings suggest that an extended follow-up period of at least three years may have reduced and/or prevented alcoholism several years after their release from the military. Presently, the VAC Rehabilitation Program aims to help veterans and their families acquire professional help in order to handle problems, particularly medical, psychosocial, and vocational issues, interfering with the veteran's ability to transition successfully to civilian life; notably, family members are able to contribute to the veteran's rehabilitation program.[20] In the Canadian literature, a potential order for practitioners to best manage the care of veterans transitioning to civilian life has been suggested.[21] They suggested that transition issues should be addressed; starting with interpersonal re-adjustment, followed by emotional and social needs, as addressing these issues first would likely ease the transition to the civilian labour force. This approach for these types of programs and services would be beneficial for reducing or preventing homelessness among the veteran population by easing the transition experience to civilian life.[22] In regards to future directions, there is a need to research the efficacy of such VAC counselling programs for veterans. In addition, future longitudinal research studies are needed to aid veterans and their families over the long-term and to re-adapt existing programs and services to changing circumstances. There is a need for future research to understand the experience of homelessness among the veteran population within the context of the veteran culture and to develop a transition model that situates the veteran culture as the overarching framework for testing. [23]

In regards to their present situation of homelessness, many of the veterans recommended that VAC outreach counselors should come to the shelters to identify veterans and to discuss eligibility for benefits or a pension. Currently, VAC has launched three projects — in Montreal, Vancouver and Toronto — specifically geared to find and help homeless vets, and is partnering with veteran, mental health and community groups. Follow up studies are needed to determine if this outreach approach is effective for assisting the homeless veteran population in regards to VAC services and benefits. All the veterans stated that they were different than the rest of the homeless population because of their service in the military. They felt that fellow veterans understood and could support each other more so than the general homeless population. Therefore, the majority felt that there should be shelters or transitional housing designed for veterans to deal not only with alcohol and drug addiction but mental illnesses including post-traumatic stress disorder caused by service in the military. Currently, Cockrell House in Colwood, near Victoria, B.C., is the only transitional house for homeless veterans. In 2009, the project was spearheaded by the local Legion with funding from the federal government, individuals and veteran and regimental groups. Evaluation studies are needed to determine the long-term effectiveness of transitional housing for veterans.

CONCLUSION

The veterans in this study became homeless many years after their release from the military. Alcoholism, other drug addictions and mental health problems were some of the major issues identified by the participants that lead ultimately to homelessness. The preliminary findings from this study suggest that there is a need for education among DND and VAC personnel for the early detection of alcohol abuse and other drug addictions prior to and immediately following veterans' release from the military. Alcohol and /or other drugs were used to cope with many problems that occurred while transitioning to civilian life. The difficulty in transitioning to civilian life was one of the major findings that emerged from this study. DND and VAC need to evaluate transitional programs to determine their effectiveness to reduce and/or prevent homelessness among the veteran population. Regardless of the circumstances that lead to homelessness, veterans in this study deserve to be followed up by VAC counselors to thoroughly determine eligibility for benefits and/or a pension. According to a Canadian military historian, it is not surprising, that whenever injury and illness among military personnel are perceived as being due to personal failings of any kind, support for MVHC decreases.[24]

> Your responsibility for the rest your life is to avoid anything that will make you deviate from the responsibility you have for your fellow warriors who still live and, in turn, for the rest of humanity. …You have to get your back up Finn. You have to get mad as hell and start fighting back for what you know is truly right. Begin by helping all the other shopping cart soldiers you find. In helping them come back to life, you will be healing America.[25]

The above excerpt from Shopping Cart Soldiers was written by a Vietnam veteran who had been shattered by his experiences in the war, suffered from PTSD and ended up an alcoholic and homeless for 10 years in the streets of San Francisco. He felt anger and sadness every time he saw a homeless Vietnam veteran pushing a shopping cart through American streets.[26]Homeless veterans are straddling the line between death and life. They are survivors unable to claim their survival. The central character Finn asks the Nazarene, the Christ figure that carries the pain Finn has caused, "Why?" The Nazarene explains Finn's survival mission and gives him the boon or elixir that the mythic hero is to take back from his adventure to help his fellow man. Finn was spared in order to take on the responsibility for his Band of Brothers for the rest of his life.[27]

Like Finn, Canadian society needs to make a social covenant to care for the homeless veteran population. In the context of MVHC, a social covenant is often taken to be a solemn promise by governments and the Canadian people to provide adequate, and if necessary increasing, levels of support to veterans. It is usually perceived to be enduring and unchangeable.[28]However, such commitments have become more like a social contract than a covenant.[29] In this context, a social contract can be seen as a commitment that, while durable, is subject to modification over time according to prevailing circumstances.[30] The Canadian government, DND and the VAC have not maintained a social covenant with their homeless veterans. It is time for the Canadian public to speak out about this moral imperative to provide at the very least affordable housing and services to those who served our country.

Note: Adding the percentages together may not yield in 100% due to rounding the numbers.

	Age	Years of Service	Time Spent Homeless in the Last Year	Total Time Homeless	Years since Released from Forces	Time since 1st Homeless episode
Average	52.4	7.11	185.88 days	5.71 years	24.25	8.58 years
Minimum	30	0.33	5 days	1 month	2	1 month
Maximum	87	25	365 days	32.08 years	64	39 years

Table 20.1: Age, Years of Service and History of Homelessness.

Housing	Shelter	Housed	Street/NFA
Percentage	62.5	31.3	6.3
Education	**High School**	**University/College**	**Grade School**
Percentage	56.3	31.3	12.5

Table 20.2: Housing and Education.

Canadian Forces	Regular Force	Reserve Force
Percentage	84.4	15.6

Table 20.3: Forces.

Ethnicity	Canadian	American	Aboriginal	British
Percentage	71.9	15.6	9.4	3.1
Marital Status	**Separated/Divorced**	**Single**	**Widowed**	**Married/Common Law**
Percentage	43.8	40.6	12.5	3.1

Table 20.4: Ethnicity and Marital Status.

[1]M. Cunningham, M. Henry and W. Lyons, *Vital Mission: Ending Homelessness Among Veterans* (Washington, DC: National Alliance to End Homelessness, Homelessness Research Institute, 2007).

[2]Chamberlain, C. and MacKenzie, D., Australian Census Analytic Program: Counting the homeless 2006 http://www.abs.gov.au/AUSSTATS/subscriber.nsf/log, accessed 5 November 2009.

[3]Johnsen, S., Jones, A., and Rugg, J., "The Experience of Homeless Ex-service Personnel in London," *The University of York Research Report*, 2008, http://www.york.ac.uk/inst/publications/PDF/HomelessExServiceinLondon.pdf, accessed 30 September 2009.

[4]M. Robertson, "Homeless Veterans: An emerging problem?" In *The Homeless in Contemporary Society*, eds. R.E. Green, S.B. White and R.D. Gingham (Beverly Hills, CA: Sage, 1987); R. Rosenheck, C. Leda, L.K. Frishman, J. Lam, and A. Chung, "Homeless Veterans," *Homelessness in America: A reference Book*, eds. A.Z. Phoenix and J. Baumohl: Oryx Press, 1996), 97-108; R.C. Tessler, and D.L. Dennis, "Mental illness among homeless adults: A synthesis of recent NIMH funded research," *Research in Community and Mental Health*, eds. J.R. Greenley and P.J. Leaf (Greenwich, CT: JAI Press, 1992), 3-54.

[5]M. Cunningham, M. Henry and W. Lyons, *Vital Mission: Ending Homelessness Among Veterans* (Washington, DC: National Alliance to End Homelessness, Homelessness Research Institute, 2007); R. C. Tessler, R. Rosenheck, and G. Gamache, "Gender differences in self-reported reasons for homelessness," *Journal of Social Distress and the Homeless* 10, 3 (2001): 243-254; R. C. Tessler, R. Rosenheck, and G. Gamache, "Comparison of homeless veterans with other homeless men in a large clinical outreach program," *Psychiatric Quarterly* 73, 2 (2002): 109-119.

[6]Johnsen, S., Jones, A., and Rugg, J., "The Experience of Homeless Ex-service Personnel in London," *The University of York Research Report*, 2008, http://www.york.ac.uk/inst/publications/PDF/HomelessExServiceinLondon.pdf, accessed 30 September 2009.

[7]Canadian Forces, *CCHS supplement: Briefing document* (Ottawa: Statistics Canada, 2003).

[8]S.L. Ray, "The experience of contemporary peacekeepers healing from trauma," Nursing Inquiry 16, 1 (2009a): 53-63; S.L. Ray, "Contemporary treatment approaches for trauma from the perspective of peacekeepers," Canadian Journal of Nursing Research 41, 2 (2009b): 114-182.

[9]S.L. Ray, "The experience of contemporary peacekeepers healing from trauma," *Nursing Inquiry* 16, 1 (2009a): 53-63; S.L. Ray, "Contemporary treatment approaches for trauma from the perspective of peacekeepers," *Canadian Journal of Nursing Research* 41, 2 (2009b): 114-182; S. L. Ray and M.Vanstone, "The impact of PTSD on veterans' family relationships: An interpretative phenomenological inquiry," *International Journal of Nursing Studies* 4, 6 (2009): 838-847.

[10]Chamberlain, C. and MacKenzie, D., *Australian Census Analytic Program: Counting the homeless* 2006 http://www.abs.gov.au/AUSSTATS/subscriber.nsf/log, accessed 5 November 2009; Johnsen, S., Jones, A., and Rugg, J., "The Experience of Homeless Ex-service Personnel in London," *The University of York Research Report*, 2008, http://www.york.ac.uk/inst/publications/PDF/HomelessExServiceinLondon.pdf, accessed 30 September 2009; United States Department of Veterans Affair, "Community Homelessness Assessment, Local Education and Networking Group (CHALENG) for Veterans," *The Fourteenth Annual Progress Report on Public Law 105-114, Services for Homeless Veterans Assessment and Coordination*, 2008, http://www1.va.gov/homeless/docs/CHALENG_14th_annual_Rpt_7-7-08.pdf, accessed 30 September 2009.

[11]P. Strogan, *Homeless Veterans: A discussion paper* (Ottawa: Veterans Affairs Canada, 2009).

[12]M. Van Manen, *Researching lived experience* (3rd ed) (London, ON: The Althouse Press, 1998).

[13]M. Van Manen, *Researching lived experience* (3rd ed) (London, ON: The Althouse Press, 1998); M. Merleau-Ponty, "Phenomenology of perception" trans. M. Smith (New York, NY: Routledge, 1962); M. Ray, "The richness of phenomenology: Philosophical, theoretical, and methodological concerns," *Critical issues in qualitative methods*, ed. J. Morse (Thousand Oaks, CA: Sage, 1994), 177-133.

[14]Johnsen, S., Jones, A., and Rugg, J., "The Experience of Homeless Ex-service Personnel in London," *The University of York Research Report*, 2008, http://www.york.ac.uk/inst/publications/PDF/HomelessExServiceinLondon.pdf, accessed 30 September 2009.

[15]Johnsen, S., Jones, A., and Rugg, J., "The Experience of Homeless Ex-service Personnel in London," *The University of York Research Report*, 2008, http://www.york.ac.uk/inst/publications/PDF/HomelessExServiceinLondon.pdf, accessed 30 September 2009.

[16]M. Cunningham, M. Henry and W. Lyons, *Vital Mission: Ending Homelessness Among Veterans* (Washington, DC: National Alliance to End Homelessness, Homelessness Research Institute, 2007); R. C. Tessler, R. Rosenheck, and G. Gamache, "Gender differences in self-reported reasons for homelessness," *Journal of Social Distress and the Homeless* 10, 3 (2001): 243-254; R. C. Tessler, R. Rosenheck, and G. Gamache, "Comparison of homeless veterans with other homeless men in a large clinical outreach program," *Psychiatric Quarterly* 73, 2 (2002): 109-119.

[17]C.J. Frankish,and S.W. Hwang, "Homelessness and Health," *Canadian Medical Association Journal* 164, 2 (2001): 229-33.

[18]Canadian Institute for Health Information, *Improving the health of Canadians: Mental Heatlh and homelessness* (Ottawa: CIHI, 2007); A. Cheung S.W. and Hwang, "Risk of death among homeless women," *Canadian Medical Association Journal* 170, 8 (2004): 1251-52; S.W. Hwang, R. Wilkins, M. Tjepkema, P.J. O'Campo, and J.R. Dunn, *Mortality among residents of shelters, rooming houses, and hotels in Canada: 11 year follow-up study*, 2009, doi: 10.1136/bmj.b4036; W.H. Martens, "A Review of Physical and Mental Health in Homeless Persons," *Public Health Review* 29 (2001): 13-22.

[19]M. Rossignol, *Afghanistan: Military personnel and operational stress injuries* (Ottawa: Parliamentary Information and Research Service, 2007).

[20]Veterans Affairs Canada. Rehabilitation, 2006, http://www.vac-acc.gc.ca/client/sub.cfm?source=forces/nvc/programs/rehab, accessed 10 November 2009.

[21]M.J. Westwood, T.G. Black, and H.b. McLean, "A re-entry program for peacekeeping soldiers: Promoting personal and career transition," *Canadian Journal of Counselling* 36, 3 (2002): 221-232.

[22]M.J. Westwood, T.G. Black, and H.b. McLean, "A re-entry program for peacekeeping soldiers: Promoting personal and career transition," *Canadian Journal of Counselling* 36, 3 (2002): 221-232.

[23]S.I. Ray and K.Heaslip, "Canadian military transitioning to civilian life: A discussion paper," *Journal of Psychiatric and Mental Health Nursing* 18, 3 (2011): 198–204.

[24]A. English, "Leadership and Operational Stress in the Canadian Forces," *Canadian Military Journal* 1, 3 (2000): 33-38.

[25]J. Mulligan, *Shopping Cart Soldiers* (Willimantic, CT: Curbstone Press, 1997), 185.

[26]J. Mulligan, *Shopping Cart Soldiers* (Willimantic, CT: Curbstone Press, 1997), 185.

[27]J. Mulligan, *Shopping Cart Soldiers* (Willimantic, CT: Curbstone Press, 1997), 185.

[28]J. Sacks, *The address of the Chief Rabbi of Britain to a major conference of the worldwide Anglican Communion highlights the salient differences between a convenant and a contract*, 28 July 2008, www.chiefrabbi.org/UploadedFiles/Articals/lambethconference28july08.pdf, accessed 6 February 2011.

[29]Veterans Affairs Canada, Canadian Forces Advisory Council, *" Honouring Canada's Commitment:'Opportunity with Security' for Canadians Forces Veterans and their Families in the 21st Century" Disussion Paper* March 2004, http://www.veterans.gc.ca/eng/sub.cfm?source=information-canadian-forces, accessed 6 February 2011.

[30]A. English, "Not written in stone: Social covenants and resourcing military and veterans' health care in Canada," (presented, Military Veterans Health Research Forum, Royal Military College of Canada (RMC) and Queen's University, Kingston, Ontario: November 15-17, 2010).

CHAPTER 21

Social Suffering in the Military and Possible Uses for the Creative Arts

Julie Salverson, PhD, Cultural Studies Programme, Queen's University

ABSTRACT

The creative arts offer resources and methodologies to reconnect the individual with the community in a therapeutics of integrated wellness. Research in this field can form the basis of a prevention program targeting the isolation that personnel and their family can experience as a consequence of trauma. How does an individual and family live through a rupture in the fabric and meaning of their lives and then not remove the trauma, or hide the disfigurement, but live with it? This paper offers several case studies of programs with groups dealing with displacement, trauma, and violence: workshops with military students; a play developed with youth for the Canadian Red Cross on anti-personnel landmines; a theatre process with refugees; a theatre research project in South Africa. The discussion is framed in theory about the personal and social costs of listening and bearing witness, and the difficulty of limiting options for how traumatized individuals self-define and narrate their lives. Drama, storytelling and the creative arts provide environments of witness and support so that working through the impact of trauma is not an isolated task left up to an individual and a family, but a social challenge for which all Canadians are responsible.

SOCIAL SUFFERING IN THE MILITARY AND POSSIBLE USES FOR THE CREATIVE ARTS

This paper addresses creative arts based research, education, community support, health care, and advocacy. The creative arts have a lot to offer the many faceted challenges the military is facing today. What follows are a few specific stories designed to capture the imagination and suggest the kinds of things the arts – visual art, music, dance, creative writing and theatre – can offer. These examples are intended to provide an additional resource, extension or support to other methods for addressing social suffering.

Over the past thirty years, I have worked with a number of groups, including refugees, assault victims, stroke survivors, adolescents inside the corrections system, kids on the street. This sample has included adults, children, and families. Almost always the groups have never done drama, almost always people say, "It won't work with my community!" and always – I've never come across an exception – always it does work. People like to express themselves, to tell stories. The creative arts offer additional vocabularies for finding out what people's experience is, giving them skills to share those experiences and tell others - their broader community, their school, their neighbourhood, or you the researcher - who they are, what they love, where they hurt and what they need.[1]

Much of my work has been with communities dealing with displacement, trauma, and violence.[2] How does a man, a woman, a family, or a community, live through a ghastly rupture in the fabric of skin and sense and order and meaning of their lives – and then not remove the trauma, or hide the disfigurement, but live with it? How do we make sure suffering the effects of trauma is not an isolated journey but a social challenge? Drama, storytelling, narrative and the creative arts provide places to create communities of witness and support. I am writing this paper as a theatre practitioner working with researchers. I am going to give some examples of what this work looks like, interspersed with some analysis about how it works.

For 15 years, I have been invited every fall by the Royal Military College of Canada Department of English Studies to give a theatre and story making workshop for first through fourth year students. I bring members of my Queen's University drama class with me. The two groups show each other stereotypes and assumptions each have about the other. They laugh. They ask questions. The Queen's students say everyone thinks they are rich and only want to drink. The RMCC students say everyone thinks they are brainwashed and only want to fight. Then the stories get more layered, more complex, and truer. One military student says, "When I go home for Christmas everyone thinks I'm the same. I'm not." Another talks about visiting a local restaurant with his girlfriend and being refused service because he is in uniform. Talk about making a play to show people in Kingston, ON, about what it means to be in the Canadian military, and who these young people really are.

In 1997, the Canadian Red Cross commissioned me to write a play about antipersonnel land mines, to be performed by youth groups and schools across Canada. When finished, the play was also performed in the United States and Thailand. The occasion of the first performance was the Ottawa, ON, conference where the first international treaty banning the production and implementation of mines was signed. The initial exploration for the play was done with student teachers in a course on drama across the curriculum taught at the University of British Columbia. For three weeks, the class learned all they could about land mines and turned their research into images, scenes, songs, bits of text. Then my co-writer Patricia Fraser and I went away and wrote the play we called "Boom". It is about a young Canadian high school student named Roger who meets a girl named Ana. Ana is Croatian and comes from Bosnia. Ana lost her father to a land mine. She wants to be Canadian, to be a scientist, and she doesn't want to talk about her homeland but, instead, tries to control her trauma by designing a land clearance device that will rid the earth of land mines. When Roger tries to befriend her and approaches her world, he finds his own becoming disrupted. Overwhelmed, he says: "Why should I have to listen to this? I'm not even finished grade twelve? I have enough to worry about, land mines are not my problem."

This project asked the question, "What does it really mean for Canadian-born teenagers and teachers to meet the reality of land mines? What is involved in preparing to be a witness, to meet with testimony? As writers and educators, Fraser and I wrote a play that put the witness on stage with the survivor and explored what both were going through, with all their contradictions, with all the things that are taboo to say, feel, think. Most importantly, we tried to show what it meant for these two characters to meet and risk beginning a difficult friendship without judgment. It was our hope that the audiences and the youth groups who worked on the play encountered these questions, made this journey of discovery for themselves.

Yale scholar Ora Avni has written that we need to take seriously what it means not only to speak, but also to listen to accounts of violence. When a reservist or a soldier returns home, to whom can she or he speak? How will anyone understand? Avni describes a character in the Elie Wiesel story "Night". Moshe has been taken from his home by the Nazis, survived the murder of his convoy of foreign Jews and returns to warn the others. However, those to whom he returns do not, and more importantly, cannot believe him. Accepting his story would disrupt the very foundations of what they understand to be human. Moshe's return to town is an attempt to reaffirm ties with the human community of his past, whose integrity was put into question by the incomprehensibility of what he had witnessed. Listening to your story will change the world I live in, and I do not want my world to change.

Avni says it is essential that Moshe speak not just privately to a friend, but publicly to the community network to which he seeks readmission. "Only by having a community integrate his dehumanizing experience into the narratives of self-representation that it shares and infer a new code of behaviour based on the information he is imparting, only by becoming part of this community's history can Moshe hope to reclaim his lost humanity."[3]

What is true for Wiesel's character is true for soldiers returning home to Canada. If the community's job is to shift our understanding of what makes sense in this world and what this world IS - both beautiful and terrible—we must take seriously the cost of listening. To be a witness – as a spouse, a child, a parent, a neighbour – involves both hearing someone's story and allowing our attitudes and behaviours to be changed by it. This is only possible if, first, we allow ourselves and others to be afraid to know, afraid to hear, and risk the anger our fear of listening can bring in survivors.

This kind of project is about education, about developing in people the capacity to hear and be changed by what they hear. The capacity also to see survivors as complex, full subjects who are much more than their injury.

One of the dynamics in work with the creative arts is an expansion of the possible narratives survivors of trauma and their families can use to interpret and frame their experience. Canadian researchers Brett Smith and Andrew Sparks describe a group of men who have suffered spinal cord injuries as having few narrative options for re-telling their testimonies. They use as an example a study that analyzed three disability magazines in the U.S. The plots, events and characters in these stories of men with SCI fell into three categories:

1) commitment to battle
2) heroic qualities
3) heroic action

These magazines act as narrative scripts for newcomers to the world of injury and can be inspirational or confining. To the extent that these narratives reinforce, rely and actively cultivate a particular model of masculinity, they may hinder the transformative potential of disability. Transformative not in the sense of triumph, but in the sense of moving through trauma and being allowed to become a new person, whose self is not continually referencing what the researchers call 'heroic masculinity'. "Problems arise when people become fixated on one kind of body and sense of self in situations where the restitution and hero narrative are not appropriate."[4] Having the narrative resources to contemplate options for re-telling their life stories - to re-imagine or re-invent themselves- is not easy. This is the kind of thing that can be explored, played with, in a creative arts situation.

I worked with the Jesuit Centre for Social Faith and Justice in Toronto, ON, to create a play with refugees. This time it was people with direct experience of trauma sharing and staging their stories. The group talked, exchanged images and music, made scenes and created a play and a video called "Are the Birds in Canada the Same?" The play toured for several weeks to community centres across Toronto, playing for audiences of refugees who had arrived anywhere from one week to several years previously. The play was well received, and many people said "Yes, this was true for me" about many moments in the show. "This makes us feel heard," people said. The Centre then hired me to spend a year giving workshops to groups who either worked with refugees directly, or, had little knowledge of refugee issues. In both circumstances the video became a helpful resource to 'speak refugee stories' while the workshop – also incorporating drama – allowed helping professionals, teachers, ministers and the wider public to confront their own stereotypes, ask questions and analyze where their assumptions about what a refugee is come from. In the workshops the helpers could admit their frustrations and confusions and tackle together – using drama – the impasses they faced and the problems they encountered.

The last example is a project I did with my colleague here at Queen's University, Dr. Rosemary Jolly. Dr. Jolly` is working on issues around HIV, gender based violence and AIDS in South Africa. Last year I worked with her research team to develop a drama workshop process in which rural Zulu South African boys and men – and groups of women – could investigate the dynamics in their communities and families. Part of the goal of drama in this case is to find out how the community members define their lives; their problems, but also their resources, their desires. Four researchers flew to Kingston from South Africa – together with the Kingston, ON, based research team – to develop and learn to facilitate a one-day workshop process that would allow participants to create images from their own lives and then play with and change those images. When I asked Dr. Jolly what she wanted from this process, she said that in South Africa there is a lot of drama work but most of it is about education or therapy. She said that if the people in the villages where her team was going got even a whiff of that – educators or researchers wanting to judge them and change them – they'd have nothing to do with it. What she wanted, instead, was a process of investigation and play that was, fundamentally, about witnessing, about listening. About letting the participants speak.

To sum up, there some key elements inside a drama or creative arts process: exchanging stories without judgment/imagining multiple narratives for framing your sense of self and trying those narratives out/witnessing and being witnessed/ experiencing oneself inside the network of one's community and beyond the definition of one's injury. Drama engages both the private and the public human being and allows room for what evades language or definition. It is communal, it can't be done alone but its process can invite a deeper and more complex self; and, perhaps most importantly, give permission to be that self.

[1]See for example: Julie Salverson, "Community Engaged Theatre and Performance," *Critical Perspectives on Canadian Theatre in English* 19, ed. Ric Knowles (Toronto: Playwrights Canada, 2011); Tim Prentki and Sheila Preston, *The Applied Theatre Reader*, eds, (New York: Routledge, 2008); Jan Cohen-Cruz, *Engaging Performance: Theatre As Call and Response*, (New York: Routledge), 2010.

[2]For examples of theatre and drama and military trauma: Patrick Healy, "The Anguish of War Explored by Sophocles," *The New York Times* (New York), 11 November 2009; Andrew Pomykal, "Role Play Scenarios Add Awareness to Suicide Awareness Training," *Fort Hood Sentinel* (Fort Hood, Texas), 9 July 2009, www.forthoodsentinel.com/story.php?id=1318, accessed 26 May 2011; Michael St. Clair Balfour, "The Difficult Return: Contexts and Developments in Drama-Based Work with Returned Military Personnel," *Applied Theatre Researcher* 10 (2009): 1-11; James Miller and David Read Johnson, "Drama Therapy In The Treatment Of Combat-Related Post-Traumatic Stress Disorder," *The Arts in Psychotherapy* 23, 5 (1997): 383-395; D. Golub, "Symbolic expression in post-traumatic stress disorder: Vietnam combat veterans in art therapy," *The Arts in Psychotherapy* 12 (1985): 285-296.

[3]Ora Avni, "Beyond Psychoanalysis: Elie Wiesel's Night," *Historical Perspective, Auschwitz and After: Race, Culture, and "the Jewish Question" in France*, ed. Lawrence D. Kritzman, (New York: Routledge, 1995), 212.

[4]Brett Smith and Andrew C. Sparks, " Men, Sport, and Spinal Cord Injury: Identity Dilemmas, Embodied Time, and the Construction of Coherence," *Unfitting Stories: Narrative Approaches To Disease, Disability, and Trauma*, eds. Valerie Raoul, Connie Canam, Angela D. Henderson and Carla Patrson (Waterloo: Wilfred Laurier Press, 2007), 194.

CHAPTER 22

Income Study: Regular Force Veteran Report

Mary Beth MacLean, MA, Linda Van Til, PhD, James Thompson, MD, Alain Poirier,
Jill Sweet, MSc, David Pedlar, PhD, Veterans Affairs Canada, Research Directorate;
Jonathan Adams, CGA, Veterans Affairs Canada, Audit and Evaluation Division;
Kerry Sudom, PhD, Catherine Campbell, MA, Department of National Defence,
Director General Military Personnel Research and Analysis;
Brian Murphy, MES, and Claude Dionne, BSc, Statistics Canada, Income Statistics Division.

ABSTRACT

The objective of the Income Study was to examine family income using Statistics Canada's low income measure (LIM); and describes veteran income trends and income differences between sub-populations within a larger population of veterans. Statistics Canada linked together DND records for 36,638 Regular Force veterans released between January 1, 1998 to December 31, 2007 to the general family tax records from 1997 to 2007 and produced tables based on this record linkage. Non Veterans Affairs Canada (VAC) clients accounted for the majority (68%) of the Regular Force veteran study population. Overall, the post-release income of Regular Force veterans (not including the impact of VAC programs) declined by 10% compared to their income during service. Females experienced the greatest decline in income (30%), followed by the medically released (29%) while subordinate officers experienced an increase in income (27%). While 15% had ever experienced low income post-release, for those released at the youngest age group (15 to 19) and involuntary releases, this rate was more than double. VAC clients had experienced greater declines in income post-release than non-clients. Post-release, veterans on average experience a decline in income. VAC programs reach the groups with the largest declines. Small numbers of veterans experience low income. Unfortunately, most low income veterans are not clients of VAC.

INCOME STUDY: REGULAR FORCE VETERAN REPORT.

Income can be an important determinant of health and satisfaction with life after release from the military. Studies of Veteran income have included only small subsets of veteran populations and have measured satisfaction with income or absolute income rather than relative income. No studies have examined continuity of income pre- and post-release for a large population of veterans.

This paper summarizes the initial findings of the income part of the Life After Service Studies (LASS) program of research. The Income Study is one part of the LASS conducted by VAC, DND (Chief Military Personnel) and Statistics Canada.[1] LASS also currently includes a population health survey (STCL, Survey on Transition to Civilian Life), and a mortality and cancer study (CF-CAMS). LASS was created to evaluate the NVC programs, and to fill gaps in the research on military to civilian transition in Canada and other countries. The studies focus on four research questions:

1. Re-establishment: How are Canadian Forces personnel doing after transition to civilian life in terms of income, health, well-being, disability, and other determinants of health?
2. Program Reach: Are existing transition/re-establishment programs reaching those in need?
3. Unmet Needs: Are there unmet needs that call for new/revised programs?
4. Program Effectiveness: How do VAC clients and non-clients compare in terms of income, health (well-being), disability and other determinants of health?

The Income Study analyzes incomes pre- and post-transition from military service for four populations of personnel released from the CF from 1998 to 2007: (1) Regular Force veterans excluding re-enlisted[2]; (2) Regular Force veterans including re-enlisted; (3) Primary Reserve veterans excluding re-enlisted; and (4) Primary Reserve veterans including re-enlisted. This initial report includes an analysis of the incomes for the first group, i.e., Regular Force veterans excluding those re-enlisted. The objectives of this report are to describe:

1. The study populations;
2. The tax file record linkage and linkage rates;
3. The income trends, sources of income including Employment Insurance and social assistance and prevalence of low income among CF veterans; and
4. Differences in income trends according to demographic group, service characteristics (e.g. rank), VAC client status NVC client, DP client and non-client) and specific VAC program participation (Rehabilitation Program and Disability Benefit program).

Background

Income as a Determinant of Health

Factors which influence population health are called the determinants of health and include income, social status, social support networks, education, employment/working conditions, social environments, physical environments, personal health practices and coping skills, healthy child development, biology and genetic endowment, health services, gender, and culture.[3]

In general, higher socioeconomic status has been associated with better health. However, in wealthy countries like Canada, the distribution of income in a given society may be a more important determinant of population health than the total amount of income earned by society members.[4]

Over the last 10 years, the literature on income as a determinant of health has continued to evolve. However, weaknesses remain in Canadian research studies on income and health. A 2003 review of the published literature on the relationship between income inequality and health outcomes[5] concluded that while most studies indicate a significant association between income inequality and health outcomes there are many inconsistencies in the methods used. These inconsistencies include the method of measuring income inequality and the health outcomes assessed which have included mortality, self-reported health and psychological distress. Raphael *et al.* (2005)[6] examined 241 Canadian research studies on income and health and found gaps in Canadian knowledge concerning the roles that income and its distribution play in Canadians' health. The gaps included poor conceptualization of income and the means by which it influences health, the lack of longitudinal studies, and the lack of linked databases that allow for analysis of how income contributes to health.

Some studies support the threshold effect hypothesis which suggests the existence of a threshold of income beyond which adverse impacts on health begin to emerge.[7] While no such threshold exists in Canada, two measures of low income are produced regularly by Statistics Canada; the low income cut-off (LICO) and the low income measure (LIM) which are both measured at the family level and take into account family size.[8] These measures are designed to identify populations in economically straightened circumstances who may be at risk of poverty and have some measure of social consensus in Canada.

Recent studies have examined the pathway from low income to poor health using longitudinal data. Orpana *et al.* (2007)[9] used the Statistics Canada National Population Health Survey (NPHS) data and found that individuals living in households with combined incomes of less than $20,000 were almost three times more likely to experience a decline in self-rated health than people with the highest incomes. More recently, another study using the NPHS data[10] showed that stressors play an important role in the relationship between household income and psychological distress.[11] Lower-income individuals had greater prevalence of stressors in their lives, "such as job strain, financial problems, personal stress, and problems with relationships, neighbourhoods or children."

CANADIAN FORCES INCOME AND INCOME POLICY

Given the importance of income as a determinant of health, income and its effects on the quality of life of military members and veterans has been a major policy concern of both the CF and VAC. In the 1990s, concerns about the lower salaries of CF personnel compared to those of the Canadian Public Service resulted in a move to increase incomes within the CF. A substantial increase in pay for non-commissioned members and officers was implemented in 1996 in order to begin addressing this discrepancy in incomes. During the 1997-1998 Quality of Life hearings of the Standing

Committee on National Defence and Veterans Affairs (SCONDVA), one of the main concerns expressed by CF members and their families was compensation and benefits.[12] This issue became one of the five "pillars" that support the quality of life of CF personnel and their families. It was determined that military service is unique from other occupations in Canada, and the compensation and benefits received by serving members must adequately reflect their skills, experience, as well as the unique nature of the military. In particular, it was determined that basic military pay should be enhanced to reflect the loss of personal freedom, frequent postings that cause disruption to personnel and their families, periods of prolonged separation from families, and overtime (i.e., the "Military Factor"). Thus, the 1990s saw substantial improvements in the economic quality of life of CF personnel. The gap between military and comparable Public Service incomes was closed in 1999, and pay increases to reflect the Military Factor were also achieved at this time.[13]

While CF personnel have experienced steady increases in income since the late 1990s, civilian earnings have remained constant.[14] The pay adjustments and increases that occurred in the late 1990s coincide with the changes in demographic composition of the military in the past 20 years, reflecting an older and more highly educated CF population. In addition to the pay increases of the 1990s, higher earnings of CF personnel compared to the civilian population may be a result of the various allowances that many individuals receive in addition to their salary, such as hazard, paratroops, or submarine. Within the CF, differences in income are apparent according to service characteristics and demographics, with higher incomes among higher-ranking members, officers, and males (who have greater representation at the higher ranks and have on average participated in more deployments).[15]

In addition to the changes in demographic composition of the CF, a trend that has occurred in Canadian society is the increased prevalence of dual-income families. Research within DND to assess the impact of military life on spousal income and employment, and income comparisons of military and civilian families, is currently being carried out.[16] Data from the US suggests that military spouses are more highly educated yet earn lower wages than their civilian counterparts.[17] In the only DND study focused specifically on spousal income and employment,[18] it was found that the proportion of dual-income families in the CF exceeded that of the general population, although on average, spousal employment income and total CF family income were lower than that of a comparable civilian group of Public Service employees. Characteristics of military life, such as posting and deployment history, may have an impact on family income, since frequent moves of location and the disruption of normal family life that occur with frequent deployments may result in employment limitations for spouses. For example, qualitative data collected within DND has suggested that it may be difficult for spouses of military personnel to obtain employment, acquire seniority, and receive promotions when they experience frequent moves.[19] As well, in a survey of Regular Force CF members, it was reported that it takes a significant amount of time for many CF spouses to obtain employment when posted, which translates into lost income during the time of searching for employment. Once employed, over half of the respondents reported that their spouses were earning less than in their previous posting.[20] It is unknown whether any impact of military life on family income remains present once the military member transitions to civilian life. For families with a history of frequent moves, it is possible that the accumulated loss of spousal earnings over the span of the CF member's career may result in lower earnings that extend into retirement, compared to the general population. It should be kept in mind that the issue of impacts on spousal income does not apply to all veterans as many veterans either never marry or marry after release, especially those who release at a young age.

The CF recognizes that for some occupations, educational requirements are higher than they were in the past, and many ill and injured personnel transitioning to civilian employment must upgrade their education or certifications in order to obtain gainful employment. The CF/DND offers educational benefits to ill and injured individuals who are medically releasing from the Regular Forces or Primary Reserves through an Educational Reimbursement (ER) program. For eligible individuals, reimbursement can be made for expenses (tuition, books, etc.) during an approved period of study in which academic qualifications are being upgraded. Personnel selection officers (PSOs), in consultation with the casualty management team, Director Military Careers Administration (DMCA), and Integrated Personnel Support Centre (IPSC) staff, coordinate initial educational upgrading for CF members facing medical release. An Individual Learning Plan (ILP) is developed for ill and injured members detailing the educational program being sought and the funding required. Once the educational program is completed, PSOs coordinate with representatives from the SISIP during transition from the ER program to vocational rehabilitation programs, at which time financial support from the educational reimbursement program ceases. SISIP is a suite of programs developed to financially support CF personnel and their families, including life and long-term disability (LTD) insurance, vocational rehabilitation, financial counselling and planning, and loans for financial distress and educational assistance. These programs are available to personnel while in the CF as well as following release. In addition to the educational reimbursement program, the CF Transition Assistance Program provides assistance to medically releasing CF members in making the transition to civilian employment by matching job openings of potential employers with individual skills.

For Regular Force and full-time Reserve personnel releasing from the CF, assistance in the transition to civilian employment is also offered through the SCAN program. This program offers counselling, seminars, and workshops in areas including financial planning, disability pensions and benefits administered by VAC, SISIP benefits available after release, career development and transition, and job search training. The seminars and workshops are administered at varying time points throughout the members' career, so that individuals are fully informed of their entitlements should they decide to transition to civilian employment.

VETERANS AFFAIRS CANADA POLICY ON INCOME

VAC has had a long history of providing income support benefits to veterans of the First and Second World Wars and the Korean War. First introduced in 1930, the purpose of the War Veterans Allowance Act was to provide income support for certain aged or permanently unemployable wartime veterans who, due to the intangible effects of wartime service, became unable to maintain themselves and their families. It was recognized at the time that not all veterans whose post-war incomes were affected by wartime service would be eligible for benefits provided under the Pension Act of 1919. Over the years eligibility was expanded and the War Veterans Allowance (WVA) program was harmonized with the Guaranteed Income Supplement (GIS). By the mid 1980s, the number of allowance program recipients totalled approximately 90,000 and the annual client expenditure was about $454 million dollars.[21] Today less than 6,000 veterans and survivors of veterans receive WVA.

While CF veterans are not eligible for WVA, they are eligible for disability benefits, earnings loss while participating in the Rehabilitation Program[22] and the Canadian Forces Income Support (CFIS) benefit if they have completed the Rehabilitation Program and cannot find work. CFIS and the Rehabilitation program were both introduced in 2006 as part of the suite of New Veterans Charter Programs under the Canadian Forces Members and Veterans Re-establishment and Compensation Act. However, eligibility for these programs is restricted to those with service-related conditions.[23] The exception is the Career Transition Services program that is available to all who are releasing. Today, less than 10% of CF veterans are in receipt of benefits from VAC, few have used Career Transition Services and the income support needs of the wider veteran population are largely unknown.

The New Veterans Charter programs were part of the response to the 1998 SCONDVA report. The programs are aimed at supporting military member re-integration into civilian life and were supported by research conducted by VAC as part of the Review of Veterans Care Needs (RVCN). In 1999, the RVCN conducted a survey of 1,968 CF clients of a total of 18,500 CF clients to determine their health needs. The findings suggested that CF clients are economically vulnerable, by career interruptions, the nature and severity of their disability, or low education.[24] More recent studies in the US have found that early retirement (less than 15 years) is associated with slightly lower measures of life satisfaction in general and in particular lower levels of satisfaction with their financial situations than those who retired later.[25] Another US study found that the extent to which expectations of civilian work, financial, and family aspects of life were met emerged as significant predictors of satisfaction and adjustment after military retirement.[26]

Previous veteran studies have tended to rely on self reported incomes measured at one point in time and in absolute terms or measured satisfaction with income. However, those with high incomes could have low satisfaction with finances, having more to do with expectations of income rather than real or perceived income inequality. As well, these studies have included only small sub-sets of the veteran population (for example VAC clients, US officers or US Naval officers). Very little is known about the larger population of releasing veterans. The aim of the income study is to fill some of the gaps in research on post-military veteran and family income by: (1) examining income over time (continuity of income); (2) measuring relative income and family income using Statistics Canada's low-income measure (LIM); and (3) describing income trends and income differences between sub-populations within a larger population of veterans.

METHOD

Study Population

As of March 2009, there were an estimated 686,000 CF personnel and former personnel living in Canada, including 592,000 veterans[27] and 94,000 still serving personnel.[28]   As of March 2009, about 58,000 (8%) of these CF veterans and personnel were VAC clients. The vast majority of VAC CF clients were disability benefit clients (those in receipt of a disability award under the New Veterans Charter [CFMVRCA] and/or a disability pension paid under the *Pension Act*). Of the 58,000 VAC CF clients, almost one-quarter, or 14,000, accessed New Veterans Charter (NVC) programs.[29]

Data on releases were extracted from DND Human Resources Management System to create the study population. DND implemented a new national system in 1998 for the Regular Force and by 2002 the system started capturing data on Primary Reserve personnel.   At the time of the study income data was not available after 2007. Therefore, the study population included releases from January 1, 1998 to December 31, 2007. Four populations were derived from this data for the tables produced by Statistics Canada:

(1) 36,638 Regular Force veterans excluding re-enlisted members (42,591 releases less 5,953 who re-entered the CF and were still serving as of November 2009);

(2) 42,591 Regular Force veterans including re-enlisted members

(3) 12,018 Primary Reserve veterans excluding re-enlisted members (20,831 releases less 8,813 who re-entered the CF and were still serving as of November 2009); and

(4) 20,831 Primary Reserve members including re-enlisted members.

The first group, the Regular Force veterans excluding re-enlisted members is the subject of this report.

Various client status groupings were studied by merging VAC administrative data into the income data set. The types of clients are as of March 2009:

- NVC clients (VAC clients who used programs under the New Veterans Charter including Disability Awards,[30] Rehabilitation, Earnings Loss, Career Transition Services, Canadian Forces Income Support and Health Insurance);
- DP clients (VAC clients in receipt of Disability Pension but not NVC programs); and
- Non-clients (veterans not using any VAC programs).

SERVICE AND DEMOGRAPHIC VARIABLES

The following variables were derived from the DND Human Resources Management System data:

- Age at release derived from date of birth;
- Gender;
- Length of service derived from enrollment year and release dates;
- Release type (involuntary, medical, voluntary, retirement age and service complete);
- Release year;
- Rank at release (senior officer, junior officer, subordinate officer, senior NCM, junior NCM, private and recruit);
- Branch (Army, Navy, Air Force) and;
- Province of residence at release.

The tax data provided province of residence as of December 31, 2007.

RECORD LINKAGE

The study population data were record linked to the general family file (T1FF) tax records data from 1997 to 2007 using the social insurance numbers (SIN) contained on both datasets. The T1FF data cover all persons who completed a T1 tax return for the year of reference or who received Canada Child Tax Benefits (CCTB), their non-filing spouses (including wage and salary information from the T4 file), their non-filing children identified from three sources (the CCTB file, the births files, and an historical file) and filing children who reported the same address as their parent. Development of the small area family data is based on the census family concept. The census family includes parent(s) and children living at the same address and persons not in census families.[31]

The following income indicators were included in this report:

1. Total income and earnings expressed in 2007 constant dollars;
2. Income from following sources: wage, self-employment, investment and government transfers expressed in 2007 constant dollars (excludes VAC Disability Benefits and includes a small amount of VAC Earnings Loss benefits);
3. Rates of receipt of Employment Insurance (EI) and Social Assistance (SA) or GIS;
4. Prevalence of low income using the Statistics Canada before-tax LIM that establishes a threshold income each year by family size; and
5. Share of Veteran income to family income.

Since the time period covered includes multiple years of income data, all income amounts were expressed in 2007 constant dollars. Low-Income Measures (LIMs) are a relative measure of low income. LIMs are a fixed percentage (50%) of adjusted median family income where *adjusted* indicates that economies of scales have been taken into account. A census family is considered to be low-income when their income is below the Low-Income Measure (LIM) for their family type and size. As the thresholds are adjusted each year no inflation adjustment is required.

Transfers received from the VAC Disability Benefits Program would not be included in the T1FF data as both disability pensions and awards including related special awards such as attendance allowance are non-taxable and need not be reported to the Canada Revenue Agency. However, earnings loss paid by VAC would be included as earnings.

Results

The majority of the 36,638 Regular Force veterans in the study population released at age 35 and older (61%). This population was predominately male but 12% were female. Almost half had served 20 years or more making them eligible for a CF Superannuation annuity. In the first part of the release period, the number of releases was generally between 3,300 and 3,600 each year but increased to over 4,000 in 2006 and to almost 5,000 in 2007. Over half of the population released voluntarily (56%), 24% released for medical reasons, 7% had completed their service term, 6% had reached retirement age and 6% released involuntarily. Over half released as junior and senior non-commissioned members (58%), 16% released as recruits, 8% as senior officers, 7% as junior officers, 7% as privates and 4% as subordinate officers. Half of the population released from the Army, 29% from the Navy, 17% from the Air Force and for 5% the data was missing. Over half of the population enrolled in the 1970s and 80's. Over half of the population released in either Ontario and Quebec (51%), 20% in Atlantic Canada, 13% in Alberta, 9% in British Columbia and the remainder in other provinces and territories including a few who released in other countries.

The characteristics of VAC clients and non-clients differed in many ways. Both NVC clients and Disability Pension (DP) clients were more likely than non clients to be older, to have served for longer periods of time, released for medical reasons, released at higher ranks, and released from the Army than non-clients. Over three-quarters of both NVC and DP clients were aged 35 and older at release compared to half of non-clients. More than half of both NVC and DP clients served for 20 years or more, compared with less than half of non-clients. Over half of both NVC and DP clients were medically released compared to just 9% of non-clients. Over 90% of both NVC and DP clients released at the junior NCM rank or above compared to 70% of non-clients.

There were also important differences between NVC clients and DP clients. DP clients tended to be older and have served for longer periods of time than NVC clients. Some 86% of DP clients were aged 35 and older at release compared to 77% of NVC clients and 70% of DP clients served for 20 years or more, compared with 58% of NVC clients.

Of the entire cohort, 92% had income tax records on the Statistics Canada income dataset for the release year. The match rates for the release year were higher for clients than non clients: 97% for NVC clients; 95% for DP clients; and 90% for non clients. As the match rates decline with each year following release, the analysis of post-release income focused mainly on veterans who reported income in the release year and each of the first three years post release (n=21,436).

Average income in the year prior to release was $62,300 in 2007 constant dollars (Figure 22.1). Average total income increased in the release year to over $80,000 and then declined in the first year post release to less than $60,000. Total income then steadily increased over the nine years post-release and eventually surpassed pre-release income but not until after six years post-release.

The spike in total income in the release year was mainly due to other income which included severance pay, which is based on years of service.[32] The reduction in average post-release income was mainly due to a decline in earnings income. In the first year post-release, the average pension income (mainly CF Superannuation) was $19,500 and this remained fairly stable over the remaining years. Government transfer income which includes Old Age Security and Canada Pension Plan also increased post-release from $600 to $1,700. Over the longer-term, rising earnings eventually resulted in post-release income greater than pre-release income.

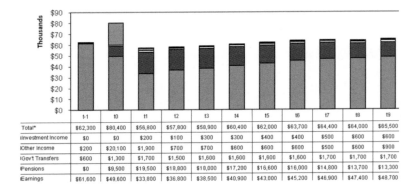

	t-1	t0	t1	t2	t3	t4	t5	t6	t7	t8	t9
Total*	$62,300	$80,400	$56,800	$57,800	$58,900	$60,400	$62,000	$63,700	$64,400	$64,000	$65,500
Investment Income	$0	$0	$200	$100	$300	$300	$400	$400	$500	$600	$600
Other Income	$200	$20,100	$1,900	$700	$700	$600	$600	$600	$500	$600	$900
Gov't Transfers	$600	$1,300	$1,700	$1,500	$1,600	$1,600	$1,600	$1,600	$1,700	$1,700	$1,700
Pensions	$0	$9,500	$19,500	$18,800	$18,000	$17,200	$16,600	$16,000	$14,800	$13,700	$13,300
Earnings	$61,600	$49,600	$33,800	$36,800	$38,500	$40,900	$43,000	$45,200	$46,900	$47,400	$48,700

Note: Total income is the before tax income of the veteran expressed in 2007 constant dollars. It includes income from taxable market income (including VAC Earnings Loss Benefits) and government transfers but does not include non-taxable VAC Disability Benefits.

Figure 22.1:Total averageincome by source and year.

The highest prevalence of receipt of Employment Insurance (EI), Social Assistance (SA) or Guaranteed Income Supplement (GIS) and low income was in the year following release (Figure 22.3). Prevalence rates for all three indicators declined each year after. The rate of receipt of EI spiked at 17% in the year following release and then declined to 12% and 15% in the following years. The prevalence of low household income was 4% in the pre-release year which is roughly comparable to the rate for the general population working full-time for a full year 6% for 2008.[33] After rising to almost 7% in the year following release, the prevalence fell to below the pre-release level by the seventh year post-release. Even at the peak of 7%, post-release rates of low income were lower than the rate of 13% for workers and 16% for non-workers in the overall general population. The rate of receipt of SA or GIS was relatively low compared to receipt of EI. In the year prior to release less than 1% of veterans were in receipt of social assistance. This grew to only 1.2% in the release year and the 1.3% in the year following release. The rate then declined and was again below 1% by the fifth year post-release.

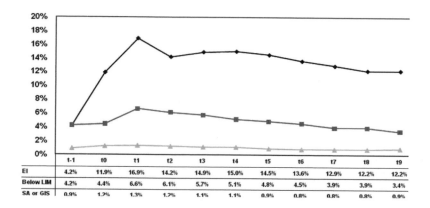

	t-1	t0	t1	t2	t3	t4	t5	t6	t7	t8	t9
EI	4.2%	11.9%	16.9%	14.2%	14.9%	15.0%	14.5%	13.6%	12.9%	12.2%	12.2%
Below LIM	4.2%	4.4%	6.6%	6.1%	5.7%	5.1%	4.8%	4.5%	3.9%	3.9%	3.4%
SA or GIS	0.9%	1.2%	1.3%	1.2%	1.1%	1.1%	0.9%	0.8%	0.8%	0.8%	0.9%

Note: Low income measure is before tax. EI in the year prior to release would include mainly those in receipt of maternity or paternity benefits.

Figure 22.2: Veterans in receipt of EI or SA/GIS and prevalence of low income by year.

VAC clients experienced the greatest declines in income post-release at 32% for NVC clients, 19% for DP clients compared to 4% for non clients (Figure 22.3). NVC clients and non clients were more likely to have ever received EI and to experience low income than DP clients. Given that 68% of the population were non-clients and non-clients were more likely to experience low income than the total population (17% compared to 15%), most veterans (75%) who experienced low income post-release were not clients of VAC.

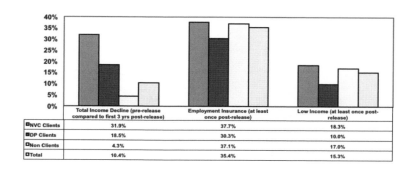

	Total Income Decline (pre-release compared to first 3 yrs post-release)	Employment Insurance (at least once post-release)	Low Income (at least once post-release)
NVC Clients	31.9%	37.7%	18.3%
DP Clients	18.5%	30.3%	10.0%
Non Clients	4.3%	37.1%	17.0%
Total	10.4%	35.4%	15.3%

Figure 22.3: Total Average Income, Employment Insurance and low income by client status.

Some groups with the highest declines were more likely to be VAC clients. For example, 75% of the medically released and 47% of those who served 10 to 19 years were VAC clients compared to the average of 32% (Table 22.1). These groups were also more likely to be NVC clients.

The groups with the highest rates of receipt of EI were less likely to be clients. For example, 60% of Newfoundland residents had received EI at least one year post-release, however 26% were VAC clients compared to the average of 32%. However, the reverse was not always true. For example veterans released as senior officers had the lowest EI rate but were also less likely to be VAC clients.

Those released at age 15 to 19 experienced the highest rate of low income at 41%, however less than 1% were VAC clients compared to 32% of the entire population. Those released involuntarily experienced the second highest rate of low income post-release. However, this group was less likely to be VAC clients than the average for the entire population. Also, since 68% were non-clients and 17% of non-clients experienced low income, there are many veterans experiencing low income who receive no benefits from VAC.

Population	% of Pop	Change	% Clients
Income Change (pre-release year compared to average first 3 yrs post-release) -10%			
Increase			
Subordinate Officers	4%	+27%	4%
Recruits	16%	+1%	6%
Sask. resident	2%	+1%	21%
Largest Declines			
Females	12%	-30%	32%
Medically released	24%	-29%	75%
Served 10 to 19 yrs	14%	-21%	47%
Employment Insurance (at least once post-release) 35%			
Lowest Rates			
Senior Officers	8%	8%	27%
Aged 55+ at release	5%	15%	39%
Reached Retirement Age	6%	15%	31%
Highest Rates			
Newfoundland resident	2%	60%	26%
Privates	7%	59%	10%
Recruits	16%	58%	6%
Low Income (at least once post-release) 15%			
Lowest Rates			
Aged 55+ at release	5%	1%	39%
Aged 50 to 54 at release	8%	2%	41%
Reached Retirement Age	6%	2%	31%
Highest Rates			
Aged 15-19 at release	4%	41%	0.5%
Involuntarily released	6%	37%	12%
Recruits	16%	35%	6%

Table 22.1: Income Change,Employment Insurance and low income and reach.

CONCLUSION

Non VAC clients accounted for the majority (68%) of the Regular Force veteran study population. Overall, the post-release income of Regular Force veterans (not including the impact of VAC programs) declined by 10% compared to their income during service. Females experienced the greatest decline in income (30%), followed by the medically released (29%) while subordinate officers experienced an increase in income (27%). While 15% had ever experienced low income post-release, for those released at the youngest age group (15 to 19) and involuntary releases, this rate was more than double. VAC clients had experienced greater declines in income post-release than non clients. Post-release, veterans on average experience a decline in income. VAC programs reach the groups with the largest declines. Small numbers of veterans experience low income. Unfortunately, most low income veterans are not clients of VAC.

[1]M.B. MacLean, L. Van Til, J.M. Thompson, D. Pedlar, A. Poirier, J. Adams, S. Hartigan, and K. Sudom, *Life After Service Study: Data Collection Methodology for The Income Study and The Transition to Civilian Life Survey*, veterans Affairs Canada Research Directorate Technical Report, April 29, 2010:79.

[2]"Veteran" is defined as former CF personnel. Re-enlisted are personnel who released from the CF and subsequently re-enlisted and were still serving as of November 2009.

[3]Public Health Agency of Canada, "What makes Canadians Healthy or Unhealthy?" *The National Health Forum*, accessed May 5, 2010, http://www.phac-aspc.gc.ca/ph-sp/determinants/determinants-eng.php#income.

[4]Federal, Provincial and Territorial Advisory Committee on Population Health, "Toward a Healthy Future: Second Report on the Health of Canadians" (prepared for, the Meeting of Ministers of Health, Charlottetown, P.E.I., September 1999).

[5]J.A. Macinko, L. Shi, B. Starfield, and J.T. Jr. Wulu, "Income inequality and health: a critical review of the literature," *Med Care Res Rev* 60, No.4 (2003): 407-52.

[6]D. Raphael, J. Macdonald, R. Colman, R. Labonte, K. Hayward, and R. Torgerson, "Researching Income and Income Distribution as Determinants of Health in Canada: Gaps between Theoretical Knowledge, Research Practice, and Policy Implication," *Health Policy* 72 (2005): 217-232.

[7]N. Kondo, G. Sembajwe, I. Kawachi, R.M. van Dam, S.V. Subramanian, and Z. Yamagata, "Income inequality, mortality, and self rated health: meta-analysis of multilevel studies," *BMJ* 339, B4471(2009): 339.

[8]Heather M. Orpana, Louise Lemyre, and Ronald Gravel, "Income and psychological distress: The role of the social environment," *Statistics Canada Health Reports*20, 1, Catalogue 82-003-XWE (2009): 21-28.

[9]H.M. Orpana, L. Lemyre, and S. Kelly, "Do stressors explain the association between income and declines in self-rated health? A longitudinal analysis of the National Population Health Survey," *International Journal of Behavioral Medicine* 14, 1 (2007):40-47.

[10]Heather M. Orpana, Louise Lemyre, and Ronald Gravel, "Income and psychological distress: The role of the social environment," *Statistics Canada Health Reports* 20, 1, Catalogue 82-003-XWE (2009): 21-28.

[11]Psychological distress is characterized by anxiety or a depressed mood, and may indicate more serious disorders such as clinical depression.

[12]Standing Committee on National Defence and Veterans Affairs, *Moving forward: A Strategic Plan for Quality of Life Improvements in the Canadian Forces*, National Defence, (1998).

[13]Standing Committee on National Defence and Veterans Affairs,*2000 Annual Report to the Standing Committee on National Defence and Veterans Affairs on quality of life in the Canadian Forces*, National Defence, (2000).

[14]J. Park, "A profile of the Canadian Forces. Statistics Canada catalogue 75-001-X," *Perspectives*(2008):17-30.

15##J. Park, "A profile of the Canadian Forces. Statistics Canada catalogue 75-001-X," *Perspectives*(2008):17-30.

[16]J. Coulthard and J. Dunn, *Canadian Forces spousal/partner employment and income project: research framework and methodology*, DGMPRA Technical Memorandum, 2009.

[17]Margaret C. Harrell, Nelson Lim, Laura Werber Castaneda and Daniela Golinelli. *Working Around the Military: Challenges to Military Spouse Employment and Education*. Santa Monica, CA: RAND Corporation, 2004. http://www.rand.org/pubs/monographs/MG196.

[18]S. Truscott , *Military spousal employment and loss of income*. Operational Research and Analysis, Directorate of Social and Economic Analysis, ORA Project 712, 1995.

[19]K. Sudom and S. Dursun, *The relationship study: qualitative findings*. Department of National Defence, DRDC CORA Technical Report 2006-36, (2006).

[20]J.E.M. Ewins, *CF Household Survey*, Reaction Research Report 00-1. Director Human Resources Research and Evaluation, (2000).

[21]L. Malone, *War Veterans Allowance Program: An historical perspective - 1930 to 2009*. Veterans Affairs Canada internal report, (2009).

[22]Those who participated in the Rehabilitation Program but have been found to be Totally and Permanently Incapacitated for work may continue with extended earnings loss until age 65.

[23]Service-relationship in this context includes those with career ending conditions (medically released) eligible for the VAC Rehabilitation Program and those eligible for VAC Disability Benefits.

[24]V.W. Marshall, R.A. Matteo, and M.M. Mueller, *Canadian Forces clients of Veterans Affairs Canada: Employment status, career and retirement planning issues*. Report prepared for Veterans Affairs Canada,2000.

[25]R.T. Graves, "A comparative study of the life satisfaction of early retirement military officers," *Dissertation, Graduate Studies of Texas A&M University*, 2005, http://repository.tamu.edu/handle/1969.1/2581.

[26]M.A. Taylor, K.S. Shultz, P.E. Spiegel, R.F. Morrison, and J. Greene, "Occupational attachment and met expectations as predictors of retirement adjustment of naval officers," *Journal of Applied Social Psychology* 37, No.8 (2007):1697 1725.

[27]Includes 313,000 Regular Force Veterans (former personnel) and 279,000 Primary Reserve Veterans. Source: VAC Corporate Information System, 2009.

[28]Source: National Defence, *Report on Plans and Priorities* (2008-09). Includes approximately 68,000 Regular Force FTEs and 26,000 Primary Reserves (paid strength).

[29]The NVC clients are defined as those in receipt of at least one of the NVC programs (Disability Awards, Rehabilitation, Earnings Loss, Canadian Force Income Support, Health Insurance, and Career Transition Services).

[30]Includes veterans also in receipt of a disability pension.

[31]Statistics Canada, Annual Estimates for Census Families and Individuals (T1 Family File), accessed June 21, 2010, http://www.statcan.gc.ca/cgi-bin/imdb/p2SV.pl?Function=getSurvey&SDDS=4105&lang=en&db=IMDB&dbg=f&adm=8&dis=2, accessed 14 April 2011.

[32]Average other income in the release year was $3,740 for those with less than 10 years service, $10,056 for those with 10 to 19 years of service and $32,048 for those with 20 years of service or more.

[33]Source: Population below the before-tax LIM derived from the Statistics Canada Survey of Labour and Income Dynamics (SLID), 2008. SLID includes serving members and veterans. Note that the comparison covers differing time periods as SLID is a cross-sectional survey covering income for 2008 whereas the income data for this report is longitudinal in nature and as such the pre-release year includes income from 1997 to 2006.

CHAPTER 23

"Soldier On" The Construction, Deconstruction and Reconstruction of the Cyborg Soldier/Tactical Athlete

Stephanie Cork, MA Candidate, Queen's University

ABSTRACT

The contemporary soldier is argued to be "cyborged" by the emergent "postmodern war".[1] This hybridization occurs both in conflict overseas and on the homefront in another type of war, against ableist Canadian society. Analyzing the literal deconstruction and then reconstruction of the modern soldier after acquired disability, this research looks to further assert that the disabled body, a casualty of war, makes use of advanced biomedical innovations in the way of prosthetics to itself transcend essential humanness.[2] Using a sociological analysis of the construction of rehabilitation discourses, the researcher intends to place documented experiences of acquired disability along a spectrum of resiliency among casualties, specifically amputees. It becomes evident, through an analysis of literature, that some amputees embrace the way in which technology can improve their condition, from day-to-day activities to excellence within elite sport. Conversely there are also others who wish only to return to their former state. This piece looks to interrogate the social forces that act upon military bodies through the military discourses of the "tactical athlete" that often govern rehabilitation goals.[3]

"SOLDIER ON" THE CONSTRUCTION, DECONSTRUCTION AND RECONSTRUCTION OF THE CYBORG SOLDIER/TACTICAL ATHLETE

Pertti Joenniemi has aptly noted that, "...new and increasingly rich vocabularies are needed now that war exists as a plurality. Modernity has lost control in a dual sense: War is neither disappearing nor taking expected forms".[4] The difficulty in defining modern war demands an exploration of the conceptual paradigm deemed "postmodern war".[5] Its postmodern character distinguishes war, in the current era – by fragmentation, flexibility, and fluidity.[6] Modern warfare, Derek Gregory indicates, "...has become unfixed, its concepts un-moored" but it is more than a theoretical conception; "the new slipperiness has the most acutely material consequences".[7] Focusing on the life course of landmines, Gregory emphasizes how the vestiges of contemporary warfare remain long after the 'end' of the conflict itself. He explores the harsh reality of aftermath, where both soldiers and civilians are still harmed by technologies of, "...'slow violence'" such as, "...landmines, cluster bombs and other unexploded ordnance".[8] Bodies, in this context, are painted as a "political concept/space" as ethereal subjects marred by the remnants of war.[9] Emily Grabham uses the term "flagging" to refer to the scaring (physical and emotional) that remains long after the battles have been fought.[10] In this piece, the "flagged" bodies are military casualties who have lost limbs and must cope with that loss long after their term of service ends. Paradoxically, it is new technologies that both maim and then reframe mangled bodies and tissues as advanced prosthetics flag the body technologically.

POSTHUMAN WAR, POSTMODERN BODIES

Science and technology in the postmodern world has fused a new, intimate interface between the human (soldier) and machine, as material and digital technologies erase fundamental separations in human life. One of the most significant innovations for organic corporeality is the emergence of cybernetics.[11] Advanced cybernetic interface on military fronts to curb the loss of life and limb; troops are, "cyborged" into "... advanced systems of sensing and surveillance from air and space platforms, systems of information management, and weapons systems revolving around pilotless aircraft, robotic vehicles and precision-guided weapons".[12] The postmodern mechanization of war establishes the reality of the 'cyborg' soldier.[13] This soldiering body, Christina Masters argues, holds significant potential: "Neither old nor new, neither worldly nor out-of-this-world, neither entirely man nor machine, the cyborg soldier represents the, 'juncture of ideals, metals, chemicals, and people that makes weapons of computers and computers of weapons and soldiers'".[14] Donna Haraway's *Cyborg Manifesto* uses the "ironic political myth" of the cyborg body to emphasize the degree to which the modern human form is integrated into the mechanical and digital world.[15] Haraway argues that this immersion into new technologies that serve as extensions of self, has created, "hybrid[s] of machine and organism," in other words, 'cyborgs'.[16] Haraway extends the cyborg trope to the everyday lives of everyone in the postmodern world. However, no other forms embody such a trope, as directly as soldiering bodies within the modern military establishment. While technology expands human potential and increases human control, the cyborg image also stirs fears and uncertainty as technology is increasingly wired into our everyday lives.[17] Cyborg bodies can thus be viewed as bodies that challenge stringent conceptions of corporeal limitations.[18] Furthermore, modern soldiers, unlike civilians, are constructed as cyborgs in a dual-fashion. Primarily they are heavily armed for combat with the latest technological innovations. However, as Chris Hables Gray emphasizes, "technology has rendered human bodies in war incredibly vulnerable even as it has integrated them into cyborgian (human-machine) weapon systems".[19] That vulnerability is flagged in the body living with acquired disability that is 'cyborged' with modern prosthetics to overcome the costs of war. It is this simultaneous strength and vulnerability that characterizes the dialectic of the cyborg soldier, a body under constant stress. The story of the modern soldier is therefore characterized by these cyborg elements; understood as the visceral material reality of contemporary warfare. The disabled soldiering body becomes a prime example of the integration of advanced technologies into a unique lived experience, both within and beyond the fronts of "postmodern" conflicts.[20] External prosthetic technologies, such as planes, tanks and ships protect and destroy the human form, whereas bionic and static prosthetic technologies are provided to injured veterans, in an attempt to augment fallible flesh.[21]

The disabled body, itself, is often described as being in conflict, "...visually repulsive; helpless; pathetic; dependent; too independent; plucky, brave and courageous; bitter, with chips on [their] shoulders; evil (the 'twisted mind in a twisted body'); mentally retarded; endowed with mystical powers; and much else".[22] Therefore, there are many spaces throughout historic and contemporary societies where these bodies have been relegated to the margins. The same was true of sport until technology ushered in cyborg corporeality, creating new possibilities for athletes with physical limitations. The biographies of Parlympians Oscar Pistorius and Aimee Mullins, who each hold coveted spaces in mainstream society, demonstrate this transformation.[23] Pistorius is the celebrity focus in a number of Nike commercials, and Mullins is an actor, activist and model, appearing on the runway for Alexander McQueen and in print and live-media advertisements for Kenneth Cole New York.[24] These normalized performances demonstrate the ability of such deviant bodies to both transgress and conform to standardized binaries of ability/disability. These performances often receive the label of 'supercrip,' which denotes the extreme examples of near 'superhuman' abilities showcased by bodies considered disabled. It is this level of extreme ability, which gives them acceptance within the mainstream. However, what becomes clear, when comparing the supercrip with more typical experiences of disability, is that cases such as Pistorius and Mullins are by no means standard. Ronald J. Berger has emphasized that: "The 'supercrip' athlete is often derided as a figure that is antithetical to the interests of people with disabilities".[25] This criticism lies within the consequences of normalizing disability, and the expectations then placed on all disabled bodies, when such exceptional cases are held up as the acceptable standard. As a result, even though the Paralympic Movement has enabled disabled bodies to step into the limelight of high performance sport, this is not an all-inclusive paradigm. The supercrip "... negotiates the terms under which some disabled athletes may enter" but this does not denote the full acceptance of all non-normative frames.[26] Such structures are, of course, not solely detrimental to the project of equal civil rights, but in the case of exceptional performances, there is a need to recognize the individual, and not generalize the experiences of one body to all bodies. Such exercises in tokenism do nothing to further the cause of different ability, and it is therefore important to recall that all disabled bodies experience daily life differently. Further, the dangerous realities of high-performance sport are not appealing to everyone, though some can, and will engage in such activities.[27] However, in the contemporary era, what has furthered the engagement of such bodies within the competitive arena is the proliferation of advanced prosthetic technologies.

The issue of *National Geographic* from January 2010 featured an article entitled "bi-on-ics." The focus of the piece was on recent advances made in bionic prosthetic technologies, which have truly redefined the limits of the body. The point was illustrated through a comparative timeline showing the advances made from the traditional arm prosthesis with only three movements, to the Proto 1, of seven, to the newest "Modular Prosthetic Limb," which allows up to twenty-two movements.[28] Other advancements showcased in the piece included the cochlear implant, bionic vision, skin and Power Knees; all pieces of equipment that far surpass historic examples of assistive technology.[29] Amanda Kitts, a woman featured in the article, is a test subject for the bionic arm technology that she only wishes to take home with her. The article poises her body as a idealized space for such technologies, stating, "Kitts is one of 'tomorrow's people,' a group whose missing or ruined body parts are being replaced by devices embedded in their nervous systems that respond to commands from their brain".[30] Kitts' missing right arm, lost in a car accident, is compared to the housing for "dangling telephone wires, severed from a handset" which can be mechanically restored.[31] The bionic arm magnifies existing nerve endings that were damaged in the accident, permitting Kitts' severed nerves to interact with the artificial limb. The prosthesis becomes an extension of her organic self: "I don't really think about it. I just move it".[32] Kitts' body showcases the reality of the modern cybernetic interface, replacing damaged organic materials (i.e. nerves and missing tissue) with the mechanical substitute. Though Kitts' narrative highlights a civilian experience, the article further demonstrates the potentialities of such innovations for returning casualties; the cyborg soldier on the homefront.[33] A second body highlighted in the piece, is that of Lieutenant Colonel Greg Gadson of the US Army, who is regaining function, "...by meshing my 43-year-old body with a machine..." specifically the new Power Knees.[34] This merger has enabled Gadson to do many activities a double above the knee (ATK) amputee could not have dreamt of only a few years ago. These cases vividly demonstrate the contemporary place of cyborg bodies. In the wake of postmodern war, military bodies are flagged with both the scars of battle and modern assistive prostheses.

The products showcased in National Geographic merely demonstrate the cybernetic side of contemporary technological innovation. However, there are a series of high-performance sport pieces, such as Swiss designer, Richard Stark's "Neptune" swim fin, and Össur's ATK and below the knees (BTK) prosthetics including the infamous Flex-Foot© worn by both South African sprinter Oscar Pistorius, and American Paralympic Athlete Aimee Mullins, that truly redefine ability.[35] These technologies allow the disabled body to enter arenas of performance that were impossible just a few years ago. Such technical innovations give truth to the claim that, "...missing a limb, needn't mean missing much," promising a, "life without limitations".[36] As Gray notes, such slogans engage with a posthuman future, as "...with the cyborg in general, the idea and the reality of the posthuman offers us an opportunity to do better than the human".[37] These modern prosthetic technologies illustrate how the disabled body can be poised within an era of postmodern war, as posthuman bodies. This construction demonstrates the emergence of the soldier as cyborg, not only as troops in the field, but as disabled veterans (and those who remain in service) that return to the homefront to wage war on their own fractured frames. These are of course optimistic success stories, and as "bi-on-ics" comes close, Todd Kuiken, a physician and biomedical engineer at the Rehabilitation Institute of Chicago, reminds us that these technologies "…are still crude, like a hammer, compared with the complexity of the human body. They can't hold a candle to Mother Nature".[38] With this further engagement of disabled bodies within the competitive arena, comes the Paralympic Games, which also showcase the shared histories of both high-performance sport and the military. The emergence of contemporary prostheses has permitted a further transgression of able/disabled boundaries of the Olympic and Paralympic Games.[39]

The inception of the Paralympic Games arose out of the influx of individuals with Spinal Cord Injury (SCI) on the homefront, in the wake of the Second World War.[40] Initially, individuals who survived the war had returned home with injury, only to live, "…two or three years at the utmost as a rule".[41] This was due to complications such as sepsis and pressure sores which, "…were considered inevitable" by medical professionals.[42] Involvement in sport was seen to dramatically increase the stability of individuals, enabling them to have access to a more normal and healthy lifestyle. Sir Ludwig Guttmann, a German neurosurgeon and the founder of the modern Paralympic Games, encouraged the involvement of sport within his rehabilitation program. Guttmann's belief was that sport would speed both physical and mental rehabilitation.[43] Initially entitled the Stoke Mandeville Games, after the facility where Guttmann labored; in the fall of 1944 patients competed in their first competitive event, wheelchair polo. Based on this early success, Guttmann declared in 1948 that the Stoke Mandeville Games would become truly international – the disabled equivalent of the Olympic Games. Guttmann's prediction was realized when, in 1960, the first Paralympic Games took place and Pope Paul XXIII declared that Guttmann was, "the de Coubertin[44] of the paralyzed!"[45] The historic success of involving sport within the rehabilitation of disabled bodies instigated a redefinition of the potentialities of life after acquired disability, and more specifically the perception of both a 'good' and long life for individuals after acquired disability. The military body, living with acquired disability in contemporary society is included in recreational and elite arenas, away from traditional rehabilitation programs. These goals and expectations of athleticism are embodied within the Canadian Soldier On/Sans Limites program, "A proactive, front-line, multi-disciplinary physical activity and sport based program designed to improve quality of life of ill and injured military personnel, still active and retired, and their families".[46] Many prominent service men and women have taken advantage of the program by taking part in a number of competitive sports ranging from sledge hockey to rally racing.

The intimate relationship between military bodies and sportsmen and women is no coincidence. The criteria for excellence in each arena are extremely similar as George Orwell noted in his short essay, "The Sporting Spirit." Sport, Orwell wrote, "is war minus the shooting".[47] The same values, which are paramount within the sporting arena, are also embodied within military life. This can be seen very clearly in the expectations of corporeal discipline. Michel Foucault deemed soldiers the 'docile body' in his work Discipline and Punish.[48] This moniker was not meant to express softness but rather the hard corporeal strength and discipline of the soldiering body. Foucault saw the abilities of soldiers, as superior to civilians, viewing military physicality as easily recognizable, "...an erect head, a taut stomach, broad shoulders, long arms, strong fingers, a small belly, thick thighs, slender legs and dry feet, because a man of such a figure could not fail to be agile and strong...".[49] Citing J. Montgommery's work from 1636, Foucault brings the timeless image of the military figure into the contemporary era. These strong bodies with precise and disciplined movements imply a mechanistic physicality, an articulation that relates directly to the reality of the modern cyborg soldier.[50] It is for this reason that the military amputee provides a centrally important link between sport and war. These bodies have become central to biomedical advances, being both strong and determined, and therefore, provide the medical establishment with a well-equipped group of willing test subjects.[51] Jeffrey Gambel, the chief of Walter Reed Veterans Hospital in Washington DC, notes that: "These are unique young adults who we regard as tactical athletes. They are otherwise healthy young people who have suffered devastating injuries. We use all of our energies to help them recover to do whatever they want to do".[52] Therefore these brave men and women serve as extremely dedicated and disciplined test subjects, and with the right access seem to be able to re-define what life after acquired disability is, and can become.[53] The soldiering body is 'flagged' therefore not only with the physical scars of war but with the intervention of the state.[54] Therefore, each damaged body is encouraged within the rehabilitation model to engage as deeply as possible. The ideal of the 'tactical athlete,' is most clearly supported within rehabilitation models that include a 'sports model' ideology, such as the programs offered by Soldier On/Sans Limites. This sports model itself,

> [e]merges out of innovations in orthopedic and rehabilitative medicine that emphasize the linkage of biomechanical interventions, life-style wellness education, and occupation or work specific training. Patients are often referred to as 'tactical athletes' and emphasis is laid on restoring them to their preinjury levels of functioning.[55]

Therefore, a look into the intersection of these social histories and the discourses that surround idealized corporeality helps to place the military body, with acquired disability, in the contemporary Canadian context. The loss of a limb, in combat, is now accompanied by expectations of full rehabilitation. This ideal, of the 'tactical athlete,' therefore resonates quite clearly with the close historical ties of sport and military, and further can be used as the seminal point on which to paint an emergent spectrum of resiliency.

CHAPTER 23

War after War: Tactical Athletes Soldier On

Thomas Hobbes' vision of the dark realities of daily life, as 'nasty brutish and short,' can be translated to his perception of war itself.[56] Hobbes highlights the tense, "tract of time" in which combatants are not poised at their weapons (or weapons systems) but rather are insitu, waiting for the enemy to attack.[57] This not only characterizes war on the front, but another kind of battle; one characterized by the biological, the social and the psychological. This is the battle, against the body, within rehabilitation as captured in a W5 special on Captain Trevor Greene: "My army comrades helped me win my war, and my rehab comrades helped me win my peace".[58] All casualties have an extremely difficult path to follow on the way back towards full health; however, it is the loss of a limb, in combat that can be seen as one of the most severe injuries encountered. Further, this physical loss can be accompanied not only by environmental barriers, but the emotional stress of loss and phantom pain. Research on military-specific experiences has documented a spectrum of resiliency, demonstrating the treacherous terrain that is navigated on the homefront.

Though advanced prosthetic technologies have enabled civilians to participate within a vast array of activities it is their military counterparts who are encouraged to climb a far steeper slope of high performance athleticism. A close reading of Seth Messinger's work demonstrates that not all patients will respond similarly to the situation now thrust upon them. His work illustrates the existence of a spectrum where some patients agree and fully embody the goal of tactical athletes, whereas others set down their own path. Messinger's comparison of two military bodies, Henry Bare and Ronald Eiger, from the Walter Reed Clinic, demonstrate two opposed responses to the loss of a limb. Messinger elaborates on the diversity of reaction based on each individual's involvement within the clinic, both in their rehabilitation programs and the interactions with other patients. Bare a patient in his mid-twenties, demonstrates a less content candidate, his experience characterized by what both Bare himself and Messinger identify as a sense of, "powerlessness".[59] This sense of lost agency, during the accident in the field, translated to a negative view around rehabilitation. In Bare's words, when citing the incident, "There was no need for it. It was a [local] holiday. We didn't have to be out".[60] These sentiments propelled an "aloof" disposition at the Walter Reed Clinic, with Bare rarely engaging in group activities. Even though his time there was defined as being extremely successful, exemplified in the mastery of his prosthetics; after leaving the clinic Bare reported that he did not often use his prosthetic arm, and chose to do very little on his own. Just before leaving the facility, he stated, "I don't feel like I can do anything anymore".[61] Though Bare would score quite highly on a scale measuring rehabilitative success from the position of the practitioners, it is clear that his inability to cope with his changed life circumstances left him with a sense of loss, for both the limb and the life he had once enjoyed. Bare's experiences with the ideal of the tactical athlete and his disavowal of the rehabilitation discourses would place him at one end of the spectrum marked by his a poor relationship with the 'sports model,' and therefore a disassociation with the ideal of tactical athlete. Bare's unwillingness to embrace his acquired disability left him with extremely negative views towards his future.

In stark contrast to Bare, lies Eiger's story, which can be seen as one of a more focused and contented patient. Eiger, a man in his thirties, with a wife and two children, remembers the experience – where his arm and part of his face were damaged – quite differently than Bare. Eiger describes one of his first thoughts in the aftermath of the incident, as, "'shit, there goes my golf game," demonstrating a different conception of agency over Bare.[62] Eiger's ability to recognize the changed state his body had now engaged in commanded agency in uncontrollable circumstances. This recognition of his changed body permitted him to engage in a more productive rehabilitation process, especially psychologically. Even though Eiger was more severely injured than Bare, he was able to engage in almost all areas he desired. Further, Bare left the army, whereas Eiger continued in service, avidly using his prosthetic limb. He was equally successful at learning how to maneuver his prosthetic devices in the clinic, but also spent most of his social time away from the clinic, and with his family. It is arguable that Eiger could have been more engaged in the process. However, he clearly engaged with external forces, due to the commitments that he had to his family. These choices further demonstrate the wide spectrum of coping strategies engaged with by military bodies. Eiger's attitude clearly denotes a much more positive outlook on his acquired disability. This separates Eiger from Bare, placing him on the opposite end of a spectrum of resiliency. These two cases therefore can scale along with further case studies. Of course, this spectrum is merely a heuristic device, meant to distinguish the differential reactions to life after acquired disability. The descriptions of these patients demonstrate this tone, though Messinger himself further admits to the complexity of their respective social, psychological and physical barriers. His piece reinforces sociological conception of an emergent 'spectrum of resiliency,' wherein individuals respond differently to their situation based on differential lifestyle factors.

CONCLUSION

The emphasis within this piece on the concept of postmodern war is meant to articulate the centrality of an historical materialist perspective. This analysis can be understood through the role of technological innovation that has brought on a new typology of warfare, both on the front, and at home. The cyborging of bodies, through war machines or prosthetic technology is leading to the proliferation of new breed of soldier, those that are simultaneously created and destroyed by this intimate technological interface.[63] This contemporary challenge comes with expectations from the therapeutic side of the military establishment. Therefore even though rehabilitation efforts are fraught with dialectical desires and expectations, of both the patient and the rehabilitation 'experts,' there is a shared desire for the reconstruction of bodies, to grasp at lost normalcy.[64] A 'spectrum of resiliency' emerges when engaging with independent narratives of rehabilitation. This spectrum is derived from the individual's compliance or denial of the standard of the 'tactical athlete.' Messinger's ethnographic work compares the intersection of personal, situational, environmental and social factors (though it requires further depth) that arguably contributed to these cases' acceptance or rejection of the program goals in their daily lives.[65] The subjects chosen for close analysis were similar, but as Messinger noted: "The similarities in their ages and injuries might suggest that they would have similar outcomes, but in fact while they both achieved good clinical outcomes, measured against other considerations they fared quite differently".[66] Messinger's study therefore emphasizes the unique experience each soldier can undertake even if injuries seem similar. It is this philosophy that governs the Soldier On/Sans Limites program; and it is this type of narrative analysis that requires replication in the Canadian context. MCpl Paul Franklin, as cited by Dr. Stéphanie A.H. Bélanger at the November 2010 Military and Veteran Health Research Forum, has been quoted stating, "I did not lose two legs to shred paper".[67] This sentiment further articulates the position in which so many casualties agree, in the sense that they wish, and deserve to engage in all activities; in a similar fashion to their pre-injury bodies; and finally, that there should be the appropriate government and societal support to do so.

[1]C. H. Gray, "Posthuman Soldiers in a Postmodern War," *Body & Society,* 9, 4 (2003): 216.

[2]D. Haraway, "A Cyborg Manifesto: Science, Technology, and Socialist-Feminism in the Late Twentieth Century," in Simians, *Cyborgs and Women: The Reinvention of Nature* (New York: Routledge, 1991), 149-181; T. Magdalinski, *Sport Technology and the Body* (Abingdon, Oxon, LN: Routledge, 2008); C. H. Gray, "Posthuman Soldiers in a Postmodern War," *Body & Society* 9, 4 (2003): 216; C. Masters, "Cyborg soldiers and militarised masculinities", *Eurozine* (2010), http://www.eurozine.com/articles/2010-05-20-masters-sv.html, accessed 26 May 2011.

[3]S. D. Messinger, "Incorporating the Prosthetic: Traumatic, Limb-Loss, Rehabilitation and Refigured Military Bodies," *Disability and Rehabilitation,* 1-5, (2009).

[4]P. Joenniemi, "Toward the End of War? Peeking Through the Gap," *Alternatives* 33 (2008); 235.

[5]D. Gregory, "War and Peace," *Transactions of the Institute of British Geographers* 35, 2 (2010); P. Joenniemi, "Toward the End of War? Peeking Through the Gap," *Alternatives* 33 (2008); 235.

[6]C. H. Gray, "Posthuman Soldiers in a Postmodern War," *Body & Society* 9, 4 (2003): 216; C.H. Gray, *Postmodern War* (New York, NY: Guilford Press, 1997).

[7]D. Gregory, "War and Peace," *Transactions of the Institute of British Geographers* 35, 2 (2010): 159.

[8]D. Gregory, "War and Peace," *Transactions of the Institute of British Geographers* 35, 2 (2010):157.

[9]T. Atkinson, *The Body* (Palgrave MacMillan, 2005), p.81; E. Grabham, "'Flagging' the Skin: Corporeal Nationalism and the Properties of Belonging," *Body & Society* 15 (2009).

[10]E. Grabham, "'Flagging' the Skin: Corporeal Nationalism and the Properties of Belonging," *Body & Society* 15 (2009), 64.

[11]A. Bousquet, *The scientific way of warfare: order and chaos on the battlefields of modernity* (London: Cambridge University Press, 2009), 122.

[12]D. Gregory, "War and Peace" *Transactions with the Institute of British Geographers.* 35 (2010): 160.

[13]C. Masters, "Cyborg soldiers and militarised masculinities", *Eurozine* (2010), http://www.eurozine.com/articles/2010-05-20-masters-sv.html, accessed 26 May 2011.

[14]C. Masters, "Cyborg soldiers and militarised masculinities", *Eurozine* (2010), http://www.eurozine.com/articles/2010-05-20-masters-sv.html, accessed 26 May 2011, p. 3.

[15]Donna Haraway, "A Cyborg Manifesto: Science, Technology, and Socialist-Feminism in the Late Twentieth Century," in *Simians, Cyborgs and Women: The Reinvention of Nature* (New York: Routledge, 1991), 149.

[16]Donna Haraway, "A Cyborg Manifesto: Science, Technology, and Socialist-Feminism in the Late Twentieth Century," in *Simians, Cyborgs and Women: The Reinvention of Nature* (New York: Routledge, 1991), 149.

[17]C. Masters, "Cyborg soldiers and militarised masculinities", Eurozine (2010), http://www.eurozine.com/articles/2010-05-20-masters-sv.html, accessed 26 May 2011; L.S. Watermeyer, "Cyborg anxiety: Oscar Pistorius and the boundaries of what it means to be human", *Disability & Society*, 23 2 (2008): 187-190.

[18]T. Magdalinski, *Sport Technology and the Body* (Abingdon, Oxon, LN: Routledge, 2009), 33.

[19]C. H. Gray, "Posthuman Soldiers in a Postmodern War," *Body & Society* 9, 4 (2003): 216; C.H. Gray, *Postmodern War* (New York, NY: Guilford Press, 1997), 216.

[20]C. H. Gray, "Posthuman Soldiers in a Postmodern War," *Body & Society* 9, 4 (2003): 216; C.H. Gray, *Postmodern War* (New York, NY: Guilford Press, 1997).; C. Masters, "Cyborg soldiers and militarised masculinities", *Eurozine* (2010), http://www.eurozine.com/articles/2010-05-20-masters-sv.html, accessed 26 May 2011; L.S. Watermeyer, "Cyborg anxiety: Oscar Pistorius and the boundaries of what it means to be human", *Disability & Society* 23 2 (2008): 187-190.

[21]C. H. Gray, "Posthuman Soldiers in a Postmodern War," *Body & Society* 9, 4 (2003): 216; C.H. Gray, *Postmodern War* (New York, NY: Guilford Press, 1997); D. Haraway, "A Cyborg Manifesto: Science, Technology, and Socialist-Feminism in the Late Twentieth Century", In *Simians, Cyborgs and Women: The Reinvention of Nature* (New York: Routledge , 1991), 149-181.

[22]A.T. Sutherland, *Disabled We Stand* (Bloomington, IN: Indiana University Press, 1981), 6.

[23]Oscar Pistorius (personal web page), *Oscar Pistorius*, 2011, Video, accessed from http://www.oscarpistorius.com/; TED (personal web page), *Speakers Aimee Mullins: Athlete and Actor*, Video, 2011, accessed from http://www.ted.com/speakers/aimee_mullins.html.

[24]Oscar Pistorius (personal web page), *Oscar Pistorius*, 2011, Video, accessed from http://www.oscarpistorius.com/; TED (personal web page), *Speakers Aimee Mullins: Athlete and Actor*, Video, 2011, accessed from http://www.ted.com/speakers/aimee_mullins.html.

[25]Ronald J. Berger, "Disability and the Dedicated Wheelchair Athlete: Beyond the "Supercrip" Critique," *Journal of Ethnography* 37, 6 (2008): 647.

[26]F. Moola and E. Norman, "Bladerunner or Boundary Runner?" in Oscar Pistorius, "Cyborg Transgressions, and Strategies of Containment", *Sport in Society, forthcoming* (2010), 6.

[27]T. Magdalinski, *Sport Technology and the Body* (Abingdon, Oxon, LN: Routledge, 2009), 271.

[28]J. Fischman, "Bi-on-ics," *National Geographic*, January (2010), 42-43.

[29]J. Fischman, "Bi-on-ics," *National Geographic*, January (2010), 42-43.

[30]J. Fischman, "Bi-on-ics," *National Geographic*, January (2010), 39.

[31]J. Fischman, "Bi-on-ics," *National Geographic*, January (2010), 39.

[32]J. Fischman, "Bi-on-ics," *National Geographic*, January (2010), 43.

[33]J. Fischman, "Bi-on-ics," *National Geographic*, January (2010), 53.

[34]J. Fischman, "Bi-on-ics," *National Geographic*, January (2010), 53.

[35]M.E. Moola and F. Norman, "Bladerunner or Boundary Runner?"; Pistorius, *Oscar Pistorius*; Össur, Americas, Video, 2010, accessed from http://www.ossur.com/?PageID=12501, accessed 10 November 2010.

[36]M. Aguilar, "Sea Legs." *Wired* (2010), 112; Össur (company website), Americas, http://www.ossur.com/?PageID=12501, accessed 10 November 2010

[37]C.H. Gray, *Postmodern War* (New York, NY: Guilford Press, 1997), 225.

[38]J. Fischman, "Bi-on-ics," *National Geographic*, January (2010), 53.

[39]Pistorius was banned from competing in the 2008 Beijing Olympic Games due to a perceived advantage of his prosthetic limbs. See J. Christie, "Bionic Supermen of Sport", *The Globe and Mail*, 24 November 2009; S. Bailey, *Athlete First: A History of the Paralympic Movement* (West Sussex, England: Wiley, 2008); T. Magdalinski, *Sport Technology and the Body* (Abingdon, Oxon, LN: Routledge, 2009), 271.

[40]S. Bailey, Athlete First: *A History of the Paralympic Movement* (West Sussex, England: Wiley, 2008); D. Legg, T. Fay, M.A., Hums and E. Wolff, "Examining the Inclusion of Wheelchair Exhibition Events within the Olympic Games 1984-2004", *European Sport Management Quarterly*, 9, 3 (2009): 247.

[41]S. Bailey, Athlete First: *A History of the Paralympic Movement* (West Sussex, England: Wiley, 2008), 15.

[42]S. Bailey, Athlete First: *A History of the Paralympic Movement* (West Sussex, England: Wiley, 2008), 15.

[43]S. Bailey, Athlete First: *A History of the Paralympic Movement* (West Sussex, England: Wiley, 2008), 15.

[44]Baron Pierre de Coubertin is credited with the original ideals of the Modern Olympic Games; R. Beamish and I. Ritchie, Fastest, *Highest, Strongest: A Critique of High-Performance Sport* (New York and London: Routledge Taylor & Francis Group, 2996), 49.

[45]S. Bailey, Athlete First: *A History of the Paralympic Movement* (West Sussex, England: Wiley, 2008), 24.

[46]G. Legacé, *Soldier On/Sans Limites*, Presentation at Military and Veteran Health Research Forum, Kingston, Ontario, November 2010.

[47]G. Orwell, *The Sporting Spirit* (London, GB: Tribune, 1945).

[48]M. Foucault, *Discipline and Punish: The Birth of the Prison* (New York: Pantheon, 1979).

[49]M. Foucault, *Discipline and Punish: The Birth of the Prison* (New York: Pantheon, 1979..

[50]C. Masters, "Cyborg soldiers and militarised masculinities", *Eurozine* (2010), http://www.eurozine.com/articles/2010-05-20-masters-sv.html, accessed 26 May 2011.

[51]Gray, "Posthuman Soldiers in a Postmodern War"; M. Janofsky, "Redefining the Front Lines in Reversing War's Toll," *New York Times*, 2004, accessed from http://www.nytimes.com/2004/06/21/us/redefining-the-front-lines-in-reversing-war-s-toll.html; C. Masters, "Cyborg soldiers and militarised masculinities", *Eurozine* (2010), http://www.eurozine.com/articles/2010-05-20-masters-sv.html, accessed 26 May 2011; S. D. Messinger, "Incorporating the Prosthetic: Traumatic, Limb-Loss, Rehabilitation and Refigured Military Bodies," *Disability and Rehabilitation*, 1-5, (2009).

[52]Janofsky, "Redefining the Front Lines in Reversing War's Toll".

[53]Foucault, *Discipline and Punish*.

[54]Grabham, "'Flagging' the Skin".

[55]S. D. Messinger, "Incorporating the Prosthetic: Traumatic, Limb-Loss, Rehabilitation and Refigured Military Bodies," *Disability and Rehabilitation*, 1-5, (2009), 1.

[56]T. Hobbes, *Leviathan* (London, GB: C.J. Clay and Sons Cambridge University Press Warehouse, 1904); E. Hobsbawm *Age of Extremes The Short Twentieth Century* 1914-1991 (London, GB: Great Britain Abacus A Division of Little, Brown and Company, 1995)

[57](Hobsbawm, 1995, p.226)

[58]Trevor Greene, "W5: Capt. Trevor Greene, In His Own Words," *CTV*, Video, 4 December 2010, accessed from http://www.ctv.ca/CTVNews/WFive/20101201/w5-trevor-greene-soldier-amazing-recovery-102101/

[59]S. D. Messinger, "Incorporating the Prosthetic: Traumatic, Limb-Loss, Rehabilitation and Refigured Military Bodies," *Disability and Rehabilitation*, 1-5, (2009), 2.

[60]S. D. Messinger, "Incorporating the Prosthetic: Traumatic, Limb-Loss, Rehabilitation and Refigured Military Bodies," *Disability and Rehabilitation*, 1-5, (2009).

[61]S. D. Messinger, "Incorporating the Prosthetic: Traumatic, Limb-Loss, Rehabilitation and Refigured Military Bodies," *Disability and Rehabilitation*, 1-5, (2009), 4.

[62]S. D. Messinger, "Incorporating the Prosthetic: Traumatic, Limb-Loss, Rehabilitation and Refigured Military Bodies," *Disability and Rehabilitation*, 1-5, (2009), 4.

[63]Gray, "Posthuman Soldiers in a Postmodern War".

[64]S. D. Messinger, "Incorporating the Prosthetic: Traumatic, Limb-Loss, Rehabilitation and Refigured Military Bodies," *Disability and Rehabilitation*, 1-5, (2009).

[65]S. D. Messinger, "Incorporating the Prosthetic: Traumatic, Limb-Loss, Rehabilitation and Refigured Military Bodies," *Disability and Rehabilitation*, 1-5, (2009).

[66]S. D. Messinger, "Incorporating the Prosthetic: Traumatic, Limb-Loss, Rehabilitation and Refigured Military Bodies," *Disability and Rehabilitation*, 1-5, (2009), 2.

[67]S. Bélanger, *Soldiering Identity*, Presentation at Military and Veteran Health Research Forum, Kingston, Ontario, November 2010.

CHAPTER 24

Life After Service Studies: A Program of Population Health Research at VAC

*Linda VanTil, DVM, MSc(Epi), MaryBeth MacLean, MA, James Thompson, MD, David Pedlar, PhD,
Research Directorate, Veterans Affairs Canada*

ABSTRACT

Life After Service Studies (LASS) is a program of population health research with the goal of improving the health of veterans in Canada, by understanding the ongoing effects of military service. The LASS program has several defining characteristics. The study population is Canadian veterans, defined as former CF (Regular or Reserve) personnel, regardless of their length of service, and regardless of their status as clients of VAC. Their health is broadly defined as physical, mental and social well-being, with and without illness and infirmity. LASS includes disability as the functional impact of barriers related to health impairment. Determinants of health include income, social support, education, employment, personal health practices, and access to health services. Changes that take place over the veterans' life course are important to consider in assessing the health of a veteran population. LASS partners are VAC, the Department of National Defence/Canadian Forces, and Statistics Canada. The first LASS projects are the Survey of Transition to Civilian Life, and the Income Study. The LASS program of research is a vital resource to provide the research evidence-base for future policy directions that will prepare VAC to meet veterans' health needs in the future.

LIFE AFTER SERVICE STUDIES: A PROGRAM OF POPULATION HEALTH RESEARCH AT VAC

"Life After Service Studies (LASS)" is a program of population health research with the goal of improving the health of veterans in Canada, by understanding the ongoing effects of military service. Population health "examines the interrelated conditions and factors that influence the health of populations over the life course, identifies systematic variations in their patterns of occurrence, and applies the resulting knowledge to develop and implement policies and actions to improve the health and well-being of those populations."[1]

BACKGROUND

Since WWI, Canadian research on the health of veterans has focused on those receiving care and benefits from VAC and its predecessor agencies. The most recent of these was the Veteran Care Needs Study in 1997-99. This study found that VAC clients had lower self-reported health than Canadians, and their use of prescription drugs, loss of mobility and need for personal help increased with age while their income decreased with age.[2] Further examination of post-Korean War male clients of VAC described them as economically vulnerable by career interruptions, or the nature and severity of their disability,[3] or low education,[4] and had more long-term health problems (especially back pain, arthritis, depression) than the general population.[5] These male peacekeeping clients of VAC had increased health care utilization if they had depression or PTSD,[6] but treatment was more likely for depression and alcohol problems that for PTSD.[7] The results of the Veteran Care Needs Study supported transformation of VAC programs over the past ten years, but this work did not include veterans who were not VAC clients.

Limiting research on clients presents a challenge for VAC, demonstrated by Figure 24.1. Of the estimated 750,000 veterans in Canada, 17% are VAC clients.[8] VAC clients are unlikely to be representative of Canadian veterans, since they have contacted VAC, been assessed as eligible for benefits, and are receiving financial, health and/or re-establishment benefits.

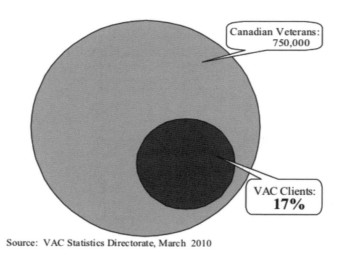

Source: VAC Statistics Directorate, March 2010

Figure 24.1: Canadian veteran population, 2010.

Canadian population health studies of veterans that include both VAC clients and non-clients are rare. There were five such studies over the past 30 years, described in Table 24.1. These studies have provided estimates of Canadian veteran populations, and other useful findings. However, these studies did not differentiate between veterans who are VAC clients or non-clients, and were not designed toprovide the data necessary to forecast participation rates for existing and future VAC programs.

Study	Population	Findings
Aging and Independence Survey, 1991	Phone survey of community-dwelling Canadians aged 45+ (n=20,000). War veteran identifier (n=1,948).	War Veterans and non-veterans had similar rates of self-reported general health. War Veterans were more likely to be married and had higher rates of disability and activity limitations than non-veterans.[19]
General Social Survey (c6), 1991	Phone survey of community-dwelling Canadians aged 15+ (n=12,000). War veteran identifier if age 50+ (n=672).	War Veterans and non-veterans had similar rates of self-reported general health, and likelihood of being married. War Veterans had higher rates education and of activity limitations than non-veterans.[20]
Gulf War Veterans, 1997	Mail survey 6 years after conflict, using DND HR files: n= 3,113 CF with GW service (73% RR); n= 3,439 CF without GW service (controls 60% RR)	The deployed cohort (still-serving and released) had a higher prevalence of ill health than the control group, including psychoneurological dysfunction and musculoskeletal complaints; symptoms of chronic fatigue, anxiety, PTSD and respiratory diseases.[21]
Canadian Persian Gulf Cohort Study, 2003	9 year follow-up record linkage n= 5,117 CF with GW service (deployed); n= 6,093 CF without GW service (control)	No significantly different mortality and cancer incidence between the deployed and control cohorts (cohorts include both still-serving and released). Mortality risk from all causes 50% lower for the military cohorts compared to the general population.[22]
CCHS (c2.1), 2003	Phone survey of community-dwelling Canadians aged 15+ (81% RR); war veteran identifier if age 65+ (n=2,742); post-Korean War veteran identifier if age 18+ (n=3,281).	Veterans more often reported arthritis, activity limitation, and asthma than the general population, however Veterans more often reported lower levels of life stress and higher rates of influenza vaccination.[23]

Table 24.1: Population health studies of Canadian vetern, prior to 2010.

LASS PROGRAM OF RESEARCH

Starting in 2010, VAC began a program of population health research called "Life After Service Studies". The goal of LASS is to improve the health of veterans in Canada, by understanding the ongoing effects of military service. The program of research requires multiple studies to answer questions such as:

- How healthy are veterans?
- How does their health change over time?
- How does their health compare to Canadians?
- How does the health of clients compare to other veterans?
- How does the health of deployed compare to not deployed?
- What opportunities can support the health of veterans?

The LASS program has several defining characteristics. The study population is Canadian veterans, defined as former Canadian Forces Regular or Reserve personnel,[9] regardless of their length of service. The study population includes both veterans who are VAC clients, and non-clients. Their health is broadly defined as physical, mental and social well-being, with and without illness and infirmity.[10] LASS includes disability as the functional impact of barriers related to health impairment. LASS determinants of health include income, social support, education, employment, personal health practices, and access to health services. Changes that take place in over the veterans' life course are important to consider in assessing the health of a Veteran population. The framework of core concepts is further described in another report.[11] Most LASS projects are a partnership between Veterans Affairs Canada, the Department of National Defence/Canadian Forces, and Statistics Canada.

CURRENT LASS STUDIES

Several LASS projects are currently underway. The LASS Survey of Transition to Civilian Life (STCL) was a telephone survey of over 3,000 Regular Force veterans released from 1998 to 2007. Details of the methodology are described by MacLean *et al* (2010).[12] The survey content is based on the Health Indicator Framework[13] to address the major research questions of re-establishment, program reach, and unmet needs. For the first time, differences between veterans who are VAC clients compared to non-clients were quantified. In STCL, 28% of clients had excellent or very good perceived health, compared to 70% of non-clients; similar discrepancies were found for back problems (64% vs. 30%), arthritis (45% vs. 13%), depression or anxiety (39% vs. 11%), and a difficult adjustment to civilian life for 42% of STCL clients compared to 17% of STCL non-clients.[14]

The LASS Income Study was a database linkage study of 40,000 veterans released from 1998 to 2007. Details of the methodology are described by MacLean *et al* (2010).[15] The study examined their pre- and post-release income. Regular Force veterans in the study experienced declines in income from pre- to post-release of 4% for non-clients, and larger declines of 22% for VAC clients. 17% of non-clients had experienced low household incomes at least one year post-release, compared to 12% of clients.[16]

The Canadian Forces Cancer and Mortality Study[17] is a broader study of both still-serving and released military personnel enrolled between 1972 and 2007. This study is a database linkage to Canadian mortality and cancer data. The study is led by the Department of National Defence, and will provide findings that will inform the LASS program of research.

FUTURE LASS STUDIES

Future LASS studies need to consider a longitudinal design to overcome the limitations of point-in-time cross-sectional studies, and to provide ongoing information on the life course dynamics of veterans. The first of these will be the Veteran Health Initiative within the *Canadian Longitudinal Study of Aging*.[18]

Building on the current LASS studies, VAC is planning to broaden its research by surveying both Reserve and Regular Force veterans, covering a longer release period, and increasing the scope of research questions. Taking a lifecourse approach, this program of research will help determine the impacts of military service on family members and set the stage for ongoing follow up of VAC clients and non-clients. Researchers are invited to participate in development of future studies and analysis of existing studies.

Conclusion

By implementing a comprehensive population health research strategy, VAC will have the information needed on both the 17% of veterans who are VAC clients, and the 83% of Canadian veterans who are potential future clients. The ongoing nature of this research will furnish VAC with a clear picture to assess veteran health, and subsequently providing:

- The data to evaluate the effectiveness of existing programs;
- The evidence to modify programs to suit client needs; and
- The research evidence-base for future policy directions and VAC strategic planning.

The "Life After Service Studies" program of research is a vital resource to provide the research evidence-base for future policy directions that will prepare VAC to meet veterans' health needs in the future.

---

[1]Federal, Provincial and Territorial Advisory Committee on Population Health, *Toward a Healthy Future: Second Report on the Health of Canadians*. Prepared for the Meeting of Ministers of Health, Charlottetown, P.E.I., (September 1999), Cat. No: H39-468/1999E, http://www.phac-aspc.gc.ca/ph-sp/report-rapport/toward/pdf/toward_a_healthy_english.PDF, accessed 1 February 2011..

[2]Statistics Canada, *Veterans' Care needs Survey, Report on Findings*, Minister of Industry, 1998, Cat No: 89-554-XPE.

[3]V.M. Marshall, R.A. Matteo, M.M. Mueller, *Canadian Forces Clients of Veterans Affairs Canada*: Employment *Status, Career and Retirement Planning Issues*, Veterans Affairs Canada, (2000).

[4]V.M. Marshall, R.A. Matteo, *Canadian Forces Clients of Veterans Affairs Canada: Risk Factors for Post-Release Socioeconomic Wellbeing*, Veterans Affairs Canada, 2004.

[5]G.J.J. Asmundson, *VAC Canadian Forces Survey Analysis*, Report prepared for Veterans Affairs Canada, (2000).

[6]J. Elhai, D. Richardson and D. Pedlar, "Predictors of General Medical and Psychological Treatment Use Among a National Sample of Peacekeeping Veterans with Health Problems," *J Anxiety Disorders* 21, 4 (2006): 580-589.

[7]J. Yarvis, P. Bordnick, C. Spivey and D. Pedlar, "Subthreshold PTSD: a comparison of depression, alcohol and physical health problems in Canadian peacekeepers with different levels of traumatic stress," *Stress, Trauma & Crisis* 8, 2-3 (2005): 195-213.

[8]124,200 Veteran clients: VAC Statistics Directorate estimates for March 2010.

[9]New Veterans Charter, *Canadian Forces Members and Veterans Re-establishment and Compensation Act*, (2005), http://www2.parl.gc.ca/HousePublications/Publication.aspx?pub=bill&doc=C-45&parl=38&ses=1&language=E&File=143, accessed 1 February 2011.

[10]World Health Organization, "Preamble to the WHO Constitution as adopted by the International Health Conference." Presented to International Health Conference, New York, NY, June 19-22, 1946; signed on 22 July 1946 by the representatives of 61 States (Official Records of the World Health Organization, 2: 100) and entered into force on 7 April 1948.

[11]M.B. MacLean, L. Van Til, J.M. Thompson, D. Pedlar, A. Poirier, J. Adams, S. Hartigan and K. Sudom, *Life After Service Study: Data Collection Methodology for The Income Study and The Transition to Civilian Life Survey*, Veterans Affairs Canada Research Directorate Technical Report, (2010), 1-79.

[12]M.B. MacLean, L. Van Til, J.M. Thompson, D. Pedlar, A. Poirier, J. Adams, S. Hartigan and K. Sudom, *Life After Service Study: Data Collection Methodology for The Income Study and The Transition to Civilian Life Survey*, Veterans Affairs Canada Research Directorate Technical Report, (2010), 1-79.

[13]Statistics Canada, *Health Indicators*, Statistics Canada and the Canadian Institute for Health Information, (2008), Cat No: 82-221-XIE.

[14]J.M. Thompson, M.B. MacLean, L. Van Til, K. Sudom, J. Sweet, A. Poirier, J. Adams, V. Horton, C. Campbell, and D. Pedlar, *Survey on Transition to Civilian Life: Report on Regular Force Veterans*, Research Directorate, Veterans Affairs Canada,Charlottetown, and Director General Military Personnel Research and Analysis, Department of National Defence, (2011a), 1-103.

[15]M.B. MacLean, L. Van Til, J.M. Thompson, D. Pedlar, A. Poirier, J. Adams, S. Hartigan and K. Sudom, *Life After Service Study: Data Collection Methodology for The Income Study and The Transition to Civilian Life Survey*, Veterans Affairs Canada Research Directorate Technical Report, (2010), 1-79.

[16]M.B. MacLean, L. Van Til, J.M. Thompson, A. Poirier, J. Sweet, J. Adams, K. Sudom, C. Campbell, B. Murphy, C. Dionne and D. Pedlar, *Income Study: Regular Force Veteran Report*, Veterans Affairs Canada, Research Directorate and Department of National Defence, Director General Military Personnel Research and Analysis, 2011, 1-70.

[17]M. Carew, E. Rolland, J. Whitehead, C. Dubiniecki, L. Bogaert, J. Born, L. VanTil and J. Thompson, *Epidemiological Protocol for the Canadian Forces Cancer and Mortality Study*, Department of National Defence, CF Health Services Group and Veterans Affairs Canada, Research Directorate, (July 2010), 1-96.

[18]P. Raina, C. Wolfson, S.A. Kirkland, L.E. Griffith, M. Oremus, C. Patterson, H. Tuokko, D. Hogan, A. Wister, H. Payette, K. Brazil and H. Shannon, "The Canadian Longitudinal Study on Aging (CLSA)," *Canadian Journal on Aging* 28, 3 (2009): 221-229.

[19]M.B. MacLean, *Survey on Aging and Independence: Health and social variable comparison of veterens and non-veterens*, Veterans Affairs Canada 1996a, Statistics Unit, (October 1996).

[20]M.B. MacLean, *General Social Survey Cycle 6, 1991: Health and social variable comparison of veterens and non-veterens*, Veterans Affairs Canada 1996b, Statistics Unit, Corporate Planning Division, (November 1996).

[21]Goss Gilroy, *Health Study of Canadian Forces personnel involved in the 1991 conflict in the Persian Gulf*, Report prepared for Gulf War Illness Advisory Committee, Department of National Defence, (1998), http://www.forces.gc.ca/site/Reports/Health/study1_e.asp, accessed 1 February 2011.

[22]Statistics Canada, *Canadian Persian Gulf Cohort Study: Detailed Report*. Report prepared for the Gulf War Veterans Cohort Study Advisory Committee, Department of National Defence., (2005), http://www.forces.gc.ca/health/information/pdf/engraph/canadian_persian_war_detailed_report_e.pdf, accessed 1 February 2011.

[23]J.M. Thompson, J. Sweet and D. Pedlar, *Preliminary analysis of the CCHS 2.1 National Survey of the Health of Canadian Military Service Veterans*, Veterans Affairs Canada Data Report, (September 2008), 1-24.

.

CHAPTER 25

Results of a File Review of 350 Clients who have Participated in the Veterans Affairs Canada Rehabilitation Program, *New Veterans Charter Evaluation*

Marlee Franz, OT Reg (Ont), Occupational Therapist, External Health Professional

ABSTRACT

The New Veterans Charter (NVC) helps Canadian Forces (CF) veterans and families who face challenges to re-establishment created by disability or health problems. As part of a comprehensive evaluation of the NVC, a file review of 350 clients who participated in the Rehabilitation Program was conducted to provide an overall assessment of level of functioning and progress for clients. The sample population consisted of clients who entered the NVC Rehabilitation Program between April 1, 2006 and October 31, 2009 and participated in the program for at least six months. The analysis explicitly describes clients' level of functioning when they apply, the types of barriers identified, and if level of function changed as a result of services and interventions provided. The appropriateness of case plan actions, gaps that impact progress and differences among client groups (e.g. male/female, pre/post NVC, families or reservists) were addressed. On the whole, for the sample clients, the Rehabilitation Program provided appropriate services to address the needs of CF veterans that face challenges to re-establishment and allowed the majority to make overall progress with functioning and the attainment of suitable employment. This supports the overall desired outcome of the NVC to facilitate the transition from military to civilian life.

RESULTS OF A FILE REVIEW OF 350 CLIENTS WHO HAVE PARTICIPATED IN THE VETERANS AFFAIRS CANADA (VAC) REHABILITATION PROGRAM, *NEW VETERANS CHARTER EVALUATION*

The unique needs of the recently released Canadian Forces (CF) veterans and their families have necessitated a change to the programs available to them. Previously, the focus was on the treatment of a pensioned condition and not the broader focus on the re-establishment of a veteran from the military to the civilian world. Clients require assistance to transition from a career in the CF to civilian employment. Some clients also require support to address injuries sustained during service including OSI, chronic pain and permanent disability.

NVC was implemented in 2006 to help Canadian Forces veterans and their families who face challenges to re-establishment in civilian life created by disability or health problems. The overall desired outcome of the NVC is to assist CF members, veterans and their families in making the successful transition from military to civilian life.

As part of a comprehensive evaluation of the NVC, a review of 350 Rehabilitation Program files was carried out to provide an overall assessment of the level of functioning and progress for clients who participated in the NVC Rehabilitation Program. The purpose of the Rehabilitation Program is to provide former CF members with a client-centred approach to restore physical, psychological, social and vocational functions to an optimal level following injury or illness. The following describes the four components of the Rehabilitation Program:

Medical Rehabilitation is designed to stabilize client functioning, *reduce* symptoms and *restore* basic physical and psychological functioning to the extent possible.

Psycho Social Rehabilitation is designed to *restore* independent functioning and *promote* adaptation to permanent disabilities that impact on daily activities at home and in the community.

Vocational Rehabilitation is designed to *identify* and *achieve* an appropriate *occupational goal* for a person with a physical or a mental health problem, given their state of health and the extent of their education, skills and experience.

Vocational Assistance applies to the medically released CF member and/or spouses of eligible veterans or survivors of deceased Regular Force veterans or members. It is a more streamlined process for persons who do not have a disability. The goal is to *find suitable employment*. A plan is developed and is based on the person's previous education, skills and experiences.[1]

SCOPE AND OBJECTIVES

The file review and analysis was done to provide an evaluation of progress for medical, psycho social and vocational rehabilitation and to assess outcomes for clients who participated in the Rehabilitation Program. The main focus of the file review and analysis describes:

i)   Level of functioning when clients apply to the Rehabilitation Program
ii)   The identified barriers for clients
iii) Change in clients' level of function as a result of interventions provided to clients
iv) If the case plan actions to address the barriers are appropriate
v)   Any gaps that impact on progress of a client's level of functioning
vi) Any differences among client groups (e.g. male/female, pre/post NVC, families or reservists)

Further elaboration on these issues determined the extent to which CF members, veterans and their families were successful at making the transition from military to civilian life. The results also provide further information on the extent to which NVC clients are experiencing optimal functional status, if they are participating actively in the civilian workforce, generally if they are able to meet basic needs, and if they can participate in or are integrated into their community as a result of access to comprehensive health care and rehabilitative services.

ESTABLISHED REHABILITATION FRAMEWORKS

A frame of reference (or framework) is a mechanism for linking theory to practice. This file review used principals from the Person, Environment and Occupation Model[2] as well as the International Classification of Functioning, Disability and Health (ICF) [3]to guide clinical thinking. The NVC Rehabilitation Program aims to restore physical and psychological, social and vocational functions. This recognized interplay among a client's bio-psycho-social and environmental elements is consistent with the Person, Environment, Occupation (PEO) Model put forth by Law, et al., (1996).[4]

The key messages from the PEO model are the *interaction* among several components, the effects and influences of the *environment* as well as *client-centered practice*, all of which are essential to the provision of services to clients served by the NVC programs. Figure 25.1a illustrates the convergence of the three spheres, referred to as "occupational performance", which is how a person manages their everyday activities (or life roles) at home, school/work or at play/leisure. For clients in the Rehabilitation Program, the goal is to re-establish from military life into civilian roles in the workplace, community and family.

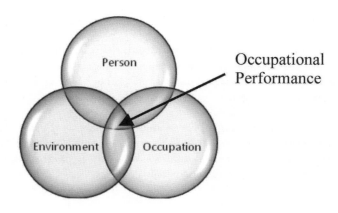

Figure 25.1a: Person, Environment, Occupation Model

Figure 25.1b illustrates that changes to occupational performance, or the performance of life roles, (convergence of spheres) is a consequence of variances in person, environment and occupation. For Rehabilitation Program clients, the effects of intervention (or case planning) to change a client's environment or occupation or the response of the person to adapt to a change in function can maximize occupational performance or "fit". This is essential to good client outcomes.

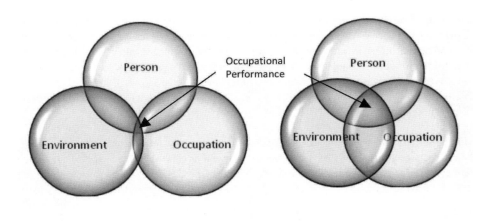

Minimal Fit   **Maximize Fit**

Figure 25.1b: Effects of Intervention to Change Occupational Performance

In this analysis, the ICF, Disability and Health (ICF) facilitated the classification and organization of the domains of the baseline assessment and the Rehabilitation Record of Decision (RROD) in determining barriers clients have in re-establishing from the military into a civilian world.

The ICF uses a representation of functioning and disability (Figure 25.2) to depict the interactive relationship between health conditions and contextual factors. Since an individual's functioning and disability occur in a context, the ICF includes consideration of environmental and personal factors.

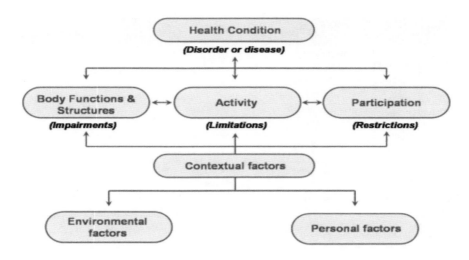

Figure 25.2: International Classification of Functioning, Disability and Health.

World Health Organization, 2001

As described by Stucki, G., *et al.*, (2007),[5] the ICF is based on a bio-psycho-social model. "Functioning" is made up of *"body functions and structures* and *activities* and *participation"* and is viewed in relation to the physical or mental health condition as well as personal and environmental factors ("contextual factors"). "Disability" (the decline or absence of "Function") includes impairments, limitations in activities and restrictions in participation.

POPULATION AND SAMPLING METHODOLOGY

The population for this file review consisted of clients who entered the Rehabilitation Program between April 1, 2006 and October 31, 2009 and participated in the program for at least six months. Table 25.1 illustrates how this population was then divided into the following seven mutually exclusive groups to allow for stratification of the sample.

	Stratified Population	% of Total Population	Weighted Average	Actual Sample
Veterans or Reservists with a completed rehabilitation plan.	486	15%	55	80
Veterans who released before 2006 with an active rehabilitation plan.	1,211	36%	128	97
Veterans who released after 2006 with an active rehabilitation plan.	849	28%	96	73
Reservists with an active rehabilitation plan.	146	5%	17	25
Survivors / Spouses with an active rehabilitation plan.	66	2%	7	25
Veterans or Reservists identified as TPI.	265	9%	30	25
Veterans or Reservists with a cancelled rehabilitation plan.	151	5%	17	25
Totals	3,084	100%	350	350

Table 25.1: Sample stratification.

As is normally used for health research, this was a descriptive sample which allows for analysis of the sample's characteristics and a comparison among groups but does not allow for results to be generalized to the entire client population. A random stratified sample of 350 clients was drawn which is approximately 10% of the total population and is the largest sample that could be reviewed within available resources.

It was determined that a minimum of 25 clients per stratified population was necessary to develop any conclusions about a specific group. As illustrated in the table above, using a weighted average to draw the sample would have resulted in some stratified groups with less than 25 sample clients. As a result, a minimum of 25 clients was randomly selected for the Reservists, Survivor/Spouse, TPI and Cancelled groups. Additionally, given the intent of the review was to assess achievement of outcomes, the sample of clients who have completed a rehabilitation plan was increased to 80 clients, thus reducing the sample size for veterans with an active rehabilitation plan to 97 clients before 2006 and 73 after 2006. Finally, in order to perform some gender based analysis a quota of female veterans was drawn from those who participated in the Rehabilitation Program. In total, 61 female veterans and 25 survivors/spouses were randomly selected as part of this review, which was 86/350 or 25% of the file sampl

LIMITATIONS

The findings from the client files were summarized for review using these established rehabilitation frameworks. The following documentation was reviewed: client notes, case plans, assessment reports and progress updates prepared by VAC staff as well as reports prepared by health and vocational rehabilitation professionals. All information reviewed for each file was taken from the Client Service Delivery Network (CSDN) system and from VAC's regional files.

The analysis was limited to information that was documented in CSDN or on the client's file. VAC policy and business process dictate that all relevant information to complete this analysis should be stored in these areas. If information was not documented in CSDN or on the client's file it was not captured or commented on.

RESULTS

Level of Baseline Functioning. What do clients look like when they come to the Rehabilitation Program? Overall, the sample of clients reviewed presented to the Rehabilitation Program with a varied profile. The majority were married or common-law, had at least high school education and qualified for services through the "Rehabilitation Need" gateway. An exceptionally high proportion (83%) of sample clients reported pain at baseline functioning. Age ranges and length of service varied considerably. At least half of the sample clients self reported a significant mental health issue, a high stress level and presented with a type of OSI. The reasons these clients accessed the Rehabilitation Program were divided almost equally among the need for medical/psychosocial stabilization, the need for vocational rehabilitation and concurrent needs in medical/psychosocial and vocational areas.

As seen in Figure 25.3, approximately three quarters of the sample clients were injured at least 5 years or more before applying to the NVC. However it was noted that many of these injured members continued to serve while injured and were therefore supported by the Department of National Defence during this time.

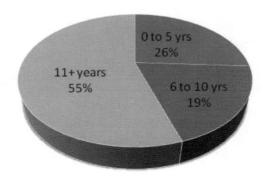

Figure 25.3: Injury date to application to the Rehabilitation Program.

Date of Release from the CF was used to look at how long it took for clients to access the Rehabilitation Program following release. Figure 25.4 demonstrates that approximately 1/3 of the clients accessed the Rehabilitation Program within the first year of their release. An additional 1/3 accessed services within 5 years of their release date with percentages dwindling the longer a client was released.

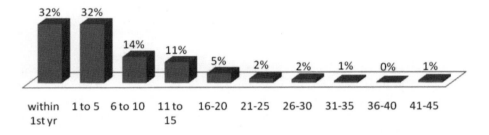

Figure 25.4: Number of years between leaving CF (release date) and applying to the Rehabilitation Program.

Of the sample clients, 60% of the clients (202 files) applying for the Rehabilitation Program had SDA service (Figure 25.5).

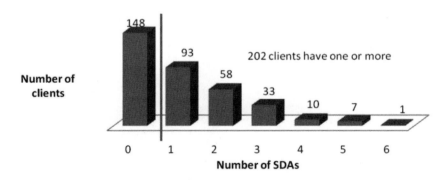

Figure 25.5: SDA service.

The most common areas for SDA service varied depending on service period and reflect the active areas of theatre during a client's career. Figure 25.6 highlights the most prevalent SDAs for clients in this sample.

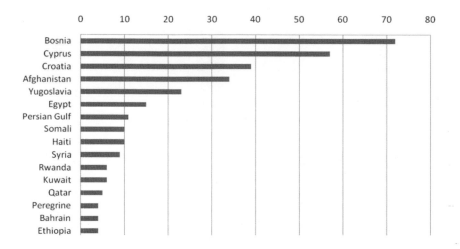

Figure 25.6: Most Prevalent Special Duty Areas for clients who applied to the Rehabilitation Program.

Based on the types of situations and conditions many clients are faced with when serving in an SDA, there is an assumption that there may be a higher percentage of mental health conditions for clients who serve in an SDA and that the number of cumulative SDAs may contribute to a higher incidence of mental health conditions. There is an affirmative relationship between having SDA service and a higher incidence of OSIs. However, for the sample clients, there was no correlation between the *number* of SDAs served and a *higher incidence* of OSIs. There was also no correlation for the sample clients between the *number of SDAs* served in and *number of barriers* to re-establishment.

Depicted in Figure 25.7, as a self-report, 57% of the clients in the sample reported only "Fair" or "Poor" Mental Health when accessing services. Similarly, half (51%) of the clients in the sample reported the degree of Stress in their lives as "Quite a bit" or "Extreme". A significantly high percentage (83%) of clients in the sample reported Pain upon initial presentation to the Rehabilitation Program with back/neck, lower extremities (knees, hips, ankles, and feet) and multiple sites accounting for 90% of the complaints.

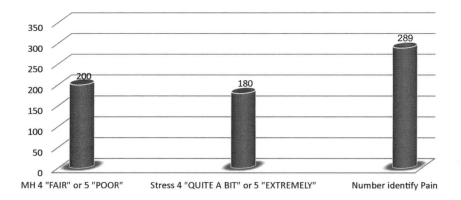

Figure 25.7: Self Report of Mental Health, Stress and Pain upon access to the NVC.

BARRIERS TO RE-ESTABLISHMENT

A barrier to re-establishment in civilian life is that which limits or prevents the client's reasonable performance of his/her roles in the workplace, home or community. Barriers are assessed by rating a client's ability to perform a standard set of roles. This includes rating the client's ability to manage personal care such as eating, bathing, dressing, grooming, etc., rating a client's ability to perform life skills such as housekeeping, meal preparation, shopping, laundry, to use transportation and the telephone, to manage money and mange personal relationships and finally, assessing the impact of the health condition on family roles, community participation and employability.

Table 25.2 outlines the barriers to re-establishment and provides examples of difficulties as well as the corresponding Level of Functioning and Barrier Severity Rating: [6]

Barrier to Re-establishment	Level of Functioning	Barrier Severity Rating
ADL Difficulties with personal care e.g. washing, dressing, eating, toileting, taking medications, etc.	Independent, Occasional assistance, Minimal supervision	Minimal
	Intermittent daily supervision/assistance	Moderate
	Significant supervision/assistance , Total care	Severe
IADL Difficulties with activities around the house or in the community e.g. Housekeeping, preparing meals, shopping, banking, etc.	Independent, Occasional assistance, Minimal supervision	Minimal
	Intermittent daily supervision/assistance	Moderate
	Significant supervision/assistance, Total care	Severe
Family Roles Difficulty performing role as a spouse /partner or parent	Performs role as spouse/partner 80-100% of the time.	Minimal
	Performs role as spouse/partner 40-60% of the time.	Moderate
	Performs role as spouse/partner less than 40 % of the time.	Severe
Community Participation Difficulties participating in hobbies, leisure or community activities	Participates in activities at least once a week.	Minimal
	Participates in activities at least once or twice a month.	Moderate
	Unable to or does not participate in activities	Severe
Vocation Roles Difficulties with work	Work ready but difficulty finding a job.	Minimal
	a) Not work ready OR b) Has difficulties on the job or in keeping a job	Moderate
	Unable to work	Severe
Physical Environment Physical environment limits ability to do personal care, activities around the house or family roles	Physical environment limits performance of ADL IADL or Family Roles less than 20% of the time.	Minimal
	Physical environment limits performance of ADL IADL or Family Roles 40-60 % of the time.	Moderate
	Physical environment limits performance of ADL IADL or Family Roles less than 60-100% of the time.	Severe

Table 25.2: Quantifying barriers to re-establishment.

As seen in Figure 25.8, 92% of the clients presented to the Rehabilitation Program with a barrier in vocational roles meaning they were unable to work, had difficulty on the job or keeping a job or were not work ready. These numbers mean that 322/350 clients were not participating in the civilian workforce in an optimal way. The next most common barriers that clients presented with were in IADL, Community

Participation and Family Roles. These clients had difficulties completing activities around the house or in the community, participating in hobbies, leisure or community activities and difficulty performing their role as a spouse/partner or parent. Barriers in the Physical Environment and performance of personal care (ADL) had the least representation at 14% each.

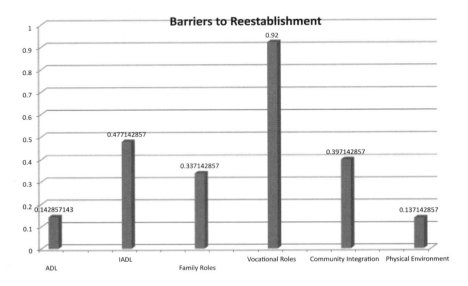

Figure 25.8: Barriers to re-establishment.

This next graph (Figure 25.9) illustrates that for the sample clients, there was no correlation between the *number* of barriers and the ability to make *overall progress*.

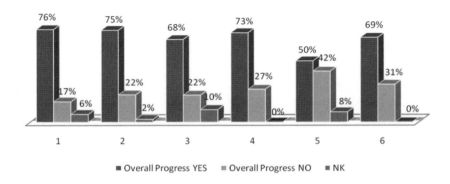

Figure 25.9: Overall progress and number of barriers.

This speaks to client variability. The ability of a client to re-establish will depend on the interplay among their health condition, activity level and participation as well as environmental/personal factors and is *not dependent on the numbers of barriers*. This finding highlighted that there is no correlation between the number of barriers a client presents with and the ability to make overall progress. Some clients present with multiple barriers and still make overall progress while other clients that present with only one barrier may have significant difficulty with transition to the civilian world.

The ability to make progress to overcome or compensate for a barrier(s) depends on a variety of factors, including the extent of the *health condition* (e.g. "mild", "moderate" or "severe" PTSD or depression), the impact of the *impairment(s)* in body functions (e.g. attention, memory, ability to concentrate) , body structures (e.g. mild brain damage from a blast injury) and how this affects the client's activities (problem solving, using transportation, caring for self, managing finances) and participation in their life roles(i.e., as worker, spouse/partner, parent, coach, friend, hobbyist, etc). Contextual factors, made up of environmental and personal factors also play a part in this client's successful reintegration.

Clients' Change in Level of Functioning as a Result of the Rehabilitation Program

For many sample client files, disengagement or a time two assessment was not consistently done so change in functioning over time was often difficult to gauge. Much of this information was not known.

Of the clients reviewed that self reported fair to poor mental health, the majority had a case plan to address mental health in some capacity. In addition, the support from a partner/spouse or at least high school education both positively influenced the clients' success in the Rehabilitation Program.

Of the six barriers to re-establishment, a very high percentage (92%) of the sample clients identified a vocational barrier upon entry into the Rehabilitation Program. More than one quarter of these clients improved and half showed no change in barrier, meaning they were at least maintained. The next most common barriers noted were in IADL, Community Participation and Family Roles. Improvements in these three types of barriers were negligible which means that when an IADL, Community or Family Barrier was identified, limited change occurred as a result of being on the Rehabilitation Program. IADL needs were usually addressed by providing funding for house and grounds keeping and Community and Family interactions were generally not well described at baseline so reassessment of these needs was difficult and imprecise. ADL and Physical Environment barriers were only noted infrequently and limited improvements in these domains were noted.

For the sample clients that are still participating in the Rehabilitation Program (220 clients with an active rehabilitation plan), most have been receiving services for about 18-24 months. For approximately half of this group, it was not anticipated that they would meet medical, psycho social and/or vocational goals in the next six to twelve months. They will likely require ongoing long term support to maximize function and/or prevent deterioration.

For clients who did not make overall progress, Case Managers have access to the Interdisciplinary Team (IDT), Regional Rehabilitation Officer (RRO) and Regional Mental Health Officer (RMHO) functional specialists for input and direction. However all of these services appeared to be under-utilized for the sample files. Similarly, for clients in the sample that applied to the Rehabilitation Program with an OSI, linkages to the OSI clinics and OSISS programs were done in less than half the files.

Of the entire sample of 350 files, 71% of the clients made overall progress after receiving services through the Rehabilitation Program. With the exception of the Cancelled group, all subgroups, including a comparison of Male/Female files, showed a similar trend of overall progress and had in common that they were married, had at least high school education and made progress with vocational barriers. As would be expected, the Completed group showed a higher level of overall progress when compared to the entire sample and these clients had approximately twice the success rate (75%) with vocational barriers when compared to the overall sample (38%).

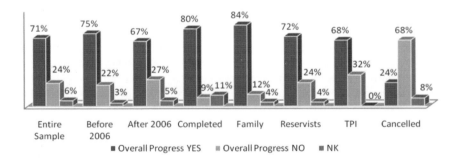

Figure 25.10: Overall progress – comparison among groups.

The majority of clients with an active rehabilitation plan also demonstrated overall progress, although to a lesser degree since active case planning is still in progress.

APPROPRIATENESS OF CASE PLAN ACTIONS TO ADDRESS THE BARRIERS

Case plan actions to address client barriers were not well articulated in many of the sample files as there was no consistent reporting format and in some cases, the case plan addressed an issue (e.g. improve sleep quality) that did not directly relate to one of the six barriers. It was difficult to measure change in a client's functioning or the effect of a case plan action as although there usually was a Case Manager assessment to measure baseline functioning, there is no established tool to capture change in the impact or severity of a barrier at a second point in time.

Case plan documentation ranged in degree of detail and measurability and although the "SMART" (Specific, Measureable, Attainable, Realistic and Timely) format for goal setting was aspired to, very few goals were crafted in this manner. The frequency that a case plan was monitored also varied with some files being updated regularly (biweekly, monthly) and other having large gaps of up to a year or more between entries. It was therefore a challenge to measure if case plan actions were appropriate to address a client's specified barrier(s) as there were many variables that made this unrealistic to measure.

GAPS THAT IMPACT PROGRESS OF A CLIENT'S FUNCTIONING

"Gaps" are interpreted largely as something the NVC Rehabilitation Program failed to do or provide. Gaps in services were identified in 124/350 (35%) of the files. Of these 124 files, management in Head Office was notified in 70 cases or 56% of the time for further actioning. The most common reasons were the lack of active case management or follow-up and the need for more frequent case monitoring to track issues and move case plans forward.

Of the remaining 54 files, several clients did not appear ready to address mental health issues or ready to accept recommendations such as attending counselling or seeking treatment. All issues were not resolved or addressed. However, limited community resources often prevented further action or the client did not wish to pursue. There appeared to be several instances where there was limited access to appropriate professionals to address long standing mental health conditions such as depression. In many communities there was limited access to psychiatrists for mental health medication and symptom management.

Referencing the ICF model, this lack of progress can be attributed in part to the severity of health condition and its impact on functioning as well as to contextual factors, such as a client's motivation, level of support to engage in case planning, a client's physical location where access to appropriate professionals and services may be limited, or travel to access services is impractical.

Re-establishment with respect to Family Roles and Community Participation was not as well understood. There was a lack of descriptive documentation in the baseline assessment so reassessment of these needs and of a client's functioning was difficult and imprecise. A well defined tool to describe and quantify these barriers in a meaningful way is necessary.

Following participation in or completion of a SISIP sponsored vocational retraining program, most of the clients presented to the VAC Rehabilitation Program with a vocational barrier. This suggests that the chosen field for retraining was not suitable given a client's pensioned or awarded condition(s). This overlap of resources could be better addressed.

For sample clients who self reported a significant mental health issue or concern ("fair" or "poor" mental health), almost one third did not have a specific case plan to address mental health functioning. Access to VAC functional specialists (RRO, RMHO) to assist Case Managers with case planning for files that are not progressing or for clients who present with mental health challenges was largely underutilized.

Similarly, for clients that presented to the Rehabilitation Program with a moderate to severe barrier in Family Roles, less than half had case plans that identified the need for family services. Many families experience the impact of the challenges that come with the transition from military to civilian life. When re-establishment is complicated by significant physical and/or mental health conditions or involuntary career loss, the family often needs support to endure and thrive in redefined roles. One possible explanation for this lower than expected number of case plans to address Family roles is that the clients often present with multiple issues, many which require stabilization. Further work with the family may not be considered until the client's main needs have been addressed.

DISCUSSION AND PROFESSIONAL PERSPECTIVE

Overall, the NVC Rehabilitation program provided suitable services to meet the needs of released CF veterans in the file review. Sample clients presented with divergent psychosocial profiles and needs. Most sample clients identified a vocational barrier upon application to the Rehabilitation Program and case planning often addressed stabilization of medical and psychosocial needs and/or the restoration of functioning to identify and achieve appropriate occupational goals. Sample clients that completed the Rehabilitation Program had approximately twice the success rate with vocational barriers when compared to the whole sample. They were likely able to secure suitable gainful employment and re-establish in a work environment.

An exceptionally high proportion of clients identify pain when they access the Rehabilitation Program. Pain does not appear to be well understood, addressed or consistently incorporated into case planning. The concept of a "pain clinic" or referral to a "pain specialist" appears to be ill-defined. Clinics vary in focus and treatment philosophy from a single consult with an anesthesiologist to a full assessment by "multidisciplinary" teams with various combinations of rehabilitation specialists (e.g. Occupational Therapist (OT,) Physiotherapist (PT), pharmacist, psychologist, recreation therapist, nurse, etc). There is also the community based approach of the Progressive Goal Attainment Program (PGAP). The waiting lists for consultation appointments and clinics are often lengthy (some over one year, depending on geographic location).

The influence of pain on a client's functioning is not well understood nor is its impact on a client's barriers. Further understanding and education to VAC staff and clients on the components, benefits and scope of a referral to address "pain" is essential to affect outcomes. There may be a need for a care path approach for the Case Manager to better understand the options available and the hierarchy of interventions that can be recommended. Overarching this is the need for local District Office pain resources as well as the need for an internal VAC specialist similar to the RRO or RMHO or even a designated VAC affiliated pain clinic (similar to the OSI clinic model).

A very interesting finding was that there was no correlation in the analysis between the number of barriers a client presents with and the ability to make overall progress. This finding supports the PEO Model and ICF, Disability and Health framework principals that it is the INTERPLAY of factors and not necessarily the types of factors or numbers of factors that influence how a client is functioning and ultimately how they have success with re-establishment into civilian life.

The ability to make progress to overcome or compensate for barriers depends on a variety of factors including the extent of the health condition, the *impact* of impairments on a client's *activities* and *participation* in their life roles such as worker, spouse/partner, parent, coach, friend, hobbyist, etc.

Good client outcomes can be achieved when case plan goals are collaborative and client-centered and communication is clear regarding the anticipated outcomes and what the Case Manager and client can effect change on through the Rehabilitation Program. As the Rehabilitation Program is holistic, all the barriers that have been identified should be clarified, actioned and monitored. Perhaps, based on the initial screening of the client and the completion of the RROD, several barriers may appear to exist but in reality, they are only barriers if the client feels they are. Perhaps a self rating system could be considered so the client can identify real (and not externally perceived) barriers.

In reviewing files that showed overall progress, when the desired outcomes were specific and measurable and established resources available, clients appeared to be serviced expediently and progress and outcomes could be quantified. Also, when clients were given specific responsibilities to action, outcomes were more easily measured. A suggestion for further improvement may be to look at case planning care paths (such as a flow chart) to assist with decision making to ensure all relevant avenues are explored.

To improve on the things that are done well in the Rehabilitation Program, perhaps a "Best Practice" or "Things that are Working" forum can be established for the sharing of best practices from successful cases with good outcomes or as a resource for ideas on challenging cases. As the expanded and enhanced case management role is key to the delivery of the Rehabilitation Program ongoing professional development will be pivotal to keep abreast of evolving roles, scopes and obligations and innovations.

FINAL CONCLUSIONS

Overall, 71% of the sample clients reviewed made overall progress after receiving services through the Rehabilitation Program. Clients who showed overall progress tended to be married, have at least high school education and demonstrated the greatest improvements in vocational barriers. Most of the client who completed the Rehabilitation Program made overall progress and 75% of them demonstrated improvements in their vocational barriers compared to 38% of the overall sample. For clients with an active rehabilitation plan, while not to the same degree, the majority made overall progress to date and are still working on active case plan issues.

Overall, for the sample clients, the Rehabilitation Program provided appropriate services to address the needs of CF veterans that face challenges to re-establishment and allowed the majority to make overall progress with functioning and the attainment of suitable employment. This supports the overall desired outcome of the New Veterans Charter to facilitate the transition from military to civilian life.

[1]Veterans Affairs Canada, *New Veterans Charter Evaluation Plan* (Canada: VAC, 2009), 1-10.

[2]Law, M., Cooper, B., Strong, B., Stewart, D., Rigby, P., and Letts, L. "The Person-Environment-Occupation Model: A Transactive Approach to Occupational Performance," *Canadian Journal of Occupational Therapy* 63, 1 (1996): 9-23.

[3]World Health Organization, *International Classification of Functioning, Disability and Health* (Geneva: WHO, 2001).

[4]Law, M., Cooper, B., Strong, B., Stewart, D., Rigby, P., and Letts, L. "The Person-Environment-Occupation Model: A Transactive Approach to Occupational Performance," *Canadian Journal of Occupational Therapy* 63, 1 (1996).

[5]Stucki, G., Cieza, A., and Melvin, J., "The International Classification of Functioning, Disability and Health: A Unifying Model for the Conceptual Description of the Rehabilitation Strategy," *J Rehabil Med* 39 (2007): 279-285.

[6]Veterans Affairs Canada, *Rehabilitation Program Eligibility Decision Making Guide* (Canada: VAC, 2006), Annex A.

CHAPTER 26

The Canadian Primary Care Sentinel Surveillance Network: Opportunities for Collaboration on Veteran's Health[1]

Richard Birtwhistle, MD, MSC, FCFP, CPCSSN Chair, Department of Family Medicine, Queen's University;
Anita Lambert-Lanning, MLS, The College Of Family Physicians of Canada;
The Canadian Primary Care Sentinel Surveillance Network

Abstract

The health of military veterans and their families is affected by the individual's military experience. There is evidence that veterans are at increased risk of a number of chronic diseases. In Canada, many of these veterans do not maintain contact with Veteran's Affairs Canada after they leave active duty and therefore are lost to follow-up. A potential collaboration with the Canadian Primary Care Sentinel Surveillance Network (CPCSSN) may be a way of providing longitudinal de-identified health information on military veterans. CPCSSN is a network of nine primary care practice based research networks (PCPBRN) in six provinces in Canada. Its aim is to have representation across the country in five years. Each PCPBRN recruits primary care physicians with electronic medical records to provide de-indentified patient health data on a quarterly basis to study chronic disease in Canada. CPCSSN has been funded by the Public Health Agency of Canada for five years as a way to collect longitudinal information on the development, management and outcomes of people with chronic disease. This paper describes CPCSSN and the methodological requirements for using de-identified primary care health data to study chronic disease in veterans and consideration of family health.

The Canadian Primary Care Sentinel Surveillance Network: Opportunities for Collaboration on Veteran's Health

There are approximately 593,800 veterans in Canada who served in operations other than WWII or the Korean War. Roughly 91% of these veterans are not clients of Veteran's Affairs Canada (VAC).[2] This leaves a large number of people with military service whose health status is unknown and lost to follow-up by VAC. Thompson *et al.* have conducted a cross sectional study of Canadian veterans and found that about 17% of veterans who were not clients of VAC had a difficult transition to civilian life and that most of those who had a clinically diagnosed chronic disease attributed it to their military service.[3] There is evidence from studies conducted in the United States,[4] and Australia,[5] that the health of veterans' may be different than that of the general population particularly in the prevalence of chronic disease. Little information exists concerning the state of veterans' health and their medical care in Canada. Filling this gap will provide valuable information for planning and prevention and for determining whether military service is a risk factor for the development of chronic disease.

The CPCSSN is a potential organization that could contribute to the understanding of veterans health.

The Canadian Primary Care Sentinel Surveillance Network

CPCSSN was established in 2008.[6] It is a network of nine PCPBRN across Canada. Each network has recruited family physicians from their region who use electronic medical records (EMR) in their practice. This study extracted de-identified patient health data from these EMR. Each PCPBRN has a director, full-time data manager and part-time research assistant. There are presently 140 family physician practices with approximately 132,000 patients contributing de-identified patient health information to a central repository on a quarterly basis. We extracted this data from seven different EMR products across the country. The extraction process has been developed as a unique application for each EMR system. The health information that we collect and integrate into a common database includes patient demographics such as age and sex, diagnosis or health condition, risk factors, laboratory results, procedures, referrals and medications prescribed. Although we collected data on all patients in the practice, we are focused on the following chronic conditions: chronic obstructive lung disease, dementia, depression, diabetes, epilepsy, hypertension, Parkinson's disease and osteoarthritis. Patient identifiers such as name, address and health card number were stripped from the data before the information left the practice site and each patient was given a unique CPCSSN number. The extracted data was cleaned at the regional network and then uploaded to the central repository. Data transmission is encrypted and highly secure. All data is stored at a secure site at Queen's University.

Veterans Health and the Life Cycle

Military service generally happens in early adulthood. There is increasing evidence that this experience, especially for those who served in a combat role, has effects that ripple long after the members are discharged back to civilian life. As an example, Ikin *et al.* found that Australian veterans from the Korean War had poorer health related and psychosocial quality of life than a comparable group of men with no exposure, and this continued late into life. They also found that veterans of lower rank or who had more combat exposure had lower quality of life.[7] There are calls for longitudinal studies of current veterans' health[8] and with these studies, CPCSSN would be able to follow veterans in practice over time. In the Canadian context, there are many veterans who served in peacekeeping roles in the Balkans and elsewhere as well as combat in Afghanistan. We have the opportunity to understand the effects on their health over time.

Chronic Disease in Veterans

A number of papers have described increase prevalence of chronic disease in veterans. These disorders and diseases include, but are not limited to, post-traumatic stress disorder (PTSD),[9] diabetes,[10] hypertension, depression, and chronic obstructive lung disease.[11] There is also evidence that military personnel and veterans have a higher degree of risk factors such as excessive smoking and alcohol consumption.[12] As well, former military personnel are at a greater risk of multiple co-morbidity and increased mortality rates.[13] There is an understood value, in following the health of this population, to try to understand the effects of military experience, particularly exposure to combat, on the development of disease.[14]

What about Veterans' Families?

A number of studies have demonstrated that partners and families of veterans can be at increased risk of disease or disorders, particularly those of veterans with mental health disorders like PTSD. Studies of Vietnam veterans' families in both the US and Australia showed increased prevalence of psychological disorders in partners of veterans and an increased risk of intimate partner violence (IPV).[15] There is also evidence that children of veterans may be at increased risk for emotional disorders especially when both parents have a mental illness.[16] There is increasing recognition that family physicians could play an important role in the care of veterans and their families but these physicians need to be better informed about the unique situations in which these families find themselves.[17]

Issues with doing Surveillance of Veteran's Health

There are a number of issues that would have to be addressed before developing a veterans 'cohort' surveillance study using primary care EMR data.

1. Researched estimates on the number of veterans found in a single family practice are limited. There are about 32,000 family physicians across the country, which, if veterans were evenly distributed in practices, would result in about 20 veterans per practice. However there may be clustering of veterans in certain cities. Estimates of sample size are required.
2. In order to identify those who served in the military who qualify, a standard definition of 'veteran' would be required.
3. A unique field within the EMR database would have to be developed to record veteran status or prior military service. Most EMRs have a field for occupation and this would be a useful place for this data so that it is recorded in a routine way.
4. Estimating the denominator for the veteran population to calculate rates would be a requirement for such studies.

5. A method for identifying veteran's family members would need to be developed.
6. CPCSSN is a surveillance network that does not require patient consent to collect de-identified patient data. This approach to the use of de-identified patient health data has been approved by Research Ethics Boards (REB) across the country. Collecting information about veterans in the sentinel practice should fall under the same ethics and privacy requirements because no individual Veteran would be identified however, this would need to have REB approval. Collecting de identified health data on family members would need REB approval and may require explicit consent.

SUMMARY

Despite recent concern about confidentiality of health issues of Canadian veterans,[18] CPCSSN's de-identified approach to data collection could support the sensitive de-identified collection of data that could provide a unique window on this population in a sensitive manner. It is important for the military to understand health issues for military veterans throughout their life courses because there is evidence that these individuals are at increased risk of chronic disease, which may or may not be related to their occupational exposures. It may also be useful to track family health as it relates to the increased rate of IPV and emotional health problems in both partners and children. CPCSSN could provide a unique way of following veteran's health over time and provide data on chronic diseases for this group that is otherwise unavailable.

[1]We would like to acknowledge the assistance of Dr. James Thompson who reviewed the paper and our co-investigators in CPCSSN Drs. Marshall Godwin, Wayne Putnam, Marie-Thérèse Lussier, Michelle Griever, Moira Stewart, Alan Katz, Neil Drummond and Donna Manca.

[2]J.M. Thompson et al., Survey on Transition to Civilian Life: Report on Regular Force veterens, Research Directorate; Veterans Affairs Canada, and Director General Military Personnel Research and Analysis; Department of National Defence, 04 January 2011, 18.

[3]J.M. Thompson et al., Survey on Transition to Civilian Life: Report on Regular Force veterens, Research Directorate; Veterans Affairs Canada, and Director General Military Personnel Research and Analysis; Department of National Defence, 04 January 2011, 9.

[4]B.I. O'Toole, S.V. Catts, S. Outram, K.R. Pierse, J. Cockburn, "Factors associated with civilian mortality in Australian Vietnam veterans three decades after the war," Mil Med. 175, 2 (2010): 88-95; J.A. Boscarino, "Posttraumatic stress disorder and mortality among U.S. Army veterans 30 years after military service," Annals Epidemiology 16, 4 (2006): 248-56.

[5]L.K. Richardson, B.C. Frueh, R. Acierno, "Prevalence estimates of combat-related post-traumatic stress disorder: critical review," Aust N Z J Psychiatry 44, 1 (2010): 4-19.

[6]R. Birtwhistle, K. Keshavjee, A. Lambert-Lanning, et al., "Building a pan-Canadian primary care sentinel surveillance network: initial development and moving forwar," J Am Board Fam Med 22, 4 (2009): 412-422.

[7]J.F. Ikin, M.R. Sim, D.P. McKenzie, K.W.A. Horsley, E.J. Wilson, W.K. Harrex, et al., "Life satisfaction and quality in Korean War veterans five decades after the war," Journal of Epidemiology and Community Health 63, 5 (2009): 359-365.

[8]S. Chatterjee, A. Spiro, L. King, D. King and E. Davison, "Research on Aging Military veterans lifespan Implications of Military Service," PTSD Research Quarterly 20, 3 (2009): 1-2.

[9]K. Ginzburg, T. Ein-Dor and Z. Solomon, "Comorbidity of posttraumatic stress disorder, anxiety and depression: A 20-year longitudinal study of war veterans," *Journal of Affective Disorders* 123, 1-3 (June 2010): 249-257.

[10]D.R. Miller, M.M. Safford, L.M. Pogach, "Who Has Diabetes? Best Estimates of Diabetes Prevalence in the Department of Veterans Affairs Based on Computerized Patient Data," *Diabetes Care* 27, 5 (2004): B10-B21.

[11]W. Yu, A. Ravelo, T. Wagner, C. Phibbs, A. Bhandari, S. Chen and P. Barnett, "Prevalence and Costs of Chronic Conditions in the VA Health Care System," *Medical Care Research and Review* 60, 3 (2004): 146S-167S.

[12]W.H. Thompson and S. St-Hilaire, "Prevalence of Chronic Obstructive Pulmonary Disease and Tobacco Use in Veterans at Boise Veterans Affairs Medical Centre," *Respiratory Care* 55, 5 (2010): 555-560.

[13]T.A. Lee *et al.*, "Mortality rate in veterans with multiple chronic conditions," *J Gen Intern Med* 22, 3 (2007): 403–407.

[14]A.C. Justice *et al.*, "Veterans Aging cohort study (VACS): overview and description," *Med Care* 44, 8 Suppl 2 (2006): S13–S24; K.B. Chesbrough, M.A. Ryan, P. Amoroso, J.R. Boyko, G.D. Gackstetter, T.I. Hooper, J.R. Riddle, G.C. Gray and the Millennium Cohort Group, "The millennium cohort study: a 21 year prospective cohort study of 140,000 military personnel," *Military Medicine* 167, 6 (2002): 483-88.

[15]H. Peach, "Australia's Vietnam Veterans--a review," *Australian family physician* 35, 8, (2006): 619-622.

[16]H. Peach, "Australia's Vietnam Veterans--a review," *Australian family physician* 35, 8, (2006): 620.

[17]R. Hinojosa, M.S. Hinojosa, K. Nelson and D. Nelson, "Veteran family reintegration, primary care needs and the benefit of the patient-centered medical home model," *J Amr Board Fam Med* 23, 6 (2010): 770-774.

[18]P.C. Hébert and B. Sibbald, "Protecting privacy of health information for those who serve and protect us," *CMAJ* 182, 17 (2010): E755, www.ncbi.nlm.nih.gov/pubmed/20961997, Epub 2010 Oct 20.

CHAPTER 27

From Military to Civilian Healthcare:
What are the Challenges for Healthcare Managers?

*Brenda J. Gamble, PhD and Olena Kapral, BHSc, Faculty of Health Sciences,
University of Ontario Institute of Technology*

ABSTRACT

Healthcare reform requires the implementation of interprofessional collaboration (IPC). Interprofessional teams (IPTs) include frontline providers (e.g., nurses, physiotherapists, doctors, physician assistants, etc.) who deliver direct patient care. However, a lack of management support has been identified as one of the key barriers to the implementation of IPTs. What are the views of managers on the skills/competencies needed to manage in the next five to ten years? Are the skills/competencies identified by managers those required to manage interprofessional teams? These are important questions for military healthcare managers who must navigate between the military and civilian environment, ensuring military personnel have access to healthcare services and programs. Canadian College of Health Leaders' members were surveyed between January and June 2010 to determine their views on the skills/competencies required to successfully manage in healthcare. Respondents identified the following skills/competencies: systems thinking; human resources; interpersonal and people skills; flexibility; change management; and communication skills. While CCHL respondents reported they were not directly managing IPTs, they are aware of the skills/competencies that support the implementation of IPC. Strategies to implement IPC must incorporate both top down and bottom up approaches with a clear understanding of how both managers and frontline workers can work together to facilitate the coordination of care.

FROM MILITARY TO CIVILIAN HEALTHCARE: WHAT ARE THE CHALLENGES FOR HEALTHCARE MANAGERS?

The Canadian Forces Health Services Group (CF H Svcs Gp) strives to ensure that the men and women who serve our country have access to high quality and safe healthcare services. The CF Surgeon General's report "Building On Our Strategy"[1] highlights key initiatives and achievements of the CF H Svcs Gp in providing healthcare services both abroad (e.g., Afghanistan) and at home. In fact, the CF H Svsc Gp is referred to as Canada's 14th healthcare system.[2] One strategy utilized by the CF H Svcs Gp is to liaise with a variety of organizations, healthcare professionals and administrative managers in the civilian sector (e.g., Health Canada, provincial regulatory bodies, scientific conferences, healthcare workers, training institutions, etc).[3] These partnerships serve a variety of purposes including (but not limited to) education/training, research and the delivery of services and programs. Essential to successful partnerships between the military and civilian sectors is an awareness of the existing challenges that are common and unique to both sectors.

One way to capture the perceived challenges and necessary skills/competencies within the civilian sector is to ask healthcare managers from across Canada about their views on these matters. The Canadian Institute of Health Research Team in Community Care and Health Human Resources (CIHR Team) collaborated with the Canadian College of Health Leaders (CCHL)[4] to conduct a national survey of CCHL members to determine their views on the skills/competencies that will be required to manage healthcare services successfully within the next five to ten years. CCHL is a national professional organization representing health leaders across Canada working in a variety of healthcare sub-sectors.

POLICY QUESTION

Healthcare reform requires the implementation of interprofessional care. Many jurisdictions both nationally and internationally[5] have identified interprofessional collaboration (IPC) as a top healthcare reform priority for the delivery of safe, coordinated and efficient patient centred care,[6] and as a means to enhance the working conditions of healthcare workers.[7] Interprofessional care is "the provision of comprehensive health services to patients by multiple health caregivers who work collaboratively to deliver quality care within and across settings".[8] For many observers, coordination across professional and organizational boundaries is seen as key to collaborative care (e.g., healthcare, social care and rehabilitation) in both the hospital and the community sectors.[9]

Healthcare service delivery is based on the efforts of a number of different healthcare workers who provide either direct patient services (e.g., assessment, monitoring, treatment, etc.) and/or indirect patient services (leadership, quality improvement, system coordination, etc.)[10] across a variety of healthcare sectors (e.g., community, primary care clinics, the home, emergency departments and hospitals). These healthcare workers include both regulated and non-regulated workers, as well as informal caregivers[11] working collaboratively on teams and/or individually to deliver services.

Healthcare managers, who are non-regulated healthcare workers with training and expertise in a wide range of both general and specialized skills (e.g., business, clinical, etc), are also an integral part of the healthcare workforce.[12] Although healthcare managers may not provide direct services, they work behind the line of care providing indirect services that facilitate health encounters between patients and other healthcare workers.[13] Managers play a very important role in hospitals and other health institutions in terms of structural, financing, planning and professional issues.[14] A central role played by healthcare managers is to facilitate change as healthcare delivery focuses on a model of patient centred care regardless of where services are delivered.

A number of barriers to the provision and delivery of interprofessional care have been identified including internal organizational barriers, cultural barriers, different management styles[15] and the division of authority between key stakeholders.[16] However, the lack of management support has been identified as one of the key barriers to the implementation of interprofessional collaboration.[17] According to Engel and Gursky (2003) "appropriate management practices will balance professional independence with interprofessional interdependence."[18] It would seem then, that managers can play a key role in breaking down a number of the barriers to interprofessional collaboration by facilitating the opportunity for healthcare workers to work in a collaborative manner in an environment that supports mutual respect for each healthcare worker's skills and knowledge.

What then are the views of managers on the skills/competencies necessary to manage in the next five to ten years? Are the skills/competencies identified by managers those required to manage interprofessional teams?

SURVEY OF CANADIAN COLLEGE OF HEALTH LEADERS CCHL MEMBERS

METHOD

As noted above, the CIHR Team partnered with the CCHL to conduct a national survey of all CCHL members (N=2984) including active members (n=2247), students (n=76), corporate memberships (n=338) and non-active members (i.e., honourary, retired, etc.) (n=323). Data was collected using a self-administered electronic questionnaire distributed by email using the survey software SurveyMonkey between January and June 2010. The CCHL sent an email invitation to all their members asking for their participation in the study. The invitation included the consent form and a link to the questionnaire. By clicking on the link to the questionnaire participants indicated their willingness to participate in the study. This English questionnaire included a total of 26 questions with items on employment characteristics (i.e., sector and type of work), clinical background, views on leadership skills (open-ended question) and demographic characteristics. The survey tool was constructed in collaboration with health administration educators/scholars from health administration programs at the undergraduate (Ryerson University) and the graduate level (University of Toronto) approved by the Association of University Programs in Health Administration. The study received ethics approval from the Research Ethics Boards at the University of Ontario Institute of Technology and the University of Toronto.

Descriptive trends, based on close-ended questions were analyzed using the statistical software SAS. The responses for the open-ended question, "What do you feel are the top five skills/competencies needed to lead/manage successfully within the next 5 –10 years" were mapped against the NCHL competency model[19] and then compared to the Canadian Interprofessional Competency Framework (CICF).[20]

RESULTS

The findings presented are based on 513 responses representing a 17.2% response rate. It is important to note that CCHL reports that 2247 of their members are active. If this number is taken into consideration as the N, the response rate would increase to 23% which is acceptable rate for electronic surveys.[21] The majority of respondents were female (65.8%). Table 27.1 provides a breakdown of the respondents by age category. 61.7% of the respondents were between 45-59 years of age. The majority of respondents currently, or most recently worked in, Ontario (57.2%), followed by British Columbia (18.4%) and Western Canada (16.6%) (Figure 27.1). The geographical distribution of respondents is very similar to the CCHL membership distribution across Canada (e.g., Ontario at 55.4%, British Columbia at 16.4%, Western Canada at 15.9%).

Age Category	N	Percentage of Respondents
<29 years of age	18	3.75
30-34 years of age	22	4.58
35-39 years of age	33	6.88
40-44 years of age	49	10.21
45-49 years of age	80	16.67
50-55 years of age	106	22.08
55-59 years of age	110	22.92
60-64 years of age	43	8.96
65 + years of age	19	3.96
Total	480	100
Missing=33		

Table 27.1. Age distribution

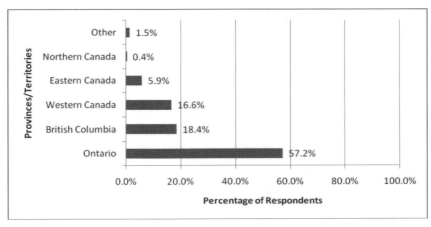

Missing=36

Figure 27.1: Geographical distribution of respondents.

There are 83.9% currently working in healthcare with the hospital/institutional sector (41.4%) the predominant place of employment. Very few of the CCHL members work in the community sector (Figure 27.2).

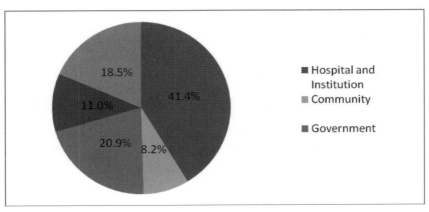

Missing=15

Figure 27.2: Comparison of place of employment

A total of 77.6% hold a management position and identify work place responsibility as either management (21.2%), management and planning (20.5%), planning (7.2%) or clinical and management (28.7%) (Figure 27.3).

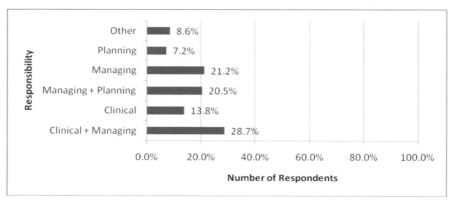

Missing=10

Figure 27.3: Workplace responsibility

The majority of respondents (56.8%) have a clinical background. Of those with a clinical background, 59.4% have a nursing background. Very few of the respondents directly manage frontline healthcare workers. When asked if they thought a clinical background was necessary to manage, 52.2% of respondents disagreed and 19.0% answered neutral. However, 95.6% agree that learning from, with, and about healthcare professions is advantageous when it comes to succeeding in a management position.

No consensus (either agreement or disagreement) existed over whether the skills to manage in healthcare are the same as in other industries. When asked about whether the skills/competencies required to manage in the hospital are the same as in the community there was also no consensus (Figure 27.4).

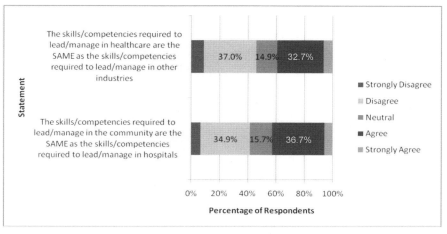

Missing=15

Figure 27.4: Comparison of views on skills/competencies.

CCHL members were asked to list the top five skills/competencies needed to manage successfully within the next five to ten years. Broad base trends were identified using the NCHL's competency model which resulted in the identification of five aggregated categories. Table 27.2 illustrates the categories and the corresponding skills/competencies identified. While very few of the CCHL respondents directly manage frontline healthcare workers, they recognize the importance of the behavioural and social (non-technical) skills/competencies associated with IPC (Table 27.2).

Categories	NCHL Skills/Competencies
Systems Thinking	Community orientation, organizational awareness and strategic orientation
Human Resources, Interpersonal and People Skills	Collaboration, human resources, management, impact and influence, interpersonal understanding, talent development and team leadership
Flexibility	Interpersonal understanding, organizational awareness and self development
Communication Skills	Communication Skills (facilitate group interaction)
Change Management	Change leadership (identify areas of change and express vision for change)

Table 27.2. Respondents' views on the skills/competencies needed to lead/manage within the next 5-10 years

Discussion

Although healthcare reform promotes the coordination of care across organizational sectors (i.e., shift in the site of care from hospital to the community), few if any of the CCHL respondents are supporting these attempts by working in the community sector (Figure 27.2). This lack of support may be due to a number of factors including, for example, the perceived unattractiveness of the community sector in terms of the lack of career opportunities, working conditions, funding (e.g., lack of public funding) and financial incentives (e.g., salary differentials).[22]

As noted above, the results show no overall consensus about whether the skills/competencies needed to manage in the community are the same as those needed in the hospital sector. However, with few working in the community sector (Figure 27.2), many do not have the experience or the educational background[23] on which to make an informed decision.

There is very little consensus among CCHL respondents about whether a clinical background is necessary to manage. This issue is compounded by the observation that few of those surveyed who possess a clinical background either a) manage those with a similar background, or b) manage other workers with a different clinical background. Clearly, the majority of those surveyed are not directly involved in the management of interprofessional care delivery models. Considering the majority of respondents identified their position as a top-level manager (60.8%) this is not a surprising result. However, these managers do recognize, that in order to succeed in their positions, it is important to learn from, with, and about other healthcare professions; a model of learning that supports interprofessional collaboration.

What is interesting are the views about the skills/competencies needed to manage in the next five to ten years. The results when mapped against the NCHL's competency model clearly illustrate that these healthcare managers agree with the NCHL's view on the skills/competencies needed to manage in the future. However, are these the skills/competencies required to manage interprofessional teams? The Canadian CICF identifies six interrelated interprofessional competency domains: role clarification; patient/client/family/community-centred; team functioning; collaborative leadership; interprofessional communication, and; dealing with interprofessional conflict. A comparison of the skills/competencies identified by CCHL members to the CICF competency domains illustrates that these leaders/managers are in fact supportive of the skills/competencies needed to implement the policy direction that supports interprofessional collaboration.

CONCLUSION AND RELEVANCE TO THE CF H SVCS GP

From the perspective of the CF H Svcs Gp the findings of the CIHR Team study illustrate the demographic and employment characteristics as well as the views on the skills/competencies of CCHL respondents. The findings should prove essential, and helpful to the CF H SVCS Gp, in the development of strategies to form successful partnerships with the civilian sector. While healthcare reform requires the implementation of IPC, the unanswered questions deal directly with the coordination and integration of care regardless of the site of delivery. The answers to the following questions are of high importance to the CF H Svcs Gp when partnering with the civilian sector. If not these healthcare managers, who is responsible for the coordination and integration of patient care? Is this an additional role and should it even be an expectation of frontline workers? If this is the case, when and where do these healthcare workers acquire skills/competencies necessary to carry out this role? What does this mean for frontline workers in terms of workload responsibility?

Part of the solution is recognizing that both clinical and managerial leadership is necessary to facilitate change.[24] The delivery of coordinated and efficient patient care is highly dependent upon frontline healthcare workers who must, on a daily basis, make decisions that affect the patient's experience. Managers can support the implementation of reform by providing the resources (e.g., time, funding) needed to facilitate change. Clearly to the CF H Svcs Gp and the civilian sector, it is of great importance that strategies incorporate both top down and bottom up approaches with a clear understanding of how both managers and frontline workers can work together to facilitate the coordination and integration of care regardless of the site of delivery.

It is recommended that a similar study be conducted to determine the views of healthcare managers in the CF H Svcs Gp on the skills needed to manage in the next five to ten years. This study should determine whether the challenges are the same or different than those identified by CCHL members. The study should also examine how healthcare workers in the military healthcare system working on IPTs are supported to practice IPC. Whether similar challenges exist for healthcare managers and frontline workers in the CF H Svcs Gp, the findings suggest that the implementation of IPC requires role clarity and coordination at all levels, including those healthcare workers who provide indirect care. Failure to address this issue could result in burnout of frontline healthcare workers providing direct patient care as they take on the additional role of coordinating care. Clearly, a healthcare workforce, be it in the civilian sector or the CF H Svcs Gp, will want to ensure the healthcare workforce is properly supported at all levels.

ACKNOWLEDGEMENTS

Funding and support for this research project was provided by The CIHR Team in Community Care and Health Human Resources (CIHR grant number 79849). We would like to thank our co-investigators: Raisa Deber, Winston Isaac and Tina Smith, for invaluable advice; any errors cannot be attributed to them. We would particularly like to thank our research partner, Linda O'Rourke, Vice President, Professional Standards & Leadership Development, Canadian College of Health Leaders, who assisted us in identifying the sampling frame, encouraging responses, and dissemination of the results

[1]Canadian Forces Health Service Group [CF H Svcs Gp], "The Surgeon General's Report 2010: Building On Our Strategy," (2010), http://www.forces.gc.ca/health-sante/pub/sgr-rmc-2010/default-eng.asp, accessed 11 April 2011.

[2]G.P. Marchildon, "Introduction" In *Health Systems in Transition: Canada*, 7th ed., edited by Sara Allin and Elias Mossialos (Copenhagen, Denmark: WHO Regional Office for Europe on behalf of the European Observatory on Health Systems and Policies, 2006), 1-19.

[3]CF H Svcs Gp,, "The Surgeon General's Report 2010: Building On Our Strategy," (2010), 42, http://www.forces.gc.ca/health-sante/pub/sgr-rmc-2010/default-eng.asp, accessed 11 April 2011.

[4]Canadian College of Health Leaders formerly known as the Canadian College of Health Service Executives

[5]C.P. Herbert, "Changing the culture: interprofessional education for collaborative patient-centred practice in Canada," *Journal of Interprofessional Care* 19, S1 (2005): 1-4, doi: 10.1080/13561820500081539, accessed 11 April 2011; HealthForceOntario, *Interprofessional Care Steering Committee [ICSC], Interprofessional care: a blueprint for action in Ontario*, (July 2007), http://www.healthforceontario.ca/WhatIsHFO/AboutInterprofessionalCare/ StrategicImplementationCommittee.aspx, accessed 11 April 2011; J. Liaskos, A. Frigas, K. Antypas, D. Zikos, M. Diomidous and J. Mantas, "Promoting interprofessional education in health sector within the European interprofessional education network," *International Journal of Medical Informatics* 78, 1 (2008): S43-S47, doi:10.1016/j.ijmedinf.2008.08.001, accessed 11 April 2011; J. Meuser, T. Bean, J. Goldman and S. Reeves, "Family Health Teams: A new Canadian interprofessional initiative," *Journal of Interprofessional Care* 20, 4 (2006): 436-438, doi: 10.1080/13561820600874726, accessed 11 April 2011.

[6]S. Mickan, S.J. Hoffman and L. Nasmith, "Collaborative practice in a global health context: Common themes from developed and developing countries," *Journal of Interprofessional Care* 24, 5 (2010): 492-502, doi: 10.3109/13561821003676325, accessed 11 April 2011; G.M. Russell, S. Dabrouge, R. Geneau, L. Muldoon and M. Tuna, "Managing chronic disease in Ontario primary care: The impact of organizational factors," *Annals of Family Medicine* 7, 4, 309-318, doi: 10.1370/afm.982, accessed 11 April 2011.

[7]Canadian Medical Association, "Achieving Patient-Centred Collaborative Care," CMA Policy Statement, Canadian Medical Association, 2008, http://policybase.cma.ca/dbtw-wpd/Policypdf/PD08-02.pdf, accessed 11 April 2011; Mickan, Collaborative practice in a global, 492-502.

[8]*Interprofessional care: a blueprint for action in Ontario*, (July 2007), 7, accessed from http://www.healthforceontario.ca/WhatIsHFO/AboutInterprofessionalCare/StrategicImplementationCom mittee.aspx

[9]R.B. Saltman, A. Rico and W.G.W. Boerma, *Primary care in the driver's seat?: organizational reform in European primary care* (Glasgow, UK: Bell & Bain Ltd., 2006), http://www.euro.who.int/__data/assets/pdf_file/0006/98421/E87932.pdf, accessed 11 April 2011.

[10]R.T. Fox, D.H. Fox and P.J. Wells, "Performance of first-line management functions on productivity of hospital unit personnel," *Journal of Nursing Administration* 29, 9 (1999): 12-18, doi: 10.1097/00005110-199909000-00005, accessed 11 April 2011.

[11]Canadian Institute for Health Information [CIHI].*Canada's Health Care Providers* (Ottawa, CA: Canadian Institute for Health Information, 2007), http://secure.cihi.ca/cihiweb/products/hctenglish.pdf, accessed 11 April 2011.

[12]World Health Organization [WHO]. *The World Health Report 2006 - working together for health*. Geneva, Switzerland: World Health Organization, (2006a), http://www.who.int/whr/2006/en/index.html, accessed 11 April 2011.

[13]C. Engel and E. Gursky, "Management and interprofessional collaboration," in *Interprofessional collaboration: From policy to practice in health and social care, 1st ed.*, edited by A. Leathard (New York, NY: Brunner-Routledge, 2003), 44-55; World Health Organization [WHO], "Copenhagen, Denmark: World Health Organization European Region," (2006b), http://www.euro.who.int/document/E88365.pdf, accessed 11 April 2011.

[14]C.M. Flood, D. Sinclair and J. Erdman, "Steering and rowing in health care: The devolution option?" *Queen's Law Journal* 30, (2004): 156-204, http://papers.ssrn.com/sol3/papers.cfm?abstract_id=1144891, accessed 11 April 2011.

[15]J.H.V. Gilbert, "Interprofessional learning and higher education structural barriers," *Journal of Interprofessional Care* 19, S. 1, (2005): 87-106, doi: 10.1080/13561820500067132, accessed 11 April 2011.

[16]D. Irvine, "The changing relationship between the public and the medical profession," *Journal of the Royal Society of Medicine* 94, 4, (2001): 162-169, http://www.pubmedcentral.nih.gov/articlerender.fcgi?artid=1281385, accessed 11 April 2011.

[17]J. Ovretveit, *Cooperation in Primary Health Care (Uxbridge: Brunel Institute of Organisation and Social Studies, 1990).*

[18]C. Engel and E. Gursky, "Management and interprofessional collaboration," in *Interprofessional collaboration: From policy to practice in health and social care, 1st ed.*, edited by A. Leathard (New York, NY: Brunner-Routledge, 2003), 49.

[19]National Centre for Healthcare Leadership [NCHL], "NCHL Health Leadership Competency Model," 2011. http://www.nchl.org/static.asp?path=2852,3238, accessed 11 April 2011,

[20]L. Bainbridge, C. Orchard and V. Wood, "Competencies for Interprofessional Collaboration," *Journal of Physical Therapy Education* 24, 1 (2010): 6-11, http://www.ipe.uwo.ca/Administration/teachings/Competencies for Interprofessional Collaboration.pdf, accessed 11 April 2011.

[21]Don A. Dillman, Jolene D Smyth and Leah Melani Christian, *Internet, mail, and mixed-mode surveys: The tailored design method, 3rd ed.* (Hoboken, NJ, US: John Wiley & Sons Inc., 2009).

[22]C.J. Evashwick, J. Frates and D.F. Fahey, "Long term care: an essential element of health administration education," *Journal of Health Administration Education* 25, 2 (2009): 95-108.

[23]Evashwick *et al.*, "Long term care," 95-108.

[24]C. Ham, "Improving the performance of health services: The role of clinical leadership," *The Lancet* (2003): 1978-1980. http://image.thelancet.com/extras/02art8342web.pdf, accessed 11 April 2011.

CHAPTER 28

An Informal Buddy Support System for Canadian Forces Reservists and their Families

Donna Pickering, PhD, and Tara Holton, DRDC Toronto

ABSTRACT

During a deployment, Canadian Forces members have a variety of support requirements that need to be met in order to ensure they remain connected with home and family. This role is fulfilled for Regular Force members by their unit's rear-party located at their home base in Canada. One of the duties of the rear-party is to address any family or personal matters that individual unit members experience during their deployment. However, Reservists typically do not receive this type of unit support when they deploy. The main objective of this research was to obtain a better understanding of an 'informal buddy support system' that was developed to provide peer support to deploying Reservists and their families. System implementers, deploying Reservists, and buddies were asked about their experiences and knowledge of the system. Overall, participants indicated that this type of system would be of benefit to all Reservists deploying. Findings are presented in relation to the current and suggested organization of the system; specific requirements for an effective buddy-to-deployed-member relationship; the unique needs of deployed Reserve members and their families; benefits and challenges associated with this informal support system; and recommendations are made for improving the system.

AN INFORMAL BUDDY SUPPORT SYSTEM FOR CANADIAN FORCES RESERVISTS AND THEIR FAMILIES

Military deployments by their nature are stressful on both the deploying member and their family. Indeed, deploying members have a variety of support requirements which need to be met in order to ensure that they remain connected with home and family and can address any family or work related issues that arise in their absence. Within the Canadian context, Canadian Regular Force members usually deploy as a unit, and the unit's rear-party located at their home base in Canada, provides for their support requirements. One of the duties of the rear-party is to address any family or personal matters that individual unit members experience during their deployment. Reservists and other CF members not deployed with their unit (Sharpe & English, 2006),[1] typically do not receive this type of unit support when they deploy, placing them at potentially higher risk for negative stress-related health outcomes. Reservists not only face many of the same stressors as Regular Force members, they are also subjected to stressors unique to Reservists such as lack of accessibility to deployment-related services due to distance to nearest military base, inadequate administrative support, and a military system geared primarily to Regular Force members (i.e., having to schedule deployment related appointments during normal working hours when the Reservist would be working at their civilian job).[2] In light of this shortcoming in the system, some Commanding Officers (CO) have decided to informally provide assistance to members of their Reserve units. More specifically, a rear-party advocate system has been developed as a means of providing support to deployed Reservists. Using this approach, a deployed Reservist is matched with a non-deployed member of the same unit and the non-deployed member takes on the role of the rear-party providing assistance to the deployed member and his/her family. This non-deploying member is colloquially known as 'the buddy.' This terminology was extended to the rear-party advocate system as a whole, which is commonly referred to as 'the buddy system.'

The purpose of this chapter is to discuss the informal support system that was developed to assist Reservists and their families with any deployment-related issues they may experience. Informal support refers to support that is unfunded, local, and non-mandated. This contrasts to formal support services that are officially offered by Chief of Military Personnel including, health and dental services, and those offered by Military Family Resource Centres (MFRC). The implications of this informal support system are discussed within the broader context of protecting and caring for the psychological, social, and physical health and well-being of Reserve members and their families not only during a deployment but over their life course. Before continuing with a discussion of this informal support system itself, it is important to first provide some background on the unique deployment-related stresses Reserve members may experience. This will allow for some context for the reader to ground their understanding of the development, implementation, and evaluation of the 'buddy system' for Canadian Forces (CF) Reservists.

THE RESERVE EXPERIENCE

Aside from the typical deployment related stressors experienced by members, Reservists also experience stressors that are unique to the Reserve experience. Recent research by McKee and Powers (2008)[3] undertaken to better understand the issues and concerns of CF Reservists suggests that Reservists are under-resourced, in part due to a lack of administrative support.[4] Further, it was found that Reserve members' understanding of the CF can be limited in that they do not always know where to obtain certain information or how to retrieve it, particularly with respect to pay and pension related issues.[5] Of note, many Reservists indicated that the administration of pay and benefits was a source of stress not only during their deployment but also post-deployment and that this stress was due in large part to not having a contract in place prior to starting pre-deployment training.[6] Specifically, when they deploy, Class A (employed part-time with their unit) and Class B (employed on duties of a temporary nature when it is not practical to employ members of the Regular Force) Reservists sign a contract that lasts the length of their deployment. During this time, the Reservist's class changes to 'C,' and they receive the same pay and benefits as a Regular Force member. If the Reservist has a full-time, non-indeterminate position (known as a Class B annotated A or established position) with the CF after they return they become a

Class B Reservist, otherwise they return to part-time status, i.e., Class A. It is during this transition period where pay and benefit related issues can arise such as those reported in McKee and Power's (2008) research.[7] Additional stress ensues if the Reservist was not able to secure a job post-deployment. In particular, for Class B Reservists, the position held prior to deployment may be given to another Reservist while the member is deployed. If the deployed member was unable to secure post-deployment employment prior to the end of their deployment they may face the added stress of looking for a job after returning to Canada.[8]

Work-life conflict is another type of stress that is typically experienced by Reservists. In particular, Reservists face time restrictions which are the result of their many commitments, and which are exacerbated by the way in which the CF is organized. This is particularly the case for Class A Reservists who typically have a job or attend university/college and work on a part-time basis for their Reserve unit. This employment with their unit takes the form of training one evening a week or two full days a month during the training year, extending from September to April. In the context of the deployment cycle, work-life conflict can interfere with the Reservist's ability to complete their post-deployment screening and any necessary administrative paperwork. This process needs to be completed immediately after the Reservist returns from their deployment. Scheduling a time for these activities may be challenging as these appointments are typically set during regular working hours. However, getting time off from their civilian job to do so may be difficult for Class A Reservists who indicated that they felt "neglected and forgotten" and did not receive the necessary post-deployment follow-up.[9]

This issue is exacerbated by the fact that unlike their Regular Force counterparts, Reservists, in particular Class A Reservists, spend the majority of their time with individuals who are unfamiliar with the experience of deployment. Consequently, they may have limited opportunities to share their experiences with individuals similar to themselves.[10] This reduces the Reservist's ability to assess how their post-deployment readjustment to their family, friends and work compares with that of their military peers.[11] It also limits the opportunities for their military superiors and peers to observe whether they may be experiencing any ongoing deployment-related emotional or behavioural problems.[12] This issue is compounded by the fact that their civilian co-workers and supervisors do not have the training to recognize whether they are experiencing any difficulties adjusting.[13]

The families of Reservists also face additional stresses associated with being a part of two worlds, one military and the other civilian. As Smith (2010) states, [14] many Reservist families may tolerate or accept the fact that their family member is involved on a part-time basis with the military; however, they typically identify themselves as being civilian, and not a military family. They usually do not reside on a military base and thus they may not have the benefit of experiencing the support of other military families.[15] This is a concern as military families are undoubtedly in a better situation than their civilian counterparts to understand the deployment-related issues the family may encounter.

Thus, there is an obvious need to ensure that the pre-, during and post-deployment health and welfare of Reservists and their families is being taken care of and this is one area where an informal buddy support system would be of benefit. This chapter will document the informal buddy support system developed for deploying Canadian Forces Reservists and their families. Given the varied nature in which this support system was taken up within participating units, the main objective of this research is to better understand this support system and what it can offer Reservists and their families. This involved investigating: 1) the ways in which the system had been set up; 2) how buddies were matched with deploying Reserve members; 3) the role of the buddy in supporting the deploying Reservist and their family; 4) benefits and limitations of the system and; 5) possible recommendations for improving this system.

Method

Participants

Participants consisted of 24 individuals who were: 1) Individuals involved in the implementation of the informal buddy support system; 2) Reservists deploying, or who had returned from deployment, and were matched with a buddy; 3) Reservists who served as buddies; 4) Reservists deploying or who had deployed and were not matched with a buddy.

With five age categories spanning 20-54 years, the 30-34 year category comprised half of the participants, and the 20-24 year category comprised almost a third. Sixty-two percent of the sample consisted of junior non-commissioned members while 38% were senior non-commissioned members. Thirty-one percent of participants were married or living common law with no dependents, 38% were married or living common law with dependents, and 31% were single (i.e., includes divorced, widowed, or separated individuals). Twenty-five percent of participants had five or fewer years of military service, 12% had six to ten years of military service, 44% had eleven to fifteen years of military service, while 19% had 16 years or more of military service. Forty-four percent of participants reported not having deployed on any United Nations (UN)/NATO tours, 38% reported being on one UN/NATO tour, while 18% reported being on two or more UN/NATO tours.

Also, although not formally included as participants in this research, individuals involved in formally supporting deploying military members and their families were consulted. They were asked about their experiences with Reservists and their families, what they thought the Reservists' unique support needs were, and what types of support their organization provided. This provided the context with which to better understand how the informal buddy support system relates to the more formal support systems available to deploying Reservists and their families.

Individuals involved in the implementation of the system were interviewed about their roles and knowledge of the system. Reservists who had served or were serving as buddies, and Reservists who had deployed either with or without a buddy, all participated in a focus group session and then completed a brief survey. Individuals who were unable to attend the focus group session were interviewed at a later date. At the end of their interview they completed a survey. As participants involved with the informal buddy support system, they were asked questions regarding the support needs of Reservists and their families, their knowledge and experience with the system, how the matching of buddies with deploying members occurred, their thoughts regarding the benefits and weaknesses of the system, along with any suggestions regarding improvements to the system.

Focus Group/Interview Data Analysis

A content analysis was conducted on the focus group and interview data using conventional qualitative data-analytical tools and techniques. Specifically, NVivo8, a qualitative research software package created by QRS International (Melbourne, Australia) was used to identify and categorize themes and issues pertaining to specific interview/focus group questions as well as themes and issues that emerged from the focus groups and interviews. The analysis involved two stages.

The first stage involved a preliminary analysis of the data to determine the structure of the coding scheme. This process was done using a modified Delphi technique. The Delphi process as applied to this setting can be described as a consensus based method of aggregating opinions of a team or set of experts.[16] The co-authors and a member of the data-collection support staff met on two occasions to discuss and debate the coding scheme. Consensus was achieved on the second meeting, resulting in a coding scheme. This coding scheme was applied to a few of the interviews and focus groups to ensure that the coding scheme was able to capture all of the themes emerging from the data and that there were not gaps (i.e., data that is not able to be coded using the existing coding scheme). The adequacy of the initial coding scheme was assessed in two subsequent meetings at which time modifications were introduced. This more refined coding scheme was then imported into NVivo8.

For the second stage of the analysis, all the interviews and focus groups were analyzed by two individuals using the refined coding scheme. One individual coded all of the interviews while another individual also independently analyzed them. The same procedure was applied to the analysis of the focus groups. Each individual's analysis was then merged into one final document.

Survey Analyses

The sample size only permitted descriptive data analyses to be performed on the survey data. For each open-ended survey question, the responses participants provided to the question were grouped into broad categories and then the number of responses in each category was calculated. In the case of closed-ended questions, frequency counts of the various responses to each category were calculated. For instance, Reservists were asked to indicate the types of support their buddy had provided them with during their deployment. A list of the types of support (i.e., tangible aid, reassurance) the individual may have received from their buddy during their deployment was provided. They then checked off all of the response alternatives that applied. The frequency that individuals reported receiving each of the different types of support was calculated. This then allowed a preliminary assessment of the different types of support received to be made.

Results

Interview and Focus Group Results

The following results pertain to the six main themes, and their respective subthemes, that emerged from the content analysis of the interview and focus group data. The three largest, i.e., most prominent, themes pertained to the flexible set up and use of the system, the nature of the relationship the buddy has with the deployed Reservist, and the nature of the relationship the buddy has with the family. The three other themes were the benefits of the informal buddy support system, the issues associated with use of the system, and recommendations for establishing and using the system.

Flexible Set-up and Use

The largest theme pertained to what the implemented buddy system looked like or thoughts about what it could look like. The most consistent comments participants made about the system centered on the necessity for the informality of the system. They indicated that the system was informally implemented within their unit and that they preferred it that way. As one participant said, "If you try to formalize it too much...I don't think it will be as effective." The other comment that was frequently mentioned by participants was the need for flexibility of the system. As one participant noted, "... it all depends, every case is different so you can't make a model to fit every situation." In fact, there was no typical way in which the system had been set up across units. In some units the focus of the system was primarily the deploying Reservist while in others the informal buddy system was a part of a larger family support system set up by the unit.

Nature of Relationship with Buddy

The focus of this theme was the nature of the buddy's relationship with the deployed member. This included comments regarding the frequency of contact and type of contact. Participants reported a wide variety of ways in which buddies and deploying Reserve members were matched. Many participants reported having a pre-existing friendship with their buddy, while some reported having a buddy assigned to them, and still others had an experienced senior Reserve unit member serve as their buddy. Many participants indicated, irrespective of how they were matched with their buddy, the importance of having a pre-existing relationship. One participant who served as a buddy on more than one occasion indicated that, "…the one fellow that I did have a pre-existing relationship with, there was a lot more contact, and it was a lot more deep and much more detailed."

The type and frequency of contact between the buddy and the deployed Reservist was partially determined by accessibility of phones and the internet. The most common method Reservists used to maintain contact with buddies was via the internet, i.e., e-mail or Facebook. Many participants reported limited time on the phone so this means of communication was typically reserved for contacting families back home. A minority of individuals sent letters or postcards. Care packages were also sent by buddies to the deployed member. Many participants indicated that communication between buddies and the deployed Reservist was informal, and simply involved saying "hi" and asking how things were. Some described the buddy as a link between the deployed member and their Reserve unit back home.

Nature of Relationship with Family

Next to the nature of the relationship buddies have with their paired Reservist, the buddy's relationship with the deployed member's family also emerged as an important theme. Some participants reported having pre-existing contact with the deploying member's family while others did not know the family well. The benefits of having a pre-existing relationship with the family were noted by one participant, "…the benefit lies in that the buddy has a close connection with the actual family which works well if your buddy in Reserve life is your friend in civilian life, so the family feels comfortable dealing with them."

A few participants indicated that families were not really a part of the system, and that the system focused on the deploying Reservist. Others commented that some families do not really want to be contacted, by the buddy, or by the military in general. This partially influenced the amount of contact the buddy had with the family.

Participants provided many examples of the types of support provided by the buddy. These included assistance with chores, social outings, providing information, and listening to concerns the family had, for instance about the welfare of their deployed family member. It was remarked by a few participants that the buddy connected the unit with the family and vice versa. As one participant said about their buddy, "...he was like the middle man between.... my family and the unit."

BENEFITS

The benefits from the informal buddy support system emerged as one of the major themes. Participants mentioned benefits of the system as viewed from the deploying Reservist, their family, the Reserve unit, and the buddy. Some commented that individuals lacking an adequate social network would benefit the most from this system.

The main benefit of the system as expressed by participants was the reduction of stress for deploying Reservists and their family. As one participant said with respect to the deployed Reservist, "I guess they're always worried about how things are going at home, so it's a bit of a reassurance that there's somebody there to help keep an eye on things and help out."

As for the families, one participant noted, "...the families...they benefit from the, lower level of stress because they know, if they need anything, they have a number to call... .and somebody will help them."

Another benefit that the deployed Reservist and their family experience is a sense of connection, of being cared for. This was reflected in a comment made regarding the benefits of having a buddy, "Like, you leave and there's still people there wondering hey what's up, what are you doing, that's not your immediate family."

With respect to the family members, one participant said, "...they need to feel connected...to the military and to... the member. And that's...one of the primary roles of the buddy system, is to keep them connected."

The major benefit of the system for the Reserve unit is that of communication. More specifically, the buddy provides a means for the Reserve unit to keep in contact with the Reservist during their deployment, and also post-deployment. This was reflected in the following comment made by one participant, "....we could use that person to get hold of them if there was something we needed to pass on and get some information we needed..."

The buddy also connects the unit with the deployed member's family. Additional ways in which the system could be of benefit, as noted by a few participants, are in assisting Reservists to reintegrate, and by contributing to retention.

ISSUES

This theme focused on the challenges or drawbacks associated with the informal buddy support system. One of the issues mentioned by the buddies was that they have other work-related responsibilities that needed to get done. Some participants reported having limited time to complete their duties and acting as a buddy would be another responsibility for them. Participants mentioned that obtaining greater support from the Canadian Forces, in the form of extra time and funding to run the program (i.e., additional Class A funding to support the buddy for the extra time required to fulfill their role and funding to provide the necessary oversight of the program) would be useful. However, there was a concern about increased expectations that might accompany such support. This concern is exemplified in the statement made by one participant, "Funding is very tricky because… once you start funding the program then it has to be…measurable and it has to produce results."

Another concern was the stress that might be experienced by the buddy as a result of carrying out their role. Participants provided a variety of possible sources of stress including the family of the deploying Reservist not wanting to communicate with anyone in the military, the buddy not being able to answer questions that the family has because, for example, they do not have access to the required information, or if something happens to the deployed member. Acknowledging the important role played by buddies, some participants indicated that buddies deserve more recognition for their contribution than they typically receive. It was felt that this could assist in recruiting future buddies. As one participant said about recognizing buddies:

> It doesn't take anyone any time, money or energy at all to do it. But it's to recognize a person. And I think it's important because it makes the person feel like they did a good job, if of course they did a good job, it makes other people go, "If I did that job, I would get recognized too."

The last concern pertained to buddies not being able to fulfill their role. Examples provided when this might occur are: when the buddy leaves the unit or the military during a deployed member's tour, or when demanding commitments keep them from their buddy role. As one participant commented on this type of situation, "That can be difficult because you have to remember that they may start with a certain peer or buddy who may leave when they're on their tour."

SYSTEM SET-UP AND USE RECOMMENDATIONS

The last major theme pertained to the recommendations made regarding the set up and use of the informal buddy support system. The first set of recommendations put forth by many participants involved ensuring the system remains flexible while at the same time providing it more structure. For example, allowing deploying Reservists to "opt out" of the system but ensuring on paper they have a buddy in case they unexpectedly require assistance.

The need to provide resources to better support the system was mentioned by participants. People were one type of resource mentioned. One participant discussed the use of a facilitator to aid in the organization of the system. Another mentioned inviting a variety of experts to come in to informally visit the unit and talk about relevant topics:

> A support person, such as career counselor, or mental health counselor, or a psychologist, to just come out every once in while, we'll take them around and introduce them to the people, and they can have informal discussions with them about different things.

Others mentioned it would be useful for the members of the unit if recently deployed individuals would share their experiences. Another set of recommendations focused on support for buddies. For example, participants mentioned providing buddies with key contact numbers. Because of limited time, eliminating lengthy training for buddies was stressed by some participants. Otherwise, this might be a disincentive for buddies who volunteer for the role. The idea of having a 'back up buddy' or greater number of peer support members per deploying Reservists was discussed by some.

Improving communication was another recommendation. More specifically, units should provide more opportunities for buddies to meet with the deploying member's family before deployment. As one participant said:

> ...I think it would be easier if we had...some form of direct communication that was started by the unit before they went over as opposed to just like, "Here, you're the buddy, you know, talk to the family if you feel like it."

Also, some participants indicated that greater communication about the informal buddy support system needs to be provided to deploying Reservists and their families.

SURVEY RESULTS

After completing a focus group or an interview, participants completed a survey involving both open-ended and closed-ended survey questions. Questions that required more detailed answers were asked using an open-ended survey format.

The survey questions were of two types, ones focused on the informal buddy support system and those more general in nature, asking about Reservists' deployment and post-deployment experiences. The latter were asked in a survey should participants not wish to discuss these experiences openly in a group setting. Participants were asked open-ended questions regarding the suitability of individuals to be buddies. More specifically, they were asked: 1) what specific groups or types of individuals would make the best buddies and 2) what groups and types of individuals would not make good buddies.

Overwhelmingly, participants said that the best person to be a buddy would be someone who is friends with the deploying Reservist and if possible, also knows the deploying member's family. Experience or a previous deployment was also seen to be a desirable characteristic in a buddy. With respect to characteristics that would not contribute to an effective buddy, the three most reported responses were: 1) individuals who were assigned to be a buddy (i.e., non voluntary); 2) someone who did not have a pre-existing relationship with the member deploying; and 3) someone without experience (i.e., lack of deployment experience, lack of life experience).

Reservists who deployed and individuals who served as buddies were also asked open-ended questions about who benefits from having a buddy. In particular, they were asked: 1) what specific groups or types of individuals would benefit the most from having a buddy and 2) what specific groups or types of individuals would benefit the least from having a buddy. The four most mentioned groups that participants indicated would benefit the most from having a buddy were: 1) individuals who lacked a support network; 2) individuals going on their first deployment; 3) new members, young Reservists (i.e., with parents, not partnered); and 4) individuals with concerns about their upcoming deployment. Also noted, although to a lesser degree, were individuals with a young family and Regular Force Augmentees (i.e., a Regular Force member posted to a different unit for an overseas deployment. The individual is not permanently posted with this unit/headquarters). Thus, Regular Force Augmentees, who deploy by themselves or only a few at a time, face many of the same issues as do Reservists. With respect to individuals who would benefit the least, the two most cited groups were individuals who have strong, stable support networks and individuals who have been on many deployments.

Reservists who had buddies were also asked about the type of support they received during their deployment. Complementarily, buddies were asked about the types of support they provided to the deployed Reservists with whom they were matched. The main type of support Reservists indicated their buddy provided while they were deployed was advice and information (i.e., 80% of respondents). Advice and information was also tied with reassurance as being the main type of support buddies reported providing during deployment (i.e., 71% of respondents). Following advice and information, reassurance was the most received type of support during deployment (i.e., 60% of respondents).

Discussion

Individuals involved in the informal buddy support system reported that the system would be of benefit to deploying Reservists and their families. However, when asked who would benefit the most from this system, participants reported that Reservists who lack an adequate support network, who are going on their first deployment, or who are inexperienced (i.e., new or young) would receive the most benefit. This informal buddy support system fills a gap in the Reservists' larger support network. This is clearly evidenced in following statements:

> I think the Reserve soldier has very very little expectations that they're going to be supported when they go away.

> ...and there is no support for them; so I think the expectation that has been brought up has been there isn't any support.

One of the strengths of the buddy support system is that it empowers Reservists to support one another. In fact, Reservists are in the best position to understand their unique needs and the needs of their families. In addition, the buddy typically has a pre-existing relationship with the deploying member and his/her family so they have a better understanding of their support needs and preferences compared to more formalized support resources. This understanding can be further enhanced were the buddy to have a pre-deployment conversation with the family about their preferences regarding: 1) type of contact (i.e., e-mail, phone, in person), frequency of contact (i.e., once a week, bi-monthly, monthly), and type of support desired (i.e., information, someone to talk to about concerns, assistance with chores, someone to socialize with). Understanding the preferences of the family is important since unwanted support or the wrong type of assistance, is not only unhelpful but can in fact be an additional source of stress to the family.[17]

Location of Formalized Support Systems Inhibits Usage by Reservists and their Families

Aside from understanding the unique stresses experienced by Reservists and their families, the fact that Reservists and their families typically do not reside on base and may live some distance away from the base can contribute to them not receiving the deployment-related support they may require.[18] MFRC located across Canada, are an example of a formalized support resource. One of their roles is to assist families of deploying military members by providing them with deployment related information, support services, etc. Although the MFRCs undoubtedly provide invaluable support to a number of military families, typically they are located on military bases. This poses difficulties for many Reserve force families who for the most part do not reside on military bases (CIOR, 2007; Smith, 2010).[19] In fact, they may not reside in the local area where the MFRC exists. Accordingly, attending support groups, information sessions, or making use of available child care services may not be possible for Reservists' families. This is where an informal buddy support system can be of benefit.

The difficulty of accessing these more formalized support resources and the benefits of a peer support system such as an informal buddy support system is clearly evidenced by the following participant's comment:

> …we don't have resources centres that we can go to….They would be made available, in a centralized location, but in our case I have Reserve soldiers… And for them to come in and make use of that resource, is…time from their day…So, most of the support network for us simply becomes friendships that develop between people in the unit, and their families.

Accordingly, if one of the criteria suggested in matching a buddy with a Reservist and his/her family is that the buddy be located in the same local area as the family, this would enable the buddy to have more contact with the family. Since they may already be familiar with the family, they would be able to provide more individualized support than formalized support resources such as an MFRC.

FLEXIBILITY AND INFORMALITY OF THE SYSTEM

One of the consistent messages to emerge from this research is that individuals want the buddy system to remain informal and that it be able to be adapted to suit the needs of different Reserve units. For the system to be of most benefit it has to be adapted and used in a way that is most advantageous for each unique Reserve unit.

IMPORTANCE OF PRE-EXISTING RELATIONSHIP

Matching a buddy with a deploying Reservist based on a pre-existing relationship, in particular having a friendship, was deemed the most desirable way to match individuals. Whenever possible, this matching should be done on a voluntary, and not on an assigned, basis. As one participant said, "…if you appoint your buddy…you're telling him, you gotta do this for me. You want somebody who is gonna say, 'Hey I'll do it for you.' "

This is important since the buddy is not a paid position. The individual in the role of a buddy does this on their own time (i.e., visiting the family) and it is important to make sure that it is not viewed as an obligation. If so, the person may be resentful of having one more task assigned to them and thus may not invest as much of their time and effort in the role as someone who voluntarily chose to be a buddy.

Having the buddy be familiar with the family prior to the Reservist deploying was also considered to be important. Ensuring the buddy has an opportunity to meet with the family pre-deployment enables a level of comfort to develop so that the family is not hesitant about contacting the buddy when they require assistance. It also allows both parties to discuss preferences regarding the amount and type of contact. A few participants felt that this process could be facilitated by the Reserve unit. More specifically, organizing pre-deployment events would allow the families of deploying Reservists to meet their buddies and become more familiar with the unit.

BENEFITS OF THE SYSTEM

The informal buddy support system benefits the deploying Reservist, their family, the buddy and the Reserve unit. For Reservists deploying, concern about the welfare of their family is one of the many stresses they may experience during their deployment. This stress is reduced by having someone, their buddy, "check in" on their family, ensure they are doing well, and assist them with any problems they may have. It also may make them feel more closely connected to their home Reserve unit as their buddy provides a mechanism through which their home unit can keep in contact with them and their family. As well, the buddy is seen as someone they can talk to back home, outside of their family. They understand them in a way their family does not (i.e., they can talk to their buddy about deployment and redeployment issues they may not want to talk to their family about). Their buddy is viewed as someone who cares about their welfare.

Taking care of any administrative issues that might arise during the Reservist's deployment is another form of support that the buddy can provide. In fact, approximately 80% of Reservists who deployed indicated that their buddy had provided them with advice and information during their deployment. Some buddies even reported assisting their deployed member in finding a job post-deployment. In one instance, the buddy completed the necessary job-related paperwork for the deployed Reservist. This is not surprising considering the fact that some participants mentioned they had limited access to the internet during their deployment. Although assistance in finding a job may seem to be beyond the typical expectations for someone in the role of a buddy, there were participants who reported not having a job when they returned. This was a source of stress for them and undoubtedly is a stress unique to Reservists.

For the family of the Reservist, knowing that there is someone they can contact if they need anything can reduce some of the stress they may be experiencing. What is also important is that the buddy can be contacted outside of the military's operating business hours if needed. The buddy can assist them with a variety of support needs (i.e., chores, listening to concerns, providing information, socialization) thus providing a sense of being cared for and supported.

The main benefit the system has for the deployed member's home unit is that it provides them with a way to communicate with the Reservist and their family. More specifically, the buddy is able to convey information that the unit may want the deployed member's family to know including upcoming events or deployment-related information.

With respect to the buddies' role in connecting the Reserve unit with the deployed Reservist, one participant commented:

> The buddy system or the advocate system is really a lot of times our only contact with that Reservist while he deploys....the minute they go on pre-deployment training we've lost contact with them....When we send someone away for a year we basically lose contact with them...even when they come back on leave they're going to want to spend quality time with their families. They're not going to want to come down and see us...

Thus, the buddy is able to bridge this gap by enabling the home Reserve unit to contact the deployed Reservist if they need to pass on any important information or if the Reservist needs information or assistance from their home unit. This role would normally be fulfilled by the rear-party system in the case of Regular Force members. Also, post-deployment, the buddy enables the Reserve unit awareness of how the Reservist is reintegrating.

Accordingly, the buddy, because of their relationship to the member they were matched with (i.e., typically a pre-existing friendship), can have a role to play in the reintegration process. They are in a position to know if their friend is experiencing problems, and be attuned to behaviour that is out of character for their friend. As one participant said, "...that's where I could see the buddy system coming in insofar as having somebody to gauge how you're doing emotionally and so on."

Further, participants indicated that it is during the reintegration phase of the deployment cycle that the Reservist may particularly need the support of their buddy. More specifically, many of the participants who had deployed indicated that it had been important during their deployment for them to receive support from their deployed friends/co-workers and that they received the most amount of support from these individuals. While perhaps not unexpected, there are some potential drawbacks associated with the strong connections Reservists may make with the individuals they deploy with. In many instances, Reservists do not deploy as a unit but instead they deploy as Augmentees (i.e., they augment Regular Force units). Thus, connections are developed during pre-training and are maintained as they work side-by-side with the Regular Force members with whom they deployed. However, relationships become severed post-deployment after the Reserve Force members return to their home unit. This was clearly exemplified in the following statement made by a participant:

...it was hard because, when we got off the plane...it was literally, "Reg Force this way, Reserves this way." ...it was literally ...you were whisked away and then like, "I just lived with these guys for seven and a half months"... I haven't seen them since...we didn't say goodbye...we couldn't even exchange....a cell number.

It is during the reintegration phase of the deployment cycle when the Reserve member is adjusting to life back home, that one of their most important sources of support is lost. This is where the potential benefits of the informal buddy support system may serve to fill that gap.

Buddies can also benefit from their participation in the informal buddy system. As one participant said:

> ...for the buddies...I think they feel like they had a significant role, not only in being able to help out a friend while he's deployed—but also to help in the larger mission that we're involved with....and I think they have a lot of personal satisfaction from caring for the family members.

Thus, although the buddy expends time, which is already limited, to assist the deploying Reservist and their family, they reap many benefits from this role.

SYSTEM LIMITATIONS

There are two main limitations of the system with respect to its current implementation. First, Reservists have many demands for their time. Participants said that they already have many duties that need to be completed during the time available to them in the course of their work hours with their Reserve unit. Thus, the informal buddy support system, although important, was seen by some as yet another duty they were tasked with.

Other limitations of the system with respect to its current implementation are first, the possible stress that buddies may experience as a consequence of their role (e.g., managing unexpected events such as injury of the deployed member, difficult family) and second, a lack of planning should a buddy no longer be able to function in their role. These concerns were taken into account when recommendations were developed for improvement of the system.

SYSTEM RECOMMENDATIONS

System recommendations can be classified into five main categories. The first category focuses on recommendations regarding how the system should be structured. The second category focuses on need for resources to further enhance system functioning.

The third set of recommendations focuses on who would be best suited to the role of a buddy. The fourth set of recommendations highlights the importance of providing recognition for the contribution made by buddies. The last set of recommendations outline a way forward with respect to implementing the findings of this research.

System Structure. Keeping the system informal and flexible in order to best meet the needs of individual Reserve units is essential. However, there is a need for increased system structure. For instance, ensuring the system starts during the pre-deployment phase of the deployment cycle and continues on into the post-deployment reintegration phase of the cycle. One participant described the ideal system in the following way, "It's formal enough that people know what's expected of them, but informal enough that it's still very flexible."

Another recommendation put forth is for more than one buddy per deploying member, i.e., the need for a 'back up buddy' in case a buddy is unable to fulfill their role. Finally, ensuring that participation in the system is voluntary is also important.

Providing Resources. It is necessary to have support from all levels of the organization for the informal buddy support system. Providing resources is one way of supporting the system. An example of one such resource is having experts (i.e., psychologists, career counselors) informally visiting Reserve units. They would speak with unit members about issues such as what to expect during the reintegration process which would assist buddies and returning members in better identifying OSIs).

Another valuable resource is the knowledge and experience gained by two groups of Reservists. The first group is individuals who have recently returned from a deployment. They could share their deployment experiences with other members of their unit. Similarly, individuals who served as a buddy in the past are also a valuable resource. As one participant said, 'You could learn from their experiences.' This would be particularly useful for less experienced Reservists in the role of a buddy.

Having someone acting in the role of a facilitator would aid in the organization of the system. One of the functions of the facilitator could be to arrange meetings where buddies could meet to discuss any issues they may be experiencing. If the issue is of a more sensitive nature, the buddy could meet one-on-one with the facilitator.

There is also a need to provide buddies with a brief one or two page document summarizing information to assist them in their role. Important contact numbers should be included as well as advice on how to best communicate with families. As one participant said, this advice could state: "You know, you might not want to say this", or "This would be a good thing to say", or "If this happens…then a very reassuring thing to do is this."

Who the buddy should consult if they encounter a situation they do not know how to handle also needs to be included. This would not only save the buddy time but would assist in alleviating some of the anxiety they may experience.

Effective Buddies. Aside from providing individuals serving as buddies with the resources to better enable them to carry out their role, it is equally important to ensure that individuals who volunteer to be buddies have the necessary pre-requisites to be effective buddies. Some of the characteristics used by participants to describe individuals who would make the best buddies are: maturity, reliability, good communication skills, having a pre-existing relationship with the deploying Reservist, and if possible their family. Characteristics used to describe individuals who would not make the best buddies are: assigned and lack of deployment-related experience. Although it may not always be possible to find individuals who possess all of the characteristics associated with the best buddies and are willing to volunteer to be someone's buddy, it would be desirable to select individuals with as many of these attributes as possible.

Buddy Recognition. Another recommendation is that buddies receive recognition for their contribution. This serves two purposes. First, it thanks the buddy for their time and effort which is important since serving as a buddy is a voluntary role. Second, it can assist in the recruitment of buddies in the future thus aid in sustaining the system.

Unit Specific Program. The final recommendation is that the results of this study be used to develop a unit specific informal buddy support program to meet the needs of individual Reserve units. This meets the needs of individual Reserve units who clearly indicated at a 'one size fits all' approach to implementing an informal buddy support system would not be desirable.

In summary, an informal buddy support system, such as was discussed in this chapter, enables the CF to better protect the health and well-being of Reservists and their families. This system provides them with an important source of support during the deployment cycle which can lessen the negative effect of deployment-related stress. This includes deployment-related stressors typically experienced by deploying military members and those that are unique to Reservists.

[1] G.E. Sharpe and Allan English, *Observations on the Association between Operational Readiness and Personal Readiness in the Canadian Forces*, Defence Research and Development Canada – Toronto, report CR 2006-072,(31 March 2006): 43-48, 50-51.

[2] Captain McNary, R. Carman, President, Interallied Confederation of Reserve Officers (CIOR), (letter report, CIOR 2007 *Symposium Summary - Post Deployment Care of Reservists*, Riga, Latvia, November 28, 2007), 1; H. Smith, "Operational stress and retention," Journal of Military and Strategic Studies 12, 4 (2010): 60.

[3] B. Mckee and Sergeant S.A. Powers, *The Canadian Forces Reserve Force Study* 2008, Defence Research and Development Canada – CORA, report TN 2008-051, (1 December 2008).

[4] M. McFadyen, *Special Report to the Minister of National Defence*. Reserved Care: An Investigation into the Treatment of Injured Reservists, National Defence and Canadian Forces Ombudsman, (April 2008), 6, 55, http://www.ombudsman.forces.gc.ca/rep-rap/sr-rs/rc-str/doc/rc-str-eng.pdf., accessed 26 May 2011.

[5] B. Mckee and Sergeant S.A. Powers, *The Canadian Forces Reserve Force Study* 2008, Defence Research and Development Canada – CORA, report TN 2008-051, (1 December 2008), 7-8.

[6] B. Mckee and Sergeant S.A. Powers, *The Canadian Forces Reserve Force Study* 2008, Defence Research and Development Canada – CORA, report TN 2008-051, (1 December 2008), 11.

[7] B. Mckee and Sergeant S.A. Powers, *The Canadian Forces Reserve Force Study* 2008, Defence Research and Development Canada – CORA, report TN 2008-051, (1 December 2008), 11.

[8] B. Mckee and Sergeant S.A. Powers, *The Canadian Forces Reserve Force Study* 2008, Defence Research and Development Canada – CORA, report TN 2008-051, (1 December 2008), 11.

[9] B. Mckee and Sergeant S.A. Powers, *The Canadian Forces Reserve Force Study* 2008, Defence Research and Development Canada – CORA, report TN 2008-051, (1 December 2008), 11-12.

[10] J. Philipp, "Army Reserve suicides up in 2010: Increase tied to seclusion, lack of peer support," *Epoch Times*, (20 January 2011): 2, http://www.theepochtimes.com/n2/content/view/49657, accessed 26 May 2011; H. Smith, "Operational stress and retention," *Journal of Military and Strategic Studies* 12, 4 (2010): 60.

[11] H. Smith, "Operational stress and retention," *Journal of Military and Strategic Studies* 12, 4 (2010): 60.

[12] J. Philipp, "Army Reserve suicides up in 2010: Increase tied to seclusion, lack of peer support," *Epoch Times*, (20 January 2011): 2, http://www.theepochtimes.com/n2/content/view/49657, accessed 26 May 2011; H. Smith, "Operational stress and retention," *Journal of Military and Strategic Studies* 12, 4 (2010): 60.

[13] McNary, "CIOR 2007 Symposium Summary," 2; H. Smith, "Operational stress and retention," *Journal of Military and Strategic Studies* 12, 4 (2010): 60.

[14] H. Smith, "Operational stress and retention," *Journal of Military and Strategic Studies* 12, 4 (2010): 61.

[15] B. McNary, CIOR 2007 Symposium Summary, 5; Laura W. Castaneda, Margaret Harrell, Danielle Varda, Kimberly Hall, Megan Beckett, and Stefanie Stern, "Deployment Experiences of Guard and Reserve Families: Implications for Support and Retention," *RAND National Defense Research Institute* (2008): 139-177. http://www.rand.org/pubs/monographs/2008/RAND_MG645.pdf, accessed 26 May 2011; H. Smith, "Operational stress and retention," Journal of Military and Strategic Studies 12, 4 (2010): 61.

[16] J.W. Murry Jr. and James O. Hammons, "Delphi: A versatile methodology for conducting qualitative research," *Review of Higher Education* 18, 4 (1995): 423-436.

[17] T.C. Antonucci, Hiroko Akiyama, and Jennifer E. Lansford, "Negative effects of close social relations," *Family Relations* 47, 4 (1998): 379-384; Karen S. Rook, "The negative side of social interaction: Impact on psychological well-being," *Journal Personality and Social Psychology* 46, 5 (1984): 1097-1108.

[18] B. McNary, "CIOR 2007 Symposium Summary," 7-8; H. Smith, "Operational stress and retention," *Journal of Military and Strategic Studies* 12, 4 (2010): 60.

[19] . McNary, "CIOR 2007 Symposium Summary, 1,5; H. Smith, "Operational stress and retention," *Journal of Military and Strategic Studies* 12, 4 (2010): 61.

CHAPTER 29

The Impact of Musculoskeletal Conditions on the Canadian Forces

Lieutenant-Colonel Peter Rowe, PT, MRSc, CD and Major Luc J. Hébert, PT, PhD, CD,
Directorate of Medical Policy, Canadian Forces Health Services Group Headquarters

ABSTRACT

The Canadian Forces Health Services (CFHS) invests significant resources annually in the management of musculoskeletal conditions (MSKC). This is evident in all aspects of health services delivery and ultimately CF operational readiness, as we see the impact of MSKC on absenteeism at work and medical releases. The purpose of this work is to provide a broad and strategized review of the impact of MSKC on the CF with the objectives of: 1) developing support for a strategic plan of capturing necessary information; 2) sharing information to facilitate integrated approaches for positive clinical outcomes; and 3) developing integrated performance measurement strategies. A review of the academic literature was conducted. Clinical data from various CFHS sources was analyzed. The triangulation of data from these multiple sources was used to provide a much broader and clearer perspective of the impact of MSKC in the CF. High health service utilization rates, expenditures and high musculoskeletal injury rates are detailed as well as the implications on the operational readiness of the CF. Statistics confirm that MSKC are a leading cause of morbidity in the modern armies of the world. The use of a multiple sources approach allows us to weight the true value of MSKC on operational readiness relative to other health problems and medical conditions. The evidence suggests that the impact of MSKC in the CF may be much greater than expected. A more integrated musculoskeletal management program could lead to improved clinical outcomes.

THE IMPACT OF MUSCULOSKELETAL CONDITIONS ON THE CANADIAN FORCES

It has been reported in the literature by many military forces, including the Canadian Forces (CF), that musculoskeletal (MSK) injuries are a leading cause of morbidity and one of the most prevalent sources of disability among military personnel.[1] Bergman & Miller reported that in 1998, MSK conditions and injuries were the leading causes of medical discharges and were responsible for 70% of medical discharges from the British Army.[2] Similarly, Bell, Schwartz, Harford, Hollander & Amoroso (2008) found that disability risks in the US Army were seven times higher in 2005 than they were in 1980 and that MSK disability is the fastest growing category for disability in the US Army.[3] Darakjy, Marin, Knapik and Jones (2006) followed a US Armour Brigade during a 37-day operational training phase and reported that 11.2% of the brigade sought medical care during the training period and that MSK injuries were the leading reason for seeking healthcare.[4]

While many of these reports confirm that injuries are a leading health concern, it has also been suggested that these data may still markedly underestimate the magnitude of the injury problem.[5] As an example, Hauret, Jones, *et al.* express that depending on the definition of injury that is used, often only hospitalizations or acute traumatic injuries (Chapter 17, ICD-9-CM) are often captured.[6] Reports of this nature may be missing an entirely different component of injuries that are not classified as traumatic injuries. These may include repetitive or cumulative trauma conditions, also known as repetitive strain or overuse injuries that are often diagnosed during out-patient visits rather than hospitalizations. These injury-related MSK conditions are classified in Chapter 13 of the ICD-9-CM[7] as Diseases of the Musculoskeletal System and Connective Tissue and also include conditions such as overuse tendonitis's, meniscal derangements of the knee, recurrent shoulder dislocations and spinal strains as common examples. In their study, they investigated the incidence of injury-related MSK conditions that included both outpatient and inpatient consultations for active duty, non-deployed US Department of Defence, combined services (Air Force, Army, Navy, Marines) personnel. Hauret, Jones, *et al.* reported 743,547 injury-related MSK conditions (Rate: 628 per 1000 person-years) and added that when combined with traumatic injuries, the overall incidence was close to 1.6 million injuries per year.[8]

Considering the similarities between the CF and NATO armies with regard to demographic profiles, training and types of mission of the past decade, we believe that there may be a similar situation in the CF with respect to incidence and impact of MSK conditions. Although not much literature exists on injury rates in the CF, a closer look at the preliminary data available from various sources is now suggesting that as with other militaries of the world, the management of MSK conditions may be an underestimated burden to the CF Health Services (CFHS) and a significant challenge to CF Operational Readiness. Thus, the main purpose of this paper is to provide an initial broad and strategized review of the impact of MSK conditions on the CF. Secondary objectives are: 1) to develop support for a strategic plan of capturing necessary information pertaining to MSK conditions; and 2) to use this information to facilitate integrated approaches for positive clinical outcomes and developing integrated performance measurement strategies.

METHOD

A review of the most recent academic literature on other militaries of the world was conducted and used to obtain the most current estimates of the magnitude of the problem of MSK conditions. This was followed by the identification and review of all other potential sources of data available within the CF Health Services. To optimize the use of this sparse CF data available, a triangulation from these multiple sources was used to provide an initial broad perspective of the impact of MSK conditions in the CF.

The information obtained from this review on MSK conditions was used: 1) to present the problem of MSK conditions in the modern Armies and most specifically in the CF; 2) to estimate the magnitude of this problem relative to the other injuries and diseases; and, 3) to describe its impact on operational readiness.

RESULTS

The problem of MSK conditions in the modern Armies

A number of recent publications were found pertaining to injuries in modern armies. Jones, Canham-Chervak, Canada, Mitchener, & Moore (2010) reviewed 2000-2006 US Armed Forces Health Surveillance Center data for non-deployed active duty personnel.[9] As per the recommendations of Hauret, Jones et al., they looked at both traumatic injuries and injury-related MSK conditions and found that injuries resulted in more than 1.95 million medical encounters in 2006.[10] They also reported that the Department of Defence injury rate was over 1600 injury-related visits per 1000 service person years and that the low back was the most commonly affected body part followed by the knee, shoulder and neck. They concluded that "injuries are the biggest health problem of the military services for which medical care is sought."[11]

Reynolds et al. conducted a comparison of non-combat injuries in Infantry, Artillery, Construction Engineers and Special Forces Soldiers.[12] They found the highest injury rates to be in the infantry, construction engineers and artillery personnel and the lowest in the Special Forces. However, they also found that the average light-duty days was higher for injuries sustained by the special forces personnel and attributed this to the fact that this group had a higher incidence of more serious traumatic injuries such as fractures, tears/ruptures and dislocations. The authors attributed this to the fact that Special Forces personnel likely had greater exposure to higher risk activities such as parachuting, running and climbing with packs. Their study also found that the lower extremities and the low back were the most commonly injured areas and that the most common causes were duty-related fitness training, sports and marching with packs.

Although the CF currently does not yet have a systematic process for the surveillance and tracking of medical encounters, it has been estimated that 35-45% of sick parade visits (walk-in medical care appointments) pertain to MSK conditions.[13] Furthermore, beyond this primary care on sick parade, the evidence of medical care sought for MSK conditions manifests in several areas of health services delivery including booked medical appointments, orthopaedic surgical services, diagnostic imaging services, physiotherapy services, specialist consultations and pharmaceutical supplies, including both medications and orthoses, such as custom foot orthotics. A review of potential existing data within the CF identified several other key sources of evidence to help estimate the impact of MSK conditions on the health and operational readiness of the CF. These included the Canadian Forces Health and Lifestyle Information Survey

(CFHLIS) data, CFHS medical discharge data, CF Physiotherapy continuous quality improvement (CQI) database data, CF Physiotherapy workload measurement data and CF Blue Cross expenditure data.

The CF recently completed the report for the CFHLIS 2008/2009.[14] The CFHLIS is a population health survey intended to guide the prioritization of health resource allocation; the planning, implementation, and evaluation of health promotion and disease prevention programs; and the monitoring and effectiveness of health care interventions. Several key details pertaining to MSK injuries were contained within the report. For example, 22.7% of respondents reported suffering from a repetitive strain injury in the past year that was serious enough to limit their normal activities. The most common body parts injured were the lower back (36.2%), followed by the thigh/knee (31.7%) and then the shoulder/upper back (25.8%). With respect to acute injuries, 20.7% of CF respondents reported sustaining an acute injury in the previous year that was serious enough to limit their normal activities. The most common acute injuries reported were sprains/strains of the hip, knee, ankle and foot, followed by back injury. Sports and physical training followed by military training activities were the most common causes of both repetitive strain injuries and acute injuries. When asked to identify Chronic conditions (>6 months) that had been diagnosed by a health professional, 40.7% of conditions were MSK related, comprised of back (17.7%), other MSK (16.2%) and Arthritis (6.8%). In terms of the impact of MSK on CF deployability, for those who responded that they were unable to deploy in the past two years, the main reason reported was MSK related injury (32%) followed by family issue (17%).

THE MAGNITUDE OF MSK CONDITIONS AND ITS PROFILE

As seen in Figure 29.1, information (from November 2009 to February 2010) provided by the CFHS GP HQ,[15] Directorate of Medical Policy demonstrates that approximately 53% of medical releases from the CF are for MSK conditions. Of those service personnel medically discharged for MSK conditions, 27% were due to lower extremity conditions (mostly the knee), 21% were due to spinal disorders (mostly the lumbar spine) and 5% were due to upper extremity conditions (mostly the shoulder).

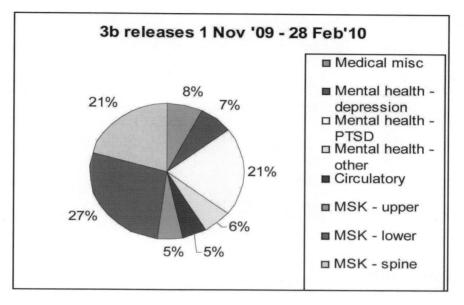

Figure 29.1: CF medical release data

Canada. Department of National Defence. Canadian Forces Health Services. "Medical Release data extraction" *Directorate of Medical Policy- Medical Standards Section*, (2010).

More current supportive data pertaining to the impact of MSK conditions in the CF was available from CF Physiotherapy workload statistics.[16] This physiotherapy utilization data showed that 19,862 CF personnel accessed CF physiotherapy and attended more than 101,000 appointments for MSK conditions. This figure represents almost 30% of the CF Regular force population. To add further to the physiotherapy utilization data, Blue Cross expenditure data indicates that an additional 5,711 military personnel were referred to off-base physiotherapy and attended 62,771 physiotherapy appointments.

In 2000, a CF Physiotherapy CQI Database was developed and piloted as physiotherapy services surveillance system. It allowed the CF Physiotherapy Services to capture valuable injury demographics on a case-by-case basis. Two separate trials of the physiotherapy CQI database were conducted that provided interesting and relevant data. One trial examined the MSK injury profiles observed by CF military physiotherapy officers during the CF peacekeeping mission in Bosnia from 2000-2004.[17] Interestingly, this study reported that on average 28.3% of the Canadian soldiers deployed to Bosnia during a 6-month period consulted with a physiotherapy officer. Not surprisingly, injuries to the lower extremity (41.8%) were the leading reason for physiotherapy consultation, followed by injuries to the spine (28.5%) and the upper extremity (21.5%). In addition, the knee was the most affected body part in the lower extremity, followed by the low back in the spinal conditions and the shoulder in the upper extremity. The second trial of the CF Physiotherapy CQI database was conducted across eight CF locations (Edmonton, Halifax, Cold Lake, Valcartier, Kingston, Ottawa, Petawawa and Bosnia) from 2002-2004. Overall, as indicated in Table 29.1, from the statistics compiled across all locations, the lumbar spine (17.6%), knee (17.2%), ankle (12.2%), and shoulder (11.2%) conditions were by far the most frequent MSK injuries contributing to 58.2% of all the cases reported.

Percentage of MSK Conditions according to body area										
MSK Condition	Bosnia	Cold Lake	Edmonton	Halifax	Kingston	Ottawa	Petawawa	Valcartier	TOTAL Percentage	SD
Shoulder	17.3	13.6	8.5	13.0	12.5	16.8	14.4	7.6	**11.2**	3.3
Elbow	2.9	3.7	1.9	5.1	3.6	7.5	2.9	3.1	**3.2**	1.6
Wrist	1.9	1.5	2.2	3.0	3.6	3.7	2.1	2.0	**2.2**	0.8
Hand	1.9	0.7	1.7	4.0	0.0	4.7	2.5	0.5	**1.8**	1.6
Other Upper Limb	2.1	3.3	0.4	0.8	0.0	0.9	0.6	0.2	**0.8**	1.0
Hip	0.8	2.6	4.1	3.6	3.6	1.9	2.9	2.2	**2.9**	1.0
Knee	18.7	9.5	18.6	13.8	25.0	11.2	20.2	17.5	**17.2**	4.7
Ankle	15.2	9.5	12.3	8.3	12.5	6.5	14.4	13.3	**12.2**	2.9
Foot	6.9	16.1	14.5	9.3	12.5	4.7	5.4	10.9	**10.7**	3.9
Other Lower Limb	5.6	2.2	4.4	5.1	8.9	3.7	6.0	3.0	**4.4**	2.0
Cervical Spine	5.6	12.8	8.1	8.9	1.8	10.3	5.1	10.8	**8.6**	3.4
Thoracic Spine	2.4	2.2	4.0	1.4	1.8	3.7	1.8	3.9	**3.0**	1.0
Lumbar Spine	16.0	17.9	16.8	19.0	14.3	17.8	19.8	17.2	**17.6**	1.6
Sacro-iliac Spine	2.1	0.7	1.2	0.8	0.0	0.0	0.2	1.0	**1.0**	0.7
Other spine	0.0	0.4	0.2	3.0	0.0	0.9	0.0	0.8	**0.7**	0.9
Post-op	0.0	3.3	0.9	0.4	0.0	5.6	1.6	4.9	**2.2**	2.1
Other conditions	0.5	0.0	0.0	0.2	0.0	0.0	0.0	0.8	**0.3**	0.3
Other diseases	0.0	0.0	0.0	0.4	0.0	0.0	0.0	0.3	**0.1**	0.2
TOTAL	100	100	100	100	100	100	100	100	**100**	

Table 29.1: Percentage of MSK conditions according to anatomical area and Base.

Canada. Department of National Defence. Canadian Forces Health Services. "The use of a systematic process to reduce MSK injuries in the CF: comparisons of MSK injury profiles between the three CF environments, bases with different training requirements, and MOSIDs". *Surgeon General's Health Research Program: Quality of Life Reports.* (2005).

The Impact of MSK Conditions on Operational Readiness

Two recent US Army studies were found that provided interesting perspectives on the impact of MSK conditions on operations in Afghanistan and Iraq.[18] Cohen *et al.* reviewed the medical evacuation data of 34 006 personnel from January 2004 to December 2007 and found that disease and non-battle-related injuries were the leading cause of soldier attrition in modern warfare.[19] They reported that MSK and connective tissue disorders (24%), combat injuries (14%), neurological disorders (10%), psychiatric diagnoses (9%) and spinal pain (7%) were the leading reasons for medical evacuations from the deployed settings. Of further note, Cohen *et al.* found that there was a low rate of return to duty for MSK and connective tissue disorders, particularly of the spine and suggested interesting parallels between emotional distress of combat operations and spinal pain.[20]

Hauret, Taylor *et al.* (2010) reviewed 31,197 air medical evacuation files from October 2001 to December 2006 and also found that non-battle injuries were the leading reason for medical evacuations from Afghanistan (36%) and Iraq (35%).[21] Additionally, they confirmed that the vertebral column was the most affected body area followed by the lower extremity and that the low back was the most commonly affected body part followed by the knee and then the shoulder. Hauret, Taylor *et al.* also identified that the three main causes of injury were sports and physical training, followed by falls and jumps, followed by motor vehicle-related incidents.[22]

In their survey of 696 active-duty soldiers on limited duty due to MSK injuries, Jennings, Yoder, Heiner, Loan, & Bingham (2008) reported that almost 75% were unable to perform all of the US Army common military tasks and 50% were unable to perform their jobs in a deployed work setting.[23] Our CFHLIS data supports these findings by capturing that MSK conditions were the largest reason for personnel not being able to deploy during the previous 2 years. This is consistent with another US Army study by Konitzer, Fargo, Brininger and Reed (2008) that found that soldiers reported increased back, neck and upper extremity pain during deployment and that the wearing of individual body armour was the primary aggravating factor.[24] Furthermore, 18% of their respondents, reported difficulties with firing their weapons due to MSK pain. Further support for the impact of MSK conditions on deployments is evidenced by Rowe and Carpenter's (in press) work that describes the experiences of physiotherapy officers deployed to Afghanistan.[25]

Discussion

The findings in this paper add to the understanding of MSK conditions in military populations and confirm that the incidence and impact of MSK-related injuries are a growing concern amongst the modern militaries of the world. Similar to other studies, our CF findings support that military-related activities including physical fitness training, sports and military training were the most common cause of injuries and also that knees and backs, followed by shoulders are the most commonly affected body parts in military personnel.[26]

With respect to the CFHLIS data, it is worth noting that where 23% of CF personnel reported suffering from repetitive strain injuries in the previous year, that by comparison, only 14% of the general Canadian population reported repetitive strain injuries.[27] Similarly for acute injuries, the CFHLIS percentage for acute injuries was 21%, when Statistics Canada showed 13% for general population. It has been evidenced in the literature that the day-to-day tasks of military personnel are very different from those of the general civilian population.[28] Hollander and Bell reported that US soldiers were in physically demanding jobs that put them at increased risk of injury and disability. The higher injury rates in a military population may be due to the unique nature of their job, environmental factors, equipment, time-constraints and the need to perform under pressure.[29] Asymmetric working postures, frequent reaching, load carrying, repetitious tasks, heavy material handling and exposure to vibration are all risk factors that put them at a higher risk of developing MSK overuse injuries.[30]

The impact of not properly addressing MSK conditions could be more detrimental than realized. As depicted above, MSK conditions occur at high rates in all settings of the military, right from Basic Recruit training through to operational tasks in deployed settings. If not adequately managed, MSK conditions can lead to temporary or permanent medical conditions that limit deployability and operational readiness. Permanent medical conditions may result in medical discharges which then necessitate increased resources for the recruitment and training of new and inexperienced recruits. In the deployed setting, MSK conditions result in increased medical evacuations and subsequently decreased force strength when personnel are unable to perform their operational military duties.

We believe that an economic analysis of the financial impact of MSK conditions on the CF would be staggering. Beyond the direct day-to-day healthcare costs of managing MSK conditions in terms of medical consultations, specialist consultations, physiotherapy, orthotics and bracing, diagnostic imaging and pharmaceutical expenditures, there would also be high indirect costs related to the burden of MSK conditions. These indirect costs would be associated with the decreased ability of CF personnel to exercise due to their MSK conditions. The resulting reduced physical fitness of injured soldiers would lead to more failed fitness tests, increased weight gain and greater risks for developing long-term cardio-vascular conditions. CFHLIS (2008-2009) data does confirm that CF personnel are trending towards less activity and increased obesity.[31] This scenario has the potential to spiral further downwards as overweight personnel are at increased risk to re-injure themselves while training to meet military physical fitness testing standards. In reality, little is known about the full cost impact of MSK conditions on the CF. However, it would be very logical and rational to assume that with the high incidence of MSK conditions in the CF, that there are significant annual expenditures on the direct medical care of our service personnel. Furthermore, it is important to keep in mind that MSK conditions not only have an impact on the operational readiness of a fighting force but also represent a significant financial challenge in terms of provision of health services, medical pensions and replacement recruitment and training.

LIMITATIONS OF THE STUDY

Several limitations must be considered in interpreting these findings. Firstly, it is important to recognize the difficulties in data availability within the CFHS. While an integrated electronic health record is in development, it has not been fully developed and is not yet available to provide the reporting required with respect to quality injury surveillance. Several other initiatives, including an Injury Surveillance Database are under way within CFHS that may enhance the information that will be available. However, these may also have challenges of national administration, comprehensiveness and reporting capability.

Also, physiotherapy utilization statistics as well as Physiotherapy CQI database statistics only capture personnel who were either referred to physiotherapy or accessed directly. This could possibly lead to an under-estimation of the impact of MSK conditions since an unknown number of personnel with MSK conditions may never access physiotherapy services as they may be managed directly by other healthcare providers.

Moreover, our review of literature and CF utilization data does not include the comprehensive rehabilitation care provided to our complex rehabilitation cases returning from Afghanistan with significant, poly-trauma battlefield injuries. While the number of this population is fortunately small, they nevertheless deserve and require an extensive amount of healthcare resources, aimed towards maximizing their return to optimal function.

Despite the limitations noted above, the data that were available are certainly enough to demonstrate that MSK conditions are undoubtedly causing a very high burden to the health and operational readiness of the CF. It is therefore critically necessary to more accurately capture data on the impact of MSK conditions on the CF and to strategize and develop programs aimed to better manage and prevent their negative effects on the CF.

RECOMMENDATIONS

It is believed that a comprehensive and integrated MSK management program is required to meet the current challenges of the high incidence of MSK conditions in the CF. Such an integrated MSK program would require the following:

1. A robust, national injury surveillance system.
2. Increased clinical resources in key areas such as physiotherapy resources; both in-garrison and on deployments.
3. Enhanced injury prevention capabilities.
4. A supported research division with the objective of setting research priorities relevant to CF population.

While the CFHS currently has initiatives under way to address these requirements, now is the time to ensure that MSK conditions are recognized as a burden to the health of the CF so that greater priority is given to initiatives in this area of healthcare.

The CFHS needs a more comprehensive and user-friendly electronic surveillance system. An injury surveillance system is currently in trial at Canadian Forces Base Valcartier and once developed and proven, will need to be implemented nationally as quickly as possible at all locations and intake points where patients may present for their first medical consultation for new conditions. This will provide the most comprehensive information regarding the types of injuries in the CF as well as the most common causes. Since physiotherapists are becoming more and more recognized as integral subject matter experts in the area of MSK care, more resources should be invested in this area as well.[32] A physiotherapy CQI database is in development but needs greater support to achieve a national roll-out capability. Such a database will provide the CFHS with patient demographics and MSK profiles and provide a capability for results-based, clinical outcomes for performance measurement. Ultimately, the data captured from such a database would provide physiotherapy managers with the necessary information required to develop evidence-based clinical pathways for the most common conditions to maximize the efficiency and monitor effectiveness of physiotherapy services.

In terms of resources, physiotherapists have a specialized skill-set that can directly influence the outcomes of MSK management both in terms of earlier access to medical treatment, as well as injury prevention.[33] We must maximize clinical physiotherapy services and resources, both in-garrison and in the deployed setting. In-garrison physiotherapy services have been shown to be more cost efficient than off-base services yet on-base services are understaffed. Our analysis of CF physiotherapy utilization date from 2009, demonstrated that patients assessed at on-base physiotherapy clinics only required an average of five follow-up treatment appointments.[34] By comparison, patients that were assessed at off-base physiotherapy clinics required an average of 11 follow-up treatment sessions. While more investigation would be required to determine the reasons for this difference, it is evident that these six additional off-base appointments would likely result in an additional two to three weeks of limited duty restrictions and lost manpower. Moreover, the cost of these additional appointments of $240 - $300 per patient would result in an additional estimated expenditure of $1.4 million to $1.7 million for the 5,711 CF personnel treated off-base in 2009. Additional in-garrison physiotherapy staffing would help maximize the efficient use of on-base physiotherapy services.

On bases, military soldiers training for operations have been compared to athletes training for competition.[35] The CF Physiotherapy profession is developing a military sports physiotherapy approach aimed towards keeping soldiers healthy and on the field of battle. On operations, this becomes even more important as the closer soldiers are treated to the front-line, the more likely they will be to remain fit for duty. Based on this model, more physiotherapy support would be beneficial in-garrison as well as on deployed operations.

With respect to physiotherapy in the deployed setting, Rowe and Carpenter (in press) described the excessive workload placed on deployed military physiotherapists in Afghanistan.[36] Davis, Machen, & Chang (2006) reported on the US Army's tremendous success with their co-location of army physical therapists with orthopaedic surgeons in their combat support hospitals and they recognized the need to have more physical therapists further forward at the Level I and II echelons of care.[37] Furthermore, Rhon *et al.* positively described the role of the Army Physical Therapist as part of the Brigade Combat Team.[38] In their experience, early access to care prevented injuries from becoming chronic and reduced medical evacuations, thus conserving force strength. Rhon *et al.* also detailed that physical therapists that have deployed more forward with the troops have also played active roles in injury prevention.[39] The CFHS need to consider the benefits of placing additional physiotherapy officer resources on deployed operations in the Role 1.

Hauret, Jones *et al.* (2010) suggest that recognized injury profiles can be reduced through targeted injury prevention initiatives.[40] While injury prevention work is currently underway, more resources are required. CF Physiotherapists on bases and Force Health Protection colleagues are actively working together to develop and implement injury prevention strategies related to running and fitness training, ankle injuries, ergonomic education and low back pain education programs. Better educated and better conditioned personnel will be stronger and more resilient to the physical stresses that may lead to injuries. An enhanced injury prevention cell and dedicated physiotherapy, human resources could increase the speed and scope of new injury prevention program initiatives.

Our final recommendation pertains to the importance of the on-going development of a military-specific health research capability. To this end, the CF Surgeon General has recently introduced such a CF health research strategy aimed towards developing an organizational culture of research that will both generate and utilize evidence from health research. Our objective is to ensure that MSK injuries become a research priority to the CFHS, so that enough attention and resources are given to the increasing and often unrecognized burden of MSK injuries on the CF population. Research initiatives in this area can be used to investigate key areas of MSK management that could lead to improved treatments through clinical pathways and guidelines or injury prevention programs and policy developments that meet the unique needs of the CF.

Conclusion

This compilation of evidence presented suggests that the impact of MSK conditions in the CF may be greater than realized. Our own internal statistics confirm that MSK conditions are a leading cause of morbidity in the CF, as similar to other modern militaries of the world. High health service utilization rates, increasing medical expenditures and high MSK injury rates support our views that MSK conditions have a significant impact on the CF. This is evident in all aspects of health services delivery including primary care on sick parade, orthopaedic surgical services, diagnostic imaging services, physiotherapy services, pharmaceutical supplies including braces and orthoses, medical review boards and ultimately operational readiness. It is believed that a more integrated musculoskeletal management program with a multi-pronged team approach could lead to improved clinical outcomes and efficiencies in this area.

[1] B.P. Bergman and S.A. Miller, "Unfit for further service: Trends in medical discharge from the British Army 1861-1998," *Journal of Royal Army Corps* 146, 3 (2000): 204-211; M. Feuerstein, S.M. Berkowitz and C.A. Peck, "Musculo-skeletal disability in U.S. Army personnel: prevalence, gender and military occupational specialties," *Journal of Occupational Environmental Medicine* 39 (1997): 68-78; L.J. Hebert and P.R. Rowe, "The lessons learned from the Canadian Forces physiotherapy experience during the peacekeeping operations in Bosnia," *Military Medicine* 172, 8 (2007): 829-834; K.R Kaufman, S. Brodine, and R. Shaffer, "Military training-related injuries: Surveillance, research and prevention," American Journal of Preventative Medicine 18, 3S (2000): 54-63; T.J. Songer and R.E. LaPorte, "Disabilities due to injury in the military," *American Journal of Preventative Medicine* 18 (2000): 33-40; V.M. Mattila, J. Parkkari, H. Korpela and H. Pihlajamaki, "Hospitalisation for injuries among Finnish conscripts in 1990-1991," *Accident Analysis and Prevention* 38, 1 (2006): 99-104.

[2] B.P. Bergman and S.A. Miller, "Unfit for further service: Trends in medical discharge from the British Army 1861-1998," *Journal of Royal Army Corps* 146, 3 (2000): 200-211.

[3] N.S. Bell, C.E. Schwartz, T. Harford, I.E. Hollander and P.J. Amoroso, "The changing profile of disability in the U.S. Army: 1981-2005," *Disability and Health Journal* 1, 1 (2008): 14-24.

[4] S. Darakjy, R.E. Marin, J.J. Knapik and B.H. Jones, "Injuries and illnesses among armor brigade soldiers during operational training," *Military Medicine* 171, 11 (2006): 1051-1056.

[5] K.G. Hauret, B.H. Jones, S.H. Bullock, M. Canham-Chervak and S. Canada, "Musculoskeletal Injuries: Description of an under-recognized injury problem among military personnel," *American Journal of Preventative Medicine* 38, 1S (2010): S61-S70.

[6]K.G. Hauret, B.H. Jones, S.H. Bullock, M. Canham-Chervak and S. Canada, "Musculoskeletal Injuries: Description of an under-recognized injury problem among military personnel," *American Journal of Preventative Medicine* 38, 1S (2010):S62.

[7]K.G. Hauret, B.H. Jones, S.H. Bullock, M. Canham-Chervak and S. Canada, "Musculoskeletal Injuries: Description of an under-recognized injury problem among military personnel," *American Journal of Preventative Medicine* 38, 1S (2010): S62.

[8] K.G. Hauret, B.H. Jones, S.H. Bullock, M. Canham-Chervak and S. Canada, "Musculoskeletal Injuries: Description of an under-recognized injury problem among military personnel," *American Journal of Preventative Medicine* 38, 1S (2010): S64-S66.

[9]B.H. Jones, M. Canham-Chervak, S. Canada, T.A. Mitchener and S. Moore, "Medical Surveillance of injuries in the U.S. Military: Descriptive epidemiology and recommendations for improvement," *American Journal of Preventative Medicine* 38, 1S (2010): S42-S60.

[10]B.H. Jones, M. Canham-Chervak, S. Canada, T.A. Mitchener and S. Moore, "Medical Surveillance of injuries in the U.S. Military: Descriptive epidemiology and recommendations for improvement," *American Journal of Preventative Medicine* 38, 1S (2010): S44.

[11]B.H. Jones, M. Canham-Chervak, S. Canada, T.A. Mitchener and S. Moore, "Medical Surveillance of injuries in the U.S. Military: Descriptive epidemiology and recommendations for improvement," *American Journal of Preventative Medicine* 38, 1S (2010): S59.

[12]K. Reynolds, L. Cosio-Lima, M. Bovill, W. Tharion, J. William and T. Hodges, "A comparison of injuries, limited-duty days, and injury risk factors in infantry, artillery, construction engineers and special forces soldiers," *Military Medicine* 174, 7 (2009): 702-708.

[13]Canada. Department of National Defence. Canadian Forces Health Services, "Surgeon General's Report - 2010," *Government of Canada*, from http://www.forces.gc.ca/health-sante/pub/sgr-rmc-2010/default-eng.asp, accessed 20 April 2011.

[14]Canada. Department of National Defence. "Canadian Forces Health and Lifestyle Information Survey- 2008/2009," *Directorate of Force Health Protection*, http://www.forces.gc.ca/health-sante/pub/hlis-sssv/pdf/20082009-rgf-res-eng.pdf, accessed 20 April 2011.

[15]Canada. Department of National Defence. Canadian Forces Health Services. "Medical Release data extraction" *Directorate of Medical Policy- Medical Standards Section*, (2010).

[16]Canada. Department of National Defence. Canadian Forces Health Services " Physiotherapy Workload Statistics 2009" *Directorate of Medical Policy, Physiotherapy Section*, (2010).

[17]L.J. Hebert and P.R. Rowe, "The lessons learned from the Canadian Forces physiotherapy experience during the peacekeeping operations in Bosnia," *Military Medicine* 172, 8 (2007): 829-834.

[18]K.G. Hauret, B.J. Taylor, N.S. Clemmons, S.R. Block and B.H. Jones, "Frequency and causes of non-battle injuries air evacuated from Operations Iraqi Freedom and Enduring Freedom, U.S. Army, 2001-2006," *American Journal of Preventative Medicine* 38, 1S, (2010): S94-S107; S.P. Cohen, C. Brown, C. Kurihara, A. Plunkett, C. Nguyen and S.A. Strassels, "Diagnoses and factors associated with medical evacuation and return to duty for service members participating in Operation Iraqi Freedom or Operation Enduring Freedom: a prospective cohort study," *Lancet* (2010): 301-309, http://www.ncbi.nlm.nih.gov/pubmed/20109957, accessed 14 April 2011.

[19]S.P. Cohen, C. Brown, C. Kurihara, A. Plunkett, C. Nguyen and S.A. Strassels, "Diagnoses and factors associated with medical evacuation and return to duty for service members participating in Operation Iraqi Freedom or Operation Enduring Freedom: a prospective cohort study," *Lancet* (2010): 309, http://www.ncbi.nlm.nih.gov/pubmed/20109957, accessed 14 April 2011.

[20]S.P. Cohen, C. Brown, C. Kurihara, A. Plunkett, C. Nguyen and S.A. Strassels, "Diagnoses and factors associated with medical evacuation and return to duty for service members participating in Operation Iraqi Freedom or Operation Enduring Freedom: a prospective cohort study," *Lancet* (2010): 308, http://www.ncbi.nlm.nih.gov/pubmed/20109957, accessed 14 April 2011.

[21]K.G. Hauret, B.J. Taylor, N.S. Clemmons, S.R. Block and B.H. Jones, "Frequency and causes of non-battle injuries air evacuated from Operations Iraqi Freedom and Enduring Freedom, U.S. Army, 2001-2006," *American Journal of Preventative Medicine* 38, 1S, (2010): S97.

[22]K.G. Hauret, B.J. Taylor, N.S. Clemmons, S.R. Block and B.H. Jones, "Frequency and causes of non-battle injuries air evacuated from Operations Iraqi Freedom and Enduring Freedom, U.S. Army, 2001-2006," *American Journal of Preventative Medicine* 38, 1S, (2010): S104.

[23]B.M. Jennings, L.H. Yoder, S.L. Heiner, L.A. Loan and M.O. Bingham, "Soldiers with musculoskeletal injuries," *Journal of Nursing Scholarship* 40, 3 (2008): 268-274.

[24]L.N. Konitzer, M.V. Fargo, T.L. Brininger and M.L. Reed, "Association between back, neck, and upper extremity musculoskeletal pain and the individual body armor," *Journal of Hand Therapy* 21, 2 (2008): 143–149.

[25]P.R. Rowe and C. Carpenter, "The recent experiences and challenges of military physiotherapists deployed to Afghanistan- A qualitative study," *Physiotherapy Canada* (in press 2011).

[26]B.M. Jennings, L.H. Yoder, S.L. Heiner, L.A. Loan and M.O. Bingham, "Soldiers with musculoskeletal injuries," *Journal of Nursing Scholarship* 40, 3 (2008): 268-274.

[27]Statistics Canada, "Public use micro data file (PUMF): Integrated derived variable (DV) and grouped variable specifications," *Canadian Community Health Survey* (CCHS) Cycle 4.1(2007/8), Government of Canada, (2008).

[28]I.E. Hollander and N.S. Bell, "Physically demanding jobs and occupational injury and disability in the U.S. Army," *Military Medicine* 175, 10 (2010): 705-712.

[29]Bergman and Miller, "Unfit for further service," 204-211; S.M. Berkowitz, M. Feuerstein, M.S. Lopez and C.A. Peck, "Occupational back disability in U.S. Army personnel," *Military Medicine* 164, 6 (1999): 412-418.

[30]S.M. Berkowitz, M. Feuerstein, M.S. Lopez and C.A. Peck, "Occupational back disability in U.S. Army personnel," *Military Medicine* 164, 6 (1999): 415; M. Feuerstein, S.M. Berkowitz and C.A. Peck, "Musculoskeletal disability in U.S. Army personnel: prevalence, gender and military occupational specialties," *Journal of Occupational Environmental Medicine* 39 (1997): 73-74.

[31]Canada, Department of National Defence, Canadian Forces Health Services, "Canadian Forces Health and Lifestyle Information Survey- 2008/2009," *Directorate of Force Health Protection.* http://www.forces.gc.ca/health-sante/pub/hlis-sssv/pdf/20082009-rgf-res-eng.pdf, accessed 20 April 2011.

[32]J.D. Childs, J.M. Whitman, M.L. Pugia, P.S. Sizer, T.W. Flynn and A. Delitto, "Knowledge in managing musculoskeletal conditions and educational preparation of physical therapists in the uniformed services," *Military Medicine* 172, 4 (2007): 440-445; D.I. Rhon, N. Gill, D. Teyhen, M. Scherer and S. Goffar, "Clinician perception of the impact of deployed physical therapists as physician extenders in a combat environment," *Military Medicine* 175, 5 (2010): 305-312.

[33]D.I. Rhon, "A physical therapist experience, observation and practice with an infantry brigade combat team in support of Operation Iraqi Freedom," *Military Medicine* 175, 6 (2010): 442-447.

[34]Canada, Department of National Defence, Canadian Forces Health Services, "Physiotherapy Workload Statistics 2009"

[35]B.H. Jones and J. Knapik, "Physical Training and Exercise-Related injuries: Surveillance, research and injury prevention in military populations," *Sports Medicine* 27, 2 (1999): 111-125.

[36]P.R. Rowe and C. Carpenter, "The recent experiences and challenges of military physiotherapists deployed to Afghanistan- A qualitative study," *Physiotherapy Canada* (in press 2011).

[37]S. Davis, M.S. Machen and L. Chang, "The beneficial relationship of the collocation of orthopedics and physical therapy in a deployed setting: Operation Iraqi Freedom," *Military Medicine* 171, 3 (2006): 220-223.

[38]D.I. Rhon, N. Gill, D. Teyhen, M. Scherer and S. Goffar, "Clinician perception of the impact of deployed physical therapists as physician extenders in a combat environment," *Military Medicine* 175, 5 (2010): 309-311.

[39]D.I. Rhon, N. Gill, D. Teyhen, M. Scherer and S. Goffar, "Clinician perception of the impact of deployed physical therapists as physician extenders in a combat environment," *Military Medicine* 175, 5 (2010): 309-310.

[40]K.G. Hauret, B.H. Jones, S.H. Bullock, M. Canham-Chervak and S. Canada, "Musculoskeletal Injuries: Description of an under-recognized injury problem among military personnel," *American Journal of Preventative Medicine* 38, 1S (2010): S67.

[41]Canada. Department of National Defence. Canadian Forces Health Services. "Medical Release data extraction" *Directorate of Medical Policy- Medical Standards Section*, (2010).

[42]Canada. Department of National Defence. Canadian Forces Health Services. "The use of a systematic process to reduce MSK injuries in the CF: comparisons of MSK injury profiles between the three CF environments, bases with different training requirements, and MOSIDs". *Surgeon General's Health Research Program: Quality of Life Reports.* (2005).

CHAPTER 30

Wheelchair Skills Training for Trainers and Manual Wheelchair Users

R. Lee Kirby, MD, FRCPC, and Cher Smith, BScOT, Sponsor/host:
Lieutenant-Colonel M.H. Besemann, B.Sc. MD FRCPC Diploma Sport Medicine,
Head of Rehabilitation Medicine, Canadian Forces Health Services
Group Headquarters-Health Services Delivery

ABSTRACT

A didactic presentation intended for a broad stakeholder audience combined with a practical session providing firsthand experience to a range of caregiver and manual wheelchair user skills, are intended to focus therapists on training issues by learning "tricks of the trade" and motor-skillslearning principles. Very favourable workshop follow-up exercises have been the encouragement for partner funders to facilitate this workshop for at least two additional jurisdictions to occur in 2009Q4.

WHEELCHAIR SKILLS TRAINING FOR TRAINERS AND MANUAL WHEELCHAIR USERS

Research evidence has been accumulating that demonstrates the safety and superior efficacy of a formal approach to wheelchair skills training for wheelchair users and their caregivers. The Wheelchair Skills Program (WSP), available free on the Internet (www.wheelchairskillsprogram.ca), includes useful evaluation and training tools to help practitioners translate this research evidence into clinical practice. The low-tech, high-impact WSP is designed to help practitioners optimize the safety and maneuverability challenges that face wheelchair users and their caregivers.

The measurement properties of the Wheelchair Skills Test (WST) have been documented.[1] The WST has been found to be safe, practical, reliable, valid and useful. The WST has been used as a screening or outcome measure in a number of studies. The relationships between the objective WST and the questionnaire version (WST-Q) have been reported.[2] The correlations between the total WST and WST-Q scores were found to be excellent, although the WST-Q scores were slightly higher. The objective WST is a measure of wheelchair-skill capacity, whereas the WST-Q can be used to assess either capacity or performance.

Regarding the Wheelchair Skills Training Program (WSTP), we initially completed two randomized controlled trials on wheelchair users, one on wheelchair users admitted for initial rehabilitation[3] and one on wheelchair users in the community.[4] In both, we found that the WSTP was safe, practical and resulted in significantly greater improvements (2-3 fold) in wheelchair skills performance than standard care. In a third randomized controlled trial, on occupational therapy students, we found that the WSTP resulted in significantly greater improvement (2-3 fold) in wheelchair skills than a standard undergraduate occupational therapy curriculum[5] and that these skills were retained nine to twelve months later. In a later pilot study in a rehabilitation centre,[6] we provided less than 50 minutes of training on wheelchair-handling skills to caregivers of wheelchair users. We found that the WSTP was an effective way to improve caregiver skills and that these skills were retained. We have also conducted studies focusing on optimizing the training of specific skills.[7] Routhier et al., have translated the WSP into Canadian French and have replicated our study on the WSTP in the rehabilitation-centre setting.[8] Mountain et al., have demonstrated the positive effect of the WSTP using powered wheelchairs for patients with stroke and additional work on powered wheelchairs is underway.[9] We have also explored use of the WSP in long-term-care settings[10] and less resourced or post-conflict settings (e.g. India, Jordan and Bosnia).[11]

On September 9, 2008, Dr Besemann and members of his team visited the Nova Scotia Rehabilitation Centre in Halifax and participated in a WSP mini-workshop designed specifically for them. Over the succeeding year, Dr Besemann recognized that the WSP might meet the need of some military personnel and veterans who had mobility problems. He contacted the WSP group and invited them to organize this workshop.

Learning Objectives

On completion of the 1-hour didactic presentation, general-audience attendees will be able to:
1. Explain the rationale, elements and the research evidence regarding the components of the Wheelchair Skills Program (WSP) for manual wheelchairs. operated by their users.
2. Describe the practical steps involved in conducting wheelchair skills training.

On completion of the 3-day workshop, trainer attendees will be able to:
1. Explain the rationale, elements and the research evidence regarding the components of the Wheelchair Skills Program (WSP) for manual wheelchairs operated by their users.
2. Describe the practical steps involved in conducting wheelchair skills training.
3. Demonstrate appropriate assessment, spotting and training techniques.
4. Implement the WSP in their own settings.

On completion of the 2-day workshop, wheelchair-using attendees will be able to:
1. Briefly describe the components of the WSP for manual wheelchairs operated by their users.
2. Describe the practical steps involved in conducting wheelchair skills training.
3. Demonstrate appropriate approaches to the safe performance of wheelchair skills within their capabilities.
4. Describe a plan for refining and extending their wheelchair-skill repertoires.

METHOD

BRIEF DESCRIPTION OF WORKSHOP

The workshop included a 1-hour didactic introduction to the WSP including wheelchair video demonstrations, the WSP principles and a brief summary of the current body of the evidence. This presentation occurred on Day 1 during the lunch break between practical sessions. The presentation was relevant for a broad audience, including administrators and other stakeholders.

The practical component of this workshop on Days 1-3 was relevant for therapists who have interactions with people who are wheelchair users and their caregivers. The practical portion of the schedule provided trainer-participants with an opportunity to experience a range of caregiver and manual wheelchair user skills including spotting techniques and assessment methods, but focused on training issues (both the 'tricks of the trade' and motor-skills learning principles).

On Days 2 and 3, the focus turned to wheelchair-using participants. The trainers from Day 1 assisted the workshop faculty in assessing and training the wheelchair users.

Dates of Session. September 13-15, 2010.
Length. 3 days.

Responsibilities of the Faculty

The faculty:
1. Worked with representatives of the host institution(s) to customize the workshop to meet the needs of the intended audiences.
2. Prepared needed materials.
3. Designed and delivered the curriculum to meet the objectives.
4. Provided a summary of the workshop evaluation results.

Responsibilities of the Sponsor/Host

The sponsor/host provided the local arrangements, as specified below:
1. Advertised the workshop as needed.
2. Identified trainer and wheelchair-using participants.
3. Distributed pre-workshop information to the participants as needed.
4. Arranged for the printing and distribution of handouts provided by the faculty.
5. Arranged for and provided lunch and coffee-break refreshments for faculty and participants.
6. Booked space and arranged equipment for the workshop activities.
7. Arranged for the use of wheelchairs. These were needed for all of the trainer-

participants. For this workshop, we confined ourselves to manual wheelchairs. For Day 1, we needed one wheelchair for every two trainer-participants. About half of the wheelchairs were be of the modular lightweight type with folding frames and removable footrests. The others were rigid-frame ultra light wheelchairs. All had cushions that fit the wheelchairs. A range of seat sizes was needed to accommodate people of different sizes.

8. At the beginning of Days 1 and 2, the participants for that day registered and signed waivers.
9. Participants were provided with nametags.

TRAVEL
Faculty arrived Sunday afternoon, September 12, 2010, to meet the logistician and review the facilities and wheelchairs. Faculty returned to Halifax on the evening on September 15.

EVALUATION AND CERTIFICATES
At the close of Day 3, the participants completed workshop evaluation forms. At the closing session, certificates of participation were distributed.

RESULTS

Mailing address	Ottawa region: 17 PQ: 1 Petawawa: 1 Alberta: 1
Affiliated with Canadian Forces	5/20
Sex	M: 6/20, F: 14/20
Age (yrs) (n = 19)	Mean 36.3 yrs, range 20-50 yrs
How many years experience do you have working with wheelchairs and wheelchair users? (n = 19)	Mean 11.1 yrs, range 0.5-27 yrs
Which of the following descriptions apply to you (tick all that apply): Only those ticked are shown	
• Wheelchair user	6
• Occupational therapist	10
• Physical therapist	3
• Therapy aid	1 (OT assistant)
• Physician	1
Which of the following reasons account for you doing this on-line education program (tick all that apply):	
• Interest	16
• Job requirement	7
• Other (specify)	2

Table 30.1: Summary of REGISTRATION data. (N = 20 unless otherwise indicated)

In response to the instructions "Please tick a box for each question, in the table below, scoring as follows: 1 = "Extremely not", 2 = "Somewhat not", 3 = "Neutral", 4 = "Somewhat so" and 5 = "Extremely so".

Did you find the session:	Total score	%
Useful?	89/90	99%
Relevant?	88/90	98%
Easily tolerated?	87/90	97%
Understandable?	88/90	98%
Enjoyable?	89/90	99%
Inspiring?	89/90	99%

Table 30.2. Evaluation of the workshop, N = 18.

* See Annex 30.A for additional questionnaire responses.

DISCUSSION

The Workshop was completed as planned and appears to have met its objectives. The participants enjoyed the experience and perceived it as useful. A low-tech, high-impact intervention such as the WSP appears to be highly suitable for military personnel, veterans and civilian populations in Canada and around the world, including less-developed nations and post-conflict zones.

Specifically we recommend that:

1. The "made in Canada" WSP be implemented at the Ottawa Rehabilitation Centre.
2. The Canadian Military endorse and promote the WSP at:
    a. All of the sites where its military personnel and veterans receive rehabilitation care.
    b. Sites in conflict and post-conflict zones where civilians receive rehabilitation care.
    c. Sites where its NATO allies offer rehabilitation care.

ACKNOWLEDGEMENTS

We thank the Canadian Forces for funding and the Ottawa Rehabilitation Centre for hosting the event. This workshop would not have been possible without the efforts of Lieutenant Colonel M.H. Besemann of the Canadian Forces and Karen St Germain of the Ottawa Rehabilitation Centre. We also thank Pauline Godsell and Amy Passmore of the Canadian Forces for their help.

Individual Skills for Manual Wheelchairs Operated by Wheelchair Users. N = 15.			
Version #	Individual Skills	n	%
1.	Rolls forward 10m	8	53
2.	Rolls forward 10m in 30s	5	33
3.	Rolls backward 5m	4	27
4.	Turns 90° while moving forward L&R	5	33
5.	Turns 90° while moving backward L&R	5	33
6.	Turns 180°in place L&R	2	13
7.	Maneuvers sideways L&R	11	73
8.	Gets through hinged door in both directions	8	53
9.	Reaches 1.5m high object	1	7
10.	Picks object from floor	5	33
11.	Relieves weight from buttocks	9	60
12.	Transfers from WC to bench and back	3	20
13.	Folds and unfolds wheelchair	7	47
14.	Rolls 100m	2	13
15.	Avoids moving obstacles L&R	2	13
16.	Ascends 5° incline	8	53
17.	Descends 5° incline	9	60
18.	Ascends 10° incline	10	66
19.	Descends 10° incline	10	66
20.	Rolls 2m across 5° side-slope L&R	8	53
21.	Rolls 2m on soft surface	9	60
22.	Gets over 15cm pot-hole	12	80
23.	Gets over 2cm threshold	10	66
24.	Ascends 5cm level change	10	66
25.	Descends 5cm level change	10	66
26.	Ascends 15cm curb	14	93
27.	Descends 15cm curb	11	73
28.	Performs 30s stationary wheelie	9	60
29.	Turns 180° in place in wheelie position L&R	8	53
30.	Gets from ground into wheelchair	11	73
31.	Ascends stairs	13	87
32.	Descends stairs	12	80

Table 30.3. Post-training response to q uestion "Which of the following skills did you learn something new about or improve upon?"

Abbreviations and symbols: WC = wheelchair, L&R = includes performance on both left and right

ANNEX 30.A - ADDITIONAL QUESTIONNAIRE RESPONSES

In response to the instructions **"Please tick a box for each question, in the table below, scoring as follows**: 1 = "Extremely not", 2 = "Somewhat not", 3 = "Neutral", 4 = "Somewhat so" and 5 = "Extremely so".

Duration of the session (pick one):
- too short: 0/18 = 0%
- just right: 18/18 = 100%
- too long: 0/18 = 0%

Would you recommend it to others?
- Yes: 18/18 = 100%
- No: 0/18 = 0%

Question: Can you think of anything we neglected to include?
Answers:
- No. Practice worked well
- Not really as so much was new to me but maybe more considerations re applications to populations with cognitive impairments
- Some reference to power when relevant
- No not really
- How to make a spotter strap
- Potentially ask/review wheelchair parts and …theory at the beginning of the workshop
- No
- Nothing! You thought of everything and have excellent reference material easily accessible
- No, you have been very thorough
- No
- It would have been nice to have at least one copy of the manual to see. It would also be nice to have a short time (1-2 hours) on power wheelchair

Question: What did you find most helpful?
Answers:
- Experiencing all mobility issues. Learning how to teach
- Boot camp style worked for clinical. Practicing the skills myself was useful in learning. Having clients present how they perform skills and then seeing a pass can have a variety of ways to complete
- Experience learning. Trying things and then talking about them
- Everything! Raised body awareness, great hands on training
- Everything! Being able to try all the "tricks" in a safe environment. Clear

explanations from the instructors and demonstration. Knowing that stairs are not an obstacle for wheelchair users

- The videos, repeated demonstrations and all the practice
- The break down of doing a wheelie
- Alternative ways to training
- Being around wheelchairs again (its been many years) and around highly skilled wheelchair participants and trying all the skills myself – spotting straps and spotters obviously most helpful
- Going up and down curbs
- To learn the progressions in all the tasks, as we teach it to our clients
- Being able to actively participate alongside clients
- Practical chance to trial skills ourselves and then see clients learn the skills
- Learning how to go up curbs
- Combination of individual mobility over barriers and caregiver assistant
- The clear description of each skills and how to grade them. Having an objective assessment for evidence based practice
- Learning the wheelie
- Learning how to lift the wheelchair onto the back wheels

Question: What did you find least helpful?
Answers:
- Nothing
- I think it would have been great to have more wheelchair users
- I learned something new from all the skills taught! I can't think of anything that was not helpful
- Maybe the lecture…I'm not a very good auditory learner…but the handout is a good as a reference
- Picking up objects from the floor
- Early Skills – rolling straight, reaching objects – but I think these are definitely still needed as they may be overlooked as easy to others in different situations
- No concerns
- Wheeling over distances
- Everything was helpful
- Having people at the same skill level
- Basic wheelchair pushing lesson

Question: Any other comments on how we could improve this practical session?
Answers:
- Great stuff. Great teachers
- No – it worked well
- Great job!
- No. it was great
- Have mother nature improve the weather

- Good all around course
- It was a great sessions, well done. For clients to break into two smaller groups initially to help with comfort level. It looked intimidating for them when they are "tested" for the skills especially the basic ones.
- To be offered in French
- Ensure instructor is able to demonstrate lessons on a wheelchair (rather than simply describe)

[1]R.L. Kirby, J. Swuste, D.J. Dupuis, D.A. MacLeod, and R. Monroe, "Wheelchair Skills Test: Pilot Study of a New Outcome Measure," *Arch Phys Med Rehabil* 83 (2002), 10-18; R.L Kirby *et al.*, "The Wheelchair Skills Test (version 2.4): Measurement Properties," *Arch Phys Med Rehabil* 85 (2004), 794-804. F. Routhier F *et al.*, "Inter-rater and test-retest reliability of the French-Canadian Wheelchair Skills Test (Version 3.2): Preliminary Findings," Proceedings of the Annual Meeting of RESNA, (Phoenix, AZ, June 15-19, 2007); N.J. Lindquist *et al.*, "Reliability of the Wheelchair Skills Test (WST) Version 4.1 for Manual Wheelchair Users," *Arch Phys Med Rehabil* (under review 2011).

[2]A.M. Newton, R.L. Kirby, A.H. MacPhee, D.J. Dupuis and D.A. MacLeod, "Evaluation of Manual Wheelchair Skills: Is Objective Testing Necessary or Would Subjective Estimates Suffice?" *Arch Phys Med Rehabil* 83 (2002), 1295-9; A.D. Mountain, R.L. Kirby and C. Smith, "The Wheelchair Skills Test: validity of an algorithm-based questionnaire version," *Arch Phys Med Rehabil* 85 (2004), 416-23.

[3]A.H. MacPhee *et al.*, "Wheelchair Skills Training Program: A Randomized Clinical Trial on Wheelchair Users Undergoing Initial Rehabilitation," *Arch Phys Med Rehabil* 85, (2004), 41-50.

[4]K.L. Best, R.L. Kirby, C. Smith and D.A. MacLeod, "Wheelchair Skills Training for Community-Based Manual Wheelchair Users: A Randomized Controlled Trial," *Arch Phys Med Rehabil* 86 (2005), 2316-2323.

[5]A.L. Coolen *et al.*, "Wheelchair skills training program for clinicians: a randomized controlled trial with occupational therapy students," *Arch Phys Med Rehabil* 85 (2004), 1160-7.

[6]R.L. Kirby *et al.*, "The Wheelchair-Handling Skills of Caregivers and the Effect of Training," *Arch Phys Med Rehabil* 85 (2004), 2011-9.

[7]R.L. Kirby *et al.*, "Effect of a high-rolling-resistance training method on the success rate and time required to learn the wheelchair wheelie skill: A randomized controlled trial," *Am. J. Phys. Med. Rehabil.* 87 (2008), 3; R.L. Kirby, S. Bennett, C. Smith, K. Parker and K. Thompson, "Wheelchair Curb Climbing: Randomized Controlled Comparison of Highly Structured And Conventional Training Methods," *Arch Phys Med Rehabil* 89 (2008), 2342-8.

[8]W.S.T-F. Routhier *et al.*, "Measurement Properties of the French-Canadian Version of the Wheelchair Skills Test: Preliminary Results," Proceedings 21st Canadian Seating and Mobility Conference, (October 4-6, 2006), 116-119.

[9]A.D. Mountain *et al.*, "Ability of People with Stroke to Learn Powered Wheelchair Skills: A Pilot Study," *Arch Phys Med Rehabil* 91 (2010), 596-601.

[10]C. Smith, *Wheelchair Skills in the Long-term-care Setting*, Dalhousie University Master's Thesis, (2009).

[11]R.L. Kirby and R.A. Cooper, "Applicability of the wheelchair skills program to the Indian context," *Disabil. Rehabil.* 29 (2007), 11-12.

CONTRIBUTORS

This section is organized by chapter, with each paragraph representing all major contributors for each article.

Commodore H.W. Jung, OMM, CD, joined the Canadian Forces in 1981. He completed his medical training at the University of Toronto and the Toronto East General and Orthopaedic Hospital. Commodore Jung has been posted to CFB Esquimalt and on HMCS PROVIDER as the ship's Medical Officer, to Lahr and Baden in Germany, as Base Surgeon, and as the Senior Medical Officer to the Canadian Air Task Group (Middle East) Qatar, serving through the air campaign of the 1991 Persian Gulf War. During his five-year tenure at Canadian Forces Europe, he was a member of the NATO Tactical Evaluators. He also completed a tour as a medical Detachment Commander at and National Defence Headquarters Medical Inspection Room. In 1995, he was posted to Air Command Headquarters in Winnipeg. During his tenure at Air Command, he assumed multiple roles that included the posts of the Command Flight Surgeon and A1 Medical Operations. He was also posted to Maritime Forces Pacific Headquarters in Esquimalt as the Maritime Pacific Surgeon, and to NDHQ as the Maritime Command Surgeon and Medical Advisor to the Chief of Maritime Staff. Commodore Jung was appointed to the Order of Military Merit in 2001. Subsequently, Commodore Jung assumed responsibilities as Director Health Services Operations, Director Health Services Personnel and Deputy Surgeon General at the Canadian Forces Health Services Group HQ. Commodore Jung was also the principle officer responsible for achieving Canadian Medical Association recognition of Physician Assistants as a health care professional in Canada. He was promoted to his current rank in June 2009 and appointed Surgeon General, Commander of the Canadian Forces Health Services Group and Queens Honourary Physician. Commodore Jung completed his Masters of Arts in Leadership from the Royal Roads University in 2005. He is a graduate of National Securities Studies Program at the Canadian Forces College.

David Pedlar, PhD, is the Director of Research at the National Headquaters of Veterans Affairs Canada in Charlottetown (2000-present). He holds an MSc in Gerontology from the University of Southern California and a PhD in Social Welfare from Case Western Reserve University. He was a Canada-US Fulbright Scholar, Rotary Foundation Scholar and co-recipient of an International Psychogeriatric Association/Bayer Research Award in Psychogeriatrics. He holds university affiliations in Medicine at Dalhousie University and Nursing at the University of Prince Edward Island. He has been responsible for many research studies conducted at Veterans Affairs Canada and investigator in a number of CIHR funded studies. He was a Co-Director of the PEI study centre in two waves of the Canadian Study of Health and Aging. He conducts applied research and publishes and speaks on topics in the fields of military and veteran health and continuing care for seniors. **James Thompson, MD,** is Research

Directorate Medical Advisor at Veterans Affairs Canada. Prior to medicine, he served in the Canadian Forces Reserve infantry and was a research biologist in Canada's Department of Fisheries and Oceans. Prior to Veterans Affairs, he practised Family Medicine and Emergency Medicine in Alberta where he was Director of the Alberta Family Practice Research Network, and practised Emergency Medicine in Prince Edward Island. He served as Chief of a multi-hospital Rural Department of Family Medicine in the David Thompson Health Region in Alberta, and Chief of the Department of Emergency Medicine in Charlottetown. Jim held faculty appointments at the University of Calgary and Dalhousie University. He researches in the field of military and police veterans' health and has a particular interest in weighing expert opinion and scientific evidence to support policy and programs.

Physical Health

Major Vivian McAlister, Commander Ray Kao, Major Brian Church, Lieutenant-Colonel Markus Besemann, and Lieutenant-Colonel Robert Stiegelmar are medical officer specialists with 1 Canadian Field Hospital, Canadian Forces Medical Service. Collectively they have deployed over 20 times on Canada's overseas missions such as those to Afghanistan or Haiti. In Canada, they are posted to teaching hospitals in London, Ottawa and Edmonton.

An internationally recognized surgical leader in orthopaedics and trauma, **David Pichora, MD,** is a pioneer in the use of motion analysis techniques for documenting patterns of disease in upper extremities. As a member of the Kingston General Hospital orthopaedic trauma service, he has undertaken extensive clinical outcome studies in the management of multiple traumas, and pioneered the world's first computer-assisted distal radius osteotomy. He is also a Professor cross-appointed in the Department of Mechanical and Materials Engineering at Queen's University. **Tim Bryant, PhD,** is internationally recognized for fundamental studies of biomechanics of the knee and for studies undertaken with U.S. and European companies in fundamental analysis of total knee replacement designs. His main areas of research are in joint biomechanics, prosthetic materials for orthopaedics, design of biomedical devices, and measurement of task-related fitness parameters in occupational settings. He is a Professor in the Department of Mechanical Engineering and cross-appointed to the Department of Surgery and the School Kinesiology and Health Studies. **Randy Elis, PhD,** is recognized nationally and internationally as a leader in image-guided surgery techniques and leads the Kingston General Hospital Image Guided Surgical Suite project in computer-assisted therapies. Dr. Ellis is a Professor at Queen's University at Kingston. His primary Queen's University appointment is in the School of Computing, and he is also appointed as a Professor in the Department of Mechanical Engineering and as a Professor in the Department of Surgery. John Rudan, MD, is recognized internationally for his work in the areas of total joint surgery as well as computer-assisted orthopaedic surgery. He is one of the innovators responsible for the development of the Kingston General Hospital OR2010, one of the world's first computer-enhanced surgical suites. He also holds a number of patents as a co-inventor. He is currently the Head of the Department of Surgery at Queen's University and a senior Principal Investigator at the Human Mobility Research Centre.

Brendon Gurd, PhD, is an Assistant Professor within the school of Kinesiology and Health Studies where he has recently established the Muscle Biochemistry Lab. Dr. Gurd's research includes the study of exercise capacity and muscle metabolism in healthy young, older and overweight/obese individuals. Specifically, Dr. Gurd studies the ability of regular physical activity, including interval training, to improve exercise capacity and skeletal muscle mitochondrial content in these diverse populations. **Jasmin K Ma, BSc(Cand)** is an undergraduate student in the school of Kinesiology and Health Studies at Queen's University. She has been working in the Muscle Biochemistry Lab for the past year and is actively researching the efficacy of different modes of interval training at improving aerobic fitness, muscular strength, and mitochondrial capacity.

Alain Beaulieu, PhD, graduated in computer engineering from the Royal Military College of Canada. He was an officer in the Electrical and Mechanical Engineering Branch of the Canadian Army for 28 years. He was employed as a field officer and engineer for a wide variety of Army systems. He is an assistant professor in the Electrical and Computer Engineering Department at RMC. Alain has research interests in biomedical engineering and completed for his PhD on Safety of Computer Guided Surgery.

Danielle Salmon, PhD(Cand), completed her MSc (Exercise Physiology) at the University of Regina, with her thesis topic that examined the role of exercise therapy in the treatment of chronic neck pain and dysfunction in helicopter aircrew in the Canadian Forces Military. Danielle is currently a doctoral (PhD) student in the School of Physical Education at the University of Otago in Dunedin, New Zealand. Her area of research examines the effects exercise training on cervical muscle function and pain, and its application to occupational injuries and sports performance. **Michael Harrison, PhD,** recently completed his PhD in the area of night vision goggle induced neck strain and injury in helicopter aircrew in the Canadian Forces Military. He is currently a medical student, with an interest in aviation medicine. **Donald Sharpe, PhD,** is an Associate Professor in the Faculty of Arts, Department of Psychology at the University of Regina. Dr. Sharpe's current research interests include applications of quantitative approaches (eg. meta-analyses, structural equation modeling) and research methodology. He teaches introductory and advanced statistical courses. **Darren Candow, PhD,** is an Associate Professor in the Faculty of Kinesiology & Health Studies and is the Gerontology Graduate Coordinator, Centre on Aging and Health at the University of Regina. Dr. Candow supervises the Aging Muscle and Bone Health Laboratory, and serves on the editorial board for the Journal of Aging and Physical

Activity and the Journal of the International Society of Sports Nutrition. Dr. Candow's research program involves the development of effective resistance training and nutritional intervention strategies for improving properties of aging muscle and bone health. **Wayne Albert, PhD,** is a Professor and Dean of Faculty of Kinesiology at the University of New Brunswick. Dr. Albert's major research focus pertains to occupational biomechanics (ergonomics) and the prevention of musculoskeletal injuries in the workplace as well as general low back health, with research projects including: 1) assessing the neuromuscular demands placed on military helicopter pilots when using night-vision equipment mounted to their helmets; 2) injury concerns in offshore industries workers that must deal with moving environments; 3) cumulative loading concerns associated with automotive assembly to musculoskeletal 4) biomechanical stresses of city transit workers; 5) lifting biomechanics programs in long term care facility workers; and 6) effects of fatigue on lifting technique. **Patrick Neary, PhD,** is a Professor in the Faculty of Kinesiology & Health Studies at the University of Regina. His current research explores the mechanism(s) associated with cerebral, skeletal, and cardiac muscle fatigue during exercise, and factors related to muscle strain and dysfunction in aviation aircrew. His research program has been funded by NSERC, CIHR and the Department of National Defence.

Yushan Wang, PhD, moved to Canada after receiving his MD degree in China. He obtained his Ph.D. from Dalhousie in Pharmacology/Neuroscience in 2000. Dr. Wang completed his Post-doc training at the University of Toronto for one and a half years and at the University of British Columbia for another one and a half years, specializing if glutamate receptor trafficking and neurodegeneration. He then started his work as a Defence Scientist at DRDC Suffield, where he conducted research on the effect of nerve agents and biological toxins on the central nervous system (6 publications). Due to Dr. Wang's recent interest in the mechanisms of blast-induced neurotrauma (BINT), he is currently investigating the role of glutamate receptor trafficking in BINT.

Ayush Kumar, PhD, is an Assistant Professor in the Faculty of Health Sciences at UOIT, where he studies bacterial pathogens exhibiting multidrug resistance (MDR) and a protein family known as resistance-nodulation-cell division (RND) family. Efforts in his laboratory are focused towards understanding the mechanisms of function and regulatory pathways of these proteins in pathogens like *Acinetobacter baumannii* and *Pseudomonas aeruginosa* in order to aid in designing effective drug therapy

Ann Nakashima, MASc, is a Defence Scientist in the Individual Behaviour and Performance Section at DRDC Toronto. She has a B.Sc. (hons) in Physics and an M.A.Sc. in Mechanical Engineering from the University of British Columbia. Her research interests include communication and performance in noise, hearing conservation and physical performance in stressful operational environments. **Oshin Vartanian, PhD,** obtained his Ph.D. in experimental psychology at the University of Maine, followed by a postdoctoral fellowship in cognitive neuroscience at York University and a visiting fellowship at DRDC Toronto, where he is currently a Defence Scientist. He is the recipient of the Daniel E. Berlyne Award from the American Psychological Association's Division 10 for outstanding research by a junior researcher, and holds an Adjunct Assistant Professor position in the Department of Psychology at the University of Toronto. **Fethi Bouak, PhD,** is a Defence Scientist and the Head of the Performance Group in the Individual Behaviour and Performance Section, DRDC Toronto. His interest and work include underwater life and work support systems covering the range from CF divers to submariners, and measuring and optimizing CF personnel physical and mental performance in austere operational environments. **Kevin Hofer, MA,** obtained both his B.Sc. in human biology and his B.A. in psychology from the University of Guelph, followed by an M.A. in psychophysiology from York University. He is currently the Technical Group Leader of the Joint Operational Human Sciences Centre at DRDC Toronto. His involvement in Defence R & D focuses on managing resources for human performance projects. **Bob Cheung, PhD,** is the Senior Scientist and Scientific Advisor for the Joint Operational Human Sciences Centre, DRDC Toronto. His academic background includes: Hon B.Sc. in Physiology and Mathematics, B.Ed. in Biology and Mathematics, from the University of Toronto, M.Sc. and Ph.D. in Neurophysiology specializing in vestibular physiology and psychophysics, from the University of Toronto/York University. He has published over 90 refereed scientific journal papers, book chapters, and NATO proceedings. His research interests are in spatial orientation, primary blast wave injury and the vestibular system, and cognitive and physiological performance in general.

Mental Health

Colonel Rakesh Jetly, OMM, CD, MD, FRCPC, is the senior psychiatrist in the Canadian Forces. He is currently the Psychiatry and Mental Health Advisor to the Surgeon General. In a career that spans more than 20 years he has deployed to the Middle East, Rwanda and twice to Kandahar. Colonel Jetly has presented nationally and internationally on issues such as PTSD and other military mental health issues.

Kate St. Cyr, MSc, is a research associate at the Parkwood Hospital Operational Stress Injury clinic in London, Ontario. Her research interests include health-related quality of life, psychiatric epidemiology, and social determinants of health. She is also interested in comorbid psychiatric illness and suicidality amongst military personnel. **Maya Roth, PhD,** is a psychologist (in supervised practice) at the Parkwood Hospital Operational Stress Injury Clinic in London, Ontario. Her clinical practice centres on assessment and both individual and group treatment of mood and anxiety disorders related to military service, and other sequelae of service, such as chronic pain. Dr. Roth's research examines treatment outcomes in chronic pain and post traumatic stress disorder, as well as pain and psychological distress at end of life. **Don Richardson, MD, FRCPC;** Adjunct Professor, Department of Psychiatry- University of Western

Ontario. Dr. Richardson is the consultant psychiatrist for the National Centre for Operational Stress Injuries, veterans Affairs Canada and for the Parkwood OSI Injury Clinic in London, Ontario. He has more than 15 years experience in the assessment and treatment of veterans and Canadian Forces members suffering with PTSD and other operational stress injuries. His research interests include risk factors for PTSD, health care utilization, treatment outcomes monitoring and quality of life assessment of veterans suffering from psychiatric illnesses. His research has been published in numerous peer-reviewed journals. **Alexandra McIntyre-Smith, PhD,** is a psychologist (in supervised practice) at the Parkwood Hospital Operational Stress Injury clinic in London, Ontario. She works with Canadian Forces members and their family members, providing diagnostic assessment and individual psychotherapy. Dr. McIntyre-Smith completed her undergraduate training at McGill University and her graduate training at the University of Western Ontario. Her research interests focus on the health and wellbeing of CF members; recent research projects include the impact of somatic complaints on quality of life and sexual function among CF members. **Nancy Cameron** has been a clinical nurse specialist at the Parkwood Hospital Operational Stress Injury clinic in London, Ontario since 2006. She is interested in qualitative research, and specializes in providing therapeutic services to spouses of Canadian Forces members and providing psychoeducation to family members and community partners, such as local and provincial police forces and other mental health service providers.

Sandra Pickrell Baker, MA, holds a Master of Arts in Family Studies and Gerontology From Mount Saint Vincent University and a Master of Social Work degree (Dalhousie University). Her interest in family's experience of trauma led to her research of secondary traumatic stress in female partners of military veterans diagnosed with post traumatic stress disorder. With her understanding of family systems and the adaptation and adjustment necessary in the family unit to navigate times of challenge, Sandra's practice focuses on assisting families and individuals experiencing trauma, to cultivate their innate resilience and strength. **Deborah Norris, PhD,** is an Associate Professor within the Department of Family Studies and Gerontology at Mount Saint Vincent University. Informed through her background in family studies and critical theory, Dr. Norris has developed a research program over the past twenty years that focuses on the strength and capacities of military families. Specific research interests include the everyday lives of female military partners experiencing the cycle of deployment and pathways to resilience for military members, veterans and their families throughout the life course.

Alla Skomorovsky, PhD, is a defence scientist with Defence Research and Development Canada, currently assigned to the Conditions of Service team, part of the DGMPRA. She holds a PhD in Psychology from Carleton University in Ottawa. With DND since 2005, Alla has conducted research on individual characteristics influencing psychological well-being and job performance of CF members as well as the resilience factors among military families. **Kerry Sudom, PhD,** is a defence scientist with Defence Research and Development Canada, currently assigned to the Psychosocial Health Dynamics team, part of the Director General Military Personnel Research and Analysis (DGMPRA). She holds a Master of Science and a PhD in psychology from Carleton University in Ottawa. With DND since 2005, Kerry has conducted research on the impacts of military life on families, as well as the well-being of CF members and veterans.

Shannon Gifford, PhD, is a Registered Psychologist who has worked at the Operational Stress Injury Clinic at Parkwood Hospital in London, Ontario, since 2006. She is also a Clinical Adjunct at the University of Waterloo. **James Hutchinson, PhD** received his Ph.D. in Clinical Psychology from Washington State University in 2009. His research thus far has focused on the relationship between personality and cardiovascular health. Dr. Hutchinson is currently a staff Psychologist with the Trillium Health Centre Specialty Hand Program in Toronto, in addition to his work in private practice. **Maggie Gibson, PhD,** is a Registered Psychologist in Ontario and has provided psychological services to the Veterans Care Program, Parkwood Hospital, St. Joseph's Health Care, London, Ontario, since 1993. She is an Associate Investigator with the Aging, Rehabilitation and Geriatric Care Research Program of the Lawson Health Research Institute and an Adjunct Professor in both the Department of Psychology and the Division of Geriatric Psychiatry, University of Western Ontario. She contributes geropsychology expertise to national and international committees and task forces, including initiatives sponsored by the Canadian Coalition for Seniors Mental Health, the Alzheimer Society of Canada, the Public Health Agency of Canada and the International Psychogeriatric Association.

SOCIAL HEALTH

Allan English, PhD has taught undergraduate and graduate courses at the Royal Military College of Canada as well as courses in senior officer professional military education at the Canadian Forces College, Toronto. He is currently an adjunct associate professor in the History Department at Queen's University, where he teaches Canadian military history. He has been a member of a number of committees that have advised Veterans Affairs Canada, the Department of National Defence, and the RCMP on issues related to operational stress injuries.

Amy Buitenhuis, BScE, BA(Cand) is a research assistant for the Canadian Disability Policy Alliance at Queen's University. Her research focuses on improving health policy related to people with disabilities in Canada. She has a Bachelor of Science in Engineering and a Bachelor of Arts in Geography. She is beginning a master's degree in geography at the University of Toronto. **Alice Aiken, CD, PhD, MSc, BScPT, BSc(Kin),** is an assistant professor in the Physical Therapy Program of the School of Rehabilitation Therapy at Queen's University in Kingston, Canada. She does health services / health policy research in the area of innovative models of care and disability policy. She lectures in clinical orthopedics, and is the Director of the Canadian Institute for Military and Veterans Health Research. Dr. Aiken is the current president of the Board of Directors of the Canadian Physiotherapy Association. She received her PhD and Master's from Queen's University in Kingston, her Physical Therapy degree at Dalhousie University in Halifax, Nova Scotia and a BSc in Kinesiology at the University of Ottawa. She also proudly served in the Canadian military for 14 years.

Stéphanie A.H. Bélanger, PhD is a professor at the French Department of the Royal Military College of Canada (2008). Her research focus on the representation of the warrior through Just War Theories and Testimonies and she is the author of the recently published book *Guerres, sacrifices et persécutions* on the representation of warriors and just war theory (Paris: Editions l'Harmattan, 2010). She is also co-editor of two other collectives published by the Canadian Defence Academy Press, Transforming Traditions (2010) and Le Leadership des femmes dans les Forces canadiennes (2009). She is co-chair of the Kingston Diversity Advisory Group for Persons with Disabilities and she is the Associate Director of the Canadian Institute for the Military and Veteran Health Research. She serves as a logistics officer in the Naval Reserve (2004).

Susan L. Ray, PhD is an Associate Professor at the School of Nursing, Faculty of Health Sciences, with a cross appointment to Psychiatry at the Schulich School of Medicine & Dentistry, University of Western Ontario (UWO). She is an Associate Scientist at the Lawson Health Research Institute. Dr. Ray received her BScN from the University of Toronto, her MScN and Post Masters NP from UWO and her PhD from the University of Alberta. Her research focuses on the impact of psychological trauma and testing interventions for PTSD on military personnel, the refugee population and male survivors of abuse.

From Queens University, **Julie Salverson's, PhD,** current research, writing and performance interests include: Canada's involvement in the development of the atomic bomb (continuing work from a SSHRC funded project with Peter Van Wyck, Concordia University); the comedic and absurd as approaches to witnessing violence beyond an aesthetic of injury and spectacle; the relationship between aesthetics and ethics in translating stories of violence; creative non-fiction and its place in scholarship; the role of the imagination in learning and development.

Mary Beth MacLean, MA, received a BA in economics from University of Prince Edward Island (UPI) and a Masters Degree in Economics specializing in health economics in the late 1980s. She worked as a health economist and policy and evaluation analyst for the Alberta Health, Statistics Canada, the Patented Medicine Prices Review Board and Health Canada prior to moving back home to PEI in 1995. In these roles Mary Beth developed case-mix funding for acute care hospitals in Alberta, wrote papers on the measurement of hospital productivity, regional variations in surgical rates, surgical rates among the elderly, pharmaceutical cost and price control mechanisms internationally, economic impact of pharmaceutical price controls in Canada and developed a survey on transition homes for the Federal Family Violence Initiative. She has worked for Veterans Affairs Canada since this time as an economist with the Statistics Directorate and as director of Statistics. She worked on the Modernization Task Force which developed the specific programs for the New Veterans' Charter, generating cost estimates and actuarial projections that found that it was a least cost neutral in the longer-term to provide the proposed wellness programs and disability awards in place of monthly pensions. One year later she was working on the Veterans' Health Services Review that proposed to extend benefits to veterans and survivors not currently eligible. She joined the Research Directorate of VAC in 2008. Her research interests include case-mix measurement and funding, economic evaluation and in particular the economic evaluation of comprehensive rehabilitation, population health, poverty and low income as a determinant of health, the development of nominal rolls, and measuring transition outcomes.

Stephanie Cork, MA(Cand), is a Master's Candidate from Queen's University whose interests lie in the intersections of sport, rehabilitation, military and disability discourses. She currently works as a Teaching Assistant for an Introductory Sociology course at Queen's, and in her spare time works on event planning (such as Queen's Annual (Dis)Ability Awareness Month) and is an editor for the new Queen's Publication *Able*.

Program Description

Linda VanTil, DVM, MSc(Epi), received her Doctor of Veterinary Medicine from the University of Guelph in 1985, and her Master of Science in Epidemiology from the University of Prince Edward Island in 1990. She spent 14 years as Epidemiologist with the Prince Edward Island Department of Health. In the past 3 years, she has been working on population health research at Veterans Affairs Canada.

For 20 years **Marlee Franz., OT Reg (Ont)** has provided Occupational Therapy services, predominately in the community. Since 2004, she has worked as the District OT for VAC providing expert opinion and advice to their Interdisciplinary Team members. In 2010 she conducted a file review of VAC clients who participated in the Rehabilitation Program as part of an evaluation to determine the extent to which VAC is assisting Canadian Forces members, veterans and families transitioning from military to civilian life.

Richard Birtwhistle, MD, MSC, FCFP, CPCSSN, is a family physician and professor of Family Medicine and Community Health and Epidemiology and is currently Director of the Centre for Studies in Family Medicine at Queen's University. His clinical research interests have been in the primary care of hypertension, chronic disease management and the evaluation of primary care models. Since 2008 his main research interests is as principal investigator for the Canadian Primary Care Sentinel Surveillance Network which is a national project funded by the Public Health Agency of Canada to develop a network of primary care practitioners using electronic medical records to collect data on chronic disease in patients across the country. **Anita Lambert-Lanning, MLS,** is a health research librarian and project manager of the Canadian Primary Care Sentinel Surveillance Network based in the research department at the national offices of the College of Family Physicians of Canada (CFPC) in Mississauga where she is also the manager for the National Research System (NaReS). She began working with family medicine researchers to operationalize nation-wide research projects involving CFPC members in 2002.

Brenda Gamble, PhD, received her PhD in medical sciences from the University of Toronto in 2006 and is an Assistant Professor in the Faculty of Health Sciences at the University of Ontario Institute of Technology (UOIT). She is an Adjunct Professor in the School of Health Services Management at Ryerson University and holds a status position as an Assistant Professor in the Faculty of Medicine at the University of Toronto. Brenda's research focuses on allied health professionals, healthcare leaders and medical laboratory services. **Olena Kapral, BHSc** completed a Bachelor Degree in Health Sciences, specializing in Kinesiology, at the University of Ontario Institute of Technology in April 2011. During the course of her studies, Ms. Kapral has worked as a research assistant for the Faculty of Health Sciences. She has also worked on several projects with the Canadian Institutes for Health Research Team in Community Care and Health Human Resources. Ms. Kapral's research interest include interprofessional collaboration, health policy, and health human resources.

Donna Pickering, PhD, is a Research Scientist at Defence Research and Development Canada - Toronto. She holds a PhD in social and personality psychology, specializing in the role of stress and coping on health and well-being. Her research at DRDC Toronto focuses on resilience, post-deployment reintegration, social support, work-life balance/conflict, and readiness.

Lieutenant-Colonel Rowe, MRSc, CD, has been a Military Physiotherapy Officer in the Canadian Forces since 1988 and has served postings at CFB Calgary, 4 Wing Cold Lake, 8 Wing Trenton, CFB Halifax and NDHQ Ottawa. He recently completed his Master in Rehabilitation Sciences at the University of British Columbia and currently works in at Canadian Forces Health Services Group Headquarters in Ottawa, as the National Physiotherapy Practice Leader. **Major Luc Hébert, PhD, CD** is a physiotherapist with the Canadian Forces Primary Reserve List and he served in the Regular Forces from 1982 to 1996. He completed a Master Degree in Biomedical Sciences at Montreal University in 1989, and he obtained a PhD degree in Experimental Medicine at l'Université Laval in 2001. He is a researcher with the Quebec provincial rehabilitation network and the National Defence of Canada. One of his research interests has been on the variables that best explain and predict musculoskeletal injuries as well as on the factors limiting physical performance, most specifically muscle strength. Since May 2000, Dr Hébert has been the National Physiotherapy Training Director for the Canadian Forces Health Services Group Headquarters.

R. Lee Kirby, MD, FRCPC is a Professor in the Division of Physical Medicine and Rehabilitation at Dalhousie University in Halifax, Nova Scotia, Canada. Over the past 30 years, he has authored or co-authored over 125 papers in peer-reviewed journals, 10 textbook chapters and over 250 minor publications (mostly abstracts and proceedings of presentations to scientific meetings). He has presented numerous symposia on wheelchair safety, stability and performance to such organizations as RESNA, the International Seating Symposium and the American Academy of Physical Medicine and Rehabilitation. **Cher Smith, BScOT,** is an occupational therapist who is the Wheelchair Coordinator at the Queen Elizabeth II Health Sciences Centre and an adjunct professor in the School of Occupational Therapy at Dalhousie University in Halifax, Nova Scotia, Canada. She has completed a MSc thesis in Kinesiology at Dalhousie University. She has been involved in clinical work, education and research about wheelchairs for over 10 years. In 2002, she was acknowledged for her work at the Canadian Seating and Mobility Conference, being awarded the prestigious Phil Mundy Award. She has provided workshops on seating and mobility and has presented symposia on wheelchair skills at the Canadian Seating and Mobility Conference, the International Seating Symposium and RESNA.